Laos

**Northern
Laos**
(p77)

**Luang
Prabang &
Around**
(p44)

**Vientiane,
Vang Vieng
& Around**
(p140)

**Central
Laos**
(p182)

**Southern
Laos**
(p205)

Austin Bush, Bruce Evans, Nick Ray

RICE PADDIES NEAR LUANG NAMTHA P116

PRESSDIGITAL/GETTY IMAGES ©

KIM BRIERS/500PX ©

TAK BAT P51

KENGPHOTOSTOCK/SHUTTERSTOCK ©

TAT KUANG SI P76

Contents

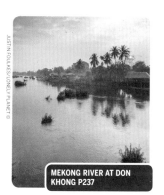

Welcome to Laos

Vivid nature, voluptuous landscapes and a vibrant culture collide with a painful past and optimistic future to make Laos an enigmatic experience for the adventurous.

An Authentic Asia

Laos cherishes many of the traditions that have disappeared in a frenzy of development elsewhere in the region. It's hard to believe somnolent Vientiane is an Asian capital, and there's a timeless quality to rural life, where stilt houses and paddy fields look like they are straight out of a movie set. Magical Luang Prabang bears witness to hundreds of saffron-robed monks gliding through the streets every morning in a call to alms, one of the region's iconic images. Intrepid travellers will discover a country untainted by mass tourism and Asia in slow motion.

A Kaleidoscope of People

Laos is one of the most ethnically diverse countries in the region, reflecting its geographic location as a crossroads of Asia. The hardy Hmong people live off the land in the remote mountains of the north, Kahu and Alak elders in the south still have traditional face tattoos, and the Katang villagers of central Laos sleep with forest spirits. Whether it is the cities of the lowlands or the villages of the highlands, Laos offers wonderful opportunities for local interaction. However, change is coming as a new high-speed railway will cut across the country, criss-crossing some of these isolated communities.

Fifty Shades of Green

With its dark and brooding jungle, glowing emerald rice fields, and glistening tea leaves that blanket the mountains, the landscape in Laos changes shades of green like a chameleon. But it's not just the luscious landscapes that are green: when it comes to ecotourism, Laos is leading the way in Southeast Asia. Protected areas blanket the landscape, and community-based trekking initiatives combine these spectacular natural attractions with the chance to experience the 'real Laos' with a village homestay, helping contribute to the local community and preserve the environment.

Eclectic Asia

Travellers rave about Laos for a reason. Adventure seekers can lose themselves in underground river caves, on jungle ziplines or while climbing karsts. Nature enthusiasts can take a walk on the wild side and spot exotic animals such as gibbons or elephants. Culture lovers can explore ancient temples and immerse themselves in Lao spiritual life. Foodies can spice up their lives with a Lao cooking class or go gourmand in the French-accented cities. And if all this sounds a little too strenuous, then unwind with a spa session or yoga class. Eclectic Laos caters for everyone.

Why I Love Laos

By Nick Ray, Writer

I first came to Laos as a backpacker in 1995 and quickly succumbed to the incredible beauty of the natural landscapes and the warm-hearted welcome. There have been many memorable trips since and this enigmatic country still charms. On this trip, I headed north to the mysterious Vieng Xai Caves and took some long boat trips on the Nam Ou from beautiful Nong Khiaw to reach remote Phongsali Province. However, it is Luang Prabang that really leaves an impression thanks to its enticing combination of historic temples, living culture, evolving cuisine scene and rural upcountry adventures.

For more about our writers, see p320

Above: Xieng Khuan (p145)

Laos

ELEVATION
1250m
1000m
750m
500m
250m
0

0 — 100 km
0 — 50 miles

Zipline Adventures
Whiz through the jungle on ziplines (p130)

Trekking
Hike through the jungle of Nam Ha NPA (p88)

Luang Prabang
Be charmed by the country's historic heart (p44)

Vieng Xai Caves
Experience history in a wartime cave hideout (p95)

River Trips
Cruise down the Mekong on a river boat (p90)

Vang Vieng
Go on an adventure amid stunning scenery (p170)

CHINA

MYANMAR (BURMA)

VIETNAM

HANOI

Haiphong

Gulf of Tonkin

SOUTH CHINA SEA (EAST SEA)

Mong La

Mengla

Muang Sing

Muang Mom

Chiang Saen

Huay Xai (Houayxay)

Pha Udom

Nam Kan NPA

BOKEO

Kok

Xieng Nam Ha NPA

Veng Phoukha

Vieng Phukha

LUANG NAMTHA

Luang Namtha (Namtha)

Boten

Boun Tai

PHONGSALI

Phongsali

Ou Tai (Muang Nyot Ou)

Nam Ou (Muang Khua)

Phu Den Din NPA

Pang Hok

Muang Khua

Dien Bien Phu

Tay Trang

Son La

Nong Khiaw

Vieng Kham

LUANG PRABANG

Luang Prabang

Muang Houn

Hongsa

Muang Ngeun

Huay Kon

Nan

SAINYABULI (SAYABOURY)

Sainyabuli (Sayaboury)

Pak Beng

Nam Tha

Mekong

UDOMXAI

Muang Xai

Udomxai (Muang Xai)

Muang Khoun

Phu Khoun

Kasi

Vang Vieng

VIENTIANE

Phon

Nam Ngum

SAISOMBUN

Nam Et/Phou Louey National Park

HUA PHAN

Sam Neua (Xam Neua)

Vieng Xai

Na Meo

Nam Sor

Nam Sam NPA

Muang Kham

XIENG KHUANG

Phonsavan

Muang Khoun (Old Xieng Khuang)

Nong Haet

Nam Can

Phu Bia (2820m)

BORIKHAMSAI

Nam San

Nam Ngum

Ca

Vinh

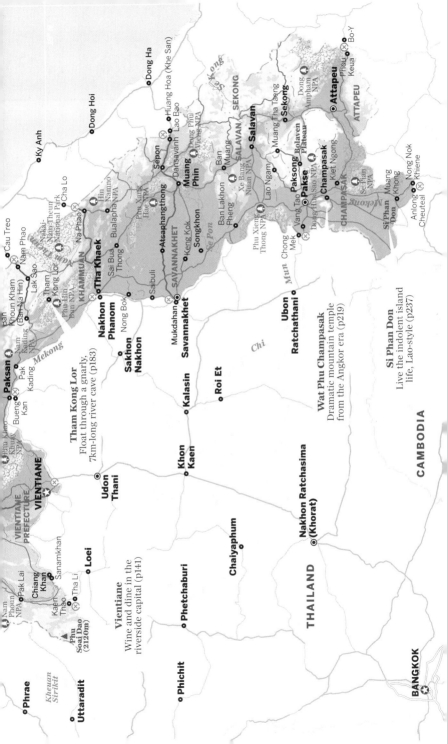

Cau Treo
Ky Anh
Dong Hoi
Dong Ha
Dong Hoa (Khe San)
Huang Hoa (Khe San)
Lao Bao
Cha Lo

Se Kong
Bo-Y
Phou Keua
Bo-Y

Attapeu
Dong Ampham NPA

ATTAPEU

Nam Phao
Cau Treo

Ban Khoun Kham
Nam Kading NPA
Lak Sao

Tham Kong Lor (Ban-Na Hin)
Phu Hin Bun NPA

Nakai-Nam Theun National Park

Na-Phao

Hin Namno NPA

Tha Khaek

Sepon
Dansavanh
Muang Phin
Ban Muang
Muang Tha Taeng

SEKONG
Sekong

SALAVAN
Salavan
Xe Bang Nuan NPA
Lao Ngam

Dong Phu Vieng NPA
Phu Xang Hae NPA

Bualapha
Atsaphangthong
Keng Kok
Songkhon
Se Pon

SAVANNAKHET

Sai Bua Thong

Saibuli

KHAMMUAN

Nakai

Paksan
Nam Kading
Pak Kading
Bueng Kan

Mekong

Phu Xieng Thong NPA

Chong Mek

Vang Tao
Pakse
Paksong
Bolaven Plateau
Klet Ngong
Dong Hua Sao NPA

Champasak
CHAMPASAK

Mun
Mekong

Phu Khieu Khuay NPA

VIENTIANE
VIENTIANE PREFECTURE

Nong Bok
Nakhon Phanom

Sakhon Nakhon

Mukdahan
Savannakhet

Chi

Kalasin

Roi Et

Ubon Ratchathani

Se Piane NPA
Si Phan Don
Muang Khong
Nong Nok Khiene
Anlong Cheuteal
Muang Don

Nam Poun NPA
Pak Lai
Sanamkhan

Phrae

Uttaradit

Kheuan Sirikit

Chiang Khan
Kaen Thao
Tha Li

Phu Soai Dao (2120m)

Loei

Sanamkhan

Phetchaburi

Phichit

Chaiyaphum

Khon Kaen

Udon Thani

Tham Kong Lor
Float through a gnarly, 7km-long river cave (p183)

Vientiane
Wine and dine in the riverside capital (p141)

Nakhon Ratchasima (Khorat)

THAILAND

Wat Phu Champasak
Dramatic mountain temple from the Angkor era (p219)

Si Phan Don
Live the indolent island life, Lao-style (p237)

CAMBODIA

BANGKOK

Laos'
Top
10

Luang Prabang

1 Bordered by the Mekong River and the Nam Khan (Khan River), this timeless city (p45) of temples is the stuff of travel legends: rich in royal history, saffron-clad monks, stunning river views, world-class cuisine and some of the best boutique accommodation in the region. Hire a bike and explore the tropical peninsula's backstreets, take a cooking class or just ease back with a restful massage at one of the many affordable spas. Prepare to adjust your timetable and stay a little longer than expected.

Top: Wat Xieng Thong (p49)

Si Phan Don

2 Laos' hammock-flopping mecca has been catering to weary travellers for years. While these tropical islands (p237) bounded by the waters of the Mekong are best known as a happy haven for catatonic sun worshippers, more active souls are spoilt for choice. Between tubing and cycling through paddy fields, grab a kayak, spot rare Irrawaddy dolphins, and then round off your day with a sunset boat trip. Don't miss a side trip to the largest falls in Laos, the mighty Khon Phapheng (pictured), often referred to as the Niagara Falls of Laos.

Vientiane

3 Meandering along the banks of the Mekong, Vientiane (p141) is surely Southeast Asia's most languid capital. The wide streets are bordered by tamarind trees and the narrow alleys conceal French villas, Chinese shophouses and glittering wats. The city brews a heady mix of street vendors, wandering Buddhist monks, fine cuisine, boutique hotels and a healthy vibe that sees visitors slinking off for spa treatments and turning their time to yoga and cycling. It may not have Luang Prabang's looks, but Vientiane has a certain charm all of its own.

Left: Pha That Luang (p145)

Vang Vieng

4 The riverine jewel in Laos' karst country, Vang Vieng (p170) sits under soaring cliffs beside the Nam Song (Song River) and is the undisputed adventure capital of Laos. Since the party crowd moved on, tranquillity reigns again with more family-oriented visitors dropping in to soak up such well-organised activities as hot-air ballooning, trekking, caving and climbing. And don't forget the original draw: tubing down the river. Where once there were only budget guesthouses and same-same traveller cafes, now they have been joined by smarter boutique hotels and restaurants serving delicious food.

5

Trekking & Homestays

5 Laos is famous for its wide range of community-based treks, many of which include a traditional homestay in a local ethnic minority village for a night or more. Trekking is possible all over the country, but northern Laos is one of the most popular areas. Luang Namtha (p118) is the most accessible base for ecotreks in the Nam Ha NPA, one of the best-known trekking spots in the Mekong region, and there are lots of local homestays available in Lanten, Khmu and Tai Daeng communities.

Top: Lanten woman near Luang Namtha

Vieng Xai Caves

6 This is history writ large in stone. An area of outstanding natural beauty, Vieng Xai (p95) was home to the Pathet Lao communist leadership during the US bombing campaign of 1964–73. Beyond the breathtaking beauty of the natural caves, it is the superb audio tour that really brings the experience alive. When the bombers buzz overhead to a soundtrack of Jimi Hendrix you'll be ducking for cover in the Red Prince's lush garden. It's a long, hard journey to this remote corner of the country, but well worth the effort.

Tham Kong Lor

7 Imagine your deepest nightmare: the snaggle-toothed mouth of a river cave beneath a towering limestone mountain, the boatman in his rickety longtail taking you into the heart of darkness. Puttering beneath the cathedral-high ceiling of stalactites in this extraordinary 7.5km-long underworld (p183) in remote Khammuan Province is an awesome experience. You'll be glad to see light at the end of the tunnel. The village of Ban Kong Lor is now the most convenient base for visiting the cave, after an influx of guesthouses and small resorts in the last few years.

8

9

River Trips

8 River trips (p90) are a major feature of travel through Laos. One of the most popular connects Luang Prabang and Huay Xai, the gateway to the Golden Triangle, via Pak Beng. From local boats to luxury cruises, there are options to suit every budget, including floating through sleepy Si Phan Don in the far south. Beyond the Mekong, other important rivers such as the Nam Ou connect places as diverse as Nong Khiaw and Muang Khua (for Phongsali). It's also possible to kayak some of these regional rivers on multiday trips.

Wat Phu Champasak

9 Not as majestic as the temples of Angkor, but just as mysterious, this mountainside Khmer ruin (p219) has both the artistry and the setting to impress. Once part of an important city, it now sits forlorn on the side of Phu Pasak. You'll discover something special at each level as you walk up to the summit, where the views are vast and the crowds are thin. Other related ruins can be found in the rice paddies and the forest down below.

Zipline Adventures

10 Laos has really emerged as the zipline capital of Asia, with high wires criss-crossing the jungle and karst landscape from the far north to the deep south of Laos. The original zipline adventure is the Gibbon Experience (pictured; p130), which spans the forest valleys of the lush Nam Kan NPA. There are now many other world-class ziplines in Laos, including the Nong Khiaw Jungle Fly, the Green Jungle Park in Luang Prabang, the Tad Fane Zipline on the Bolaven Plateau and the Mekong Fly over a Mekong waterfall. Adrenaline adventures await.

Need to Know

For more information, see Survival Guide (p285)

Currency
Lao kip (K)

....

Language
Lao, French, ethnic minority languages

....

Visas
Thirty-day tourist visas are readily available on arrival at international airports and most land borders.

....

Money
The official national currency in Laos is the Lao kip (K), but Thai baht (B) and US dollars (US$) are also commonly accepted.

....

Mobile Phones
Roaming is possible in Laos but is generally expensive. Local SIM cards and unlocked mobile phones are readily available.

....

Time
Indochina Time (GMT/UTC plus seven hours)

When to Go

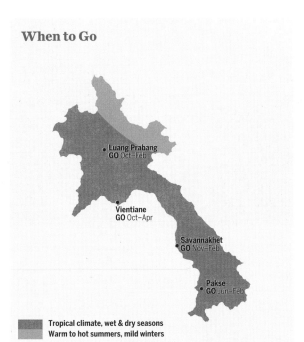

Luang Prabang
GO Oct–Feb

Vientiane
GO Oct–Apr

Savannakhet
GO Nov–Feb

Pakse
GO Jun–Feb

Tropical climate, wet & dry seasons
Warm to hot summers, mild winters

High Season
(Nov–Mar)

➡ Pleasant temperatures in much of Laos, though it's cold in the mountains.

➡ The best all-round time to visit.

➡ Book accommodation in advance during the peak Christmas and New Year period.

Shoulder Season
(Jul & Aug)

➡ Wet in most parts of Laos with high humidity, but the landscapes are emerald green.

➡ Popular time for European tourists to visit from Italy or Spain, plus backpacking students with a long summer break.

Low Season
(Apr–Jun, Sep & Oct)

➡ April and May brings the hot season to Laos when the thermostat hits 40°C.

➡ September and October can be very wet, but some incredible cloud formations accompany the deluge.

Useful Websites

Ecotourism Laos (www.eco
tourismlaos.com) Focusing on
trekking and other ecotourism
activities.

Hobo Maps (http://hobomaps.
com) Up-to-date maps and
transportation details, mostly
regarding northern Laos.

**Lao National Tourism Admin-
istration** (www.tourismlaos.org)
Mostly up-to-date travel information from the government.

We Are Lao (https://wearelao.
com) Popular website covering
all things travel-related in Laos.

RFA (Radio Free Asia; www.rfa.
org/english/news/laos) Un-
biased, censorship-free news.

Important Numbers

To dial listings from outside
Laos, dial your international
access code, the country code
and then the number (minus
'0', which is used when dialling
domestically).

Laos' country code	☏	856
International access code	☏	00
Ambulance	☏	195
Fire	☏	190
Police	☏	191
Tourist Police	☏	192

Exchange Rates

Australia	A$1	5885K
Canada	C$1	6523K
Euro zone	€1	9500K
Japan	¥100	8050K
Thailand	10B	2803K
UK	UK£1	10,595K
US	US$1	8610K
Vietnam	10,000d	3690K

For current exchange rates, see
www.xe.com.

Daily Costs

**Budget:
Less than US$50**

➡ Cheap guesthouse room:
US$5–10

➡ Local meals and street eats:
US$2–4

➡ Local buses: US$2–3 per
100km

**Midrange:
US$50–US$150**

➡ Air-con hotel room:
US$12–50

➡ Decent local restaurant
meal: US$5–10

➡ Local tour guide per day:
US$25

**Top End:
More than US$150**

➡ Boutique hotel or resort:
US$50–500

➡ Gastronomic meal with
drinks: US$15–50

➡ 4WD rental per day:
US$60–120

Opening Hours

Bars & Clubs 5pm to 11.30pm
(later in Vientiane)

Government Offices 8am to
noon and 1pm to 5pm Monday
to Friday

Noodle Shops 7am to 1pm

Restaurants 10am to 10pm

Shops 9am to 6pm

Arriving in Laos

Wattay International Airport
Buses and jumbos run to/from
Vientiane's airport. Taxis/mini-
buses cost a flat fare of US$7/8.
The airport is just 6km from the
centre of the city.

**Luang Prabang International
Airport** The airport is about
4km from the old town and
taxis to/from the airport cost a
standardised 50,000K.

**Savannakhet International
Airport** Jumbos cost 30,000K
from the airport, but drivers
may start higher.

Pakse International Airport A
săhm-lór or tuk-tuk to the airport, about 8km north of town,
will cost about 40,000K.

Getting Around

Transport in Laos is generally
very good value, but journeys
can take a lot longer than distances on a map might suggest.

Air Laos has an extensive
domestic flight network and this
can save considerable time on a
short visit.

Boat Rivers are the lifeblood
of Laos, making boat journeys
an important element of the
transport network.

Bus Laos has some smart buses
operating on major routes out
of Vientiane, but venture into
remote areas and vehicles are
as old as the hills.

Car For those with a more
flexible budget, a rented car with
driver is the smoothest way to
cover a lot of ground in a limited
amount of time.

For much more on
getting around,
see p293

PLAN YOUR TRIP NEED TO KNOW

Accommodation

Find more accommodation reviews throughout the On the Road chapters (from p44)

PRICE RANGES

The following price ranges refer to a high-season double room with attached bathroom, unless otherwise stated.

$ less than US$25 (200,000K)

$$ US$25–75 (200,000–600,000K)

$$$ more than US$75 (600,000K)

Accommodation Types

Guesthouses Legally speaking a guesthouse in Laos has fewer than 16 rooms. Facilities are improving across the country, but the most inexpensive places might still have cold-water showers or simple Lao-style bathing.

Homestays Homestays are invariably in rural areas, cost little and provide a chance for travellers to experience local life, Lao style. Food will be simple fare, usually two dishes and sticky rice. Sleeping will probably be under a mosquito net on a mattress on the floor.

Hostels There aren't many hostels in upcountry Laos, but there are plenty in popular tourist locations.

Hotels Small and medium-size hotels oriented towards Asian business and leisure travellers and tour groups exist in the larger cities. This is also where you'll find the few top-end hotels with better decor, more facilities and personalised service.

Resorts The term 'resort' in the Lao context may be used for any accommodation situated outside towns or cities. It does not imply, as it usually does in many other countries, the availability of sports activities, a spa and other similar features.

Best Places to Stay

Best on a Budget

In places such as Don Det in southern Laos or Muang Ngoi Neua in northern Laos there are guesthouses consisting of simple bamboo-thatch huts with shared facilities, costing as little as US$3 a night. Staying in a village home is becoming increasingly popular, costs little and provides a chance for travellers to experience local life, Lao style.

➡ Aham Backpackers Hostel (p65), Luang Prabang

➡ Alisa Guesthouse (p210), Pakse

➡ My Box (p152), Vientiane

➡ PVO Hostel (p152), Vientiane

Best for Families

Vientiane offers some good accommodation with swimming pools, and outside of Luang Prabang's old town are family-oriented eco-resorts, waterfalls, boat trips, farm visits and, for older kids, mountain biking and ziplining. Extra beds are not that common outside of the smarter hotels in the main centres, so prepare to share double or twin beds or plan ahead for rooms with connecting doors or adjacent rooms.

➡ Kong Resort (p176), Vang Vieng

➡ Nakorn Cafe Guest House (p217), Champasak

➡ Thongbay Guesthouse (p61), Luang Prabang

Best for Solo Travelers

There aren't many hostels in upcountry Laos, but there are plenty in popular tourist locations. Violence against women travellers is extremely rare, but if travel-

BARTOSZ HADYNIAK/GETTY IMAGES ©

ling solo, it may be useful to team up with other travellers on long overland journeys into remote areas of the country. If you're feeling lonely, consider a stint at a rural homestay: villages are full of kids, and you'll be billeted with a family.

➡ Fan Dee (p60), Luang Prabang

➡ Hostel Savan Cafe (p199), Savannakhet

➡ Kingfisher Ecolodge (p224), Kiet Ngong

➡ Sailomyen Hostel (p155), Vientiane

Best for Nature Lovers

In Laos, the term 'resort' is often used to describe any accommodation situated outside towns or cities. Alternatively, if you're looking for something more budget friendly, there are an increasing number of homestay options all over the country, particularly in or near National Protected Areas (NPAs).

➡ Nong Kiau Riverside (p100), Nong Khiaw

➡ Spring River Resort (p187), Tham Kong Lor

➡ Tayicseua Guesthouse (p227), Paksong

➡ Vieng Tara Villa (p176), Vang Vieng

Booking

It's worth booking in advance in popular destinations like Luang Prabang and Vientiane during peak-season months of November to February and around Lao New Year in April.

Lonely Planet (lonelyplanet.com/hotels) Find independent reviews, as well as recommendations on the best places to stay – and then book them.

Agoda (www.agoda.com) Asia-based booking website with lots of properties of all prices ranges.

Airbnb (airbnb.com) At press time, there were a couple hundred listings in Laos.

Booking.com (booking.com) Yes, Laos is included here; includes several hostel listings.

Culture Trip (theculturetrip.com) the Laos pages here include accommodation recommendations of just about every price range.

Hostelworld (hostelworld.com) Online portal for budget/backpacker-oriented accommodation with properties in the country's larger cities.

Travelfish (travelfish.org) Independent, reliable reviews of budget accommodation in Southeast Asia, including Laos.

What's New

Laos isn't exactly known for it's breakneck pace of life, but the country is changing. In particular, options for travellers have expanded notably in the last few years, ranging from a handful of new hotels and man-made attractions to the opening of natural areas that were formerly off-limits.

Laos Buffalo Dairy

Try your hand at milking a buffalo on a tour of this responsible farm outside Luang Prabang (p76) before sampling the organic produce on offer such as tasty cheeses, fresh yoghurt and ice-cream in a range of zesty flavours. The buffaloes are mainly rented from local farmers who have never previously used their milk and some of the income goes towards farmer and animal health benefits, as well as free English lessons for local students.

Nahm Dong Park

Explore the verdant landscape of this new park (p75), located 10km southwest of Luang Prabang. The highlights are the treetop walk and ziplines, but you can also explore the forest, plunge into the water-falls and pools here or even dig into some local-style arts and crafts, including including making mulberry paper or a Thai-Leu dreamcatcher or Hmong embroidery. There is also an excellent Lao restaurant and teahouse with a stunning valley view. Overnight camping is possible in the dry season months of November to March.

E-Mountain Biking

Let this outfit (p57) take you on an e-mountain biking adventure in the rice-fields and local ethnic villages (including a couple of river crossings) in the country-side around Luang Prabang. Combine with some kayaking or stand-up paddleboarding (SUP) action on the Nam Khan, and overnight excursions are also offered with camping or a stay at the attached lodge.

LOCAL KNOWLEDGE

WHAT'S HAPPENING IN LAOS

Austin Bush, Lonely Planet writer

Undoubtedly the most newsworthy event in Laos these days is the construction of the vast intra-regional railway linking Kunming in China to Vientiane, begun in late 2016 and scheduled for completion in 2021. Once completed, the railway should have far-reaching consequences for Laos, not least of which is cementing strong economic and political links with China.

The environment remains one of the biggest issues in Laos, and although country's current leaders have made some progressive moves such as a total ban on logging, they continue to capitalise on the country's natural resources in a sometimes tragic effort to become the 'battery of Southeast Asia'. A case in point is the 2018 Attapeu dam collapse, which killed at least 100 people and displaced more than 6000. Laos is thought to have as many as 140 dam projects planned, including nine along the Mekong, the latter a cause of much consternation for downstream neighbours Cambodia and Vietnam who rely on the river for irrigation and fish stocks.

Carpe Diem

Seize the day and enjoy a meal at this impressive gourmet restaurant (p76) set among the natural swimming pools and lower falls of Tat Kuang Si, just outside Luang Prabang. The menu is heavily French accented with frog's legs, filet de boeuf and filet mignon, but there are vegie and kids options as well. It's hard to envisage a more beautifully situated restaurant in all of Laos.

Nong Khiaw Jungle Fly

Discover some natural highs around the karst scenery of Nong Khiaw with a day of adventures on this new zipline (p98), which also includes some 'Tarzan swings,' abseiling and trekking through the bamboo forest. Expect quality equipment and an emphasis on safety from the professional English-speaking guides.

Homestays in Hin Namno NPA

Recently opened to tourism is this immersive cultural experience in Central Laos, which offers the chance to see some of the more remote and rugged parts of Hin Namno NPA. The surrounding area is stunning, and hikes include activities such as viewing wildlife and visiting waterfalls, underwater rivers and caves, including one that allegedly housed 3000 Viet Cong soldiers in the 1970s. Your host is the end-of-the-road village of Ban Thongxam, home to 379 Yoy people.

Cycling around Tham Kong Lor

An NGO-supported community initiative has set up bike rental on the Natane (p186) side of Tham Kong Lor offering a fun way to explore some absolutely beautiful countryside. Homestay accommodation is available in the village.

Southern Ziplines

The new zipline (p245) – located at Don Khon, part of Si Phan Don – doesn't just cross the Mekong, it crosses the raging torrent of the Tat Somphamit waterfall. Or zip across the valley of the amazing twin Tat Fan waterfall at a height of 250m. The company also runs kayaking dolphin-watching tours in the high season.

LISTEN, WATCH AND FOLLOW

@everydaylaos People-centred Instagram feed.

Lao National Radio (lnr.org.la) Government-controlled radio broadcasts.

Lao Star (laostartv.la) The country's entertainment-heavy television station.

New Mandala (newmandala.org) Deep-dive stories on Southeast Asian current events, including Laos.

Vientiane Times (vientianetimes.org.la) Government mouthpiece, but one of few sources of information on Laos in English.

FAST FACTS

Food trend Thai and Vietnamese junk food

Ethnic groups officially recognized by government 49

Average annual GDP growth over past decade 7.5% (highest in the world)

Pop 7.2 million

≈25 people per sq km

Newly Discovered Waterfalls

In Attapeu Province, Tat Sae Pha waterfall (p233) is being pushed as the one of the most beautiful waterfalls in Laos, but it is only accessible by motorbike or 4WD. The nearby Tat Sae Pong Lai waterfall is no less spectacular. A guesthouse and restaurant had been built here and access roads improved in preparation for opening it up to tourism, but the 2018 Attapeu Dam collapse effectively washed away everything that had been built and put the project back to square one. At the time of research rebuilding efforts were underway.

Scoot Flights to Singapore

Both Luang Prabang and Vientiane are now connected directly to Singapore via Scoot (www.flyscoot.com), one of the region's leading budget airlines.

If You Like...

Outdoor Activities

Vang Vieng An adventure playground for adrenaline activities such as river tubing, kayaking, caving, climbing and cycling. (p171)

Luang Prabang It's not all about culture here, with mountain biking, trekking, kayaking, ziplining and waterfalls all on tap in the surrounding countryside. (p53)

Khammuan Province The karst limestone peaks are home to deep caves and soaring overhangs. (p183)

Bolaven Plateau Impressive waterfalls, motorcycle trips and the Treetop Explorer zipline adventure. (p225)

Luang Namtha Gateway to northwest adventures such as trekking, cycling, kayaking and, further down the jungle trail, the Gibbon Experience. (p116)

Phongsali Province Rugged yet rewarding hill-tribe country in one of the most authentic trekking destinations in the region. (p105)

Culinary Experiences

Vientiane The culinary capital of the country, with Lao home cooking, characterful cafes and Med-inspired fusion cuisine. (p141)

Luang Prabang Dine on the Mekong side of the peninsula for sunsets or on the Nam Khan (Khan River) for sophisticated set menus. (p45)

Luang Namtha Luang Namtha has several excellent restaurants that specialise in ethnic minority cuisine. (p116)

Savannakhet Relatively unknown but up-and-coming destination for Lao food, especially for street food at breakfast and lunch. (p200)

Tamarind Learn the art of Lao cuisine in Luang Prabang at the atmospheric lakeside pavilion of Tamarind restaurant. (p55)

River Trips

Huay Xai to Luang Prabang One of the more conveniently accessed river trips in Laos, with an overnight stop at the dramatically situated town of Pak Beng. (p72)

Si Phan Don With a name that means 'Four Thousand Islands', it's not surprising that boat trips feature strongly in this beautiful southern stretch of the Mekong in Laos. (p237)

Tham Kong Lor A river trip with a difference, passing through a 7km cave that is straight out of Greek mythology. (p183)

Vang Vieng River tubing on the Nam Song is a young backpacker rite of passage, but there are kayaking trips here too. (p170)

Off the Beaten Track

Vieng Xai Caves These underground caves were the Pathet Lao's base during the US bombing campaign. (p95)

Phongsali Province The remote far north of Laos is the location for some of the most authentic hill-tribe village treks in the country. (p105)

Khammuan Province This rugged central province is peppered with karst limestone peaks and rewards two-wheeled adventurers prepared to head off-piste on the Loop. (p190)

Nam Nern Night Safari A night-time boat tour through Nam Et/Phou Louey National Park spotlighting for wildlife and tigers – fingers crossed! (p96)

Old Temples

Luang Prabang The royal city is home to more than 30 gilded wats, including the soaring roofs of Wat Xieng Thong. (p45)

Wat Phu Champasak The ancient Khmers once held sway over much of the Mekong region and Wat Phu was one of their hilltop temples. (p219)

Vientiane The Lao capital is home to some fine temples, including Pha That Luang, the golden stupa that is the symbol of a nation, and Wat Si Saket,

Top: Tat Fan waterfalls (p225), Bolaven Plateau

Bottom: Produce at a market in Luang Prabang (p44)

which houses thousands of revered Buddha images. (p141)

That Ing Hang Built in the mid-16th century, this elegant *thâat* is one of the holiest religious structures in southern Laos. (p198)

Memorable Markets

Handicraft Night Market Night markets, day markets; they come in every flavour in Luang Prabang, including the handicraft night market and an affordable food market. (p71)

Morning Market This local market in the back alleys of old town Luang Prabang is one of the most vibrant in the country in the first few hours after dawn. (p66)

Sam Neua's Main Market This huge market has some interesting textiles from this remote region, as well as proving a crossroads for imported goods from China and Vietnam. (p91)

Talat Dao Heuang The largest market in Laos is packed to the gunnels with goods including silk textiles and local handicrafts. (p207)

Wellness Centres

Luang Prabang The spiritual home of wellness in Laos, there are lots of impressive spas at the leading hotels and resorts in town. (p45)

Vientiane The capital is home to some sumptuous spas, some international standard fitness centres and a yoga school. (p141)

Champasak Home to the eponymous Champasak Spa which helps create a sustainable living for young women in this small town. (p216)

Nong Khiaw Get in shape with a yoga session at Mandala Ou Spa or a scrub at Sabai Sabai Spa. (p97)

Month by Month

January

This is peak tourist season in much of Laos. It's a pleasantly chilled time to be in the main centres and downright cold at higher altitudes in the north.

⭐ International New Year

A public holiday in sync with embassy and aid workers resident in Laos, it has been adopted as an excuse to celebrate among the younger population in urban areas.

⭐ Vietnamese Tet & Chinese New Year

Celebrated in Vientiane, Pakse and Savannakhet with parties, fireworks and visits to Vietnamese and Chinese temples. Chinese- and Vietnamese-run businesses usually close for several days.

⭐ Bun Khun Khao

The annual harvest festival takes place in mid-January and sees local villagers perform ceremonies offering thanks to the land spirits for their crops.

February

The weather is usually still relatively cool and dry at this time and it can even snow at altitude in places like Phongsali. Chinese and Vietnamese New Year often fall this month.

⭐ Makha Busa

Also known as Magha Puja or Bun Khao Chi, this full-moon festival commemorates a speech given by Buddha to 1250 enlightened monks. Chanting and offerings mark the festival, and celebrations are most fervent in Vientiane and at Wat Phu Champasak. (p222)

March

Things are starting to warm up and this can be a good time to step up to the higher altitudes of Xieng Khuang, Sam Neua and Phongsali.

⭐ Bun Pha Wet

This is a temple-centred festival in which the Jataka (birth tale) of Prince Vessantara, the Buddha's penultimate life, is recited. This is also a favoured time for Lao males to be ordained into the monkhood.

April

April is the hottest month of the year when the thermometer hits 40°C. It is also the month to celebrate the Lao new year, the biggest festival in the calendar.

⭐ Bun Pi Mai

Lao new year is the big one. Houses are cleaned and Buddha images are washed with lustral water. Locals soak one another (and tourists) with water. Markets, shops and restaurants close down for a public holiday from 14–16 April.

May

Events go off with a bang this month, as rockets are fired into the sky. 'Green' (low) season kicks in and prices drop accordingly. Like April, this can be one of the hottest months in the calendar.

 Visakha Busa

Visakha Busa (also known as Visakha Puja) falls on the 15th day of the sixth lunar month: the day of the Buddha's birth, enlightenment and *parinibbana* (passing away). Countrywide celebrations are centred on the wat, with candlelit processions by night.

Bun Bang Fai

The Rocket Festival is a pre-Buddhist rain ceremony celebrated alongside Visakha Busa. It can be one of the wildest festivals in the country, with music, dance and processions all culminating in the firing of bamboo rockets into the sky.

July

The wet season is starting to kick in with some heavy rains, but it only pours for a short time towards the end of each day, making this a lush time to explore.

Bun Khao Phansa

Also known as Khao Watsa, this full-moon festival is the beginning of the traditional three-month 'rains retreat', during which Buddhist monks are expected to base themselves in a single monastery. Many young men enter the monkhood temporarily at this time.

August

Summer holidays in Europe see a mini peak during the off season, which

brings French, Italian and Spanish tourists, as well as university students to the country. The landscapes are dazzling green thanks to the fertile rice fields.

Haw Khao Padap Din

This sombre full-moon festival sees the living pay respect to the dead. Many cremations take place – bones being exhumed for the purpose – and gifts are presented to the Buddhist order (Sangha) so monks will chant on behalf of the deceased.

October

It is all about river action this month. Witness the memorable sight of floating candles drifting down the river in communities across the country before a burst of adrenaline-fuelled dragon boat racing in major towns.

Bun Awk Phansa

At the end of the three-month rains retreat, monks are presented with robes and alms bowls. The eve is celebrated with the release of small banana-leaf boats carrying candles and incense in a ceremony called Van Loi Heua Fai.

Bun Nam

In many river towns, including Vientiane and Luang Prabang, boat races are held the day after Awk Phansa. In smaller towns races are postponed until National Day (2 December) so residents aren't saddled with two costly festivals in two months. (p151)

November

Peak season begins in earnest thanks to the monsoon season drawing to an end and temperatures becoming pleasant. With the surge in visitor numbers, accommodation prices rise once more.

Bun Pha That Luang

The That Luang Festival, centred around Pha That Luang in Vientiane, lasts a week and includes fireworks, music and drinking. Hundreds of monks receive alms and floral offerings and the festival ends with a candlelit procession circling That Luang. (p151)

December

Christmas may not be a big Lao festival, but it certainly sees a lot of foreign visitors arrive in the country. Book ahead and be prepared to pay top dollar during festive week.

Lao National Day

This public holiday on 2 December celebrates the 1975 victory over the monarchy with parades and speeches. Lao national and Communist hammer-and-sickle flags are flown.

Luang Prabang Film Festival

This festival in early December sees free screenings at several venues around town. The focus is on the blossoming work of Southeast Asian production houses and all films have English subtitles. (p59)

Itineraries

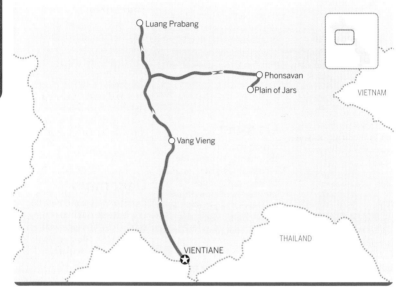

 A Week in Laos

Start out your classic Laos adventure in **Vientiane**, the atmospheric Lao capital. There are few must-see sights beyond a handful of temples, but the Mekong riverside setting is dramatic and there are some excellent cafes, restaurants and bars to enjoy, plus some of the best shopping in the country.

Head north to **Vang Vieng**. Once a sort of backpacker Xanadu where anything goes, it has reinvented itself as the adventure centre of Laos with caving, rock climbing, ziplining, kayaking, mountain biking and trekking, not forgetting the infamous river tubing that put this place on the map.

Continue north on Rte 13, making a side trip to **Phonsavan**, gateway to the **Plain of Jars** and its mysterious vessels, one of the more popular destinations in Laos.

The highlight of this trip is **Luang Prabang**, the historic capital of Lan Xang and a worthy Unesco World Heritage Site. Plan a few days here to soak up the timeless atmosphere of the old town, including the *tak bat* (dawn call to alms) for the city's many monks. Save some time for outdoor adventures, with waterfalls, mountain-bike trails, kayaking trips and jungle treks all on offer.

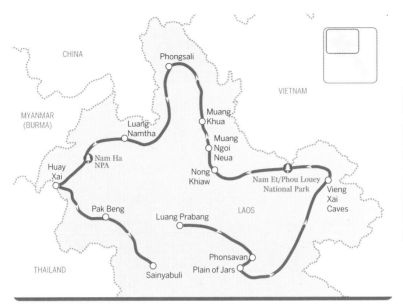

 ## Hit the North

Northern Laos is one of the most popular regions of the country for adventure activities, coupled with an authentic dose of ethnic-minority lifestyles. Right at the heart of the region lies Luang Prabang, the perfect place to start or finish a road trip through the remote north.

Lovely **Luang Prabang** is a destination in itself. Spend your time exploring the old town and its myriad temples, traditional buildings and galleries, cafes and shops.

Head southeast from Luang Prabang to **Phonsavan**, the base from which to see the impressive **Plain of Jars**. It is then time to leave the tourist trail and head to the **Vieng Xai Caves**. The setting is spectacular amid the karst caves and the historic audio tour is one of the most compelling experiences in Laos.

Swinging west, head to the remote protected area of **Nam Et/Phou Louey National Park** for a night-time wildlife-watching safari. Continue to **Nong Khiaw**, a beautiful village on the banks of the Nam Ou (Ou River) with striking limestone crags looming all around. This is the embarkation point for an adventurous trip to Phongsali Province, including beautiful boat trips to the small villages of **Muang Ngoi Neua** and **Muang Khua** en route. **Phongsali** is considered the most authentic trekking destination in Laos and it is possible to experience homestays with Akha villagers.

Head on to **Luang Namtha**, a friendly base for some northwesterly adventures. Trek into the **Nam Ha NPA** or try a cycling or kayaking trip in the countryside beyond.

From Luang Namtha head down to **Huay Xai**, a Mekong River border town and gateway to the Gibbon Experience. If time is tight, bail out here, but it is better to continue the loop back to Luang Prabang by river. The two-day boat trip from Huay Xai to Luang Prabang via **Pak Beng** is one of the most conveniently accessible river trips in the country.

Or take just a one-day boat trip to Pak Beng and then leave the river behind to head to **Sainyabuli** and the superb Elephant Conservation Center on the Nam Tien lake. This can also be visited out of Luang Prabang.

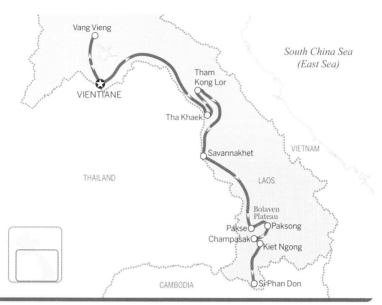

2 WEEKS Central & Southern Laos

This classic southern route takes you through the heartland of lowland Lao culture, a world of broad river plains planted with rice and shaded by wooden houses on stilts.

Start in **Vientiane**, the country's capital, and soak up the sights, shopping, cuisine and nightlife, as things get quieter from here. Make a side trip to the backpacker mecca of **Vang Vieng**, surrounded by craggy, cave-studded limestone peaks.

Head south to **Tha Khaek**, the archetypal sleepy town on the Mekong, and then east on Rte 12 to explore the caves of the Khammuan limestone area, where some of the best rock climbing in the country is on offer. Alternatively, go full tilt and explore the Loop by motorcycle all the way around, stopping at the incredible river cave of **Tham Kong Lor**.

Continue south to **Savannakhet** for a taste of how Vientiane looked before it received a makeover from the Lao government and international aid money. Explore the somnolent streets of old French architecture and and dip into virtually the entire spectrum of Lao cuisine at decades-old stalls.

Roll on southward to **Pakse**, gateway to the **Bolaven Plateau**, location of many impressive waterfalls, including Tat Fan, where you can try an adrenaline-fuelled zipline adventure 300m above the treetops. Pass through the coffee capital of **Paksong** before heading to beautiful Tat Lo, a great place to hang out and swim in the falls, or do some treks through local villages.

Champasak town is a more relaxed alternative to Pakse and is the base for seeing Laos' most important archaeological site, Wat Phu Champasak, an Angkor-style temple ruin spread across the slopes of sacred Phu Pasak.

Continuing on, consider stopping at the village of **Kiet Ngong** to try bird-spotting in the nearby forest and wetlands. This is a logical stop on the route south to **Si Phan Don** (Four Thousand Islands), an archipelago of idyllic river islands where the farming and fishing life have not changed much for a century or more. Swing in a hammock and relax for a while, but be sure to take in the thundering rapids of Tat Somphamit and the grandest of the Mekong's waterfalls, Khon Phapheng. From here, move on to Cambodia or head to Thailand via Pakse and Chong Mek.

Cycling near Vang Vieng (p170)

Plan Your Trip

Outdoor Adventures

Dense jungles, brooding mountains, endless waterways, towering cliffs and hairpin bends: the potential for adrenaline-fuelled adventures in Laos is limitless. Whether you prefer to scale the heights of lofty peaks or plumb the darkness of extensive caves, Laos will deliver something special.

PLAN YOUR TRIP OUTDOOR ADVENTURES

When to Go
November to February

This is the cool, dry season and considered the best time for activities like trekking, cycling and motorbiking. Trekking in higher altitude places like Phongsali may be better in spring or autumn, as the winter can be very cold at 1500m, but it is a great time of year to trek in central and southern Laos.

March to May

Temperatures regularly hit 40°C during the hot season. Common sense dictates that this is a good time to go underground and do some cave exploring around Vang Vieng or Tha Khaek or cool off with some kayaking on the Nam Ou (Ou River) or tubing on the Nam Song (Song River).

June to October

The wet season is the time for water-based activities such as rafting or kayaking, as even the smaller rivers have a bit more volume at this time of year. The waterfalls are at their grandest at this time and some may be more difficult to access.

transport, accommodation and park fees, start at about US$25 per person per day for larger groups. For more specialised long treks into remote areas, prices can run into several hundred dollars. In most cases you can trek with as few as two people, with per-person costs falling with larger groups.

Where to Go

Nam Ha NPA (p117) Luang Namtha has developed an award-winning ecotourism project for visits to local ethnic-minority villages in the national park.

Phongsali Province (p105) Explore fascinating hill-tribe terrain in one of the most authentic trekking destinations in the region. Mountainous and chilly in winter, multiday treks include traditional homestays with the local Akha people.

Phu Hin Bun NPA (p183) A karst of thousands, this national park offers sublime scenery with towering limestone peaks and snaking rivers.

Se Pian NPA (p224) Community-run trekking trips provide easy access to some deep forest.

Hin Namno NPA (p194) One of the most rugged protected areas in Laos has opened its doors to visitors.

Dong Phu Vieng NPA (p204) Cut directly through one of Laos' more diverse natural areas and stay at remote Katang villages.

Trekking

Trekking in Laos is all about exploring the National Protected Areas (NPAs) and visiting the colourful ethnic-minority villages, many of which host overnight trekking groups. Anything is possible, from half-day hikes to week-long expeditions that include cycling and kayaking. Most treks have both a cultural and an environmental focus, with trekkers sleeping in village homestays and money going directly to some of the poorest communities in the country. There are now a dozen or more areas you can choose from. Less strenuous walks include jungle hikes to pristine waterfalls and village walks in remote areas. The scenery is often breathtaking, featuring plunging highland valleys, tiers of rice paddies and soaring limestone mountains.

Treks are mostly run by small local tour operators and have English-speaking guides. Prices, including all food, guides,

Cycling

Laos is slowly but steadily establishing itself as a cycling destination. For hard-core cyclists, the mountains of northern Laos are the ultimate destination. For those who like a gentler workout, meandering along Mekong villages is memorable, particularly in southern Laos around Si Phan Don.

In most places that see a decent number of tourists, simple single-speed bicycles can be hired for around 10,000K per day. Better mountain bikes will cost from 40,000K to 80,000K per day or US$5 to US$10. Serious tourers should bring their own bicycle. The choice in Laos is fairly limited compared with neighbouring Thailand or Cambodia.

Several tour agencies and guesthouses offer mountain-biking tours, ranging in duration from a few hours to several weeks.

Where to Go

Luang Namtha (p116) Cycle through ethnic-minority villages.

Luang Prabang (p45) Biking is a great way to get around the old town or explore some of the surrounding countryside.

Si Phan Don (p237) Cycle past peaceful rice paddies and raging waterfalls.

Udomxai (p111) Three-day cycle challenge to Chom Ong Caves.

Pakse (p207) Take a serene one-day bike trip along the Mekong to Don Kho island.

Vientiane (p150) Not to be overlooked, the capital is a great city for cycling: flat, compact and with relatively light traffic.

Motorbiking

For those with a thirst for adventure, motorbike trips into remote areas of Laos are unforgettable. The mobility of two wheels is unrivalled. Motorbikes can traverse trails that even the hardiest 4WD cannot follow. It puts you closer to the countryside – its smells, people and scenery – compared with getting around by car or bus. Just remember to watch the road when the scenery is sublime. Motorbiking is still the mode of transport for many Lao residents, so you'll find repair shops everywhere. If you're not confident riding a motorbike, it's comparatively cheap to hire someone to ride it for you. For those seeking true adventure there is no better way to go.

In addition, public transport is fairly undeveloped in some regions, with your only choices being to either go by motorbike or hire a car or tuk-tuk.

Where to Go

The Loop (p190) Tame the back roads of uncharted central Laos in this motorbike circuit out of Tha Khaek.

Bolaven Plateau (p225) Explore off-the-beaten-path places in southern Laos, taking in some great waterfalls and coffee plantations.

West Vang Vieng (p177) Delve deep into the limestone karsts that pepper the west bank of the Nam Song with this scenically stunning motorbike ride.

Boat Trips, Kayaking & Tubing

With the Mekong cutting a swathe through the heart of the country, it's hardly surprising to find that boat trips are a major drawcard here. There are also opportunities to explore small jungled tributaries leading to remote minority villages.

Kayaking has exploded in popularity in Laos in the past few years, particularly around Luang Prabang, Nong Khiaw, Vang Vieng and Si Phan Don; all popular destinations for a spot of paddling. Kayaking trips start from around US$25 per person and are often combined with cycling.

Tubing down the river has long been a popular activity in Vang Vieng and is now a more sedate affair with the clampdown on riverside bars, rope swings and aerial runways.

SAFETY FOR HIKERS

➡ Don't stray from established paths, as there is unexploded ordnance (UXO) in many parts of the country.

➡ Hire a local guide; they're inexpensive, speak the language and understand indigenous culture. What's more, you'll be giving back to the local community.

➡ Dogs can be aggressive; a stout stick can come in handy.

➡ Invest in a pair of boots with ankle support.

➡ Carry a mosquito net if trekking in malarial zones of the region.

➡ Leeches can be a problem once the rains kick in. Wear quality socks and repellent for protection.

➡ Carry water-purification tablets if you have a weak constitution.

➡ Take along some snack bars or energy snacks to avoid getting riced out on longer treks.

Rock climbing near Tha Khaek (p188)

Where to Go

Huay Xai to Luang Prabang (p126) Down the mighty Mekong from the Golden Triangle via Pak Beng to the old royal capital of Laos.

Nong Khiaw to Muang Ngoi Neua (p97) A short but very sweet ride passing through a striking landscape of karst limestone.

Si Phan Don (p237) A kayak trip or boat is the only way to see the Four Thousand Islands, where the Mekong spreads its girth to around 13km.

Tham Kong Lor (p183) Cruise through this otherworldly 7km cave system – the Lao answer to the River Styx.

Vang Vieng (p170) Go with the flow on the Nam Song in the tubing capital of Laos.

Ziplining

Ziplining has quite literally taken off in Laos. The Gibbon Experience (p130) in Nam Kan NPA pioneered the use of ziplines to glide through the forest where the gibbons roam. Now, cords are going up at an astounding pace in forests across the country.

Ecotourism pioneer Green Discovery (p209) offers a zipline experience for thrill-seekers in southern Laos. Its Tree Top Explorer tour is an exciting network of vertiginous ziplines passing over the semi-evergreen canopy of the south's Dong Hua Sao NPA. Green Discovery is also building a new zipline over the karst peak of Phou Phaman in Khammuan Province.

Vang Vieng, Nong Khiaw and Udomxai have also all emerged as zipline centres, with several companies offering aerial adventures through jaw-dropping mountainous terrain.

And not to be outdone, southern Laos has added two exciting new ziplines to its repertoire at Tad Fane Resort (p227) and Tat Somphamit (p241).

Where to Go

Gibbon Experience (p130) Fly like a gibbon near Huay Xai with Laos' ziplining pioneer.

Green Jungle Park (p76) Zip through a verdant forest on the outskirts of Luang Prabang.

Nong Khiaw Jungle Fly (p98) Glide through the bamboo forests or do the canopy walks or 'Tarzan swings' near Nong Khiaw.

A bear at the Tat Kuang Si Bear Rescue Centre (p76)

Where to Go

Vang Vieng (p171) More than 200 rock-climbing routes – many of them bolted – up the limestone cliffs, plus some impressive caves to explore.

Vieng Xai Caves (p95) Underground base and wartime capital of the Pathet Lao, these caves are set beneath stunning limestone rock formations.

Tham Kong Lor (p183) This river cave is not for the faint-hearted, but offers one of the most memorable underground experiences in Laos.

Tham Lot Se Bang Fai (p194) The most impressive of Khammuan's cave systems; a river plunges 6.5km through a limestone mountain and can only be explored between January and March.

Green Climbers Home (p190) Set in soaring karst country outside Tha Khaek, this camp offers all levels of climbs.

Animal Encounters

While wildlife-spotting may not be quite as straightforward as on the Serengeti, it's still possible to have some memorable encounters in Laos.

Where to Go

Elephant Conservation Center (p136) Learn about the life of the Lao elephant at this superb conservation centre near Sainyabuli.

Si Phan Don (p237) The freshwater Irrawaddy dolphin is one of the rarest mammals on earth, with fewer than 100 inhabiting stretches of the Mekong, and only three left in this region. View them in their natural habitat off the shore of Don Khon in southern Laos.

Nam Nern Night Safari (p96) The Nam Et/Phou Louey National Park is the last official home of tigers in Laos, and this exciting night trip by boat uses torchlight to scope out forest animals coming to the river to drink.

Tat Kuang Si Bear Rescue Centre (p76) Tat Kuang Si is a must-visit destination thanks to its iconic menthol-blue waters, plus the chance to see Asiatic Wild Moon bears saved from the wildlife trade.

Nakai–Nam Theun National Park (p195) This park is particularly good for wildlife-watching, and activities such as night viewing and camera traps are being developed.

Nam Kat Yorla Pa (p113) Pair ziplining with rock climbing at this forest resort near Udomxai.

Vang Vieng Challenge (p174) Unleash your inner child on a gruelling obstacle course by Vang Vieng.

Mekong Fly (p245) Soar across the raging rapids of Tat Somphamit.

Tad Fane Zipline (p226) Test your nerves on Laos' highest zipline.

Rock Climbing & Caving

When it comes to organised climbing, Vang Vieng and Tha Khaek have some of the best climbing in Southeast Asia, along with excellent instructors and safe equipment. Climbing costs from about US$25 per person in a group of four and rises for more specialised climbs or for instruction.

Real caving of the spelunker variety is not really on offer unless undertaking a professional expedition. However, there are many extensive cave systems that are open to visitors.

Lát

Eat & Drink Like a Local

Lao food doesn't have the high profile, or indeed the variety and depth, of the more famous cuisines of neighbouring China, Thailand and Vietnam. However, it has influenced its neighbours, and some dishes that you may have thought of as Thai, such as *sôm dam,* are actually Lao in origin.

The Year in Food

Traditionally the Lao food year revolved around the rainy season, when farmers make the most of the monsoon's abundant waters to plant rice. In restaurants, however, there is little seasonal variation. Fish are abundant year-round.

Rainy season (July–October)

Rice-planting time. The first rains bring out *maang môw* (flying termite larvae), which swarm out of the ground and are collected to be cooked up in omelettes. Bullfrogs and other kinds of frogs will also turn up in markets.

Cool season (November–February)

Rice is harvested, and if you're lucky you may find some *kòw môw* (green, unripe rice), which is roasted with coconut milk into a delicious sweet. Watermelons and papayas are in season.

Hot season (March–June)

This is when many of Laos' distinctive fruits ripen, with *mahk móoang* (mangoes) and *mahk mêe* (jackfruit)in abundance. *Mahk tooa-lêean* (durians) can also be found.

Food Experiences

Meals of a Lifetime

Doi Ka Noi (p161) Vientiane spot with a changing menu of dishes ranging from Lao standards to regional specialities.

Coco Home Bar & Restaurant (p101) Leafy riverside oasis in Nong Khiaw, with typical local dishes as well as duck in orange sauce.

Tamarind (p68) 'Mod Lao' cuisine with an à la carte menu in Luang Prabang.

Dyen Sabai (p68) One of Luang Prabang's top destinations for fabulous Lao food.

Khambang Lao Food Restaurant (p160) This long-standing Vientiane restaurant is the ideal introduction to Lao food.

Ping Kai Napong (p192) Specialises in grilled chicken, but also does a wide range of Lao cuisine, in Tha Khaek.

Daolin Restaurant (p211) Popular and lively restaurant with great food and service in downtown Pakse.

Dare to Try

Numerous frogs and insects, such as crickets and red ants' eggs are readily seen at markets, although less common in restaurants. One insect dish that is surprisingly tasty is giant water bug chilli paste *(jaaou mâang dah)*. The male of the species has an aromatic fragrance that adds a touch of sweetness to a chilli paste. You may end up trying it without knowing, as it's often used in chilli sauces.

Local Specialities

Láhp is the most distinctively Lao dish, a delicious spicy salad made from minced beef, pork, duck, fish or chicken. Another famous Lao speciality is *đạm màhk hung* (known as *sôm dam* in Thailand); a salad of shredded green papaya mixed with garlic, lime juice, fish sauce, land crab or dried shrimp and, of course, chillies by the handful.

Noodles

In villages and urban areas, noodles are more commonly found. The standard Lao breakfast is *fĕr* (rice noodles), usually served floating in a broth with vegetables and a meat of your choice. Other popular noodle dishes are *kòw Þûn* (thin rice noodles), generally eaten with a spicy curry-like broth or a clear pork broth, and *kòw Þeeak sèn,* sometimes just called *kòw Þeeak* (thick rice- and tapioca-flour noodles), served in a slightly viscous broth with crispy-fried pork belly or chicken. *Mee* (traditional Chinese egg noodles) is another favourite, as is the Vietnamese *băn kŭan* (freshly steamed rice noodles), filled with minced pork, mushrooms and carrots.

Sticky Rice

Laos runs on sticky rice, and Lao people proudly refer to themselves as *lòok kòw něeo* (sticky rice children). Especially in rural areas, sticky rice forms the basis to just about every meal.

Baguettes

In main centres, French-style baguettes (*kòw jee*) are a popular breakfast food. Sometimes they're eaten with condensed milk, or with kai (eggs) in a sandwich that also contains Lao-style pâté and vegetables.

Drinks

Beerlao remains a firm favourite with 90% of the nation. It's growing in stature on the international scene and is very popular with travellers. Officially illegal *lòw-lów* (Lao liquor or rice whisky) is a popular drink among lowland Lao.

Drinking water is simply called *nâm deum*, whether it's boiled or filtered. All water offered to customers in restaurants or hotels will be purified, and purified water is sold everywhere. Check that the ice in any drink originated from purified water.

Chinese-style green tea is the usual ingredient in *nâm sáh* or *sáh lôw*, the weak, refreshing tea traditionally served free in restaurants. For Lipton-style tea, ask for *sáh hôrn* (hot tea).

A LAO MEAL

A typical Lao meal consists of sticky rice, something grilled, such as fish or chicken, some steamed vegetables and a chilli paste. Sometimes there is also a soup (*òrm*), which is eaten throughout the meal. Take a small amount of rice and, using one hand, work it into a bite-sized ball before dipping it into the food. Many restaurants sell set meals, which do not usually have a 'sweets' course. These are usually bought in markets and eaten as snacks.

Baguettes

Vegetarian & Vegan Food

Almost all Lao dishes contain some sort of animal product, be it fish sauce, shrimp paste or lard. There are very few dedicated vegetarian or vegan restaurants in Laos, but traveller-oriented restaurants and cafes usually have some vegetarian dishes available. The best all-round phrase to learn is 'I only eat vegetables' or '*kòy gin ðaa pak*' in Lao.

Where to Eat

Laos has a great range of dining options in the cities, but the choice dries up quickly in remote areas.

Restaurants These range from local hole-in-the-wall spots and street markets to sophisticated international bistros. Most cuisines are covered in Vientiane and Luang Prabang.

kòw pûn (p35)

Cafes A legacy of the French, Laos has a sophisticated coffee culture. The best cafes are found in Luang Prabang and Vientiane, but larger towns have good options too.

Beer gardens A lot of larger restaurants in provincial Laos double as beer gardens by night. Beware there may be karaoke involved.

Courses & Tours

Bamboo Tree Cooking Class (p57) Based in Luang Prabang, Linda teaches how to make a half dozen typical Lao dishes.

Forest Retreat Laos (p119) Cooking classes are offered among other activities at this Luang Namtha ecotourism outfit.

Gecko Tours & Cooking Class (p103) Muang Ngoi Neua outfit offering cooking classes that include working with the restaurant's organic garden.

Lao Experiences (p150) Cooking classes held in the owner's home in Vientiane.

Mr Vieng Coffee & Homestay (p229) Fun and friendly homestay on a coffee plantation near Tat Lo.

Mystic Mountain Coffee (p227) Simple lodgings near Paksong, with a focus on tours of the coffee plantation.

Tamarind (p55) Join a one-day cooking course at this top-notch outfit in Luang Prabang.

Tang Kin (p150) Nok and her mother offer cooking classes at their home-based school in Vientiane.

Plan Your Trip
Family Travel

Travelling with children in Laos can be a lot of fun as long as you come prepared with the right attitude. The Lao people adore children and will shower attention on your offspring, who will find playmates and a temporary nanny service at practically every stop.

Keeping Costs Down

Accommodation

Southeast Asians tend to travel in groups, so hotels and even guesthouses will often have a family room or two, equipped with several beds. And although they're not standard in Laos, larger hotels might be able to provide a cot for kids, sparing you the expense of paying for another room.

Activities

Water-based activities, in particular, are free or very cheap in Laos, so take advantage of the country's abundance of rivers, waterfalls and swimming pools. Some of the country's ziplines offer reduced rates for kids. Consider boat trips as a way to double down on transport and fun.

Eating

Although kids might find some of the food in Laos challenging, the ubiquitous sticky rice and fruit are easy, delicious, nutritious and cheap. There's an entire repertoire of cheap, non-spicy menu items – bland soups, mild stir-frys – meant for kids, and most Lao people will suggest these dishes by default.

Children Will Love...

Adventures

Tham Kong Lor, Ban Kong Lo (p183) A family-friendly journey boat trip to the centre of the earth through this 7km river cave system.

Vang Vieng (p11) A fun, easy kayak or tube down the Nam Song River taking in the stunning karst scenery along the way.

Nong Khiaw Jungle Fly, Nong Khiaw (p98) Kids will love the 'Tarzan swings' and gliding over the bamboo forests around Nong Khiaw.

Gibbon Experience, Huay Xai (p130) This iconic family-friendly zipline adventure includes a night in a treehouse in a protected area.

Animal Encounters

Tat Kuang Si Bear Rescue Centre, Luang Prabang (p76) The whole family can meet Sun and Moon Bears in this wildlife protection centre at the beautiful Kuang Si Falls.

Laos Buffalo Dairy, Luang Prabang (p76) Kids can learn to milk a buffalo, help feed and wash buffaloes and meet the resident rabbits at this working farm.

Elephant Conservation Center, Sainyabuli (p136) Stay overnight at the leading elephant conservation centre in Laos where kids can learn all about these noble creatures.

Waterfalls

Tat Kuang Si, Luang Prabang (p76) The most iconic (and photographed) waterfall in Laos thanks to its turquoise waters with plenty of small swimming holes that are perfect for kids.

Nahm Dong Park, Luang Prabang (p75) This spectacular series of waterfalls in the jungle is also a base for lots of child-friendly activities like mulberry paper-making and dream catcher classes.

Khon Phapheng, Si Phan Don (p241) The largest waterfall in Southeast Asia should impress the kids providing you haven't already visited Victoria, Iguazu or Niagara falls.

Tat Somphamit, Si Phan Don (p241) Older kids can literally fly over the Mekong on this zipline that crosses a Mekong waterfall.

Tat Lo, Bolaven Plateau (p229) A popular waterfall with some family-friendly swimming holes under the falls.

Food

Băn Kŭan Freshly steamed rice noodles, filled with minced pork, mushrooms and carrots is probably one of the most child-friendly noodle dishes in Laos.

Kòw Jee French-style baguettes are eaten with condensed milk, or eggs in a sandwich – perfect for picky eaters.

Sticky Rice Everybody loves this Lao staple.

Fruit Bananas, papayas, mangoes, pineapples... You probably won't find it a challenge to get your kids to indulge in Laos' amazing buffet of fruit.

Region by Region

Luang Prabang

Rural-feeling bungalows, such as those at Thongbay Guesthouse (p61), are great for kids. Beyond the beautiful old town are family-oriented eco-resorts.

Children of all ages will love Tat Kuang Si (p76) and Tat Sae (p75) for the natural swimming pools and ziplines; the former also offers a fascinating glimpse of Asiatic Wild Moon bears in their impressive sanctuary (p76), as well as the Kuang Si Butterfly Park (p75). Green Jungle Park (p76) will have adventurous kids flying through the forest like monkeys on ziplines and rope courses. Boat trips on the Mekong, such as to Pak Ou Caves (p74), are a nice diversion for budding explorers.

Older children will enjoy the activities on offer around town like cycling or kayaking. The younger ones can spend some

time on the playground and ziplines at the ABC School (p54).

Northern Laos

Nong Khiaw is popular thanks to its striking scenery and close proximity to Luang Prabang. Kids will love the activities at Nong Khiaw Jungle Fly (p98), while the boat journey from Huay Xai to Luang Prabang is a relaxing option.

Vientiane, Vang Vieng & Around

Small by the standards of Asian megacities, Vientiane is not such a daunting prospect for families. Many midrange hotels now have swimming pools and there is even the Ocean Park (p156) water park in town. Common Grounds (p160), with its indoor play room and kid-friendly menu, is one of the most family-friendly cafe/restaurants we've come across anywhere.

Vientiane's sights are not particularly noteworthy for children, but they should appreciate the surreal sculptures of Xieng Khuan (Buddha Park) (p145) and clambering around the larger monuments. Alternatively, the city's cooking lessons or guided tour outfits such as Tuk Tuk Safari (p151) may be able to create kid-appropriate lessons or excursions.

Vang Vieng offers some good accommodation with swimming pools – Kong Resort (p176) is a great example. But the real draw for kids here is the stunning scenery and some soft adventures in the countryside beyond.

Central Laos

Tham Kong Lor (p183) is memorable for older children, but long journeys and fewer child-friendly sites means this is one region that could be skipped.

Southern Laos

This is a rewarding area for adventurous families to explore thanks to waterfalls on the Bolaven Plateau, such as Tat Lo (p229), or those of Si Phan Don, including Khon Phapheng (p241) and Tat Somphamit (p241). Nakorn Cafe Guest House (p217), in Pakse, is a particularly family-friendly place to stay.

Good to Know

Look out for the ⛲ icon for family-friendly suggestions throughout this guide.

Facilities Child-safety seats for cars, high chairs in restaurants or nappy-changing facilities in public restrooms are few and far between in Laos, pretty much limited to a handful of places in Vientiane or Luang Prabang.

Health For the most part parents needn't worry too much about health concerns, although it pays to lay down a few ground rules – such as regular hand-washing or using hand-cleansing gel – to head off potential medical problems. Children should be warned not to play with animals encountered along the way, as rabies is disturbingly common in Laos.

Nappies Bring a supply of nappies if your child wears size 3 or larger. And don't forget to pack a sufficient supply of any specialised baby products, such as nappy rash cream to combat the humidity, when travelling in rural areas.

Sleeping Cots are not that common outside of the smarter hotels in the main centres, so prepare to share double or twin beds or plan ahead for rooms with connecting doors or adjacent rooms. Luang Prabang's old town is good for couples and independent travellers, but there are not many heritage hotels with swimming pools, so consider staying a little further out to cool off after a long day.

UXO Do not let children stray from the path in remote areas of Laos. Unexploded ordnance (UXO) remains an everyday threat in some regions and children are usually the most common victims, as the the small cluster bombs could look like toys.

Walking In the cities, footpaths can be crowded with vendors, making it tricky to navigate a larger pushchair or pram, so something more compact is smarter.

Useful Resources

Lonely Planet Kids (www.lonelyplanetkids.com) Loads of activities and great family travel blog content.

Travelfish (travelfish.org) Great general resource on travel in Southeast Asia, with country-specific advice for traveling with kids in Laos.

Wild Junket (wildjunket.com) A mum making her way to every country in the world – including Laos.

World Travel Family (worldtravelfamily.com) With specific advice for Southeast Asia.

Kids' Corner

Say What?

Hello.	ສະບາຍດີ sábai-dĕe
Goodbye.	ສະບາຍດີ sábai-dĕe
Thank you.	ຂອບໃຈ kòrp jai
My name is ...	ຂ້ອຍຊື່ ... kòy seu...
What's your name?	ເຈົ້າຊື່ຫຍັງ jôw seu nyăng

Did You Know?

- Laos is landlocked, it does not touch the ocean.
- The widest waterfall in the world is in Laos.

Have You Tried?

Durian
The king of fruit.

Regions at a Glance

For many short-stay visitors, Luang Prabang is their Laos experience. And a mighty impressive one it is too, thanks to its glittering temples, traditional architecture and sophisticated culinary scene. Laos' other main city, its capital Vientiane, may be bucolic for an Asian city, but it hits home on the charm stakes, with attractive cafes, stylish restaurants and lively little bars.

Beyond lies northern Laos, a landscape of towering mountains and dense forests that is home to extensive national parks, rare wildlife and some of the most colourful minorities in the region.

The middle of the country is one of the least travelled regions. Some of the most dramatic cave systems in Asia are found here, together with spectacular scenery and crumbling colonial-era towns. Head south to live life in the slow lane. The Mekong islands of Si Phan Don suck people in for longer than expected, and there is a real buzz on the Bolaven Plateau – not just from the coffee.

Luang Prabang & Around

Food
Activities
Shopping

Wining & Dining

World-class dining is on the menu, with many impressive eateries set in beautifully restored colonial-era properties. As the evening moves on, there are some bohemian little bars and swanky watering holes.

Outside Luang Prabang

It's not all temples and monks in Luang Prabang, despite the iconic imagery. Just beyond the 'burbs lie action and adventure, including inviting waterfalls, mountain-bike trails and ziplines.

Art & Antiquities

The night market is lit up with fairy lights and draws visitors to browse its textiles and trinkets. Around town are art galleries and antique shops that reward the curious shopaholic.

p44

Northern Laos

Adventure
Boat Trips
History

Massive Jungle

The jungle really is massive in northern Laos. This region is home to rewarding national parks and the best trekking in the whole country, not to mention cycling, kayaking and ziplining.

All Aboard

The Mekong meander from the Golden Triangle down to lovely Luang Prabang is one of the most iconic river trips in the region. Smaller rivers reward with fairy-tale scenery, particularly the Nam Ou around Nong Khiaw.

On the Trail of War

The convoluted history of modern Laos comes alive here. Discover the Vieng Xai Caves where the Pathet Lao based their underground government, or explore the Plain of Jars, one of the most contested areas in in the 1960s.

p77

Vientiane, Vang Vieng & Around

Food
Activities
Shopping

Fine Dining

Vientiane's spectrum of global cuisine ranges from Italian to Japanese. But perhaps its ace card is its chic French restaurants, so redolent of Indochina they could make the Seine glow green with envy.

Healthy Living

Vientiane has great bike tours, yoga classes, running clubs, swimming pools and, come the early morning, free Mao-style mass exercises by the Mekong riverfront.

Tailor-Made Shopping

Expect tasteful locally sourced soap shops and silk boutiques hawking made-to-measure chemises, boho dresses and pashminas. You can still buy lacquer Tintin prints or old Russian watches if that's your thing.

p140

Central Laos

Caves
Architecture
Adventure

Going Underground

Central Laos is honeycombed with caves ranging from small, Buddha-ornamented grottoes with swimmable green lagoons, to monstrous river caves, such as Tham Kong Lor, which is cloaked in preternatural darkness.

Colonial-Era Towns

French colonials left not just boules and baguettes here, but also some elegant architecture, still seen today in cities like Tha Khaek and Savannakhet, and ranging from beautifully restored to ghostly decrepit.

Two-Wheeled Touring

Hit the Loop on a motorbike or, if training for the Tour de Laos, bicycle, and experience sublime scenery and destinations a world away from the tourist trail of mainstream Southeast Asia.

p182

Southern Laos

Rivers
Activities
Adventure

Mekong Islands

Zoning out in Si Phan Don is the quintessential southern Laos experience, but do prise yourself away from your hammock to engage with laid-back locals or kayak around this sublime slice of the Mekong.

Walks & Waterfalls

Jungle walks in a clutch of national parks lead to minority villages, crumbling temples and some of Laos' highest waterfalls. Combine your trek with a village homestay for the ultimate experience.

Bike Trips

Southern Laos is ripe for exploration by mountain bike or motorbike. New pavement has spread beyond the main highways making exploration easier than ever, including on the legendary Ho Chi Minh Trail.

p205

On the Road

Luang Prabang & Around

Why Go?

It's hard to imagine a more whimsical confection of delights than you find in lantern-strung Luang Prabang and its gorgeously green surrounding countryside. This is a region in which old-world colonial-era charm meets jungle adventure.

Over the last 25 years Luang Prabang has seen a flood of investment, with once-leprous French villas being revived as fabulous boutique hotels, and some of the best chefs in Southeast Asia moving in. The population has swollen, and yet still the peninsula remains as sleepy and friendly as a village, as if time has stood still here.

Beyond the evident history and heritage of the old French town are aquamarine waterfalls, top trekking opportunities, meandering mountain-bike trails, kayaking trips, river cruises and outstanding natural beauty, the whole ensemble encircled by hazy green mountains.

Best Places to Eat

➡ Tamarind (p68)

➡ Bouang Asian Eatery (p67)

➡ Dyen Sabai (p68)

➡ Khaiphaen (p68)

➡ Paste (p68)

Best Places to Stay

➡ Apsara (p61)

➡ Fan Dee (p60)

➡ La Résidence Phou Vao (p66)

➡ Satri House (p64)

➡ Cold River Guesthouse (p60)

When to Go
Luang Prabang

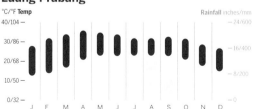

Nov–Feb The ideal season to visit weather-wise, but it's also peak tourist season.

Mar–May Hot season with some hazy skies, but some people like to join in the Pi Mai celebrations.

Jun–Oct The wet season sees numbers, as well as prices, plummet.

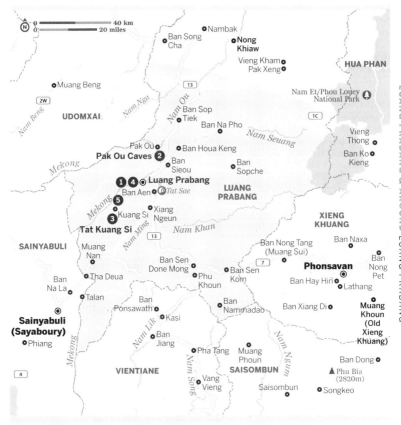

Luang Prabang Highlights

1 Luang Prabang
Watching the dawn call to alms as locals give their daily offering to the monks.

2 Pak Ou Caves (p74)
Cruising up the Mekong River to this holy site brimming with Buddha images.

3 Tat Kuang Si (p76)
Plunging into menthol-blue waters, some of the most beautiful in all of Laos.

4 Wat Xieng Thong (p49)
Marvelling at the sweeping roof of the oldest and most beautiful temple in Luang Prabang's centre.

5 Laos Buffalo Dairy
(p76) Try your hand at milking a buffalo down on the farm or just sample the delicious cheese and ice cream.

LUANG PRABANG

♪ 071 / POP 67,000

Luang Prabang (ຫລວງພະບາງ) slows your pulse and awakens your imagination with its combination of world-class comfort and spiritual nourishment. Sitting at the sacred confluence of the Mekong River and the Nam Khan (Khan River), nowhere else can lay claim to this Unesco-protected gem's romance of 33 gilded wats, saffron-clad monks, faded Indochinese villas and exquisite fusion cuisine.

History

Legend has it that Luang Prabang's founder was Phunheu Nhanheu, a sexually ambiguous character with a bright-red face and a stringy body. His/her ceremonial effigies are kept hidden within Wat Wisunarat, only appearing during Pi Mai (Lao New Year), but models are widely sold as souvenirs.

Known as Muang Sawa (Muang Sua) from 698, then Xiang Dong Xiang Thong (City of Gold) from the 11th century, a city-state here passed between the Nanzhao (Yunnanese), Khmer and greater Mongol empires over several centuries. It flourished at the heart of Lan Xang, following that kingdom's creation in 1353 by Khmer-supported conqueror Fa Ngum. In 1512, Lan Xang's King Visoun accepted the Pha Bang, a celebrated Buddha image, as a gift from the Khmer monarchy. The city was renamed in its honour as Luang (Great/Royal) Prabang (Pha Bang).

Although Viang Chan (Vientiane) became the capital of Lan Xang in 1560, Luang Prabang remained the main source of monarchical power. When Lan Xang broke up following the death of King Suriya Vongsa in 1695, one of Suriya's grandsons set up an independent kingdom in Luang Prabang, which competed with kingdoms in Vientiane and Champasak.

From then on, the Luang Prabang monarchy was so weak that it was forced to pay tribute at various times to the Siamese, Burmese and Vietnamese. The reversal of China's Taiping Rebellion caused several groups of 'Haw' militias to flee southern China and reform as mercenary armies or bandit gangs. The best known of these was the Black Flag Army which devastated Luang Prabang in 1887, destroying and looting virtually every monastery in the city. In the wake of the attack, the Luang Prabang kingdom chose to accept French protection, and a French commissariat was established in the royal capital.

The French allowed Laos to retain the Luang Prabang monarchy. Luang Prabang quickly became a favourite post for French colonials seeking a refuge as far away from Paris as possible. Even during French Indochina's last years, prior to WWII, a river trip from Saigon to Luang Prabang took longer than a steamship voyage from Saigon to France.

The city survived Japanese invasion and remained a royalist stronghold through the Indochina wars, as such avoiding the US bombing that destroyed virtually every other northern Lao city. Through the 1980s, collectivisation of the economy resulted in a major exodus of business people, aristocracy and intelligentsia. With little money for or interest in conserving the city's former regal-colonial flavour, Luang Prabang became a ghost of its former self. But after 1989, the return of private enterprise meant that long-closed shops reopened and once-dilapidated villas were converted into hotels and guesthouses. The city received Unesco World Heritage status in 1995, accelerating the process, raising the city's international profile and, in principle, ensuring that any new development in the old city remains true to the architectural spirit of the original. Such has been the city's international popularity in the 21st century that in some quarters, guesthouses, restaurants, boutiques and galleries now outnumber actual homes.

⊙ Sights

Thanon Sisavangvong & Around

★ **Phu Si**   HILL

(ພູສີ; Map p52; 20,000K; ⊘ 6am-7pm) Dominating the old city centre and a favourite with sunset junkies, the 100m-tall Phu Si (prepare your legs for a steep 329-step ascent) is crowned by a 24m gilded stupa called **That Chomsi** (ທາດຈອມສີ; Map p52; admission incl with Phu Si). Viewed from a distance, especially when floodlit at night, the structure seems to float in the hazy air like a chandelier. From the summit, however, the main attraction is the city views.

Beside a flagpole on the same summit there's a small remnant anti-aircraft cannon left from the war years.

Ascending Phu Si from the northern side, stop at **Wat Pa Huak** (ວັດປ່າຮວກ; Map p52; admission by donation; ⊘ daylight hours). The gilded, carved front doors are usually locked but an attendant will open them for a tip. Inside, the original 19th-century murals show historic scenes along the Mekong River, including visits by Chinese diplomats and warriors arriving by river, and horse caravans.

Reaching That Chomsi is also possible from the southern and eastern sides. Two such paths climb through large **Wat Siphoutthabat Thippharam** (ວັດສີພຸດຕະບາດ; Map p52; ⊘ daylight hours) **FREE** to a curious miniature shrine that protects a **Buddha Footprint** (ຮອຍພະບາດພະພຸດທະເຈົ້າ; Map p52) **FREE**. If this really is his rocky imprint, then the Buddha must have been the size of a brontosaurus. Directly southwest of here a series of gilded Buddhas are nestled into rocky clefts and niches around Wat Tham-mothayalan (ວັດຖໍ້າໂມໄທຍາລານ; Map p52; ☉daylight hours); this monastery is free to visit if you don't climb beyond to That Chomsi.

Royal Palace
MUSEUM

(ພະຣາຊວັງຫໍຄຳ, Ho Kham; Map p52; ☑071-212068; Th Sisavangvong; 30,000K; ☉8-11.30am & 1.30-4pm, last entry 3.30pm) Evoking traditional Lao and French beaux-arts styles, the former Royal Palace was built in 1904 and was home to King Sisavang Vong (r 1904–59), whose statue stands outside. Within are tasteful, decidedly sober residential quarters, with some rooms preserved much as they were when the king's son (and successor) was captured by the Pathet Lao in 1975. A separate outbuilding displays the five-piece Royal Palace Car Collection (Map p52; entry incl in Royal Palace fees).

No single treasure in Laos is more historically resonant than the Pha Bang, an 83cm-tall gold-alloy Buddha. To find it, head to Wat Ho Pha Bang (ວດຫໍພະບາງ; Map p52; entry incl in Royal Palace fees) in the southeast corner of the palace gardens.

Inside the museum, footwear and photography are not permitted and you must leave bags in a locker room to the left side of the main entrance. An audio tour is also available to visitors if you prefer a self-guided explanation.

Wat Mai Suwannaphumaham
BUDDHIST TEMPLE

(ວັດໃຫມ່ສຸວັນນະພູມອາຮາມ; Map p52; Th Sisavangvong; 10,000K; ☉8am-5pm) Wat Mai is one of the city's most sumptuous monasteries, its wooden *sĭm* sporting a five-tiered roof in archetypal Luang Prabang style, while the unusually roofed front verandah features detailed golden reliefs depicting scenes from village life, the Ramayana and Buddha's penultimate birth. It was spared destruction in 1887 by the Haw gangs who reportedly found it too beautiful to harm. Since 1894 it has been home to the Sangharat, the head of Lao Buddhism.

LUANG PRABANG IN...

Two Days

After breakfasting on coffee and croissants at Le Banneton (p68), immerse yourself in the old town of Luang Prabang with a stroll around the temples and historic buildings. Make sure you include the striking temple of Wat Xieng Thong (p49) and the Royal Palace, where you can see the fabled Pha Bang Buddha statue, as well as some of the small alleyways that link the Mekong and Nam Khan riverfronts. Try lunch at Tamarind (p68) on the slow-flowing Nam Khan and dinner after sunset on the banks of the mother Mekong. On your second day, rise early to observe the tak bat (p51) as the monasteries empty of their monks in search of alms (to avoid the scrum of photographers on the main road, follow it through the peninsula's interior). Continue to the lively morning market (p66) before taking a boat trip upriver to the Pak Ou Caves (p74). Round things off with a good-cause Lao dinner at Khaiphaen (p68) followed by a night on the town at buzzing Utopia (p69).

Four Days

Once you've explored the old town and the headline attractions, it's time for an adrenaline buzz or some cultural immersion. For adrenaline seekers, choose from hiking, biking or kayaking in the surrounding countryside. Tiger Trail (p59) or Green Discovery (p59) are reliable tour operators to hook up with. For more culture than adventure, consider a cooking class at Tamarind (p55) or Bamboo Tree (p57), a weaving class at Ock Pop Tok (p57), or a visit to the excellent Traditional Arts & Ethnology Centre (p50). Definitely try a gastronomic blowout at one of the classy international restaurants in town such as Tangor (p67) or Paste (p68). Still want more? Check out La Pistoche (p54) for the equivalent of a beach experience in town. And if you want an epic day trip that includes lots of diverse experiences, consider beautiful Tat Kuang Si (p76) waterfalls with a stop at the family-friendly Laos Buffalo Dairy (p76) and a side trip to the ziplines and canopy walks of Nahm Dong Park (p75).

Luang Prabang

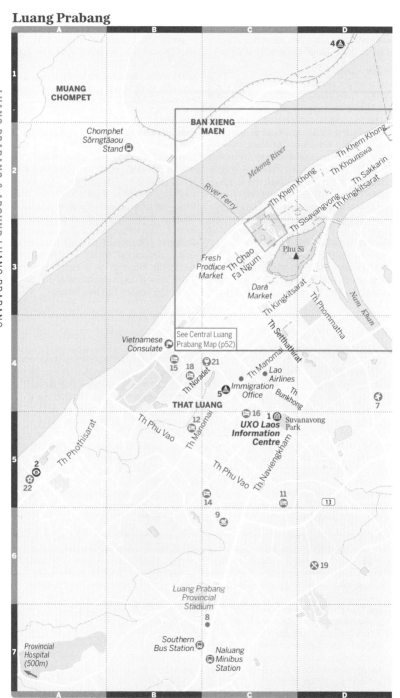

MUANG CHOMPET

Chomphet Sŏrngtǎaou Stand

BAN XIENG MAEN

Mekong River

River Ferry

Th Khem Khong

Th Khem Khong

Th Khounswa

Th Sakkarin

Th Sisavangvong

Th Kingkitsarat

Fresh Produce Market

Th Chao Fa Ngum

Phu Si

Dara Market

Th Kingkitsarat

Th Phommatha

Nam Khan

Th Setthathirat

See Central Luang Prabang Map (p52)

Vietnamese Consulate

15 18 21

Th Noradet

Th Manomai

Lao Airlines

5 Immigration Office

Th Bunkhong

THAT LUANG

7

Th Phothisarat

Th Phu Vao

12

Th Manomai

16 1 Suvanavong Park

UXO Laos Information Centre

Th Naviengkham

2

22

Th Phu Vao

14

11

13

9

19

Luang Prabang Provincial Stadium

8

Southern Bus Station

Naluang Minibus Station

Provincial Hospital (500m)

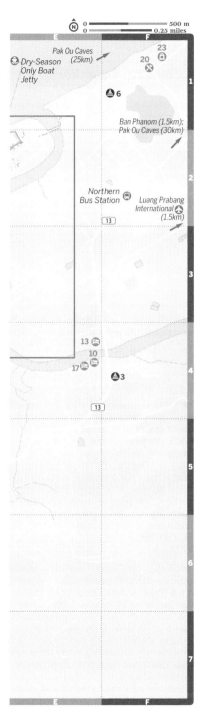

Luang Prabang

Mekong Riverfront & Around

A series of lanes and narrow linking passages run down to the enchanting Mekong riverfront with its shuttered colonial-era house-fronts, river-facing terrace cafes and curio shops.

★Wat Xieng Thong   BUDDHIST TEMPLE
(ວັດຊຽງທອງ; Map p52; off Th Sakkarin; 20,000K; ⊙6am-6pm) Luang Prabang's best-known monastery is centred on a 1560 *sĭm*. Its roofs sweep low to the ground and there's a stunning 'tree of life' mosaic set on its western exterior wall. Close by are several stupas and three compact little chapel halls called *hŏr*.

Wat Xieng Thong

Hŏr Đại, shaped like a tall tomb, houses a standing Buddha. The **Hŏr Đại Pha Sai-nyàat**, dubbed La Chapelle Rouge – Red Chapel – by the French, contains a rare reclining Buddha.

Fronted in lavish gilt work, the **Hóhng Kép Mîen** stores a ceremonial carriage, festooned with red-tongued *naga* designed to carry the golden funeral urns of Lao royalty.

Heuan Chan Heritage House   ARCHITECTURE
(ເຮືອນຈັນ ເຮືອນມໍລະດົກ; Map p52; Th Xotikhoumman; entry to compound free, museum 15,000K; ⊙9am-9pm) Footpaths lead back from the commercial main drag into a little oasis of palm-shaded calm around Heuan Chan, an authentic traditional longhouse on tree-trunk stilts that acts as a small museum on the lifestyle of Luang Prabang, a cafe, handicraft centre and more. There are also cooking classes to learn about Lao desserts, bamboo crafts and the chance to dress up in traditional local costumes for a photo op.

The Information Centre has computers on which you can peruse a series of photos and descriptions of the city's numerous Unesco-listed historic buildings.

Wat Xieng Mouane   BUDDHIST TEMPLE
(ວັດຊຽງມວນ; Map p52; Th Xotikhoumman; ⊙8am-5pm) FREE In the old quarter, Wat Xieng Mouane's ceiling is painted with gold *naga* and the elaborate *háang thien* (candle rail) has *naga* at either end. With backing from Unesco and Greece, the monks' quarters were restored as a classroom for training young novices and monks in the artistic skills needed to maintain and preserve Luang Prabang's temples, including

woodcarving, painting and Buddha-casting, all of which came to a virtual halt after 1975.

Nam Khan Riverfront & Around

Wat Pakkhan   BUDDHIST TEMPLE
(ວັດປາກຄານ; Map p52; Th Sakkarin; ⊙daylight hours) FREE Dated 1737 but rebuilt a century ago, Wat Pakkhan has a simple, appealingly archaic look with angled support struts holding up the lower of its two superposed roofs. Across the road, the ochre colonial-era villa that now forms **Unesco offices** (Map p52; Th Sakkarin) was once the city's customs office.

Wat Souvannakhili   BUDDHIST TEMPLE
(ວັດສຸວັນນະຄິລີ, Wat Khili; Map p52; off Th Sakkarin; ⊙daylight hours) FREE The most prominent building of Wat Souvannakhili looks more like a colonial-era mansion than a monastery, but the small *sĭm* is a classic of now-rare Xieng Khuang style.

South of Phu Si

Two of Luang Prabang's most historically important temples lie amid palms in pleasant if traffic-buzzed grounds, offering glimpses towards Phu Si.

★**UXO Laos Information Centre**   MUSEUM
(ສູນຂໍ້ມູນຂ່າວສານປະເທດລາວກ່ຽວກັບການເກັບກູ້ລະເບີດທີ່ບໍ່ທັນແຕກ; Map p48; ☑020-22575123, 071-252073; www.uxolao.org; off Th Naviengkham; admission by donation; ⊙8am-noon & 1-4pm Mon-Fri) The sobering UXO Laos Information Centre helps you get a grip on the devastation Laos suffered in the Second Indochina War and how nearly 40 years later death or injury from unexploded ordnance (UXO) remains an everyday reality in several provinces. If you miss it here, there's a similar centre in Phonsavan.

TAEC   MUSEUM
(ສູນສິນລະປະພື້ນເມືອງແລະຊົນເຜົ່າ, Traditional Arts & Ethnology Centre; Map p52; ☑071-253364; www.taeclaos.org; off Th Kitsarat; 25,000K; ⊙9am-6pm Tue-Sun) 🖋 Visiting this professionally presented three-room museum is a must to learn about northern Laos' various hill-tribe cultures, especially if you're planning a trek. There's just enough to inform without overloading a beginner, including a range of ethnic costumes and the permanent exhibition, 'Seeds of Culture: From Living Plants

LOCAL KNOWLEDGE

TAK BAT: THE MONKS' CALL TO ALMS

Daily at dawn, saffron-clad monks pad barefoot through the streets while pious towns-folk place tiny balls of sticky rice in their begging bowls. It's a quiet, meditative ceremony through which monks demonstrate their vows of poverty and humility, while lay Buddhists gain spiritual merit by the act of respectful giving.

Although such processions (called *tak bat*) occur all over Laos, old Luang Prabang's peaceful atmosphere and extraordinary concentration of mist-shrouded temples mean that the morning's perambulations along Th Sakkarin create an especially romantic scene. Sadly, as a result, tourists are progressively coming to outnumber participants. Despite constant campaigns begging visitors not to poke cameras in the monks' faces, the amateur paparazzi seem incapable of keeping a decent distance. Sensitive, nonparticipating observers should follow these guidelines:

➡ Stand across the road from the procession or better still watch inconspicuously from the window of your hotel (where possible).

➡ Refrain from taking photos or at best do so from a considerable distance with a long zoom. Never use flash.

➡ Maintain the silence (arrive by bicycle or on foot; don't chatter).

If it's genuinely meaningful to you, you may take part in the ceremony – meaningful in this case implies not wanting to be photographed in the process. Joining in takes some preparation and knowledge to avoid causing unspoken offence. Don't be pushed into half-hearted participation by sales-folk along the route. Such vendors contribute to the procession's commercialisation and many sell overpriced, low-grade rice that is worse than giving nothing at all. Instead, organise some *kao kai noi* (the best grade sticky rice) to be cooked to order by your guesthouse. Or buy it fresh-cooked from the morning market before the procession. Carry it in a decent rice-basket, not a plastic bag. Before arriving, dress respectfully as you would for a temple (covered upper arms and chest, skirts for women, long trousers for men). Wash your hands and don't use perfumes or lotions that might flavour the rice as you're handing it out.

Once in situ, remove your shoes and put a sash or scarf across your left shoulder. Women should kneel with their feet folded behind them (don't sit) while men may stand. Avoid making eye contact with the monks.

to Handicrafts'. TAEC sits within a former French judge's mansion that was among the city's most opulent buildings of the 1920s. There's a cafe and a shop selling handicrafts and pictorials.

The shop has a second branch (p71) in town. Sign up at either location for half-day workshops (from US$12) on Khmu bamboo weaving, Hmong embroidery or Katu backstrap weaving.

Around Town

A short bike ride south of the city brings you to quiet streets peppered with wats, of which the oldest is Wat Manorom.

Ock Pop Tok Living
Crafts Centre   ARTS CENTRE
(ສູນຫັດຖະກຳຜ້າໄໝອອກພົບຕົກ, OPT; Map p48; 071-212597; www.ockpoptok.com; 125/10 Ban Saylom; 8am-6pm) FREE Set serenely

close to the Mekong, this beautiful, traditionally styled workshop, where weavers, spinners and batik makers produce top-quality fabrics, offers free tours every half-hour. There's also a great riverside Silk Road Cafe serving drinks and excellent Lao food. Or try a cup of the surprisingly pleasant worm-poo tea, a unique infusion made from silk-worm droppings. Better still, why not try a bamboo weaving course (p57). There is also a beautiful boutique and a handful of elegant boutique rooms available on-site.

Wat Manorom   BUDDHIST TEMPLE
(ວັດມະໂນລົມ, Wat Mano, Wat Manolom; Map p48; Th Pha Mahapatsaman; daylight hours) FREE Winding lanes to the west lead to Wat Manorom, set amid frangipani trees just outside what were once the city walls (now invisible). This is possibly the oldest temple site in Luang Prabang and the *sǐm* contains

Central Luang Prabang

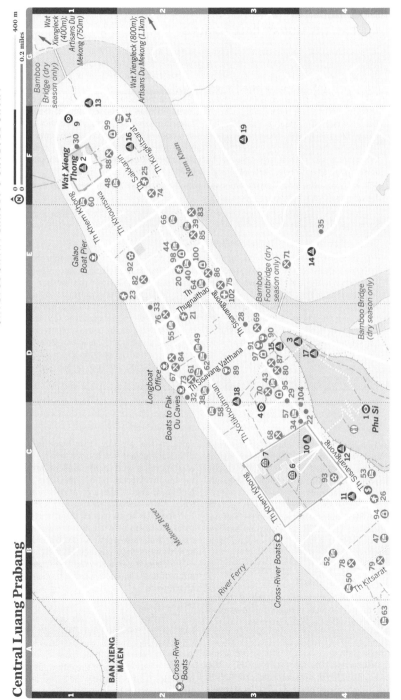

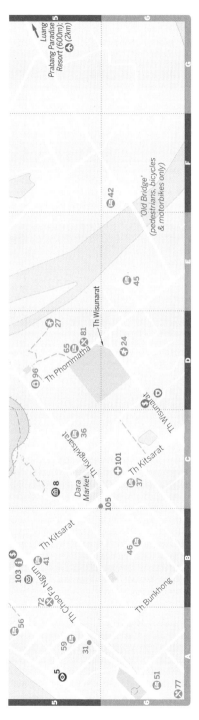

a sitting 6m-tall bronze Buddha originally cast in 1372. During the 1887 devastation the statue was hacked apart, but surviving elements were reconstituted in 1919; the missing limbs were replaced with concrete falsies covered in gold leaf in 1971.

🏃 Activities

Some of the most popular activities in Luang Prabang are based in the countryside beyond, including trekking, cycling, motocross, kayaking and rafting tours. In Luang Prabang itself, it's all about temple-hopping, cookery classes and cycling.

Luang Prabang Yoga   YOGA

(Map p52; www.luangprabangyoga.org; classes 60/90min 40,000/60,000K; ⊙ classes at 7.30am & 5pm) Slow down, unwind and sync your spirit to the city's relaxed vibe with yoga classes taught at serene locations, from lush riverside garden decks at daily Utopia (p69) to rooftop sunset views. The city's yoga cooperative keeps up-to-date information on classes and venues on its website. In our experience this is a well-run network of qualified teachers. All levels welcome.

Luang Prabang Yoga also runs relaxing three-day yoga retreats at the delicious Mandala Ou Resort (p99) in Nong Khiaw; see www.laosyogaretreats.com.

Big Brother Mouse   VOLUNTEERING

(BBM; Map p52; ☑ 071-254937; www.bigbrother mouse.com; Th Phayaluangmeungchan; ⊙ classes 9-11am & 5-7pm) 🌿 Home-grown initiative dedicated to improving literacy among kids in Laos, from cities to remote villages. Hang out at the BBM office and read to, or with, the kids who attend. If you're travelling in Laos, buy some books to take with you when you go to remote villages. It's an inspiring place.

Lao Red Cross   MASSAGE, SPA

(Map p52; ☑ 071-252856; Th Wisunarat; sauna 15,000K, traditional/aromatherapy massage per hour 50,000/80,000K; ⊙ 1-8pm) 🌿 This traditional blue Lao house was the original place to come for a sauna and massage before all the fancy spas arrived. It might be no frills, but well-trained staff give first-rate massages and there's a terrific sauna infused with medicinal plants that will clear your respiratory system like Vicks vapour rub!

Donations go directly to improving the lives of the poorest villages in Laos.

Central Luang Prabang

Khopfa Cruise
CRUISE

(Map p52; ☑ 020-92100012; www.khopfa-mekong-cruise.com; Th Khem Khong; US$15; ◷ daily departures winter 4.30pm, summer 5.15pm) A new arrival on the sunset cruise scene, Khopfa offers a comfortable boat with two upper decks for river breeze and views. Sophisticated snacks such as olives, cold cuts and cheese platter are available, as well as the obligatory cold drinks.

Crazy Golf
PLAYGROUND

(ABC School; Map p48; ☑ 020-56920137; adult/child incl golf 30,000/15,000K, playground only 10,000K; ◷ 10am-8pm) A good spot to bring younger children who are not impressed with gilded wats. As well as the eponymous 13-hole crazy golf, you'll find a trampoline, zipline, jungle gym, slides, swings, carousel, sandbox and seesaw. There's also food available.

La Pistoche
SWIMMING

(Map p48; www.lapistochepool.wordpress.com; Ban Phong Pheng; 30,000K; ◷ 10am-11pm; ⊕) The perfect medicine for landlocked Laos, La Pistoche offers several swimming pools and a small water park set amid a spacious garden in the suburbs south of town. Entry includes *petang* (Lao version of pétanque) and water volleyball if you're feeling active. Generous happy hours from noon to 7pm mean there's a bit of a hippy-trippy vibe by day.

If you've got kids with you, it's quiet enough during the day to bring them here to cool down.

L'Hibiscus Massage
MASSAGE

(Map p52; ☑ 030-9235079; Th Sakkarin; foot massage from 60,000K; ◷ 10am-10pm) Set in a former gallery in an old French building, Hibiscus is prettier than the offerings on the main street and wafts chilled tunes through its silk-draped walls while you get pummelled to perfection.

Children's Cultural Centre VOLUNTEERING
(Map p52; ☑ 071-253732; www.cccluangprabang.weebly.com; Th Khounswa; ⏱ 9-11.30am & 2-5pm Tue-Fri, 8-11.30am & 2-5pm Sat Sep-May, closed Sat Jun-Aug) Providing after-school and weekend activities for Lao children to learn about Lao culture and traditions and develop skills that encourage healthy lifestyles and cultural preservation. Traditional music, drama, storytelling, singing and a variety of arts-and-crafts activities are on offer. Drop in to the centre to find out about leading a class or donating supplies.

There are also **performances** on Thursdays and Saturdays between December and early March, the proceeds of which help fund the centre's activities. Check the website for the latest schedule.

Courses

Luang Prabang is an inspiring place to learn something new, whether it's rice farming at Living Land (p57), dyeing and weaving at Ock Pop Tok (p57), or learning to cook a few Lao staples at Bamboo Tree (p57) or Tamarind. Some weavers in Ban Xang Khong offer informal courses on request.

★**Tamarind** COOKING
(Map p52; ☑ 020-77770484; www.tamarindlaos.com; Ban Wat Nong; full-day/evening course 285,000/215,000K) Join Tamarind at its lakeside pavilion for a day's tuition in the art of Lao cuisine, meeting in the morning at its restaurant before heading to the market for ingredients for classic dishes such as *mok phaa* (steamed fish in banana leaves). Evening classes don't include a market visit.

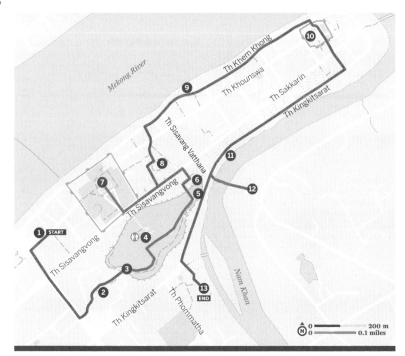

Town Walk
Old Luang Prabang

START MORNING MARKET
END UTOPIA
LENGTH 4.5KM; FOUR TO FIVE HOURS

This walk meanders through the heart of the historic city in a leisurely half-day, assuming plenty of stops. We suggest starting bright and early to miss the afternoon heat on Phu Si, and avoiding Tuesday to fit in with museum opening times. But if you accept that it's the overall atmosphere and cafe scene that makes Luang Prabang special rather than any particular sights, the walk can work any time.

After an early stroll through the ❶ **Morning Market** (p66) and a local breakfast, arrive at ❷ **TAEC** (p50) where you can peruse the excellent little exhibition on northern Laos' ethnic mosaic. Suitably fuelled, try to weave your way through the untouristed little maze of residential homes to reach the southern flank of ❸ **Phu Si** (p46). Climb to ❹ **That Chomsi** (p46) before the day gets too hot. Or, if the air looks too hazy for city views, continue instead around the hill via Buddha's

oversized ❺ **footprint** (p46) and descend to the main commercial street through ❻ **Wat Siphoutthabat Thippharam** (p46). If you can arrive by 11am, visit the ❼ **Royal Palace Museum** (p47) to see how Lao royalty lived until 1975 and the Pha Bang Buddha statue. Afterwards meander through the palm-shaded footpaths of ❽ **Xieng Mouane area** to reach the ❾ **Mekong waterfront** with its inviting cafes and Lao-French colonial-era houses. If you didn't already explore them at dawn after the monks' alms procession, dip into a selection of atmospheric wats as you wander up the spine of the peninsula. Don't miss the most famous monastery of all, ❿ **Wat Xieng Thong** (p49). Stroll back, taking in a stretch of the lovely ⓫ **Nam Khan waterfront** and, in the dry season, cross the bamboo bridge for a well-deserved lunch at delightful ⓬ **Dyen Sabai** (p68). If the bridge isn't there (June to November), or you are walking in the afternoon, seek the winding path to ⓭ **Utopia** (p69) for a drink and peaceful views of the Nam Khan.

Ock Pop Tok   COURSE
(Map p48; ☎071-212597; www.ockpoptok.com; 125/10 Ban Saylom; half-/full-day bamboo-weaving course US$26/42, Hmong Batik class US$52/69, 3-day natural dyeing & weaving course US$158; ☉8.45am-4pm) ◢ Learn to weave and dye your own scarf and textiles or take a half-day bamboo-weaving course at Ock Pop Tok. Teachers are master craftspeople, you get to keep your handiwork and lunch is included. Situated 2km past Phousy market; a free tuk-tuk will pick you up and bring you back.

Weaving Sisters   WEAVING CLASSES
(Map p52; ☎020-58178875; weaving.sisters@gmail.com; per person 300,000-370,000K; ☉9am-8pm) Unlike many of the other weavers in Luang Prabang, these two sisters are from the Katu minority in southern Laos and specialise in backstrap weaving, which can be adapted to anything from belts to camera straps to headbands. The classes include some tea and fruits and are proving popular with visitors.

Backstreet Academy   HANDICRAFTS
(www.backstreetacademy.com; US$22-33) ◢ Expanding across Southeast Asia, Backstreet Academy offers a range of immersive experiences with local crafts people so visitors can learn a new skill. In Luang Prabang, they offer bow crafting and knife making for would-be jungle survivalists and woodcarving and weaving for something more sedate.

Bamboo Tree Cooking Class & Restaurant   COOKING
(Map p52; ☎020-22425499; bambootreelpb@live.com; Th Sakkarin; cookery class 200,000-250,000K; ☉9am-10pm) Chef Linda will teach you how to cook five or six Lao dishes, such as *láhp* (minced pork salad with shallots and coriander), at Bamboo Tree's spacious and airy restaurant. Morning classes run from 9am to 2pm, while evening classes (which don't include a market visit and are cheaper) go from 5pm to 8pm. Vegetarian options are available.

If you're not a student it also makes a great spot for lunch or dinner (mains 40,000K). By night it's enchanting, strung with glowing paper lanterns and laced with delicious aromas.

Tours
Luang Prabang has an abundance of travel agents vying for your patronage for half- to multiday tours. Tours to waterfalls and the Pak Ou Caves are particularly popular and prices are generally competitive (typically around 130,000K for the full day), but it still pays to shop around. The Pak Ou Caves and Tat Kuang Si are an odd combination, given that the sites are in opposite directions, but the advantage is that the vehicle to the Kuang Si waterfalls should be waiting when you return to the agency office from your boat trip. Note that tour prices don't include entry fees.

★Living Land   CULTURAL
(☎020-55199208; www.livinglandlao.com; Ban Phong Van; tours per person 344,000K; ☉8.30am-noon; 🚗) ◢ About 5km out of Luang Prabang, on the road to Tat Kuang Si, is this brilliant rice-farm cooperative, where you can spend half a day learning how to plant and grow sticky rice, the ubiquitous dish of Laos. This includes prepping the paddy with gregarious water-buffalo Rudolph – expect to be knee-deep in glorious mud! You'll never taste rice in the same way. Kids love it.

Living Land helps educate children in disadvantaged families in the local community.

E-bike Adventures   MOUNTAIN BIKING
(Map p52; ☎071-211152; www.ebike-laos.com; half day US$59, full day with SUP/kayaking & lunch US$103) ◢ Enjoy a village and jungle romp on a state-of-the-art e-mountain bike in the beautiful countryside around Chateau Orientale, an opulent ecolodge located on the Nam Khan, with the option of an overnight stay. The ride takes in ricefields, local ethnic villages and a couple of river crossings, so prepare to get down and dirty if it rains (though they also offer professional protective gear).

Mountain-bike rides can be combined with kayaking on the river or stand up paddleboarding. Overnight excursions and combination activities are also offered with camping or a stay at the lodge. There are some great family rooms that can be combined to offer villa living on the riverside.

🛈 ELEPHANT INTERACTIONS
There are lots of elephant camps located around Luang Prabang, but many of them promote elephant riding, which can be harmful to the animal. For the best elephant interaction experience in Laos, make a short overnight side trip to the Elephant Conservation Center (p136) in Sainyabuli. However, Mandalao (p58) offers responsible and recommended elephant interactions closer to Luang Prabang for those with limited time on their hands.

CROSSING THE RIVER

Across the Nam Khan

In the dry season, once water levels have dropped significantly, a pair of bamboo foot-bridges (2000K) are constructed, making for easy access to the Nam Khan's east bank and its semi-rural neighbourhoods. When the river is high (June to November), the bridges disappear.

Crossing the southern bamboo bridge, climb steps past the highly recommended garden cafe Dyen Sabai (p68), emerging beside Wat Punluang (ວັດພັນຫຼວງ; Map p52; Ban Phan Luang; ⊙ daylight hours) FREE. The road to the left leads to Watpakha Xaingaram (ວັດປ່າຂາໄຊຍະຮາມ; Map p52; ⊙ daylight hours) FREE with its ruined shell of a temple, and Wat Xiengleck (ວັດຊຽງເຫຼັກ; Map p48; ⊙ daylight hours) FREE, in an Angkorian-style state of atmospheric dilapidation. Half a kilometre beyond, Ban Xang Khong has a 400m-strip of old houses and craft boutiques where you can watch weavers and papermakers at work and buy their work. The most striking gallery-workshop is Artisans Du Mekong (p71), behind a giant 'tusk' gateway, with its pleasant cafe.

Across the Mekong

For a very different 'village' atmosphere, cross the Mekong to Muang Chomphet. To get there, take a cross-river boat (p74; 10,000K) from behind the Royal Palace. Boats depart once they have a handful of passengers. Alternatively, boatmen at various other points on the Luang Prabang waterfront will run you across to virtually any point on the north bank for around 20,000K per boat. If water levels allow, a good excursion idea is to hire such a boat to the Wat Longkhun (ວັດລອງຄຸນ; Map p48; Ban Xieng Maen; 10,000K; ⊙ 8am-5pm) jetty then walk back via Ban Xieng Maen to catch an upstream cross-river boat (Map p52; one-way 15,000K). However, reaching Wat Longkhun by boat isn't always practicable due to seasonally changing sandbanks.

Above the ferry landing on the other side, a branch of Jewel Travel Laos (Map p52; ☑ 020-55687663; www.jeweltravellao.com; Sisavangvong Rd, Ban Xieng Muen; ⊙ 8am-4pm; 🛜) rents mountain bikes (per day 50,000K). However, you'll need neither bike nor map to visit the series of attractive monasteries that are scattered east along the riverbank from the traffic-free village of Ban Xieng Maen.

Mandalao
WILDLIFE

(Map p52; ☑ 030-5664014; www.mandalao tours.com; Th Sisavangvong; US$80-130; ⊙ 8.30am-5.30pm; 🚻 🐘) Mandalao offers a range of nonriding elephant encounters on the banks of the Nam Khan about 15km from Luang Prabang. There are seven elephants resident in the Mandalao sanctuary and visitors can choose from a challenging 'Into the Wild' morning trek to a more gentle 'Communicating with Elephants'. Full day tours are also available and all tours include a delicious organic Lao set lunch.

Shompoo Cruise
BOATING

(Map p52; ☑ 071-213189; www.shompoocruise. com; Th Khem Khong; cruise incl breakfast & 2 lunches US$130) An excellent way to see the Mekong in style from a comfortable longboat, and less expensive than other operators offering the same trip, Shompoo runs two-day cruises between Huay Xai and Luang Prabang. Departures are from the Galao Boat Pier (p72). If leaving from Huay Xai, a guide will meet you at the Thai border.

Luang Say Cruise
BOATING

(Mekong Cruises; Map p52; ☑ 071-252553; www. luangsay.com; 50/4 Th Sakkarin; cruise US$303-506; ⊙ 8.30am-7pm) The most luxurious way to travel the Mekong on two-day trips to/from Huay Xai on the Thai border. Its boats are stunning romantic affairs with wood accents and great service. Last-minute bookings at the office can shave more than 50% off the listed price. Departs from the Galao Boat Pier (p72).

White Elephant Adventures
HIKING

(Map p52; ☑ 030-5789120; www.white-elephant-adventures-laos.com; 44/3 Th Sisavangvong; ⊙ 8am-9.30pm) 🌿 White Elephant is hailed for its relationships with remote Hmong and Khamu villages, allowing a deeper insight into their way of life on well-planned two- or three-day trekking experiences. Look out for the BMW motorbike and communist flag to find its office on the main drag.

Mekong River Cruises BOATING

(Map p52; ☑071-254768; www.cruisemekong.com; 22/2 Th Sakkarin, Ban Xieng Thong; 6-day all-inclusive cruise per person from $1080; ◎8.30am-6pm Mon-Fri) Offers an upmarket way to explore the Mekong River with 11-day cruises from Vientiane to the Golden Triangle, six-day cruises between Vientiane and Luang Prabang, and six-day round-trip journeys to/from Luang Prabang visiting the highlights of the area. Apart from lazing on the deck of the new Mekong Pearl, there are luxurious onboard massages and numerous offshore excursions.

Green Discovery OUTDOORS

(Map p52; ☑071-212093; www.greendiscoverylaos.com; 44/3 Th Sisavangvong; ◎8am-9pm) The daddy of ecotourism in Laos offers safety-conscious kayaking, trekking, mountain biking and multiday trips north. Staff speak good English, kit is safety conscious and the company is owned by a Lao ecotourism expert who recycles some of the profit back into conservation.

Sa Sa Sunset Cruise CRUISE

(Map p52; ☑020-95198933; www.facebook.com/sasacruiselaos; Th Khem Kong; 2hr cruise incl 1 drink 85,000K; ◎daily departures winter 4.30pm, summer 5.15pm) Easily the best budget cruise in town with two-hour sunset trips along the Mekong each evening in a comfortable longboat. Add in the cheap drinks and the 10,000K chicken skewers and you have all the makings for an affordable night out on the river.

Tiger Trail HIKING

(Map p52; ☑071-252655; www.laos-adventures.com; Th Sisavangvong; tours from US$50; ◎8am-9pm) Tiger Trail offers hikes through Hmong and Khamu villages, cultural bike tours and off-road mountain biking. All tours can be tailored to include kayaking, rafting or mountain biking.

★ Festivals & Events

The two most important annual events in Luang Prabang are Pi Mai in April, when Luang Prabang is packed to the gills with locals armed with water pistols (book accommodation well in advance), and boat races during Bun Awk Phansa in October.

Pi Mai CULTURAL

(Lao New Year; ◎Apr) Large numbers of visitors converge on Luang Prabang for this 'water throwing' festival in April. Be careful of your camera getting soaked and prepare to be drenched! Advance bookings around this time are recommended.

Bun Awk Phansa CULTURAL

(End of the Rains Retreat; ◎Sep/Oct) Bun Awk Phansa sees boat races on the Nam Khan in September or October. Buddhists send little boats made of banana leaves with lit candles inside downriver by night, chiefly to send the bad luck of last year away, and to also make thanks to Mother Mekong and the sentinel *naga* who dwell within her watery arms. Pure magic.

Luang Prabang Film Festival FILM

(LPFF; www.lpfilmfest.org; ◎Dec) At the start of every December, the Luang Prabang Film Festival hand-picks the best new films from 10 Southeast Asian countries, with screens set up alfresco all around the city. Better still, it's free.

🛏 Sleeping

For sybarites looking to recapture the comforts of old Indochine, Luang Prabang has world-class hotels and stunning boutique belles, plus impressive ecolodges and resorts in the surrounding lush countryside. Midscale bargains can be found in clean simple guesthouses, and loads of hostels and super basic digs make for good budget options. In high season, prices rocket and availability is low. Old town peninsular accommodation generally comes at a premium but is more peaceful.

Thanon Sisavangvong & Around

Bou Pha Guesthouse GUESTHOUSE $

(Map p52; ☑071-020450; Th Sisavangvong; r 60,000-100,000K; ❄🛜) This takes us back to old-school 1990s Luang Prabang with an old house in the heart of the city offering rooms for less than a tenner. The cheapest rooms have a shared bathroom and fans while the more expensive upstairs rooms include a street view and air-con.

Indigo House BOUTIQUE HOTEL $$

(Map p52; ☑071-212264; www.indigohouse.la; Th Sisavangvong; r US$60-70; ❄@🛜) A contemporary boutique property bookending the old town peninsula, Indigo House has open-plan staircases leading to well-appointed rooms with a bold indigo colour scheme throughout. Breakfast is included at the excellent little Indigo Cafe downstairs, which is invitingly open to nonguests, plus there's even a rooftop bar.

Nora Singh Guesthouse   GUESTHOUSE **$$**
(Map p52; ☎ 071-212035; off Th Sisavangvong; r 150,000-250,000K; ❄️ 🛜) In the verdant skirts of Phu Si, this fragrant guesthouse has seven clean rooms with lowered beds, white and ochre walls hung with tapestries, and private hot-water bathrooms. Central but peaceful.

Phounsab Guesthouse   GUESTHOUSE **$$**
(Map p52; ☎ 071-212975; Th Sisavangvong; r 150,000-350,000K; ❄️ 🛜) Slap-bang in the heart of the old-city's commercial centre, the Phounsab's newer rooms are set back off a narrow courtyard and the great-value front ones are big and breezy with wooden trim and polished floorboards. Other perks include private balconies and en suite, helpful management and the night market begins almost outside your front door.

Burasari Heritage Hotel   BOUTIQUE HOTEL **$$$**
(Map p52; ☎ 071-255031; www.burasariheritage.com; Th Sakkarin; r from US$150; ❄️ 🛜) This romantic bijou belle is stunningly tasteful with Indochinese style; think pendulums ticking away on walls covered with vintage Lao B&W photography, slatted wood mother-of-pearl-inlay furniture, rosewood floors, fragrant linen and chandeliers. The air-con units have been boxed in, preserving the conceit that you have travelled back 100 years. A leafy brick-floored garden lies behind.

Villa Santi   HISTORIC HOTEL **$$$**
(Map p52; ☎ 071-252157; www.villasantihotel.com; Th Sakkarin; r US$129-289; ❄️ 🛜 🏊) This striking old royal building has three very different personalities. The original 19th-century villa, once home to King Sisavang Vong's wife, has just six vast 'royal' suites, plus an upstairs breakfast room with an enviable road-view terrace. The standard rooms are in a central annexe behind, while the majority are in a well-appointed 'resort', 5km south of town.

Auberge les 3 Nagas   BOUTIQUE HOTEL **$$$**
(Map p52; ☎ 071-253888; www.3-nagas.com; Th Sakkarin; r US$175-300; ❄️ @ 🛜) Luang

Prabang style was minted at this boutique hotel, bookended by mango trees and a burgundy 1950s Mercedes. The 100-year-old Lao-style building brims with old-world atmosphere and offers palatial suites sporting sink-to-sleep four-poster beds, tanned-wood bathrooms and a modern Asian design fusing colonial-era French roots.

Avani+ Luang
Prabang Hotel   BOUTIQUE HOTEL **$$$**
(Map p52; ☎ 071-262333; www.avanihotels.com/en/luang-prabang; r US$195-495; ❄️ @ 🛜 🏊) This stylish property, originally the brainchild of Aman Resorts' founder Adrian Zecha, is right in the centre of town and set around a courtyard garden with one of the only swimming pools in the old quarter. Rooms are impressively finished in minimalist style.

Nam Khan Riverfront & Around

⭐ **Fan Dee**   GUESTHOUSE **$**
(Sa Sa Lao; Map p48; ☎ 020-55357317; www.sasalao.net; Ban Vieng Mai; dm US$5-9, r US$25-35; 🛜) 🌿 Like a luxury ecoresort for the budget crowd, this jungly oasis of thatch-roofed bungalows boasts an array of on-site activities, from cooking classes to mud baths on decks overlooking the Nam Khan. Wood-built bunks hold some of the comfiest dorm beds in town, while many of the private rooms have bamboo walls that open to reveal stunning river views.

Perks include a self-wash laundry area, hammocks strewn about landscaped gardens, weekly bonfires and free shuttles to/from the city centre (an otherwise 2km walk).

Cold River Guesthouse   GUESTHOUSE **$$**
(Map p52; ☎ 071-252810; www.coldriverluangprabang.com; Ban Meuana; US$31-66; ❄️ 🛜) Tucked away near the Nam Khan, this welcoming, family-run guesthouse is a home away from home in Luang Prabang. Rooms are beautifully decorated in tribal motifs from Passa Paa, include contemporary bathrooms and the owners strive for zero-use of disposable plastic. Rates include breakfast and substantial discounts are available for direct bookings.

Oui's Guesthouse   GUESTHOUSE **$$**
(Map p52; ☎ 020-54349589, 071-252374; Th Kingkitsarat; r US$25-45; 🛜) In a peaceful setting at the end of the peninsula facing the Nam

Khan, it's so quiet here you can almost hear the breeze. Downstairs rooms are simple wood-ceiling affairs with tile floors, ethnic curtains and swish bathrooms. For an extra 10 bucks you can get an upstairs room with verandah and riverine views.

Luang Prabang Paradise Resort HOTEL **$$**
(Map p48; ☑071-213103; Rte 13; r US$50-80; ❄❄❄) Near the Nam Khan, but a long way out of town over the new bridge, this is a relaxing place to stay for those who want to get away from it all. Sun-filled bungalows are nicely finished with polished teak floors and colourful bed rugs, and bathrooms are huge. Outside there's a swimming pool bedecked by swaying palms.

Thongbay Guesthouse GUESTHOUSE **$$**
(Map p48; ☑071-253234; www.thongbay-luang prabang.com; r US$45-65; ❄❄) Subtle lighting and immaculately managed foliage intersperse the Thongbay's close-packed, wood-and-thatch bungalows, most of which overlook the Nam Khan. Facilities include balconies, minibars and good tiled bathrooms with step-in showers. The downside is an isolated location on an unpaved backstreet near the new bridge, so it's a 20-minute walk from town or 20,000K by tuk-tuk.

Villa Senesouk HOTEL **$$**
(Map p52; ☑071-212074; www.luangphabang. com/senesouk; Th Sakkarin; r US$30-60; ❄❄) The morning monks' procession passes right outside the cheaper rooms. The upper ones are brighter and share a balcony with a wat view. Wood-panelled rooms have full mod cons, with the upstairs options offering additional space. Rooms out back are more expensive.

★**Apsara** BOUTIQUE HOTEL **$$$**
(Map p52; ☑071-254670; www.theapsara.com; Th Kingkitsarat; r incl breakfast US$105-185; ❄❄) Apsara commands fine views of the sleepy Nam Khan. Its Indochinese lobby is peppered with silk lanterns and the bar springs from an old classic film, while each of the open-plan rooms is individually designed. From its turquoise walls to its coloured glass Buddhas, everything about this place screams style.

Rates plummet out of season.

Bel Air Boutique Resort RESORT **$$$**
(Map p52; ☑071-254699; www.lebelairhotels.com; r US$80-180; ❄❄❄) Bel Air has had a total facelift from the foundations up and now looks more like one of the colonial-era resorts that punctuate the old town. Thanks to its location on the opposite side of the Nam Khan, it's set in spacious grounds with a swimming pool, river views and beautifully manicured lawns, plus the rates are great value.

Mekong Riverfront & Around

Pack Luck Villa BOUTIQUE HOTEL **$$**
(Map p52; ☑071-253373; Th Thugnaithao; r US$40-70; ❄❄) This impressive little boutique hotel has an eclectic feel of dark woods, paper lanterns, chrome fans and Persian rugs; by night, subtle lighting picks out flecks of gold leaf on its wine-red walls. Rooms are a little tight, but the three with upper balconies overlook the monks' morning meander. Downstairs is the popular Pack Luck Liquor wine bar.

GIVING SOMETHING BACK

There are several ways in which travellers can give back to the local community in Luang Prabang.

Big Brother Mouse (p53) Travellers can buy books here to distribute to local children. As well as promoting literacy, the idea is that it's more beneficial for visitors to hand out books than candy.

Luang Prabang Library (Map p52; ☑071-254813; www.communitylearninginternational. org; Th Sisavangvong; ⊙8am-5pm) ✐ Collects donations to provide local books for a mobile library that sails to remote villages.

Children's Cultural Centre (p55) Seeks donations of virtually anything recyclable or resalable to provide after-school activities for kids.

Lao Red Cross (p53) Travellers can donate used, washed clothing or even give blood, a precious commodity in Laos as anywhere.

River Life

The Mekong River is the lifeblood of Laos. It's like an artery cutting through the heart of the country, while other important rivers are the veins, breathing life into the landscape and providing transport links between remote landlocked communities. For many Lao people, the river is not just part of their life, it is their life.

1. Luang Prabang (p44)
A child mooring the family houseboat on the Mekong River.

2. Near Vang Vieng (p170)
Nam Song flowing past mountain landscape.

3. Si Phan Don (p237)
Local fisherman on the Mekong River.

4. French Bridge (p244)
Connecting Don Det and Don Khon.

5. Si Phan Don (p237)
Travelling on the Mekong River.

Apple Guesthouse
GUESTHOUSE **$$**

(Map p52; ☑ 071-252436; www.appleguest
houselaos.com; off Th Khem Khong; r US$20-
60; ❀ 🛜) This small guesthouse gets high
marks for its amiable English-speaking
owners, 24-hour front desk and shaded up-
stairs balcony where you can meet fellow
travellers. There's also free tea and coffee all
day. Most rooms have lovely teak walls, but
try for the upstairs ones, which get more
sunlight.

Villa Chitdara
GUESTHOUSE **$$**

(Map p52; ☑ 071-254949; www.villachitdara.com;
Th Khounswa; r US$45-65; ❀🛜) The monks'
alms procession at dawn passes directly by
Villa Chitdara, set amid a verdant garden in
the heart of the old town. It's a charming,
house-proud base to explore the peninsula.
Rooms include TVs, hot water and safes.
The friendly owners speak eloquent French
and are warmth personified.

Villa Champa
GUESTHOUSE **$$**

(Map p52; ☑ 020-99208886; villachampa@ya
hoo.com; Th Sisavang Vatthana; r US$15-50; ❀🛜)
This tastefully renovated traditional house
has a prime location between the Mekong
River and the old temple district. The nine
rooms include air-con, TV and minibar, plus
some more traditional Lao textiles to com-
plete the picture. Fresh and airy, this is a
good peninsula option.

Manichan Guesthouse
GUESTHOUSE **$$**

(Map p52; ☑ 020-22444722; www.manichan
guesthouse.com; off Th Khem Khong; r 120,000-
350,000K; ❀🛜) Run by Andy and Venus,
Manichan is big on personality and warmth,
with air-con rooms and terrific breakfasts,
including crêpes, homemade jams and
wholemeal bread, fruit salads and yoghurt.
Upper rooms share a bathroom worthy of a
boutique hotel, plus a wide terrace with Phu
Si views, while ground-floor rooms have en
suite bathrooms with screened showers.

Luang Prabang River Lodge
HOTEL **$$**

(Map p52; ☑ 071-253314; Th Khem Khong; r
US$25-50; ❀🛜🐾) This shuttered coloni-
al-era corner house has an alluring patio
draped in floral vines and punctuated with
some old bomb casings. Interiors have clean
lines and restrained decor, with wood floors,
white walls and cable TV. A few rooms offer
Mekong views. It's one of a few places in
town that welcomes pets.

Lao Wooden House
GUESTHOUSE **$$**

(Map p52; ☑ 071-260283; www.laowooden
house.com; Th Khounswa; r incl breakfast US$25-
60; ❀🛜) This friendly guesthouse-hotel is
typical of the neat, pseudo-traditional buildings that have popped up in this part of the
old quarter recently. Wood-heavy rooms
enjoy TV, desk, fridge, waffled quilts and
silence! Only six rooms; there's also a front
yard to chill in.

Khoum Xiengthong Guesthouse
GUESTHOUSE **$$**

(Map p52; ☑ 071-212906; Th Sisalernsak; r US$20-
50; ❀🛜) There's a subtle whiff of Indo-chic
here and the stone-floored, white-walled
rooms, although showing their age, enjoy
golden tapestries and chrome fans. Rooms
2 (lower floor) and 5 (upper floor) are vast
and include four-poster beds and stylish
modern en suites.

★ Satri House
HISTORIC HOTEL **$$$**

(Map p48; ☑ 071-253491; www.satrihouse.com;
off Th Phothisarat; r US$170-450; ❀🛜🏊) This
beautiful compound of villas (one is the
former house of the Lao Red Prince) boasts
stunning rooms with huge beds, fine furniture and a decorative flair unmatched
by any other boutique in the city. Imagine
pathways through lush gardens lit by statues of Indian gods, ornamental lily pools, a
stunning jade swimming pool and a maze of
Indo-chic corridors. The spa is terrific.

Victoria Xiengthong Palace
HISTORIC HOTEL **$$$**

(Map p52; ☑ 071-213200; www.victoriahotels.asia;
Th Khem Khong; r US$105-300; ❀@🛜🏊) This
former royal residence has a striking setting
overlooking the Mekong River next to Wat
Xieng Thong. The 26 rooms are luxuriously
appointed and include open-plan Mekong
suites with grandstand views and two-sto-
rey suites with their own private plunge
pools and lounges.

Sala Prabang
HOTEL **$$$**

(Map p52; ☑ 071-254087; www.salalaoboutique.
com; 102/6 Th Khem Khong; r incl breakfast
US$80-155; ❀🛜) Housed in an old French
villa and another seven buildings in the immediate neighbourhood, Sala's rooms have
lime-washed walls, guacamole-coloured
linen and hardwood floors, and are separated from the bathrooms by Japanese-style
screens. There are many variations of room
size so make sure you shop around. Beautiful throughout, this is a tasteful option.

Ban Hoxieng & Around

Compact, pretty and generally good value, Ban Hoxieng is a delightful little network of formerly residential lanes tucked behind the main post office, to the southwest of the intersection of Th Chao Fa Ngum and Th Kitsarat, with a great concentration of relatively central choices. There are more than 20 guesthouses in the alley that runs from Joma Bakery Cafe (p69) to the river.

Phonemaly Guesthouse GUESTHOUSE $
(Map p52; 071-253504; Th Hoxieng; r from 100,000K; ※ �
) Close to the night market, this pair of traditionally styled wooden houses has very much the feel of a real home yet all the conveniences of a well-run guesthouse. The best timber-clad rooms are upstairs. Obliging family owners ensure a free supply of bananas, coffee and water refills, plus decent air-con and wi-fi.

Sayo Naga Guesthouse GUESTHOUSE $$
(Map p52; 071-212484; www.sayoguesthouse. com; Th Wat That; r US$20-50; �
) Guarded by *naga*, this serene white, green-shuttered house boasts atmospheric rooms with polished wood floors, bathroom, mozzie nets, fine furniture and balcony. Add to this bedside lamps and Hmong throws and it seems a fair steal. There are also small rooms in a separate block at the back of the garden, but skip these and go for the house.

Villa Pumalin BOUTIQUE HOTEL $$
(Map p52; 071-212777; www.villapumalin.com; Th Hoxieng; r incl breakfast US$29-65; ※ �
) Rosewood steps lead across a tiny carp pool on the way up to this hotel, which has superbly finished rooms that combine stylish bathroom fittings with semi-traditional woodwork interiors and top-quality linens. The best room (201) has a private balcony with glimpses of the Mekong. For more privacy and better views, grab a room upstairs.

Maison Dalabua BOUTIQUE HOTEL $$$
(Map p52; 071-255588; www.maisondalabua. com; Th Phothisarat, Ban That Luang; r US$65-145; ※ �
) Set in spacious grounds that include a vast pond dotted with water lilies and an inviting swimming pool, Maison Dalabua is a real hideaway. The 15 rooms are in an attractive building and include flat-screen TVs and generously proportioned beds, choice furnishings and a sense of space. More expensive rooms include a bathtub.

South of Phu Si

A selection of budget and lower-midrange places south of Phu Si are generally less atmospheric, but there's a cluster of good bars nearby. Bigger hotels, some aimed at package tours and Thai/Chinese groups, are mostly further south, notably along Th Phu Vao. Few are original enough to warrant the out-of-centre location.

Aham Backpackers Hostel HOSTEL $
(Map p52; 030-2136027; Th Kingkitsarat; dm 25,000-40,000K) A real budget crashpad, Aham offers fan-cooled dorm beds in compact rooms at rock-bottom prices. Somehow the rates include breakfast, which makes it an even better deal. Staff are friendly and helpful and it's close to some of the restaurants and bars on the south side of Mt Phu Si.

Villa Sayada HOTEL $
(Map p52; 071-254872; Th Phommatha; r 150,000-220,000K; ※ �
) This nine-room minihotel offers generously sized cream and cloud-white rooms, with hung fabrics, handmade lamps and decent hot showers. There are small private balconies with pleasant views. Find it opposite Wat Wisunarat.

Davita Boutique Hotel BOUTIQUE HOTEL $$
(Map p52; 071-212088; www.davitaboutique hotel.com; Th Kingkitsarath, Ban Thongjalem; US$50-65; ※ �
) This charming backstreet boutique hotel offers 28 rooms set around a small garden courtyard with tropical foliage and a small pond. Rooms include a small terrace or balcony and offer the key box-tickers like air-con and hot-water bathrooms.

Amantaka LUXURY HOTEL $$$
(Map p52; 071-860333; www.amanresorts.com; Th Kitsarat; ste from US$1000; ※ �
 ☖) You can imagine Graham Greene writing under a wood-blade fan in the wicker-accented restaurant of this beautifully renovated French colonial-era building. Flanked by manicured lawns, a centrepiece jade swimming pool and dreamy spa and gym, suites here are capacious, with living room, four-poster beds and most featuring a private pool in their back garden. Surely Luang Prabang's finest hotel?

Substantial discounts are available in the low season.

Around Town

Hillside Resort RESORT $$

(☎ 030-5717342; www.hillsidelaos.com; r US$55-90; ❄ 🛜 🏊) Twelve kilometres south of Luang Prabang, Hillside Resort has eight bungalows and a family unit, plus plenty of activities on tap, including board games, volleyball, *petang* and a swimming pool. Top set-up and exceptional value at these prices.

Lao Spirit Resort RESORT $$

(☎ 030-5140111; www.lao-spirit.com; r US$100-160) Lao Spirit is on the banks of the river 13km east of Luang Prabang and has a convivial collection of thatched cottages on sturdy brick stilts. Interiors have antique furniture and rosewood floors and the views are stunning. Trekking and kayaking available.

Villa Suan Maak GUESTHOUSE $$

(Map p48; ☎ 071-252775; www.villasuanmaak.com; Th Noradet; r incl breakfast US$25-50; ❄ 🛜) This family-run guesthouse in a homely colonial-era villa has upstairs rooms featuring local fabrics and views across the quiet patch of garden. Newer downstairs rooms are tacked around the old house and are well appointed. A generous breakfast is included at the restaurant, known as The Kitchen, which is renowned for serving some of the best German food in town.

⭐La Résidence Phou Vao LUXURY HOTEL $$$

(Map p48; ☎ 071-212530; www.belmond.com/la-residence-phou-vao-luang-prabang; r incl breakfast US$160-460; ❄ @ 🛜 🏊) With its stunning hilltop grounds, seamless service and stylish wood rooms, Luang Prabang's first luxury hotel minted revivalist Indo-chic. The infinity pool reflects distant Phu Si and is flanked by a top-notch Franco-Lao restaurant. The Mekong Spa is spectacular and has won several global awards. No other hotel has such a spectacular view of the city and mountains. Bliss!

Free use of bikes and free limo shuttle to the city five minutes away.

Sofitel Luang Prabang SPA HOTEL $$$

(Map p48; ☎ 071-260777; www.accorhotels.com; Ban Mano; r from US$250; ❄ 🛜 🏊) This former governor's residence hides a paradise of mature palms and exotic flowers within its high walls, the highlight of which is a stunning cherry-tiled swimming pool. Rooms are huge, with battleship-grey walls, fine art and walk-in showers. In a fan-cooled pavilion the Governor's Grill turns out terrific Western food, and there's also a world-class spa.

Luang Say Residence LUXURY HOTEL $$$

(Map p48; ☎ 071-260891; www.luangsayresidence.com; Ban Phonepheng; ste incl breakfast US$175-395; ❄ @ 🛜 🏊) Conjuring the colonial-era heyday of Luang Prabang, this sophisticated all-suite hotel consists of six French-accented buildings set amid verdant gardens a short tuk-tuk ride southwest of the city. Furnishings are sumptuous and there's an inviting swimming pool. The Belle Epoque Restaurant is considered one of the top dining destinations in town.

If you're here around Christmas time (when it's *really* cool), head to the 1861 Bar decked out like a hunting lodge with a fire and plenty of malt whiskies.

Le Sen Boutique Hotel BOUTIQUE HOTEL $$$

(Map p48; ☎ 071-261661; www.lesenhotel.com; 113 Th Manomai; r US$105-239; ❄ @ 🛜 🏊) This stylish boutique hotel southwest of town is exceptional value when compared with some of the heritage hotels crammed into the old quarter. Rooms are well appointed with modish bathrooms and flat-screen TVs, and all face the inviting central swimming pool and Jacuzzi. Extra touches include a well-equipped gym and free use of bicycles. Staff are super friendly and the place is well organised.

🍴 Eating

After the privations of the more remote areas in Laos your stomach will be turning cartwheels at the sheer choice and fine execution of what's on offer here. Aside from some very fine Lao restaurants, the gastro scene is largely French. Luang Prabang also has a terrific cafe culture, with bakeries at every turn.

Self-caterers should check out the **morning market** (Map p52; Ban Pakam; ⏱ 5.30am-4pm Sat-Mon).

Thanon Sisavangvong & Around

Night Food Stalls LAO $

(Map p52; ⏱ 6-10pm; 🖉) Food stalls emerge at dusk on a narrow street behind the tourist office with illuminated communal tables to sit at. There's no better place to taste a wide variety of cheap, well-cooked local food.

There are plenty of vegetarian stalls offering a range of dishes for just 15,000K. Whole roast fish stuffed with lemongrass is a bargain at around 25,000K.

★ Bouang Asian Eatery FUSION $$

(Map p52; ☏ 020-55632600; Th Sisavangvong; mains 35,000-65,000K; ⊙ 11.30am-9.30pm Mon-Sat; ☞ ☛) This attractive eatery on the main drag puts a smile on your face with its colourful chairs, funky light fixtures and mural-covered wall. The hand-written menu of exceptional (and affordable) 'Lao revision' food includes intriguing fusions like gnocchi green curry and cinnamon-pork stew. The plating is as playful as the vibe.

Novelty Cafe CAFE $$

(Map p52; ☏ 020-55195023; 126 Th Sisavangvong; mains 25,000-75,000K; ⊙ 8am-10.30pm; ☞ ☛) One of the most popular cafes on the main strip, Novelty offers some delectable coffees, novel teas (their pun, not ours!) and delicious fruit shakes. It is a favourite spot for brunch with fresh pastries and a bistro-style menu of global dishes on the dinner menu. There is an impressive selection of vegan dishes available. Highly recommended.

Coconut Garden LAO, INTERNATIONAL $$

(Map p52; ☏ 071-252482; www.elephant-restau.com/coconutgarden; Th Sisavangvong; mains 29,000-95,000K, set menus 80,000-150,000K; ⊙ 7.30am-10pm; ☞ ☛) Excellent set menus (including a veggie option) span five top-quality Lao dishes, allowing a single diner to create the subtle palate of flavours that you'd normally only get from a feast with many people. Coconut Garden has front and rear yards, and is a great spot for lunch or dinner. International favourites are also available.

Le Café Ban Vat Sene FRENCH $$

(Map p52; www.elephant-restau.com/cafeban vatsene; Th Sakkarin; mains 50,000-75,000K; ⊙ 7.30am-10pm; ✻ ☞) Luang Prabang's most stylish stop for afternoon tea and scones. Fans whirr above a serenely lit bar, while the dessert cabinet purrs at you like a calorific temptress – think éclairs, lemon tart and raspberry mousse. Beef steak, salads, pizza, and grilled chicken and perch are also on the menu. Eat outside or within the cool interior.

Yuni Yupoun INTERNATIONAL $$

(Map p52; ☏ 020-57773636; Th Sisavangvong; mains 30,000-70,000K; ⊙ 9am-11pm; ☞) *Yuni*

yupoun means 'here or there' and pays tribute to world flavours from every corner of the globe, including Peru, Greece, Senegal, Lebanon and more. The mezze platter is a popular entry point for Med comfort food or there are more unexpected flavours like Indian butter chicken and a Canadian poutine, the original dirty fries. Happy hour is midday to 7pm.

Tamnak Lao LAO $$

(Map p52; ☏ 071-252525; Th Sakkarin; mains 40,000-75,000K; ⊙ 9am-4pm & 6-10pm; ☛) Plenty of Lao and Luang Prabang options served in an archetypal half-timbered house with sturdy arched balconies overlooking the street. Service is obliging but it often fills out with international tour groups. Try the freshwater fish.

Café Toui FUSION $$

(Map p52; www.cafetoui.com; Th Sisavang Vatthana; mains 50,000-80,000K; ⊙ 7am-10pm; ☞ ☛) Elegant and bijou, Café Toui is a delight of Lao cuisine. Great service and an Asian fusion menu with standout dishes such as *mok phaa* and zingy *láhp*, plus an inviting sampler menu.

Tangor FUSION $$

(Map p52; ☏ 071-260761; www.letangor.com; Th Sisavangvong; mains 35,000-135,000K; ⊙ 11am-11pm; ☞) Atmospheric with its low-lit interior of dark woods and tangerine-coloured walls peppered with old travel posters, Tangor boasts a menu of beautifully crafted fusion food, blending the best of seasonal Lao produce with French cuisine. Dishes include beef tenderloin, pork filet mignon and tapas, and there's a decent wine selection. Finish it off with a Cuban cigar.

Nam Khan Riverfront & Around

Pha Khao Lao LAO $

(Map p52; ☏ 030-9061120; www.phakhaolao.com; Th Phommatha; mains 20,000-70,000K; ⊙ 7am-10pm; ☞ ☛) Based on the Lao concept of a shared dining table, this local restaurant is earning a loyal following thanks to its delicious home-cooked-style food that includes a generous vegetarian selection. Noodles come in many shapes and sizes here and you can request a level of chilli to suit your palate. The lunches are an absolute bargain at 20,000K a plate.

Xieng Thong Noodle-Shop

LAO $

(Map p52; Th Sakkarin; noodle soup 15,000K; ⏰7am-2pm) The best *kòw ʔɛ̀eak sèn* (round rice noodles served in a broth with pieces of chicken or deep-fried crispy pork belly) in town is served from an entirely unexotic shopfront well up the peninsula. Popular with Chinese and Korean tourists, it usually runs out by 2pm.

Le Banneton

BAKERY $

(Map p52; 030-5788340; Th Sakkarin; meals 20,000-60,000K; ⏰6.30am-8.30pm) It's the softness of the melt-in-your-mouth pastry that keeps us coming back to our favourite bakery in Luang Prabang, which serves *pain au chocolat* (chocolate croissant), pizza, terrine, baguette sandwiches, salads, crêpes and more. The ceiling is a maze of arabesques, there's a cool fan at every turn, and the white walls are offset by a passing blur of orange outside – monks from the monastery opposite.

Located on the peaceful end of the peninsula; you'll need to get here early before the croissants run out!

★Tamarind

LAO $$

(Map p52; 071-213128; www.tamarindlaos.com; Th Kingkitsarat; mains 35,000-55,000K, set dinner 120,000-160,000K; ⏰10am-10pm; 🛜) On the banks of the Nam Khan, mint-green Tamarind has created its very own strain of 'Mod Lao' cuisine. The à la carte menu boasts delicious sampling platters with bamboo dip, stuffed lemongrass and *meuang* (DIY parcels of noodles, herbs, fish and chilli pastes, and vegetables). There's also buffalo *láhp* and Luang Prabang sausage. Deservedly popular.

★Dyen Sabai

LAO $$

(Map p52; 020-55104817; www.dyensabai restaurant.wordpress.com; Ban Phan Luang; mains 35,000-65,000K; ⏰8am-11pm; 🛜) One of Luang Prabang's top destinations for fabulous Lao food. The eggplant dip and fried Mekong riverweed are as good as anywhere. Most seating is on recliner cushions in rustic open-sided pavilions. It's a short stroll across the Nam Khan bamboo bridge in the dry season or a free boat ride at other times. Two-for-one cocktails between noon and 7pm.

Rosella Fusion

FUSION $$

(Map p52; www.facebook.com/rosellafusion; Th Kingkitsarat; mains 30,000-60,000K; ⏰9am-10.30pm) Established by a former Amantaka

(p65) bartender, this riverside restaurant offers an innovative selection of affordable fusion flavours. Try the steak and pepper sauce. The owner is particularly proud of his bargain cocktails, so consider dropping by for a sundowner before dinner.

★Paste

FUSION $$$

(Map p52; 071-254670; www.pastelaos.com; Apsara Hotel, Th Kingkitsarat; mains 120,000-280,000K; ⏰11am-10pm; 🛜) Offering a Lao fusion menu inspired by the recipes of royal chef Phia Sing and sprinkled with some magic dust from Michelin-starred Thai chef Bongkoch 'Bee' Satongun, Paste brings fine dining to Luang Prabang. Try crunchy cured rice balls with sour sausage and clear curry with beef ribs, or the signature Bangkok Paste dish: yellow curry with blue swimmer crab.

There are several tasting menus for those wanting to embark on a gastronomic journey to discover the best in traditional Lao cuisine with a twist.

🍴 Mekong Riverfront & Around

Saffron Coffee

CAFE $

(Map p52; www.saffroncoffee.com; Th Khem Khong; mains 20,000-40,000K; ⏰7am-8pm Mon-Fri, 7.30am-5pm Sat & Sun; ❄🛜) 🍃 The beans at this hip riverfront cafe are sustainably sourced from the micro coffee plots of nearby hill tribes, while profits are reinvested in the community. The result: amazingly rich coffee you'll feel good about drinking. There's an entire menu of alternative brews (cold drip, Aeropress etc) alongside yummy breakfasts and panini sandwiches. Ask about weekly coffee tours and tastings.

★Khaiphaen

LAO $$

(Map p52; 030-5155221; www.tree-alliance.org/our-restaurants/khaiphaen.php; Th Sisavang Vatthana; mains 30,000-55,000K; ⏰11am-10.30pm Mon-Sat, kitchen closes 9.30pm; 🛜🍴) 🍃 Khaiphaen is a popular training restaurant run by NGO Friends International that operates a network of inspired venues across the region. The menu is Lao with a creative twist and includes buffalo carpaccio, five spices pork belly and a pea and apple eggplant curry. The shakes are also creative. And do save space for the delicious desserts. Happy hour runs 3pm to 6pm.

Popolo

INTERNATIONAL $$

(Map p52; 020-98996858; Th Khounswa; mains 35,000-85,000K; ⏰11am-11pm; 🛜🍴) Pitching itself as a 'cantina convivial', Popolo is the brainchild of the team from the ever-popular Tangor (p67). Set in an old, exposed-brick building along quiet Th Khounswa, it still manages to draw a crowd to sample its creative cocktails and delicious Med-inspired menu that includes wood-fired pizzas, beef carpaccio and the Groovy Veggie, a vegan salad.

Blue Lagoon   INTERNATIONAL **$$**
(Map p52; www.blue-lagoon-restaurant.com; Th Ounheun; mains 75,000-140,000K; ☺10am-10pm; ⊛) A favourite with expats for its lantern-festooned walls, leafy patio and jazz-infused atmosphere. The menu features Luang Prabang sausage, pasta, boeuf bourguignon, salads and very tasty *láhp*.

Big Tree Cafe   KOREAN, INTERNATIONAL **$$**
(Map p52; www.bigtreecafe.com; Th Khem Khong; mains 35,000-65,000K; ☺9.30am-9pm Mon-Sat; ⊛⊘) Big Tree Cafe's Korean food is considered the best in the city and it's always packed with Koreans, as well as aesthetes who come to see photographer Adri Berger's work in the **gallery** (Map p52; ✎ 020-77776748; www.adriberger.com/general/luang-prabang; ☺9.30am-9pm Mon-Sat; ⊛) upstairs. Eat inside or out on the terrace in the leafy, restful garden. There's also a choice of Western and Japanese dishes.

L'Elephant Restaurant   FRENCH **$$$**
(Map p52; www.elephant-restau.com; Ban Wat Nong; mains 80,000-250,000K; ☺11.30am-10pm; ✳) L'Elephant serves some of the most sophisticated cuisine in the city in a renovated villa with wooden floors, stucco pillars, stencilled ochre walls and bags of atmosphere. The Menu du Chasseur (265,000K) includes terrines, soups, duck breast and other Gallic specialities. The buffalo steak tartare is amazing.

Ban Hoxieng & Around

Joma Bakery Cafe   BAKERY **$**
(Map p52; www.joma.biz; Th Chao Fa Ngum; mains 30,000-45,000K; ☺7am-9pm; ✳⊛) This haven of cool with comfy chairs and a contemporary vibe is one of the city's busiest bakeries. It offers delectable comfort food in the form of soups, salads, bagels, creative coffees and wholesome shakes. Oh, and mocha, coconut, carrot and chocolate cakes, plus doughnuts! There's a second branch on Th Kingkitsarat overlooking the Nam Khan.

Manda de Laos   LAO **$$$**
(Map p52; ✎ 071-253923; www.mandadelaos.com; 10 Th Norrassan; mains 80,000-180,000K; ☺noon-10.30pm; ⊛) This stunning restaurant is set in a beautiful lantern-festooned garden flanking a lily pond that is pretty by day, but enchanting by night. The menu of classic Lao cuisine includes a fun DIY *láhp* to make using a medley of herbs and spices, as well as delicious offerings such as slow-cooked duck, grilled river fish and chicken curry.

Around Town

Tea House   TEAHOUSE **$**
(Map p48; ✎ 020-77773224; www.facebook.com/teahouse.luangprabang; Ban Xang Khong; mains 15,000-45,000K; ☺8am-5pm) Located in the weaving village of Ban Xang Khong, the Tea House specialises in organic herbal teas from all over Laos, including 400-year-old tea from Phongsaly Province and a host of health-inducing teas like rosella and turmeric. High-season tea-tasting sessions are available, as well as excellent-value Lao food with a smattering of international dishes.

Secret Pizza   ITALIAN **$$**
(Map p48; ✎ 020-56528881; www.facebook.com/pizzasecret; Ban Nasaphanh; mains 50,000-60,000K; ☺from 6.30pm Tue & Fri) All right, so the secret is out, but it's well worth sharing. Long the preserve of Luang Prabang residents, host Andrea prepares wood-fired pizzas, classic lasagne and homemade gnocchi in the garden of his lovely home. Profiteroles round things off nicely, plus a fine bottle of Italian wine. Signposted from the main road; it's at the end of Soi 3 off Rte 13.

Drinking & Nightlife

The main stretch of Th Sisavangvong northeast of the palace has plenty of drinking places, including some appealing wine bars. The main hub for drinkers is just south of Phu Si on Th Kingkitsarat. Legal closing time is 11.30pm and this is fairly strictly enforced with the exception of a few out-of-town nightclubs and the notorious, late-night bowling – drunk bowlers, be warned not to drop the ball on your toes!

★**Utopia**   BAR
(Map p52; www.utopialuangprabang.com; ☺8am-11pm; ⊛) Lush riverside bar with peaceful views of the Nam Khan; think recliner cushions, low-slung tables and leafy nooks. Chill over a fruit shake, burger or breakfast (mains

30,000K to 60,000K), play a board game or volleyball, or just lose yourself in a sea of candles come sunset. Brilliantly designed with faux Khmer ruins and creeper vines, this is surely the city's liveliest outdoor bar.

Luang Prabang Yoga (p53) runs regular morning classes here; check the website for the schedule.

★Icon Klub   BAR
(Map p52; www.iconklub.com; Th Sisavang Vatthana; ☉5.30-11.30pm; 🛜) A beatnik boudoir more than a club, Icon pays homage to an older era and offers some of the best cocktails in town, including the devilish absinthe martini. A sculpted angel rises out of the wall and there are poetry slams, jam sessions and kick-ass tunes from Patti Smith to Tom Waits.

Luang Prabang Motorcycle Club   BAR
(Map p52; ☑020-98870254; Th Sakkarin; ☉3-11pm) It's worth venturing further up the peninsula after dark to discover this little gem. It's not a hardcore biker bar, but a lovely little hole-in-the-wall serving creative cocktails, cold Beerlao and a good range of international comfort food. Enquire about motorbike tours, as it is run by Nila, one of Laos' only female motorbike tour guides.

Maolin Tavern   TAVERNA
(Map p52; ☑020-91558252; www.facebook.com/maolintavern; Th Sisavangvong; ☉10am-11.30pm; 🛜) A popular spot in the heart of the old town, this bar draws a local crowd thanks to a diverse selection of international beers, including some potent Belgian options, plus a mix of cocktails. The menu includes some cold cut and cheese platters for grazing.

Bar 525   BAR
(Map p48; ☑071-212424; www.525cocktailsandtapas.com; Th Noradet; ☉4.55-11.30pm; 🛜) Parked down a quiet street, there's nothing retiring about this chic, urban bar. Sit outside stargazing on the terrace, inside at the long bar in low-lit style, or chill in the comfy lounge. Cocktails galore, glad rags, stunning photography on the walls and a sophisticated crowd. Snacks like buffalo sliders and quesadillas are also available. Prices match the ambience.

Chez Matt   BAR
(Map p52; Th Sisavang Vatthana; ☉7pm-late; 🛜) Ox-blood walls, low lights and a handsome bar glittering with polished crystal, this candlelit haunt is central and peaceful, adding a dash of upscale sophistication to the city's nocturnal landscape. With its cocktails, French and Italian wine cellar and chilled music, this makes for a good spot to dress up in your finest before going somewhere swish for dinner.

☆ Entertainment

Garavek Storytelling   THEATRE
(Map p52; ☑020-96777300; www.garavek.com; Th Khounswa; tickets 50,000K; ☉6.30pm) *Garavek* means 'magical bird', and this enchanting hour-long show – comprising an old man dressed in tribal wear playing a haunting *khene* (Lao-style lyre) alongside an animated storyteller (in English) recalling local Lao folk tales and legends – takes your imagination on a flight of fancy. Held in an intimate 30-seat theatre. Book ahead in high season.

Moonlight Cinema   CINEMA
(Map p48; www.ockpoptok.com/visit-us/whats-on; Ock Pop Tok Living Crafts Centre, 125/10 Ban Saylom; ticket incl return tuk-tuk & dinner adult/child 70,000/50,000K; ☉6.15pm selected Fri; 🛜) The latest films are shown at the Ock Pop Tok centre on selected Fridays at 7pm, screened after 6.30pm dinner. Tuk-tuk is included; pick-up is from in front of the Joma Bakery Cafe (p69) on Th Chao Fa Ngum at 6.15pm. Book via email.

Phralak-Phralam Theatre   DANCE
(Map p52; www.phralakphralam.com; Royal Palace Grounds, Th Sisavangvong; tickets 100,000-150,000K; ☉shows Mon, Wed, Fri & Sat, 6pm Oct-Mar, 6.30pm Apr-Sep) The misleadingly named Royal Lao Ballet puts on slow-moving traditional dances accompanied by a 10-piece Lao 'orchestra'. Performances last about 1¼ hours and include a Ramayana-based scene. It's well worth reading the typewritten notes provided at the entrance to have an idea of what's going on. If all the seats are full (rare), guests who bought the very cheapest tickets could end up standing.

🛍 Shopping

The best areas for shopping are Th Sisavangvong and the Mekong waterfront, where characterful boutiques selling local art, gilded Buddhas, handmade paper products and all manner of tempting souvenirs abound. Silver shops are attached to several houses in Ban Ho Xieng, the traditional royal silversmiths' district. And don't forget the night market where you'll find a cornucopia of handicrafts.

★**Handicraft Night Market**   MARKET
(Map p52; Th Sisavangvong; ⏰5.30-10pm) Every evening this tourist-oriented but highly appealing market assembles along Th Sisavangvong and is deservedly one of Luang Prabang's biggest tourist lures. Low-lit, quiet and devoid of hard selling, it has myriad traders hawking silk scarves and wall hangings, plus Hmong appliqué blankets, T-shirts, clothing, shoes, paper, silver, bags, ceramics, bamboo lamps and more.

Prices are remarkably fair but cheaper 'local' creations sometimes originate from China, Thailand or Vietnam – as a rule of thumb, if it's a scarf or bed runner, those with perfectly smooth edges are factory-made copies.

Naga Creations   JEWELLERY
(Map p52; ☎071-254400; Th Sisavangvong; ⏰10am-10pm) One of the first jewellery shops to open in Luang Prabang, Naga Creations takes its inspiration from tribal motifs around Laos combined with an international eye for semi-precious stones from around the world. The result is some unique fusion pieces that will certainly catch the eye.

Passa Paa   ARTS & CRAFTS
(Map p52; ☎030-5252471; www.passa-paa.com; Th Sisavangvong; ⏰8am-9pm) This Hmong-inspired textile studio means 'language of the cloth' and it weaves an expressive tale combining geometric tribal motifs with everyday items such as cushions, bags and artwork.

TAEC Shop   ARTS & CRAFTS
(Map p52; www.taeclaos.org; Th Sakkarin; ⏰9am-9pm) This shop sister to the TAEC (p50) museum is a safe way to buy the finest handicrafts made in Laos – be it clothes, bags or bed runners – in the knowledge they are not fakes and your purchase is directly benefiting local people. They make the perfect presents to take home.

Artisans Du Mekong   ARTS & CRAFTS
(Map p48; Ban Xang Khong; ⏰9am-4pm) This place houses a collection of beautifully made crafts from local villages in the area. There's also a chilled cafe for tea, coffee or a snack.

Queen Design Lao   CLOTHING
(Map p52; queendesignlao@gmail.com; Th Sakkarin, 1/17 Ban Khili; ⏰10am-6pm Mon-Sat; 🛜) This stylish Aussie-run boutique has a choice selection of hand-woven linen, silk and cotton dresses, chemises, skirts, and beach shawls made by Chris Boyle, a renowned designer

RETAIL THERAPY WITH A CONSCIENCE: ARTICLE 22 BOMB JEWELLERY

Named after the Declaration of Human Rights, these exquisite collectibles (http://article22.com) are designed by a well-known jeweller from New York, and are made from war scrap recycled into necklaces and bangles, the proceeds of which go directly towards supporting training and employment of unexploded ordnance (UXO) survivors. The pieces are crafted in rural Laos then sent to New York for final touches. Beautiful earrings, rings and necklaces cost from US$50 upward to US$500. Sold exclusively by Queen Design Lao.

in Oz. Most are one-off pieces. As well as pashminas and scarves, it also sells organic face scrubs and wooden designer glasses, and is the main distributor for Article 22 Bomb Jewellery.

Ma Te Sai   ARTS & CRAFTS
(Map p52; www.matesai.com; cnr Th Kingkitsarat & Th Phommatha; ⏰8.30am-8.30pm) The name means 'where is it from' in Lao, and all the silk, paper and gift items in this attractive boutique come from villages around Luang Prabang. A great selection of silk pashminas, cool T-shirts and linen chemises.

Luang Prabang Artisans   ARTS & CRAFTS
(Map p52; ☎020-55571125; www.facebook.com/luangprabangartisanscafe; off Th Sisavangvong; ⏰9am-6pm Mon-Sat, to 9pm Oct-Apr; 🛜) Located in a 100-year-old wooden home on a narrow lane running from the main street, this great little shop sells handicrafts like naturally dyed cushions, soft toys, and silk purses and scarves. There is a small on-site cafe for dropping after the shopping, with great juices and Lao food and a pretty shaded terrace where you can eat and relax.

Ock Pop Tok Boutique   CLOTHING, HANDICRAFTS
(Map p52; ☎071-254406; www.ockpoptok.com; Th Sakkarin; ⏰8am-9pm) Ock Pop Tok works with a wide range of different tribes to preserve their handicraft traditions. Fine silk and cotton scarves, chemises, dresses, wall hangings and cushion covers make perfect presents. Hop across Th Sakkarin to visit Ock Pop Tok's newer **Heritage Shop** for

more classical textiles. Weaving courses (p57) are also available.

Information

DANGERS & ANNOYANCES

Luang Prabang is an incredibly safe and intimate city, but of course there are always exceptions.

→ Beware of buying drugs; you'll probably be offered them by tuk-tuk drivers, but given they may well be undercover cops and the fine is around US$500 if you get caught, it's not worth it.

→ If you have a security box in your room, use it.

→ Beware, too, of leaving valuables out in hostels; theft does sometimes point towards the owners, as it does occasionally to other travellers.

MEDICAL SERVICES

Chinese Hospital (Map p52; ☏ 071-254026; Ban Phu Mok; ☉ 24hr) Modern medical equipment and supplies, but sometimes short of trained personnel.

Pharmacie (Map p52; Th Sakkarin; ☉ 8.30am-8pm) Stocks basic medicines. On weekends, hours are variable.

Provincial Hospital (☏ 071-254027; Ban Phou Mock; doctor's consultation 200,000K, overnight stays 400,000K) This hospital is OK for minor problems but for any serious illnesses consider flying to Bangkok or returning to Vientiane and neighbouring hospitals across the Thai border. Note that the hospital in Luang Prabang charges double for consultations at weekends or anytime after 4pm. Doctors recommend you arrive with a worker from your guesthouse who can help with translations.

MONEY

There are lots of ATMs in town. Several tour companies on Th Sisavangvong offer cash advances on Visa or MasterCard for around 3% commission. They'll also change money but rates tend to be poor.

BCEL (Map p52; Th Sisavangvong; ☉ 8.30am-3.30pm Mon-Fri) Changes major currencies in cash, has a 24-hour ATM and offers cash advances against Visa and MasterCard.

Lao Development Bank (Map p52; Th Wisunarat; ☉ 8.30am-3.30pm Mon-Fri) Has a 24-hour ATM.

Minipost Booth (Map p52; Th Sisavangvong; ☉ 8.30am-9pm) Changes most major currencies at fair rates and is open daily.

TOURIST INFORMATION

Provincial Tourism Department (Map p52; ☏ 071-212487; www.tourismluangprabang.org; Th Sisavangvong; ☉ 9-11.30am & 1.30-3.30pm Mon-Fri; ☎) General information on festivals and ethnic groups. Also offers some maps and leaflets, plus information on buses or boats on a high-tech touchscreen computer. Great office run by helpful staff.

VISAS

Immigration office (Map p48; ☏ 071-212435; Th Pha Mahapatsaman; ☉ 8-11.20am & 2-4pm Mon-Fri) It's usually possible to extend a Lao visa for up to 30 extra days (20,000K per day) if you apply before it has expired. You'll need one passport-sized photo. Pick-up is the following day at 3pm.

Getting There & Away

AIR

There has been a boom in international routes into the city ever since **Luang Prabang International Airport** (LPQ; ☏ 071-212173; www.luangprabangairport.com; ☎) got a smart new building and an expanded runway in 2013. Bangkok Airways (www.bangkokair.com) and Air Asia (www.airasia.com) both fly daily to Bangkok, while the latter also serves Kuala Lumpur. **Lao Airlines** (Map p48; ☏ 071-212172; www.laoairlines.com; Th Pha Mahapatsaman; ☉ 8am-noon & 1-5pm Mon-Fri) serves Vientiane several times daily, as well as Pakse, Chiang Mai and Hanoi once daily. It also has frequent flights to Jinghong and Chengdu in China. Vietnam Airlines (www.vietnamairlines.com) flies to both Siem Reap (codeshare with Lao Airlines) and Hanoi daily. Budget airline Scoot (www.flyscoot.com) now connects Luang Prabang to Singapore. It is easy to buy tickets through **All Lao Travel** (Map p52; ☏ 020-55571572, 071-253522; www.alllaoservice.com; Th Sisavangvong; ☉ 8am-9pm).

BOAT

Though not always the quickest way to travel, journeying by river allows you to slow down and take in the city and surrounding country from a different angle.

Pak Beng & Huay Xai

For slowboats to Pak Beng (130,000K, nine hours, 8.30am), it will likely be cheaper and easier to buy tickets from an agent in town than to take a tuk-tuk to the navigation office (☉ 8-11am & 2-4pm) at the slowboat landing, located an inconvenient 10km north of the city in Ban Done-mai. Through-tickets to Huay Xai (250,000K, two days) are also available, but you'll have to sleep in Pak Beng. This allows you to stay a little longer in Pak Beng should you like the place.

The more upscale Luang Say Cruise (p58) departs on two-day rides to Huay Xai from the **Galao boat pier** (Map p52; Th Khem Khong) near Wat Xieng Thong. Rates include an overnight stay at the Luang Say Lodge in Pak Beng. A cheaper alternative is Shompoo Cruise (p58), a two-day cruise aboard a smart boutique boat; accommodation in Pak Beng is not included.

Fast, uncomfortable and seriously hazardous speedboats can shoot you up the Mekong to Pak Beng (190,000K, three hours) and Huay Xai (310,000K, seven hours). Boats depart when full with six or seven passengers, so your best bet is to arrive at the **speedboat landing** (next to the slowboat landing in Ban Donemai) at around 8am and form a group.

Thailand's Golden Triangle

From June to February, Mekong River Cruises (p59) makes lazy eight-day trips from Luang Prabang to Thailand's Golden Triangle on an innovative two-storey German–Lao riverboat with a small sun deck and 15 cabins in which you sleep as well as travel.

BUS & MINIBUS

Predictably enough, the **Northern Bus Station** (Map p48; ☏ 071-252729; Rte 13) and **Southern Bus Station** (Bannalaung Bus Station; Map p48; ☏ 071-252066; Rte 13, Km 383) are at opposite ends of town. Several popular bus routes are duplicated by minibuses/minivans from the **Naluang minibus station** (Map p48; ☏ 071-212979; Rte 13), diagonally opposite the latter.

For less than double the bus fare, another option is to gather your own group and rent a comfortable six-seater minivan. Prices include photo stops and you'll get there quicker. Directly booked through the minibus station, prices are about 1,000,000K to Phonsavan or Vang Vieng and 800,000K to Nong Khiaw, including pick-up from the guesthouse.

Sainyabuli & Hongsa

Buses to Sainyabuli depart from the Southern Bus Station. The Tha Deua bridge over the Mekong River has reduced the journey time to Sainyabuli to two hours or so by private vehicle. There is also a direct minibus service to the Elephant Conservation Center (p136) in Sainyabuli, which picks you up outside the post office and is included in the price of your tour. For Hongsa, the new bridge means it is easiest to travel to Sainyabuli and connect from there.

Nong Khiaw & Sam Neua

An alternate route for Nong Khiaw and Sam Neua leaves from the Northern Bus Station. Take the *sŏrngtăaou* (pick-up trucks fitted with benches in the back for passengers; 40,000K) at 9am, 11am and 2pm or the 8.30am bus that continues to Sam Neua (140,000K, 17 hours) via Vieng Thong (120,000K, 10 hours). Another Sam Neua–bound bus (from Vientiane) should pull in sometime around 5.30pm.

BUSES FROM LUANG PRABANG

DESTINATION	STATION	COST (K)	DISTANCE (KM)	DURATION (HR)	DEPARTURES
Huay Xai	Northern	120,000	475	15	5.30pm
Huay Xai (VIP)	Northern	145,000	475	15	7pm
Luang Namtha	Northern	100,000	310	9	9am, 4pm
Luang Namtha (minibus)	Naluang	110,000	310	8	8.30am
Nong Khiaw	Northern	40,000	142	4	9am, 11am, 2pm
Nong Khiaw (minibus)	Naluang	55,000	142	3	9.30am
Phonsavan (minibus)	Naluang	110,000	262	8	9am
Phonsavan (ordinary/express)	Southern	95,000/105,000	262	10/9	8.30am
Sainyabuli	Southern	60,000	118	3	9am, 2pm
Sam Neua	Northern	150,000	390	17	8.30am, 5.30pm
Udomxai	Northern	60,000	193	6	9am, noon, 4pm
Vang Vieng	Southern	95,000	185	7	9.30am
Vang Vieng (minibus)	Naluang	110,000	185	6	8.30am, 9.30am, 10am, 2pm, 3pm
Vieng Thong	Northern	120,000	275	10	8.30am, 5.30pm
Vientiane	Southern	110,000	384	9	10 daily btwn 6.30am & 7.30pm
Vientiane (sleeper)	Southern	150,000	384	9	8pm, 8.30pm
Vientiane (minibus)	Naluang	155,000	384	9	7am, 11am

China

The sleeper bus to Kunming (500,000K, 24 hours) in China departs from the Southern Bus Station (p73) at 7am, sometimes earlier. Pre-booking, and checking the departure location, is wise.

Vietnam

Head to the Naluang minibus station (p73) for buses to Dien Bien Phu (200,000K, 10 hours, leaves 6.30am) and Hanoi (350,000K, 24 hours, leaves 6pm) in Vietnam.

🛈 Getting Around

Compact Luang Prabang is easily walkable and best appreciated on foot. Bicycles come in handy for reaching some further-afield attractions, while tuk-tuks are needed for the airport, boat landings and bus stations.

BICYCLE

A satisfying way to get around is by bicycle. Numerous shops and some guesthouses have hire bikes for 15,000K to 30,000K per day.

Be careful to lock bicycles and motorbikes securely and don't leave them on the roadside overnight. Note that the peninsula's outer road is one-way anticlockwise: signs are easy to miss. Although you'll see locals flouting the rule (and riding without helmets), police will occasionally fine foreigners.

BOAT

Numerous boats to Pak Ou Caves (Map p52) depart between 8.30am and lunchtime; buy tickets at the easily missed little **longboat office** (Map p52; Th Khem Khong; ⊙8am-3pm). **Banana Boat Laos** (Map p52; ☑071-260654; www.bananaboatlaos.com; Ma Te Sai, Th Phommatha) offers better-organised boat trips for those who aren't worried about every last kip; boats leave from behind Wat Xieng Thong. There are also handy **cross-river boats** (Map p52; one-way 10,000K) connecting the old town with the rural west bank of the Mekong.

BUS

E-Bus is an electric zero-emission tuk-tuk (green and yellow) that used to circulate around the old town as a form of public transport, but now acts like a normal tuk-tuk. Prices are generally a fraction of what the old-school tuk-tuks charge, at about 10,000K for a short hop or 20,000K to the bus stations. Simply wave one down as it passes by.

The company also offers an **E-Bus Tour** (Map p48; ☑071-253899; www.laogreengroup.com; tour US$40, child under 10 free; ⊙tours 8.30am-12.30pm & 1-4.30pm), which takes passengers around the city on a guided visit to local attractions.

CAR & MOTORCYCLE

Motorcycle rental typically costs 120,000K per day. **KPTD** (Map p52; ☑071-212077; Th Kitsarat; semi-automatic 100,000K, automatic 120,000K, 250cc dirt bikes per day US$70; ⊙8am-5pm) has a wide range of bikes available, including Honda Waves (semi-automatic), Honda Scoopy (automatic) and a thoroughly mean Honda CRF (US$70) for motocross riders only. **Motolao** (Map p52; ☑020-54548449; www.motolao.com; Th Chao Fa Ngum; ⊙8.30am-5pm) rents Honda 250cc motorbikes.

SŎRNGTĂAOU

Located on the opposite side of the Mekong to Luang Prabang, about 400m up from the river, the Chomphet sŏrngtăaou stand (Map p48) serves local villages only.

TAXI-VAN

Taxi-vans at the airport charge a standardised 50,000K into the city centre (4km away) for one to two people. These will cost a bit more if three or four people share the ride. From town back to the airport you might pay marginally less.

TUK-TUK

Luang Prabang has no motorbike taxis, only tuk-tuks charging a standardised 50,000K from the airport into town. These will cost more if more than three people share the ride. From town back to the airport you might pay marginally less.

Around town, locals often pay just 5000K for short tuk-tuk rides, but foreigners are charged a flat 20,000K per hop. To the slowboat landing or speedboat landing reckon on at least 50,000K for the vehicle.

AROUND LUANG PRABANG

The countryside surrounding Luang Prabang's protected area is home to aquamarine waterfalls, top trekking opportunities, meandering mountain-bike trails, kayaking trips and river cruises.

North of Luang Prabang

Pak Ou Caves   ຖ້ຳປາກອູ

Where the Nam Ou (Ou River) and Mekong River meet at Ban Pak Ou, two famous **caves** (Tham Ting; cave 20,000K, return boat tickets per person/boat 65,000/300,000K; ⊙boats depart 8.30-11am) in the limestone cliff are crammed with myriad Buddha images. In the lower cave a photogenic group of Buddhas are silhouetted against the stunning riverine backdrop. The upper cave is a five-minute climb up steps (you'll need a torch), 50m into the rock face. Buy boat tickets from the longboat office in Luang Prabang.

Most visitors en route to Pak Ou stop at the 'Lao Lao Village' **Ban Xang Hay**, famous for its *lòw-lów* (whisky). The narrow footpath-streets behind the very attractive (if mostly new) wat are also full of weavers' looms, colourful fabric stalls and a few stills producing the wide range of liquors sold.

An alternative is to go by road to Ban Pak Ou (30km, around 150,000K return for a tuk-tuk) then take a motor-canoe across the river (20,000K return). Ban Pak Ou is 10km down a decent unpaved road that turns off Rte 13 near Km 405.

East of Luang Prabang

Ban Phanom & Beyond
ບ້ານພະນົມ/ສຸສານທມູທິດ

If you climbed Phu Si you'll surely have spied a large octagonal stupa painted a dazzling golden hue near the 'New Bridge'. This is the 1988 **Santi Chedi** (ສັນຕິເຈຕິ, Peacefulness Pagoda; Map p48; donation expected; ⊙ 8-10am & 1.30-4.30pm Mon-Fri), whose five interior levels are painted with all manner of Buddhist stories and moral admonitions.

It's on a gentle rise, 1km off Rte 13 beside the road to **Ban Phanom**, a prosperous weaving and handicrafts village less than 1km further east. A mostly unpaved road initially follows the Nam Khan east and south, looping round eventually after 14km to **Ban Kok Gniew**, the 'pineapple village' at Km 372 on Rte 13, just 500m short of the turning to Tat Sae waterfall. The road is dusty and gently hilly but quiet and scenic with some attractive karst scenery and several points of interest.

Around 6.5km from Ban Phanom, and less than 2km further along the road from the **tomb of Henri Mouhot** (ສຸສານ ຫານຣີ ເຮັນຣີ ມູຮ໋ອດ), the French explorer and naturalist, are the mural-daubed old wat and gilded stupa of **Ban Noun Savath** (ບ້ານບຸນສະຫວາດ). The scene is especially photogenic in afternoon light with a large karst-hump mountain forming a perfect backdrop.

Tat Sae
ນ້ຳຕົກຕາດແສ

The wide, multi-level cascade pools of this menthol-hued **waterfall** (ຕາດແສ; 20,000K, child under 8 free; ⊙ 8am-5.30pm) 15km southeast of Luang Prabang are a memorable sight from August to November. Unlike Tat Kuang Si, there's no single long-drop centrepiece and they dry up almost completely by February. But several year-round gimmicks keep visitors coming, notably a loop of 14 **ziplines** (☑ 020-54290848; per person 300,000K) that allow you to 'fly' around and across the falls.

Part of the attraction of a visit is getting here on a very pleasant seven-minute boat ride (20,000K per person return, 40,000K minimum) that starts from Ban Aen, a peaceful Lao village that's just 1km east of Rte 13 (turn east at Km 371.5). A 30-minute tuk-tuk from Luang Prabang costs up to 150,000K return, including a couple of hours' wait.

West of Luang Prabang

Nahm Dong Park

This beautiful area of private **park** (ສວນນ້ຳດົງ; ☑ 030-5609821; www.nahmdong. com; Nahm Dong Reservoir; entry 20,000K, 2/3 activities US$23/33, ziplining US$23; ▣) ✐ lies about 10km southwest of Luang Prabang in the rolling jungle-clad hills around town. Explore the forest, plunge into the waterfalls and pools here or dabble in some of the many activities on offer, including making mulberry paper, a Thai-Leu dreamcatcher or Hmong embroidery. For more of an adrenaline buzz, try the treetop walk and ziplines. There is also an excellent Lao restaurant and teahouse with a stunning valley view.

Kuang Si Butterfly Park

Just 300m before the Kuang Si waterfall, **Kuang Si Butterfly Park** (ສວນແມງກະເບື້ອກວາງຊີ; www.facebook.com/laos.kuang. si.butterflypark; adult/child 40,000/20,000K; ⊙ 10.30am-4.30pm) ✐ was opened in 2014 as a breeding sanctuary for Laos' myriad butterflies. Open to travellers, you can wander the beautiful gardens on a tour, as well as having your feet nibbled by miniature fish at the foot spa. Great fun for kids. There's also a cafe here with special entry and cake combination tickets available.

Tat Kuang Si   ຕາດກວາງຊິ

Thirty kilometres southwest of Luang Prabang, **Tat Kuang Si** (ຕາດກວາງຊິ; 20,000K; ⊙8am-5.30pm) is a many-tiered waterfall tumbling over limestone formations into a series of cool, swimmable turquoise pools; the term 'Edenic' doesn't do it justice. When you're not swinging off ropes into the water, there's a public park with shelters and picnic tables where you can eat lunch. Don't miss the **Tat Kuang Si Bear Rescue Centre** (ສູນກູ້ໄພຫມີຕາດກວາງຊິ; www.freethebears.org; Tat Kuang Si; admission incl with Tat Kuang Si ticket; ⊙8.30am-4.30pm) **FREE**, where wild Asiatic moon bears, confiscated from poachers, are given a new lease of life.

Many cheap eateries line the entrance car park at the top end of the Khamu village of Ban Thapene, selling everything from local snacks to grilled chicken and fish. Alternatively, **Carpe Diem** (☑020-98676741; www.carpediem.la; Tat Kuang Si; mains 45,000-175,000K; ⊙9am-5pm; ✐⊕) ⬤ is a French restaurant set in thatched pavilions dotted about the lower falls of Kuang Si.

Visiting Kuang Si by hired motorcycle is very pleasant now that the road here is decently paved and allows stops in villages along the way. By bicycle, be prepared for two long, steady hills to climb. A tuk-tuk from Luang Prabang costs 150,000K for one person, and 50,000K per person in a group of three, so it's best to get a group together. A private minivan will cost 350,000K.

Laos Buffalo Dairy

Set up by Australian pioneers with no prior experience in farming, the **Buffalo Dairy** (ຟາມນົມຄວາຍຢູ່ລາວ; ☑030-9690487; www.laosbuffalodairy.com; farm tours 50,000-100,000K; ⊙9.30am-5.30pm) ⬤ is now producing a range of delicious cheese and dairy products. Visitors can tour the working farm with English-speaking guides, learning how to milk a buffalo, help wash the pampered

'Ferdinand' and meet the resident rabbits. Ice cream and cakes are also on sale here, as well as a cheese platter.

It is located 23km from Luang Prabang on the road to Kuang Si.

Green Jungle Park

Thirty-two kilometres west of the city, **Green Jungle Park** (ສວນປາດິງຂງວ; ☑071-253899; www.laogreengroup.com; Ban Pakleuang; park entry US$3, ziplining & ropes courses US$30-65, trekking US$35, return boat transfer from Luang Prabang 10,000K; ⊙9am-4.30pm) ⬤ is a slice of natural paradise reclaimed from a rubbish dump and uses the forest and a stunning cascade as its backdrop for a spectacular cat's cradle of ziplines (900m), monkey bridges and rope courses. Also here are a cafe, flower gardens and natural swimming pools, an organic produce market and an elephant-viewing area where ex-logging jumbos can socialise.

To reach the park, you catch the comfy boat from behind the Royal Palace in Luang Prabang; you'll ride downriver for 30 minutes, then be taxied the rest of the way by road.

Pha Tad Ke Botanical Garden

As relaxing as a trip to the spa, this **botanical garden** (ສວນພຶດສາຂາດຜາຕັດແກ; Map p52; ☑071-261000; www.pha-tad-ke.com; adult/child US$25/10; ⊙8am-6pm Thu-Tue), opened in 2017 as the first in Laos, is a serene spot to read, take a stroll or perfect some yoga poses. The entry price, although steep, includes an orchid talk (11am or 3pm), a one-hour bamboo handicraft workshop (10am or 2pm) and free herbal-tea tastings in a cafe overlooking a lotus pond.

Boats depart from a dock in Ban Wat That (across from Pha Tad Ke's downtown reception office) between 9am and 4pm; it's a 15-minute ride down the Mekong to the park.

Northern Laos

Best Places to Eat

➡ Lao Falang Restaurant (p85)

➡ Coco Home Bar & Restaurant (p101)

➡ Bamboo Lounge (p121)

➡ Riverside Restaurant (p104)

➡ Souphailin Restaurant (p114)

Best Places to Stay

➡ Mandala Ou Resort (p99)

➡ Luang Say Lodge (p134)

➡ Luang Namtha Inn (p119)

➡ Nong Kiau Riverside (p100)

➡ Nam Kat Yorla Pa (p114)

Why Go?

Whether it's for trekking, cycling, kayaking, ziplining or a family homestay, a visit to northern Laos is for many the highlight of their trip. Dotted about are unfettered, dense forests home to big cats, gibbons and a cornucopia of animals, with a well-established ecotourism infrastructure to take you into their heart.

In the north you will also find a tapestry of vividly attired ethnic tribes unlike anywhere else in Laos.

Here the Land of a Million Elephants morphs into the land of a million hellish bends and travel is not for the faint-hearted, as roads twist and turn through towering mountain ranges and serpentine river valleys.

Most northern towns are functional places, rebuilt after wholesale bombing during the 20th-century Indochina wars. But visitors aren't here for the towns; it's all about the rural life. River trips are a wonderful way to discover the bucolic scenery at a more languid pace.

When to Go
Luang Prabang

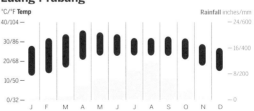

Nov–Feb The ideal season to visit, with little rain and clear skies, but chilly at higher altitudes.

Mar–May Blazing heat at lower altitudes, with lots of haze from slash-and-burn cultivation.

Jun–Oct The wet season; accommodation is cheap but humidity is high.

Northern Laos Highlights

1 Gibbon Experience (p130) Soaring through the jungle canopy on ziplines to remote tree houses on this unforgettable adventure near Huay Xai.

2 Nam Ou (p90) Karsting away on a boat ride or kayak trip down the Nam Ou (Ou River) between Muang Ngoi Neua and Nong Khiaw.

3 Phongsali (p108) Learning about the local lifestyle in homestays on a tribal trek in this remote region that's home to some of the oldest tea plantations in the world.

4 Vieng Xai Caves (p95) Discovering the history of the incredible limestone landscape where the Pathet Lao hid from US aerial assault.

5 Plain of Jars (p86) Exploring Xieng Khuang's mysterious archaeological sites where ancient burial jars are scattered across the windswept hills.

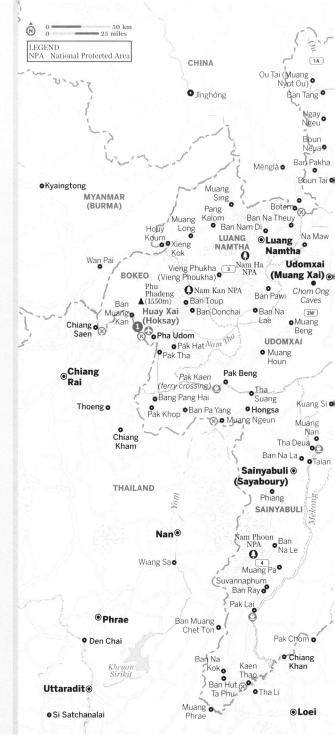

ⓘ Getting There & Away

The state of roads linking the north to the rest of Laos is steadily improving. By far the easiest, most popular and most spectacular is Rte 13 from Luang Prabang to Vang Vieng. The alternative, via Sainyabuli and Pak Lai, is now paved but less scenic. A third possibility, Rte 10 from Muang Khoun to Paksan, is now in good shape, but there are still some lingering security concerns along certain remote stretches. Finally, the hellish ordeal on what was an ulcerous and dangerously slippery road from Udomxai to Phongsali is now completely sealed, but sadly just as serpentine!

ⓘ Getting Around

Road journeys in northern Laos are slow and exhausting. Only the key major routes are asphalted and these are generally very narrow and winding. Wet season sees occasional landslides and secondary roads become as slippery as ice.

Bus/Sŏrngtăaou (pick-up trucks fitted with benches in the back) These link most major towns, but are slow going on the long and winding roads.

Car/Minivan A good option for those with more money (think US$100 per day), but less time.

Motorcycle Great for adventurous riders with experience as the scenery is stunning.

Riverboat A delightful, if slower, alternative to road travel. Think twice before opting for a 'speedboat': like a surfboard with a strap-on car engine.

XIENG KHUANG & HUA PHAN PROVINCES

Long and winding roads run in seemingly endless ribbons across these green, sparsely populated northeastern provinces towards the mysterious Plain of Jars and the fascinating Vieng Xai Caves. Both are truly intriguing places to visit if you're en route to or from Vietnam. Those with the time can add stops in Nong Khiaw and Vieng Thong. The latter is a gateway to the Nam Et/Phou Louey National Park and its 'tiger treks'. Almost anywhere else in either province is completely off the tourist radar.

The altitude, averaging more than 1000m, ensures a climate that's neither too hot in the hot season, nor too cold in the cool season. In December and January, a sweater or jacket is appropriate at night and in the early morning when seas of cloud fill the populated valleys and form other-worldly scenes for those looking down from passes or peaks.

History

Xieng Khuang's world-famous giant 'jars' along with Hintang's mysterious megaliths indicate a well-developed Iron Age culture of which historical knowledge is astonishingly hazy. Whoever carved those enigmatic monuments had long since disappeared by the 13th century when Xieng Khuang emerged as a Buddhist, Tai Phuan principality with a capital at today's Muang Khoun. Both provinces spent subsequent centuries as either independent kingdoms or part of Vietnamese vassal states known as Ai Lao and Tran Ninh. In 1832 the Vietnamese captured the Phuan king of Xieng Khuang, publicly executed him in Hué and made the kingdom a prefecture of Annam, forcing people to adopt Vietnamese dress and customs. Chinese Haw gangs ravaged the region in the late 19th century, pushing both provinces to accept Siamese and French protection.

Major skirmishes between the Free Lao and the Viet Minh took place from 1945 to 1946, and as soon as the French left Indochina, the North Vietnamese started a build-up of troops to protect Hanoi's rear flank. By the end of the 1960s the area had become a major battlefield. With saturation bombing by American planes obliterating virtually every town and village, much of the population had to live for their protection in caves, only emerging in 1973. At Vieng Xai, the most important of these caves also sheltered the Pathet Lao's Communist leadership.

North Vietnamese troops did their share of damage on the ground as well, destroying once-magnificent Muang Sui and much of royalist-held western Xieng Khuang Province. After the conflict, infamous *samana* re-education camps appeared, notably in eastern Hua Phan, to 'rehabilitate' and punish former royalists with a mixture of hard labour and political indoctrination. Many continued into the 1980s and the possibility that a *samana* still remains near Sop Hao has never been officially confirmed nor denied. Meanwhile, decades after the conflict, unexploded ordnance (UXO) remains very widespread, especially in central and eastern Xieng Khuang, threatening local lives for generations to come.

UXO & WAR JUNK

During the Indochina wars, Laos earned the dubious distinction of becoming the most heavily bombed nation per capita in world history. Xieng Khuang Province was especially hard hit and even today, innumerable scraps of combat debris remain. Much of it is potentially deadly UXO, including mortar shells, white phosphorous canisters (used to mark bomb targets) and assorted bombs. Some of the most problematic UXO comes from cluster bombs, 1.5m-long torpedo-shaped packages of evil whose outer metal casing was designed to split open lengthwise in mid-air, scattering 670 tennis-ball-sized bomblets ('bombies') over a 5000-sq-metre area. Once disturbed, a bombie would explode, projecting around 30 steel pellets like bullets, killing anyone within a 20m radius. Over 40 years after bombing ceased, almost one person a day is still injured or killed by UXO in Laos, 40% of them children. Tens of millions of bombies remain embedded in the land, causing an ever-present danger to builders, farmers and especially young children, who fatally mistake them for toys. And for impoverished villagers, the economic temptation to collect UXO to sell as scrap metal has caused numerous fatalities. Despite valiant ongoing clearance efforts, at current rates it would take an estimated 150 years to deal with the problem.

Cluster-bomb casings, which were not themselves explosive, have meanwhile found a wide range of more positive new uses. In some places you can see them reused as architectural features, feeding troughs, pots for growing spring onions or simply as ornaments around houses or hotels.

If you find any war debris, don't be tempted to touch it. Even if it appears to be an exhibit in a collection, beware that some hotels display war junk that's never been properly defused and might remain explosive. Even if it isn't live and dangerous, the Lao legal code makes it illegal to trade in war leftovers of any kind. Purchase, sale or theft of any old weaponry can result in a prison term of between six months and five years.

Phonsavan ໂພນສະຫວັນ

🎵 061 / POP 49,000

Phonsavan is a popular base from which to explore the Plain of Jars. The town itself has an unfinished feel and is very spread out, with its two parallel main boulevards stretching about 3km east–west. Fortunately, a very handy concentration of hotels, restaurants and tour agents is crammed into a short if architecturally uninspired central 'strip'. But the town is best appreciated from the surrounding hills, several of which are pine-clad and topped with small resorts. Keep an eye out too for wooden powder-blue Hmong cottages on the mountain roads with firewood neatly stacked outside.

The region has long been a centre of Phuan language and culture (part of the Tai-Kadai family). There's also a strong Vietnamese presence.

◉ Sights

About 1km apart at the southern edge of town are two hilltop **memorials** (open sunrise to sunset) to Pathet Lao and Vietnamese soldiers lost in the war.

★ UXO Information Centre (MAG)

CULTURAL CENTRE

(🎵 061-211010; www.maginternational.org/laos; donations encouraged; ⊗10am-8pm) FREE Decades after America's Secret War on Laos, unexploded bombs and mines remain a devastating problem throughout this region. Visit the thought-provoking UXO Information Centre, run by British organisation MAG (Mines Advisory Group) that's been helping to clear Laos' unexploded ordnance since 1994. The centre's information displays underline the enormity of the bomb drops, and there are also examples of (defused) UXO to ponder. Donations are encouraged: US$15 pays for the clearing of around 10 sq metres and a commemorative T-shirt.

Late-afternoon screenings show the powerful documentaries *Bomb Harvest* (4.30pm; www.redlampfilms.com/films-2/bomb-harvest-2), *Surviving the Peace* (5.50pm) and *Bombies* (6.30pm; www.bullfrogfilms.com/catalog/bombie.html). They are distressing but important, as they show the full scale of the trauma, from footage of US bombers in action to the ongoing casualties of their horrific legacy.

Phonsavan

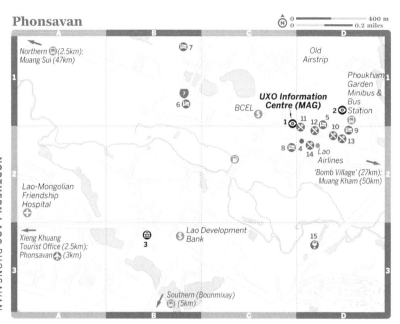

Phonsavan

◎ Top Sights
1 UXO Information Centre (MAG) C1

◎ Sights
2 Fresh Food Market D1
3 Xieng Khouang Provincial Museum B3
Xieng Khouang UXO-Survivors'
    Information Centre .... (see 1)

◆ Activities, Courses & Tours
Lao Falang Travel Service ....(see 5)
4 Sousath Travel D2

◉ Sleeping
5 Anoulack Khen Lao Hotel.......................D1

6 Favanh Mai Hotel.....................................B1
7 Hillside Residence B1
8 Jennida Guesthouse II...........................C2
9 Kong Keo Guesthouse D2

✖ Eating
10 Bamboozle Restaurant & Bar...............D2
11 Cranky-T Café & Bar D2
12 Lao Falang Restaurant..........................D2
13 Nisha Restaurant....................................D2
14 Simmaly Restaurant D2

◉ Drinking & Nightlife
15 Barview...D3

Xieng Khouang
Provincial Museum   MUSEUM
(ຫໍພິພິດຕະພັນແຂວງຊຽງຂວາງ;   15,000K;
⊙9-11.30am & 1.30-4pm Tue-Sun) One of the
most interesting provincial museums in
Laos, Xieng Khouang Provincial Museum
was funded with help from the German
government. Downstairs are lots of detailed
presentations about the Plain of Jars and
the ancient history of the Xieng Khuang
kingdom. Upstairs you'll find displays on
more recent Lao history and the US bombing campaign that so devastated Xieng

Khuang Province. Also includes some fascinating exhibits on the province's different
ethnic communities.

Xieng Khouang UXO-Survivors'
Information Centre   CULTURAL CENTRE
(www.laos.worlded.org;   donations encouraged;
⊙8am-4pm Mon-Fri) ◆ FREE This UXO information centre and colourful, upbeat shop
sells silk laptop bags, purses and handicrafts made by UXO survivors. Aside from
displays including bomb parts and harrow-
ing stories of recent victims, there's also a

wealth of information on the Secret War and the different kinds of UXO that still present a danger in Laos today. Ask to see the video *Surviving Cluster Bombs*. Note that 90% of your donations go towards the treatment of UXO survivors.

Mulberries   FARM
(ปั้ลา; ☎ 021-263371; www.mulberries.org; Ban Li; ☉ 8am-4pm Mon-Sat) `FREE` This is a fair-trade silk farm that offers interesting free visits including a complete introduction to the silk-weaving process from cocoon to colourful scarves. If you're feeling inspired you can sign up for a half-day dyeing or weaving course (US$20). Find the farm off Rte 7 just west of the main bus station.

Fresh Food Market   MARKET
(☉ 6am-5pm) This market stocks exotic fruits you won't typically see elsewhere in Laos, such as Chinese pear. Other local delicacies include *nok qen dąwng* (swallows stored whole in jars until they ferment) and *hét wâi* (wild matsutake mushrooms), which grow around Xieng Khuang and fetch high prices in Japan. Bring your camera.

🏃 Activities & Tours

Several agents on the main drag and virtually every guesthouse will be ready to slot you into a one-day Plain of Jars tour visiting the three main sites. The going rate is 150,000K including a noodle-soup lunch and entry fees. This price is contingent on there being at least seven fellow passengers.

Other advertised tours include trips to places such as Muang Khoun, Tham Piu or nearby hot springs, but these rarely garner enough customers for prices to be competitive. Try gathering your own group.

★ Sousath Travel   TOURS
(☎ 020-22967213; rasapet_lao@yahoo.com; Rte 7; ☉ 8am-8pm) Sousath is the man who helped open the Plain of Jars to tourists, and the trips run by his son, Mr Nouds, are the most informative in town. Extremely knowledgeable about the region, Mr Nouds can also organise tours of the Ho Chi Minh Trail, homestays in Hmong villages and multiday treks (including the Phakeo Trek).

For war obsessives he can plan trips to Long Tien, the clandestine runway in the Saisombun jungle created by the CIA during the Secret War. He also rents bikes (20,000K) and scooters (manual/automatic 80,000/100,000K).

Lao Falang Travel Service   ADVENTURE
(☎ 020-23305614; Rte 7; 1-day all-inclusive trip US$150) Run by a dependable Italian guy, this outfit operates multiday and one-day motorbike tours, of which 70% to 85% are spent off-road (depending on your confidence). A one-day tour typically includes Jar Site 1, the Russian Tank and Muang Khoun. Dinner is included at the excellent Lao Falang Italian restaurant (p85). Experienced guides ensure you don't go beyond your comfort zone.

Lone Buffalo   VOLUNTEERING
(☎ 020-77159566; www.facebook.com/lonebuffalo; Highway 1D) Named after Manophet 'Lone Buffalo', a visionary community leader, this nonprofit is dedicated to providing free English classes to rural youth, as well as filmmaking workshops and football coaching. There are several ways to help out, from coaching the football team on weekends to purchasing the students' guide to Phonsavan or buying Lone Buffalo T-shirts at restaurants in town.

Those with professional skills, including photography or sports coaching, who would be interested in running a workshop for the school kids are also encouraged to get in touch, as are English teachers willing to make a longer-term commitment.

🛏 Sleeping

Rooms in Phonsavan span basic guesthouse digs to midrange hotel rooms. Booking ahead is not usually necessary, nor is air-conditioning. There are also several smarter lodge-style hotels spread around town, including some imperiously perched atop pine-clad hills.

In Town

★ Kong Keo Guesthouse   GUESTHOUSE $
(☎ 020-285858; dm 50,000K, d in outside block 80,000K, bungalows 120,000K; 🛜) Run by the charming and extremely knowledgeable Kong, the seven-berth dorm is slightly cramped, but the outdoor block has large clean rooms with mint-green walls and private bathrooms. More spacious are the six bungalows dotted about the garden. The UXO-decorated restaurant-bar has occasional barbecues, and Kong runs highly recommended tours to the Plain of Jars.

PHAKEO TREK

Organised through Phonsavan agencies or the Xieng Khuang Tourist Office, the excellent two-day **Phakeo Trek** combines many essential elements of the Xieng Khuang experience. On the long first day, hike across secondary forested mountain ridges to a three-part jar site with about 400 ancient jars and jar fragments, many moss-encrusted and shaded by foliage. The trek then descends into the roadless Hmong village of Ban Phakeo, whose shingle-roofed mud-floor homes huddle around a central rocky knoll. A purpose-built, Hmong-style guest shack provides a basic sleeping platform with space for eight hikers. There's no electricity. The next day, the hike descends into attractive semi-agricultural valleys then climbs up the cascades of a multi-terraced waterfall to arrive in the famous 'Bomb Village', which no longer has many bombs after extensive clearance work.

Jennida Guesthouse II   GUESTHOUSE $
(✆020-28590001; d/tw 80,000K; ☞) Don't be put off by the surreal sight of the Snow White and the Seven Dwarfs statues in the courtyard car park, as the spacious 42 rooms here are great value for money. The room decoration is tidy if simple and all rooms include a ceiling fan and attached bathroom. There is a handy minimart out front for essential supplies.

Anoulack Khen Lao Hotel   HOTEL $$
(✆061-213599; www.anoulackkhenlao.com; Rte 7; d/tw incl breakfast 250,000-500,000K; ✳☞) This glass Lego tower has some of the best rooms in town, with wood floors, thick mattresses, white linen, cable TV, fridges, kettles and swish hot-water en suites. There's a great restaurant with panoramic views of Phonsavan on the 5th floor with free wi-fi. Conveniently the hotel also has a lift, so it is worth the extra spend.

🏠 Around Town

Pukyo Guesthouse   GUESTHOUSE $
(✆020-59556276; pukyoguesthouse@gmail.com; d/tw 100,000K; ☞) Almost more a homestay than a guesthouse, this pad is run by a friendly Belgian-Lao couple. While the location is a little inconvenient for downtown, it's handy for the airport and the owners will run guests into town to explore the restaurants and bars. Super clean and spacious rooms, plus a little cafe-bar in the main house.

Auberge Plaine des Jarres   LODGE $$
(✆020-23533333; auberge_plainjars@yahoo.fr; d/tw incl breakfast US$40-50; ☞) Perched on a pine-clad hilltop on the outskirts of town, this atmospheric lodge feels more Alpine than Lao and has undergone a much-overdue renovation. Rooms are set in individual cabins and include simple touches like Lao textiles and a log fireplace in winter. The bar-restaurant is a welcome retreat on a cool winter night.

Favanh Mai Hotel   HOTEL $$
(✆061-211555; favanhmaihotel@yahoo.com; d/tw 200,000-300,000K; ✳☞) Boasting some of the smartest accommodation in Phonsavan, this large pile offers 69 rooms featuring hard-polished floors, smart TVs, minibar and well-appointed hot-water bathrooms. VIP rooms are available for 300,000K if you're feeling very important and there's also a lift.

Hillside Residence   HOTEL $$
(✆061-213300; thehillsideresidence@gmail.com; Ban Tai; d/tw incl breakfast US$25-30; ☞) Set in a lush little garden, this replica half-timbered mansion looks like it belongs in a colonial-era hill town in Myanmar. Rooms are petite but attractive with all the trimmings, including blankets for the cool season. There's a shared upper sitting terrace and some upstairs rooms have their own balconies. Free wi-fi plus a friendly owner.

Vansana Plain of Jars Hotel   HOTEL $$
(✆061-213170; www.vansanahotel-group.com; d/tw 400,000-500,000K) Opulent by Phonsavan standards, this grand hotel occupies its own small summit above town. Large, comfortable rooms have plush carpeting, chunky TVs, minibars, tasteful decor and big tubs in the bathrooms. Each also has a small balcony with great views over town. The place is somewhat tired and in need of a little love, however.

✕ Eating & Drinking

Phonsavan has a sprinkling of quality Western restaurants. For a more local touch, regional specialties include *hét wâi* (wild matsutake mushrooms) or *nok ąen dạwng* (fermented swallows); try the fresh food market (p83). In case you want to avoid a surprise, note that several Vietnamese restaurants serve *thit chó* (dog).

By night Phonsavan is a very sleepy place. If you want a party, you'll have to start it yourself, but there are a couple of restaurants that double as drinking holes.

Nisha Restaurant   INDIAN $
(☑ 020-98266023; Rte 7; meals 20,000-40,000K; ⊙ 7am-10pm; 🗟 🍴) Cream-interiored Nisha is set in a simple shophouse, but the real colour is found in its excellent cuisine. The menu includes all the usual suspects like tikka masala and rogan josh, curries and a wide range of vegetarian options. However, it's the perfect application of spice and the freshness of the food that'll keep you coming back.

Simmaly Restaurant   LAO $
(Rte 7; meals 20,000-40,000K; ⊙ 6am-9pm) Serves up a tasty line of rice dishes, noodles and spicy meats, including steaming *fĕr* (rice noodles). The pork with ginger is memorable.

Lao Falang Restaurant   ITALIAN $$
(☑ 020-23305614; mains 50,000-120,000K; ⊙ 7am-4pm & 5-10.30pm; 🗟 🍴) This spacious, stylish and impeccably clean Italian restaurant is run by a friendly Genoese native who speaks four languages. Highly recommended for alchemising sirloin steak, lamb and giant prawns into various delicious incarnations, plus its handmade pasta (carbonara and bolognese), thin-based pizza and homemade ice cream. Great wine selection from the homeland as well.

It can also make takeaway ham, chicken, tuna or veggie sandwiches (from 7am to 10am) for long bus journeys.

Cranky-T Café & Bar   FUSION $$
(☑ 030-5388003; www.facebook.com/CrankyT Laos; Rte 7; mains 35,000-130,000K; ⊙ 7am-10.30pm Mon-Sat, to 5pm Sun, happy hour 4-7pm; 🗟) Cranky-Ts has a stylish red-wine-coloured and exposed-brick interior, with the eponymous owner creating mouthwatering salads, sashimi, smoked-salmon crêpes and hearty fare like NZ sirloin with mash to fill you up after trekking the jar sites. Add to this cinnamon muffins, brownie cheesecake and a good selection of cocktails (35,000K), and you may spend much of the day here.

Bamboozle Restaurant
& Bar   INTERNATIONAL $$
(☑ 030-9523913; www.facebook.com/Bamboozle RestaurantBar; Rte 7; meals 20,000-60,000K; ⊙ 7-10.30am & 3.30-10.30pm, kitchen closes 9.30pm; 🗟) 🍴 True to its name, with bamboo walls plus pretty lanterns strung from its ceiling, Bamboozle dishes up thin-crust pizza, salads, pasta dishes, good-sized cheeseburgers and flavoursome Lao cuisine. Add to this chilled beers and a rock-and-roll soundtrack and it's a winner. A percentage of the profits goes towards the Lone Buffalo (p83), which supports the town's youth.

Barview   BAR
(⊙ 8am-11pm) Try this simple shack for sunset beers over the rice-paddy fields. Locals gather here to play guitars and munch on barbecued meat.

ℹ Information

DANGERS & ANNOYANCES
Don't underestimate the dangers of UXO in this most heavily bombed of provinces.

MEDICAL SERVICES
Lao-Mongolian Friendship Hospital (☑ 061-312166) May be able to assist with minor health concerns.

MONEY
Currency exchange is available at **Lao Development Bank** (☑ 061-312188; ⊙ 8.30am-3.30pm Mon-Fri), at **BCEL** (☑ 061-213297; Rte 7; ⊙ 8.30am-3.30pm Mon-Fri) and from several travel agents. There are three ATMs along Rte 7.

TOURIST INFORMATION
Xieng Khuang Tourist Office (☑ 061-312217; www.xiengkhouangtourism.com; ⊙ 8-11.30am & 1.30-4pm) Located in the middle of nowhere near the airport, this helpful office has English-speaking staff, a small exhibit and souvenirs recycled from war junk. Pick up free maps for Phonsavan and Xieng Khuang district, plus the brochure 'Hidden Stories of Xieng Khoung' for alternative ideas on things to do aside from the jar sites.

Many tours include a stop here on the way to the jars to view the pile of war remnants stored behind the office.

❶ Getting There & Away

Airline and bus timetables usually call Phonsa-van 'Xieng Khuang', the name of the province, even though that was originally the name for nearby Muang Khoun.

AIR

Lao Airlines (☑ 020-22228658; www.laoair lines.com) (from US$75) and Lao Skyway (from 399,000K) both have daily connections be-tween Phonsavan (Xieng Khuang) Airport and Vientiane. Lao Airlines operates a weekly flight to/from Luang Prabang in peak season. The airport is about 3km west of the town centre.

BUS

Longer-distance bus tickets pre-sold by travel agencies typically cost around 20,000K to 40,000K more than standard fares but include a transfer to the confusingly named **Northern Bus Station** (☑ 030-5170148), located 4km west of the centre, also sometimes known as the Pro-vincial Bus Station. From here Vietnam-bound buses depart to Vinh (160,000K, 11 hours) at 6.30am on Tuesday, Thursday, Friday and Sun-day, continuing seasonally on Mondays to Hanoi (320,000K). For Vientiane (110,000K, 11 hours) there are air-con buses at 7am, 8am, 10.30am, 4.30pm, 6.30pm and a VIP bus (130,000K) at 8.30pm. These all pass through Vang Vieng, to where there's an additional 7.30am departure (95,000K). The sleeper here (150,000K) leaves at 8pm. For Luang Prabang (10 hours) both minivans (95,000K) and VIP buses (120,000K) depart at 8.30am and 6pm. There's an 8am bus to Sam Neua (80,000K, eight to 10 hours) and a 6pm sleeper (100,000K), plus two Vientiane–Sam Neua buses passing through. A 7.30am bus is timetabled to Paksan (100,000K, 10 hours) on the new road.

The **Southern (Bounmixay) Bus Station** (Highway 1D), 4km south of town, has a 6.45am bus every other day to Savannakhet (150,000K) that continues on to Pakse (170,000K). Buses to Paksan (80,000K, eight hours) via the newly completed road depart daily at 5.30am. Local buses and *sŏrngtǎaou* also depart for Muang Khoun (20,000K, hourly).

Phoukham Garden Minibus & Bus Station, in the east-central side of town (by the tour-ist strip), has minibuses leaving at 8.30am for Luang Prabang (110,000K), Vang Vieng (100,000K) and Nong Khiaw (150,000K), with 5am, 8am and 5pm minibuses for Vientiane (130,000K). There's also a VIP bus for Vientiane (130,000K) leaving from here at 7pm. Local bus-es and *sŏrngtǎaou* depart from here for Muang Kham (25,000K, two hours, hourly), and Nong Haet (35,000K, four hours, four daily).

These are the three main terminals, though competing bus stations sprout like beanstalks in

Phonsavan, so there may be alternative options for the destinations listed above.

❶ Getting Around

Tuk-tuks cost from 15,000K for a short hop to about 30,000K to the airport and the best place to find them is around the **Phoukham Garden Minibus & Bus Station** (☑ 020-99947072; Th Xaysana; ⊙7am-8pm). Lao Falang Travel Ser-vice (p83) rents 100cc and 150cc motorbikes (100,000K to 150,000K), ideal for reaching a selection of jar sites. Fill up at the **petrol station** in town.

Chauffeured six-seater vans or 4WDs can be chartered through the minibus station (or most guesthouses); you're looking at US$200 to Sam Neua or Luang Prabang.

Plain of Jars   ທົ່ງໄຫຫິນ

Mysterious giant stone jars of unknown ancient origin are scattered over hundreds of hilly square kilometres around Phonsa-van, giving the area the misleading name of Plain of Jars. Remarkably, little is known about the Austro-Asiatic civilisation that created them, although archaeologists esti-mate they date from the Southeast Asian Iron Age (500 BCE to 200 CE) and were likely used for elaborate burial rituals.

Smaller jars have long since been carted off by collectors but around 2500 larger jars, jar fragments and 'lids' remain. As the region was carpet-bombed throughout the Indochina wars, it's miraculous that so many artefacts survived. Only nine of the 90 recorded jar sites have so far been cleared of UXO, and then only within relatively limited areas. These sites, and their access paths, are delineated by easily missed red-and-white marker stones: remain vigilant.

Sites 1, 2 and 3 form the bases of most tour loops.

Phonsavan is the closest base from which to take day trips here. For food, your best bet is also to head back to Phonsavan.

History

Lao folklore tells of a race of giants ruled by a powerful king named Khun Jeuam who ordered his people to make jars here to brew and store rice wine for celebrations of their victories on the battlefield. Modern archae-ologists believe that the bone fragments, beads and burnt charcoal found in and around the jumbo-sized jars suggest that they were instead used as part of an elaborate funeral ceremony (for normal-sized people). French archaeologist Madeleine Colani was the first to float this theory in the early 1930s, though it wasn't given too much credence until further archaeological research could begin anew in the 1990s once the region was finally safe to visit. Alternatively looted and carpet bombed over the years, very little remains today of the burial offerings that may have once been hidden in these rolling hills.

There are believed to be nearly 90 recorded jar sites in Xiangkhouang Province, each with as many as 300 stone ruins between 1m and 2.5m tall. Researchers think the sites may have been chosen for their magnetic properties, as the jars seem to attract lightning (while the local airport in Phonsavan appears to have an abysmal record of plane crashes!). Some 80% of the jars were carved from quarried sandstone, with the rest made of granite, limestone or conglomerate rock. Archaeologists have found smaller jar sights in Assam, India, southern China and Vietnam, suggesting that the Austro-Asiatic people who created these stone structures may have migrated along a trade route across Asia, reaching the height of their civilisation when they hit Laos.

The first jar sites didn't open to the public until 1992 following a bootstraps effort by locals to remove UXO. Six years later, Unesco initiated a decades-long project to safeguard the archaeological ruins, promote safe (and sustainable) tourism, and get the site on the World Heritage List, to which it was inscribed in 2019. Today, the Plain of Jars is the most popular attraction in the region.

Sights

While the jars at Sites 2 and 3 aren't as large or as plentiful as at Site 1, they have their own charm. They're set in very different locations; the journey to reach them offers glimpses of some typical local villages.

Jar Site 1 ARCHAEOLOGICAL SITE
(Thong Hai Hin; 15,000K) The biggest and most accessible, Site 1 features over 300 jars relatively close-packed on a pair of hilly slopes pocked with bomb craters. The biggest, **Hai Jeuam**, weighs around 25 tonnes, stands more than 2.5m high and is said to have been the mythical victory cup of Khun Jeuam. The bare, hilly landscape is appealing, although the views of Phonsavan

Plain of Jars

Sights
1 Jar Site 1.................................A2
2 Jar Site 2.................................A3
3 Jar Site 3.................................A3
4 Mulberries.............................A2

Activities, Courses & Tours
Lone Buffalo....................(see 7)

Sleeping
5 Auberge Plaine des Jarres..........A2
6 Khoun Guesthouse & Restaurant....B3
7 Pukyo Guesthouse.................A2
8 Vansana Plain of Jars Hotel........A2

airport seem discordant. There is a cafe, a gift shop and toilets near the entrance.

Pay your entrance fee at the small **Plain of Jars Visitor Centre**, which offers an informative museum-style display on the history of the jars and theories relating to their use.

Jar Site 2 ARCHAEOLOGICAL SITE
(Hai Hin Phu Salato; 10,000K) Site 2 is a pair of hillocks divided by a shallow gully that forms the access lane. This rises 700m from the ticket desk in what becomes a muddy slither in wet conditions. To the left in thin woodlands, look for a cracked stone

DON'T MISS

TREKKING IN NORTHERN LAOS

Northern Laos has won prizes for its 'ecotrekking' system, pioneered in Luang Namtha and Nam Ha NPA. Registered agencies pledge to return a significant (and stated) percentage of profits to the villages visited and to abide by sensible ecologically friendly guidelines. Visiting remote off-road villages without a guide is of dubious legality. Fortunately, guides and any necessary trekking permits can usually be arranged very quickly by local agencies, often the evening before departure. Costs excluding transport are typically around US$50 to US$75 per person per day if alone, falling to US$25 per person for a larger group. Agencies don't generally compete directly so comparing product is more relevant than comparing prices. Employing freelance guides might be cheaper but is discouraged as they'll rarely make contributions to village development funds. Visit the excellent website www.ecotourismlaos.com for more information. The following list is a generalised overview of what differentiates the various trekking centres.

Phongsali (p108) Nowhere is better for striking out into truly timeless villages where traditional clothing and arcane animist beliefs are still commonplace, particularly in the remote Akha communities. Many homes retain picture-book thatched roofs, at least for now. Virgin-forest treks are also possible near Boun Neua.

Luang Namtha (p116) Treks are very well organised and have numerous options, some combining trekking with other activities such as biking and kayaking. Forest hikes to Nam Ha NPA 'jungle camps' are especially popular. To reduce pressure on any single host village, most agents have unique routes. However, this inadvertently adds to the complexity of deciding just what you actually want to see and where you'll find it. Not all routes are equally inspiring. Ask how deep the trek goes into the forest to ensure you don't end up with a lightweight, peripheral experience.

Vieng Phukha (p122) A much less commercial starting point for Nam Ha forest treks.

Muang Sing (p123) Guided or DIY visits to colourful and relatively accessible Akha villages. The trekking scene has died off considerably, but there's still one very good operator here.

Udomxai (p111) A specialist agency makes Udomxai a popular centre for mountain biking, with some itineraries combined with treks.

Muang Khua (p105) Limited options include a one-day trek visiting an Akha Pala village (where some local women wear colourful semi-traditional clothing), with plenty of views en route but minimal forest.

Phonsavan (p81) One unique trek combines a mossy archaeological site, accommodation in a roadless Hmong village and an ascent of a multistage waterfall. It's a fascinating walk, but don't expect to see people in traditional dress in this area.

Muang Ngoi Neua (p102) Easy DIY day walks to pretty villages or very inexpensive group treks with freelance guides, some including scenic boat trips.

Nong Khiaw (p97) Try the '100 waterfalls' tour, a walk *in* a stream, following it upward through a series of cooling limestone cascades, to a summit.

urn through which a tree has managed to grow. To the right another set of jars sits on a grassy knoll with panoramas of layered hills, paddies and cow fields.

Basic cold drinks are available at the ticket booth.

Jar Site 3
ARCHAEOLOGICAL SITE

(Hai Hin Lat Khai; 10,000K) The 150-jar Site 3 sits on a hillside in pretty woodland near Ban Lat Khai village. The access road to Lat Khai leads east beside a motorbike repair hut just before Ban Xiang Di (Ban Siang Dii). The ticket booth is beside a simple local restaurant that offers *fěr* (rice noodles; 30,000K). The jars are accessed by a little wooden footbridge and an attractive 10-minute walk (or wade, depending on the season) through rice fields.

🛏 Sleeping & Eating

Phonsavan is the closest base from which to take day trips here.

Likewise, for food, your best bet is to head back to Phonsavan.

ℹ️ Getting There & Away

All three main jar sites can be visited by rented motorbike from Phonsavan in around five hours, while Site 1 is within bicycle range. Site 1 is just 8km southwest of central Phonsavan, 2.3km west of the Muang Khoun road (1D): turn at the signed junction in Ban Hay Hin. For Sites 2 and 3, turn west off the Muang Khoun road just past Km 8. Follow the paved road for 10km/14km to find the turnings for Sites 2/3, then follow muddy tracks for 0.5/1.8km, respectively.

Alternatively, sign up the night before to join one of several regular guided minibus tours. It really is worth the extra money to hear the war stories and get some context on both the jars and their creators. Most throw in a noodle-soup lunch at Site 2 or 3 and a quick stop to see the lumpy rusting remnant of an armoured vehicle in a roadside copse at Ban Nakho: its nickname, the 'Russian Tank', exaggerates the appeal.

Muang Khoun ເມືອງຄູນ

📱 061 / POP 4000

The region's ancient capital, Muang Khoun was ravaged in the 19th century by Chinese and Vietnamese invaders, then so heavily bombarded during the Second Indochina War that by 1975 it was almost completely abandoned. However, a handful of aged monuments survived as ruins and the town slowly redeveloped, although it is very much a village in comparison to the new capital Phonsavan. It's certainly not a must-see but might be worth the detour for those staying a few days in the region.

A good asphalt road from Phonsavan (30km north) passes through some attractive rice-terrace villages, several sporting Phuan-style houses built of sturdy timbers. Buying the Muang Khoun Visitor's Ticket (10,000K; available at various sights in the area) supports ongoing maintenance efforts.

⊙ Sights

The main historic sights are a trio of historic stupas, all walking distance from the Khoun Guesthouse. One is directly behind in the grounds of the colourfully rebuilt active monastery, **Wat Si Phoum**. The other two are on a facing ridge, accessed via the brick-and-mud lane that climbs opposite the guesthouse, petering out into a narrow footpath. The 1576 **That Foun** (also called

That Chomsi) is around 25m tall and built in the Lan Xang/Lanna style. It now has a distinct lean to its spire and you can climb right through a hole that was made by 19th-century Chinese Haw marauders, who tunnelled in to loot the priceless Buddha relics enshrined within. A five-minute walk around the easy ridge track brings you to the stubbier remnants of the Cham-built 16th-century stupa **That Chom Phet**.

The main road continuing east swerves south just before Km 30 after **Wat Phia Wat**. Of Wat Phia Wat's original 1582 building just the base platform and a few brick columns survived a devastating 1966 bombing raid. But these columns photogenically frame an age-greyed, shell-shocked Buddha with a whiplash smile.

The unpaved road continuing east passes the small, very degraded **Jar Site 16** after about 5km. This road becomes increasingly difficult and finally dead-ends some 12km beyond at **Ban Thalin**, an interesting village without any commercial facilities that's used as the starting point for the Phakeo Trek.

🛏️ Sleeping & Eating

We recommend bringing your own packed lunch if you're here visiting independently from Phonsavan. Otherwise there are a few *fĕr* (rice noodle) stands scattered around Muang Khoun's market.

Khoun Guesthouse & Restaurant   GUESTHOUSE **$**
(📱 061-212464; Rte 10, Km 29; d/tw 50,000-90,000K; 🛜) Set in a garden, this is the town's sole accommodation option. The 50,000K rooms are cell-like at best but the 90,000K rooms are larger and include TV and hot water. The restaurant has an English-language menu of Lao staples; some tour groups stop here for lunch.

ℹ️ Getting There & Away

Buses to Phonsavan (20,000K, 45 minutes) depart throughout the day. By motorbike it's possible to visit Muang Khoun plus the three main jar sites in one long day.

Sam Neua ຊຳເໜືອ

📱 064 / POP 18,000

While Sam Neua (Xam Neua) is something of a nostalgic Soviet oddity, with its well-spaced concrete modernity, spartan

ⓘ RIVER TRIPS

Until the 1990s, riverboats were an essential form of intercity passenger transport in Laos. Today villagers in roadless hamlets still travel by river, while several longer-distance routes remain possible thanks in significant part to tourist interest. On riverboats the journey is an attraction in itself.

Mekong Slowboats

Huay Xai–Pak Beng or Pak Beng–Luang Prabang (one day) Both sectors are very pleasant one-day rides. Boats are designed for 70 passengers but are sometimes seriously overcrowded. The seats are usually very hard, but you can get up and walk around. There's a toilet on board and usually a stall selling snacks and overpriced beer.

Huay Xai–Luang Prabang (two days) Travel in relative luxury with Luang Say Cruise or Shompoo Cruise. Both run boats that are similar in size to the Mekong slowboats but carry a maximum of 40 passengers. The Luang Say Cruise is not for the budget traveller, but includes meals, sightseeing stops and excellent overnight accommodation at the Luang Say Lodge.

Mekong Speedboats

Huay Xai–Luang Prabang (one day) Scarily fast, dangerous and excruciatingly uncomfortable if you're not small and supple. It's also best to avoid this trip when river levels have dropped after the wet season, giving boatmen less clearance of the underwater pillars of rocks.

Nam Tha Boats

Luang Namtha–Huay Xai or Ban Na Lae–Huay Xai longboat (one day) You can now only take the boat as far as Ban Phaeng, where a dam has recently been built; from here you are picked up and driven the remaining route to Huay Xai. What was a two-day experience is now just a day, though you still have around eight hours of puttering downriver. The journey starts in Luang Namtha where you are driven by car to Ban Na Lae to board the boat.

Hat Sa–Muang Khua This is no longer possible since the Nam Ou (Ou River) was dammed, although **Muang Khua–Nong Khiaw** (six hours) still sees boats leave Muang Khua every morning, passing through Muang Ngoi Neua (five hours) before arriving in Nong Khiaw, and taking you through the country's most spectacular karst scenery. However, it is necessary to change boats to pass a large dam about one hour north of Muang Ngoi Neua.

Nong Khiaw–Luang Prabang (one day) Due to the damming of the Nam Ou, the boat trip to Luang Prabang was not possible at the time of research but, like the other dam-affected river trips, it may be available in sections in the future, and will involve hopping in and out of vehicles and boats to accommodate the obstacles. Otherwise, it is possible to sign up for kayaking trips in Luang Prabang and Nong Khiaw that include short but beautiful sections of the river.

communist monument and old boys with Muscovite hats, the real draw is the stunning countryside in which it sits. The town is a logical transit point for visiting nearby Vieng Xai or catching the daily bus to Vietnam, and remains one of Laos' least-visited provincial capitals. It is perched at an altitude of roughly 1200m, so some warm clothes are advisable in the dry winter period, at least by night and until the thick morning fog burns off. From April to October, the lush landscapes are contrastingly warm and wet.

The eye-widening, photogenic produce markets here are worth visiting for their colourful ethnic diversity.

⊙ Sights

Apart from two modest old stupas that somehow survived the wartime bombs, the main road seems brash and modern.

However, just metres away, the **suspension bridge** provides enchanting river scenes.

Food Market
MARKET
(⊙6am-6pm) The fascinating food market is well-stocked with fresh vegetables and meats, some rather startling. Field rats are displayed cut open to show the freshness of their entrails. Banana leaves might be stuffed with squirming insects. And there's plenty of dead furry wildlife that you'd probably prefer to see alive in the forests.

Suan Keo Lak
Meung Monument
MONUMENT
(ສວນແກວຫຼັກເມືອງ) At the town's central junction stands the bizarre Suan Keo Lak Meung Monument. Four hooked concrete pincers hold aloft a glittery disco ball that is intended to celebrate Sam Neua's folk-song image as an 'indestructible jewel'. However, the effect is unintentionally comic, with its backing of half-hearted fountains and a frieze full of communist triumphalist soldiers.

Main Market
MARKET
(⊙dawn-dusk) The main market is predominantly stocked with Chinese and Vietnamese consumer goods. However, some fabric stalls here carry regional textiles, and jewellers sell antique coins and silverware used for tribal headgear.

🛏 Sleeping

There's a surplus of run-of-the-mill guesthouses in town, with many budget options just across the river from the market.

Xayphasouk Hotel
HOTEL **$**
(☎064-312033; xayphasoukhotel@gmail.com; d/tw 150,000-200,000K; 🏵🛜) Still the smartest hotel in Sam Neua, the huge lobby-restaurant is woefully underused, but the rooms are very comfortable for such a remote region of Laos. All include piping-hot showers, flat-screen TVs, tasteful furnishings and crisp linen. Even the President of Laos stays here if he is in town!

Phonchalern Hotel
HOTEL **$**
(☎064-312192; d/tw 80,000-110,000K; 🏵🛜) This palatially sized hotel has a mix of rooms; some are dark and uninviting while those facing the river are full of light and have a communal balcony out front. Rooms have fridges, TVs and clean en suites. Downstairs there's a lobby the size of a bowling alley. It's a sure bet for one night.

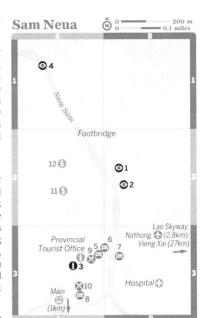

Sam Neua

It was the first place in Sam Neua to install a lift.

Sam Neua Hotel
HOTEL **$**
(☎064-314777; snhotel_08@yahoo.com; d/tw 100,000-200,000K; 🏵🛜) Located over the bridge on the same side as the main market, this well-maintained hotel has 17 rooms

GETTING TO VIETNAM: NA MEO TO NAM SOI

Getting to the border If going to the Nam Soi (Vietnam)/Na Meo (Laos) border crossing (Km 175; 7am to 11.30am and 1.30pm to 5.30pm), the easiest transport option is to take the daily direct bus (sometimes minibus) between Sam Neua and Thanh Hoa (180,000K, 10 hours) that passes close to Vieng Xai but doesn't enter town. It departs twice daily at 8am and 10am. Pre-purchase your ticket at the main bus station to avoid overcharging. 'Through tickets' to Hanoi still go via Thanh Hoa with a change of bus.

At the border Westbound, note that the Lao border post isn't a town. There are a few simple restaurant shacks but no accommodation and no waiting transport apart from the bus travelling from Thanh Hoa to Sam Neua, which passes by around 2pm.

Laos visas (p291) are available on arrival at this border but Vietnamese visas are not, so plan ahead if heading east.

Moving on Once in Thanh Hoa, there's a night train to Hanoi departing at 1.20am and arriving very early (around 5am). Alternatively, there is a morning train at 8.25am (arriving at 12.30pm). Tickets should cost US$14 but foreigners are often asked for significantly more.

complete with fresh linen, pine furniture, satellite TV and en suite bathrooms with hot water.

Bounhome Guest House GUESTHOUSE $
(☑ 064-312223, 020-2348125; s/d with fan 60,000/80,000K, d with air-con 100,000K; ❋ 🛜) Next to the bridge, this guesthouse has compact rooms with tiled floors, fans and low-set beds with fresh linen and blankets. You'll be glad to use their powerful hot showers.

🍴 Eating & Drinking

There are a number of restaurants to eat at in Sam Neua – they're nothing fancy but serve good local grub. Impromptu barbecued offerings are available on street corners after dark. During the day check out the food market (p91).

There is very little to get excited about come evening, when the place becomes something of a ghost town. A Beerlao and good conversation with a fellow traveller at any of the local restaurants is your best bet.

★ Yuni Coffee CAFE $
(☑ 020-52221515; https://yunicoffeeco.com; mains 30,000K; ⏱ 7.30am-5.30pm Tue-Sat, 8am-2pm Sun) If you're missing standard lattes your caffeine privations are over – this place is a blessing for coffee snobs. In a spacious location with a modern industrial look and a choice selection of breakfast items and casual Western fare, as well as top-notch locally grown coffee, Yuni is the only way to kick-start your day.

Dan Nao Muang Xam Restaurant LAO $
(mains 15,000-45,000K; ⏱ 7am-9.30pm) This hole-in-the-wall spot is hardly brimming with atmosphere, but it has the most foreigner-friendly menu in town in English. Breakfast includes cornflakes and a delicious *fĕr* (rice noodle soup). Dinner includes some excellent rice and soup combinations, plus a steak with al dente vegetables arranged star-like around the plate. It also serves decent portions of *láhp*, fried-rice variations and omelettes.

Chittavanh Restaurant LAO $
(mains 25,000-50,000K; ⏱ 7am-9pm; 🌶) Savouring a delicious Chinese fried-tofu dish makes it worth braving the reverberant clatter of this cavernous hotel restaurant where vinyl tablecloths have been nailed into place. Locals like to eat here as well, which is always a good sign.

ℹ Information

MEDICAL SERVICES
Hospital (☑ 064-312858; ⏱ 24hr)

MONEY
BCEL (⏱ 8am-3.30pm Mon-Fri) Has an ATM and exchanges most major currencies.

Foreign Exchange (⏱ 7am-6pm) Fabric stalls in the main market exchange Vietnamese dong faster than the banks and are open at weekends.

Lao Development Bank (☑ 064-312171; ⏱ 8am-4pm Mon-Fri) A 24hr ATM and money exchange located on the main road, 400m north of the bus station on the left.

TOURIST INFORMATION

Provincial Tourist Office (☏ 064-312567; hp_pto@yahoo.com; ⊙8-11.30am & 1.30-4pm Mon-Fri) A helpful provincial tourist office with English-speaking staff on hand.

❶ Getting There & Away

AIR

Sam Neua's little **Nathong Airport** is 3km east of the centre towards Vieng Xai. **Lao Skyway** (☏ 020-99755556, 064-314268; www.laoskyway.com; Nathong Airport; ⊙8am-4pm) runs morning flights on light aircraft to Vientiane (from 899,000K) Tuesday to Saturday. All too frequently the flights get cancelled just before departure. A new, larger airport is under construction. It has been plagued by delays and question marks over the large costs involved, but may open during 2020.

BUS

Sam Neua has two bus stations. Schedules change frequently so double-check and certainly don't rely on timetables printed on tourist maps and noticeboards.

Main Bus Station

The **main bus station** (☏ 064-314270) is on a hilltop 1.2km south of the central monument, just off the Vieng Thong road. From here buses leave to Vientiane (190,000K, 20 hours) via Phonsavan (100,000K, 10 hours) at 10am, 1pm, 3pm and 5pm. An additional 7.30am Vientiane bus (190,000K) goes via Vieng Thong (60,000K, five hours), Nong Khiaw (140,000K, 12 hours) and Luang Prabang (150,000K, 17 hours). There are also daily minibuses to Luang Prabang (130,000K to 150,000K, 15 hours) at 7.30am and 4pm. Finally there is a Vieng Thong bus (50,000K) at 7.30am and 4pm.

Nathong Bus Station

The **Nathong bus station** is 1km beyond the airport on the Vieng Xai road at the easternmost edge of town (a tuk-tuk here costs 20,000K). There is now just one daily bus to Vieng Xai (20,000K, one hour), which leaves at 9.30am and continues to Sam Tai (Xamtay; 40,000K, five hours).

❶ Getting Around

Tuk-tuks are hard to find beyond the main bus station, but they often circle the Suan Keo Lak Meung Monument looking for passengers.

The best way to get around and to enjoy the stunning scenery en route to Vieng Xai is to hire a cheap scooter and do it yourself. Unfortunately, the one rental shop in town closed and none of the restaurants or guesthouses

have proper licences to rent scooters. If you're willing to take the risk, however, you'll find some low-quality motorbikes for rent at restaurants for 100,000K.

Those wishing for a little more comfort when getting about locally or heading to Vieng Xai can hire one of the many taxis in town.

Alternatively, go to the provincial tourist office and ask them to call a **Sam Neua driver** (☏ 020-5627510, 020-55982644; taxi rental to Vieng Xai Caves one-way/return 150,000/250,000K) (020-5627510 or 020-55982644) to take you to Vieng Xai. They offer round-trips including wait time, or can just drop you by the caves office if you're planning to stay overnight.

Around Sam Neua

It doesn't take much effort to get into some timeless rural villages around Sam Neua. For random motorcycle trips you might try heading south from the hospital for a few kilometres or heading north up the unpaved lane directly to the right-hand side of Wat Phoxaysanalam. The latter winds its way after 11km to **Ban Tham**, just before which there's an inconsequential **Buddha cave** (to the left around 100m before the school and shop). But more appealing are rice-terrace valleys around 4km out of Sam Neua where two picturesque villages across the river each sport spindly, old, greying stupas. With a decent motorbike it's easy to do a day trip to Vieng Xai or a longer side trip to Hintang via Tat Saloei.

Sam Neua to Vietnam

The scenic route via fascinating Vieng Xai is open to foreigners, Vietnamese visas permitting. It's narrow but paved and offers a feast of varied views. The best incorporate giant teeth of tree-dappled karst outcrops backing bucolic valleys layered with rice terraces. Several villages en route, including **Ban Piang Ban** (Km 144.5), specialise in basket-making and bamboo crafts. Across the river at Km 169 is a 'steel cave' where knives and agricultural tools were made on an almost-industrial scale during the Second Indochina War.

Turn south at Km 164 for the recently asphalted spur road to **Sam Tai** (Xamtay), famous for producing magnificent textiles. It has a couple of guesthouses should you feel like getting well off the beaten track to investigate. Public access to the remote **Nam Sam NPA** beyond is not currently permitted.

Sam Neua to Nong Khiaw

From Sam Neua, Rte 6 runs along winding mountain ridges passing **Hintang Archaeological Park** and meeting Phonsavan-bound Rte 1C at minuscule Phoulao (Ban Kho Hing), 92km west of Sam Neua, where kilometre markings reset. West of Phoulao the green mountains become much more heavily deforested until reaching the boundary of the **Nam Et/Phou Louey National Park**, which is best visited from Vieng Thong, and is a convenient place to break the journey. The long descent towards **Nong Khiaw** lasts many kilometres and offers some glimpses of superb scenery.

⊙ Sights

Hintang
Archaeological Park   ARCHAEOLOGICAL SITE
(ສວນຫີນ, Suan Hin) Almost as mysterious as Xieng Khuang's more famous jars, this unique, unfenced collection of **standing stones** is thought to be at least 1500 years old. Spindly stones up to 3m tall are interspersed with **disks** that formerly covered funerary sites. With some over a metre in diameter, these 'families' of stones do have a certain magic. Chartered tuk-tuks from Sam Neua will ask around 500,000K return.

Access is up a rough, rutted track that cuts south from Rte 6 at Ban Phao (Km 35.3), 57km from Sam Neua. This track can be impractically muddy for vehicles after any rain. The main site is right beside the track after 6km, around 800m beyond the obvious radio-mast summit. Some 2km back towards the main road, an orange sign points to the Keohintang Trail, which allows more intrepid visitors to seek out lesser-known megalith groups hidden along a partially marked two-hour hiking trail. Take the narrow rising path, not the bigger track that descends towards Ban Nakham. If you don't get lost, the trail should emerge back onto Rte 6 at Ban Tao Hin (Km 31.5), a tiny village without any facilities.

When driving between Sam Neua and either Phonsavan or Nong Khiaw, allow two hours extra for the very slow detour to the main site. Using public transport it is necessary to walk to and from Rte 6. Practicalities work out best if visiting between Sam Neua and Phonsavan: starting with the Vieng Thong–bound minibus, you'll have around six hours for the walk before the last Phonsavan/Vientiane-bound bus rumbles past.

Tat Saloei   WATERFALL
(Phonesai Waterfall; 10,000K) This impressive series of cascades forms a combined drop of almost 100m. It's briefly visible from eastbound Rte 6 roughly 1km after Km 55 (ie 36km from Sam Neua), but easy to miss westbound. There are some small local cafes and restaurants on the roadside here, plus what looks like a ticket booth, although no one was charging for entry at the time of writing.

Vieng Xai   ວຽງໄຊ
♩ 064 / POP 4000

The thought-provoking 'bomb-shelter caves' of Vieng Xai are set amid dramatic karst outcrops and offer a truly inspirational opportunity to learn about northern Laos' painful 20th-century history. Imagine Vang Vieng, but with a compelling historical twist instead of happy tubing. Or think of it as Ho Chi Minh City's Cu Chi Tunnels cast in stone. The caves were shrouded in secrecy until they were opened to the world in 2007.

History

For centuries the minuscule hamlet of Long Ko sat peacefully here, lost amid deep ancient forests and towering karst outcrops. But in 1963, political repression and a spate of assassinations in Vientiane led the Pathet Lao leadership to retreat deep into the Hua Phan hinterland, eventually taking up residence in the area's caves. As the US Secret War gathered momentum, surrounding villages were mercilessly bombarded. Horrified and bemused, locals initially had no idea of who was attacking them, nor why. For safety, they retreated into the vastly expanded cave systems, more than 450 of which eventually came to shelter up to 23,000 people. As the war dragged on, cave sites came to host printing works, hospitals, markets and even a metalwork factory. The 1973 ceasefire allowed the refugees to tentatively emerge after almost a decade in the caves and construct a small town here. Indeed, until December 1975, it was the de facto capital of the Pathet Lao's Liberated

Territories. The town was named Vieng Xai as that had been the secret code name of future president Kaysone Phomvihane while in hiding here. Decades later, many of Vieng Xai's cave sites still retain visible signs of their wartime roles, making the complex one of the world's most complete revolutionary bases to have survived from the Cold War period.

◉ Sights

Twin roads run 1km south off Rte 6 to the busy market area. Beyond, the town retains the quiet, wide avenues and well-spaced houses of Kaysone's 1973 'capital', interspersed with artificial lakes, trees, flowers and several karst outcrops.

★ Vieng Xai Caves   CAVE

(ຖ້ຳວຽງໄຊ; ☑ 064-315022; entry incl audio tour 60,000K, bicycle rental per tour/day 15,000/30,000K; ⊙ 9am-noon & 1-4pm) Joining a truly fascinating 18-point tour is the only way to see Vieng Xai's seven most important war-shelter cave complexes, set in beautiful gardens backed by fabulous karst scenery. A local guide unlocks each site while an audio guide gives a wealth of first-hand background information and historical context. The **Kaysone Phomvihane Cave** still has its air-circulation pump in working order and is the most memorable of the caves.

Tours leave from the cave office at 9am and 1pm. If you want a tour outside of these two times, you'll have to pay a 50,000K surcharge per group.

Tham Nok Ann   CAVE

(ຖ້ຳນົກແອນ, Nok Ann Cave; 10,000K; ⊙ 8am-5pm) Tham Nok Ann is a soaring well-lit cavern through which a river passes beneath awesome rock formations. It's dripping, creepy and very atmospheric, with a set of stairs leading up to an adjacent cave complex that once housed a Vietnamese military hospital. You could previously take a boat trip deeper into the cave, like a mini Tham Kong Lor experience with some huge jellyfish-like rock formations visible, but in recent years it has only been open for viewing on foot due to limited visitor numbers.

Look for a signpost on the main road about 5km before Vieng Xai and follow the small track around to the right until it dead-ends at an entrance booth and small suspension bridge.

🛏 Sleeping & Eating

There isn't a great selection of eating establishments in Vieng Xai and many have run out of food by 8pm. By 9pm the town is in hibernation. Several *fĕr* shops in the market serve rice and cheap noodle dishes until around 5pm.

Sailomyen Guesthouse   GUESTHOUSE $

(☑ 020-56596688; d 70,000K; ⍲) Built on stilts atop a serene artificial lake with a communal balcony that's perfect for daydreaming. The rooms may be small, with wonky carpeted floors, but there are hot showers, fans and mosquito nets. And did we mention the view? Picture jungle-clad hills with watercolour reflections.

Thongnaxay Guesthouse   GUESTHOUSE $

(☑ 030-99907206; d 60,000K; ⍲) Close to the caves, this little guesthouse has six super-fresh rooms with pink walls, private bathrooms, fans, clean linen and double beds. Oh, and rather nice views of the karsts.

Naxay II Guesthouse   GUESTHOUSE $

(☑ 064-314330; d/tw 80,000K; ⍲) Opposite the cave office, these bamboo-accented bungalows are set around a manicured garden backed by an impressive split-toothed crag. Beds are comfy, hot water flows, lino floors are clean and fans keep you cool, but overall the bungalows are showing their age. They also have private verandas and bathrooms.

Chitchareune Hotel   HOTEL $$

(☑ 030-5150458; d/tw 120,000K, ste 250,000K; ❄⍲) This white monolith sits immediately south of Vieng Xai market and has clean air-con rooms with above-average furniture and stylish en suites. The parking lot doubles as the bus station for Vieng Xai so it is a convenient spot for arrival or departure.

★ Sabaidee Odisha   INDIAN $

(☑ 020-55577202; mains 15,000-45,000K; ⊙ 7am-9pm; ⍲) Don't be fooled by the less-than-impressive exterior, cement floor and bare walls of this hole-in-the-wall joint, for the food is terrific. Prepared fresh and with care, it comes with a smile and the menu offers different levels of spiciness. As well as Indian, there are rice dishes and *láhp*. You'll be mopping your plate with their pillow-soft naan.

The owner is a rare English-speaker in town and will happily help lost tourists find the caves or sort out motorbike rentals. It's

NAM ET/PHOU LOUEY NATIONAL PARK

In the vast **Nam Et/Phou Louey National Park** (ນ້ຳແອດ/ສອບສາຫາລະບະແຫ່ງຊາດພູເລີຍ), rare civets, Asian golden cats, river otters, white-cheeked crested gibbons and the utterly unique Lao warty newt (*Paramesotriton laoensis*) share 4200 sq km of relatively pristine forests with a dwindling number of tigers. Approximately half of the park is an inaccessible core zone. The remaining area includes 98 ethnic-minority hamlets. Two-day wildlife-watching excursions have been pioneered to the park's remote Nam Nern field station, a roadless former village site where a campsite and surrounding walking trails have been professionally cleared of UXO.

Trips are organised by the Nam Et/Phou Louey National Park office in Vieng Thong, and contacting them well in advance is advisable since there's a limit of two departures per week. Night safaris cost 1,200,000K per person for a group of four, and include guides, cooks, food and camping equipment, with a significant proportion of your fee going into village development funds. The price also includes the 90-minute boat ride from Ban Sonkhua, around 50km east of Vieng Thong on Rte 1.

in the northernmost corner of the Vieng Xai market, facing the main road.

ℹ️ Information

Vieng Xai Cave Tourist Office (☏ 064-315022; ⊙ 8-11.30am & 1-4pm) Organises all cave visits, rents bicycles and has maps and a useful information board. Located around 1km south of the market; there's even a display case full of old Lenin busts and socialist iconography.

ℹ️ Getting There & Away

There is just one daily bus to Sam Neua (20,000K, one hour) leaving at approximately 3pm from the bus station. Buses between Sam Neua and Thanh Hoa (one bus daily to each) can be flagged down on Rte 6. The bus for Thanh Hoa (180,000K) should pass by around 8.45am, while the bus for Sam Neua (20,000K) passes through around 4pm.

Visiting Vieng Xai by rented taxi from Sam Neua (p93) (including return) costs around 250,000K per vehicle.

Vieng Thong   ວຽງທອງ

☏ 064 / POP 4000

The original name of Vieng Thong was Muang Hiam, a Tai Daeng word meaning 'watch out' and this name still appears on most road markers. Back when tigers roamed the surrounding forests it was relevant, but these days only a handful may survive in the enormous Nam Et/Phou Louey National Park, on whose vast doorstep Vieng Thong sits. While the town is highly forgettable, the park is not and should be visited through the Nam Et/Phou Louey

National Park office at Vieng Thong Visitors' Center.

Vieng Thong has a clutch of guesthouses and food stalls, and if you're travelling between Nong Khiaw and Sam Neua, stopping here for a night makes the 10-hour journey more palatable. The dazzling green rice fields around town are photogenic and short walks or bicycle rides can take you to pretty Tai Daeng, Hmong and Khamu villages.

🏃 Activities

★ **Nam Nern Night Safari**   SAFARI
(www.namet.org/namnern; night safaris per person in group of 2 & up 1,500,000K) 🌿 Nam Nern Night Safari is a 24-hour, boat-based tour in the Nam Et/Phou Louey National Park. Highlights of the trip include a night-time boat ride 'spotlighting' for tigers, gaurs and white-cheeked gibbons. Seeing a tiger is unlikely but there's hope of spotting sambars and barking deer. Sleeping is at an ecolodge overlooking the Nam Nern. The price includes a fireside dinner.

Book through the Nam Et/Phou Louey National Park office in Vieng Thong.

The Nests   WILDLIFE WATCHING
(www.namet.org/wp/en; 2-day trek per person in group of 2 & up 1,500,000K, 3-day trek per person in group of 2 & up 2,100,000K) 🌿 The Nam Et/Phou Louey National Park office offers the chance to go on The Nests: two- and three-day treks with accommodation in cosy spherical baskets hanging from trees. This also involves wildlife-viewing from an observation tower at Poung Nied salt lick,

which attracts animals such as the rare sambar deer.

🛏 Sleeping & Eating

There's a handful of basic guesthouses in town.

Dorkkhounthong Guesthouse GUESTHOUSE $
(🌙 064-810017; d/tw 50,000-80,000K; ❄) The most appealing of Vieng Thong's limited options, this guesthouse is located right in the centre of the small town. Very clean, decent-sized rooms have hot showers, netted windows and comfortable beds. There's a pleasant 1st-floor sitting area and attractive views across riverside fields from the rear terrace.

Dokchampa Guesthouse GUESTHOUSE $
(🌙 064-810005; d with/without bathroom 60,000/40,000K; 🛜) This small guesthouse has basic rooms with mosquito nets, hot-water showers and squat toilets. The owners offer a few traveller-friendly services such as free wi-fi and bicycles for rent (30,000K per day).

Tontavanh Restaurant LAO $
(mains 20,000-40,000K; ⊙7am-8pm) This typical-looking local eatery serves unexpectedly appetising food and even has a menu in concise English.

ℹ Information

Nam Et/Phou Louey National Park Office
(🌙 064-810008; www.namet.org; ⊙8am-noon & 1-4.30pm Mon-Fri) The Nam Et/Phou Louey National Park office (in the Vieng Thong Visitors' Center, at the northwestern edge of Vieng Thong) organises award-winning Nam Nern Night Safaris to find the park's wildlife; you're taken by boat into the core zone of the protected area, incandescent eyes following you from towering jungle, followed by a picnic and homestay.

ℹ Getting There & Away

Westbound buses arrive from Sam Neua around noon, continuing after lunch to Nong Khiaw (60,000K, five hours), Pak Mong and Luang Prabang (130,000K, nine hours). Eastbound, the best choice for Sam Neua is the 7am minibus (40,000K, six hours), as the two Sam Neua through-services (from Luang Prabang/ Vientiane) both travel the road largely by night.

The bus station is 300m along Rte 6 from the market at the eastern edge of town.

MUANG NGOI DISTRICT

Tracts of green mountains are attractive wherever you go in northern Laos. But at Nong Khiaw and tiny Muang Ngoi Neua, the contours do something altogether more dramatic. At both places, vast karst peaks and towering cliffs rear dramatically out of the Nam Ou (Ou River), creating jaw-droppingly beautiful scenes. Both villages make convenient rural getaways from Luang Prabang and are accessible by riverboat from Muang Khua. Nong Khiaw also makes an excellent rural rest stop between Luang Prabang and Vieng Thong or Sam Neua.

Nong Khiaw ໜອງຂຽວ
🌙 071 / POP 4000

Nong Khiaw is a traveller's haven in the truest sense, offering pampering, good food, decent accommodation and bags of activities with established adventure-tour operators. Nestled on the west bank of the Nam Ou (the river almost currentless since the building of the dam upstream), spanned by a vertiginous bridge and bookended by towering limestone crags, it's surely one of the most photogenic spots in Laos. On the river's scenic east bank (officially called Ban Sop Houn) is the lion's share of guesthouses and restaurants.

Be aware that Nong Khiaw is alternatively known as Muang Ngoi (the name of the surrounding district), creating obvious confusion with Muang Ngoi Neua, a 75-minute boat ride further north.

⊙ Sights

At dusk a fabulous star show turns the indigo sky into a pointillist canvas subtly outlining the riverside massifs. Whether you're stationed at one of the town's two viewpoints, Pha Daeng Peak or Sleeping Woman (p98), or just rubbernecking at these extraordinary karsts from ground level, you'll be manually shutting your jaw.

Pha Daeng Peak Viewpoint VIEWPOINT
(จุดຊົມວິວຜາແດງ; Pha Daeng Peak, Ban Sop Houn; 20,000K; ⊙5am-6pm) Reached by a testing though thoroughly doable 1½-hour walk on a decent path up Pha Daeng mountain, directly above the town, this viewpoint offers an unforgettable panorama. Drink up the sunset view (but bring a strong torch for your descent) or head here at 6am to

witness the valley below veiled in mist, with the mountain peaks painted gold.

Pay the admission fee to the guy in the kiosk at the bottom. You'll find him by a sign and an old bombshell on the left side of the road.

Sleeping Woman Viewpoint VIEWPOINT
(จุดຂึ້ນอิอมาๆมอม, Pha Nang None Mountain View; ☑️ 020-55377400; Rte 1C, heading northwest from Nong Khiaw, roughly 1km out of town; 15,000K; ⊘ 7am-6pm) This viewpoint rivals that of Pha Daeng Peak Viewpoint (p97) for its widescreen drama of surging karsts and mountains, with the boats on the river far below like floating blue crayons. It's an hour's climb up a marked pathway, and while another route down is offered it's not sufficiently marked, so it's wise to descend by the same path.

If you're here for sunset, on the way back down head to Hive Bar (p101) opposite the entrance to grab a cold drink on the terrace.

Tham Pha Thok CAVE
(ຖ້ຳຜາທອກ; 10,000K; ⊘ 7.30am-6.30pm) Around 2km east along Rte 1C, Tham Pha Thok is a series of caves in a limestone cliff where villagers and Pathet Lao eluded bombing during the Second Indochina War. The first cave is around 30m high and accessed by wooden stairway. Continue to the second, somewhat-claustrophobic cave, 300m along a dark passage through the cliff.

We recommend bringing your own torch rather than renting a weak one.

🏃 Activities & Tours

There are several ecotourism outfits in Nong Khiaw that offer trekking, cycling, paddleboarding and kayaking around the area.

⭐ Nong Khiaw
Jungle Fly ADVENTURE SPORTS
(☑️ 020-22256151; http://nongkhiawjunglefly. com; Lao Outdoor Travel, Rte 1C; half/full-day tour US$37/49; ⊘ 8.30am-5pm) This highly recommended new adventure park 10km out of town offers half-day and full-day tours that include canopy walks, 'Tarzan swings' and zipping through the jungle on 10 lines up to 400m long. There's also abseiling and trekking through the bamboo forest. Expect quality equipment and an emphasis on safety from the professional English-speaking guides.

Full-day trips run from 9am to 5pm, while half-day trips go from 8.30am to 1pm and 12.30pm to 5pm. You depart from (and return to) the Laos Outdoor Travel office by the bridge in Nong Khiaw.

Sabai Sabai MASSAGE
(☑️ 020-58686068; Ban Sop Houn; body massage 60,000K, oil massage 70,000K, steam bath 25,000K; ⊘ 9am-8pm) Set in a peaceful Zen-style garden, this wooden house is the perfect spot to restore the spirit and aching limbs with treatments like traditional Lao massages and herbal steam baths.

🛏 Sleeping

In the low season, accommodation prices are definitely negotiable. Nong Khiaw offers mainly budget options, plus a few boutique beds.

Ou River House GUESTHOUSE **$**
(☑️ 020-59945500; d 150,000-180,000K; 🛜) Located in a floating barge on the Nam Ou, this place is definitely one-of-a-kind in Nong Khiaw. It offers six simple fan-cooled rooms with attached bathrooms and a small terrace out front for soaking up the impressive views. There is a little cafe-restaurant on site that's popular with Lao customers.

It is possible to swim in the river directly from the deck.

Delilah's Place HOSTEL **$**
(☑️ 020-54395686; www.delilahscafenongkhiaw. wordpress.com; Main St; dm/d 40,000/60,000K; 🛜) Delilah's Place has clean shared-bathroom rooms and cosy dorms with mozzie nets, super-thick mattresses and safety lockers. There's also a great little traveller cafe to 'carb-up' before activities, so one-stop-shop Delilah's is deservedly the main traveller hub in town. Thanks to the goodwill of exuberant owner Harp, it is also a great resource for travel information.

Sunrise Guesthouse GUESTHOUSE **$**
(☑️ 020-22478799; Rte 1C, Ban Sop Houn; bungalows 60,000-150,000K; ❋🛜) Showing their age now, these tightly packed, termite-worn wooden bungalows are the polar opposite of luxury, but have stunning views of the river and bridge. There are four newer bungalows with relatively swish bathrooms, one of which has air-con. There's also a decent cafe with Western breakfasts and Lao fare.

Nong Khiaw

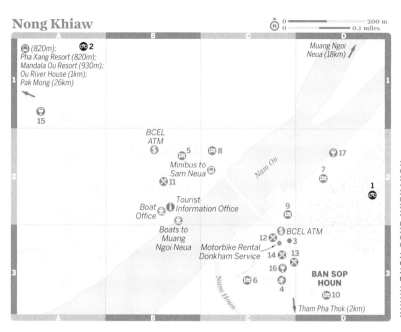

Nong Khiaw

Namhoun Guesthouse GUESTHOUSE **$**
(☏030-5533439; Ban Sop Houn; bungalows 60,000-100,000K; ❋ 🛜) Namhoun's cheaper bungalows are set around a small garden behind the family house. Much better are the more expensive riverside bungalows facing the Nam Ou. All rooms have mosquito nets and balconies with compulsory hammocks.

Sengdao Chittavong Guesthouse GUESTHOUSE **$**
(☏030-9237089; Rte 1C; bungalows 60,000-80,000K, d/tw 150,000-200,000K; 🛜) This family-run spot sits in splendid isolation on

the west bank and has wooden bungalows with rattan walls, mozzie nets, clean linen and balconies, located in a garden looking out onto the river. Even closer to the water is a new block of more upscale air-con rooms. Popular with families; there's also a restaurant with river-garden views.

★**Mandala Ou Resort** BOUTIQUE HOTEL **$$**
(☏030-5377332; www.mandala-ou.com; d/tw US$43-68; 🛜 ❋) ✿ This stunning boutique accommodation in cinnamon-coloured chalets – six facing the river – has imaginative features like inlaid glass bottles in the walls that allow more light, contemporary

bathrooms and swallow-you-up beds. The owners are friendly and there's a terrific Thai and Western menu, the town's only pool and a yoga deck used by Luang Prabang Yoga (p53), which runs monthly retreats here.

There's also a herbal sauna, which is perfect for the cooler winter nights. Find it just a short stroll from the bus station.

★**Nong Kiau Riverside** GUESTHOUSE $$
(☑020-55705000; www.nongkiau.com; Ban Sop Houn; d/tw incl breakfast US$35-55; @🛜) 🚲 Bungalows here are romantically finished with ambient lighting, wooden floors, woven bedspreads and mosquito nets. Each includes an attractive bathroom and

balcony for blissful river views of the looming karsts. There's an excellent restaurant serving Lao food with a mouth-watering breakfast buffet. It also has mountain bikes for hire. Discounts are available on room rates in the low season.

View Point Resort HOTEL $$
(☑030-4463686; viewpointresortlaos@gmail. com; d/tw US$35-60; ❄🛜) Looming large above town, this property offers some of the best panoramic views in Nong Khiaw. The 10 rooms are attractively finished with imported bed linen and upscale bathroom amenities. More convenient if you have a private vehicle – it involves a notable climb for those without wheels.

ⓘ **SENSITIVE TREKKING**

When visiting tribal villages it is important to learn slightly different etiquette according to each local culture. The following notes focus particularly on the Akha, as Akha women's coin-encrusted indigo traditional clothing make their villages popular trekking targets while their animist beliefs are also some of the most unexpected.

Shoes & feet Entering an ethnic Lao home it would be rude not to remove shoes, but in mud-floored dwellings of Hmong, Akha and some other tribal peoples, it is fine to keep them on. However, still avoid pointing feet at anyone.

Toilets If there's a village toilet, use it. When in the forest be sure to dump away from watercourses. But in remote villages with no toilets at all, check with the guide as to the local custom: although trekking etiquette usually dictates burying faeces, in some villages the deposit will be gobbled up greedily by the local pigs so shouldn't be wasted! Nonetheless, please do carry out used toilet paper, tampons etc, however unpleasant that might seem.

Photos While many hill-tribe boys are delighted to be photographed, most village women run from a camera. Asking permission to snap a passing stranger often results in refusal, which should be respected. However, if you're staying in a village homestay, your hosts may be happy for you to take a few snaps.

Gifts If you want to give gifts, consider fruit and vegetable seeds or saplings that continue to give after you've left. Always ask the guide first if it's appropriate to give anything and if so, only give directly to friends or to the village chief.

Beds In trekking villages it is common to sleep in the house of the village chief. In traditional Akha homes all the men sleep on one raised, curtained platform, most of the women on another (which it is taboo to visit). To make space for visitors, most men move out for the night to sleep in other houses, leaving the guide, trekkers and maybe a village elder or two to snuggle up in a line in the male section. Bringing a sleeping bag gives a greater semblance of privacy. Note that female trekkers count as 'honorary men'.

Spirits The spirit world is every bit as lively in hill-tribe cultures as it is in other Lao cultures and it would be exceedingly bad form for a visitor to touch a village totem (Tai Lü villages), a spirit gate (Akha) or any other taboo item. Ask the guide to explain and don't even think of dangling yourself on an Akha swing (*hacheu*).

Women & babies Akha mothers believe that covering both breasts will attract harm to their newborn offspring. Eating stones while pregnant is another custom, while the Akha attitude that twins are unlucky is common.

Pha Xang Resort HOTEL **$$**
(☎071-810014; d/tw from 250,000K; ❄ 🛜) About 1km out of town, Pha Xang is hardly a resort, more a collection of comfy A-frame rattan bungalows with wood floors, white walls and en suites dotted around a manicured garden. The staff's English is limited, but the peace and sense of nature here is not, making it a serene spot to take in the karsts.

It is conveniently located opposite the bus station.

🍴 Eating

Nong Khiaw has a foodie scene developing on both sides of the Nam Ou, though don't expect Luang Prabang levels of sophistication.

Vongmany Restaurant LAO **$**
(Ban Sop Houn; mains 20,000-50,000K; ⊙8.30am-10pm) This large, open rattan-and-wood restaurant serves very tasty locally sourced Lao food. The *láhp* here will put a bounce in your taste buds, while the buffalo steak is delicious, and the steamed fish and river shrimp are full of flavour.

Delilah's Place INTERNATIONAL **$**
(Main St; mains 15,000-50,000K; ⊙7am-10pm; 🛜) With Bach floating across the wood floors and a herd of African elephants thundering silently towards you on the mural, Delilah's satisfies your comfort cravings with amazing homemade Key lime pies, apple crumbles and ice cream, as well as hearty breakfasts of eggs, smoky bacon and pancakes. There's a nightly movie at 8.30pm.

Deen INDIAN **$**
(Ban Sop Houn; mains 15,000-50,000K; ⊙7am-10pm; 🛜) A superbly friendly Indian eatery with wood-fired naan bread, freshly made tandoori dishes, zesty curries and a homely atmosphere, Deen is deservedly packed every night.

CT Restaurant & Bakery LAO **$**
(Rte 1C, Ban Sop Houn; mains 20,000-40,000K; ⊙7am-10pm; 🛜) At the end of the bridge, this place has the best view in town. CT has a Western-friendly menu of pasta, pancakes, breakfasts, sandwiches and tasty staple Lao dishes. It also offers takeaway sandwiches for trekking.

★**Coco Home Bar & Restaurant** INTERNATIONAL **$$**
(☎020-23677818; Main St; mains 25,000-70,000K; ⊙8am-11pm; 🛜) Run by Sebastien and Chok, this leafy riverside oasis has a great menu, with dishes like papaya salad, mango sticky rice, *mok phaa* (steamed fish in banana leaves) and duck in orange sauce. It's arguably the best place in town to delight your taste buds. Eat in the lush garden or upstairs on the terrace.

🍷 Drinking & Nightlife

Q Bar BAR
(☎020-99918831; Rte 1C, Ban Sop Houn; ⊙7am-11.30pm; 🛜) Chilled Q sits on the main road with an ox-blood, rattan interior, a little roof terrace, good tunes and a friendly owner. Cocktails are 35,000K to 40,000K, with a two-for-one happy hour from 5pm to 7pm. If hungry, you can transform your tabletop into a barbecue grill and cook up a traditional Lao meal.

Watering Hole BAR
(☎030-9546046; riverside lane; ⊙8am-10pm) Set on pontoons, this peaceful, semi-alfresco Lao bar-restaurant relies on the soothing river view as its wallpaper, and dishes up cold Beerlao for the ultimate riverside sundowner. There's a decked area from where you can go swimming or kayaking (rentals 100,000K) in the gentle Nam Ou.

Hive Bar BAR
(☎030-5377990; Rte 1C; ⊙7am-11pm; 🛜) Located 1km out of town (heading towards Pak Mong), Hive Bar is run by a friendly Lao, has a downstairs disco and karaoke for those inclined, plus a chilled terrace to sink a beer and watch the sunset explode in pinks and oranges behind the karsts. Great indie tunes; happy hour is from 6pm to 7.30pm.

ℹ️ Information

BCEL has two 24-hour ATMs: one at the end of the bridge on the Ban Sop Houn side, and another 100m after the bridge on the road heading to Pak Mong.

The **Tourist Information Office** (⊙8-11am & 2-4pm Mon-Fri), located above the boat landing, is rarely open. Much better is reliable Harp at Delilah's Place (p98); a one-stop travel resource for bus and boat tickets and also decent budget digs.

Getting There & Away

BOAT

Riverboat rides are a highlight of visiting Nong Khiaw. However, since the Nam Ou was dammed, the trip to Luang Prabang is no longer possible. **Boats to Muang Ngoi Neua** (25,000K, 1¼ hours) leave at 11am and 2pm (in high season extra departures are possible), taking you through some of the most dramatic karst country in Laos. The 11am boat continues all the way to Muang Khua (150,000K, seven hours) for connections to Phongsali or Dien Bien Phu in Vietnam.

There needs to be a minimum of eight people (on all the above journeys) before the boatman leaves, otherwise you will have to club together to make up the difference. This is typically only an issue on the Muang Khua journey.

BUS & SŎRNGTĂAOU

The journey to Luang Prabang is possible in three hours but in reality usually takes at least four. Minivans or *sŏrngtăaou* (40,000K) run at 9am, 11am and 12.30pm, while air-con minibuses leave around 1.30pm (50,000K). Tickets are sold at the **bus station**, but the 11am service will wait for folks arriving off the boat(s) from Muang Ngoi. When a boat arrives from Muang Khua there'll usually be additional Luang Prabang minivans departing at around 3pm from either the bus station or **boat office** (⌚8:30-11:30am & 1-3pm).

For Udomxai, a direct minibus (50,000K, three hours) leaves at 11am. Alternatively, take any westbound transport and change at Pak Mong (25,000K, 50 minutes). For Luang Namtha, take any bus to Udomxai and change there.

Originating in Luang Prabang, the **minibus to Sam Neua** (150,000K, 11 hours) via Vieng Thong (100,000K, five hours) makes a quick lunch stop in Nong Khiaw at around 11.30am, leaving at about noon or 1pm. Another Sam Neua bus (arriving from Vientiane) passes through around 7pm. Both of these arrive at an unmarked bus stand on the Nong Khiaw side just before the start of the bridge. Try and get on the lunchtime bus as this is usually a larger vehicle compared to the cramped minibus in the evening. Plus there's the view you'll want to catch by daylight; it's one of the most beautiful mountain rides in Laos.

Getting Around

Bicycle rental makes sense for exploring local villages or reaching the Tham Pha Thok caves. Town bicycles cost 20,000K per day and mountain bikes cost 30,000K. Alternatively, hire a scooter (80,000/100,000K for a manual/automatic) from **Motorbike Rental Donkham Service** (☎030-9005476; Ban Sop Houn; ⌚8am-7pm). Tuk-tuks to the nearby bus station cost 5000K.

Muang Ngoi Neua
ເມືອງງອຍເຫນືອ

☎071 / POP 1000

Muang Ngoi Neua is deliciously bucolic; a place to unwind and reset your soul. As the Nam Ou (Ou River) slides sedately beneath the shadow of sawtoothed karsts, cows wander the village's unpaved 500m-long road, while roosters strut past villagers mending fishing nets. Packed with cheap guesthouses and eateries, here there's enough competition to keep prices down. And while hammock-swinging on balconies is still de rigueur, there's plenty more to do if you have the energy, be it short, unaided hikes into timeless neighbouring villages, exploring caves, tubing and kayaking on the now pacified Nam Ou, or fishing and mountain biking.

Sights

Ensure you're by the river come sunset to enjoy one of the most photogenic views in Laos, as the sun falls like a mellow peach beyond the jagged black cliffs. A little after dawn it's also interesting to watch locals delivering alms to monks at the rebuilt monastery, **Wat Okadsayaram**.

Phanoy Cave & Viewpoint CAVE
(ຖ້ຳພະນອຍ; 10,000K; ⌚7am-5pm) Phanoy Cave, well-signposted from the northern end of the main strip, is a cool relief on a hot day. The cave lies about halfway up a steep track that leads to a striking viewpoint over the Nam Ou and Muang Ngoi Neua below. Definitely take a torch (flashlight) for the cave as a cluster of Buddha relics lies about a 10-minute walk through a pitch-black passageway.

It's best to allow about one to two hours to see both the cave and the viewpoint. Bring water from town as there is none available at the cave or viewpoint.

Activities & Tours

Kayaking is a great way to appreciate the fabulous riverine scenery that stretches both ways along the Nam Ou. Lao Youth Travel is the most respected tour operator in town, has its own kayaks and is handily located where the boat-landing path passes by the two-storey Rainbow Guest House.

The Ou now runs very gently after being dammed, making it safer for younger kids.

Numerous freelance guides offer a range of walks to Lao, Hmong and Khamu villages and regional waterfalls. Beware of those who claim to be recommended by us (they're not!). Prices are reasonable and some visits, such as to the That Mok falls, involve boat rides. Others are easy hikes that you could do perfectly well unguided. Take a photo with your phone of the map outside Lao Youth Travel for a rough guide to the area.

★**Lao Youth Travel**   KAYAKING
(☏ 030-5140046; ⏱ 7.30-10.30am & 1.30-6pm) This long-established local outfit run by the friendly Mr Ping provides trekking, fishing and kayaking in the surrounding area. A half-day trip combining all three costs 145,000K for a group of four or more.

Gecko Tours & Cooking Class   TREKKING
(☏ 020-58886295; muangngoihandmade@gmail. com; ⏱ 7am-9pm) 🖉 The friendly team at Gecko Bar (p104) has branched out to offer tours, massages (from 60,000K) and even a cooking class (150,000K for one person, less per person for groups). The last involves a half-day trip to the restaurant's organic garden (15km away) where you'll pick ingredients and visit a nearby waterfall before returning to town to cook your dishes.

Gecko also offers a guided trek up Pha Boom, which looms above town, and can arrange trekking or biking trips to nearby villages.

🛏 Sleeping

Uniquely for such a tiny place, budget accommodation abounds and English is widely spoken, so you get the experience of a remote village without the inconvenience. The only drawback is that the accommodation is showing its age compared with up-and-coming Nong Khiaw just down the river.

Lattanavongsa Guesthouse   GUESTHOUSE $
(☏ 020-23863640; touymoy.laos@gmail.com; d/ tw from 100,000K; 🛜) Lattanavongsa offers a choice of bungalows at two locations: above the boat landing, and on the main drag in a pretty garden. Powder-blue rooms have choice art, mozzie nets, fresh linen and gas-fired showers and all have balconies. Enjoy breakfast or dinner at its idyllically situated

ⓘ **GUESTHOUSE VIEWS**

Most of the basic guesthouses have inspiring views over the Nam Ou and its multilayered karst massifs. Savouring such views from your bungalow is one of Muang Ngoi's great attractions, so think twice before choosing an inland guesthouse just to save 10,000K.

cafe above the boat landing, with unbroken cliff views. Book well ahead.

PDV Riverview Guesthouse   GUESTHOUSE $
(☏ 020-22148777; pdvbungalows@gmail.com; dm/d/tr 30,000/100,000/100,000K, bungalows 50,000-120,000K; 🛜) This place halfway down Main St offers fine riverside accommodation, with five fresh rooms and a six-berth dorm in a newer orange building with a sweeping Nam Ou panorama. The bungalows are nothing extraordinary but have great karst views and the usual balcony and hammock. Rates plummet off season.

Nicksa's Place   GUESTHOUSE $
(☏ 020-3665957; d/tw 60,000-100,000K) Overlooking the river from a pretty garden abuzz with butterflies, these seven house-proud cabanas are made of wood and stone and have en suites and mozzie nets. Each has a balcony and obligatory hammock to take in the impressive vista. Cold-water showers only, but warm management comes in the form of on-the-ball Nicksa.

Chantanohm Guesthouse   GUESTHOUSE $
(☏ 030-9737835; Ban Na; d 20,000K) This is a simple but pleasant spot to stay in the weaving village of Ban Na with its own restaurant and basic rooms with bucolic views. It's roughly a 3km walk east from the southern end of Muang Ngoi Neua. When you arrive, Mama Kham will welcome you with a soul-warming smile.

Veranda   GUESTHOUSE $
(☏ 020-23862021; bungalows 50,000-80,000K; 🛜) The five bamboo-weave bungalows here form an arc around a panoramic river view. Recently refurbished, the great-value clean rooms have hammocks, good beds and solar-heated showers. There's also a restaurant attached.

Bungalows Ecolodge   GUESTHOUSE $
(d/tr 120,000/150,000K; 🛜) Although perhaps showing their age on the outside, these

river-facing rattan-and-tin A-frame cabanas have pleasant rooms inside, with en suites and back walls that concertina into wide-screen views of the karsts from your bed. Mozzie nets, hammocks, romance – tick all the above. There's also a cosy cafe where you can rent kayaks.

Khamphan Guesthouse GUESTHOUSE $
(☑ 030-4725792; Huay Sen; d 10,000K) Has bags of rustic atmosphere, with its stilted wooden architecture and old-fashioned basic rooms. Run by a friendly Lao guy who speaks some English; food is available, as are guided walks to nearby Hmong villages. Follow the road heading out of Muang Ngoi Neua from the boat dock, heeding signs for Huay Sen.

OB Bungalows GUESTHOUSE $
(☑ 020-33863225; Ban Na; d 20,000K) Enjoying lovely karst views and the restful setting of surrounding rice fields, OB has a decidedly chilled vibe. The rooms are extremely basic, but the owner speaks a bit of English. Find it at the far end of the village of Ban Na.

Rainbow Guest House GUESTHOUSE $
(☑ 020-22957880; d/tw 80,000K; 🛜) Close to the boat ramp, this large house has clean, basic tiled-floor rooms with fresh linen and bathrooms, and a pleasant restaurant out front, the Bamboo Bar, with tasty Lao food, crêpes, curries and omelettes.

Ning Ning Guest House GUESTHOUSE $$
(☑ 030-5140863, 020-23880122; ningning_guest-house@hotmail.com; bungalows 100,000K, d/tw 300,000K; 🛜) Nestled around a peaceful garden, Ning Ning offers 10 wooden bungalows with mosquito nets, verandas, en suites, lily-white bed linens and walls draped in ethnic tapestries. There's also an impressive river-front block with a terrace restaurant and rooms that have a decidedly more upscale look and sumptuous views, but no air-con.

🍴 Eating & Drinking

Nightlife is limited in the village, but chilling over a sundowner Beerlao and watching the karsts from Riverside Restaurant is pure magic. Head to Bee Tree for a little more buzz.

★Gecko Bar & Shop LAO $
(☑ 020-58886295; muangngoihandmade@gmail.com; mains 15,000-40,000K; ☺7am-9pm; 🛜) Handmade woven gifts and tea are for sale at this delightful, memorable little cafe

(two-thirds of the way down the main drag, on your left heading south). There's a nice terrace to sit and read on, the owners are charming and the food, spanning noodles to soups, and pancakes to curries, is among the most raved about in the village.

★Riverside Restaurant LAO $
(☑ 030-5329920; meals 25,000-60,000K; ☺7am-11pm; 🛜) Since being damaged by a storm, Riverside has come back better than ever. In the evening its Chinese lanterns sway in the breeze on the decked terrace, beneath the sentinel arms of an enormous light-festooned mango tree. Riverside has gorgeous cliff views, and its menu encompasses noodles, fried dishes, *láhp* (minced meat or fish salad with shallots and coriander) and Indian fare.

Meem Restaurant LAO $
(Main St; mains 20,000-50,000K; ☺7am-9.30pm; 🛜) Halfway down Main St, welcoming Meem has wood floors and plenty of lounging cushions, and serves up flavoursome Lao and Indian fare, including delicious chicken masala, tomato curry, spring rolls and barbecued chicken and duck. By night, it has a magnetic attraction thanks to clay-pot candles and paper lanterns.

Delilah's LAO $
(mains 20,000-40,000K; ☺8am-9pm; 🛜) Serving up waffles, decent coffee, French toast, delightful desserts and fruit shakes, this cafe is the new outpost of the Delilah's empire that began in Nong Khiaw. It's a short distance down Main St on the right.

Bee Tree LAO $
(mains 15,000-35,000K; ☺11.30am-11.30pm; 🛜) Located at the end of the main drag, this restaurant-cum-beer-garden has a relaxed ambience. Choose from Lao dishes and some comfort food, or stroll here for 20,000K happy-hour cocktails between 6pm and 7pm.

Phetdavanh Restaurant & Street Buffet LAO, INTERNATIONAL $
(☑ 020-22148777; veggie buffet 30,000K, mains 30,000-45,000K; ☺buffet 7-9pm, restaurant 7am-11pm; 🛜🍴) This basic-looking restaurant runs a nightly 'all you can eat' veggie buffet (high season only), as well as serving pizzas, schnitzels, pancakes, soups, sandwiches and *shakshuka*. Try the Lao Suzy (stew with potato, carrot, eggplant and

onion). It also has rapid wi-fi, so you can eat and stream movies. Great Swedish cook.

There are also Trek mountain bikes (50,000K) and Honda dirt bikes (130,000K) for rent. Find it on a corner on the main drag, at the top of the stairs from the boat landing.

Vita Restaurant LAO **$**

(☑020-52949488; Main St; mains 20,000-40,000K; ☺8am-9pm; ☞) Fairy-lit Vita sits three-quarters of the way down the main drag on the left-hand side as you walk south, and dishes up decent *lâhp*, sandwiches and curries. There are plenty of lounging cushions for chilling and reading under a fan.

🛍 Shopping

Khao's Shop ARTS & CRAFTS

(☑020-97029526; ☺6am-8pm) Run by a friendly husband-and-wife team, this simple unnamed shop offers the best souvenirs in town. Khao makes beautiful temple-inspired stencil art, while his wife, No, creates colourful handwoven textiles. There are also used books, greeting cards, coffees and teas.

ℹ Information

Thefts from Muang Ngoi Neua's cheaper guesthouses tend to occur when over-relaxed guests leave flimsy doors and shutters unsecured or place valuables within easy reach of long-armed pincers – most windows here have no glass.

There are no banks or ATMs here so bring plenty of cash from either Muang Khua (upriver) or Nong Khiaw (downriver). In an emergency you could exchange US dollars at a few of the guesthouses but rates are unsurprisingly poor.

ℹ Getting There & Away

Boats to Nong Khiaw (25,000K, one hour) leave around 9.30am, with tickets on sale from 8am at the **boat ticket office** (☺8am-noon). At Nong Khiaw tuk-tuks wait above the boat landing for your arrival to take you to the bus station.

There is a boat from Muang Khua that runs if there is demand and it will pick up in Muang Ngoi Neua for Nong Khiaw around 1.30pm. Going to Muang Khua (120,000K, five hours), a boat leaves at 9.30am provided enough people sign up the day before on the list at the boat office. Alternatively, the 10.30am boat from Nong Khiaw will carry on to Muang Khua around midday if there are sufficient numbers; if not, people can club together to make up the difference. The first hour of the ride cuts through particularly spectacular karst scenery, but it is necessary to disembark at a major new dam,

travel around it by tuk-tuk (5000K) and continue in another boat.

A new road running alongside the Nam Ou connecting Muang Ngoi Neua to Nong Khiaw has been created. However, it is still unsealed and passes through tributaries that have not yet been bridged; pretty useless for travellers unless you can hitch a lift with a boatman who happens to be there.

PHONGSALI PROVINCE

No longer Laos, not yet China, Phongsali is a visual feast and is home to some of the nation's most traditional hill tribes. Trekkers might feel that they've walked onto the pages of *National Geographic*. For travellers, the province's most visited settlement is Muang Khua, a useful transit point linked by river to Nong Khiaw and by road to Dien Bien Phu in Vietnam. Further north the province is kept well off the standard tourist trail by arduous journeys on snaking roads that twist and turn endlessly. The only asphalt links Muang Khua to Udomxai, Phongsali and on to Mengla in China. Inconveniently, foreigners can't cross the Chinese border anywhere in the province. The road to Dien Bien Phu is now in great shape on the Lao side, but is not so great on the Vietnamese side.

Muang Khua ເມືອງຂວາ

☑088 / POP 4000

Pretty little Muang Khua is an inevitable stop when transiting between Laos and Dien Bien Phu in Vietnam, or taking the brown Nam Ou (Ou River) by boat to Nong Khiaw. While not as scenically spectacular nor as developed for the traveller as the latter, Muang Khua, with its pastel-coloured houses, still has oodles of small-town charm, set amid starburst palms where the Nam Ou and Nam Phak (Phak River) meet. The heart of the place is its wet and dry market.

If arriving from Dien Bien Phu, please relax – unlike neighbouring Vietnam, hard bargaining here is neither required nor appropriate.

👁 Sights

A short walk leads to the rustic Khamu quarter across a high, creaky **suspension bridge** (bike/pedestrian only) over the

Muang Khua

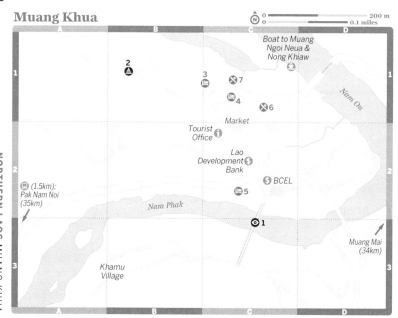

N 0 _____ 200 m
0 _____ 0.1 miles

Muang Khua

⊚ Sights
1 Suspension Bridge C3
2 Wat B1

🛏 Sleeping
3 Chaleunsuk Guesthouse C1
4 Phongpadith Guesthouse C1
5 Sensabai Guesthouse C2

✕ Eating
6 Sabaidee Restaurant C1
7 Sayfon C1

Nam Phak. An even easier stroll passes the colourful little **wat** FREE and heads into another palm-dappled village area where the road peters out. The ethnic handicrafts shop at Chaleunsuk Guesthouse sells a small but appealing range of local crafts. Photo-explanation boards describe their production and introduce the villages that your purchases support.

🏃 Activities

The tourist office organises several trekking options, including a rewarding one-day trek to the Akha Pala village of Ban Bakha (450,000K per person in a group of two).

Luang Prabang–based Tiger Trail (p59) offers six-day Akha Village 'voluntourism' experiences costing US$399.

Independent guide **Mr Khamman** (📞020-99320743) runs one- to three-day treks (one day for a group of two costs 500,000K per person).

🛏 Sleeping & Eating

There is a reasonable range of decent guesthouses and hotels in Muang Khua.

Don't expect too many culinary surprises; there are a few stands selling barbecued food and a couple of dependable restaurants where you can get decent Lao food.

Sensabai Guesthouse GUESTHOUSE $
(📞020-9998445; d 60,000K; 🛜) Overlooking the Nam Phak, the family-run Sensabai offers mint-coloured rooms with fragrant linen, TV, fan and squat toilet. There's an inviting lobby looking out over the river where you can read peacefully. It's on the main road, heading south out of town towards the bus station.

Chaleunsuk Guesthouse GUESTHOUSE $
(📞088-210847; d old block 70,000K, d/tw new block 100,000-120,000K; ❄@🛜) Chaleunsuk is popular with travellers and has house-proud, generously proportioned rooms

with large comfy beds and hot showers. Free tea is available in the ample communal sitting terrace. Next door there's a newer block with shinier rooms and upgraded TVs, although it's a little kitsch.

There is also a small shop selling hand-woven crafts and locally produced tea.

Phongpadith Guesthouse GUESTHOUSE **$$**
(☑088-213003; phongpadith.guesthouse@gmail.com; d/tw 180,000-280,000K; ❋ ☎) Towering above the other accommodation options in town, both literally and metaphorically, this guesthouse has the smartest rooms on offer, with inviting bed linen, piping-hot showers and flat-screen TVs. The 'Sweet Rooms' are more suite than sweet, but offer an ample 50 sq metres.

Sabaidee Restaurant LAO **$**
(mains 25,000-50,000K; ☺7.30am-9.30pm; ☎) This small eatery doubles as the only bar in town with a selection of more than just the ubiquitous Beerlao. The French-Lao owners offer cocktails to boat-weary travellers as well as wine by the glass and carafe. The fare is mainly Lao with some comforting home touches like homemade crêpes and fresh coffee.

Sayfon LAO **$**
(mains 25,000-40,000K; ☺7am-9pm; ☎) Set high above the river with views through the palm trees, this basic joint offers a fan-cooled interior and a wide English-language menu with Western-friendly staples like omelettes and pancakes, tasty *láhp*, noodle dishes and plenty of cool Beerlao.

ℹ Information

There are two ATMs in town. Both **BCEL** (☺8.30am-3.30pm Mon-Fri) and **Lao Development Bank** (☺8.30am-3.30pm Mon-Fri) can change major currencies such as US dollars (clean new notes only), euros, Vietnamese dong and Thai baht. Be aware that over the weekend banks are shut and ATMs may be empty, so if you're looking to catch a boat bring emergency cash.

The helpful **tourist office** (☑020-22848020; ☺8.30-11.30am & 1.30-4.30pm Mon-Fri) opposite the Sernalli Hotel can answer questions and arrange treks. If you want to book a trek out of office hours, call **Mr Keo** (☑020-22848020) to arrange a meeting, or try independent guide **Mr Khamman** (☑020-99320743). Otherwise, check out www.muangkhua.com, which has some bookable treks and the low-down on every last guesthouse in town.

ℹ Getting There & Away

Buses to Dien Bien Phu in Vietnam (60,000K) depart from outside the BCEL bank at 6am and 11am and take about four hours, including the border crossing. However, they aren't guaranteed to leave daily if there aren't enough passengers.

Muang Khua's inconvenient **bus station** (Rte 2E, 900m past Km 97) is nearly 2km west of the river towards Udomxai. Very rare tuk-tuks (10,000K per person) head out there once full from outside BCEL. Buses to Udomxai (50,000K, three hours) depart at 8.30am, 11am and 3pm. For Phongsali take the 8am *sŏrngtǎaou* to Pak Nam Noi (20,000K, one hour) and await the Udomxai–Phongsali (100,000K) bus there. It usually arrives at around 10am.

GETTING TO VIETNAM: PANG HOK TO TAY TRANG

Getting to the border Daily buses (60,000K, departing at 6am in either direction) between Muang Khua and Dien Bien Phu cross at the Pang Hok (Laos)/Tay Trang (Vietnam) border crossing 26km east of Muang Mai. The road has been entirely rebuilt on the Lao side right up to the Pang Hok border post, but is still surprisingly rough in places on the Vietnamese side. It's a picturesque route, particularly down in the Dien Bien Phu valley, which is often a blanket of emerald rice paddies. Making the trip in hops is definitely not recommended, as it will cost far more than the bus fare and it's easy to end up stranded along the way.

At the border This remote crossing sees a handful of travellers. Laos visas (p291) are available on arrival for the usual price, but you will likely be asked to pay up to 50,000K in random 'processing fees', 'tourist fees' and health checks as you pass from window to window. Vietnamese visas are definitely not available on arrival, so plan ahead to avoid getting stranded.

Moving on There are no facilities or waiting vehicles at either of the border posts, which are separated by about 4km of no man's land. From the Tay Trang side of the border it's about 31km to Dien Bien Phu.

You can no longer travel by river to Hat Sa since the damming of the Nam Ou. **Boats** run from here downriver to Muang Ngoi Neua (100,000K, five hours, 8.30am or when there are 10 people) and on to Nong Khiaw (120,000K, six hours) through stunning karst scenery.

Phongsali   ພົງສາລີ

♪ 088 / POP 8500 / ELEV 1400M

As you approach Phongsali via a sinuous mountain road, the town rears up suddenly on a ridgetop plateau. Often wrapped in mist, its atmospheric wooden Yunnanese shophouses and other buildings, spanning biscuit-brown to powder-blue, shelter below the peak of Phu Fa ('Sky Mountain'; 1625m) rising majestically in the background. The location gives the town panoramic views and a refreshing climate that can swing from pleasantly warm to downright cold in a matter of hours – expect icicles in the cold season and bring a jacket and waterproofs just in case, even in April.

The town's population is a mix of Phu Noi and Haw/Yunnanese, both long-term residents and more recent immigrants. That said, no one comes to Phongsali to experience the town, which can feel unfriendly and very untypically Lao; it's the trekking in the surrounding hill country and its vivid population of ethnic peoples that justifies the considerable effort to get here.

◉ Sights

The town's modest but distinctive old-town area includes a three-block grid of rough, stone-flagged alleys and a winding street mostly lined with traditional **Yunnanese shophouses** [FREE] whose wooden frontages recall the architecture of old Kunming. Tiny, new and functional, the **Chinese Temple** overlooks a pond, behind which is **Wat Keo** (ວັດແກວ), with its *petang*-playing monks.

Phongsali

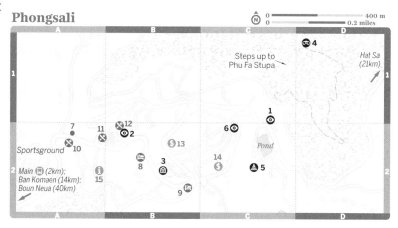

```
0 ───────────── 400 m
0 ───────────── 0.2 miles
```

Steps up to Phu Fa Stupa

Hat Sa (21km)

Sportsground

Main (2km); Ban Komaen (14km); Boun Neua (40km)

Pond

TREKKING IN PHONGSALI

Hill-tribe treks in Phongsali Province are among the most authentic and rewarding in all of Laos. Tours have a heavy emphasis on ecological and cultural sensitivity, with a sizeable chunk of fees going into development funds for the host villages. Carefully thought-out treks are offered through the well-organised tourist office. Most treks can be arranged for next-day departure, especially if you phone ahead. A popular option is the **Jungle Trek** (two short days starting from Boun Neua), visiting an Akha Phixo village as well as crossing a rare surviving stand of primary forest. Various multiday treks include boat rides up the Nam Ou (Ou River) from Hat Sa and visiting unforgettable Akha Nuqui villages linked by high ridgetop paths. One-way treks like the three-day **Nam Lan Trek** to Boun Tai can include delivery of your backpack to the destination so that you don't have to backtrack. This trek passes through Yang, Laobit, Akha Djepia and Akha Nuqui villages. However, with more than 30 stream and river crossings, it should only be attempted later in the dry season. To organise guides, phone well ahead to Phongsali's tourist office (p110) or get in touch with Amazing Phongsali Travel (p111).

Prices per person per day range from around 350,000K as part of a larger group to about 500,000K if going it alone. This includes the guide's fee, food and ultra-basic homestays in village homes. Add to this transport costs, which are widely variable depending on whether public transport or charter vehicles are used. 'Experience tours' allow you to spend more time with local communities including, perhaps, guided foraging trips to collect ingredients for the family dinner.

NORTHERN LAOS PHONGSALI

Ban Komean   VILLAGE

(ບ້ານກົມມ່ຽນ) 🍃 Phongsali's famous tea village, Ban Komean, lies 14km out of town and commands stupendous valley views that sweep nearly 360 degrees when you stand on the promontory behind the school. The tea bushes are reputedly more than 400 years old and said to be the world's oldest. A fair percentage of its authentic Phu Noi homes are set on stone-pile platforms. Rent a tuk-tuk from Phongsali (250,000K return) or hire a bike from the tourist office for 50,000K per day.

If getting here by motorbike, take the Boun Neua road, turn left directly opposite the inspirationally named Km4 Nightclub (not the asphalt road just before) then curve steadily around on the main unpaved road, keeping left at most junctions but avoiding any turn that descends into the valley.

Phu Fa   VIEWPOINT

(ພູຝ້າ, Sky Mountain; 5000K) For great views across town climb to the stupa-topped peak of Phu Fa (1625m); it's a punishing, tree-shaded climb of more than 400 stone steps. A ticket must be purchased on the last section of the ascent. An alternative descent returns to the Hat Sa road near a tea factory 2km east of town.

Cars and motorbikes can use the small road to the summit for an additional fee.

Museum of Tribes   MUSEUM

(10,000K; ⊙8-11.30am & 1.30-4.30pm Mon-Fri) This museum gives you a chance to deepen your understanding of the ethnic peoples of Phongsali Province. It contains a wealth of cultural information on animism and customs, with photos and historical background, as well as displays of the vividly coloured traditional clothing you're likely to see on your travels. If the door is locked, ask for the key from the post office across the road.

Market   MARKET

(⊙6am-5pm) Make a dawn visit to the earthy wet market (camera in hand) and thread through the labyrinthine collection of rickety stalls, with all manner of vegetables and fruit spread out on colourful display in the open area. It's a memorable experience, with its vocal Chinese vendors, exotic spices, brewing soup in forbidding cauldrons, ethnic visitors, and dogs optimistically attempting to procreate in the chaos.

🛏 Sleeping

Something of a barren choice of digs awaits you in Phongsali, which doesn't acquit itself well in welcoming travellers. All places generally have hot water, a blessing in the cold winter, but electricity is sometimes limited to a few hours a day.

Villa Amazing Maison Guesthouse
GUESTHOUSE $

(📞020-55774354; d/tw 100,000-150,000K; ❄️🛜) Despite the slightly convoluted name, this is the best-value guesthouse in town, run by the knowledgeable team from Amazing Phonsali Travel. Opened in late 2018, this place has clean, bright and spacious rooms with some nice decorative flourishes here and there.

Sengsaly Guesthouse
GUESTHOUSE $

(📞088-210165; d/tw 80,000-100,000K; 🛜) The best of three cheapies on the main drag, the Sengsaly has uber-basic 80,000K rooms with clean bedding, bare walls, tiled floors and private bathroom. Better rooms are in a newer, if overly colourful, block and come with a hot shower and veranda.

Vivaphone Hotel
HOTEL $$

(📞088-210999; vivaphonehotelphongsaly@gmail.com; unrenovated d/tw 100,000-200,000K, renovated d/tw 250,000-400,000K; ❄️🛜) Not so long ago, this hotel was on its last legs, but with new management helping to run the place, it has really turned itself around and now offers the smartest rooms in town. It is definitely worth the extra investment in the renovated rooms, which include imported bedding, smart TVs and sophisticated bathrooms.

The friendly team can also help with travel arrangements.

🍴 Eating & Drinking

Flavoursome *kòw sóy* (noodle soup with minced pork and tomato) is available from **noodle stands** (noodles 15,000K; ⊘6am-5pm) hidden away in the northwest corner of the market (p109), which is at its most interesting at dawn. The town's restaurant food is predominantly Chinese. *Đôm ʰbạh* (fondue-style fish soup) is a local specialty, notably served at simple places along the Hat Sa road (Km 2 and Km 4).

The Phongsali region, especially in Ban Komaen, is famous for Chinese-style green tea. The tourist office sells samples (along with excellent local *lòw-lów;* whisky). The pale-green tint comes from having been passed over raspberry leaves after fermentation.

Laoper Restaurant
CHINESE $

(mains 20,000-40,000K; ⊘5-10pm) Spot your dish in raw form behind the refrigerated glass counter: pork, intestines, buffalo steak and tofu, plus the day's fresh vegetables. Don't expect a menu, but point to what you want. Portions are huge so it's better to go as a couple or threesome. And be prepared for diners occasionally deconesting and spitting on the floor.

Laojhean Restaurant
LAO $

(mains 25,000-50,000K; ⊘7am-10.30pm) At this family-run noodle house the well-prepared food comes in decent-sized portions and is served with a smile. The menu's approximate English includes inscrutable offerings such as 'High-handed Pig's liver' and 'Palace Protects the Meat Cubelets'.

ℹ️ Information

MONEY
BCEL (⊘8.30am-3.30pm Mon-Fri) There is also a nearby ATM.

Lao Development Bank (⊘8.30am-3.30pm Mon-Fri) Includes an ATM, represents Western Union and changes multiple currencies to kip.

TOURIST INFORMATION
Tourist Office (📞088-210098; www.phongsali.net; ⊘8-11.30am & 1.30-4pm Mon-Fri) Helpful maps and brochures are available online (and are free from most guesthouses). To book a tour out of hours, call 📞020-22572373 or one of the mobile numbers posted on the front door.

ℹ️ Getting There & Away

Phongsali's airport is actually at Boun Neua, but the only flights available are with Lao Skyway and are not listed on their website. It is necessary to book in person at their offices and the services are often cancelled due to bad weather or fog. They operate a desk at Phongsali Airport, but it inconveniently opens only two hours before flights depart.

Phongsali's main bus station is at Km 3, west of town. A *sŏrngtăaou* runs there from the market area (10,000K) at 6.30am but only very infrequently after that, so leave plenty of time. Route 1A has finally been sealed, allowing for safer, quicker and easier passage to and from Phongsali. The daily bus to Vientiane (230,000K, more than 20 hours) leaves at 8.30am and the VIP bus (250,000K) at 2pm, passing through Luang Prabang (140,000K). Buses to Udomxai (80,000K, seven hours) leave at 8am and 2pm. There's a 7.30am bus to Luang Namtha (60,000K), and a 7am bus to Dien Bien Phu (130,000K, five hours) on the Vietnamese side. As foreigners can't cross the Chinese border at Ban Pakha, the buses to Mengla, China (7am and 1.30pm) are only useful for reaching Boun Neua (50,000K).

There's a 7.30am bus to Muang Khua (80,000K, seven hours), from where you can catch the boat to Muang Ngoi Neua and Nong Khiaw (due to river damming, it is no longer possible to catch the boat upriver from Hat Sa). Note that you cannot get to Muang Ngoi Neua or Nong Khiaw in one day and will have to overnight at Muang Khua.

ⓘ Getting Around

Amazing Phongsali Travel (☑ 088-210594, 020-55774354; www.explorephongsalylaos. com; Villa Amazing Maison Guesthouse; ⏰ 8am-5pm or later) rents small motorbikes from 100,000K per day.

Boun Neua   ບຸນເໜືອ
☑ 088 / POP 7000

A local transport hub 41km west of Phongsali, Boun Neua is a diffuse scattering of mostly newer concrete houses that has been tentatively proposed as the unlikely new provincial capital. Staying here might prove handy if connecting to Ou Tai or for those doing the Phongsali 'Jungle Trek'.

After Boun Neua (Km 41) the road to Phongsali climbs onto a ridgetop road surveying swathes of protected forests. There's a signed viewpoint 500m past Km 31, with mountain panoramas continuing for the next 15km. Baka Luang (200m beyond Km 17) is the first noticeably Phu Noi village en route, where old women still wear distinctive Phu Noi leggings.

There are a handful of guesthouses in Boun Neua.

The bus station plus a few shops and basic eateries lie around the main junction where Rte 1A to Ou Tai turns north off the Phongsali road.

Sivienkham Guesthouse   GUESTHOUSE $
(d 50,000K) Beside the bus station and market, convenient three-storey Sivienkham offers large and house-proud rooms with comfy beds, hot showers and sit-down toilets.

ⓘ Getting There & Away

For Phongsali (15,000K, 1½ hours), use the through buses from Mengla (China), Boun Tai, Udomxai or Vientiane, typically departing around 1pm and between 4pm and 6pm.

NORTHWESTERN LAOS

Northern Udomxai and Luang Namtha provinces form a mountainous tapestry of rivers, forests and traditional villages that are home to almost 40 classified ethnicities. Luang Namtha is the most developed of several traveller-friendly towns ranged around the 2224-sq-km Nam Ha NPA, with hiking, biking, kayaking and boating adventures all easily organised at short notice. Udomxai is the regional transport hub, while Boten is the one China–Laos border open to international visitors.

Udomxai   ອຸດົມໄຊ
☑ 081 / POP 37,000

Booming Udomxai (also known as Muang Xai) is a Laos–China trade centre and crossroads city, and with its cast of migrant truck drivers and Mandarin signage at every turn it certainly feels like it. The dusty, brash main street and lack of a traveller vibe puts off many short-term visitors, and you might think the highlight is the bus that spirits you out of here; however, it takes minimal effort to find the real Laos nearby. The well-organised tourist office – one of the best in the country – has many ideas to tempt you to stay longer, from cooking courses to treks through ethnic villages, ziplining and cycling. Or hop on a decent motorbike and head out in any direction and you'll quickly find attractive scenery.

Around 15% of Udomxai's population is Chinese (with many more transient workers), and the Yunnanese dialect is as common as Lao in some businesses and hotels.

⊙ Sights

Phu That Stupa   BUDDHIST TEMPLE
(ພະທາດພູທາດ; ⏰ dawn-dusk) Pretty little Phu That Stupa, a historic structure that was totally rebuilt after wartime destruction, is accessed via stairways from the main road. Religious ceremonies are held here on full-moon days.

Wat Phu That   BUDDHIST TEMPLE
(ວັດພູທາດ; ⏰ dawn-dusk) This attractive hilltop temple is one of the best spots to head to for cooler air and fabulous sunset views of the valley below. The 15m-tall gold Buddha is equally impressive.

Udomxai

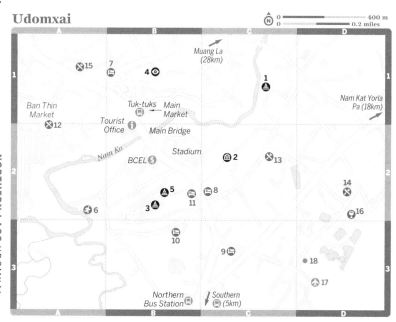

Udomxai

◉ Sights
1 Banjeng Temple C1
2 Museum...C2
3 Phu That Stupa B2
4 PMC B1
5 Wat Phu That B2

◉ Activities, Courses & Tours
6 Lao Red Cross...A2

◉ Sleeping
7 Charming Lao Hotel...............................B1
8 Lithavixay Guesthouse........................C2
9 Saylomen Guesthouse C3
10 Singha Hotel..B3
11 Villa Keoseumsack B2

◉ Eating
12 Ban Thin Market A2
   Charming Lao Coffee ....(see 7)
13 Meuang Neua Restaurant....................C2
14 Nonmengda Market D2
15 Souphailin Restaurant A1

◉ Drinking & Nightlife
16 Ming Khouan..D2

◉ Transport
17 Airport D3
18 Lao Airlines D3
   Lao Skyway ....(see 17)

PMC   WORKSHOP
(Productivity & Marketing Center of Oudomxay; ☑ 081-212803; www.facebook.com/pmc.oudom xay; ⊙ 8am-noon & 2-5pm) 🍃 FREE PMC is a small exhibition room and shop introducing local fibres such as jungle vine, and selling handmade paper products, bags and local essences. If you're wondering why it's part-funded by the UN Office on Drugs and Crime, that's because these crafts are an attempt to find non-narcotic-based commerce for former poppy-growing communities, hence its ironic nickname, the 'opium shop'.

Banjeng Temple   BUDDHIST TEMPLE
(ວັດບານແຈງ, Wat Santiphab; ⊙ dawn-dusk) Udomxai's foremost monastery is Banjeng Temple, which is modest but very attractively set on a riverside knoll. The most notable feature here is an imaginative concrete 'tree of life'. Tinkling in the breeze, its metal leaves hide a menagerie of naively crafted animal and bird statues that illustrate a local Buddha myth.

CHOM ONG CAVES

Udomxai's top tourist attraction, the extensive underground system of the **Chom Ong Caves** (ຖໍ້າຈອມອອງ) burrows more than 15km beneath a forested karst ridge near the Khamu village Ban Chom Ong, 48km from Udomxai. Often as high as 40m within, it's a veritable cathedral of a place whose first 450m have been lit with solar-powered lamps. Over millions of years the time-worn stalactites have been coated with curious crusts of minerals and sometimes studded with gravel from later wash-throughs. To gain access you'll need to borrow the gate key and pay for your entry (10,000K) at the tollbooth, and engage a guide (40,000K) in Ban Chom Ong, from which the cave entrance is an hour's walk.

The village's simple, unmarked 'guesthouse' (20,000K) is a purpose-built local-style longhouse with roll-out bedding and the relative luxury of a tap and porcelain squat in the outside shared toilets. We recommend arranging your trip through the tourist office in Udomxai, which involves a homestay where the family can prepare simple local meals.

Two- and three-day tours, including meals, an English-speaking guide and ample time to observe typical village scenes can be organised through the tourist office in Udomxai, but transport is by excruciatingly uncomfortable jeep-*sŏrngtăaou*. Two-day/one-night trips start from US$100 per person with a minimum of four people.

Museum
MUSEUM

(5000K; ⊙8-11am & 2-4pm Mon-Sat) FREE Stairways lead up from the main road to the town's two-storey museum, featuring colonial-style shutters and Asian gables. Inside, much of it is dedicated to uninspiring communist propaganda; however, you'll find some interesting ethnic clothing and tools used in rural Lao life.

🏃 Activities

The tourist office (p115) offers one-day tours around Udomxai, a city walk, one- and two-day visits to the Chom Ong Caves, plus two possible trekking routes that include Khamu or Hmong village homestays. To find potential fellow trekkers, arrive at 4pm for a 'rendezvous meeting' the day before departure. It also has well-maintained dirt bikes taking you off-road on great local adventures.

The office also offers cooking courses (100,000K per person with a minimum of four), which include shopping for ingredients. The teacher speaks better French than English.

⭐ Nam Kat Yorla Pa
ADVENTURE SPORTS

(☑020-55564359, 081-219666; www.namkatyorlapa.com; Faen village, Xay District) 🏊 Cycling, trekking, ziplining, rock climbing, abseiling, swimming, massage and shooting are all available at Udomxai Province's most popular forest resort, 17km north of Udomxai by the picturesque Nam Kat (Kat River). Lao tourists love the opportunity to dress up in traditional clothing and visit a picturesque Khamu village, meaning it is a good place to interact with them at weekends.

It also doubles as one of the most beautiful hotels in all of northern Laos.

Lao Red Cross
MASSAGE

(☑081-312391; sauna 15,000K, massage per 30min 40,000K; ⊙3-7.30pm) 🏊 On a hillock overlooking a beautiful river bend, the Lao Red Cross offers Lao Swedish-style massage and herbal saunas in a modest bamboo-matted structure. All proceeds are recycled into first-aid training in local villages.

🛏 Sleeping

Udomxai has an abundance of accommodation, including several soulless Chinese hotels in the 100,000K range. The best accommodation in the Udomxai area is to be found at the impressive Nam Kat Yorla Pa resort, about 17km from town. For an interesting rural alternative, consider staying 28km north in pretty Muang La, which is home to an exclusive boutique resort as well as some guesthouses.

Villa Keoseumsack
GUESTHOUSE $

(☑081-312170; Rte 1; d/tw 100,000-180,000K; ❄️🛜) Udomxai's best guesthouse is set back from the road in a handsome Lao house with large, inviting rooms. They come with crisp linen, decent fittings, springy beds and varnished floors. Hmong bed runners, TV, free wi-fi and a communal reading balcony finish them off. There's even complimentary toothbrushes and toothpaste.

Saylomen Guesthouse　　GUESTHOUSE **$**
(☏ 081-211377; d with fan/air-con 60,000/ 80,000K; ❄ ❂) Located off the main drag, this old guesthouse has charmless, basic rooms somewhat redeemed by mint-fresh floors and fragrant linen. Air-con rooms are a good investment in the hot season and all rooms have private bathrooms.

Lithavixay Guesthouse　　GUESTHOUSE **$**
(☏ 081-212175; Rte 1; d/tw 75,000-100,000K; ❄ ❂) An old-time traveller fave with a large lobby. Some rooms look tired but include TVs, couches and homely touches. Old showers suffer from slow drainage and service has dropped a little, but it's close to the old bus station and very central.

Singha Hotel　　HOTEL **$$**
(☏ 081-212995; singhahotel2018@gmail.com; d/ tw 150,000-370,000K; ❄ ❂) One of the newer places in town, the Singha Hotel offers 25 sparkling clean rooms with modern bathrooms and attention to detail such as towels folded as swans. Larger rooms count as 'VIP' and are almost suite-like.

Charming Lao Hotel　　BOUTIQUE HOTEL **$$**
(☏ 081-212881, 020-23966333; www.charming laohotel.com; d/tw incl breakfast US$50-150; ❄ @ ❂) An unexpected treat for Udomxai, this hotel offers tastefully furnished rooms right in the centre of town. Extra touches include flat-screen TVs with cable, coffee-making facilities, safety deposit boxes and contemporary bathrooms. The complex has a spa and a small air-con coffee shop. Staff are eager, but speak little English.

★ Nam Kat Yorla Pa　　RESORT **$$$**
(☏ 020-55564359; www.namkatyorlapa.com; Faen village, Xay District; tents US$45, d/tw US$80-150, pool ste US$360; ✦ ❂ ❂ ⛱) This stunning eco-resort is set on the banks of the Nam Kat in the lush mountains beyond urban Udomxai. Spacious rooms are built in traditional style by a babbling brook, but inside they contain all mod cons and are among the most luxurious in rural Laos. There is an inviting swimming pool and even some pool villas for the ultimate indulgence.

The cheapest rooms for less than US$100 are generally some sort of tented camp set-up – check at the time of booking.

Breakfast is usually included in the room rate and the restaurant is open to non-guests for lunch and dinner.

✕ Eating & Drinking

The **Ban Thin** (⊙ 6am-5pm) and **Non-mengda** (⊙ 6am-5pm) markets peddle vegetables, fruit and meat, including some live and dead exotica (particularly at weekends).

★ Souphailin Restaurant　　LAO **$**
(☏ 081-211147; mains 20,000-50,000K; ⊙ 7am-10pm) Don't be fooled by the modest bamboo exterior of this backstreet gem, as the tastiest Lao food in the city is served here. Friendly Souphailin creates culinary magic with her *mok phaa* (steamed fish in banana leaves), *láhp*, perfectly executed spring rolls, beef steak, fried noodles, and chicken and mushroom in banana leaf. Everything is fresh and seasonal.

Meuang Neua Restaurant　　LAO **$**
(mains 30,000-40,000K; ⊙ 7am-9pm) Festooned with lanterns and Che Guevara graffiti, this hole-in-the-wall is a 10-minute walk from the main drag. It's worth a visit for the fresh spring rolls, pancakes, juices, *pad thai* and noodle soup.

Charming Lao Coffee　　LAO **$$**
(Charming Lao Hotel; mains 45,000-60,000K; ⊙ 7am-9pm; ❂) Offering a level of aesthetic sophistication largely lacking in the city, Charming Lao has a fusion menu of barbecued pork, steamed fish, papaya salad, pasta variations and breakfast. Staff, however, speak little English and international dishes can end up as curious hybrids: carbonara with carrots and hot dog was a first for us! The garden features live music at weekends.

Ming Khouan　　BAR
(⊙ 11am-11pm; ❂) This is where it's at in Udomxai; a lively wooden and bamboo beer garden that draws a young crowd to quaff Beerlao by the crate. A decent selection of Lao food is available, including barbecued skewers, and the owner even allows drinkers to stay on after closing as long as the music stops. It's near the airport.

❶ Information

BCEL (☏ 081-211260; Rte 1; ⊙ 8.30am-3.30pm Mon-Fri) Has an ATM and changes several major currencies.

BUSES FROM NORTHERN BUS STATION

DESTINATION	PRICE (K)	DURATION (HR)	DEPARTURES
Bokeo	85,000	8	9am, 1pm
Boten	50,000	4	8am, 11.30am
Dien Bien Phu (Vietnam)	95,000	5	8.30am
Luang Namtha	40,000	2	8.30am, 11.30am, 3.30pm
Muang Khua	40,000	3	8.30am, 11.30am, 3.30pm
Muang La	70,000	4	8am
Phongsali	80,000	9	9am

BUSES (LONG-DISTANCE) FROM SOUTHERN BUS TERMINAL

DESTINATION	PRICE (K)	DURATION (HR)	DEPARTURES
Luang Prabang	60,000	7	9am, noon, 3.30pm
Muang Hongsa	110,000	7	noon
Muang Houn	30,000	3	noon, 3pm, 5pm
Nong Khiaw	45,000	4	10am
Pak Beng	40,000	4	8.30am, 10am
Pak Mong	30,000	3	1pm
Vientiane	170,000	14	11am, 2pm, 6pm
Vientiane (sleeper)	190,000	14	4pm

Tourist Office (Provincial Tourism Department of Oudomxay; ☑ 081-212483; www.oudomxay. info; ⊙ 8am-noon & 2-4.30pm) Has masses of information about onward travel, accommodation and local sights. It has free town maps and sells GT-Rider Laos maps. There are 12 different tours on offer, including the two-day/one-night tour to an impressive local cave, and three-day/two-night treks and homestays with local ethnic villages. It's best to book by email and re-confirm at the office when you arrive.

ℹ Getting There & Away

Lao Airlines (☑ 081-312047; www.laoairlines. com; ⊙ 8-11am & noon-5pm) (from US$95) and **Lao Skyway** (☑ 020-23122219; www. laoskyway.com; Udomxai Airport; ⊙ 8-11am & noon-5pm; from US$47) both fly daily to/from Vientiane. Tickets are also available from Lithavixay Guesthouse.

There are two bus stations in Udomxai: the old **Northern Bus Station** in the centre of town, and the newer Long-Distance Bus Station, aka **Southern Bus Terminal** (☑ 081-312200), 5km southwest from the centre.

An 8am minibus to Mengla (China) leaves from the Northern Bus Station. A Kunming-bound bed-bus from Luang Prabang stops at this station at around 11.30am. Booking isn't possible but the bus takes extra passengers if space allows.

ℹ Getting Around

The tourist office rents bicycles for 50,000K and motorbikes for 100,000K per day. It can help arrange chauffeured minivans from US$100 per day (negotiable).

Tuk-tuks are plentiful and cost 15,000K per person per hop within city limits.

Muang La · ເມືອງຫລາ

☑ 021 / POP 3500

Scenic Muang La, just 28km from Udomxai towards Phongsali, offers a charming rural alternative to the 'big city'. This Tai Lü village sits at the confluence of the Nam La (La River) and Nam Phak (Phak River), attractively awash with palm trees. Its central feature is a classically styled temple that hosts one of northern Laos' most revered Buddha statues, the Pra Singkham Buddha.

◉ Sights

Pra Singkham Buddha BUDDHIST STATUE
(ພະເຈົ້າສິງຄໍາ; ⊙ 8.30am-5pm) FREE Want to get rich? Afraid you might be infertile? Don't worry, just ask the Pra Singkham Buddha and your wish will be granted. For more information see the box on p116.

LOCAL KNOWLEDGE

THE LEGEND OF THE PRA SINGKHAM BUDDHA

Inlaid with precious stones, the 200kg gold-and-bronze Pra Singkham Buddha statue (p115) has an interesting history. It is said to have been created in Sri Lanka, spending time in Ayodhya, India before arriving in Laos in 868 CE. In 1355 it was reputedly one of five great Buddhist masterpieces sent out by Lan Xang founder Fa Ngum to inspire the faithful at the far reaches of his new kingdom.

However, the boat carrying the statue was sunk in a battle. Later found by a fisherman, Pra Singkham was dragged out of the water amid considerable tribulations and thereupon became the subject of a contest between residents of Muang La and Muang Khua regions. The sneaky folks from Muang Khua, downriver, suggested that the Buddha should choose for himself and set the statue on a raft to 'decide'. However, the seemingly hopeless contest went Muang La's way when the raft magically floated upstream against the current, 'proving' it belonged in La.

Kept initially in the Singkham Cave, by 1457 it had found a home in a specially built temple around which today's town of Muang La is now ranged. Like almost everything else in rural Laos, the temple was bombed to oblivion during the 20th-century Indochina wars. However, the statue had been rehidden in the Singkham Cave. By the time a new temple was consecrated in 1987, the Buddha had turned a black-green colour, apparently due to sadness at the destruction. But today he's once again a gleaming gold.

Singkham Cave
CAVE

(ຖ້ຳພະເຈົ້າສິງຄຳ) FREE The Singkham Cave, where the famous Pra Singkham Buddha statue once rested, is 3.7km west of Ban Samakisai. In Samakisai ask *'Khor kajeh tham noy?'* ('May I have the cave key please?') at the second hut south of the bridge. Then cross the bridge and take the second rough track west, just about passable by tuk-tuk or motorbike. This terminates at a collection of huts from which it's just three minutes' walk to the cave. Inside is a replica statue.

Hot Springs
HOT SPRINGS

(ບ່ຫນ້ຳອຸ່ນ; ⊙7am-5pm) FREE Wander down to the river to discover Muang La's modest hot spring that bubbles into the river when water levels are high. When levels are low, a flimsy bamboo suspension bridge allows access from the hot springs to an area where salt is produced by a mud-leeching process.

🛏 Sleeping & Eating

There are a couple of guesthouses to choose from and one or two upscale hotels.

You can either eat quick snacks at the market by the bus station or for something more salubrious pop into Muang La Resort.

★Lhakham Hotel
HOTEL $

(☑020-55555930; lhakhamhotel@gmail.com; d/tw 100,000K) Nestled on a riverbank, the Lhakham Hotel offers some of the best-value rooms in northern Laos. Furnishings are tasteful, the bathrooms include a rain shower and the river views are pretty, adding up to a steal. There's also a restaurant here. It's about 1km from the bus station.

Muang La Resort
BOUTIQUE HOTEL $$$

(☑020-22841264; www.muangla.com; 2-night package per person from US$595) The memorable Muang La Resort hides an elegant rustic refinement behind tall, whitewashed walls. It accepts neither walk-in guests nor visitors, so you'll need to prebook a package of two nights or more to enjoy the stylishly appointed half-timbered guest rooms, sauna and creatively raised open-air hot tub, all set between palms and manicured lawns.

ℹ Getting There & Away

Buses to Phongsali and Muang Khua pass through Muang La around an hour after departing Udomxai. The last bus returning to Udomxai usually rolls through at around 5pm. There's no bus station, just wave the bus down. Additional *sŏrngtǎaou* to Udomxai (20,000K) depart at around 7am and 11am if there's sufficient custom.

Luang Namtha   ຫລວງນ້ຳທາ

☑086 / POP 29,000

Welcoming travellers like no other town in northern Laos, Luang Namtha packs a powerful green hit with its selection of eco-minded tour companies catering for

Luang Namtha ⊙

Luang Nam Tha Museum (65m); Golden Stupa (1.4km)

Phou lu III Bungalows (250m)

Morning Market (200m); Pou Villa (1km)

Provincial Hospital (500m); ✈ (3km); Long-distance 🚌 (10km)

0 ━━━ 100 m
0 ━━━ 0.05 miles

NORTHERN LAOS LUANG NAMTHA

trekking to ethnically diverse villages, and cycling, kayaking and rafting in and around the stunning Nam Ha NPA.

Locally there's bags to do before you set out into the surrounding countryside, such as exploring the exotic night market, or grabbing a rental bike and tootling around the gently undulating rice-bowl valleys to waterfalls and temples. In the golden glow of sunset distant mountain ridges form layered silhouettes, and while it's not the prettiest belle architecturally speaking, the friendly vibe of Luang Namtha will grow on you.

⊙ Sights

Aside from Nam Ha NPA, there are waterfalls, temples and the night market.

★**Nam Ha NPA**   NATIONAL PARK
(ປ່າສະຫງວນແຫງຊາດນ້ຳຂ້າ; www.namha-npa. org) 🏞 The 2224-sq-km Nam Ha NPA is one of Laos' most accessible natural preserves and home to clouded leopards and possibly a few remaining tigers. Both around and within the mountainous park, woodlands have to compete with pressure from villages of various ethnicities, including Lao Huay, Akha and Khamu. Since 1999, an ecotourism masterplan has tried to ensure tour

operators and villagers work together to provide a genuine experience for trekkers while ensuring minimum impact on local communities and the environment.

Tours are limited to small groups, each agent has its own routes and, in principle, each village receives visitors no more than three times a week. Authorities don't dictate what villagers can and can't do, but by providing information on sustainable forestry and fishing practices it's hoped that forest protection will become a self-chosen priority for the communities.

Golden Stupa   BUDDHIST TEMPLE
(ພະທາດຄຳ; 5000K; ⊙8am-5pm) By far Namtha's most striking landmark, this large golden stupa sits on a steep ridge directly northwest of town. It gleams majestically when viewed from afar. Up close, the effect is a bit more bling, but the views over town are impressive.

That Phum Phuk BUDDHIST TEMPLE

(ທາດພູມພັກ; 5000K; ⊙8am-5pm) The red-gold stupa you see when first approaching the small and historic That Phum Phuk is a 2003 replica. Right beside it lies the brick-and-stucco rubble of an earlier version, blown over by the force of a US bombing raid during the Second Indochina War. Judging by the ferroconcrete protrusions, that wasn't the 1628 original either. The site is a hillock 3km northwest of the isolated Phouvan Guesthouse, on a stony laterite road that initially parallels the airfield.

An obvious set of *naga* (river serpent) stairs leads up to the stupa from a road junction in front.

Ban Nam Di VILLAGE

(ບ້ານນ້ຳດີ, Nam Dy) Barely 3km out of Luang Namtha, this hamlet is populated by Lao Huay (Lenten) people whose women wear traditional indigo tunics with purple sash-belts and silver-hoop necklaces. They specialise in turning bamboo pulp into rustic paper, using cotton screens that you'll spot along the scenic riverbanks.

At the eastern edge of the village, a three-minute stroll leads from a small car park to a 6m-high **waterfall** (2000K). You'll find it's more of a picnic site than a scenic wonder but a visit helps put a little money into village coffers. Unless the water level is really high there's no need to struggle up and over the hillside steps so ignore that sign and walk along the pretty stream. Parking costs 1000/2000/3000K for a bicycle/motorcycle/car.

Luang Nam Tha Museum MUSEUM

(ພິພິດທະພັນຫຼວງນ້ຳທາ; 020-55086368; 10,000K; ⊙8.30-11.30am & 1.30-3.30pm Mon-Fri) The Luang Nam Tha Museum contains a collection of local anthropological artefacts, such as ethnic clothing, Khamu bronze drums and ceramics. There are also a number of Buddha images and the usual display chronicling the Revolution.

⌕ Tours

For some 35km south of Luang Namtha, the pea-green Nam Tha (Tha River) flows across a series of pretty rapids tumbling between high-sided banks that are attractively shaggy with bamboo-choked forests. Luang Namtha tour agencies can organise one-day supported kayaking trips here, possibly combined with Nam Ha jungle treks. By bicycle or motorbike, the passably well-graded dirt road that runs along the river's eastern bank offers a quiet if potentially dusty way to enjoy pretty views and see some interesting minority villages without the need for hiking.

There is a self-guided cycling tour around the Namtha Valley which is a rewarding way to explore the region at your own pace. It is well signposted around and beyond town and includes a mix of ethnic villages and cultural sites. Pick up a printed route map at the Provincial Tourism Office (p121) or download a copy at http://luangnamthatourism.org.

NAM HA NPA TRIPS

Luang Namtha is a major starting point for trekking, rafting, mountain biking and kayaking trips in the Nam Ha NPA. Many of the tours stop for at least a night in a traditional village, which offers a fascinating glimpse of local life and a chance to admire the colourful clothing of the Lao Huay and Akha peoples in particular.

Treks all follow carefully considered sustainability guidelines but they vary in duration and difficulty. Kayaking is a more popular alternative in the wet season, when land trails are muddy and leeches are a minor nuisance.

Namtha agents display boards listing their tour options and how many punters have already signed up, which is very helpful if you're trying to join a group to make things cheaper (maximum eight people). If you don't want others to join you, some agents will accept a 'private surcharge' of around US$50.

There are several things to keep in mind when choosing between the dozen or so agencies in town. Be sure to ask if you will spend more time in the villages or the jungle. If it's the latter, will they take you through primary or secondary forest (and what percentage of the tour will be within the NPA)? How many hours of physical activity should you expect? If staying overnight, what will the sleeping conditions be like? Asking these basic questions will help you select the trip that's best for you.

KAO RAO CAVES

Well signed beside Rte 3, 1.5km east of Nam Eng village, is this extensive, accessible **cave system** (ຖ້ຳເກົາເລົ່າ; 10,000K), which has a 700m section open to visitors. The main limestone formations include old stalactites encrusted with crystal deposits.

Local guides accompany visitors through the cave, but speak no English and have weak torches (flashlights). Extensive lighting is already wired up, but there are often power cuts, meaning your own torch is a handy accessory. Allow around 45 minutes for the visit.

Curious corrugations in the floor that now look like great old tree roots once formed the lips of carbonate pools like those at Turkey's Pamukkale.

Hiker TREKKING
(☑ 086-212343, 020-59294245; www.thehikerlaos.com; Main St; ⊙ 8am-9pm) 🍴 This outfit is garnering some glowing feedback. Cycling and kayaking trips are available but its main focus is trekking, with one- to seven-day options; the longest one is more hard-core (eight hours' trekking per day) and promises to take you into untouched areas deep in the Nam Ha jungle, while one-day treks are much easier.

Forest Retreat Laos ECOTOUR
(☑ 020-55680031, 020-55560007; www.forestretreatlaos.com; Main St; ⊙ 8am-9pm) 🍴 Based at the Minority Restaurant (p120), this ecotourism outfit offers kayaking, trekking, homestays and mountain biking on one- to seven-day multi-activity adventures, and recruits staff and guides from ethnic-minority backgrounds where possible. It also runs a gruelling 60km one-day cycle trip to Muang Sing. Another option here is to take a cooking class.

Discovering Laos KAYAKING
(☑ 020-22990344, 086-212047; www.discoveringlaos.com; ⊙ 8am-9pm) 🍴 Specialises in kayaking and rafting trips through Khamu and Lenten villages, as well as cycling trips around Muang Sing. Also facilitates village homestays and overnights at its jungle camp on one-, two- and three-day treks.

Green Discovery ECOTOUR
(☑ 086-211484; www.greendiscoverylaos.com; Main St; ⊙ 8am-9pm) 🍴 The grandaddy of ecotourism in Laos offers a combo of boat trips, mountain biking, kayaking, homestays and one- to three-day treks in Nam Ha NPA. Safety is a given and staff are helpful. The most popular trip is a two-day walk through Nam Ha Valley combining culture and nature.

🛏 Sleeping

Popular places fill up fast during the November–February high season. It's best to book ahead.

Most lodging in Luang Namtha is in the architecturally bland northern part of town around the traveller restaurants.

Many travellers opt for a homestay experience in northern Laos and Luang Namtha is one of the most popular destinations to arrange this. Homestays can be booked through the Provincial Tourism Office (p121) or one of the local tour operators. Homestays are available in the Lanten village of Ban Nam Dee, the Khamu village of Ban Nam Ha and the Tai Daeng village of Ban Pieng Ngam.

In Town

Luang Namtha Inn GUESTHOUSE **$**
(☑ 020-5536 3699; d/tw 100,000-120,000K; ❋ 🛜) Under the same ownership as the long-running Adounsiri Guest House, this budget hotel on the main drag opened its doors in mid-2019. Included are tasteful bathrooms with hot-water showers, making it great value at current prices.

Amandra Villa GUESTHOUSE **$**
(☑ 020-98088878, 086-212407; www.amandrahotels.com; Rte 3A, Ban Nong Bua Vieng; d/tw US$12-29; ❋ 🛜) Set in a striking wooden building near the district bus station, Amandra has decent rooms with pretty bedside lanterns, satellite TV and hot water. The rattan-walled upstairs rooms are the largest, nicest and most expensive. The owner is helpful, and gives out his card so you can reach him if there are any hiccups. Bicycles are provided free of charge.

Adounsiri Guest House GUESTHOUSE **$**
(☑ 055-445532, 020-22991898; adounsiri@yahoo.com; d/tw 80,000-130,000K; 🛜) Located

down a quiet street, in the house of a friendly Lao family, rooms here have white walls draped in handicrafts with tiled floors, private bathrooms and a few sticks of furniture. The front room is fresh and welcoming with places to sit and chill. There are TVs in every room, plus free wi-fi, tea and coffee.

Manychan Guest House & Restaurant
GUESTHOUSE **$**

(☑086-312209; dm 30,000K; d with fan/air-con 70,000/100,000K; ☜) Manychan distinguishes itself not by its patchy rooms but by the warm welcome of its eponymous owner. The restaurant has a coffee machine from Italy brewing feisty cappuccinos, makes fresh bread and pastries for breakfast, and also has a terrace for dinner (mains 30,000K). Rooms are bare-walled affairs with armoire, bathroom and hot-water shower, but little else.

Thoulasith Guesthouse
GUESTHOUSE **$**

(☑086-212166; infothoulasith@gmail.com; Rte 3A; d & tw with fan/air-con from 80,000/100,000K; ✳☜) This traveller-friendly place offers clean rooms with bedside lamps, art on the walls, free tea and inviting balconies. There's also a newer block of swish rooms with bathtubs. It's set back from the main strip so makes for a peaceful spot to wind down before or after a trek.

Zuela Guesthouse
GUESTHOUSE **$$**

(☑020-22391966; www.zuela.asia; d old block with fan US$20, d/tw new block with air-con US$25-60; ✳☜) Located in a leafy courtyard, Zuela has an old block of spotless if slightly dark rooms with exposed-brick walls and en suites. The newer block has smarter rooms (some with balcony) with glazed rattan ceilings, lemon zest walls, desks and vivid local art. Besides its great restaurant, Zuela, it also offers mountain-bike and motorbike rental and tours.

Around Town

Phou Iu III Bungalows
RESORT **$$**

(☑020-22390195; www.luangnamtha-oasis-resort.com; bungalow incl breakfast 250,000-450,000K; ☜≋) This spacious resort sits in pretty, flowering gardens, although a swimming pool with waterslides and jungle gyms makes it slightly less serene for couples. Bungalows are spacious and nicely fitted out with lumber-wood beds, brick floors, fireplaces and inviting terraces. It's well signposted from the centre of town. Note that in December it's a little on the chilly side.

Boat Landing Guest House
RESORT **$$**

(☑086-312398; www.theboatlanding.laopdr.com; Ban Kone; d/tw incl breakfast US$47-60; ☜) One of the country's original ecolodges, the Boat Landing has riverside acacia groves hugging tastefully finished wooden bungalows with solar-heated showers. The cosy-but-weary rooms could do with a refresh, but the restaurant here (p121) produces some of the best Lao cuisine in the north. It is located 6km south of the new town and about 150m off the main road.

★ Pou Villa
BOUTIQUE HOTEL **$$$**

(☑086-212469; pouvillalnt@gmail.com; Khop Meaung Rd; bungalows from US$130; ✳@☜) Dramatically set on a hillside on the western edge of town, this is the most sophisticated accommodation in Luang Namtha. The small bungalows have big views and are appointed to an impressive four-star standard that is a revolution for Luang Namtha, including flat-screen TV, minibar and creature comforts like bathrobes and slippers. A swimming pool is planned for 2020.

✗ Eating & Drinking

Luang Namtha buzzes in the evenings with its lively **night market** (Rte 3A; ⊙7-11.30pm), a good place for snack grazing. Find noodle stands galore in the **morning market** (noodles 10,000K; ⊙7am-5pm).

The Classic and Bamboo Lounge, in particular, are reliable for a lively atmosphere.

Lai's Place
LAO **$**

(☑086-23939111; mains 15,000-50,000K; ⊙6.30am-9.30pm; ☜☒) No other restaurant in northern Laos offers such a tourist-friendly introduction to the region's diverse ethnic cuisines than this simple eatery with sturdy wooden tables and a small terrace. There's a long list of *jqaou* dipping sauces for sticky rice alongside traditional Akha and Tai Dam dishes like *aw lahm*, a stew of banana flower, rattan shoot, eggplant and pumpkin. Choose your level of spiciness.

Minority Restaurant
LAO **$**

(mains 25,000-50,000K; ⊙7am-10.30pm; ☜) This inviting, wood-beamed restaurant hidden down a little side alley offers the chance to sample typically ethnic dishes from the

Khamu, Tai Dam and Akha tribes, as well as *láhp,* stir-fries, chicken curry and fried fish.

Manychan Guesthouse
& Restaurant LAO $

(mains 20,000-40,000K; ⊘6.30am-10.30pm; 🛜) An inviting all-wood interior spilling out onto a fairy-lit street terrace and a menu covering a greatest hits of traveller fare keeps this place among the more popular *falang* (foreigner) venues in town. Beers arrive in coolers, the coffee has a kick and wi-fi is free.

★**Bamboo Lounge** INTERNATIONAL $$

(☑020-29643190; www.bambooloungelaos.com; mains/pizzas 40,000/75,000K; ⊘7am-11.30pm, happy hour 5-7pm; 🛜) 🖉 With its moss-green facade, this place is the favourite in town for travellers. It offers young people from remote villages employment and has donated more than 3000 books to local schools. It's alluring by night with its twinkling fairy lights, top tunes and outdoor terrace piping delicious aromas from its wood-fired oven. Myriad thin-crust pizza choices, plus regular specials like Mexican burritos.

And unusually for Laos, it's completely non-smoking.

Boat Landing Restaurant LAO $$

(☑086-312398; meals 35,000-160,000K; ⊘7am-8.30pm) The relaxing riverside setting complements some of the most authentic northern Lao cuisine on offer. From five-dish menus for two or three people to one-plate meals, the flavour combinations are divine. If you're baffled by the choice try

snacking on a selection of *jąaou* used as dipping sauces for balls of sticky rice. Located in the guesthouse of the same name.

Classic BAR

(☑020-59294245; www.facebook.com/theclass icview; ⊘3pm-midnight; 🛜) Overlooking a lily pond and the distant mountains, The Classic is a great little bar serving up purple rice beer, passion-fruit mojitos, exotic snacks and good tunes. By night its low-rise wooden tables glow under the amber lights. Run by the friendly owner of The Hiker (p119), it's a good spot to interact with locals.

ⓘ Information

MEDICAL SERVICES

Provincial Hospital (Rte 3A; ⊘24hr) This hospital can do the basics like X-rays and dishing out antibiotics. Ask for English-speaking Dr Veokham.

MONEY

BCEL (⊘8.30am-3.30pm Mon-Fri) Changes major currencies (commission-free) and has a 24-hour ATM.

Lao Development Bank (⊘8.30am-noon & 2-3.30pm Mon-Fri) Exchanges major currencies and has Western Union.

TOURIST INFORMATION

Provincial Tourism Office (☑086-211534; http://luangnamthatourism.org; ⊘8-11.30am & 1.30-4pm Mon-Fri) Helpful resource for all things local, including trekking advice, plus an excellent website that is regularly updated.

GETTING TO CHINA: BOTEN TO MÓHĀN

Getting to the border The Lao immigration post at the Boten (Laos)/Móhān (China) border crossing (7.30am to 4.30pm Laos time, 8.30am to 5.30pm China time) is a few minutes' walk north of Boten market. Tuk-tuks shuttle across no man's land to the Chinese immigration post in Móhān (Bohan) or it's an easy 1km walk.

Alternatively, take one of the growing number of handy Laos–China bus connections such as Udomxai–Mengla, Luang Namtha–Jinghong and Luang Prabang–Kunming.

At the border Northbound it is necessary to have a Chinese visa in advance. On arrival in Laos, 30-day visas (p291) are available.

Moving on From the Chinese immigration post it's a 1km walk up Móhān's main street to the stand where little buses depart for Mengla (RMB16, one hour) every 20 minutes or so until mid-afternoon. These arrive at Mengla's bus station No 2. Nip across that city to the northern bus station for Jinghong (RMB42, 2½ hours, frequent until 6pm) or Kunming (mornings only).

On the Lao side minibuses shuttle regularly in the morning from Boten to Luang Namtha (one hour, 25,000K).

BUSES FROM LUANG NAMTHA

DESTINATION	PRICE (K)	DURATION (HR)	STATION	DEPARTURES
Boten	25,000	2	district	6 daily 8am-2pm
Dien Bien Phu (Vietnam)	130,000	10	long-distance	7.30am
Huay Xai ('Borkeo')	60,000	4	long-distance	9am, 12.30pm, 4pm
Jinghong (China)	100,000	6	long-distance	8am
Luang Prabang	100,000	8	long-distance	9am, 7pm
Mengla (China)	50,000	3½	long-distance	8am
Muang Long	50,000	4	district	8.30am, 1.30pm
Muang Sing	30,000	2	district	6 daily 8am-3.30pm
Na Lae	40,000	3	district	9.30am, noon
Nong Khiaw	100,000	6	long-distance	9am
Udomxai	40,000	3	long-distance	9.30am, noon, 2.30pm
Vieng Phukha	30,000	1½	district	9.30am, 12.30pm
Vientiane	180,000-200,000	21-24	long-distance	8.30am, 2.30pm

Bamboo Lounge (p121) Produces an excellent guide to the area, which you can download online at www.luangnamthaguide.com.

ⓘ Getting There & Away

Both **Lao Airlines** (☑ 086-212072; www. laoairlines.com; ⊘ 8am-noon & 1-5pm), from US$85, and **Lao Skyway** (☑ 020-99990011; Luang Namtha Airport; ⊘ 8am-noon & 1-5pm), from US$50, fly to Vientiane daily.

There are two bus stations. The **district bus station** is walking distance from the traveller strip. The main **long-distance bus station** is 10km south of town. For buses at either station, prebooking a ticket doesn't guarantee a seat – arrive early and claim one in person.

ⓘ Getting Around

Chartered tuk-tuks charge 20,000K per person between the long-distance bus station or airport and the town centre, more if you're travelling solo, plus they may try their luck and start much higher. Most agencies and guesthouses sell ticket packages for long-distance buses that include a transfer from the guesthouse and cost around 20,000K above the usual fare.

Cycling is the ideal way to explore the wats, waterfalls, villages and landscapes surrounding Luang Namtha. There are a couple of **bike shops** (per day bicycle 10,000-25,000K; motorcycle 30,000-60,000K; ⊘ 9am-6.30pm) in front of the Zuela Guesthouse. Choose from a bicycle or motorcycle depending on how energetic you're feeling.

Vieng Phukha   ວຽງພູຄາ

☑ 086 / POP 4000

Sleepy Vieng Phukha (also spelt 'Phoukha') is an alternative trekking base for visiting the western limits of the Nam Ha NPA, notably on three-day Akha trail hikes. Such trails see fewer visitors than many from Luang Namtha and the partly forested landscapes can be magnificent, though many hills in Vieng Phukha's direct vicinity have been completely deforested.

⦿ Sights

Just 15 minutes' stroll south of Rte 3 near Km 85 but utterly hidden in thick secondary woodlands is the almost invisible site of the 1530 temple **Wat Mahapot**. What little had survived the centuries was mostly pillaged for building materials around 1977 when all the residents moved back after the war, so now all you'll see is the odd scattering of bricks poking out from a tree-choked muddy rise. Getting there involves walking along a steep V-shaped gully that once protected the **Khúu Wíeng** (ramparts) of a short-lived 16th-century 'city'. Again there's nothing but muddy banks to see but a good guide (essential) can fill in sketchy historical details and explain the medicinal uses of plants you'll encounter on a 40-minute walking tour. There are no longer local tour guides operating here, but Mr Tong Mua at Tigerman Treks (p125) in Muang Sing can take you.

Activities

Nam Ha Hilltribe Ecotrek
HIKING
(📞020-55086887; www.somhak1966.wixsite.com/ecotrek; ⊙8am-noon & 1-6pm) Run by Somhack (an experienced Khamu hunter who hung up his gun to use his tracking skills as a guide), this great outfit has multiday treks (from moderately easy to challenging) from Vieng Phukha to explore the Nam Ha NPA.

Nam Ha Ecoguide Service
Vieng Phoukha
HIKING
(📞020-55985289; www.namha-npa.org; ⊙8am-noon & 1.30-5pm) 🚶 One- to five-day treks with homestays in Nam Ha NPA.

🛏 Sleeping & Eating

Virtually all of Vieng Phukha's accommodation is in simple bungalows with cold showers. The tiny town centre consists of just three parallel streets, where you'll find a handful of guesthouses (and ecotourism outfits).

Eating is slim pickings here. Phuet Mung Khun Guesthouse has a small restaurant.

Thongmyxai
Guesthouse
GUESTHOUSE $
(📞020-22390351; d 50,000K) Just about the smartest accommodation in town, set in an attractive garden with bungalows.

Phuet Mung Khun
Guesthouse
GUESTHOUSE $
(📞020-55886089; d 60,000-80,000K; 📶) Located on a riverbank, the friendly Phuet Mung Khun Guesthouse has neat little bungalows, plus a small restaurant. The owner speaks rudimentary English.

🛈 Getting There & Away

Sŏrngtăaou for Luang Namtha (30,000K, 1½ hours) depart at around 9am and 12.30pm from the middle of town. Or you can wave down a Huay Xai–Namtha through-service (three daily).

Muang Sing   ເມືອງສິງ

📞081 / POP 9000

Bordering Myanmar and within grasp of the green hills of China, Muang Sing is a rural backwater in the heart of the Golden Triangle. Formerly on the once infamous opium trail, it's a sleepy town of wilting, Tai Lü-style houses where trekking has overtaken smuggling contraband. Hmong, Tai Lü, Akha and Tai Dam are all seen here in traditional dress at the old market (arrive at dawn), giving the town a frontier feel.

Back in the late 1990s, it was one of the must-visit destinations in Laos, but with the end of fast boat services and the clampdown on the opium trade, it has dropped off the traveller radar. Recently, a growing Chinese population has settled here, replacing rice fields with banana and rubber plantations for consumption on the other side of the border. Western travellers have spoken of being turned away from restaurants and guesthouses by Chinese operators.

History

In the late 18th century, a dowager of the Chiang Khaen principality founded the square, grid-plan citadel of Wiang Fa Ya (today's Muang Sing) along with the That Xieng Tung stupa. In 1803 this area became vassal to Nan (now in Thailand) and was largely abandoned following the deportations of 1805 and 1813. But the Chiang Khaen princes returned, moving their capital here in 1884 from Xiang Khaeng

MYSTERIOUS TOM DOOLEY

Saint or shameless self-promoter? Humanitarian or CIA pawn? More than fifty years after his early death, opinions are still divided over the 'jungle doctor' who set up his famous benevolent hospital in Muang Sing in 1958. Passionately Catholic yet dismissed from the US Navy for his sexual orientation, this complex character was cited by President Kennedy as an inspiration for the Peace Corps (founded in 1961, the year Dooley succumbed to cancer). However, his anti-communist books helped encourage the US political slide towards war in Indochina and rumours abound that the flights that brought in medical supplies to his Muang Sing base would return laden with opium. For much more, read James Fisher's flawed but detailed Dooley biography *Dr America*.

Muang Sing

the famous American 'jungle doctor' Tom Dooley set up his hospital in Muang Sing, which became the setting for a series of international intrigues.

◉ Sights

Sprinkled along the town's main street are a few classic Lao-French hybrid mansion-houses. These mostly 1920s structures have ground-floor walls of brick and stucco topped with a wooden upper storey featuring a wraparound roofed veranda. Classic examples house the tourist office and the Tribal Museum.

The **old market** (Main St), built in 1954, is all but abandoned these days. The bustling **new market** (⊙7am-10pm) is near the bus station and is very colourful first thing in the morning.

That Xieng Tung   BUDDHIST TEMPLE
(ທາດຊຽງຕຶງ) Around 6km southeast of Muang Sing, That Xieng Tung sits on a grassy plateau dotted with sacred trees, 1km up a rough access track that branches south off the Luang Namtha road 200m after Km 52. This place really comes alive at festival time (full moon of the 12th lunar month, between late October and mid-November), with a carnival atmosphere, traditional dance performances and Buddhist merit-makers offering candles and flowers around the base of the stupa.

Wat Namkeo Luang   BUDDHIST TEMPLE
(ວັດນ້ຳແກ້ວຫລວງ) Wat Namkeo Luang is one of the most visually striking monastic buildings in Muang Sing. It features an entry porch with red-tongued golden *naga* (river serpent) and an unusually tall and ornate gilded stupa. Some villagers still draw water from shaduf-style lever wells in the slowly gentrifying *bâhn* (the general Lao word for house or village) opposite. Nearby you can also find a modest Lak Bâan spirit-totem, but touching it would cause serious offence.

Tribal Museum   MUSEUM
(5000K; ⊙8.30-11.30am & 1.15-4.30pm Mon-Fri) The most distinctive of the old Lao-French buildings is home to the two-room Tribal Museum, which boasts costume displays downstairs and six cases of cultural artefacts upstairs. Watching a 40-minute video on the Akha people costs 5000K extra.

on the Mekong. This kicked off a 20-year tug of war between France, Britain and Siam, causing the principality to be split in two, with the western sector, including Muang Sing, being absorbed into French Indochina. Muang Sing rapidly became the biggest opium market in the Golden Triangle, a function officially sanctioned by the French. In 1946, parts of town were devastated by Kuomintang troops who continued to operate here well into the 1950s after losing the Chinese civil war. In 1958

TREKKING IN MUANG SING

The main reason visitors come to Muang Sing is to venture into the minority villages that dot the valley of rice paddies and sugar-cane fields surrounding the town. To do it yourself by bicycle or motorbike, start by purchasing Wolfgang Korn's helpful *Muang Sing Cultural Guide Book* from the tourist office. Its map shows major roads and labels the ethnicities of the valley's villages. To make the village-visiting experience somewhat more interactive you can engage a guide for as little as 100,000K from one of Muang Sing's ecotour agencies, which also offer a gamut of longer treks and homestay experiences.

If you've got your own wheels, the dusty, unpaved but reasonably smooth Xieng Kok road leads through a predominantly Akha district where an unusually large proportion of women wear distinctive silver 'coin' headdresses and billowing indigo blouses.

🏃 Activities & Tours

Tigerman Treks TREKKING
(☑030-5264881, 020-55467833; tigermantrek @gmail.com; Main St; 7am-7pm) 🖉 English-speaking teacher and nice guy Mr Tong Mua has long been a fixture of Muang Sing and with the slow death of the tourist office (located opposite), he's a reliable bet for general information, decent treks and homestays in the Nam Ha NPA, as well as tuk-tuk tours and cycle/trek combos. He also rents bikes (50,000K) and motorcycles (100,000K).

Phou Iu Travel ADVENTURE SPORTS
(☑081-400012; www.muangsingtravel.com; 7am-7pm) Run out of the Phou Iu II Bungalows, this decent outfit offers well-organised treks around Muang Sing. It also offers treks to the more remote Xieng Khaeng district towards Myanmar; check www.adventure-trek-laos.com for details. Other options include one- and two-day cycling tours and minority-village homestays.

🛏 Sleeping & Eating

There is not a huge range of eateries in Muang Sing. It's fair to say visitors aren't drawn here for the dining.

★ Phou Iu II Bungalows GUESTHOUSE $$
(☑086-400012; www.muangsingtravel.com; bungalows small/medium/large 150,000/250,000/350,000K) Set around an expansive garden, the biggest bungalows have fun, outdoor, rock-clad shower spaces. All rooms have comfortable beds, mosquito nets, fans and small verandas, although the rooms are cold at night during the cool season. There's an on-site herbal sauna (10,000K) and massage (50,000K per hour), plus a small restaurant serving local Lao dishes.

Couleur Cafe LAO $
(mains 25,000-60,000K; 7am-9pm) One of the few surviving restaurants in town, this is a little outpost of the former Couleur Cafe in Luang Prabang. Dishes include a host of Lao favourites, plus a few international surprises such as chicken fillet in mustard sauce and spaghetti bolognese. There is also a healthy selection of juices and shakes served in hipster jam jars.

ℹ Information

Lao Development Bank (☺8am-noon & 2-3.30pm Mon-Fri) Exchanges key currencies like US dollars, Thai baht and Chinese yuan but the rates are poor.

Tourist Office (☺8am-4pm Mon-Fri) Often understaffed so it may be closed, but there are some useful fact sheets on the walls.

ℹ Getting There & Away

From the **bus station** in the northwest corner of town, minibuses depart for Luang Namtha (30,000K, two hours) at 8am, 9.30am, 11am, 12.30pm, 2pm and 3.30pm. The bus to Muang La (40,000K) leaves at 7.30am and 1pm. *Sŏrngtăaou* depart for Muang Long (30,000K, 1½ hours) at 9am, 11am, 1pm and 3.30pm.

ℹ Getting Around

Kalao Motorcycle (per day 100,000K; 8am-5pm) rents motorbikes on the road to the morning market, but English is limited.

Tour operators and guesthouses rent bicycles (30,000K per day).

THE MIDDLE MEKONG

For many tourists the Middle Mekong region is seen merely in passing between Thailand and Luang Prabang – typically on the two-day slowboat route from Huay Xai via Pak Beng – but there's plenty to interest the more adventurous traveller. Bokeo, meaning 'Gem Mine', takes its name from the sapphire deposits in Huay Xai district, and the province harbours 34 ethnicities despite a particularly sparse population. Sainyabuli Province is synonymous with working elephants and the Elephant Conservation Center is just outside the eponymous capital. Other than in Huay Xai and Pak Beng you'll need a decent phrasebook wherever you go.

Western Sainyabuli remains particularly far off the traveller radar; places such as the dramatic Khop district are 'last frontiers' with a complex ethnic mix and reputedly high proportion of still-pristine forests.

Huay Xai ຫ້ວຍຊາຍ

☑ 084 / POP 30,000

Separated from Thailand by the mother river that is the Mekong, Huay Xai is, for many, their first impression of Laos. While that used to be a bad thing, this oddly charming town has perked up in recent years. By night, roadside food vendors take to the streets, and there are some welcoming traveller guesthouses and cafes serving tasty food.

Huay Xai was allegedly home to a US heroin-processing plant during the Secret War, but these days the only things trafficked through are travellers en route to Luang Prabang or the fabled Gibbon Experience (p130), the most talked-about adventure in the country. Yet, with day trips to nearby ethnic villages and some worthwhile voluntourism opportunities, there are passable excuses to stick around for a day or so.

◉ Sights

Huay Xai's modest tourist attractions include the Mekong views from several colourful wats.

Main Market   MARKET
(☉7am-noon) Tucked in the valley behind Fort Carnot is Huay Xai's vibrant main market.

Wat Jom Khao Manilat   BUDDHIST TEMPLE
(☉6am-6pm) One of the principal Buddhist temples in town; stairs lead up to its hilltop summit from the centre of town.

Wat Thadsuvanna
Phakham   BUDDHIST TEMPLE
(ວັດຫາດສວັນນະຜາຄຳ; ☉dawn-dusk) Commanding the rise directly above the speedboat landing, 3km south of the central area, Wat Thadsuvanna Phakham is a colourful temple featuring a row of eight gilded Buddhas demonstrating the main meditation postures and disdaining Mekong views beneath floral foliage.

Wat Khonekeo
Xaiyaram   BUDDHIST TEMPLE
(ວັດໂຄນແກ້ວ; ☉dawn-dusk) Wat Khonekeo Xaiyaram, in Ban Khonekeo, has a lavish frontage with dazzling red, gold and green pillars and doors.

Wat Keophone
Savanthanaram   BUDDHIST TEMPLE
(ວັດແກ້ວພອນສະຫວັນທະນາຣາມ; ☉dawn-dusk) Wat Keophone Savanthanaram features murals of gruesome torture scenes on the north wall of the *sĭm* (ordination hall), while on the slope above a long Buddha reclines behind chicken wire.

🏃 Activities & Tours

Anyone leaving on the slowboat to Luang Prabang will likely miss out on much of northern Laos, making a trip to the hill tribes near Huay Xai the best opportunity for a glimpse of the region's ethnic diversity. New Challenge Discovery offers treks to nearby Khamu villages. Many guesthouses offer similar tours, while Daauw Home can arrange homestays in a nearby Hmong village.

Lao Red Cross   MASSAGE
(☑084-211935; massage per hour from 50,000K; herbal sauna 20,000K; ☉1.30-9pm Mon-Fri, from 10.30am Sat & Sun) 🖉 Lao Red Cross offers Swedish-Lao massage and a traditional herbal sauna (from 4pm) in a stately old mansion beside the Mekong.

New Challenge Discovery   TREKKING
(☑020-97720313, 030-5209858; www.newchallengediscovery.com; Th Saykhong; 2-day trekking US$120 per person, 1-day kayaking US$70 per person, steep discounts for groups of 3 or more; ☉8am-5.30pm) 🖉 This raved-about company run by former Gibbon Experience guides offers authentic one- to three-day trekking tours to nearby Khamu villages on the edge of the Nam Kan NPA, as well as kayaking trips on the Mekong. Your money

LOCAL KNOWLEDGE

THE GOLDEN TRIANGLE REINVENTED

Around 5km north of Tonpheung, small Rte 3 abruptly undergoes an astonishing transformation. Suddenly you're gliding along a two-coloured paved avenue, lined with palm trees and immaculately swept by teams of cleaners. Golden domes and pseudo-classical charioteers rear beside you. No, you haven't ingested a happy pizza. This is the Golden Triangle's very own Laos Vegas, a casino and entertainment project still a work in progress, but planned to eventually cover almost 100 sq km. After 2.5km this surreal strip turns left and dead-ends after 600m at the Mekong beside another Disneyesque fantasy dome and a mini Big Ben. The huge casino here is open to all, but most of the games are aimed at Chinese or Thai gamblers and may not be familiar. Electronic roulette tables are the most accessible of the games on offer.

This area of riverfront is part of the famous Golden Triangle, where Thailand and Laos face off, with Myanmar sticking a long-nosed sand bank between the two. Boat cruises potter past from the Thai side. On the Lao bank speedboats await but foreigners can't cross the border without prearranged authorisation.

goes to support rural education projects and the empowerment of local people to restore and protect the fragile ecosystem.

🛏 Sleeping

The central drag is packed with guesthouses and many more are dotted around the edge of town. Prices can be higher than elsewhere in Laos, even though the quality is lower.

BAP Guesthouse GUESTHOUSE $
(☑084-211083; Th Saykhong; d/tw with fan 60,000, d/tw with air-con 120,000K;; ❄) Run by friendly English-speaking Mrs Changpeng, trusty BAP has 16 rooms, some with fan or air-con and private bathroom. There are four newer ones that merit a mention for their colourful quilts, wood accents, TVs and sunset views over the Mekong. The restaurant (mains 15,000K to 35,000K) is also popular for its fried-rice dishes, pasta and hearty breakfasts.

Little Hostel HOSTEL $
(☑030-5206329; https://littlehostel.wordpress.com; Th Saykhong; dm 40,000-70,000K; 🛜) Colourful furnishings stand out against the concrete floors of this otherwise bare-bones hostel with a couple of four-berth dorms. The rooms are as clean as the showers and it's a friendly place to meet fellow travellers, with a large common area and a central location on the main drag. Rates vary widely from low to high season.

Khaup Jai Guesthouse GUESTHOUSE $
(☑020-55683164; khopjailaos@gmail.com; d & tw with fan/air-con 100,000/120,000K; ❄🛜)

Khaup Jai offers clean, simple rooms with private bathrooms in a well-kept guesthouse with a friendly English-speaking owner. Fan rooms downstairs, air-con ones upstairs. Next to reception is a small tour office that can arrange transportation and tours.

Oudomphone Guesthouse 2 GUESTHOUSE $
(☑084-211308, 020-55683134; d & tw with fan/air-con 80,000/120,000K; ❄🛜) Clean and central, these digs have a pleasant breakfast cafe and spacious nondescript rooms with bathrooms. While nothing spectacular, it's one of the slightly better options in town.

Daauw Home BUNGALOW $
(☑030-9041296; http://daauwvillagelaos.com; d 80,000K, bungalows 100,000-120,000K) 🍃 Daauw Home is run by a lovely Hmong family, and your stay in a cosy bungalow near the heart of town enables you to contribute something to women's empowerment and minority rights, as this place is a grassroots initiative run by Project Kajsiab. Simple rooms and bungalows come with hammock, balcony and private bathroom.

There's a small **handicrafts shop**, and you can also **volunteer** here. It's located just off the stairs to Wat Jom Khao Manilat, halfway up on the right-hand side.

Phonetip Guesthouse GUESTHOUSE $
(☑084-211084; Th Saykhong; d/tw 40,000-100,000K; ❄🛜) The owners ensure this cheap and somewhat cheerful place smells fragrant, the sheets and floors are clean, the wi-fi works and the staff are friendly.

Huay Xai

LAOS

Slowboat
Landing

Th Saykhong

Enlargement

See Enlargement

LAOS
THAILAND

Mekong River

Th Sai Klang

Th Saykhong

Th Saykhong

Chiang Rai (107km)

Sŏrngtǎaou
to Tonpheung
& Muang Mom

Wangview Hotel (1.3km);
Speedboat Landing (2km);
Wat Thadsuvanna
Phakham (2km);
(4km);
(6km)

(4km)

The cheapest options are just beds in boxes with a shared bathroom, but there's a pleasant road-facing upstairs communal area, if you can grab a seat.

Gateway Villa Hotel GUESTHOUSE $

(084-212180; gatewaytour.laos@gmail.com; Th Saykhong; dm 84,000K, d/tw 110,000-368,000K, incl breakfast;) Gateway Villa has tastefully furnished rooms with hardwood floors, wicker chairs, TVs and comfy beds. Some rooms are more sophisticated than others and have Mekong views. You'll get a good night's sleep, an OK breakfast, fast internet and helpful English-speaking staff.

Sabaydee Guest House GUESTHOUSE $

(084-212252; Th Saykhong; d/tw incl breakfast 90,000-130,000K;) Sabaydee has unfailingly clean rooms with comfy beds, TVs, fans and en suites. Decked in bright colours and pleasant furnishings, some overlook the river. There's also a nice communal area with internet access. Bathrooms are the basic, flood-the-entire-floor type.

Huay Xai

◉ Sights
1 Main Market C4
2 Wat Jom Khao Manilat D2
3 Wat Keophone Savanthanaram C5
4 Wat Khonekeo Xaiyaram..................... B1

◉ Activities, Courses & Tours
5 Gibbon Experience C2
6 Lao Red Cross B2
7 New Challenge Discovery D2

◉ Sleeping
8 BAP Guesthouse................................. D2
9 Daauw Home....................................... D2
10 Gateway Villa Hotel............................ D2
11 Khaup Jai Guesthouse B4
12 Little Hostel D2
13 Oudomphone Guesthouse 2.............. D2
14 Phonetip Guesthouse......................... D2
15 Phonevichith Guesthouse &
   Restaurant... A1
16 Riverside Houayxay Hotel.................. D3
17 Sabaydee Guest House....................... C1
18 Thaveesinh Hotel D2

◉ Eating
Daauw ....(see 9)
19 Dream Bakery D3
20 Houy Xai Kaew Restaurant D3
21 Riverview Cafe C2
22 Terrasse Restaurant.......................... D2

◉ Drinking & Nightlife
23 Bar How D2

◉ Information
24 BCEL D2
Gibbon Experience Office ....(see 5)
25 Tourist Information Office D2

◉ Transport
26 Luang Say Cruise................................. D3
27 Shompoo Cruise...................................A2
28 Slowboat Ticket Booth....................... A1

Thaveesinh Hotel   HOTEL $
(☑084-211502;   thaveesinh.info@gmail.com;
Th Saykhong; s/d with fan 80,000/100,000K;
s/d with air-con 110,000/140,000K;   ❄🛜)
Rooms in this very central hotel are fair-
sized and clean, if chintzy thanks to the
pink floral wallpaper and lilac bedding.
Heavy wooden furniture and ornaments
decorate common areas and there's a
rooftop breakfast room. Wi-fi is patchy, so
check your connection before committing
to a room.

Wangview Hotel   BUSINESS HOTEL $$
(☑020-29121999;   wangviewhotels@gmail.com;
Th Saykham; d/tw 250,000-375,000K; ❄@🛜)
Located a couple of kilometres south of
the main strip, this is the smartest hotel
in town, offering spacious rooms at a
competitive price. More expensive rooms
include a Mekong view, but feel like they
were designed a decade or more ago for a
rush of Thai conference business that never
materialised.

Riverside Houayxay Hotel   HOTEL $$
(☑084-1211064;   riverside_houayxay_laos@hot
mail.com;   d/tw 200,000-250,000K;   ❄🛜)
Located just off the main strip and overlooking the mighty Mekong, this is the
most upmarket hotel in the centre of town,
although that's not saying much. Rooms
are spacious, hot water is on tap, plus
there's a satellite TV and a minibar.

Phonevichith Guesthouse
& Restaurant   GUESTHOUSE $$
(☑084-211765; www.houayxairiverside.com; Ban
Khonekeo; d/tw incl breakfast US$45; ❄🛜) Col-
ourful fabrics, fans and kitschy lamps add
a little character to the smart rooms, which
come with piping-hot showers and air-con.
The newer wing offers the smartest beds
in town, which are verging on 'boutique
hotel'. The main attractions are the Mekong
perch and handy proximity to the slowboat
landing. It's impossible to miss this place
thanks to its bright orange facade.

✗ Eating & Drinking

Huay Xai is livelier than most Lao towns
thanks to a steady flow of travellers to and
from nearby Thailand. The best spot to let
your hair down is in a river bar, watch-
ing the sunset turn the Mekong chocolate
orange.

★**Daauw**   LAO $
(http://daauwvillagelaos.com;   mains   20,000-
50,000K; ⏱6-10pm; 🎵) 🌿 Probably the
friendliest vibe in town; head here to soak
up sunset views on its chill-out terrace
decked in low cushions and an open-pit
fire, and choose from freshly prepared
organic Hmong food, wood-fired pizza,
plenty of vegetarian options, or whole bar-
becued Mekong fish or chicken. Linger for
laojitos if there's a crowd, a mojito made
with *lòw-lów* (rice wine).

THE GIBBON EXPERIENCE

Adrenaline meets conservation in this ecofriendly adventure in the 1060 sq km of the Nam Kan NPA, home to tigers, clouded leopards, black bears and the black-crested gibbon. The **Gibbon Experience** (📞 084-212021, 030-5745866; www.gibbonexperience. org; 2-day Express US$180, 3-day Classic or Waterfall US$305; ⊙7am-5pm) 🖉 is essentially a series of navigable 'ziplines' among pristine forest canopy.

Back in 1996 poaching was threatening the extinction of the black-crested gibbon, when Animo, a brilliantly inventive conservation-based tour group, convinced the hunters of Bokeo to become the forest's guardians. Now as guides, they earn more for their families than in their old predatory days.

The benchmark for sustainable monkey business, this two- to three-day experience is one of Laos' most unforgettable adventures, and your chance to play Tarzan; living two nights in soaring treehouses within thickly forested hills and swinging high across valleys on incredible ziplines, some more than 500m long. It's a heart-stopping, superhero experience, but you should always remain personally vigilant with your harness and karabiner, ensuring it actually closes.

There was a tragic death on one of the ziplines in 2017 when a traveller crossed cables with a GE technician, severing the man's harness. Several new safety regulations were implemented in its aftermath, including additional signage, first aid kits for guides, and the dialling down of speedier cables. Teams also cleared vegetation to increase clearance. Safety does appear to be a priority, however there are some basic precautions to consider. Should it rain, remember you need more time to slow down with your brake (a humble bit of bike tyre). It's also optional to wear a helmet, but we recommend asking for one – given the speed you travel along the cable, you wouldn't want your head to come into contact with it.

There are three options for your visit: the two-day Express, during which there's little chance of seeing the gibbons, and the three-day Classic and Waterfall. While there's a good chance you'll hear the mellow ray-gun *whoop-whoop* of the gibbon's call at dawn, seeing a gibbon is less likely (though not unheard of). That said, the gibbons are flourishing and the treehouses for the Classic and Waterfall are built close to where these magnificent arboreal athletes live. All three trips involve a serious amount of trekking, particularly the Waterfall. And should you be here when it rains heavily, you may have to abandon Animo's vehicle and walk the slippery dirt roads to reach the park. We recommend you're in good shape for all three options.

Accommodation is located in unique thatched treehouses that are spaced sufficiently far from each other so that each feels entirely alone in the jungle. Often around 40m above the ground and set in natural amphitheatres with spectacular views, the treehouses can sleep up to 16 people with bedding laid out beneath large cloth nets, although some 'honeymoon treehouses' sleep just two people. Large spiders on the walls and rats rustling in the ceilings will be your companions, too, but this is the jungle after all. Well-cooked meals consisting of rice and four accompaniments are ziplined in from one of five rustic kitchens, while coffee, tea, hot chocolate and various additional snacks are available in each treehouse. Keeping anything edible in the provided strong box is essential to avoid attracting the forest rats.

Check in at the Huay Xai **Gibbon Experience Office** (📞084-212021; www.gibbon experience.org; Th Saykhong; ⊙8am-5pm) one day before departure. Gloves (essential for using the ziplines) are provided, while spiked rubber jungle shoes (US$3) are sold across town, though they're only necessary after heavy rains. Other recommended items for your adventure include hiking boots, long socks, toilet paper, industrial-strength mozzie repellent, a torch (flashlight), water bottle and earplugs. Everything you bring must be carried on your back while hiking and ziplining (the rest of your luggage can be left in the office storeroom). There's no electricity, save the solar-powered lights, so pre-charge all your batteries and devices. And book well ahead, before you leave home, as the Gibbon Experience gets jammed up in high season.

Daauw also runs a new daytime cafe by the stairs up to Wat Jom Khao Manilat. All of the income generated by both properties goes back into Project Kajsiab, an initiative to empower Hmong women.

Dream Bakery   BAKERY $

(Th Saykhong; snacks from 11,000K, pizzas 40,000-70,000K; ☺7am-7.30pm Mon-Fri, to 6pm Sat; 🛜) This main-street cafe is a sweet spot for homemade treats like apple pie, pecan pie and blueberry pie. It's also a top choice for coffee thanks to its Gaggia machine and it does a wide range of breakfasts, snacks and sandwiches. Some of the profits are diverted to help with child education in Bokeo Province.

Terrasse Restaurant   LAO $

(mains 20,000-60,000K, set menu 40,000K; ☺8.30am-10.30pm; 🛜) This relaxing hilltop spot just off the stairs to Wat Jom Khao Manilat offers simple Lao food cooked to perfection using market-fresh ingredients, plus some international favourites. With comfy cushions and views of the tangerine sun setting over the Mekong, it makes a great spot for a long, lazy dinner. The set menu includes soup, a main and fresh fruit.

Riverview Cafe   LAO $$

(Th Saykhong; meals 40,000K; ☺6.30am-11pm; 🛜) With its rattan ceiling that has seen better days and the thirsty walls peeling, Riverview Cafe (aka Muang Ner) might not look like much. However, it's often full, so stand by and catch the aromas from the kitchen, and in no time you'll be tucking into wood-fired pizzas, burgers, stir-fries, soup noodles and very zestful *láhp*.

It's next door to the Gibbon Experience Office; stock up on a sandwich to take with you to the jungle.

Houy Xai Kaew Restaurant   LAO $$

(Th Saykhong; mains 25,000-75,000K; ☺7am-11pm; 🛜) The Mekong terrace here offers a great vantage point from which to watch the boats shuttling to and from Thailand. The menu has a wide range of Thai and Lao food, including soups, stir-fries and curries, plus Western breakfasts.

Bar How   BAR

(☑020-55167220; Th Saykhong; ☺6.30am-11pm; 🛜) Decked in old muskets and rice-paddy hats, Bar How is darkly atmospheric. By night a row of homemade *lòw-lów* (rice wine), infused with everything from blueberry to lychee, catches the low light and resembles a Victorian apothecary. It also serves pizza, steak and spring rolls (mains 30,000K to 60,000K). However, slack service means you may have to seek out staff.

ℹ Information

BCEL (Th Saykhong; ☺8.30am-4.30pm Mon-Fri) Has a 24-hour ATM, exchange facility and Western Union.

Tourist Information Office (☑084-211162; Th Saykhong; ☺8am-noon & 2-4.30pm Mon-Fri) Has free tourist maps of the town and some suggestions for excursions around the province.

ℹ Getting There & Away

For years, streams of Luang Prabang–bound travellers have piled into Huay Xai and jumped straight onboard a boat for the memorable descent of the Mekong. Today, improving roads mean an ever-increasing proportion opt instead for the overnight bus. But while slightly cheaper than the slowboat, it's far less social, less attractive and, at around 15 hours of travel, leaves most travellers exhausted on arrival.

AIR

Huay Xai's airport is oddly perched on a hillside off the city bypass, 1.5km northwest of the bus station. At the time of writing, neither Lao Airlines or Lao Skyway were offering any flight services from here.

BOAT

Slowboats to Pak Beng & Luang Prabang

Slowboats currently depart from Huay Xai at 11.30am daily. Purchase tickets at the **slowboat ticket booth** (☑084-211659) for Pak Beng (100,000K, one day) or Luang Prabang (200,000K not including accommodation, two days). Sales start at 8am on the day of travel. Avoid buying a ticket from a travel company, as it will include an overpriced tuk-tuk transfer to the pier and then a long wait for the departure.

Most boats now offer comfortable mini-van-style seats. If the boat operators try to cram on too many passengers (more than 70 or so), a tactic that really works is for later arrivals to simply refuse to get aboard until a second boat is provided.

'Luxury' Slowboats

To do the two-day river journey to Luang Prabang in more comfort, a popular alternative is the stylish 40-seat **Luang Say Cruise** (☑071-252553, 020-55090718; www.luangsay.com; cruise US$379-542, single supplement from

US$64; ⊙ 8-11.30am & 1.30-5pm Mon-Fri, 8-11.30am Sat & Sun). Packages include meals, guides, visits en route and a night's accommodation at the lovely Luang Say Lodge (p134) in Pak Beng. Departures are three or four times weekly in peak season (October to March), with prices varying according to season. There's no service at all in June or when the Mekong is too low.

Another, more affordable option is the newer **Shompoo Cruise** (☑ 020-59305555, 071-213189; www.shompoocruise.com; per person with/without accommodation from US$175/155). This is a tastefully upgraded boat that heads downstream Monday, Tuesday, Thursday and Saturday and upstream on Monday, Wednesday, Friday and Sunday. It includes two lunches and a dinner in Pak Beng. It has accommodation but tickets can be sold without, leaving travellers free to select their own place to stay.

With some patience a small group could charter their own slowboat, starting from around US$750 (highly negotiable).

Speedboats & Longboats

The **speedboat landing** (☑ 084-211457; Rte 3, 200m beyond Km 202) is directly beneath Wat Thadsuvanna Phakham, 3km south of town. Six-passenger speedboats (*héua wái*) zip thrillingly but dangerously and with great physical discomfort to Pak Beng (180,000K, three hours) and Luang Prabang (350,000K, seven hours including lunch stop), typically departing around 10.30am.

Due to a section of the Nam Tha (Tha River) being dammed, it's no longer possible to catch a boat all the way up to Luang Namtha.

BUS & SŎRNGTĂAOU

Note that Huay Xai–bound buses are usually marked 'Borkeo'. The bus station is 5km southeast of town. Buses to Luang Prabang (120,000K, 14 to 17 hours) depart at 10am and 4pm; for Luang Namtha (60,000K, four hours) they leave at 9am and 12.30pm; for Udomxai (90,000K, eight hours) there are buses at 9.30am and 1pm. For Vientiane (230,000K, 25 hours) catch the 11.30am.

Travel-agency minibuses to Luang Namtha leave from central Huay Xai at around 9am (100,000K, four hours) but still arrive at Namtha's inconveniently out-of-town bus station. **Sŏrngtăaou** to Tonpheung (30,000K, two hours) leave when full from beside the main market, very occasionally continuing to Muang Mom.

⊙ Getting Around

Bicycles (30,000K per day) are available from Little Hostel (p127), while the Gibbon Experience Office (p130) rents electric motorbikes for 50,000K per day.

Tuk-tuks charge about 20,000K per person to the airport, bus station, speedboat or slowboat landings.

Pak Beng   ປາກແບ່ງ
☑ 084 / POP 3500

A halfway riverine stop between Luang Prabang and Huay Xai (lunch for speedy longtails, overnight for slowboats), Pak Beng is short on architectural charm, but there are some good places to stay and nice spots to eat, including bakeries and Western-friendly cafes.

GETTING TO THAILAND: HUAY XAI (HOKSAY) TO CHIANG KHONG

Getting to the border Since the completion of the Thai-Lao Friendship Bridge 4 at the Huay Xai/Chiang Khong border crossing in late 2013, the former ferry-boat crossing is for locals only.

Tuk-tuks cost about 30,000K per person to the immigration post. Alternatively, many agencies in Huay Xai sell tickets to Chiang Mai or Chiang Rai that include a tuk-tuk to the border, bus across the bridge and onward transport for about the same price as doing it yourself.

At the border Lao visas (p291) are available on arrival from US$30-42 depending on nationality. A bus (25B) crosses the bridge to Thailand where a 30-day visa waiver is automatically granted to residents of most countries. There are ATMs and exchange counters at the heavily trafficked border post in Chiang Khong.

Moving on Most buses to Chiang Mai and Chiang Rai booked in Huay Xai will pick up at the border. Alternatively, buses for Chiang Rai (from 65B, 2½ hours) typically depart from Chiang Khong's bus station every hour from 6am to 5pm. **Greenbus** (☑ in Thailand 0066 53 241933; www.greenbusthailand.com) has a service to Chiang Mai at 9.45am. Several overnight buses for Bangkok (650B to 800B, 14 hours) leave at 3pm and 3.30pm.

LAND OF A MILLION ELEPHANTS

Laos was originally known as Lan Xang, the Land of a Million Elephants, yet curiously no recent statistics accurately record how many remain. Especially in Sainyabuli Province, working elephants have long been a mainstay of the logging industry, allowing tree trunks to be dragged out selectively without the clear-felling required for tractor access. Elephants are trained and worked by a *mahout* (handler) whose relationship with the animal is akin to a marriage and can last a lifetime. Elephants are generally owned by a consortium of villagers who share profits, costs and risks. To ensure a profit, owners need their animals to keep working but as a result, few working elephants have the energy for romance nor the time for a two-year maternity leave.

With Lao elephants dying more often than they're born, usually at a rate of only two births to 10 deaths, the domestic elephant could be extinct within 50 years, according to the team from the impressive Elephant Conservation Center (p136) outside town. Meanwhile, numerous retired or 'unemployed' elephants have found alternative employment in tourism, notably around Luang Prabang and Pak Beng. However, this is not an altogether happy alternative as many are overworked, having to do as many as 20 treks a day with humans on their back, particularly uncomfortable for their stickleback spine, in blistering heat, with no socialisation time and largely unvaried diets. Animal-welfare organisations recommend tourists find more elephant-friendly alternatives, such as walking with elephants, rather than opting for potentially harmful elephant rides.

The best time to enjoy this one-street town is late afternoon from on high at one of the restaurant balconies clinging to its vertiginous slope, watching the Mekong slide indolently by in a churn of gingery eddies, dramatically framed by giant boulders and sharp jungle banks.

◉ Sights & Activities

The tourist office offers treks to a Hmong village (400,000K per person in a group of four) or cooking classes (100,000K per person in a group of four), and can suggest a typical selection of local caves and waterfalls in the district to explore if you rent a motorbike. Ask at your guesthouse for a driver, as drivers around the market charge a steep 40,000K per hour.

A pleasant excursion is to cross the river by **motor canoe** (5000K) then walk for about 10 minutes diagonally right away from the river to a tiny, authentic Hmong hamlet.

Le Grand Pakbeng Resort (p135) also has a comprehensive tour program for those planning more than a one-night stop in this sleepy riverside town.

Wat Sin Jong Jaeng   BUDDHIST TEMPLE
(ວັດສິນຈົງແຈງ) Overlooking the Mekong, archaic little Wat Sin Jong Jaeng dates back to the early colonial period. Although its eaves have been entirely repainted, an old, very faded mural remains on the eastern exterior of the *sĭm* (prayer hall). Look carefully and you'll spot a moustached figure

with a hat, umbrella and big nose, presumably representing an early European visitor.

Mekong Elephant Park   WILDLIFE WATCHING
(www.mekongelephantpark.com; adult/under 12 US$20/10, privileged instants US$35-60; ⊙11am-4.30pm, privileged instants from 7am) ✦ Located across the Mekong River from Pak Beng and run in partnership with Sanctuary Pakbeng Lodge (p135), this is a small elephant centre that does not allow elephant riding, only light interaction with the four resident pachyderms. General admission is from 11am, but 'privileged instants', which allow more time to meet the elephants, are available in the morning.

General admission includes the chance to observe the elephants take a bath and sometimes an afternoon swim in the Mekong, as well as seeing them enjoying their natural habitat while chomping on the surrounding undergrowth. Mekong Elephant Park is a justifiable excuse to stay another day in Pak Beng. If you have the time and resources to visit the Elephant Conservation Center (p136) in Sainyabuli, then clearly that is the best elephant experience in Laos, but if time is more limited, this might just be the place for you.

🛏 Sleeping

With almost 20 relatively similar options within five minutes' walk of the boat dock, it's worth shopping around. Guesthouse prices generally seem to drop the further

Pak Beng

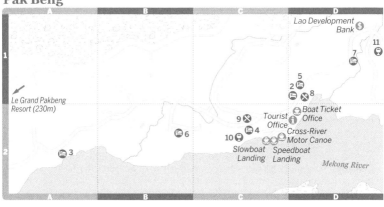

Le Grand Pakbeng
Resort (230m)

Lao Development Bank

Boat Ticket Office

Tourist Office

Cross-River Motor Canoe

Slowboat Landing   Speedboat Landing

Mekong River

Pak Beng

up the hill you go. There are now several smarter places in town, mostly strung out along the hilltops to the west of town.

Thip Phavanh Guesthouse   GUESTHOUSE $
(☏ 081-214003; d/tw with fan 80,000K, d/tw with air-con 100,000-120,000K; ❄ 🛜) One of the many guesthouses stretching up the hill from the boat dock, this stands out thanks to its friendly English-speaking owner, slightly larger than average rooms and a personal touch to the decorative elements. Upstairs rooms are a little more airy on hot days.

Monsavan Guesthouse   GUESTHOUSE $
(☏ 084-212619, 020-55771935; d/tw 130,000K; ❄ 🛜) Don't be put off by the hammer-and-sickle flag out front, as this little guesthouse on the main strip has a friendly old

owner. Bamboo-walled rooms are cleanly presented with TV, bathroom and tasteful fittings. Better still is the river-view bakery just across the street (open from 6.30am to 10pm) for fresh muffins, croissants, sandwiches and delicious shakes and coffee.

⭐ **Luang Say Lodge**   LODGE $$
(☏ 084-212296; www.luangsay.com; d/tw from US$73) Principally for the use of passengers aboard the Luang Say Cruise (p131), this traditional hardwood-and-rattan lodge has stylish bungalows in a pretty garden, overlooking a dramatic stretch of river, with fans and hot-water showers. A terrace restaurant for breakfast and dinner overlooks the Mekong. Be warned: it's a steep and sometimes slippery climb from the jetty to the hotel.

DP Guesthouse   GUESTHOUSE $$
(☏ 081-212624; www.duangpasert.com; Main St; s/d from 150,000/200,000K; ❄ 🛜) Run by a friendly Lao guy, this lively little guesthouse outstrips the competition with mint-green and orange walls and above-average rooms with nice touches like bed runners, air-con and cool tile floors and bathrooms. For an inexpensive and tasty breakfast, on-site DP Bakery serves pastries, good coffee and fruit shakes.

Mekong Riverside Lodge   BUNGALOW $$
(☏ 020-55171068; www.mekongriversidelodge. com; s/d US$30/40; 🛜) Widescreen views of the river from tastefully finished private-balcony bungalows, with stylish bathrooms, lacquered rattan walls, wood floors, fresh linen, mosquito nets and swan towel

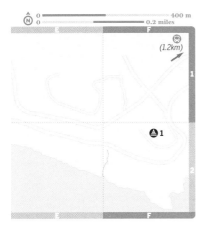

0   400 m
0   0.2 miles

(1.2km)

 1

origami. Some rooms can be combined for families with an adjoining door. Breakfast is included at Khopchaideu opposite. Good value for such sophisticated surrounds and the management are very helpful.

Le Grand Pakbeng Resort
RESORT $$$
(☏081-214035; www.legrandpakbeng.com; d/tw US$130-300; ❋@☎☒) Setting the standard for luxury accommodation in petite Pak Beng, Le Grand is a big resort located on a strategic hilltop just to the west of town. The rooms are spacious and sumptuously decorated with elegant touches, including twin sinks, a walk-in rain shower and a panoramic balcony.

There is an inviting infinity pool to take in the incredible views, an international restaurant and a walk-in wine cellar with the most extensive wine list this side of Luang Prabang. Impressive indeed.

Sanctuary Pakbeng Lodge
BOUTIQUE HOTEL $$$
(☏084-212304; www.sanctuaryhotelsandresorts.com/english/main/pakbeng; d/tw US$105-195; ❋☎) 🍃 Sanctuary Pakbeng Lodge has elegantly presented rooms with attractive interiors, Western-style bathrooms and minibars, all offering panoramic views. The bar-restaurant is a stylish spot for a sundown drink or a meal, and traditional Lao massage is also available.

Part of the profits go towards funding a healthcare initiative called Les Medicins du Pakbeng and they also support the Mekong Elephant Park (p133) across the river.

🍴 Eating

There's a string of eateries almost as long as the guesthouse strip. Most places have long menus and all charge approximately the same prices (mains 15,000K to 35,000K) for standard Lao, Thai and Western fare. By day, pick one with a good Mekong view. Most kitchens stop cooking around 9pm and by 10pm it might be a struggle just to find a beer.

DP Bakery
BAKERY $
(mains 30,000K; ⊙6.30am-8.30pm; ☎) Fresh and bursting with doughy aromas, DP is a great spot for Western or healthy fruit breakfasts. And as well as mouthwatering pastries (get here early before they go), it makes good coffee, fruit shakes and ice cream. You'll find it – surprise, surprise – in the same location as DP Guesthouse.

Khopchaideu
INDIAN $
(☏020-55171068; mains 20,000-50,000K; ⊙7am-10pm; 🍴) Located opposite the Mekong Riverside Lodge, this place serves some of the best Indian food you'll find in northern Laos. You can expect all the usual curries, as well as dishes like buffalo masala, executed with flair and sufficiently zesty spice. The English-speaking staff are charming and the view is superb. They also dish up Lao and Western food.

Hashan
INDIAN $
(mains 15,000-60,000K; ⊙7am-10pm; 🍴) By night, with its paper lanterns like glowing pupae hanging from the ceiling, this trusty old place pulls you in with its delicious aromas drifting out on to the street. Terrific Indian food includes the melt-in-your-mouth roti. Grab a table overlooking the river and browse the Lao and Western menu if you don't fancy Indian.

🍷 Drinking & Nightlife

The impressive bar-restaurant at the Luang Say Lodge is ideal for enjoying Mekong views with a sundowner such as a gin and tonic or a glass of wine. There are a couple of small bars in town for backpackers looking to party in Pak Beng, or at least have a drink or two.

Hive Bar
BAR
(Main St; ⊙5-11.30pm; ☎) It's a fair trek up the hill beyond the gaggle of guesthouses, but it's worth it to find this buzzing little bar. Bring the flyer you receive when

NORTHERN LAOS PAK BENG

ELEPHANT CONSERVATION CENTER

Set on the shores of the stunning Nam Tien lake, the **Elephant Conservation Center** (ECC; ☎020-96590665; www.elephantconservationcenter.com; 2-day discovery US$210, 3-day exploration US$280, 7-day eco-volunteering US$470) ✏ has placed Sainyabuli firmly on the visitor map. It's never been easier to visit as direct minibuses from Luang Prabang arrive here in just two hours or so, crossing a major bridge over the Mekong River at Tha Deua. However, it is important to book well in advance as numbers are strictly limited to 20 visitors per night. The centre is sometimes booked out by educational volunteer groups, so if you are set on a visit here, it's worth making enquiries ahead of time and planning this section of your trip accordingly.

Spread over 530 hectares, the centre offers visitors a unique insight into the lives of these majestic creatures in a natural setting. Life as an elephant in Laos – be it one of the remaining 400-odd left in the wild, forever on the run from ivory poachers, or one of the 400 captive elephants working in logging or elephant tourism – is not much fun. It's hard to say which is worse, giving 20 rides a day overladen with people on your back (the spine of an elephant is jagged and unsuitable to carry loads on anywhere but its neck) or trying to extract trees on dangerously steep mountain slopes. For every 10 elephants that die in Laos, only two young elephant calves are born and will make it into adulthood.

Given these depressing statistics the work of the ECC is evermore vital, paying mahouts a generous salary and medical benefits to come and live at the centre and give their females the chance to breed, and care for their baby; something the average elephant owner could not even consider as their workhorses must be constantly earning to pay for their care (estimated at US$250 per week).

There are now about 30 resident elephants at the ECC. Two calves have been born at the centre and one female elephant was pregnant at the time of research, offering great optimism for the future if the domesticated elephant population can be encouraged to breed in a natural environment once more. The longer-term goal is to release the elephants back into the wild in Nam Phoun NPA, and research work and trials are already well under way to this end.

Arriving at the centre is a memorable experience, as a small wooden boat glides through the green weeds that carpet Nam Tien lake. It's straight out of *Apocalypse Now*, and as the boat approaches the centre, visitors may see some of the resident elephants enjoying their morning bath. A two-day visit includes a guided tour of the centre and its elephant nursery to learn about the conservation work done here, including the on-site hospital, which works to

jumping off the slowboat to get a free Lao cocktail, choose your own tunes and smoke a shisha to warm up for a game of pool or the infamous beer pong.

Happy Bar BAR
(☺4-11.30pm) Offering some prime views of the Mekong River, this is a popular spot for sundowners and late drinks. Happy hour runs from 6.30pm to 8.30pm and there are plenty of games on offer like pool, beer pong and darts.

ⓘ Information

Guesthouses change money at unimpressive rates. Thai baht are also widely used here.
Lao Development Bank (☺24hr) Near the market, it has an ATM that has been known to run out of money at busy times.
Tourist Office (www.oudomxay.info; ☺7am-noon & 2-9pm) Free maps of town and can help arrange guides.

ⓘ Getting There & Away

The tiny bus station is at the northernmost edge of town, with departures to Udomxai (40,000K, four hours) at 9am and 12.30pm. There is also one morning bus to Muang Ngeun (35,000K, 1½ hours) and the Thai border, which departs when full.

The downriver **slowboat** to Luang Prabang departs between 9am and 10am (110,000K, around eight hours) with request stops possible at Pak Tha and Tha Suang (for Hongsa). The slowboat for Huay Xai (110,000K, around nine hours) departs at 8.30am.

Speedboats take around three hours to either Luang Prabang or Huay Xai, costing 200,000K per person assuming a crushed-full quota of six passengers (dangerous and highly uncomfortable, but cheaper than a 1,200,000K charter). Arriving by speedboat, local boys will generally offer to carry your bags for about 5000K (after some bargaining). If your bags are unwieldy this can prove money well spent, as when river levels are low you'll need to cross two planks safeguard the health of the resident elephants and some of the other 360 registered captive elephants in Sainyabuli Province.

If time allows, it's rewarding to immerse yourself in the work of the centre with a three-day stay. This includes the chance to observe the elephants from morning until evening, as they bathe, feed themselves and let loose in the socialisation area (you are able to watch unseen from a treehouse high above and lower observation platforms). Visitors also get the chance to watch one of the veterinary team at the hospital giving a check-up to a pachyderm in the 'medical crush' – a humane wooden structure that allows the carer to examine its feet and body without getting trodden on.

For those with a jumbo-sized interest in elephants, it is possible to volunteer for six days or more, offering an even greater insight into the lives of the elephants and their mahouts, as well as the work of the ECC, and directly contributing to the work undertaken here.

Accommodation at the centre is in basic thatched bungalows that include some electricity after dark to power LED lights for reading. The bungalows also have mosquito nets and a small veranda to relax on during the heat of the day. Bathroom facilities are shared but scrupulously clean. Those on the longer 'volunteer stay' live in a dormitory.

A newer and more comfortable lodge (additional US$100 per person) offers four spacious rooms all with en suite bathrooms. This is a good option for small groups, families or guests seeking a little more comfort. However, there is no wi-fi or internet available unless you have your own independent 3G/4G access via a mobile device.

Food and transport from and to Luang Prabang (or Sainyabuli) is included in all packages, with minivans departing Luang Prabang's post office at 8am daily and returning from ECC around 2pm. Meals are enjoyed at the welcoming restaurant, which offers a panoramic view of the lake and centre. The food is tasty Lao cuisine and a range of snacks and drinks are available on demand. However, this is a long way from the bright lights of Vientiane or Luang Prabang, so should you be craving something particular or have special dietary requirements, then plan ahead.

The ECC is not your typical tourist elephant camp. It is run by people with a passion for the animals and the proceeds generated from your visit go towards funding the centre and other elephant conservation projects around the country. The only hope for Laos' dwindling elephant population, they are a bright light in an increasingly dark landscape for wildlife conservation in the region.

and climb a steep sandbank to reach the road into town.

Get tickets at the **boat ticket office**.

Sainyabuli   ໄຊຍະບູລີ

♪ 074 / POP 32,000

One of Laos' 'elephant capitals', Sainyabuli (variously spelt Sayaboury, Sayabouri, Sayabouli, Xaignabouri and Xayaboury) is a prosperous town backed by the east by an attractive range of high forested ridges. Making a self-conscious attempt to look urban, central Sainyabuli consists of over-spaced avenues and showy administrative buildings that are surprising for their scale but hardly attractions. Starting around the tourist office and continuing south you'll find an increasing proportion of attractive wooden or part-timber structures, some with languid settings among arching palm trees. Overall it's a friendly and entirely untouristed place, but numbers are unlikely to increase dramatically with new roads, as most visitors are heading directly to the Elephant Conservation Center.

⊙ Sights

Many spots along the riverside are rendered especially idyllic thanks to the dramatic ridge of **Pak Kimin** reflected in the waters of the Nam Heung (Heung River).

Nam Tien   LAKE

(ບຶງຕຽນ) To fully appreciate the charm of Sainyabuli's setting, drive 9km southwest to Nam Tien lake, access point for the Elephant Conservation Center. A restaurant here is perched above the dam, offering views across emerald rice paddies and wooded slopes towards a western horizon where the Pak Kimin and Pak Xang ridges overlap.

Sainyabuli (Sayaboury)

Sainyabuli (Sayaboury)

The 3km asphalt road to Nam Tien branches west off the Pak Lai road 500m before the southern bus station, just before a bridge (6.5km from central Sainyabuli).

Wat Sibounheuang   BUDDHIST TEMPLE
(ວັດສີບຸນເຮືອງ) Wat Sibounheuang, the town's most evocative monastery, sports a lopsided gilded stupa and reclining Buddha in a delightful garden setting where the bare-brick ruins of the tiny original *sĭm* are reckoned to be from the early 14th century. The 'new' *sĭm* is covered in murals, including anti-adultery scenes in a style reminiscent of Matisse.

This building covers a mysterious 'hole' traditionally associated with *singkhone* spirit-ghosts who are placated in the Phaveth Festival (the 13th to the 15th day of the third Lao month) leading up to the February full moon.

Wat Sisavangvong   BUDDHIST TEMPLE
(ວັດສີສະຫວາງວົງ) More central than the other wats in Sainyabuli, Wat Sisavangvong was reportedly built by King Sisavang Vong on an older temple site.

🎊 Festivals & Events

Elephant Festival   CULTURAL
(www.elephantconservationcenter.com; ⊙mid-Feb) The Elephant Festival is a vast two-day jamboree, on the east bank of the Nam Heung, featuring music, theatre and many a beer tent as well as elephant parades and skills demonstrations. It's a popular event, though animal-welfare groups have raised concerns about some activities, including elephant riding and its impact on the health of the animals.

🛏 Sleeping

There are plenty of places to stay in town that are cheap but largely forgettable. Most visitors breeze through on their way to the Elephant Conservation Center (p136).

Santiphap Guesthouse   GUESTHOUSE $
(🖉 074-211184; 13 Northern Rd; d & tw with fan/air-con 60,000/100,000K; ❄) Currently the best choice in town, the Santiphap has a friendly English-speaking manager who is attentive to overseas guests. Clean rooms include en suite bathrooms, an armoire and a desk, although not a lot else.

Alooncheer Hotel   GUESTHOUSE $
(🖉 074-213136; d/tw with fan 60,000-80,000K, d/tw with air-con 100,000-120,000K; ❄) This sizeable Hmong-owned complex is quiet yet central. The polished wood-panelled lobby is decorated with traditional instruments and most rooms have high ceilings. Be aware that the very cheapest rooms are a significant step down in quality.

🍴 Eating & Drinking

Take yourself off to one of the riverside bars for a peaceful sundowner beer.

Nam Tiene Restaurant   LAO $
(mains 25,000-60,000K, fish by weight; ⊙6.30am-11pm) The place to be for well-made,

GETTING TO THAILAND: MUANG NGEUN TO HUAY KON

Getting to the border The Muang Ngeun (Laos)/Huay Kon (Thailand) border crossing (8am to 5pm) is around 2.5km west of Muang Ngeun junction. Several *sŏrngtǎaou* (passenger trucks) make the run from Hongsa (45,000K, 1½ hours) to Muang Ngeun.

Coming from Thailand, there's no restaurant nor any waiting transport on the Lao side, but if you can persuade the immigration officer to call for you, the afternoon *sŏrngtǎaou* to Hongsa should be prepared to collect you for a small fee.

At the border Lao visas (p291) are available on arrival at this border, payable in US dollars or Thai baht, albeit at an unfavourable exchange rate. There have been several reports of travellers on motorbikes and bicycles being denied entry into Laos, so you may want to consider a more trafficked crossing if cycle-touring. Most nationalities crossing into Thailand do not require a visa.

Moving on From the Thai side, if you don't want to walk your bags across the 1km of no-man's land you can pay 100B for a motorbike with a luggage-carrying sidecar. The Thai border post, Huay Kon, is not quite a village but does have simple noodle shops. The only public transport is a luxurious minibus (☑ 083-0243675) to Phrae (170B, five hours) via Nan (100B, three hours), departing from Huay Kon at 9.15am, 10am, 11am, noon and 3pm. Northbound buses leave Phrae five times between 5am and noon, passing by Nan on the way to the border.

well-presented food with a backdrop of beautiful reservoir views, it is worth the journey out here to the Nam Tien dam. Locals descend here at weekends and rent kooky avian-inspired pedalos.

Night Market MARKET $
(◕6-10pm) This night market near the central roundabout has food stalls for noodle soup, Lao grills, fresh fruits and *khànŏm* (traditional sweets).

Sainamhoung Restaurant LAO $$
(☑074-211171; mains 25,000-70,000K; ◕7am-10pm; 🛜) Contemplate the bamboo-banked river and the looming Pak Kimin massif as you dine on tasty Lao food. Dishes include delectable steamed fish, grilled meats and varied exotica such as fried crickets and wasps, and bamboo worms.

Beer Gardens BEER GARDEN
(◕6-11pm) There is some life beyond the dodgy and dark nightclubs in Sainyabuli and it comes in the form of a pair of lively beer gardens on the banks of the Nam Heung. They draw a young crowd with a thirst for Beerlao.

❶ Information

BCEL (◕8.30am-3.30pm Mon-Fri) Has an ATM and can change money.
Tourist Office (☑030-5180095; Sayaboury_ptd@tourismlaos.org; ◕8.30-11am & 2-4pm Mon-Fri) English-speaking staff offer free city maps, plus rental of bikes and motorcycles.

❶ Getting There & Away

The airport is beside the main Pak Lai road, around 3km south of the centre, but there were no regular flights to Vientiane (or anywhere else) at the time of writing. Luang Prabang International Airport is just 2½ hours away by road.

From the **main bus station** 2.5km north of the centre, an 11am *sŏrngtǎaou* runs to Hongsa (70,000K, three hours), continuing some days to Muang Ngeun (90,000K).

Vientiane is served via Luang Prabang and Pak Lai, both buses costing 130,000K. Services via Luang Prabang depart at 1pm and 4pm. The Pak Lai service (80,000K, four hours) departs at 9.30am and in the dry season only. Given the appallingly dusty road, this bus is a much better way to reach Pak Lai than by *sŏrngtǎaou*, which depart around 9am and noon from the **southern bus station**, a tiny stand 4km southwest of the airport. **Sakura Tour** (☑ 074-212112) offers air-con minibus connections to Vientiane (130,000K), departing at 8am, 9am and 10am daily.

The Tha Deua bridge over the Mekong River has reduced journey times to Luang Prabang to just two to three hours by minibus or private vehicle. Slower buses (60,000K, three hours) depart at 9am and 2pm. The Elephant Conservation Center (p136) runs a daily shuttle bus between Sainyabuli and Luang Prabang, departing at 8.30am in both directions, and the price is included in the overall cost of a visit to the center.

Tuk-tuks to the bus stations (main/southern 15,000/20,000K per person) depart from the main market.

Vientiane, Vang Vieng & Around

Best Places to Eat

➡ Doi Ka Noi (p161)

➡ Khambang Lao Food Restaurant (p160)

➡ Chokdee Cafe (p160)

➡ Nemnueng Sihom (p159)

➡ Suzette (p158)

➡ PVO (p158)

Best Places to Stay

➡ Hotel Beau Rivage Mekong (p157)

➡ Sailomyen Hostel (p155)

➡ Vieng Tara Villa (p176)

➡ Vayakorn Inn (p156)

➡ Hôtel Khamvongsa (p154)

➡ My Box (p152)

Why Go?

Vientiane is one of the smallest capital cities in Southeast Asia, but what it lacks in size it more than makes up for in character. Set on the banks of the mighty Mekong River, there is a palpable French influence, and it's the perfect place to recharge the batteries on an overland journey through Laos.

The urbane sophistication of Vientiane is a world away from the poetic beauty of the karst mountains of Vang Vieng and the dense jungles of Phu Khao Khuay National Protected Area (NPA).

Vang Vieng, one of Southeast Asia's leading adventure centres, is also one of the most beautiful spots in Laos. Rising up across the Nam Song (Song River), the limestone karst is a throwback to the Jurassic-era and is peppered with caves.

Throw in homestays and jungle treks around Phu Khao Khuay, the most accessible protected area in the country, and prepare to encounter some remarkable contrasts on your travels.

When to Go
Vientiane

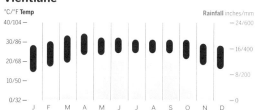

Nov–Feb A great time to visit, with the magical Bun Pha That Luang (Full Moon Festival) in November.

Mar–May Temperatures and humidity levels climb, but hotel prices fall.

Jun–Nov The monsoon brings fresh air and river festivals like Bun Awk Phansa and Bun Nam.

VIENTIANE

🖉 021 / POP 821,000

From its sleepy tuk-tuk drivers to its location on the right bank of the lumbering, lazy Mekong, this former French trading post is languid, to say the least. Indeed, despite being the capital and largest city of the Lao People's Democratic Republic, there's not a whole lot to do in Vientiane (ວຽງຈັນ). But that is also, quite honestly, its selling point.

For the traveller happy with a couple of low-key sights and lots of contemplative river watching while sipping on Beerlao, or hopping from cafe to cafe, Vientiane excels. And best of all, these pleasures are available to all budgets, be it via the city's low-cost digs and street markets, or its upscale boutique accommodation and foreign restaurants.

Even though in Vientiane the days blend into one another, once you leave you'll miss this place more than you expected.

History

Set on a bend in the Mekong River, Vientiane was first settled around the 9th century AD and formed part of one of the early Lao valley *meuang* (city-states) that were consolidated around the 10th century under the control of the Khmer empire. The Lao who settled here did so because the surrounding alluvial plains were so fertile, and initially the Vientiane *meuang* prospered and enjoyed a fragile sovereignty following the decline of Angkor.

In the ensuing centuries, Vientiane's fortunes have been mixed. At various times it has been a major regional centre; at other times it has been controlled by the Vietnamese, Burmese and Siamese.

The height of Vientiane's success was probably in the years after it became the Lan Xang capital in the mid-16th century, after King Setthathirat moved the capital from Luang Prabang. Several of Vientiane's wats were built following this shift and the city became a major centre of Buddhist learning.

It didn't last. Periodic invasions by the Burmese, Siamese and Chinese, and the eventual division of the Lan Xang kingdom, took their toll on the city.

It wasn't until the Siamese installed Chao Anou, a Lao prince who had been educated in Bangkok, on the throne in 1805 that the city received an overdue makeover. Chao Anou's public works included Wat Si Saket, built between 1819 and 1824.

Unfortunately, Chao Anou's attempts to assert Lao independence over the Siamese resulted in the most violent episode in Vientiane's history. In 1828 the Siamese defeated Chao Anou's armies and wasted no time in razing the city and carting off much of the population. Wat Si Saket, the base for the Thai invaders, was the only major building to survive, and the city was abandoned.

In 1867 French explorers arrived but it wasn't until late in the century, after Vientiane had been made capital of the French protectorate, that serious reconstruction began. A simple grid plan was laid out for the city and a sprinkling of colonial-style mansions and administrative buildings emerged. However, Vientiane was always low in the French order of Indochinese priorities, as the modest building program testifies.

In 1928 the 'city' was home to just 9000 inhabitants – many of them Vietnamese administrators brought in by the French – and it wasn't until the end of WWII that Vientiane's population began to grow with any vigour. It was a growth fed primarily by Cold War dollars, with first French and later American advisors arriving in a variety of guises.

After a couple of coups d'état in the politically fluid 1960s, Vientiane had by the early '70s become a city where almost anything went. Its few bars were peopled by an almost surreal mix of spooks and correspondents, and the women who served them.

Not surprisingly, things changed with the arrival of the Pathet Lao (PL) in 1975. Nightclubs filled with spies were the first to go and Vientiane settled into a slumber punctuated by occasional unenthusiastic concessions to communism, including low-level collectivisation and an initial crackdown on Buddhism. These days the most noticeable leftovers from the period are some less-than-inspired Soviet-style buildings.

Things picked up in the 1990s and in recent years Vientiane has seen a relative explosion of construction, road redevelopment and vehicular traffic, much of it financed by China, the country that will likely have the most significant influence on Vientiane's future.

◉ Sights

The bulk of sights are concentrated in a small area in the centre of the city. With the exception of Xieng Khuan (Buddha Park), all sights are easily reached by bicycle and, in most cases, on foot. Most wats welcome visitors, from after the monks have collected alms in the morning until about 6pm.

Vientiane, Vieng Vang & Around Highlights

1 Vang Vieng (p170)
Tubing, climbing, kayaking, cycling, motorbiking or walking through the rivers and stunning karst terrain.

2 Lao cuisine (p161)
Indulging in a culinary journey through Vientiane by sampling the country's widest array of domestic food, starting at one of its best restaurants, Doi Ka Noi.

3 Pha That Luang (p145)
Seeking out the spiritual side of Laos with a visit to one of

the principal Buddhist wats in the country.

4 Phu Khao Khuay NPA (p168) Getting off the grid with a trip to this National Protected Area, with its diverse landscape, pretty waterfalls and homestays.

5 Cafes (p160) 'Downtown' Vientiane is packed with high-quality coffee shops, a contrast with its low-intensity vibe.

In Town

★ COPE Visitor Centre
CULTURAL CENTRE

(ສູນພຶ້ນຟູຄົນພິການບແຫ່ງຊາດ; Map p146; ☑ 021-241972; www.copelaos.org; Rue Khu Vieng; donations welcome; ⊙ 9am-6pm) FREE Laos has the dubious distinction of being the most bombed country on earth, and although the Vietnam War ended more than 40 years ago, unexploded ordnance (UXO) continues to wound and kill people. COPE (Cooperative Orthotic & Prosthetic Enterprise) is the main source of artificial limbs, walking aids and wheelchairs in Laos. Its excellent Visitor Centre, part of the organisation's National Rehabilitation Centre, offers myriad interesting and informative multimedia exhibits about prosthetics and the UXOs that sadly make them necessary.

Several powerful documentaries are shown on a rolling basis in a theatre, and there's a gift shop and cafe, 100% of the proceeds of which go to supporting COPE's projects in Laos.

★ Wat Si Saket
BUDDHIST TEMPLE

(ວັດສີສະເກດ; Map p152; cnr Rue Lan Xang & Rue Setthathirath; 10,000K; ⊙ 8am-5pm, closed public holidays) Built between 1819 and 1824 by Chao Anou, the last monarch of the Kingdom of Vientiane, Wat Si Saket is believed to be the city's oldest surviving wat. And it is starting to show, as this beautiful temple is in need of a facelift. Along the western side of the cloister is a pile of Buddhas that were damaged during the 1828 Lao Rebellion.

In the *sĭm* (ordination hall) a slightly damaged Khmer-style Naga Buddha – which depicts the Buddha seated on a coiled cobra deity *(naga)* and sheltered by its multiheaded hood – is also on display just in front of the main seated Buddha; it is believed to date from the 13th century and was brought from a nearby Khmer site.

The *sĭm* is surrounded by a colonnaded terrace in the Bangkok style and topped by a five-tiered roof. The interior walls bear hundreds of Buddha niches similar to those in the cloister, as well as beautiful – but decaying – Jataka murals depicting stories of the Buddha's past lives. Portions of the Bangkok-style murals are unrestored 1820s originals, while others date from a 1913 restoration.

Wat Si Muang
BUDDHIST TEMPLE

(ວັດສີເມືອງ; Map p146; cnr Rue Setthathirath, Rue Samsenethai & Rue Tha Deua; ⊙ daylight hours)

FREE The most frequently used grounds in Vientiane are those of Wat Si Muang, the site of the *lák méuang* (city pillar), which is considered the home of the guardian spirit of Vientiane. The large *sĭm* (destroyed in 1828 and rebuilt in 1915) was constructed around the *lák méuang*, and consists of two halls.

The large entry hall features a copy of the Pha Kaeo (Emerald Buddha), and a much smaller, rather melted-looking seated stone Buddha that allegedly survived the 1828 inferno. Locals believe it has the power to grant wishes or answer troubling questions, and the practice is to lift it off the pillow three times while mentally phrasing a question or request. If your request is granted, then you are supposed to return later with an offering of bananas, green coconuts, flowers, incense and candles (usually two of each).

The pillar itself is located in the rear hall, and is believed to date from the Khmer period, indicating the site has been used for religious purposes for more than 1000 years. Today it is wrapped in sacred cloth, and in front of it is a carved wooden stele with a seated Buddha in relief.

Behind the *sĭm* is a crumbling laterite *jĕh-dii* (stupa), almost certainly of Khmer origin. In front of the *sĭm* is a little public park with a statue of King Sisavang Vong (r 1904–59).

Wat Chanthabuli
BUDDHIST TEMPLE

(ວັດຈັນທະບຸລີ; Map p152; Rue Fa Ngoum; ⊙ daylight hours) FREE This beautiful riverside wat was built in the 16th century, destroyed during the Siamese invasion of 1828 and later fully restored to its present glory. It's notable for its enormous bronze seated Buddha.

Patuxai
MONUMENT

(ປະຕູໄຊ, Victory Gate; Map p146; Rue Lan Xang; 3000K; ⊙ 8am-5pm) Vientiane's Arc de Triomphe replica is a slightly incongruous sight, dominating the commercial district around Rue Lan Xang. Officially called 'Victory Gate' and commemorating the Lao who died in prerevolutionary wars, it was built in the 1960s with cement donated by the USA intended for the construction of a new airport. Climb to the summit for panoramic views over Vientiane.

Haw Pha Kaeo
MUSEUM

(ຫໍພະແກ້ວ; Map p152; Rue Setthathirath; 10,000K; ⊙ 8am-5pm) Once a royal temple built specifically to house the famed Emerald Buddha, Haw Pha Kaeo is today a rather dusty, lacklustre national museum of religious art. It is

THE LEGEND OF WAT SI MUANG

Legend has it that a group of sages selected the site for Wat Si Muang in 1563, when King Setthathirat moved his capital to Vientiane. Once the spot was chosen, a large hole was dug to receive the heavy stone pillar (probably taken from an ancient Khmer site nearby) that would become the *lák méuang* (city pillar). When the pillar arrived it was suspended over the hole with ropes. Drums and gongs were sounded to summon the townspeople to the area and everyone waited for a volunteer to jump into the hole as a sacrifice to the spirit.

Depending on who's relating it, the legend has several conclusions. What is common to all of them is that a pregnant woman named Sao Si leaped in and the ropes were released, killing her and in the process establishing the town guardianship. Variations include her leaping in upon a horse, and/or with a diminutive monk.

However, Lao scholars think that if there is any truth to this story it is likely to have occurred much earlier than Setthathirat's time, in the pre-Buddhist Mon or Khmer periods when human sacrifice was ritually practised...and that Sao Si's legendary leap might not have been her choice at all.

across the street from the entrance to Wat Si Saket. The main hall contains a small mix of Khmer carvings, Lao Buddhas and relics from temples around town.

Wat Ong Teu
Mahawihan   BUDDHIST TEMPLE
(ວັດອົງຕື້ມະຫາວິຫານ; Map p152; Rue Setthathirath; ☉daylight hours) FREE This temple is one of the most important in Laos. It was originally built in the mid-16th century by King Setthathirat and is believed to occupy a site first used for religious purposes in the 3rd century. However, like almost every other temple in Vientiane it was destroyed in later wars with the Siamese, then rebuilt in the 20th century.

The Hawng Sangkhalat (Deputy Patriarch) of the Lao monastic order has his official residence here and presides over the Buddhist Institute, a school for monks who come from all over the country to study *dhamma* (the Buddha's teachings).

That Dam   MONUMENT
(ທາດດຳ, Black Stupa; Map p152; Rue Bartholoni; ☉24hr) FREE That Dam sits on a quiet roundabout near the centre of Vientiane. Legend has it that this stupa was once coated in a layer of gold. The gold is said to have been carted off by the Siamese during their pillaging of 1828, after which the stupa took the 'black' sobriquet in memory of the dastardly act.

However, another myth is slightly at odds with this and says That Dam is the abode of a dormant seven-headed dragon that came to life during the 1828 Siamese–Lao war and

protected local citizens, although apparently not the stupa's gold...

⊙ Around Town

★ Xieng Khuan   MUSEUM
(ຊຽງຂວັນ, Suan Phut, Buddha Park; 5000K, camera 3000K, motorbike parking 5000K; ☉8am-5pm) Located 25km southeast of central Vientiane, eccentric Xieng Khuan, aka Buddha Park, thrills with other-worldly Buddhist and Hindu sculptures, and was designed and built in 1958 by Luang Pu, a yogi-priest-shaman who merged Hindu and Buddhist philosophy, mythology and iconography into a cryptic whole. It's a bizarre, delightfully mouldy and dilapidated compound that's great for a wander and a photo op.

Bus 14 (8000K, one hour) leaves Talat Sao Bus Station every 20 minutes for Xieng Khuan. Alternatively, charter a tuk-tuk (250,000K return).

★ Pha That Luang   BUDDHIST STUPA
(ພະທາດຫລວງ; Rue 23 Singha; 10,000K, rental of long skirt to enter temple 5000K; ☉8am-5pm) Svelte and golden Pha That Luang, located about 4km northeast of the city centre, is the most important national monument in Laos; a symbol of Buddhist religion and Lao sovereignty. Legend has it that Ashokan missionaries from India erected a *tâht* (stupa) here to enclose a piece of Buddha's breastbone as early as the 3rd century BC.

A high-walled cloister with tiny windows surrounds the 45m-high stupa. The cloister measures 85m on each side and contains various Buddha images, including a serene

Vientiane

MUANG SIKHOTTABONG

MUANG CHANTHABULI

Rue Nong Buathong

Rue T2

Rue Nong Douang

21

Rue T2

Rue Dongnasok

Rue Asean

✈ 23

Alliance
International
✚ Medical Center
Rue Souphanouvong

8

Rue Sihom

22

Rue Souphanouvong

10

Rue Sithane

19
18

Rue Phanga Sy
7
17

Mekong River

THAILAND

A   B   C   D

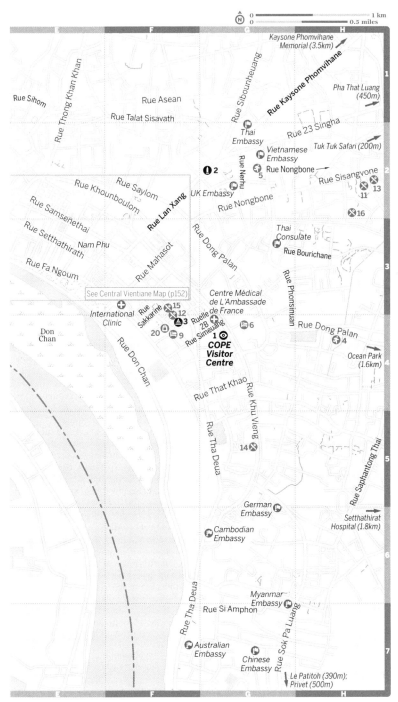

VIENTIANE, VANG VIENG & AROUND VIENTIANE

Vientiane

◎ **Top Sights**
1 COPE Visitor Centre G4

◎ **Sights**
2 Patuxai G2
3 Wat Si Muang F4

◎ **Activities, Courses & Tours**
4 Sengdara Fitness H4
5 Vientiane Yoga Studio G2

◎ **Sleeping**
6 Green Park Boutique Hotel G4
7 Hotel Beau Rivage Mekong D3
8 Khunta Residence C2
9 Mandala Boutique Hotel F4
10 Somerset Vientiane D2

◎ **Eating**
11 Amphone H2
12 Bakery By Boris F4
13 Doi Ka Noi H2
14 Kuvieng Fried Chicken G5
15 PVO F3
16 Senglao Cafe H2

◎ **Drinking & Nightlife**
17 Laodi D3
18 Naga Boat C3
19 Spirit House C2

◎ **Shopping**
20 Monument Books F4

◎ **Transport**
China Eastern Airlines .... (see 22)
21 Fuark Motorbike Service C1
Lao Airlines .... (see 23)
Lao Skyway .... (see 23)
Sixt .... (see 23)
22 Thai Airways International C2
23 Wattay International Airport A1

statue of Jayavarman VII, the great Angkor-era king who converted the state religion of the Khmer empire to Buddhism.

★ **Kaysone Phomvihane Memorial**   MUSEUM
(ຫໍພິພິດທະພັນແລະອະນຸສາວລີໄກສອນພົມວິຫານ; Km 6, Sivilay Village; 5000K; ⊙8am-noon & 1-4pm Tue-Sun) The former home of Kaysone Phomvihane, the first leader of an independent Laos, has been made into this quirky but worthwhile museum.

The house is inside the former USAID/CIA compound known as 'Six Klicks City' because of its location 6km from central Vientiane. It once featured bars, restaurants, tennis courts, swimming pools, a commissary and

assorted offices from where the Secret War was orchestrated. During the 1975 takeover of Vientiane, Pathet Lao forces ejected the Americans and occupied the compound. Kaysone lived here until his death in 1992.

Today, the house includes Kaysone's half-empty bottles of scotch, souvenirs from the Eastern bloc, running shoes, notepads and original Kelvinator air-conditioners. Even the winter coats he wore on visits to Moscow remain neatly hanging in the wardrobe. A Lao People's Revolutionary Party (LPRP) guide will show you through the house, making for a remarkably good-value experience.

Kaysone's house can be tricky to find, so it's easiest to backtrack from the nearby Kaysone Phomvihane Museum. Head back towards the city centre and turn right at the first set of traffic lights, continuing about 1km until you see the sign on your right that says 'Mémorial du Président Kaysone Phomvihane'. Alternatively, a tuk-tuk will cost around 40,000K from the centre.

★ **Kaysone Phomvihane Museum**   MUSEUM
(ຫໍພິພິດທະພັນແລະອະນຸສາວລີໄກສອນພົມວິຫານ; Rte 13; 5000K; ⊙8am-noon & 1-4pm Tue-Sun) Opened in 1995 to celebrate the late president's 75th birthday, the Kaysone Phomvihane Museum serves as a tribute to Indochina's most pragmatic communist leader. The museum is a vast Vietnamese-style celebration of the cult of Kaysone, a cult he himself never encouraged.

The museum is impossible to miss, with its mega-sized bronze statue of Kaysone out front flanked by large sculptures in the Heroes of Socialism style, complete with members of various ethnic groups and a sportsman looking like Superman. The building is a stark contrast, too, and is filled with a remarkably complete collection of memorabilia of both Kaysone and the Party. These include a mock-up of Kaysone's childhood home in Savannakhet, his desk from the French school he attended at Ban Tai, and a model of a portion of 'Kaysone Cave' in Hua Phan Province, complete with revolver, binoculars, radio and other personal effects.

It's possible to cycle here or take any transport on Rte 13 south. Alternatively, a tuk-tuk will cost around 40,000K from the centre.

Lao Textile Museum   MUSEUM
(ພິພິດທະພັນຜ້າໄໝບູຮານລາວ; ☏ 021-213467; www.laotextilemuseum2003.weebly.com; Ban Nongthatai; 30,000K; ⊙9am-4pm Mon-Sat) What

VIEWING PHA THAT LUANG

Each level of Pha That Luang (p145) has different architectural features in which Buddhist doctrine is encoded; visitors are supposed to contemplate the meaning of these features as they walk around. The first level is an approximately square base measuring 68m by 69m that supports 323 *sěe máh* (ordination stones). It represents the material world, and also features four arched *hǒr wái* (prayer halls), one on each side, with short stairways leading to them and beyond to the second level.

The second level is 48m by 48m and is surrounded by 120 lotus petals. There are 288 *sěe máh* on this level, as well as 30 small stupas symbolising the 30 Buddhist perfections *(báhlamée sǎhm-síp tat),* beginning with alms-giving and ending with equanimity.

Arched gates again lead to the next level, a 30m by 30m square. The tall central stupa, which has a brick core that has been stuccoed over, is supported here by a bowl-shaped base reminiscent of India's first Buddhist stupa at Sanchi. At the top of this mound the superstructure, surrounded by lotus petals, begins.

The curvilinear, four-sided spire resembles an elongated lotus bud and is said to symbolise the growth of a lotus from a seed in a muddy lake bottom to a bloom over the lake's surface, a metaphor for human advancement from ignorance to enlightenment in Buddhism. The entire *tâht* (stupa) was regilded in 1995 to celebrate the 20th anniversary of the Lao People's Democratic Republic (Lao PDR), and is crowned by a stylised banana flower and parasol. From ground to pinnacle, Pha That Luang is 45m tall.

began as a private museum, established by the family that runs Kanchana Boutique (p163), has subsequently become something of a Lao cultural centre. The emphasis at this leafy compound, spread across several local-style wooden buildings, is on textiles. There is a house filled with looms and antique Lao textiles representing several ethnic groups, and at other stops you can see various stages of weaving and dyeing in action.

The museum is located about 4km northeast of the city centre, in Ban Nongthatai. We do not suggest visiting without first making a reservation at Kanchana Boutique, where you can also pick up a map. Otherwise you may find the place closed.

🏃 Activities

Herbal Sauna   MASSAGE
(Map p152; ☑020-55044655; off Rue Chao Anou; ⊙1.30-9pm) Located near the river, this no-frills outfit offers Lao-style herbal saunas (20,000K) in separate rooms for men and women. In addition to the sauna it also offers Lao-style massage (per hour 100,000K).

The fee includes a cloth (for men) and towel; women must pay an additional 2000K for the rental of a sarong.

Sengdara Fitness   HEALTH & FITNESS
(Map p146; ☑021-452159; www.sengdarafitness. com; 5/77 Rue Dong Palan; ⊙6am-10pm) Sengdara has decent facilities and plenty of running machines, as well as massage (50,000K for one hour), sauna, pool and aerobics and

yoga classes. Visitors can buy a 70,000K day pass, which includes use of all equipment and the pool.

Lao Bowling Centre   BOWLING
(Map p152; ☑021-218661; Rue Khounboulom; per game with shoe hire from 11,000K; ⊙9am-2am) Bright lights, Beerlao and boisterous bowlers are what you'll find here. While the equipment is in bad shape, it's still a fun place to come later in the evening for a Lao-style night out. It sometimes stays open into the wee hours. BYO socks.

Vientiane Yoga Studio   YOGA
(Map p146; ☑020-56984563; www.vientianeyoga studio.com; off Rue Nerhu; 80min class 90,000K; ⊙10am-7pm) Hatha, vinyasa and yin yoga, as well as warrior yoga (for men) and prenatal yoga (for women), are available at this studio, located in a quiet garden down a secluded alleyway (look for signs across from Fuji Japanese Restaurant 2). Instructors Jessica, Nanci and Toshi have more than 10 years' experience. Check the website for the latest schedule.

Dalany Massage & Salon   MASSAGE
(Map p152; Rue Francois Ngin; ⊙9am-8pm) Cool, clean and professional, Dalany is an excellent central place to enjoy a foot massage (60,000K), a Lao-style body massage (60,000K) or a peppermint body scrub (250,000K), to name a few. There is also a salon for haircuts, manicures and pedicures.

A CYCLING TOUR OF VIENTIANE

Mostly flat, relatively car-free Vientiane is a great city to explore via bicycle, although it's wisest approached in the cool hours of the morning. Bikes can be hired at several places in town, including Lao Bike (p167) and Mixay Bike 2 (p167).

After fuelling up with a coffee and croissant at Le Trio (p160), head southeast along Rue Setthathirath. At the stoplight, on your right, is the **Presidential Palace** (ທຳນຽບປະທານປະເທດ; Map p152) , a vast beaux-arts-style chateau built to house the French colonial governor. Just beyond is Wat Si Saket (p144), a must-see with its thousands of Buddha figures.

Continue southeast along Rue Setthathirath for a stop at atmospheric Wat Si Muang (p144). Head northwest on Rue Simeuang, take a right on Rue Khu Vieng, and after a minute or so you'll be at the COPE Visitor Centre (p144), where you can learn about the plight of unexploded ordnance in Laos.

Head northwest on Rue Khu Vieng; if you're feeling the heat at this point, stop in for a smoothie at PVO (p158). Otherwise, proceed to the junction with Rue Lan Xang, a street sometimes (very) generously described as the 'Champs-Elysées of the East'. Turn right and head northeast until you reach the unmissable Patuxai (p144), Vientiane's 'Arc de Triomphe'.

Consider heading an additional 2km northeast for an excellent Lao lunch stop at Doi Ka Noi (p161). Otherwise, circle Patuxai, head southwest on Rue Lan Xang, take a right on Rue Samsenethai, a left on Rue Pangkham, and after crossing through **Nam Phu**, Vientiane's underwhelming fountain, you're back where you started.

Courses

Lao Experiences   COOKING
(☑ 020-55699429; www.lao-experiences.com; market tour & cooking class US$55; ⊙ 8am-1pm) Hit a local market and learn how to make Lao dishes at this homegrown outfit. The cooking courses, held in the owner's home, get good feedback, and transport is included.

Tang Kin   COOKING
(☑ 020-56788787; www.facebook.com/pg/tang kincookingclass; US$29) Let Nok and her mother teach you how to make traditional Lao dishes at their home-based, semi-outdoor school just outside of 'downtown' Vientiane.

Houey Hong Vocational Training Centre for Women   ARTS & CRAFTS
(☑ 021-560006; www.houeyhongvientiane.com; Ruelle 22, Rue Chao Anou; ⊙ 8.30am-4.30pm Mon-Sat) You can learn how to dye textiles using natural pigments and then weave them on a traditional loom at this NGO centre, run by a Lao-Japanese woman. It was established north of Vientiane to train disadvantaged rural women in the dying art of natural dyeing and traditional silk-weaving practices.

Visitors can take a guided tour (25,000K) or partake in the dyeing process (120,000K, two hours, one scarf) or weaving (280,000K, whole day). You keep the fruits of your labour. Transport to and from the centre is provided for an additional 50,000K.

Tours

Lao Disabled Women's Development Centre   CULTURAL
(LDWDC; ☑ 021-812282; www.laodisabledwomen. com; 100 Rue Tha Deua; tours 50,000-100,000K; ⊙ 9am-4.30pm Mon-Fri, weekends by appointment; 🚌 14) 🚶 FREE Run by a collective of Lao disabled women, this centre challenges the prejudices that the disabled community in Laos sometimes faces. Concentrating on abilities, the centre offers training and education to empower disabled women. It is open to drop-in visitors for free, or you can sign up for a tour (from 50,000K) to learn about recycled-paper handicrafts and weaving.

Other interactive experiences include lunch (100,000K) from the organic garden at the centre, a handicraft class (100,000K) or the chance to take part in a traditional *baasĭi* ceremony (string-tying ritual; 100,000K). There is a shop on-site where you can purchase handicrafts. Bus 14 passes this way en route to Xieng Khuan (Buddha Park; 8000K): ask the driver for '*soon pee kan*'.

Backstreet Academy   TOURS
(☑ 020-58199216; www.backstreetacademy.com) For some original local encounters, contact Backstreet Academy, a peer-to-peer travel website that specialises in connecting travellers to cultural experiences with local hosts. Choose from a *móoay láo* (kickboxing) class, a traditional dance lesson, a Lao cooking

class in a private home, a clay art class, Zen meditation and a whole lot more.

This outfit is one tour company that can definitely bring you closer to the local people and their culture.

Tuk Tuk Safari
CULTURAL

(☎020-54333089; www.tuktuksafari.com; adult/child US$75/45) This community-conscious tour company gets under the skin of Vientiane in a tuk-tuk. Tour guide Ere has several different 'safaris' and can spirit you away to a Lao market, a rice farm, Vientiane's premier weaving houses or on food-centred expeditions.

Given fair warning, the husband-and-wife team can devise specially tailored tours for people with disabilities.

✨ Festivals & Events

You can rest assured that whatever the festival, celebrations in Vientiane will be as vigorous as anywhere in the country. Whatever you do, *don't* drive or ride about in the city during festivals; drunk driving is unfortunately the norm and accidents myriad.

Pi Mai
CULTURAL

(☺Apr) Lao New Year is celebrated in mid-April with a mass water fight and tourists are considered fair game. Be warned, drunk driving and theft go through the roof at these times so remain vigilant with your driver and wallet!

Bun Nam
SPORTS

(Bun Suang Héua; ☺Oct) A huge annual event at the end of *pansăh* (the Buddhist rains retreat) in October, during which boat races are held on the Mekong River. Rowing teams from all over the country, as well as from Thailand, China and Myanmar (Burma), compete; the river bank is lined with food stalls, temporary discos, carnival games and beer gardens for three days and nights.

Vientiane is jam-packed during Bun Nam, and given how far away the boat racing is and how difficult it is to find a vantage point, we think smaller towns such as Vang Vieng and Muang Khong are better bets, though Muang Khong doesn't usually hold its festival until early December, around National Day.

Bun Pha That Luang
CULTURAL

(That Luang Festival; ☺Nov) Bun Pha That Luang, usually held in early November, is the largest temple fair in Laos. Festivities begin with a *wéean téean* (circumambulation) around Wat Si Muang, followed by a procession to Pha That Luang, which is illuminated all night for a week.

The festival climaxes on the morning of the full moon with the *dăk bàht* ceremony, in which thousands of monks from across Laos receive alms. Fireworks cap off the evening and everyone makes merit or merry until dawn. Look out for devotees carrying *Ђąhsàht* (miniature temples made from

---

VIENTIANE IN...

Two Days

Start with a coffee and croissant at Le Trio (p160) before hiring a bicycle and spinning to Vientiane's main sights, including ancient Buddha statues at Wat Si Saket (p144), Lao textiles at Talat Sao (p163) and the iconic Patuxai (p144) monument. Dive into Lao cuisine with lunch at Doi Ka Noi (p161). Top off your day with riverside cocktails at Spirit House (p161), followed by a DIY Vietnamese dinner at Nemnueng Sihom (p159).

On day two consider getting some motorised wheels and leaving the city centre to visit the concrete Buddhas and Hindu deities at Xieng Khuan (p145), or the communist monuments at Kaysone Phomvihane Museum (p148) and Memorial. On the way back stop at Pha That Luang (p145), the country's most famous Buddhist monument, for great afternoon photos. Enjoy a Belgian dinner at Chokdee Cafe (p160).

Four Days

On day three, make the delicious Vietnamese-style sandwiches at PVO (p158) your lunch. It's then a short walk to the COPE Visitor Centre (p144), where you could easily spend a couple of hours checking out the excellent exhibits and powerful documentaries. After a Lao dinner at Khambang Lao Food Restaurant (p160), head to nearby Herbal Sauna (p149) for a healthy Lao-style sweat. Rehydrate with locally made rum at Laodi (p161).

Day four can be spent at a Lao cooking course at Tang Kin or stocking up on souvenirs, such as the handmade soaps and oils at T'Shop Lai Gallery (p162).

Central Vientiane

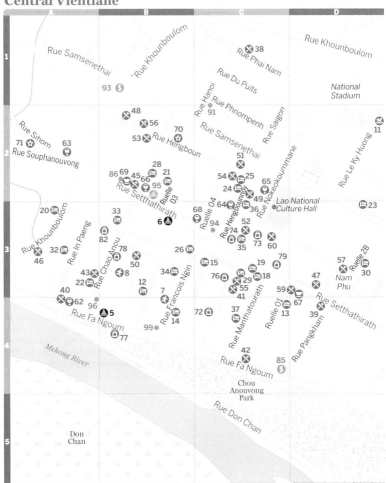

banana stems and decorated with flowers and other offerings).

🛏 Sleeping

Vientiane is bursting with a wide range of accommodation, from cheap backpacker digs to boutique hotels and monolithic corporate hotels. The cheaper end of the spectrum can be a bit dreary, although there are a few catches. There are some exceptional midrangers in town, and a few of the upscale and boutiques are worth considering.

Rue Setthathirath & Nam Phu

★ My Box   HOSTEL $
(Map p152; ☑ 030-5671199; myboxhaysok@gmail.com; Rue Chao Anou; dm incl breakfast 80,000K; 🖨 ❋ 🛜) The 12-bed dorms at this new hostel feel modern, clean and inviting. This vibe extends to the tidy, spacious common bathrooms and the lobby/cafe. And all this on a strip with a bit of a burgeoning nightlife buzz.

PVO Hostel   HOSTEL $
(Map p152; ☑ 030-5222256; www.facebook.com/PVO.Hostel; Rue Pangkham; dm incl breakfast for

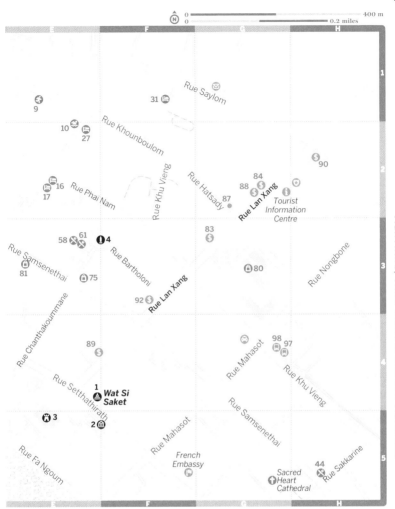

2/4 US$16/28; ❄ 🛜) This centrally located hostel offers 11 air-con dorms for two or four travellers (prices are by room, not person). Despite the odd pricing system, it works, and rooms are clean and well-maintained, although not all have windows. You can also rent bicycles (10,000K) or motorbikes (70,000K to 80,000K) here.

Hive Hostel HOSTEL **$**
(Map p152; ☎ 020-98132074; www.facebook. com/hivelao; Rue Setthathirath; dm incl breakfast 60,000K; ❄ 🛜) This hostel has a central location, a modern feel and three exceptionally cold air-con dorms with curtained-off bunks,

lockers and sparklingly clean toilets. There's a funky little cafe on the ground floor where you'll eat your (simple) breakfast.

Mixay Paradise Guesthouse GUESTHOUSE **$**
(Map p152; ☎ 021-254223; laomixayparadise@ yahoo.com; Rue Francois Ngin; s/d with fan & shared bathroom US$16/19, r with air-con & bathroom US$23/25; 🖨 ❄ 🛜) Mixay Paradise has 50 rooms with pastel-coloured walls, some of which have balconies, bathrooms and air-con; spotless floors; a bright lobby cafe with lime-green walls; and a lift. It's a good deal if you don't need character in your accommodation.

Central Vientiane

Vayakorn House HOTEL $
(Map p152; ☑021-241911; www.vayakorn.biz; 91 Rue Nokeokoummane; r US$16-22; ◉ ❋ ◈) Vayakorn has 21 clean, simple rooms (doubles, twins and cramped singles) with TV, air-con and city views. There's a welcoming lobby and very helpful staff.

Niny Backpacker HOSTEL $
(Map p152; ☑020-96043884; nguyennhotinh3103@gmail.com; Th Nokeokoummane; dm incl breakfast 40,000K; ❋ ◈) A hostel with cheerful orange walls (although not much natural light) and dorms accommodating four to 10 beds. Safety deposit lockers, free breakfast (toast and eggs) and clean facilities.

★**Souphaphone Guesthouse** GUESTHOUSE $$
(Map p152; ☑021-261468; www.souphaphone.net; off Rue Francois Ngin; r incl breakfast US$27-38; ◉ ❋ ◈) A very tidy and homey guesthouse with 25 spacious rooms, some with lots of sun, and all with fresh linen, cool tiled floors and pristine walls. If you don't need an in-house breakfast, you can chip a few dollars off the price.

Hôtel Khamvongsa HOTEL $$
(Map p152; ☑021-218415; www.hotelkhamvongsa.com; 2338 Rue Khounboulom; incl breakfast r US$50-55, ste US$70-90; ◉ ❋ ◈) Lovely French-era building lovingly reincarnated as a welcoming boutique hotel; think subtle belle-époque touches like glass-tear lightshades, chequerboard-tiled floors, and softly lit simple rooms with two-poster beds, wood floors and Indo-chic decor. Rooms on the 3rd and 4th floors have charming city views. There's also a restful courtyard and restaurant. Breakfast is a treat.

Avilla Phasouk Hotel HOTEL $$
(Map p152; ☑021-243415; www.avillaphasoukhotel.com; 57/4 Ruelle 01; r/ste incl breakfast US$35/45; ❋ @ ◈) A popular long-term stay, this place also doubles up as a good-value midrange option with spacious wood-clad rooms offering all the trimmings, including rather sensual wall art, and vast suites.

Champa Boutique Hotel BOUTIQUE HOTEL $$
(Map p152; ☑021-255866; www.champaboutiquehotel.com; 2-2 Rue Francois Ngin; r incl breakfast US$40-60; ◉ ❋ ◈ ▩) Tucked away just

off popular Rue Francois Ngin, this is a charming boutique hotel set around a courtyard swimming pool. Despite its central location in the capital, it is very peaceful and feels more like a Luang Prabang–style hideaway. That said, rooms would benefit from a touch of TLC and a splash of light.

Lani's House by the Ponds GUESTHOUSE $$
(Map p152; ☑021-215639; www.lanishousebytheponds.com; Ruelle O3; incl breakfast r US$45-65, ste US$75-80; ➜❋🌐) Down a narrow side street leading to a temple, this white art deco–accented villa evokes Indochina with its authentic Parisien chandeliers, antique furniture, lobby peppered with stunning images of old Laos, and coy carp in an ornamental pool. Unfortunately the rooms, although spacious, can feel dark, and are outfitted with frumpy, unattractive furniture.

Dhavara Boutique Hotel BOUTIQUE HOTEL $$$
(Map p152; ☑021-222238; www.dhavarahotel.com; 25 Rue Manthatourath; r incl breakfast US$100-600; ➜❋@🌐) An opulent neoclassical hotel, the Dhavara offers some of the handsomest if not

greatest-value rooms in the capital. Features include marble-clad bathrooms and parquet floors, as well as more predictable touches such as free wi-fi, a well-stocked minibar and airport pick-up.

Salana Boutique Hotel BOUTIQUE HOTEL $$$
(Map p152; ☑021-254254; www.salanaboutique.com; 112 Rue Chao Anou; incl breakfast r US$135-140, ste US$170-200; ➜❋🌐) Highly polished, wood-flavoured Salana fuses Lao and contemporary styles to add a sleek dimension to Vientiane's accommodation scene. Rooms have wood floors, ethnically inspired bed runners, soft lighting, flat-screen TVs, safety deposit boxes, rain showers and nice little touches including frangipani flowers scattered around. Some rooms have fantastic temple views.

Rue Samsenethai & Around

★**Sailomyen Hostel** HOSTEL $
(Map p152; ☑020-78374941; www.facebook.com/sailomyenhostel; off Rue Saylom; incl breakfast dm 72,000K, r 170,000K; ➜❋🌐) Honestly

SWIMMING IN VIENTIANE

There are several places in Vientiane where you can work on your stroke or simply take a cooling dip. You could try Sengdara Fitness (p149), where a day pass costs 70,000K, including the pool. Several hotels welcome nonguests, including the beautiful **Settha Palace Hotel** (Map p152; ☑ 021-217581; 6 Rue Pangkham; 160,000K; ☉ 7am-7pm), with its decadent pool and surrounding bar, or there's the public **Vientiane Swimming Pool** (Map p152; ☑ 020-55521002; Rue Le Ky Huong; adult/child 15,000/10,000K; ☉ 7am-7pm) or the private **Le Patitoh** (☑ 030-5082428; www.facebook.com/lepatitoh; 20 Rue Sithoong; swimming 30,000K; ☉ 7am-9pm Tue-Sun), a swimming pool and microbrewery that is popular with expats and Lao people in the know. **Ocean Park** (☑ 030-2819014; www.oceanparklaos.com/en; Lao-ITECC, Rue Kamphengmeuang, Ban Phonthanneua; adult/child from 20,000K; ☉ 10am-7pm Tue-Sun; ⛟), with its good range of slides, tubes, lazy river riding and more, is a good option for families on a hot day.

(and astonishingly), there's little difference between the dorms and the new block of private rooms here. All are tidy and trendy, decked out in minimalist-chic, with fluffy duvets and access to rain showers and the inviting cafe. A win-win situation.

★ Vayakorn Inn   HOTEL **$$**

(Map p152; ☑ 021-215348; www.vayakorn.biz; 19 Rue Hengbounnoy; r US$35; 🅿 � ❋ 🛜) On a quiet street just off increasingly hectic Rue Setthathirath, this tasteful, peaceful hotel is great value. Generously sized rooms are impeccably clean, with crisp linen, choice art, desks and modern bathrooms. The rooms on the upper floors have excellent city views.

Lao Poet Hotel   HOTEL **$$**

(Map p152; ☑ 021-253537; www.laopoethotel.com; Rue Hengbounnoy; incl breakfast US$60-70, ste US$185-250; 🅿 ➔ ❋ 🛜) The vibe at this new hotel – smooth concrete and lots of glass, potted plants, chunky carpets, patterned wallpaper, vintage and Lao touches – is tough to pin down, but somehow, just works. Opt for the slightly more expensive

deluxe rooms, which have bathtubs and a bit more space.

Manorom Boutique Hotel   HOTEL **$$**

(Map p152; ☑ 021-250748; manoromboutiquehotel@hotmail.com; Rue Hengbounnoy; r incl breakfast US$30; ➔ ❋ 🛜) Looming large over a small lane in the centre of town, this hotel offers exceptional value. The stylish lobby sets the tone for a well-presented Lao hospitality experience, and the rooms continue this theme with polished wood floors, silk runners and tasteful handicrafts.

Day Inn Hotel   HOTEL **$$**

(Map p152; ☑ 021-222985; dayinn@laopdr.com; 59/3 Rue Pangkham; r incl breakfast US$36-50; ➔ ❋ @ 🛜) From its inviting yellow exterior to its vintage terrazzo floors, this old-timer exudes charm. The 32 spotless rooms boast large beds, rattan furniture and a sunny, open vibe, and there's also free airport pickup and laundry service.

Moonlight Champa   GUESTHOUSE **$$**

(Map p152; ☑ 021-264114; www.moonlightchampa.com; Rue Pangkham; r incl breakfast US$29-33; ➔ ❋ @ 🛜) The 'Welcome' and 'Bon Voyage' sign at the entrance sets the tone for a friendly stay, and the nine rooms continue this theme, although the furnishings seem rooted in the '90s. Twin rooms and doubles are available, some with balconies overlooking the posh Settha Palace Hotel across the road.

★ Settha Palace Hotel   HOTEL **$$$**

(Map p152; ☑ 021-217581; www.setthapalace.com; 6 Rue Pangkham; incl breakfast r US$200-280, ste US$480; ➔ ❋ @ 🛜 ⛟) This stately building, set in grounds ablaze with flowers, is as graceful as it is relaxing. Fans whirr over marble floors so polished you can see your champagne glass in them, while service is impeccable. Rooms, particularly the larger deluxe ones, are also enchanting, with four-poster beds, desks and wood floors. Check out the kidney-shaped pool.

City Inn   HOTEL **$$$**

(Map p152; ☑ 021-281333; www.cityinnvientiane.com; Rue Pangkham; r incl breakfast US$65-100; ➔ ❋ @ 🛜) As well as offering long-term apartment stays, this place is one of the smarter midrange biz-boutique hotels in town. The contemporary lobby sets the tone for a smooth stay with the 43 rooms exhibiting some artsy flourishes, as well as practical amenities such as an iron and ironing board, and desk.

Lao Plaza Hotel HOTEL **$$$**
(Map p152; ☏ 021-218800; www.laoplazahotel.com; 63 Rue Samsenethai; incl breakfast r 1,500,000-2,000,000K, ste 3,000,000-6,000,000K; ➽ ❈ ☎ ☀) A standard for business travellers, this blandly designed marbled edifice boasts a vast international-style lobby and spacious rooms. Expect desks, fridges, cable TV, bath-tubs and silk bedheads. There's also a great pool here (120,000K for nonguests) that's perfect for sun basking and escaping the heat.

Mekong Riverfront & Around

★Hotel Beau
Rivage Mekong BOUTIQUE HOTEL **$$**
(Map p146; ☏ 021-243350; www.hbrm-laos.com; Rue Fa Ngoum; r incl breakfast US$52-69; ➽ ❈ @ ☎) This pink boutique hotel still packs a punch, with 16 unique, spacious, sunny, loft-like rooms outfitted with pastel colours, terrazzo floors, waffled bedspreads and a pleasant garden out back. Large windows and balconies provide for maximum river views.

VKS Hotel HOTEL **$$**
(Map p152; ☏ 021-219922; www.facebook.com/VongkhamseneHotel; 17/01 Rue Manthatourath; r US$27-56; ➽ ❈ ☎) The handsome exterior contrasts with the new-feeling but rather bare rooms here, the cheapest of which are a tight fit. Still, it's a relatively good-value option.

Mandala Boutique Hotel BOUTIQUE HOTEL **$$**
(Map p146; ☏ 021-214493; www.mandalahotel.asia; off Rue Setthathirath; incl breakfast r US$60-78, ste US$80; ➽ ❈ ☎) A French villa built in the 1960s is the setting here, and flashes of vivid colour and chichi flourishes such as lacquered granite floors and dark-wood furniture blend perfectly with the aesthetic of its art deco lines. Unfortunately, the rooms themselves feel rather staid by comparison. Breakfast available only for those staying two or more nights.

Sala Inpeng Bungalow BUNGALOW **$$**
(Map p152; ☏ 021-242021; www.salalao.com; Rue In Paeng; r incl breakfast US$45-55; ➽ ❈ ☎) Unlike anything else in the city, this vernal oasis of wood duplex bungalows is set in gardens spilling with tamarind and *champa* flowers.

The grander rooms display rustic chic with bathrooms and air-con. And although the cheaper rooms are small, they don't lack atmosphere.

Best Western Vientiane HOTEL **$$**
(Map p152; ☏ 021-216909; www.bestwesternvientiane.com; 2-12 Rue Francois Ngin; r incl breakfast US$60-75; ➽ ❈ @ ☎ ☀) Your instinct may be to avoid the chains, but this is a solid, if not entirely unique, choice. There's a cool, plush lobby, calm garden with pool, gym and a general sense of upscale style. Rooms, of which there are 44, are equally swanky with wood floors, snow-white linen and quality fittings.

★Ansara Hôtel BOUTIQUE HOTEL **$$$**
(Map p152; ☏ 021-213514; www.ansarahotel.com; off Rue Fa Ngoum; incl breakfast r US$140-160, ste US$190-360; ➽ ❈ ☎ ☀) Achingly beautiful Ansara is housed in a compound of colonial-chic French villas with a heavy whiff of old Indochina. There are 28 rooms set across the property, including four suites, and all are lovely, offering wooden floor, balcony, flat-screen TV, bath and refined decorations. Its alfresco dining terrace is as refined as its Gallic cuisine.

★Lao Orchid Hotel HOTEL **$$$**
(Map p152; ☏ 021-264134; www.lao-orchid-hotel.com; Rue Chao Anou; r/ste incl breakfast US$75/145; ❈ ☎) A classy, modern hotel with a swish lobby and chilled verandah cafe with a great view of the road. There are 33 welcoming rooms here with varnished wood floors, mint-fresh linen, desks, balconies, fridges and Indochinese-style furniture. Ask for a room at the front to take in the Mekong views.

Around Vientiane

Khunta Residence APARTMENT **$$**
(Map p146; ☏ 021-251199; www.khuntaresidence.com; off Rue Luang Prabang; studio/1-bed apt per month from US$1000/1300; ➽ ❈ ☎) If you're going to be here for a while, check out this cosy French-run luxury apartment complex that includes a pool and tennis court.

Green Park
Boutique Hotel BOUTIQUE HOTEL **$$$**
(Map p146; ☏ 021-264097; www.greenparkvientiane.com; 248 Rue Khu Vieng; r incl breakfast US$120-290; ➽ ❈ @ ☎ ☀) A real urban oasis, this charming boutique hotel exudes calm and escapism from the moment you enter

its dark-wood lobby and step into its lush garden abuzz with flowers and a sparkling pool, and shaded by sugar palms and frangipani trees. Rooms are super stylish and feature hardwood floors, capacious bathrooms, couches, safety deposit boxes and step-in mosquito nets.

Somerset Vientiane   APARTMENT $$$
(Map p146; ☑ 021-250888; www.somerset.com; Rue Souphanouvong; incl breakfast r 770,000-850,000K, ste 920,000-1,460,000K; ☞ ❋ @ 🛜 ⊠) For a home-like stay, check out Somerset Vientiane, a luxury apartment complex on the road to the airport. Rooms include lots of space, kitchenette, large refrigerator and balcony, and access to a pool, tennis courts and a gym. Discounted monthly rates also available.

✗ Eating

For such a small capital city, Vientiane boasts a wide range of culinary options and is an exceptional spot for fine dining on a budget.

🍴 Rue Setthathirath & Nam Phu

★PVO   VIETNAMESE $
(Map p146; ☑ 021-454663; Ruelle 2B; mains 10,000-35,000K; ⊙ 6.30am-4.30pm Mon-Sat, to 2pm Sun; 🛜 🍴) This fresh, no-frills eatery is one of the better places in town to grab lunch, and in addition to a variety of Vietnamese dishes, does some of the best *kòw jee* (Vietnamese-style baguette sandwiches) in town. Finish with the free, self-serve, dessert bar.

Bakery By Boris   BAKERY $
(Map p146; ☑ 020-77792228; www.facebook.com/bakerybyboris; Ruelle 2B; pastries 11,000-30,000K, mains 35,000-45,000K; ⊙ 7am-7pm; ❋ 🛜) With high glass ceilings and a minimalist design, this sleek cafe is like a giant fishbowl marooned in a leafy oasis next to Wat Si Muang. Paris-trained chef Boris Luangkhot makes drool-worthy macarons, croissants and homemade ice creams in flavours such as durian and passion fruit. There are also quiches, coffees and baguette sandwiches for a midday pick-me-up.

Taj Mahal Restaurant   INDIAN $
(Map p152; ☑ 020-55611003; off Rue Setthathirath; meals 15,000-65,000K; ⊙ 10am-10.30pm Mon-Sat, 4-10.30pm Sun; 🍴) Hidden down

a side street opposite the back of the Lao National Culture Hall, this unpretentious earthy joint dishes up fresh and lively curries (tasty chicken masala) and melt-in-your mouth naan. Portions are generous and you can sit semi alfresco. There's a hefty veggie selection, too.

★Ka-Tib-Khao   LAO $$
(Map p152; www.facebook.com/pg/katibkhao; Rue Setthathirath; mains 40,000-100,000K; ⊙ 10am-2.30pm & 5-11pm; ❋) Ka-Tib-Khao (Rice Basket) has a reassuringly short and delicious menu of dishes, many from the country's north. Think sheets of deep-fried Mekong River weed served with a spicy dip, lemongrass-stuffed pork and Luang Prabang–style herbal sausages, all served in a setting that manages to feel both sophisticated and traditional.

★Suzette   FRENCH $$
(Map p152; ☑ 020-58655511; www.facebook.com/suzette.vientiane; Rue Setthathirath; mains 35,000-58,000K; ⊙ 8am-9pm Tue-Sun; ❋ 🍴) This bright, contemporary-feeling place specialises in *galettes,* crêpes made with buckwheat flour. Pair yours with a dressed salad and bottle of cider, and you have one of the tastiest, best-value French meals outside of the EU.

Café Vanille   BAKERY $$
(Map p152; ☑ 021-217321; Rue Nokeokoummane; breakfast from 40,000K; ⊙ 7am-6.30pm Mon-Sat, to 1pm Sun; ❋) Get here early before some of the city's best croissants run out. The simple interior makes for a nice place to read the paper over a tart, salad, panini or quiche, or you can sit outside on the small terrace.

Benoni Café   ASIAN, FUSION $$
(Map p152; ☑ 021-213334; Rue Setthathirath; mains 40,000-60,000K; ⊙ 7am-9pm; ❋ 🛜) A stylish place on Rue Setthathirath, the menu here is Asian-fusion-meets-Italian, and includes super-fresh snacks, salads and pasta dishes.

Khop Chai Deu   ASIAN, FUSION $$
(Map p152; ☑ 021-251564; 54 Rue Setthathirath; mains 25,000-90,000K; ⊙ 8am-midnight; ❋ 🛜 🍴) In a remodelled colonial-era villa near Nam Phu, Khop Chai Deu has been a travellers' favourite for years because of its range of approachable Lao, Thai, Japanese, Indian and assorted European fare. It's also a popular bar.

★ **Pimentón** SPANISH $$$
(Map p152; ☎021-215506; www.pimenton restaurant-vte.com; Rue Nokeokoummane; mains 60,000-200,000K; ⊙11am-2.30pm & 5-10pm Mon-Sat; 🅿🛜) Pimentón, with its open fire pit and beefy menu, is all about the meat. But to be honest, we didn't make it past the lengthy and an appetising tapas menu. For a bit of everything, the set lunch (95,000K) is a wise strategy.

L'Adresse de Tinay FRENCH $$$
(Map p152; ☎020-56913434; www.facebook. com/tinay.youtisack.inthavong; off Rue Chao Anou; mains 75,000-390,000K; ⊙11.30am-10pm; 🅿🛜🚗) Alchemising an eclectic gastronomic landscape of snails and scrambled eggs, sea-bream fillet, beef tenderloin, rack of lamb and rosemary, plus to-die-for crème brûlée perfumed with Madagascan vanilla, Chef Tinay is one of the city's top chefs. Check the Facebook page for ever-changing set lunches (from 75,000K) and dinners (from 190,000K).

Rue Samsenethai & Around

★ **Nemnueng Sihom** VIETNAMESE $
(Map p152; ☎021-213990; Rue Hengboun; mains 10,000-40,000K; ⊙11am-10pm) Nemnueng Sihom is a long-standing, bustling restaurant that offers a fun eating experience. It specialises in *nǎem néuang* (Vietnamese barbecued pork meatballs) sold in 'sets' *(sut)* with *kòw Ъûn* (white flour noodles with sweet-spicy sauce), fresh lettuce leaves, mint, basil, various sauces for dipping, sliced carambola (starfruit) and green banana – sort of a DIY spring roll.

Rice Noodle – Lao Porridge NOODLES $
(Map p152; ☎020-55414455; Rue Hengboun; mains 10,000-15,000K; ⊙4pm-1am) This is a good place to sample *kòw Ъeeak sèn*, thick rice- and tapioca-flour noodles served in a slightly viscous broth with crispy deep-fried pork belly or chicken.

Kaogee Café LAO $
(Map p152; Rue Samsenethai; mains 21,000-26,000K; ⊙6.15am-6pm; 🅿🛜) Retro-themed cafe/restaurant doing the kind of sophisticated *kòw jee* you're not going to find on the streets. Other perks include a full menu of coffee drinks and a liberal blast of air-con.

Thatdam Noodle LAO $
(Map p152; ☎021-214441; mains 15,000-35,000K; ⊙8.30am-2pm) Hidden away down a side street near That Dam, this place is run by an affable Lao chef who is clearly proud of his noodle-soup creations. Duck is a speciality, but chicken, pork and fish variations are also available.

Noy's Fruit Heaven INTERNATIONAL $
(Map p152; Rue Hengboun; mains 20,000-30,000K; ⊙7am-9pm; 🛜🚗) Noy's is a homely, colourful juice bar with Chinese paper lanterns hanging from the ceiling. Stop in to pick up a few of your 'five a day' or decimate your hangover with one of its dragonfruit, coconut, mango or tomato-juice shakes (15,000K). It also turns out super-fresh fruit salads and burgers.

Ban Anou Night Market LAO $
(Map p152; Rue Phai Nam; meals 10,000-20,000K; ⊙5-10pm) Setting up on a small street every evening, this atmospheric open-air market dishes up Lao food, from grilled meats to chilli-based dips with vegetables and sticky rice. The selections represent a crash-course in the local cuisine, but note that dishes are takeaway only.

Soukviman Cuisine Lao LAO $$
(Map p152; off Rue Chanthakoummane; mains 18,000-75,000K; ⊙10am-8pm; 🅿🛜) An upscale-ish place serving a hefty, but not too large, menu of Lao dishes. Choose from salads, soups, grilled dishes and more, including daily specials, although they're only listed in Lao. A decent jumping-off point for local cuisine.

The English-language sign simply says 'Cuisine Lao'.

Korean Restaurant KOREAN $$
(Map p152; ☎020-22087080; 220 Rue Hengboun; mains 45,000-200,000K; ⊙9am-11pm; 🅿🛜) Lacklustre name aside, this Korean-run place is great for sampling what is currently the most popular foreign cuisine in Southeast Asia. Most locals go directly for the Korean barbecue (from 120,000K), but we liked the kimchi stew (45,000K), served Korean-style with heaps of side dishes.

La Cage du Coq FRENCH $$
(Map p152; ☎020-54676065; Rue Hengbounnoy; mains 50,000-130,000K; ⊙11am-11pm; 🛜) Named after the fighting-cock cages that ornately decorate the garden, this eccentric place offers a unique blend of French dishes (frog legs, coq au vin) and Lao ingredients and cooking techniques (eels, *láhp* – minced

DON'T MISS

VIENTIANE'S CAFE SCENE

The French didn't leave much in the way of infrastructure in Laos, but they did leave a population addicted to caffeine. In central Vientiane, there's a cafe (or two) on every block, although the sleepy pace of the city doesn't exactly indicate this.

Tiny, French-run, old-school-feeling **Le Trio** (Map p152; ☑020-22553552; Rue Setthathirath; ☺7am-5pm; 🛜) is probably our fave of the lot. The beans are roasted on-site (to a soundtrack of jazz), and a bag makes a clever souvenir option. For something more modern, try **TitKafe** (Map p152; www.facebook.com/titkafe; Rue Setthathirath; ☺7am-7pm Mon-Fri, 8am-7pm Sat & Sun; 🛜), where drink options include nitro cold brew (and the music options, Top 40 pop). **Naked Espresso** (Map p152; ☑020-56222269; www.naked-espresso.com; Rue Nokeokoummane; mains 28,000-48,000K; ☺7am-9pm Mon-Fri, 8am-9pm Sat-Sun; ✳🛜🍴) isn't probably much different from your local back at home (although it might actually do better coffee), and if you're missing Western-style brunch, hit **Cabana** (Map p152; 15-16 Rue Fa Ngoum; mains 30,000-50,000K; ☺7am-5pm; ✳🛜🍴). **Common Grounds** (Map p152; ☑020-78727183; Rue Chao Anou; mains 35,000-43,000K; ☺7am-8pm Mon-Sat; ✳🛜🍴🚼) has excellent coffee and a playground for kids, making it a win-win for families, while the **Scandinavian Bakery** (Map p152; www.scandinavianbakerylaos.com; Nam Phu; mains 10,000-37,000K; ☺6.30am-9pm; ✳🛜), although it's seen better days, remains a godsend for Swedes missing their daily *fika* (coffee and a sweet treat).

pork salad with shallots and coriander). It doesn't always work, but it is fun.

Lao Kitchen
LAO $$

(Map p152; ☑021-254332; Rue Hengboun; mains 20,000-79,000K; ☺11am-10pm; ✳🛜🍴) Colourful walls, alt tunes and good service complement a menu spanning stews, Luang Prabang sausage, *láhp* variations, stir-fried morning glory (water spinach), spring rolls, Mekong fish soup and palate-friendly sorbets.

Mekong Riverfront & Around

Han 3 Euey Nong
LAO $

(Map p152; Rue Chao Anou; mains 8000-25,000K; ☺8am-8pm) Cheap and tidy, this busy family-run restaurant features tasty must-have dishes like *năem kòw* (crispy balls of deep-fried rice and sour pork sausage shredded into a salad-like dish) and the delicious *kòw ƀún nâm jạaou* (thin rice noodles served in a pork broth with pork, bamboo and herbs).

★Chokdee Cafe
BELGIAN $$

(Map p152; ☑021-263847; Rue Fa Ngoum; mains 28,000-89,000K; ☺10am-midnight; 🛜) A Belgian restaurant and bar on the riverfront, Chokdee specialises in dishes from the homeland, including, of course, *moules* (mussels) and *frites* (French fries), as well as other hearty but delicious dishes for discerning gourmands. Consider the massive selection of imported Belgian beers, and you

have one of the best places in town for non-Lao food.

★Khambang Lao Food Restaurant
LAO $$

(Map p152; ☑021-217198; 97/2 Rue Khounboulom; mains 20,000-90,000K; ☺10.30am-3pm & 5-9pm; 🛜) The slightly dreary, semi-open-air dining room couldn't be a bigger contrast with the tart, spicy, bold flavours served inside. This long-standing restaurant is the ideal introduction to Lao food via dishes such as *láhp;* roasted Mekong fish; stuffed frogs; *áw lám,* described on the menu as 'spicy beef stew'; and tasty Luang Prabang–style sausage.

La Signature
FRENCH $$$

(Map p152; ☑021-213523; www.ansarahotel.com; Ansara Hôtel, off Rue Fa Ngoum; mains 60,000-480,000K, set menu 140,000-340,000K; ☺11.30am-2.30pm & 6.30-10.30pm; ✳🛜🍴) With gentle jazz drifting onto the fan-cooled terrace of glass-topped wicker tables (and upstairs in the ochre-hued restaurant), La Signature is perfect for throwing on your smart clothes and taking a romantic supper. The menu spans French/international to Lao dishes.

Around Vientiane

Kuvieng Fried Chicken
LAO $

(KFC; Map p146; Rue Khu Vieng; mains from 5000K; ☺10am-8pm) This ramshackle restaurant draws locals for the combination of deep-fried chicken (the owner allegedly 'borrowed' the recipe from the other KFC), Lao-style papaya salad and, of course, French fries. Buy a Beerlao at the shop next door and you've got one of the most satisfying meals in town.

★ Doi Ka Noi   LAO $$
(Map p146; [☎] 020-55898959; www.facebook. com/DoiKaNoi; off Rue Sisangvone; mains 40,000-60,000K; ⊘ 10am-2.30pm Tue-Thu, to 9pm Fri-Sun; ❄) It took one meal for Doi Ka Noi to become one of our favourite restaurants in Laos. With a menu that changes daily (check the restaurant's Facebook page at around 8.30am to see what's available), the dishes here range from Lao standards to regional specialities most of us have never heard of, with something to appeal both to newbies and grizzled foodies.

The dining room has a charming old-school vibe with handsome food-related photos adorning the walls.

Privet   RUSSIAN $$
([☎] 020-78097784; https://russian-restaurant-privet.business.site; Rue Sithoong; mains 22,000-250,000K; ⊘ 11am-9pm Tue-Sun; ❄ 🛜 🍽) Dumplings, *zakuski* (small dishes eaten with vodka), pickled herring, blinis and caviar – peeps, Russian food is really tasty. And even if you don't agree or haven't tried it, this lively restaurant is worth a visit just for the kitsch factor (diners are encouraged to don fur hats and take selfies in front of a mural of Moscow's Red Square).

Senglao Cafe   INTERNATIONAL $$
(Map p146; [☎] 030-5880588; Ruelle 04, Rue Sisangvone; mains 35,000-220,000K; ⊘ 11am-10pm Mon-Sat, 9am-4pm Sun; ❄ 🛜) Named after a now-defunct cinema in the centre of town, this retro-themed restaurant has a cinematic theme and restored leather chairs from the old movie hall. The fusion menu is ambitious, with an emphasis on pasta dishes. Films are shown in the garden at weekends.

Amphone   LAO $$
(Map p146; [☎] 030-5776677; off Rue Sisangvone; mains 25,000-75,000K; ⊘ 11am-3pm & 6-10pm; ❄ 🛜) Located in a refurbished suburban home, Amphone serves Lao food – from noodle soups to sticky rice – in a sophisticated setting.

🍷 Drinking & Nightlife

Vientiane is no longer the illicit pleasure palace it once was. Beerlao has replaced opium as the drug of choice and brothels are strictly prohibited.

Most bars close by midnight, apart from a few late-night stragglers. Karaoke is popular, as are live-music performances.

★ Laodi   BAR
(Map p146; www.facebook.com/rhumlaodi; Rue Fa Ngoum; ⊘ 5pm-2am) Refurbished shipping containers in front of a spooky abandoned building, riverside breezes, and local rum distilled by a Japanese resident. Laodi is hard to pin down, but easy to enjoy. And best of all, the rum, made from Lao sugar cane grown near Vientiane, is delicious; try a tasting flight, which ranges in flavour from plain to passion fruit (we like the barrel-aged 'brown' and coffee).

★ Earth   BAR
(Map p152; www.facebook.com/earthvientiane; Rue Chao Anou; ⊘ 5pm-midnight; 🛜) At first glance, Earth looks as crunchy as a bowl of organic granola, but live music, cultural events, an eclectic soundtrack, craft beers, enthusiastic locals and fun staff mean that there's something here to appeal to just about everybody. Check the Facebook page to see what's on when you're in town.

★ Spirit House   COCKTAIL BAR
(Map p146; [☎] 021-262530; Rue Fa Ngoum; cocktails 40,000-60,000K; ⊘ 7am-11pm; 🛜) This traditional Lao house facing the Mekong has a well-stocked bar and a witty, helpful menu that doubles as a crash-course in cocktails. A chilled soundtrack complements the dark woods and comfy couches of its stylish interior, or you can sit outside and gaze at the river. Hit the exceptionally fun happy hours weekdays from 4pm to 6pm.

Dresden   BAR
(Map p152; 139 Rue Nokeokoummane; ⊘ 5pm-midnight Mon-Sat) Just your typical German-themed bar as perceived through a Japanese lens and located in Laos. There's a good selection of booze (especially sake), unique insulated beer mugs, hand-chipped ice cubes and some fascinating bar snacks that bridge the culinary gap between Japan and Germany. Oddly enough, it works.

Naga Boat   BAR
(Map p146; www.facebook.com/pg/thenagaboat; Rue Fa Ngoum; ⊘ 5.30-11.30pm) Landlubbers rejoice: we've found the perfect cruise. This permanently beached vessel features stunning river views, some of Vientiane's

better cocktails, domestic and import draught beer and an implicit no seasickness guarantee.

Cocoon
COCKTAIL BAR

(Map p152; off Rue Hengbounnoy; ⊙6.30pm-2am Tue-Sun) Cocktail culture has arrived in Vientiane, and it takes the form of this dark, sleek, new bar concealed in a tiny side street. The signature drinks veer towards the fruity end of the spectrum; we'd suggest sticking to the classics.

Bor Pen Yang
BAR

(Map p152; ☑020-27873965; Rue Fa Ngoum; ⊙10am-midnight; 🛜) Overlooking mother Mekong, a cast of locals, expats, bar girls and travellers assembles at this tin-roofed, wood-raftered watering hole to gaze at the sunset over nearby Thailand. Western tunes, pool tables and a huge bar to drape yourself over, as well as international football and rugby on large flat-screen TVs.

Samlo Pub
BAR

(Map p152; ☑021-222308; Rue Setthathirath; ⊙7pm-late) Sleazy and smoky, watch Vientiane's nocturnal population emerge from the shadows like vampires as you park yourself at the bar. It often stays open later than most bars, but take care walking home in the early hours.

CCC Bar
GAY

(Map p152; ☑020-55448686; Rue Sihom; ⊙7.30pm-late) The only gay bar in town, this place draws a convivial crowd and pushes things up a notch on weekends. From 1am it attracts a mixed crowd as one of the only late-night places in the capital.

☆ Entertainment

Like everything else, Vientiane's entertainment scene is picking up as money and politics allows, but the range remains fairly limited. By law, entertainment venues must close by 11.30pm, though most push it to about midnight.

Lao Boxing
SPECTATOR SPORT

(☑020-99999992; www.facebook.com/houay hongstadium; Houayhong Boxing Stadium, off Rue Chao Anou; ⊙7pm Sat) **FREE** Bouts of Lao boxing are held every Saturday at 7pm at Houayhong Boxing Stadium, located northwest of the city centre. It's free, and unlike the matches in Bangkok, you can get right up in the action.

Wind West
LIVE MUSIC

(Map p152; ☑021-265777; Rue Sihom; ⊙6pm-1am) A roadhouse-style bar and restaurant, Wind West has live Lao and Western rock music most nights. Depending on the night it can be heaving, or completely dead, but the interior, hung with 10-gallon hats, antlers and wooden Native American statues, lends the place a folksy atmosphere.

Anou Cabaret
LIVE MUSIC

(Map p152; ☑021-213630; Anou Paradise Hotel, cnr Rue Hengboun & Rue Chao Anou; ⊙9pm-1am) On the ground floor of the Anou Paradise Hotel, the cabaret has been swinging along here for years. It's a funny place, with old crooners and a palpable 1960s feel.

🛍 Shopping

Just about anything made in Laos is available for purchase in Vientiane, including hill-tribe crafts, jewellery, traditional textiles and carvings. The main shopping area in town is along Rue Setthathirath and the streets radiating from it.

★T'Shop Lai Gallery
COSMETICS, HOMEWARES

(Map p152; ☑021-223178; www.laococo.com; off Rue In Paeng; ⊙8am-8pm Mon-Sat, 10am-6pm Sun) 🖉 Imagine a melange of aromas: coconut, aloe vera, honey, frangipani and magnolia, all of them emanating from body oils, soaps, sprays, perfumes and lip balms and more. These wonderful products are made with sustainable, locally sourced ingredients by disadvantaged women who make up the Les Artisans Lao cooperative.

There's also a fine gallery upstairs that rotates Lao and international artists' work.

★The First
GIFTS & SOUVENIRS

(Map p152; 168b Rue Samsenethai; ⊙8am-8pm) This bright-feeling shop has a broad but well-curated selection of items representing some of Laos' most reputable brands: beautiful textiles from Ock Pop Tok and Passa Paa, Lao jewellery from Serene's, soaps and other toiletries from Les Artisans Lao, rum from Laodi and chocolate from Marou.

Saoban
ARTS & CRAFTS

(Map p152; ☑021-241835; www.saobancrafts.com; Rue Chao Anou; ⊙9am-8pm) 🖉 This small shop works with over 300 artisans in 14 communities across 10 provinces of Laos, selling everything from hand-woven silk textiles to bamboo baskets and silver jewellery. There are nice descriptions of where the

ℹ SHOPPING FOR TEXTILES IN VIENTIANE

Downtown Vientiane is littered with stores selling textiles. Rue Nokeokoummane is the epicentre, but the city's main market, Talat Sao, is also a good place to buy fabrics. You'll find antiques as well as modern fabrics, plus utilitarian items such as shoulder bags (some artfully constructed around squares of antique fabric), cushions and pillows.

Several shops along Rue Samsenethai, Rue Pangkham and Rue Setthathirath sell Lao and Tai tribal and hill-tribe textiles and crafts. The Lao goods are increasingly complemented by products from Vietnam and Thailand, such as lacquer work and Buddha images. Textile and clothing places often also carry handicrafts and antiques.

products come from and who your purchase will support (mostly rural women from ethnic minorities). Prices tend to be cheaper than elsewhere in town.

Carol Cassidy Lao Textiles ARTS & CRAFTS
(Map p152; ☑021-212123; www.laotextiles.com; 108 Rue Nokeokoummane; ⊙8am-noon & 2-5pm Mon-Fri, to noon Sat, or by appointment) Lao Textiles sells high-end contemporary, original-design fabrics inspired by generations-old Lao weaving patterns, motifs and techniques. The American designer, Carol Cassidy, employs Lao weavers who work out the back of the attractive old French-Lao house. Internationally known, with prices to match.

Camacrafts ARTS & CRAFTS
(Mulberries; Map p152; www.camacrafts.org; Rue Nokeokoummane; ⊙10am-6pm Mon-Sat) 🖉 Stocks silk clothes and weavings from Xieng Khuang Province, plus some bed and cushion covers in striking Hmong-inspired designs. All of the shop's Fairtrade products come from the artisan communities it supports in rural Laos.

State Books Shop BOOKS
(Map p152; Rue Setthathirath; ⊙8am-4pm Mon-Fri) This state-run bookshop, with its faded titles in Russian and Vietnamese, is a lingering reminder of Laos' communist roots in an increasingly slick Vientiane. If you're not interested in history, there are a few English-language titles and a good selection of colourful, Lao-language children's books.

Her Works CLOTHING
(Map p152; www.herworks.la; Rue Nokeokoummane; ⊙10am-6pm Mon-Fri, noon-6pm Sat & Sun) This social enterprise-oriented shop features the work of ethnic minorities in remote corners of the country. This means chunky, colourful clothing, bags, hats and shoes with a conscience.

Kanchana Boutique ARTS & CRAFTS
(Map p152; ☑021-213467; 140 Rue Samsenethai; ⊙8am-8pm) This shop carries what is possibly the most upscale selection of Lao silk in town (the most expensive designs, some of which sell for several thousand US dollars, are kept in an adjacent room). The friendly owners also run the Lao Textile Museum (p148).

Monument Books BOOKS
(Map p146; Rue Setthathirath; ⊙9am-8pm Mon-Sat, to 6pm Sun) A great one-stop shop for glossy magazines and a tasteful range of modern classic novels, plus travel guides, thrillers and lush pictorials on Laos.

Night Market MARKET
(Map p152; Rue Fa Ngoum; ⊙6-10.30pm) Vientiane's night market lights up the riverfront with a selection of stalls hawking handicrafts and T-shirts. It doesn't quite have the atmosphere of Luang Prabang's, but nonetheless a decent place to browse and hone your haggling skills.

Dee Traditional
Antique Textiles ARTS & CRAFTS
(Map p152; ☑020-55519908; khamtanh44@hotmail.com; Rue Setthathirath; ⊙8am-9pm) It might not look much from the outside but within this chilled shop, stuffed from floor to ceiling with an array of rustic hill-tribe woven items, there are great bargains to be found.

Talat Sao MARKET
(Morning Market; Map p152; Rue Lan Xang; ⊙9am-5pm) A once-unique Vientiane shopping experience has sadly undergone a facelift: two-thirds of its world of stalls selling opium pipes, jewellery and traditional antiques have been ripped down and replaced with a bland modern mall. The original structure remains a good place for traditional Lao fabrics, but the fate of the vendors is hanging by a thread.

Mixay Boutique ARTS & CRAFTS
(Map p152; ☑ 021-216592; Rue Nokeokoummane; ⊙ 9am-8pm Mon-Sat) One of the stores worth a visit along this busy drag is the upmarket Mixay Boutique; it stocks a veritable potpourri of textiles and handicrafts from around Laos.

ℹ Information

DANGERS & ANNOYANCES
By international standards Vientiane has a very low crime rate, but there's a small risk of getting mugged.

➡ Be especially careful around the BCEL Bank on the riverfront, where bag snatchers, usually a two-person team with a motorbike, have been known to strike; common sense should be an adequate defence.

➡ Stay off the city's roads during festivals, particularly April's Pi Mai, when drunk-driving-related accidents skyrocket.

➡ Call the **Tourist Police** (Map p152; ☑ 021-251128; Rue Lan Xang; ⊙ 24hr) if you need to talk to an English-speaking police officer.

MEDICAL SERVICES
Vientiane's medical facilities can leave a lot to be desired, so for anything serious make a break for the border and the much more sophisticated hospitals in Thailand. Aek Udon International Hospital (www.aekudon.com) in Thailand can dispatch an ambulance to take you to Udon Thani. Less serious ailments can be dealt with in Vientiane.

Alliance International Medical Center (Map p146; ☑ 021-513095; www.aimclao.com; Rue Souphanouvong) This hospital treats basic ailments like broken bones and dispenses antibiotics.

Centre Médical de L'Ambassade de France (French Embassy Medical Center; Map p146; ☑ 021-214150; cnr Rue Khu Vieng & Rue Sim-euang; ⊙ 8.30am-noon & 1.30-7pm Mon-Tue & Thu-Fri, 8.30am-noon & 1.30-5pm Wed, Sat & Sun) Open to all, but visits outside regular hours by appointment only.

International Clinic (Map p146; ☑ 021-214024; Mahosot Hospital, Rue Fa Ngoum; ⊙ 24hr) Part of the Mahosot Hospital; probably the best place for not-too-complex emergencies. Some English-speaking doctors. Take ID and cash.

Setthathirat Hospital (☑ 021-351156; Rue Khamphengmuang) This hospital northeast of the city is another option for minor ailments.

MONEY
There are plenty of banks, international ATMs and licensed moneychangers in the capital.

ANZ (Map p152; ☑ 021-222700; 33 Rue Lan Xang; ⊙ 8.30am-3.30pm Mon-Fri) Main branch has ATMs; additional machines can be found on Rue Setthathirath and Rue Fa Ngoum.

Bank of Ayudhya (Krungsri; Map p152; ☑ 021-255522; 79/6 Rue Lan Xang; ⊙ 8.30am-3.30pm Mon-Fri) Thai bank with ATM machine.

Banque pour le Commerce Extérieur Lao (BCEL; Map p152; cnr Rue Pangkham & Rue Fa Ngoum; ⊙ 8.30am-7pm Mon-Fri, to 3.30pm Sat & Sun) Longest hours of any bank in town. Exchange booth on Rue Fa Ngoum and ATMs attached to the main building.

Joint Development Bank (Map p152; 75/1-5 Rue Lan Xang; ⊙ 8.30am-4pm Mon-Fri, 9am-4pm Sat & Sun) Exchange and ATM.

Krung Thai Bank (Map p152; ☑ 021-213480; Rue Lan Xang; ⊙ 8.30am-3.30pm Mon-Fri) With 24-hour ATM.

Lao-Viet Bank (Map p152; ☑ 021-251418; Rue Lan Xang; ⊙ 8.30am-4pm Mon-Fri) ATM and money exchange.

Siam Commercial Bank (Map p152; 117 Rue Lan Xang; ⊙ 8.30am-3.30pm Mon-Fri) Foreign exchange and ATM.

Thai Military Bank (Map p152; ☑ 021-216486; cnr Rue Samsenethai & Rue Khounboulom; ⊙ 8.30am-3.30pm Mon-Fri) Exchange and ATM.

TOURIST INFORMATION
Tourist Information Centre (MICT; Map p152; ☑ 021-212248; www.tourismlaos.org; Rue Lan Xang; ⊙ 8.30am-noon & 1.30-4pm) A worthwhile tourist information centre with easy-to-use descriptions of each province, helpful staff who speak decent English, as well as brochures and regional maps.

VISAS
Getting an extension on a tourist visa is easy. Go to the **Immigration Office** (Map p152; ☑ 021-212250; Rue Hatsady; ⊙ 8-11.30am & 1.30-4.30pm Mon-Fri), in the Ministry of Public Security building opposite Talat Sao, fill out a form (5000K), supply your passport and a photo, pay a 25,000K administrative fee and then an additional 20,000K per day for the extra time you want. Return the next afternoon to collect your passport.

Getting There & Away

AIR
Departures from Vientiane's **Wattay International Airport** (VTE; Map p146; ☑ 021-512165; www.vientianeairport.com; Rte 13), located around 4km northwest of the centre, are from the linked international and domestic terminals.

At research time, there were direct domestic flights between Vientiane and destinations in Laos including Luang Namtha (Namtha), Luang Prabang, Muang Khoun (Old Xieng Khuang), Pakse, Phongsali, Savannakhet, Sam Neua (Xam Neua) and Udomxai (Muang Xai); and direct international flights between Vientiane and points in China, Korea, Singapore, Thailand and Vietnam.

Two airlines service domestic routes in Laos:

Lao Airlines (Map p146; ✆ 021-513032; International Terminal, Wattay International Airport; ⏰ 5am-6pm)

Lao Skyway (Map p146; ✆ 1441; www.laoskyway.com; Domestic Terminal, Wattay International Airport; ⏰ 7am-4pm)

International airlines:

Bangkok Airways (Map p152; www.bangkokair.com; Lao Plaza Hotel, 63 Rue Samsenethai; ⏰ 9.30am-noon & 1-6.30pm Mon-Sat)

China Eastern Airlines (Map p146; ✆ 021-252888; http://en.ceair.com; Rue Souphanou-

vong; ⏰ 8.30-11.30am & 1.30-4.30pm Mon-Fri, to 11.30am Sat)

Thai Airways International (Map p146; ✆ 021-222527; www.thaiairways.com; Rue Souphanouvong; ⏰ 8am-5pm Mon-Fri)

Vietnam Airlines (Map p152; ✆ 021-252618; www.vietnamairlines.com; Lao Plaza Hotel, 63 Rue Samsenethai; ⏰ 8am-noon & 1.30-4.30pm Mon-Fri, to noon Sat)

BUS

In Laos roads are poor and buses break down, so travel times can take longer than advertised. Buses use three different stations in Vientiane, all with some English-speaking staff, relatively clear timetables and fares, plus food and drink stands.

The **Northern Bus Station** (Rue Sithong), about 2km northwest of the airport, serves all points north. **Tong Li Bus Company** (✆ 021-242657) runs a route to Kunming, in China, from here. Minivans to Vang Vieng leave from here,

GETTING TO THAILAND: THA NA LENG TO NONG KHAI

Getting to the border At the Tha Na Leng (Laos)/Nong Khai (Thailand) border crossing (6am to 10pm), the Thai–Lao Friendship Bridge (Saphan Mittaphap Thai-Lao) spans the Mekong River. The Laos border is approximately 20km from Vientiane, and the easiest and cheapest way to the bridge is to cross on the Thai–Lao International Bus (p166). It conducts daily departures for the Thai cities of Bangkok, Khon Kaen, Nong Khai and Udon Thani. Alternative means of transport between Vientiane and the bridge include taxi (400B), tuk-tuk (50,000K/300B), jumbo (200B) or the number 14 Tha Deua bus from Talat Sao Bus Station (8000K) between 5.30am and 6pm.

To cross from Thailand, tuk-tuks are available from Nong Khai's train station (30B) and bus station (60B) to the Thai border post at the bridge. You can also hop on the Thai–Lao International Bus from Nong Khai bus station (55B, 1½ hours) or Udon Thani bus station (80B, two hours), both of which terminate at Vientiane's Talat Sao Bus Station. If flying into Udon Thani, a tuk-tuk from the airport to the city's bus station should cost about 120B.

It's also possible to cross the bridge by train, as tracks have been extended from Nong Khai's train station 3.5km into Laos, terminating at Dongphosy Station, about 13km from central Vientiane. From Nong Khai there are two daily departures (10am and 5.30pm, 30B, 15 minutes) and border formalities are taken care of at the respective train stations. But in reality, unless you are a trainspotter, it is much more convenient to use the international bus or other road transport.

At the border Travellers from most countries enjoy 30-day, visa-free access to Thailand. Lao visas (30 days) are available for US$20 to US$42, depending on your nationality. If you don't have a photo you'll be charged an extra US$1, and be aware that an additional US$1 'overtime fee' is charged from 6am to 8am and 4pm to 10pm on weekdays, as well as on weekends and holidays. Don't be tempted to use a tuk-tuk driver to get your Lao visa, no matter what they tell you, as it will take far longer than doing it yourself, and you'll have to pay for the 'service'. Insist they take you straight to the bridge.

Moving on Trains from Nong Khai to Bangkok leave at 7am, 6.30pm and 7.10pm and cost from 898B for a 2nd-class sleeper ticket (11 hours).

BUSES FROM VIENTIANE

DESTINATION	STATION	COST (K)	DISTANCE (KM)	DURATION (HR)	DEPARTURES
Attapeu	Southern	140,000-220,000	812	14-24	7.15am (VIP), 9.30am (fan), 5pm (fan), 8.30pm (VIP)
Ban Kong Lor	Southern	90,000	312	8-10	10am
Bangkok (Thailand)	Talat Sao	248,000	650	12-16	6pm
Danang (Vietnam)	Southern	200,000	900	22	6pm
Don Khong	Southern	150,000	788	16-19	10.30am (fan)
Hanoi (Vietnam)	Southern	200,000	750	24	5.30pm, 6pm (Mon, Wed, Fri, Sun)
Hongsa	Northern	250,000	450	12-16	6.30am
Huay Xai	Northern	200,000-220,000	869	24	8.30am, 5pm
Khon Kaen (Thailand)	Talat Sao	50,000	197	4	8.15am, 2.45pm
Kunming (China)	Northern	7,300,000	1200		2pm, 11pm (sleeper)
Lak Sao	Southern	85,000	334	6-8	5am, 6am, 7am, 11.30am, 6.30pm
Luang Namtha	Northern	220,000	676	24	8.30am, 5pm
Luang Prabang	Northern	110,000-150,000	384	9-11	6.30am, 7am (van), 7.30am, 8am (VIP), 8.30am, 9am (van, VIP), 11am, 1.30pm, 4pm, 6pm, 7pm (van), 7.30pm (VIP), 8pm (VIP)
Nong Khai (Thailand)	Talat Sao	15,000	25	1½	7.30am, 9.30am, 12.40pm, 2.30pm, 3.30pm, 6pm
Pak Lai	Northern	90,000	213	6-8	7.30am, 9am, 11am, 1pm (all van)

though most people end up booking more expensive tourist buses from agencies in town.

The **Southern Bus Station** (Dong Dok Bus Station; Rte 13), also known as *khíw lot lák káo* (Km 9 Bus Station), is 9km out of town and serves everywhere to the south. **SDT** (☑ 020-2205352) runs buses to various points in Vietnam from this station including Danang, Hanoi and Vinh.

The final departure point is the **Talat Sao Bus Station** (Central Bus Station; Map p152; ☑ 021-216507; Rue Khu Vieng) from where desperately slow local buses run to destinations within Vientiane Province, and some more distant destinations, though for the latter you're better off going to the Northern or Southern Bus Stations. The **Thai–Lao International Bus** (Map p152)

also uses this station for its trips to Bangkok, Khon Kaen, Nong Khai and Udon Thani.

TRAIN
In 2009 tracks were extended from Nong Khai's train station across the Thai–Lao Friendship Bridge to Dongphosy in Laos, effectively forming Laos' first railway line. There are plans to extend the tracks 417km to the border with China at Boten by 2021, part of a US$7-billion plan (funded by the Chinese government) that will see the commencement of a national railway grid in the coming years. For now, however, Laos boasts a grand total of 3.5km of rolling track, making connections with Nong Khai in Thailand very inconvenient when compared with the Thai–Lao International Bus.

DESTINATION	STATION	COST (K)	DISTANCE (KM)	DURATION (HR)	DEPARTURES
Paksan	Southern	40,000-50,000	143	3-4	frequent 7am-3pm (tuk-tuk); take any bus going south
Pakse	Southern	110,000-170,000	677	8-18	frequent 10am-4pm (all fan); 5.15am, 6pm, 6.30pm, 7pm, 8pm, 8.30pm, 9pm (all VIP)
Phongsali	Northern	230,000-250,000	811	25-28	7.15am (fan), 6pm (sleeper)
Phonsavan	Northern	110,000-150,000	374	10-11	6.30am, 7.30am, 9.30am, 8pm (sleeper)
Sainyabuli	Northern	110,000-130,000	485	14-16	9am, 4pm, 6.30pm
Salavan	Southern	130,000-190,000	774	13-20	4.30pm (fan), 7.30pm, 8.30pm (VIP)
Sam Neua (Xam Neua)	Northern	190,000-210,000	612	22-24	9.30am, noon, 5pm (all VIP)
Savannakhet	Southern	75,000-120,000	457	8-11	frequent 5.30-9am or any bus to Pakse, 8.30pm (VIP)
Tha Khaek	Southern	60,000-80,000	332	5-6	4am, 5am, 6am, noon, or any bus to Savannakhet or Pakse; 1pm (VIP)
Udomxai	Northern	190,000	578	15-17	6.45am, 1.45pm, 4pm, 5pm (all VIP)
Udon Thani (Thailand)	Talat Sao	22,000	82	2½	8am, 9am, 10.30am, 11.30am, 2pm, 3pm, 4pm, 6pm
Vang Vieng	Northern	40,000-50,000	157	4	frequent 6am-5pm (van); 8.30am, 10am
Vinh (Vietnam)	Southern	150,000	460	16	8am, 6pm

ⓘ Getting Around

Central Vientiane is entirely accessible on foot. For exploring neighbouring districts, however, you'll need transport.

TO/FROM THE AIRPORT

From Wattay International Airport, taxis to the centre cost US$7 (to Vang Vieng, US$90). Only official taxis can pick up at the airport. There is a shuttle bus linking the airport and Talat Sao Bus Station in the city centre, with departures every 40 minutes between 9.15am and 9.15pm (15,000K).

BICYCLE

Cycling is a cheap, easy and recommended way of getting around mostly flat Vientiane. Loads of guesthouses and several shops hire out bikes for 10,000K to 20,000K per day. Mountain bikes are available but are more expensive at 30,000K to 40,000K; try **Lao Bike** (Map p152; ☏ 020-54674345; Rue Setthathirath; ◷ 8.30am-6pm) or **Mixay Bike 2** (Map p152; ☏ 020-77882510; Rue Chau Anou; scooter per 24hr 60,000-80,000K; ◷ 8.30am-7.30pm).

BUS

There is a city bus system, but it's oriented more towards the distant suburbs than the central district. Most buses leave from Talat Sao Bus Station. The number 14 Tha Deua bus to the Thai–Lao Friendship Bridge and Xieng Khuan (Buddha Park) runs every 20 minutes from 5.30am to 6pm and costs 8000K. Bus 44 connects with the airport (15,000K) every 40 minutes from 9.15am to 9.40pm. Bus 8 runs to

MOTORBIKE TOURING FROM VIENTIANE

Motorbike activities have been growing in popularity for several years now. It's now possible to travel on sturdy, well-maintained motocross bikes, connected by Laos' competent mobile-phone service for backup with base, and handheld GPS devices to always keep you on track. And with drop-off and luggage-forwarding facilities to your destination available, you're now able to tackle a slice of your holiday on two wheels (an alternative to duking it out on slow, overcrowded buses). Rent by the week and take in the north via the mountains of Vang Vieng, continuing on to Luang Prabang and the rest of the north before leaving your bike in Luang Prabang. Or head south to explore the karst limestone mountains around Tha Khaek and eventually leave the motorbike in Pakse.

Recommended operators that hire dirt bikes or touring bikes and offer pick-up services at the end of your trip:

Drivenbyadventure (☑ 020-58656994; www.hochiminhtrail.org; rental per day US$38-95, tours per day from US$190) Offers the most professionally maintained dirt bikes in Laos, including Honda CRF250s (US$38 per day), Honda XR400s (US$50) and KTM XCW450s (US$95).

Fuark Motorcycle Hire (Map p146; ☑ 021-261970; fuarkmotorcross@yahoo.com; Rue T2; ☺ 9am-6pm) A leading locally owned and operated motorbike-hire place that offers a range of well-maintained dirt bikes (from US$30 per day) and drop-offs at key cities around the country.

Drivenbyadventure owner Don Duvall also masquerades as mysteriously monikered Midnight Mapper (www.laosgpsmap.com), who has spent the last 10 years tirelessly mapping Laos, and you can buy his satellite map off his website and plug it into your GPS gadget. It costs US$50, and he mails you the SIM card, or can rent you a Garmin handheld GPS device for US$7 per day and plug in your coordinates so you never get lost.

the Northern Bus Station (p165) (5000K) and buses 23 and 29 to the Southern Bus Station (p166) (4000K to 7000K).

CAR & MOTORCYCLE

There are several international car-hire companies with representation in Vientiane, including **Avis-Budget** (Map p152; ☑ 020-22861415; www.avis.la; Rue Setthathirath; ☺ 8.30am-6pm Mon-Fri, to 1pm Sat & Sun) and **Sixt** (Map p146; ☑ 020-96590475; www.sixtlao.com; International Terminal, Wattay International Airport; ☺ 8am-10.30pm). Keep in mind that while a basic sedan will get you around the city, you'll need a sturdy 4WD for trips further afield.

Scooters are a popular means of getting around Vientiane and can be hired throughout the centre of town. Recommended hire places include the following:

Mixay Bike 2 (p167)

TL Motor Bike (Map p152; ☑ 020-55528299; Rue Francois Ngin; scooters per day 70,000K; ☺ 8am-8pm)

JUMBO & TUK-TUK

Drivers of jumbos and tuk-tuks will take passengers on journeys as short as 500m or as far as 20km. Understanding the various types of tuk-tuk is important if you don't want to be overcharged (and can save you arguments in addition to money). Tourist tuk-tuks are the most expensive, while share jumbos that run regular routes around town (eg Rue Luang Prabang to Rue Setthathirath or Rue Lan Xang to That Luang) are much cheaper, usually less than 10,000K per person.

TAXI

Car taxis of varying shapes, sizes and vintages can often be found stationed in front of the larger hotels, at the airport, or at the **stall** (Map p152; ☑ 021-454168; Rue Khu Vieng) across from Talat Sao. Bargaining is the general rule.

AROUND VIENTIANE

Once you've mastered the city, you're prepared for the countryside. In the area that surrounds Vientiane, this largely means the jungle and homestays of Phu Khao Khuay NPA and the backpacker magnet that is Vang Vieng.

Phu Khao Khuay NPA
ປ່າສະຫງວນແຫ່ງຊາດພູເຂົາຄວາຍ

Covering more than 2000 sq km of mountains and rivers, the underrated Phu Khao Khuay National Protected Area (NPA) is the most accessible protected area in Laos.

Treks ranging in duration from a couple of hours to three days have been developed in partnership with Baŋ Na (ບານນາ) and Ban Hat Khai (ບານຫາດໄຂ), villages on the edge of the NPA.

Phu Khao Khuay (ພູເຂົາຄວາຍ; *poo cow kwai*) means 'Buffalo Horn Mountain', a name derived from local legend, and is home to three major rivers that flow off a sandstone mountain range. It boasts an extraordinary array of endangered wildlife, including wild elephant, gibbon, Asiatic black bear, clouded leopard, Siamese fireback pheasant and green peafowl. Depending on elevation, visitors may encounter dry evergreen dipterocarp (a Southeast Asian tree with two-winged fruit), mixed deciduous forest, conifer forest or grassy uplands. Several impressive waterfalls are accessible as day trips from Vientiane.

⊙ Sights & Activities

Detailed information on trekking, accommodation and getting to and from Phu Khao Khuay NPA can be found at the Tourist Information Centre (p164) in Vientiane. Trekking in Phu Khao Khuay costs 100,000K per person per day, and you must also purchase a permit to enter the NPA (40,000K) and contribute to the village fund (50,000K). If trekking from Village Hat Khai you'll also have to pay for boat transport (100,000K per boat, up to two passengers).

Ban Na

Village guides lead one-, two- and three-day treks from Ban Na to **Keng Khani** (three to four hours one way) and through deep forest to the waterfall of **Tat Fa** (four to five hours). There is also a one-hour trek to the old elephant observation tower, passing by plantations and through the skirts of the jungle itself. The tower overlooks a salt lick, which the elephants used to visit regularly. Trekkers sleep in the tower (100,000K per person) beneath a mosquito net on a mattress, and guides cook a tasty local dinner. Even without the elephants it still makes for a fun adventure.

Wat Pha Baht Phonsan   BUDDHIST TEMPLE
(ວັດພະບາດໂພນສັນ; Tha Pha Bat; ⊙ daylight hours) FREE En route to Ban Na it's worth stopping briefly at Wat Pha Baht Phonsan, which sits on a rocky outcrop at Tha Pha Bat, beside Rte 13 about 1.5km south of Ban Na. The wat is revered for its large *pa bàht*

(Buddha footprint) shrine, monastery and substantial reclining Buddha figure. You'll recognise it by the large and well-ornamented 1933-vintage stupa.

Ban Hat Khai

Destinations accessible from Ban Hat Khai include Tat Leuk and **orchid treks** in the forest. For those with more time, a trek taking in the huge cliff, views and beautiful landscape of **Pha Luang** (three to four hours one way), and the forested areas around **Huay Khi Ling** (two to three hours one way) can also be arranged. This takes two or three days, depending on the season, and involves sleeping in the forest.

Tat Leuk   WATERFALL
(ຕາດເລິກ) FREE Tat Leuk is a small waterfall, but is a beautiful place to camp for the night. You can swim above the falls if the water isn't too shallow, and the visitor centre has some information about the area, including a detailed guide to the 1.5km-long Huay Bon Nature Trail.

The visitor centre attendant can arrange local treks for between 60,000K and 160,000K, and rents quality four-person tents for 40,000K, plus hammocks, mattresses, mosquito nets and sleeping bags for 10,000K each. There's a very basic restaurant (best supplemented with food you bring from outside), a small library of wildlife books and a pair of binoculars.

From the junction to Ban Hat Khai village, turn left and continue another 6km until you see a rough 4km road on the left, which leads to Tat Leuk.

Tat Xai & Pha Xai   WATERFALL
(ຕາດໄຊ ຜາໄຊ) FREE Tat Xai cascades down seven steps, and 800m downstream Pha Xai plunges over a 40m-high cataract. There's a pool that's good for swimming, though it can get dangerous during the wet season. Both waterfalls are accessed from Rte 13, just before Tha Bok. From the junction to Ban Hat Khai, it's 9km to Tat Xai and Pha Xai.

🛏 Sleeping & Eating

Homestay-style accommodation is available in both Ban Na and Ban Hat Khai for 40,000K per person, per night. The prices do not include transport from Vientiane and are not negotiable. All monies go to the village and NPA.

VIENTIANE, VANG VIENG & AROUND PHU KHAO KHUAY NPA

LOCAL KNOWLEDGE

ENDANGERED ELEPHANTS

The lowland farming village of Ban Na, 82km northeast of Vientiane, is home to about 600 people. The village is typical Lao, with women weaving baskets from bamboo and men tending the fields. But it was the local herd of elephants that was historically of most interest to visitors.

The farmers of Ban Na grow rice and vegetables, but several years ago they began planting sugar cane. What they didn't count on was the collective sweet tooth of the elephants in the nearby mountains. It wasn't long before these jumbos sniffed out the delights in the field below and were happily eating the sugar cane, pineapples and bananas planted around Ban Na. Not surprisingly, the farmers weren't happy. They decided the only way to get rid of the elephants was to rip up the sugar cane and go back to planting boring (and less lucrative) vegetables.

It was hoped the 30-odd elephants would take the hint and return to the mountains. Instead, they made the lowland forests, bamboo belt and fields around Ban Na their home, causing significant destruction to the environment and finances of Ban Na. The only way the villagers could continue to live with the elephants (ie not shoot them) was by making them pay their way. The result was elephant ecotourism.

The truth is that today the elephants have vanished. In 2007 there was an estimated 25-strong herd in Phu Khao Khuay National Protected Area (NPA). In 2009 five were killed – stripped of their tusks and hind legs, which suggests that they were murdered by poachers rather than local villagers. In 2010 a further two were recorded dead; according to the Lao Army, they had been electrocuted by lightning. Villagers say they have not sighted elephants for several years, so it is likely they have been killed or have fled north into more remote areas of the NPA.

Ban Na offers 10 homestays in simple wooden houses (24-hour electricity and mosquito nets with bedding are provided). Vegetarian meals are possible. For bookings contact Mr Bounathom/Mr Khampak (☑ 020-22208262), or find a Lao speaker to call ahead for you.

Ban Hat Khai is a pretty riverside village offering 11 homestays in traditional Lao houses, or in a guesthouse built especially for visitors; all include 24-hour electricity and mosquito nets. Vegetarian meals are available on request. To book a stay in Ban Hat Khai contact Mr Khammoun (☑ 020-2224 0303) or find a Lao speaker to call ahead for you.

Homestays in Ban Na and Ban Hat Khai can provide wholesome meals for 30,000K. Vegetarians are catered for, although more complicated dietary requirements may be hard to deliver.

Even if you're not interested in a trek, a stay at Ban Na or Ban Hat Khai is a fascinating insight into Lao village life.

❶ Getting There & Away

To get to Ban Na or Ban Hat Khai, hop on the Paksan-bound trucks that depart from Vientiane's Southern Bus Station (frequent from 7am to 3pm, three to four hours) or any bus headed south. For Wat Pha Baht Phonsan and Ban Na

get off at Tha Pha Bat (25,000K) near the Km 81 stone; the shrine is right on Rte 13 and Ban Na is about 1.5km north and well signposted.

For Ban Hat Khai, keep on the bus until a turn-off left (north) at Km 92, just before Tha Bok (30,000K). If you have your own transport, continue 8km along the smooth laterite road until you cross the new bridge. Turn right at the Y-intersection and it's 1km along a dirt road to Ban Hat Khai. Alternatively, villagers in Ban Hat Khai can arrange motorcycle (40,000K) or van (80,000K) pick-up from Tha Bok, if you call ahead.

Vang Vieng   ວັງວຽງ

☑ 023 / POP 21,000

Like a rural scene from an old Asian silk painting, Vang Vieng crouches low over the Nam Song (Song River) with a backdrop of serene cliffs and a tapestry of vivid green paddy fields. Thanks to the Lao government closing the river rave bars in 2012, the formerly toxic party scene has been driven to the fringes and the community is rebooting itself as an adrenaline-fuelled adventure destination. The town itself is no gem, as concrete hotels build ever higher in search of the quintessential view. But across the Nam Song lies a rural idyll; spend a few days here – hire a bike, zipline, climb a cliff, go tubing or trekking – and soak up one of the country's most stunningly picturesque spots.

◎ Sights

Vang Vieng's activities tend to be more popular than the sights, which are mainly contemporary-style monasteries. Among these, **Wat Si Vieng Song** (ວັດສີວຽງຊອງ; ⊘ daylight hours) **FREE**, **Wat Kang** (ວັດກາງ; ⊘ daylight hours) **FREE** and **Wat Si Suman** (ວັດສິສຸມັງ; ⊘ daylight hours) **FREE** are the most notable. Over the river are a couple of villages where Hmong have been relocated; these are accessible by bicycle or motorbike.

Other sights in the area are *tàm* (caves). Of the most accessible caves, most are signed in English as well as Lao, and an admission fee is collected at the entrance to each cave. The caves around Vang Vieng are spectacular, but caves come with certain hazards: they're dark, slippery and disorienting. A guide (often a young village boy) will lead you through a cave for a small fee; bring water and a torch (flashlight), and be *sure* your batteries aren't about to die. In fact, bearing in mind some of the 'lost in the darkness' horror stories that circulate, it's vital to have a spare torch.

For more extensive multicave tours, most guesthouses can arrange a guide. Trips including river tubing and cave tours cost around US$15/25 for a half-/full day.

Tham Nam   CAVE
(ຖ້ຳນ້ຳ, Water Cave; 10,000K; ⊘ 8am-5pm) Tham Nam is the highlight of the cluster of caves north of Vang Vieng. The cave is about 500m long and a tributary of the Nam Song flows out of its low entrance. As with other caves in the area, there's a zipline and basic restaurant.

In the dry season you can wade into the cave, but when the water is higher you need to take a tube from the friendly woman near the entrance; the tube and headlamp are included in the entrance fee. Dragging yourself through the tunnel on the fixed rope is fun.

Tham Hoi   CAVE
(ຖ້ຳຫອຍ; ⊘ 8am-5pm) **FREE** Located a few kilometres north of Vang Vieng, the entrance to Tham Hoi is guarded by a large Buddha figure; reportedly the cave continues about 3km into the limestone and an underground lake.

Tham Jang   CAVE
(ຖ້ຳຈັງ; entry incl footbridge fee 15,000K; ⊘ 8am-5pm) The most famous of the caves around Vang Vieng, Tham Jang was used as a bunker to defend against marauding *jẹen hór* (Yunnanese Chinese) in the early 19th century (*jạng* means 'steadfast'). Stairs lead up to the main cavern entrance.

Tham Loup   CAVE
(ຖ້ຳຫຼຸບ; ⊘ 8am-5pm) **FREE** Tham Loup, located a few kilometres north of Vang Vieng, is a large and delightfully untouched cavern with some impressive stalactites.

Tham Sang   CAVE
(ຖ້ຳຊ້າງ, Elephant Cave; 5000K; ⊘ 8am-5pm) Tham Sang, located a few kilometres north of Vang Vieng, is a small cavern containing Buddha images and a Buddha footprint, plus the (vaguely) elephant-shaped stalactite that gives the cave its name. It's best visited in the morning when light enters the cave.

Tham Phu Kham & Blue Lagoon   CAVE
(ຖ້ຳຜຸຄຳແລະຂນບອງບ້ານສິຟ້າ; Ban Na Thong; 10,000K; ⊘ 7.30am-5.30pm) Located west of Vang Vieng, the vast Tham Phu Kham is considered sacred by Lao. The main cave chamber contains a Thai bronze reclining Buddha, and from here deeper galleries branch off into the mountain. It's hugely popular largely due to the lagoon in the cave, but overdevelopment, group tourists and noisy buggies have made it an unpleasant place to swim.

🏃 Activities

Vang Vieng has evolved into Laos' number-one adventure destination, with tubing, kayaking, rafting, mountain biking and world-class rock climbing all available. You can also explore the many caves that pepper the karst limestone peaks, while ziplining is also very popular. And nowadays, the scene also includes noisy four-wheeled buggies.

Tubing

Previously, just about every visitor to Vang Vieng went tubing down the Nam Song in an inflated tractor-tyre tube, although this was less about relaxing and more about getting blasted at loud riverside bars. These days, the bars are gone, and most visitors ride kayaks or longtail boats.

If you want to go old-school, the tubing drop-off point for the original yellow route is 3.5km north of town, and depending on

VIENTIANE, VANG VIENG & AROUND VANG VIENG

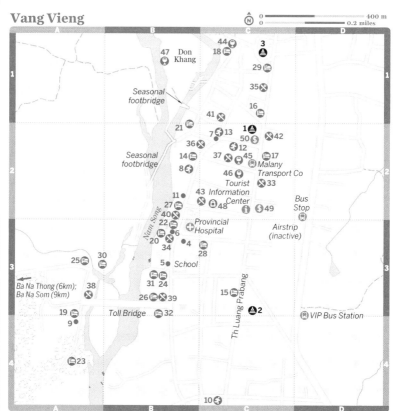

the speed and level of the river it can be a soporific crawl beneath the jungle-vined karsts, or a speedy glide downstream back to Vang Vieng. There is also a newer red tubing route through private land 4km south of town.

The **yellow tubing operators** (⊙9am-8pm) and **red tubing operators** (☑020-99223339; ⊙9am-7pm) have similar hire fees and rules, though the yellow line requires a 20,000K refundable deposit (forfeited if you lose the tube). Life jackets are available and you can rent a dry bag. Tuk-tuk services can run you to the launch points.

Whether tubing or kayaking down the Nam Song, rivers can be dangerous, and in times of high water, rapids along the Nam Song can be quite daunting. Wear a life jacket when tubing, and it's worth asking how long the trip should take (durations vary depending on the time of year) so you can allow plenty of time to get back to

Vang Vieng before dark, as it's pitch black by about 6pm in winter. Finally, don't forget that while tubing the Nam Song might be more fun when you're stoned, it's also more dangerous.

The other thing you should remember is to take something – a sarong, perhaps – to put on when you finish the trip and have to walk through town. The locals don't appreciate people walking around in bikinis or Speedos.

Kayaking

Kayaking has taken over tubing as Vang Vieng's premier water sport, and trips are typically combined with other activities such as visits to caves and villages, optional climbing, cycling, and the traverse of a few rapids (the danger of which depends on the speed of the water). There are loads of operators and prices are about US$15 per

Vang Vieng

person per day. Some of the best kayaking trips along the Nam Song are conducted by the excellent Green Discovery and involve a lot of paddling. Another useful tour operator for kayaking is the well-established VLT (☎020-55208283; www.vangviengtour.com; ⊙8am-10.30pm).

Rock Climbing

The limestone walls around Vang Vieng have gained a reputation for some of the best climbing in Southeast Asia. More than 200 routes have been identified and most have been bolted. The routes are rated between 4a and 8b, with the majority being in or near a cave. The most popular climbing spots are near **Tham Non** (Sleeping Cave), with more than 20 routes, and the tougher **Sleeping Wall** nearby, where some routes have difficult overhangs.

The climbing season usually runs between October and May, with most routes too wet at other times. However, there are some rock-shaded overhangs on Phadeng Mountain that have been bolted down (23 routes), and can still be used in the wet season.

Adam's Rock Climbing School (☎020-56564499; www.vangviengclimbing.com; half-/full-day climbing 180,000/260,000K, 2-day course US$100, private half-day climbing guide from 320,000K; ⊙8am-9pm) offers fully outfitted courses ranging in skill from beginner to advanced. Adam himself is one of the most experienced climbers in the area; his multilingual guides get good reports and equipment rental is also available.

Green Discovery (☎023-511230; www.greendiscoverylaos.com; 1-day cycling tour per person US$28-56, half-/full-day rock climbing US$39/80; ⊙8am-9pm) ⚹ conducts climbing courses (half-/full day from US$30/39), and when available, can provide a handy climbing guide to the area.

Ziplining

It's all about air and cable these days, with the jungles around Vang Vieng criss-crossed with adrenaline-inducing ziplines. The following tour outfits combine a trek, kayak, abseil or tubing session with zipping:

AK Home Tours (☑020-55033665; half-/full day 170,000/200,000K; ☺8.30am-9.30pm)

Namthip Tour (☑020-55623536; ☺7am-9pm)

TCK (☑023-511691; www.tckamazingtours.com; ☺7am-9pm)

Vang Vieng Challenge (☑023-511230; www.greendiscoverylaos.com)

Wonderful Tours (☑023-511566; www.wonderfultourslaos.la; Th Khann Muang; ☺7.30am-9.30pm)

Hot-Air Ballooning & Ultralight Flights

A ride in a hot-air balloon or ultralight is a lovely way to see the cliffs, tapestry of paddy fields and snaking river below. Departures (US$90) are at 5.40am and 4.50pm every day, weather permitting, last 40 minutes, and can be booked at several venues in town.

Other Activities

Beach-buggy tours are popular with South Korean tourists, but these activities sound a lot funkier than they actually are, once you hear the engines roaring through the landscape, disturbing the peace and leaving you chewing the dust.

★ **Blue Lagoon 3**   SWIMMING
(10,000K; ☺8am-6pm) Forget the circus that is the original Blue Lagoon (Tham Phu Kham) and head 14km further west to the Blue Lagoon 3. The azure waters are fed by a natural spring that emerges from a nearby karst limestone peak and it is still relatively quiet compared with its more infamous namesake.

Tubes are available for hire, there is a small zipline into the water, and a basic restaurant. It's usually quiet in the mornings, but can get busier in the afternoons as schoolkids come to cool off.

Vang Vieng Sauna   BATHHOUSE
(25,000K; ☺2-9pm) A family-run, local-style herbal sauna. They provide tea, soap,

bathing clothes and a towel; all you need to bring is yourself and a desire to sweat.

Yoga in Vang Vieng   YOGA
(Silver Naga; per session US$10, 2 sessions US$15; ☺7.30-9am & 5-6.30pm) Daily yoga sessions are available at the Silver Naga hotel with an experienced international yoga instructor. The price is a bit high, but the instructors are some of the best we've had in Laos. You also get free entry to Silver Naga's pool after class!

🛏 Sleeping

Vang Vieng has a relatively broad but not entirely appealing spread of accommodation. In recent years, the cheap guesthouses have been knocked down and replaced by characterless, multistorey midrange places to accommodate package tourists, and there's been an uptick in boutiques along the riverside.

If Vang Vieng town isn't your scene, head out of town for a more serene location.

In Town

Vang Vieng Rock Backpackers Hostel   HOSTEL $
(☑020-52256686; www.facebook.com/Vangvieng rockbackpackershostel; Th Luang Prabang; incl breakfast dm 40,000-60,000K, r 200,000K; ❄☎) The thumping music and flashing disco lights set the tone when you enter this party hostel, which boasts an on-site bar with a pool table and table football. The clean and traveller-friendly rooms have between four and 14 beds (including a female-only dorm), all with private sockets and lights. Avoid the ground-floor dorms if you care about sleeping.

Grand View Guesthouse   GUESTHOUSE $
(☑020-55335599; r 130,000-300,000K; ⊕❄☎) This 22-room property is nestled on the river bank overlooking Don Khang, although a new development means that the eponymous view is a bit of a misnomer. Nonetheless, rooms are spacious and tidy.

Central Backpackers Hostel   HOSTEL $
(☑020-56770677; www.vangviengbackpackers. com; Th Luang Prabang; r with fan/air-con 100,000/150,000K, tr 200,000K; ⊕❄☎) This hostel, with wedding-cake-style architecture, boasts private rooms with fan or air-con and private balcony and TV, and communal balconies to drink up the view of the cliffs.

THE THAM SANG TRIANGLE

A popular half-day trip that's easy to do on your own takes in a few worthwhile caves and swimming holes, all within a short, clearly marked walk. Begin this excursion by riding a motorcycle or taking a jumbo 13km north along Rte 13, turning left a few hundred metres beyond the barely readable Km 169 stone.

A road leads to the river, where you cross a toll bridge (10,000K) and encounter Tham Sang (p171). Continue west to Tham Nam (p171). From here a path takes you about 1km northwest to the entrances of Tham Hoi (p171) and Tham Loup (p171).

Just north of these caves is **Blue Lagoon 4** (5000K; ⊘8am-5pm), yet another spring-fed swimming stop. From there, it's an easy 1km walk back to the bridge. This loop is usually included in the kayaking/trekking/tubing combo trip run by most Vang Vieng tour operators.

There's a huge lobby with a cafe and TV, and safety lockers too (BYO lock). Not much atmosphere but decent value.

Le Jardin Organique HOTEL $
(☏023-511420; r 100,000-150,000K; ❋@☞) This place has spotlessly clean if somewhat characterless rooms with TV, air-con and en suites. Only five of the rooms have sufficient elevation to catch the jawdropping views, so make sure you ask for one.

Army Barracks Guesthouse HOSTEL $
(☏020-76818888; armybarrackshostel@gmail. com; Th Luang Prabang; dm 40,000K; r 130,000-180,000K; ❋☞) The dorms here are, not surprisingly, army themed – militantly minimalist, with camouflage sheets and green footlockers – and are more interesting than the tight, scruffy, private rooms.

Backpacker Chillao HOSTEL $
(☏030-4877186; Th Luang Prabang; dm 35,000K, r 100,000-150,000K; ❋❋@☞❋) With its new pool and ambitious plans to expand, this place is steadily upgrading itself. We hope this growth eventually reaches the dorms and rooms, which, when we visited, felt rather tired. Nonetheless, it draws a steady crowd of travellers.

★**Silver Naga** HOTEL $$
(☏023-511822; www.silvernaga.com; r incl breakfast US$65-180; ❋❋@☞❋) The handsome rooms here feature contemporary decoration and lots of nice touches like private balcony, flat-screen TV and rain shower. Staff are friendly and helpful, there is a 2nd-floor pool with a killer karst view that is open to nonguests for 50,000K, and a cafe was being added on when we were in town.

Vang Vieng Plaza HOTEL $$
(☏030-9260192; www.vangviengplazahotel. com; r incl breakfast US$40-100; ❋☞❋) This new-feeling hotel has one of the most imposing hotel lobbies in Vang Vieng. Like the lobby, the rooms are spacious and tidy, but don't have heaps of character. There's a pool that does a good job matching the aqua blue tile design theme.

Villa Vang Vieng Riverside BOUTIQUE HOTEL $$
(☏023-511460; www.villavangvieng.com; bungalow US$60-80; ❋❋☞❋) A handsome boutique hotel in a charming garden near the toll bridge. The Lao-influenced bungalows are relatively small but well appointed with tasteful furnishings and contemporary bathrooms. The swimming pool is located on the banks of the Nam Song and is open to nonguests for 30,000K per day.

Villa Nam Song GUESTHOUSE $$
(☏023-511015; www.villanamsong.com; r incl breakfast US$40-55; ❋❋☞) With serene views of the cliffs, this fine hotel sits in grounds choking on mango, palm, orchid and bougainvillea. The 16 rooms are fragrant and parquet-floored, with cream walls and high-end furniture, including vast beds. There's also a semi-alfresco restaurant featuring Asian favourites, and a wind-chimed breeze that sweeps through.

Elephant Crossing HOTEL $$
(☏023-511232; www.theelephantcrossinghotel. com; r incl breakfast US$40-50; ❋❋@☞) Elephant Crossing has 36 tight but tasteful rooms with balconies overlooking the river and karst. Hmong bed runners, wood floors, air-con, TV and fridge complete the picture, although a close look reveals that rooms

could use an update in amenities and a lick of paint. A sizable expansion was underway when we were in town.

★ **Riverside Boutique Resort**   BOUTIQUE HOTEL **$$$**
(📞 021-511726; www.riversidevangvieng.com; incl breakfast r US$110-169, ste US$305; 🛏️ 🌀 @ 🛜 🏊) Sugar-white and uberstylish, this beautiful boutique belle offers generously spaced rooms wrapped around a citrus-green pool and a verdant garden looking out onto the karsts. Rooms themselves are gorgeous with balconies, crisp white sheets, and chic decor straight from the pages of *Wallpaper*. It's located by the toll bridge.

★ **Inthira**   BOUTIQUE HOTEL **$$$**
(📞 023-511070; www.inthirahotels.com; incl breakfast r US$98-128, ste US$220; 🛏️ 🌀 @ 🛜 🏊) In new digs on the riverside, the Inthira is hands-down Vang Vieng's most sophisticated hotel. Dark steel, stained woods, terrazzo floors, vast flat-screen TVs and rain showers (and a Jacuzzi in the suites) leave the 38 rooms feeling effortlessly sleek and modern. But we suspect you'll remember the stunning views and the riverside deck and infinity pool.

Amari Vang Vieng   HOTEL **$$$**
(📞 023-511800; www.amari.com; r incl breakfast US$100-120, ste incl breakfast US$200; 🛏️ 🌀 @ 🛜 🏊) With its 60 rooms and five storeys, the new Amari literally looms over Vang Vieng. Service is, not surprisingly, at a high standard, but the rooms, although spacious and boasting amazing views, tend towards the stuffy end of the style spectrum. The vast riverside pool almost makes up for this.

🏠 Around Town

Chez Mango   GUESTHOUSE **$**
(📞 020-54435747; www.chezmango.com; bungalows 80,000-100,000K; 🛜) Located over the bridge, Mango is friendly, scrupulously clean and has seven basic but colourful bungalows (some with bathrooms) with private balconies in its flowery gardens. Shaded by trees, there's also a *sala* (open-sided shelter) to read in. Run by Noé, who also runs the excellent **Vang Vieng Jeep Tour** (noedouine@gmail.com; minimum group of 4, per person 180,000K; ⏰ 9am-4pm) from here, this is a soporific and restful spot.

Maylyn Guest House   GUESTHOUSE **$**
(📞 020-55604095; www.facebook.com/maylyn guesthouse; bungalows 60,000-120,000K, r 100,000-170,000K; 🛏️ 🌀 🛜) Over the bridge and run by gregarious Jo, this expansive, maze-like compound holds a mix of rather weathered but charming rooms and bungalows, both with and without air-con and en suite. The lush garden is a wonderland for kids and the overall vibe is relaxed and quiet.

★ **Champa Lao**   HOTEL **$$**
(📞 020-55428518; www.facebook.com/champa laobungalows; r 80,000K, bungalows 200,000-600,000K; 🌀 🛜) There's a variety of warm, cosy accommodation here, from basic fan rooms with shared bathrooms and mozzie nets in the main structure, to a string of bungalows and even the upper floor of a house. The communal garden, choked with plants, is a highlight and you can swing on a hammock while taking in the sunset and karst from its aerial balcony.

Bearlin Bungalow   BUNGALOW **$$**
(📞 020-58419000; bearlinbungalow@gmail.com; bungalows incl breakfast US$50-60; 🛏️ 🌀 🛜) A small resort set in a spotless garden on the road to the Blue Lagoon. One half of the ownership team is, unsurprisingly, German. There's meticulous attention to detail in the rooms (but no TV or refrigerator) and a menu that includes German dishes like currywurst and pork knuckle.

★ **Vieng Tara Villa**   BOUTIQUE HOTEL **$$$**
(📞 030-5023102; www.viengtara.com; bungalow incl breakfast US$80-100; 🛏️ 🌀 🛜) This boutique resort takes full advantage of its location on the west-bank riverside to deliver some of the most stunning hotel views in Southeast Asia. Choose one of the villa paddy-view rooms, which are set on stilts in the middle of lush rice fields and accessible via a wooden walkway. And even if you're not staying here, stop by for a drink at the elevated cafe.

Kong Resort   HOTEL **$$$**
(📞 020-91111235; www.facebook.com/kongresort pages; r incl breakfast 500,000-1,200,000K; 🌀 🛜 🏊) This rather wacky place blends disused – but attractive – cargo containers and a light military theme. Rooms are comfortable, if a bit cramped, and stylish – some have open-air showers – but sadly don't take

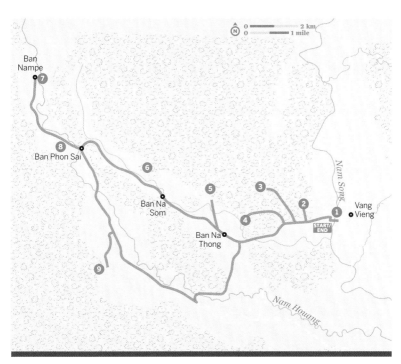

Motorcycle Tour
West Vang Vieng Loop

START MAYLYN GUEST HOUSE
END MAYLYN GUEST HOUSE
LENGTH 26KM; SIX HOURS

To get right into the heart of the limestone karsts near Vang Vieng, consider this loop by mountain bike or motorbike.

Heading west from **1 Maylyn Guest House** you'll see hand-painted signs to various caves. Worth considering is **2 Tham Pha Daeng**. There's a cave pool and the area is the best place to watch the bats stream from their caves every evening. The 2km walk to **3 Tham Khan**, approached via a rocky 1.5km side road, is probably more worthwhile than the long but claustrophobic cave.

At the village of Ban Phone Ngeun, turn right, opposite two basic shops. A road leads to a desk where the locals will collect a fee of 10,000K to take you on the steep 45-minute hike to the top of **4 Pha Ngeun**, a rocky cliff with a few basic observation decks.

Returning to the main road, keep right at the next intersection where you'll pass through the Lao Loum village of Ban Na Thong. After 2km you'll come to another fork and a sign pointing right to **5 Tham Phu Kham** (p171), also known as the Blue Lagoon. The natural pool here used to be a great place to stop for a swim, but it has been overrun with development.

Back on the main track, continue west and you'll soon be in Ban Na Som, a Hmong village. Just beyond Na Som are signs to **6 Golden Flower Cave**, a large cave with a golden hue and impressive stalactites.

Continuing west a beautiful stretch of track hugs the edge of the karsts and eventually comes to Ban Phon Sai. You have a choice now: continue 5km west through more dramatic scenery to **7 Ban Nampe**, a pretty village but nothing more, or soon start heading back east along the southern route. Either way, don't miss the nearby **8 Blue Lagoon 3** (p174), one of the most beautiful swimming spots in the Vang Vieng area, and a clever lunch stop.

About 6km southeast of Ban Phon Sai, signs point across a small bridge to a track to **9 Python Cave**, a long, visit-worthy cavern about 800m away. Once you've seen this, it's plain sailing back to Vang Vieng.

advantage of Vang Vieng's beautiful natural setting. Located on the west side of the Nam Song, via a dirt road.

✕ Eating

Vang Vieng's eating scene is, frankly, pretty dire. Although there are a couple of good local options during breakfast, cookie-cutter Lao/backpacker places dominate, and your best options are, paradoxically, Chinese or Korean.

★Tham Mada   LAO $

(mains 25,000-30,000K; ⊙ 7.30am-3pm & 5-9pm) The name here means 'normal', but there's lots that's unusual about this place. Chief among those is that the Korean owner is doing some of the better Thai-Lao food in town. Opt from a small menu that includes noodle soup, braised pork leg over rice, fried rice, and lighter dishes, all of which are prepared with care and very tasty.

★Breakfast Vendors   LAO $

(Th Luang Prabang; mains 10,000-15,000K; ⊙ 6-9am) A string of breakfast vendors sets up shop every morning serving basic but tasty Lao dishes, from noodles to rice porridge. One of relatively few places in town to get real Lao food.

Sia Po   LAO $

(mains 15,000-40,000K; ⊙ 9am-10pm) To eat with the locals, head to this open-air Lao place. An English-language menu on the wall spans pounded salads, soups and grilled dishes, or you can simply point to whatever looks good on the grill. Don't forget the sticky rice. Located on the main strip across from Vang Vieng's hospital (no roman-script sign).

Cafe Eh Eh   CAFE $

(☑ 030-5074369; breakfast 30,000-40,000K; ⊙ 6am-7pm; ❄ 🛜 🚭) Cafe Eh Eh provides a chilled (we are talking air-con here) retreat from the downtown heat of Vang Vieng, offering a small selection of freshly made cakes and coffee. Breakfast is available, and a limited selection of sandwiches. The message board outside has helpful info on town happenings.

Chantheo   LAO $

(Th Luang Prabang; mains 20,000-30,000K; ⊙ 1-9pm) In the evening, hit the strip of Th Luang Prabang where a vendor grills pork, chicken or duck, all of which are served with

platters of fresh leaves and herbs. One of the few places in Vang Vieng where locals eat.

Veggie Tables   VEGETARIAN $

(Th Luang Prabang; mains 25,000-35,000K; ⊙ 8am-10pm; 🛜 🚭) It's veggie heaven at this simple hole-in-the-wall delight. Think colourful tables, Lao life murals, and a wealth of salads, soups, spring rolls, sandwiches and tofu variations.

★Korean Restaurant   KOREAN $$

(mains 50,000-150,000K; ⊙ noon-10pm; ❄ 🛜 🚭) Initially, we were drawn in by the Bee Gees soundtrack, but were chuffed to discover that this place does some of the better foreign food in town. Let the friendly Korean owner guide you to a dish, which will inevitably be accompanied by *banchan,* an array of tart, spicy, salty and crunchy side dishes.

Chinese Expedition Force Restaurant   CHINESE $$

(mains 30,000-80,000K; ⊙ 10am-11pm) We also want to know the deal behind this restaurant's enigmatic name, but for now, we'll settle for tasty food. Flip through an iPad menu of Chinese standards such as fried vegetable dishes, dumplings, cold appetisers and more, then order up – serving sizes are massive, and the roaring stove in the kitchen and Chinese clientele are testament to this place's authenticity.

Restaurant du Crabe d'Or   INTERNATIONAL $$

(☑ 023-511726; www.riversidevangvieng.com; mains 35,000-150,000K; ⊙ noon-2pm & 6.30-9.30pm; ❄ 🛜 🚭) Set on the tasteful grounds of the Riverside Boutique Resort (p176), Vang Vieng's fanciest restaurant (a relative term) serves Western and Lao dishes, all delivered with panache.

Viman Vang Vieng   THAI, GERMAN $$

(☑ 020-58926695; mains 35,000-120,000K; ⊙ 9am-9pm) Boasts an unlikely combo of Thai and German food, with schnitzel and bratwurst alongside curry and *pad thai* on the lengthy, wandering menu. The Thai chef-owner lived in Germany before relocating to Laos, and the walls of the restaurant are covered in his abstract paintings. He's also a classically trained musician, and may opt to serenade your table.

Pizza Luka   PIZZA $$

(☑ 020-98190831; mains 50,000-70,000K; ⊙ 6-11pm Wed-Mon; 🛜 🚭) Topped with sausage, goat cheese, bacon and many more

THE DEATH OF A PARTY

Back in 1999, Vang Vieng was a little-known affair where travellers came to float on tractor inner tubes down the river, cycle through its stunning karst country and maybe smoke the odd spliff between exploring its fantastical caves. Then the word got out – Vang Vieng was Southeast Asia's next hedonistic mecca – and backpackers were marking it on their party itinerary like a sort of Thailand's Ko Pha Ngan in the mountains, one with countless blasting rave platforms along the formerly bucolic tubing route.

But behind the revelry was a darker truth: by 2011 at least 25 Western visitors (mainly Aussies and Brits) had variously died from heart attacks, drownings and broken necks, having ridden the 'deathslide' (a hastily erected zipline over a seasonally perilously low river). In 2012, after more deaths and under pressure from the Australian government, the Lao government ordered the riverside bars to close.

Since then, with drugs generally off the menu (or at least out of sight), the town has been repositioning itself from party central to the rural village it once was. For the first time in years mainstream tourists are heading to Vang Vieng, many en route to fabled Luang Prabang, stopping to kayak the Nam Song, go caving and climb the karsts. The new fear, it seems, is that the town may soon be overrun by package-tour groups that are, once again, reshaping its ephemeral identity.

ingredients, the OK wood-fired pizzas here are decked in sauces made from locally grown vegetables. Located just across the toll bridge, on the west side of Nam Song.

Drinking & Nightlife

Vang Vieng has ditched all-night parties in favour of a more chilled scene. However, there are still some late-night shenanigans at places like Sakura Bar and the weekly 'Jungle' parties.

★ **Smile Beach Bar**   BAR
(⊙9am-10pm) This mega-chill, riverside bar is a slice of the old Vang Vieng, before the buggies took over. Order a Beerlao (we don't recommend eating here) and swing in a hammock or dip your toes in the river; it's ideal for an afternoon or sunset drink and swim. Reach the bar by crossing the footbridge to Don Khang.

Smile is also the ending point for yellow-route rafting trips along the Nam Song.

★ **Earth**   BAR
(www.facebook.com/earthvangvieng; ⊙2pm-midnight; 🛜) Made from driftwood and clay, this artsy hillside bar-restaurant pipes out fine tunes to match the ambience with live music nightly from 7pm. Check out the sumptuous view of the cliffs from the lamp-lit garden, between munching on potato wedges, burgers and salads (mains 30,000K to 90,000K).

Located at the northern end of town; look for the glowing green sign.

Jungle Project   CLUB
(www.facebook.com/jungleprojectvangvienglao; incl tuk-tuk from town 40,000K; ⊙11pm-late Fri) If you want to recapture the spirit of Va Va Vang Vieng before the clampdown on the town's formerly raucous party scene, the Jungle Project parties are the easiest way to get your flashback. Friday night is the big all-nighter and it takes place at the decrepit Vang Vieng Mai Resort, about 2km north of town.

Sakura Bar   BAR
(☎020-78008555; ⊙7pm-midnight) At the time of writing, Sakura was one of the most popular bars in Vang Vieng with the largest crowds and loudest music. Expect a raucous night with shot promotions (from 8pm to 9pm and after midnight) and lots of dancing.

Gary's Irish Bar   IRISH PUB
(☎020-56115644; www.facebook.com/GarysIrishBar; ⊙9am-11.30pm; 🛜) Still one of the best bars in town thanks to its friendly, unpretentious atmosphere, live music (Mondays, Wednesdays and Fridays from 9pm), free pool and cheap grub like homemade pies, burgers and Lao fare (mains 39,000K to 49,000K). The staff are extremely knowledgeable about the area.

VIENTIANE, VANG VIENG & AROUND VANG VIENG

Heartbeat Pub CLUB

(☎020-55113366; ⏲6pm-late; 🛜) For a night out with more of a Lao flavour, head to this big beer garden and nightclub about 2km north of town. This is where the visiting weekenders from Vientiane end up for fun and frolics, and it often hosts live bands from the capital.

🛍 Shopping

Walking Street Market MARKET

(⏲6-10pm) Every evening, the street across from the Silver Naga hotel is filled with vendors selling the usual backpacker commodities.

ℹ Information

DANGERS & ANNOYANCES

Most visitors leave Vang Vieng with nothing more serious than a hangover, but this tranquil setting is also the most dangerous place in Laos for travellers. Visitors die every year from river accidents and while caving. Theft can also be a problem, with fellow travellers often the culprits. Take the usual precautions and don't leave valuables outside caves.

Drugs have been a problem in the past here, but since a government-led crackdown in 2012, they are not so widespread. But dope is still around and local police are particularly adept at sniffing out spliffs, especially late at night. If you're caught with a stash of marijuana (or anything else), the normal practice is for police to take your passport and fine you 5 million kip or more than US$600. Don't expect a receipt, and don't bother calling your embassy.

MEDICAL SERVICES

Vang Vieng's modest **Provincial Hospital** (☎023-511019) has X-ray facilities and is fine for broken bones, cuts and malaria. However, if it is more serious, you will need to get to Vientiane or Thailand.

MONEY

Agricultural Promotion Bank (Th Luang Prabang; ⏲8.30am-3.30pm) Exchanges cash, plus has an ATM.

BCEL (Th Khann Muang; ⏲8.30am-3.30pm) Exchanges cash and handles cash advances on Visa, MasterCard and JCB; also has ATMs around town.

TOURIST INFORMATION

Tourist Information Center (☎023-511707; Th Luang Prabang; ⏲8.30-11.30am & 2-4pm Mon-Fri) A useful port of call to pick up various leaflets on things to do in the area.

ℹ Getting There & Away

There are two bus stations in Vang Vieng linking the town with a handful of large cities in Laos and destinations in Cambodia, Thailand and Vietnam.

BUSES FROM VANG VIENG'S VIP BUS STATION

DESTINATION	COST (K)	DURATION (HR)	DEPARTURES
Bangkok (Thailand; bus)	270,000	17	9am & 1.30am
Chiang Mai (Thailand; bus)	350,000	17	9am & 10am
Danang (Vietnam; bus)	240,000	32	10am
Hanoi (Vietnam; bus)	220,000	28	10am
Hue (Vietnam; bus)	220,000	22	10am
Nong Khai (Thailand; bus)	90,000	5	9am
Pakse (bus)	180,000	16	1.30am
Phnom Penh (Cambodia; bus)	440,000	32	1.30am
Si Phan Don (Four Thousand Islands; bus)	240,000	20	1.30am
Siem Reap (Cambodia; bus)	440,000	36	1.30am
Tha Khaek (bus)	180,000	10	1.30am
Udon Thani (Thailand; bus)	90,000	7	9am
Vientiane (minibus)	40,000	4	10am & 1.30pm
Vientiane (bus)	40,000	4	9am & 1.30pm
Vinh (Vietnam; bus)	220,000	20	10am

BUSES FROM VANG VIENG'S NORTH BUS STATION

DESTINATION	COST (K)	DURATION (HR)	DEPARTURES
Luang Prabang (minibus)	100,000	6	9am & 2pm
Luang Prabang (bus)	90,000	7	10am
Vientiane (fan)	40,000	5	5.30am, 6am, 6.30am, 7am, 12.30pm, 2pm
Vientiane (minibus)	60,000	3-4	9am
Vientiane (bus)	50,000	3-4	10.30am & 1.30pm
Vientiane (sǒrngtǎaou)	40,000	5	frequent 7.20am-4.30pm

NORTH BUS STATION

Buses, minibuses and sǒrngtǎaou bound for Luang Prabang and Vientiane depart from the **North Bus Station** (Rte 13) about 2km north of town, although if you're coming in from Vientiane you'll most likely be dropped off at the **bus stop** (Rte 13) near the former runway, a short walk from the centre of town.

VIP BUS STATION

Departures to destinations further abroad, both in Laos (including Vientiane) and in neighbouring countries, depart from the **VIP Bus Station** (Rte 13), located just east of the town centre. Tickets can be purchased in town at **Malany Transport Co** (☒ 023-511633; Th Luang Prabang; ⊙ 8am-8pm).

Note that, for distant destinations in Laos, there's a change of bus in Vientiane; buses to Bangkok and Chiang Mai also require a change at Nong Khai.

ⓘ Getting Around

'Downtown' Vang Vieng is easily negotiated on foot. Renting a bicycle (15,000K per day) or mountain bike (30,000K per day) is also popular; they're available almost everywhere. Most of the same places also rent motorcycles from about 50,000K per day (automatics cost 80,000K). For cave sites out of town you can charter sǒrngtǎaou by the old market area near the footbridge to Don Khang: expect to pay around US$10 per trip up to 20km north or south of town.

Central Laos

Best Places to Eat

➡ Ping Kai Napong (p192)

➡ No Name Grill Place (p200)

➡ Café Chez Boune (p202)

➡ Phosy Tha Lang Restaurant (p196)

➡ Khao Sen Piak Pa Se (p192)

Best Places to Stay

➡ Spring River Resort (p187)

➡ Vivanouk Homestay (p200)

➡ Hostel Savan Cafe (p199)

➡ Sanhak Guesthouse (p191)

➡ Dongsay Hotel (p192)

Why Go?

Ever since Tha Khaek opened its French-colonial shutters to travellers and the dramatic 7km-long underworld of Tham Kong Lor became a must-see fixture on itineraries, central Laos has been enticing visitors. Thanks to its honeycomb of caves and dragon-green jungle, activities on offer run from world-class rock climbing outside of Tha Khaek to trekking in the other-worldly karst forests of Hin Namno NPA.

This part of the country claims the most forest cover and highest concentrations of wildlife, including some species that have disappeared elsewhere in Southeast Asia. With its rugged, intrepid travel, and stylish pockets of comfort in Savannakhet and Tha Khaek, central Laos makes for a great place to combine your inner Indiana Jones with a Bloody Mary.

When to Go
Savannakhet

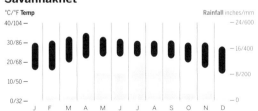

Nov–Feb The best time to visit: temperatures are balmy, paddy fields green and roads passable.

Mar–May Leading up to the monsoon, fields are bone dry and the humidity ratchets up. Avoid the south.

Jun–Nov Despite pockets of intense rain, sealed roads are still passable and the air is cool.

BOLIKHAMSAI & KHAMMUAN PROVINCES

Bolikhamsai and Khammuan straddle the narrow, central 'waist' of the country. Physically the land climbs steadily from the Mekong River valley towards the north and east, eventually reaching the Annamite Chain bordering Vietnam, via an area of moderately high but often spectacular mountains. Laid-back Tha Khaek is the logical base.

Lowland Lao dominate the population and, along with smaller groups of tribal Thais, are the people you'll mostly meet. In remoter areas the Mon-Khmer-speaking Makong people (commonly known as Bru) make up more than 10% of the population of Khammuan.

Much of the region is relatively sparsely populated and five large tracts of forest have been declared National Protected Areas (NPAs) and one a national park. These areas have become a major battleground between those wishing to exploit Laos' hydroelectricity capacity and those wishing to preserve the natural environment. They also represent an opportunity for visitors to witness some of the more pristine wilderness in mainland Southeast Asia.

Phu Hin Bun NPA & Tham Kong Lor

Phu Hin Bun NPA (ປ່າສະຫງວນແຫ່ງຊາດພູຫີນບູນ) is a huge (1580-sq-km) wilderness area of turquoise streams, monsoon forests and striking karst topography across central Khammuan. It was made a protected area in 1993 and it's no overstatement to say this is some of the most breathtaking country in the region. Exploring the NPA on foot or by boat, it's hard not to feel awestruck by the very scale of the limestone cliffs that rise almost vertically for hundreds of metres into the sky. Arguably the highlight of the NPA is Tham Kong Lor, a 7.5km river passing through the cathedral-high limestone cave.

Ban Kong Lor (Kong Lor Village) is the most convenient base for visiting the cave and has seen an explosion of guesthouses and small resorts in the last few years.

◉ Sights & Activities

At Tham Kong Lor, the ticket office doubles as an informal information centre for the cave and the surrounding area. Beyond visiting the river cave, other activities available

include short treks in the scenic countryside around Ban Kong Lor or bicycle rides to soak up the scenery. The website http://konglor-natane-cave.com/en has details about outdoor pursuits in the area.

On the Ban Natane side of the cave, bikes can be hired from 20,000K for two hours to 40,000K for a full day, and there's a (relatively) well-marked route through the countryside that takes about 1½ hours to complete.

To the north of Phu Hin Bun NPA, ecotour operator Green Discovery (p192) was at the time of research constructing an ambitious zipline and canopy walk near the **Limestone Forest Viewpoint** (ຈຸດຊົມວິວປ່າຫີນປູນ; Rte 8); check in with its website or office in Tha Khaek for details.

Khoun Kong Leng   LAKE

(ຂຸນກອງແລງ; 5000K) Nestled amid the limestone karsts of the Phu Hin Bun NPA is Evening Gong Lake. The luminescent green waters spring from a subterranean river that filters through the limestone, making the water crystal clear. Unfortunately, in recent years, development has spoiled some of the natural vibe here. It's about 50km northeast of Tha Khaek.

You must ask at the village before swimming in the lake. Once you get approval, only swim in the stream that flows from the lake, near the wooden footbridge, and not in the lake itself. Fishing is banned.

To get here from Tha Khaek, head north along Rte 13 and turn right (east) at Km 29 onto a dirt road. After 2km, turn right (south) again, and bump up over hills and through villages for 16km until you reach Ban Na Kheu. It's another 1km to the lake.

★ Tham Kong Lor   CAVING, BOATING

(ຖ້ຳກອງລໍ; cave entrance & boat trip 65,000K, parking fee 10,000K; ⊙8am-4pm) A boat trip through the other-worldly Tham Kong Lor is an absolute must. The 7.5km river cave, situated in the wilderness of Phu Hin Bun NPA, runs through an immense limestone mountain. Your imagination will be in overdrive as the boat takes you further into the bat-black darkness and the fear dial will ratchet up as if on some natural Gothic ghost ride.

A section of Kong Lor has now been atmospherically lit, allowing you a greater glimpse of this epic spectacle; your longtail docks in a rocky inlet to allow you to explore a stalactite wood of haunting pillars and sprouting stalagmites like an abandoned *Star Trek* set.

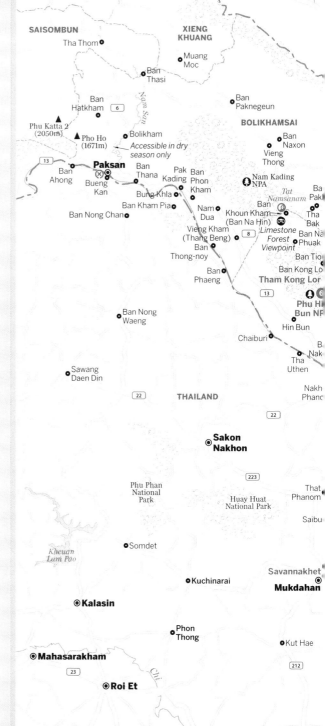

Central Laos Highlights

1 Tham Kong Lor (p183) Going underground to experience a boat trip through this incredible 7km-long limestone underworld.

2 Hin Namno NPA (p194) Exploring one of the most rugged and beautiful protected areas in the region.

3 The Loop (p190) Riding and journeying on winding roads through flooded valleys, dense jungle and jagged mountain peaks.

4 Savannakhet (p197) Soaking up the old-world atmosphere of this riverside town's colonial-era architecture.

5 Dong Phu Vieng NPA (p204) Staying in the remote villages and experiencing life in the spirit forests.

6 Phu Hin Bun NPA (p183) Trekking amid gothic limestone karsts, subterranean caves and meandering rivers.

7 Tha Khaek (p188) Charming colonial-era vibe and a superlative base for fun day trips.

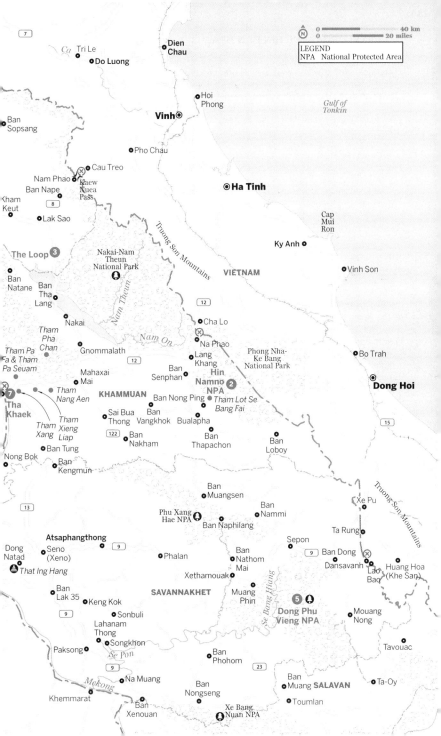

ⓘ EXPLORING PHU HIN BUN NPA

A trip out to Tham Kong Lor will give you a taste of what the NPA has to offer, but there are two more immersive ways to go deeper into this area of almost mythical Gothic peaks and snaking streams.

Khammuan Province runs five different community-based treks of varying lengths. From Tha Khaek, the popular two-day trip ($220 for two people) into the Phu Hin Bun NPA is especially good. The route includes plenty of karst scenery, a walk through Tham Pa Chan and overnight accommodation in an ethnic village. Bookings can be made through the Tourist Information Centre (p193) in Tha Khaek.

Green Discovery (p192) offers similar treks, including a very tempting three-day kayaking and cycling trip between spectacularly sheer cliffs, as the Nam Hin Bun (Hin Bun River) follows a large anticlockwise arc towards the Mekong.

Although much of Phu Hin Bun NPA is inaccessible by road, populations of key forest-dependent species have been reduced through local hunting and logging activities. Despite this, the NPA remains home to several species of primates, as well as elephants and a variety of rare species of deer. Your best chance of spotting wildlife is on a guided trek.

Boat trips through Tham Kong Lor take up to an hour each way, and in dry season when the river is low, you'll have to get out while the boatman and point man haul the wooden craft up rapids. At the other end of the cave, a brief five minutes upstream takes you to a refreshment stop. Catch your breath and then head back in for more adrenaline-fuelled excitement.

Life jackets are provided. Be sure to bring a torch (flashlight) as the ones for rent are inadequate, and wear rubber sandals; the gravel in the riverbed is sharp and it's often necessary to disembark and wade at several shallow points.

Tham Nam None   CAVING

(ຖ້ຳນ້ຳນອນ; per person 120,000K) Only recently discovered, Tham Nam None has not yet been fully explored. At 15km, it is one of the longest river caves in Laos, and it's possible to trek into the cave in the dry season. Don't venture into this cave alone; contact Spring River Resort to set up a trip and take plenty of torches and batteries.

⌂ Tours

Khammuan Province's Tourist Information Centre (p193) in Tha Khaek offers day trips to Tham Kong Lor (per person for a group of one/two/six 1,500,000/850,000/550,000K); speak to the ever-proficient Mr Somkiad. Green Discovery (p192) also runs one-day trips to Tham Kong Lor from US$70 per person and overnight trips from US$155 per person.

⌗ Sleeping & Eating

The main centre for accommodation in the greater area is Ban Kong Lor, with options ranging from homestays to one of the region's best hotels. If you're doing the Loop (p190), guesthouses and hotels can be found in Ban Khoun Kham (Ban Na Hin) and Lak Sao.

The restaurant scene in Ban Kong Lor is not the most sophisticated in central Laos, so many visitors end up eating at their guesthouse, though there is a handful of tourist-oriented restaurants.

Homestay – Ban Natane   HOMESTAY $

(☏ 030-5099071; Ban Natane; per person incl dinner & breakfast 50,000K) Homestay accommodation is available at the opposite end of Tham Kong Lor, in Ban Natane. The village is within walking distance of the drink stalls where the boats terminate, a 2km walk along the left fork. The drink vendors are more than happy to point you in the right direction. Unfortunately, you'll get charged a second time when you return through the cave.

Thongdam Guesthouse   GUESTHOUSE $

(☏ 020-5570999; Ban Kong Lor; r 60,000K, bungalow 80,000K) This compound includes a strip of concrete rooms and a row of elevated wood bungalows. The latter have more space and natural light, and balconies that look over the rice fields and karst.

Homestay – Ban Kong Lor   HOMESTAY $

(☏ 020-97015340; Ban Kong Lor; per person incl dinner & breakfast 50,000K) If you want a cultural experience, check in at the ticket booth for Tham Kong Lor for details on Ban Kong Lor's homestay program.

Chantha House GUESTHOUSE $
(📱 020-22100002; chanthahouse@hotmail.com; Ban Kong Lor; dm 35,000K, r 50,000-130,000K; ❄🛜) This Swiss-style accommodation on the main road to Kong Lor, at the start of the village, has 15 plain but well-kept rooms plus a dorm. The owners are friendly and, best of all, there are magnificent views of the cliffs.

⭐**Spring River Resort** BUNGALOW $$
(📱 020-59636111; www.springriverresort.com; Ban Tiou; bungalows US$20-45; ⊙closed Jun & Jul; P🛜) These stilted bungalows sit in an immaculately landscaped, jungle-like garden at the edge of Nam Hin Bun. The more expensive rooms have en suite bathrooms, considerably more space and private balconies to enjoy the lush river view. Easily the most charming place to stay in the region. The attached riverside restaurant (mains 35,000K to 50,000K) has a memorable setting and tasty food.

There's a clear-water creek nearby to cool off in, and you can hire kayaks.

ℹ️ Getting There & Away

The larger towns and villages in this region are connected by good-quality roads, and there are links with Vietnam, though some of the more rural roads are very poor and impassable during the rainy season.

If you're headed directly to Tham Kong Lor, from Talat Phetnamy in Tha Khaek, very slow *sŏrngtăaou* (pick-up trucks fitted with benches in the back for passengers) depart for Ban Kong Lor at 7am, 2.30pm and 3.30pm (75,000K, four hours). There's also now a direct daily bus between Vientiane and Ban Kong Lor (70,000K, seven hours), which departs at 9am or from the Southern Bus Station in the capital at 10am.

The 40km road from Ban Khoun Kham (Ban Na Hin) to Ban Kong Lor runs a largely straight path through a beautiful valley of rice fields hemmed

BORDER CROSSINGS

Getting to Vietnam: Nam Phao to Cau Treo

Getting to the border The Nam Phao (Laos)/Cau Treo (Vietnam) border crossing (7am to 7pm) is at the Kaew Neua Pass, 36km from Lak Sao. Semi-regular buses run between Lak Sao and Vinh, in Vietnam, between 10am and 2pm (150,000K). There is an exchange booth on the Lao side, though the rates aren't generous.

Coming back from Vinh in Vietnam, buses to Tay Song (formerly Trung Tam) leave regularly throughout the day (70,000d, two hours, 70km). From Tay Song, it's another 25km through some richly forested country to the border. It should cost about 170,000d (US$7.50) by motorbike or taxi, but drivers will demand several times that. Expect to be ripped off on this route.

At the border Check with a Vietnamese embassy or consulate as to whether you require a visa or not, as some Asian and European countries do not need a visa for short stays, but the majority of passport holders do. Laos issues 30-day visas at the border.

Moving on Inconveniently, the Vietnam border post is 1km up the road from the Lao border post, and once you pass this, you'll be swarmed by guys offering onward transport to Vinh. Contrary to their claims, a minibus to Vinh doesn't cost US$30 per person; about US$5 for a seat is more reasonable, though you'll do very well to get that price. A metered taxi costs about US$50, while a motorbike fare is about 320,000d. Hook up with as many other people as possible to improve your bargaining position.

Getting to Thailand: Paksan to Beung Kan

Getting to the border Few travellers use the Paksan (Laos)/Beung Kan (Thailand) border crossing (7am to 6pm) via the Mekong River. The boat (15,000K, 20 minutes) leaves when eight people show up.

At the border If you turn up at the Lao immigration office, they should process the paperwork without too much fuss, though it is very important to note that Lao visas are not available on arrival.

Moving on In Thailand buses leave Beung Kan for Udon Thani (250B, four hours), where there are onward connections to Bangkok via budget airlines or long-distance bus.

in on either side by towering karst cliffs. It's an easy one-hour motorbike or *sŏrngtăaou* ride. From Ban Kong Lor, *sŏrngtăaou* to Ban Khoun Kham (Ban Na Hin; 25,000K) depart at 10am, 1pm and 3pm.

Tha Khaek   ທ່າແຂກ

♫ 051 / POP 38,000

This ex-Indochinese trading post is a delightful melange of crumbling French villas and warped, Chinese merchants' shopfronts, with an easy riverside charm which, despite the bridge over to nearby Thailand, shows few signs of change. It's from here that you begin 'The Loop (p190)', a three-day motorbike journey through shape-shifting landscapes, and you can also use Tha Khaek as a base from which to make organised day trips to Tham Kong Lor. There are more than a dozen other caves nearby, some with swimmable lagoons, that can be accessed by scooter or tuk-tuk.

◉ Sights & Activities

Tha Khaek traces its present-day roots to French-colonial construction in 1911 and 1912 when it was a port, border post and administrative centre. Evidence of this period can be found in the slowly decaying buildings around Fountain Sq.

Most of the activities take place in the karst countryside around Tha Khaek, including clambering the karst at Green Climbers Home (p190) or exploring the many caves that pepper the jagged mountains. A day

trip to multiple caves with the Tourist Information Centre (p193) costs from 350,000K per person (for a group of six or more).

When it comes to Tha Khaek town, other than wandering the streets and soaking up the atmosphere, there's not a lot to keep you occupied. If you're looking for something (slightly) more active, then head to **Namfon Petang Field** (♫ 020-56124455; ⊙ 4-10pm) for a game of boules and a Beerlao.

Tham Pa Seuam   CAVE

(ຖ້ຳປາເຊືອມ; entry 5000K, parking 3000K) A mini Tham Kong Lor, the river cave of Tham Pa Seuam runs for 3km, spanning some impressive stalactites and stalagmites. It's conveniently only 15km from Tha Khaek. A day trip to multiple caves, including Tham Pa Seuam, with the Tourist Information Centre costs from 350,000K per person (for a group of six or more) and includes a 400m boat ride into the main chamber.

Tham Pha Chan   CAVE

(ຖ້ຳພະໄມ້ຈັນທ່ອມ, Sandalwood Buddha Cave) **FREE** Tham Pha Chan has an entrance 60m high and about 100m wide. A stream runs about 600m through a limestone karst and in the dry season it's possible to walk to the far side. At its western end there is a sandalwood Buddha image about 15m above the ground, hence the cave's name.

Not far from Tham Pha Chan is the **Nam Don Resurgence** (ຂຸນນ້ຳໂດນ), a cave where the Nam Don (Don River) emerges from the ground. It's quite a physical

DEADWOOD: ILLEGAL LOGGING IN LAOS

Laos has some of the largest remnant tracts of primary rainforest in mainland Southeast Asia. With China, Thailand and Vietnam having implemented stricter regulations to protect their own forests, Laos remains a vulnerable target for timber exploitation. The Environmental Investigation Agency (EIA) claims that the furniture industry in Vietnam has grown tenfold since 2000, with Laos facilitating the flow of its timber to enable this. An estimated 500,000 cu metres of logs find their way over the border every year. While an outwardly hard-line approach has been taken against mass logging by the government, it's the self-funded military and local officials in remote areas who can fall prey to bribes.

Forest cover fell from 70% in the 1940s to around 40% by 2010, with an annual rate of nearly 100,000 hectares disappearing every year. National Protected Areas (NPAs), which are supposed to be protected under Lao law, are prey to heavy illegal logging as they contain so much commercially valuable timber. While the valuable forest continues to disappear, the government is attempting a countrywide replantation program, but these are usually commercial timbers and not rare rainforest hardwoods. In a promising development, Lao Prime Minister Thongloun Sisoulith announced a complete logging ban in Laos, effective from 1 June 2016. Yet in the two years since this ban, exports of finished wood products from Laos have, rather paradoxically, doubled, although the government claims that the raw material comes from plantation trees rather than natural forests.

Tha Khaek

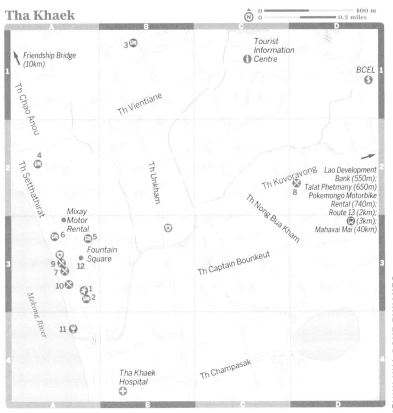

Tha Khaek

Activities, Courses & Tours
Green Discovery...........................(see 5)
1 Namfon Petang Field............................A3

Sleeping
2 Bike & Bed Hostel................................A3
3 Dongsay Hotel.......................................B1
4 Hotel Riveria...A2
5 Inthira Hotel..A3
6 Le Bouton d'Or......................................A3

Eating
7 Grilled Duck Restaurants.....................A3
8 Khao Sen Piak Pa Se...........................D2
9 Local Food Place...................................A3
10 Ping Kai Napong...................................A3

Drinking & Nightlife
11 Sabaidee Thakhek Restaurant...........A4

Transport
Mad Monkey Motorbike.............(see 12)
12 Wangwang Motor Rental.....................A3

marvel to see the water coming up and out from the cave, and the lagoon that sits at the bottom of the tall limestone karst is a beautiful swimming spot.

Unfortunately, both are accessed via a rough road that runs 20km from the junction with Rte 13. Go by motorbike, tuk-tuk or arrange an English-speaking guide through Tha Khaek's Tourist Information Centre.

Tham Xieng Liap   CAVE
(ຖໍ້າຊຽງລຽບ) **FREE** Turning off Rte 12 at Km 14 (before a bridge) you'll come across a sign pointing to this cave. Follow the dirt track south for about 400m near the village of Ban Songkhone (about 10.5km from Rte 13), to the stunning limestone cave Tham Xieng Liap, the entrance of which is at the base of a dramatic 300m-high cliff.

The cave is about 200m long and, in the dry season, you can walk/wade through and swim in the picturesque valley on the far side. *Paa faa* (soft-shelled turtles) live in the cave, while the cliffs outside are said to be home to the recently discovered *kan yoo* (Laotian rock rat). In the wet season you'll need to rent a boat (30,000K) from the Xieng Liap bridge.

Tham Pa Fa   CAVE
(Buddha Cave; entry 5000K, parking 3000K; ☉8am-noon & 1-5pm) When Mr Bun Nong used a vine to scramble up a sheer 200m-high cliff in 2004, he discovered a narrow cave mouth and was greeted by 229 bronze Buddha images. The Buddhas, ranging from 15cm to about 1m tall, were sitting as they had been for centuries facing the entrance of a cave of impressive limestone formations. Today, lights and other development have left the cave looking undoubtedly much different than when Mr Bun Nong found it.

No photographs are allowed inside the cave, but it is an atmospheric spot tended by local ascetics. It's 14km from Tha Khaek; a tuk-tuk costs 100,000K.

Tham Xang   CAVE
(ຖ້ຳຊ້າງ, Elephant Cave; 5000K) Famous for its stalagmite 'elephant head', which is found along a small passage behind the large golden Buddha, this is one of the closest caves to Tha Khaek (it's about 4km away). Bring a torch.

👉 Tours

The Tourist Information Centre (p193) runs tours in the area. Trek prices vary depending on group size, so it's worth calling reliable Mr Somkiad who runs the centre to coordinate with other travellers. As an example, a two-day trek in the Phu Hin Bun NPA for a group of four will cost a reasonable 750,000K per person. These treks typically involve a homestay. Also ask about day trips to multiple caves, including Tham Pa Seuam (p188).

Green Climbers Home   CLIMBING
(☎020-56105622; www.greenclimbershome.com; Ban Kouanphavang; courses per person 140,000-700,000K; ☉Oct-May) This efficiently run training school set in a valley in soaring karst country 18km from Tha Khaek is hugely popular, and often booked up thanks to its cosy cabanas, great food and excellent courses. It also boasts one of the easiest overhangs in the world to learn on and has beginner-, intermediate- and expert-level climbs, with more than 320 routes from class 4 to 8C.

🏃 Motorcycle Tour 'The Loop'

START THA KHAEK
END THA KHAEK
LENGTH 450KM/4-6 DAYS

The Loop, a circuit through Khammuan and Bolikhamsai Provinces – ideally including a side trip to Tham Kong Lor and perhaps even a trek in Nakai–Nam Theun National Park – has achieved mythic status with intrepid travellers. In Tha Khaek, the Tourist Information Centre can provide advice on the circuit, and DC at Mad Monkey Motorbike is a great source of information on lesser-known side trips and sights (and hires out reliable motorcycles).

It's possible to make the trip by public transport these days, but it's best done on a motorbike. Thankfully, there are now several companies in Tha Khaek hiring out motorcycles and scooters. Although you don't need a dirt bike to reach any of the places mentioned here, we recommend having some motorcycle experience; the road, although generally in good condition, is very windy and hilly in parts, and less-experienced riders have been injured or killed along the Loop.

Once you've got your wheels in ❶ **Tha Khaek** (p188), and assuming you have already spent a day heading east on Rte 12 visiting the caves and swimming spots along the way, then set out early enough to allow stops for photos, food and petrol.

North of Gnommalath, 60km from Tha Khaek, where there's petrol and basic food, you'll reach Nam Theun 2 Power Station, and its PR face, the ❷ **Nam Theun 2 Visitors Centre** (ສູນບໍລິຫານອ່າງນ້ຳເທີນສອງ; ☎020-22213855; www.namtheun2.com; ☉8.30am-noon & 1-5pm Mon-Sat) FREE. The next 23km is a disorienting corridor of pristine jungle on your left and the environmental disaster zone created by the flooding of the Nam Theun 2 Dam on the right.

Just before the road crosses the Nam Theun (Theun River) via a new bridge, you'll arrive in tiny ❸ **Ban Tha Lang** (p195), 100km from Tha Khaek, and your first overnight stop. Sabaidee Guesthouse is a decent place to stay, and Phosy Tha Lang Restaurant is probably the best place to eat along the Loop. Ban Tha Lang is also

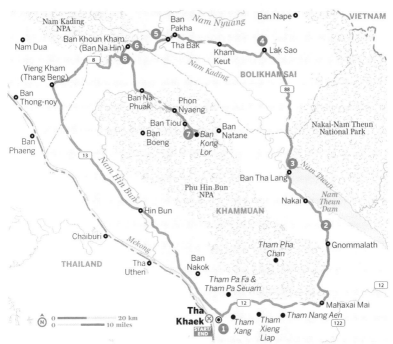

Nam Kading NPA

Ban Pakha

Nam Nyuang

Ban Nape

Nam Dua

Ban Khoun Kham (Ban Na Hin)

Tha Bak

Kham Keut

Lak Sao

Vieng Kham (Thang Beng)

8

Nam Kading

BOLIKHAMSAI

Ban Thong-noy

Ban Na Phuak

Phon Nyaeng

88

Ban Tiou

Ban Boeng

Ban Kong Lor

Ban Natane

Nakai-Nam Theun National Park

Ban Phaeng

13

Nam Hin Bun

Ban Tha Lang

Nam Theun

Nakai

Nam Theun Dam

Phu Hin Bun NPA

KHAMMUAN

Hin Bun

Chaiburi

Mekong

THAILAND

Tha Uthen

Ban Nakok

Tham Pha Chan

Gnommalath

Tham Pa Fa & Tham Pa Seuam

12

Tha Khaek

START END

1

Tham Xang

Tham Xieng Liap

Tham Nang Aen

Mahaxai Mai

12

122

N

0 — 20 km
0 — 10 miles

the jumping-off point for Nakai–Nam Theun National Park, and Sabaidee Guesthouse can arrange excursions into this impressive and recently opened protected area.

Continuing over the bridge at Ban Tha Lang, it's about 50km to Lak Sao. This stretch is stunning as you drive through the corridor between the Nakai–Nam Theun National Park and Phu Hin Bun NPA. But drive carefully; although the road is surfaced, there are lots of tight switchbacks. Take it slowly and drink up the view as you weave through another-worldly flooded valley, with its eternity of oddly angled dead trees sticking out of the water and not a soul in sight. After 17km keep straight at the junction (the left fork will take you to the Nam Theun 2 Dam site). In the dry season this stretch takes between one and two hours, depending on the number of photo stops you take.

When you finally hit ④ **Lak Sao**, there is plenty of accommodation (Phoutthavong Guest House will do in a pinch) and food, and it's also a good place if you need bike repairs. But we recommend approaching the rather dull, dusty town as a lunch stop, and continuing another 55km along Rte 8, stopping to stretch your legs at Tha Bak, where it's worth

looking at the so-called ⑤ **bomb boats** (ທ່າບັກເຮືອທີ່ເຮັດດ້ວຍຊາກລູກລະເບີດ), before proceeding to your next overnight stop, **Ban Khoun Kham** (Ban Na Hin), home to the excellent ⑥ **Sanhak Guesthouse** (☑ 020-55858159; sanhak.guesthouse@gmail.com; Ban Khoun Kham (Ban Na Hin); dm 30,000-40,000K, r 60,000-100,000K; ✿ ❋ ☏).

From a turn-off just west of Ban Khoun Kham, it's an 80km round-trip off the main loop route to Ban Kong Lor, your base for ⑦ **Tham Kong Lor** (p183), the cave that is one of the region's main attractions. The drive, an almost entirely straight shot walled by dramatic, towering karst cliffs and expansive green rice fields, is worth the trip alone.

After returning to Ban Khoun Kham, to complete the full loop would involve continuing an additional 40km west on Rte 8 then south along Rte 13 to Tha Khaek, a distance of about 150km, but honestly, the latter two thirds of this stretch aren't so scenic. If you've got the time, we'd suggest going as far west as the ⑧ **Limestone Forest Viewpoint** (p183), checking out the other-worldly view, then circling back the way you came. Because, you know, it's not only about the destination.

To get here, a tuk-tuk by day costs 100,000K. For serious climbers, **accommodation** here includes dorms (55,000K) and bungalows (from 160,000K) with hot-water showers.

Green Discovery
ADVENTURE SPORTS

(📞 051-251390; www.greendiscoverylaos.com; Inthira Hotel, Th Chao Anou; ⊙ 8am-9.30pm) Green Discovery is the country's most experienced ecotourism outfit and runs a number of interesting trips around central Laos. A range of treks and kayaking excursions in the lush Phu Hin Bun NPA are available, including Tham Kong Lor (from US$70 for a day trip to US$155 for an overnight trip). Also arranges cycling and kayaking.

This branch of Green Discovery is also the logical place to organise a trip to Hin Namno NPA.

🛏 Sleeping

Tha Khaek has a decent spread of accommodation, including a couple of worthwhile midrange options.

Bike & Bed Hostel
HOSTEL $

(📞 020-91710957; dm 55,000K; ❄ 🛜) Housed in a handsome villa, the dorms here range from four to six beds. The beds themselves are pretty standard; the real reasons to stay are the homey vibe and the communal garden where you'll want to flop down with a cool drink and a book.

Dongsay Hotel
HOTEL $$

(📞 020-56785683; r incl breakfast 190,000-386,000K; ❄ 🛜) Spacious, new-feeling rooms in a four-storey building. Perks such as friendly service, free bus station/border pick-up and one of the only hotel lifts in Tha Khaek make this one of the better midrange options in town.

Le Bouton d'Or
BOUTIQUE HOTEL $$

(📞 051-250678; boutondor-tk@hotmail.com; 89 Th Setthathirat; r incl breakfast US$45-70; ❄ @ 🛜) A somewhat over-the-top retro-renaissance hotel on the river with smart, well-finished rooms. French in accent, the riverfront rooms with balcony are a worthwhile investment. There's also a riverside restaurant where guests can enjoy breakfast.

Inthira Hotel
BOUTIQUE HOTEL $$

(📞 051-251237; www.inthira.com; Th Chao Anou; incl breakfast r US$26-36, ste US$45; ➡ ❄ @ 🛜) Set in an old French villa with a pretty facade, Inthira offers the most romantic,

stylish digs in town. That said, some of the rooms have odd and sometimes inconvenient design features, and all could use a new coat of paint.

Hotel Riveria
HOTEL $$

(📞 051-250000; www.hotelrivierathakhek.com; Th Setthathirat; r 360,000-700,000K, ste 865,000-1,030,000K; ➡ ❄ @ 🛜) Hotel Riveria has terrific views of Thailand on one side and even more dramatic vistas of the jagged karsts on the other. But this is very much a business-style hotel. Large rooms have king-sized beds, TV, fridge, bath and international-style furniture. Downstairs, there's a restaurant with a generous buffet breakfast and egg station.

🍴 Eating

Tha Khaek has a serviceable selection of eats; you don't need to stray too far from the riverfront strip to see what's available.

Khao Sen Piak Pa Se
LAO $

(Th Kuvoravong; mains from 10,000K; ⊙ 6am-4pm) Rich, garlicky bowls of *kòw ƀẹeak sèn* (noodles in a broth with chicken or deep-fried crispy pork belly), served here with wheat-and-egg noodles. A few Vietnamese dishes are also available before 10am or so. There's no English-language sign; look for the faded yellow sign across from the car wash.

Grilled Duck Restaurants
LAO $

(Th Setthathirat; mains 20,000-50,000K; ⊙ 11am-11pm) There's a strip of outdoor grilled-meat restaurants named after their cooks (Ms Noy, Ms Kay etc.), all specialising in duck. Find them on the waterfront strip directly south of the night market.

Local Food Place
LAO $

(Th Setthathirat; mains 10,000-20,000K; ⊙ 7am-7pm) Head to this busy place alongside the river if you fancy tasty Lao favourites such as *pîng kai* (grilled chicken) and sticky rice for next to no money. There are also plenty of similar stalls lining the nearby Fountain Sq promenade.

★ Ping Kai Napong
LAO $$

(Th Setthathirat; 39,000-89,000K; ⊙ 10am-10pm) Ping Kai Napong specialises in grilled chicken, but the menu is a virtual tour of Lao cuisine, ranging from salads (the duck *láhp* – minced salad with shallots and coriander – is sublime) to soups, although the English translations may not always make sense. Easily the best of the riverside places.

Drinking & Nightlife

Tha Khaek is not a nightlife place, but after a few nights on the Loop, it seems like a big city with bright lights. There are no bars as such, but quite a few restaurants that double as drinking spots by night, particularly near the Mekong River.

Sabaidee Thakhek Restaurant BAR
(Sunset; Th Setthathirat; ⊙8am-midnight; 🛜) Catching whatever breeze is going, this restaurant (mains 35,000K to 75,000K) sits right on the riverfront, and with its import beers, TV and live music, actually functions as one of the town's better bars.

ℹ Information

MEDICAL SERVICES

Tha Khaek Hospital (☑051-212084; cnr Th Chao Anou & Th Champasak; ⊙24hr)

MONEY

BCEL (Th Vientiane; ⊙8.30am-4.30pm Mon-Fri) Changes major currencies and offers cash advances on debit or credit card.
Lao Development Bank (Th Vientiane; ⊙8.30-11.30am & 1-4.30pm) Cash exchange only, plus an ATM.

POLICE

Police (☑051-212083; cnr Th Kuvoravong & Th Unkham) Avoid passing by the station on motorbike if leaving town for the Loop as the police here police here have been known to demand a fake tourist fee.

Tourist Police (☑051-213563; Fountain Sq) The police here know how to write insurance reports, if you can track down an officer.

TOURIST INFORMATION

Tourist Information Centre (☑020-55711797, 030-5300503; www.tourismkhammouane.org; Th Vientiane; ⊙8am-5pm) This excellent tourist office offers exciting one- and two-day treks in Phu Hin Boun NPA, including a homestay in a local village. There are also treks to the waterfall by Ban Khoun Kham and Tham Kong Lor (900,000K). Offers advice on journeying the Loop as well. Mr Somkiad speaks English well and is very helpful.

ℹ Getting There & Away

Tha Khaek's **bus station** (☑051-251519; Rte 13) is located about 3.5km from the town centre. Buses bound for Hanoi, Hue, Danang and Dong Hoi, in Vietnam, stop here, but the bus station staff weren't able to tell us any departure times or prices, and made clear that it's only possible to buy tickets on the bus.

Talat Phetmany (Th Kuvoravong) is the departure point for *sŏrngtăaou* to Khammuan Province interior.

ℹ Getting Around

It should cost about 30,000K to hire a jumbo (motorised three-wheeled taxi) to the bus terminal, though you'll need to negotiate. From the bus terminal, jumbos don't budge unless they're full or you're willing to fork out 50,000K or more to charter the entire vehicle. Rides around town can cost around 15,000K per person.

BUSES TO/FROM THA KHAEK

DESTINATION	DEPARTURE POINT	PRICE (K)	DURATION (HR)	FREQUENCY
Attapeu	Bus Station	90,000	10	3.30pm, 11pm
Ban Kong Lor	Talat Phetmany	75,000	4	7am, 2.30pm, 3.30pm (all *sŏrngtăaou*)
Lang Khang	Talat Phetmany	50,000	2-3	8.15am, noon (all *sŏrngtăaou*)
Nakai	Talat Phetmany	35,000	1-2	8am, 10am, noon (all *sŏrngtăaou*)
Nakhon Phanom (Thailand)	Bus Station	18,000-20,000	1½	8.15am, 9.30am, 10.30am, 11.30am, 1.30pm, 2.30pm, 4pm, 5pm
Pakse	Bus Station	70,000	6-7	8.30am
Savannakhet	Bus Station	30,000	2-3	10.30am, 11.30am, 3.30pm
Vientiane	Bus Station	60,000-80,000	6	5.30am, 6.30am, 7.30am, 8.30am, 9.15am
Vinh (Vietnam)	Bus Station	200,000	12-15	9am

A handful of places around town offer motorbike hire and most will store your luggage for free if you're doing the Loop (p190). Note that it's a common practice to hold passports until you return with the bike.

Mad Monkey (📱020-59939909; douangda vanh@yahoo.com; Fountain Sq; per day scooters 100,000K, 150-250cc dirt bikes 300,000K; ⊘8am-7pm) A great place to hire a tough, reliable motocross bike to tackle the Loop and other adventures. Mad Monkey has a couple of Honda 250cc dirt bikes and some perky 150cc Kawasaki Fox dirt bikes, plus the usual automatic and semi-automatic scooters. They're more expensive than elsewhere, but they're well maintained. The German-Lao owners are also a great source of information on the Loop.

Mixay Motor Rental (📱020-55124555; per day 70,000-120,000K; ⊘6.30am-6pm) Located in 'downtown' Tha Khaek.

Pokemongo (📱020-23431746; Thakhek Travel Lodge, Rte 13; per day 70,000-100,000K; ⊘7.30am-6pm) With reliable scooters for tackling the Loop, getting around town or exploring the closer caves.

Wangwang Motor Rental (📱020-56978535; Fountain Sq; per day 60,000-140,000K; ⊘7am-11pm) Offers a large range of motorbikes, including dirt bikes, scooters and more. If interested, you can return bikes rented here at Wangwang's sister shops in Pakse and Vientiane.

Hin Namno NPA & Around

Hin Namno NPA might just be one of the most stunning protected areas in Laos, if not in all of mainland Southeast Asia, and the experts seem to agree: combined with two linked protected zones in neighbouring Vietnam, the greater area – the largest karst region in the world – is, at the time of writing, under consideration as a bi-country Unesco Natural World Heritage site.

ℹ️ ACCESSING & EXPLORING HIN NAMNO NPA

A lack of infrastructure means that visiting Hin Namno NPA simply isn't an option for most casual visitors, although roads are slowly improving, and the authorities are (slightly) less paranoid of foreign visitors. The only way to visit the more remote parts of the park is via homestays at Ban Thongxam and Ban Nong Ping.

The park's 820 sq km spans 11 major habitat types which protect several endangered and endemic species, including the almost impossibly debonair red-shanked douc, as well as Tham Lot Se Bang Fai, thought to be one of the largest river caves in the world. Parts of the park were important conduits for the Ho Chi Minh Trail, and the area is also home to villages populated by minority groups not living elsewhere in Laos.

⦿ Sights & Activities

Activities in the area include excursions into Hin Namno NPA, visiting the river cave that is Tham Lot Se Bang Fai, and kayaking on sections of the same river. In theory, these could be approached independently, but unless you have a 4WD vehicle and speak Lao or Thai, you're going to need some help. Green Discovery (p192) and, perhaps by the time you read this, Tha Khaek's Tourist Information Centre (p193), can facilitate access to the protected area. The website www.hinnamno.org is an excellent resource for anybody considering visiting the area, and goes into great detail about many lesser yet fascinating sites.

Tham Lot Se Bang Fai   CAVE
(ຖ້ຳລອດເຊບັ້ງໄຟ) The most impressive, and yet least visited, cave in Khammuan is the amazing Tham Lot Se Bang Fai. Located in Hin Namno NPA, the cave results from the Se Bang Fai river plunging 6.5km through a limestone mountain, leaving an underground trail of immense caverns, impressive rock formations, rapids and waterfalls that have been seen by only a handful of visitors.

The cave wasn't professionally mapped until 2006, and the Canadian-American who led the expedition concluded that Tham Lot Se Bang Fai is among the largest river caves in the world. Traversing the entire cave involves eight portages and is only possible during the dry season, from January to March. Local wooden canoes can only go as far as the first portage, about 1km into the cave, making inflatable rafts or kayaks the only practical option for traversing the entire length of the cave. The website www.hinnamno.org is a terrific source of information (and legend) on the cave.

The base for visiting the cave is Ban Nong Ping, a mixed Lao Loum/Salang village about 2km downstream from the cave entrance. The village now has electricity, and has built a tourist lodge (80,000K per person), although visits are really only possible

BAN THONGXAM HOMESTAY

One of the best ways to go into the heart of Hin Namno NPA is via a homestay in the end-of-the-road village of Ban Thongxam (ບ້ານທອງຊຳ). Home to 379 Yoy people, three families (☏020-91301556) take turns hosting visitors (per person, including food, 50,000K), and can also lead excursions into the protected area (per day, two people 120,000K).

The surrounding area is, frankly, stunning, and hikes include activities such as viewing the red-shanked douc langur, an endangered and brightly coloured monkey that's considered the park's flagship animal, waterfalls, underwater rivers and caves, including one that allegedly housed 3000 Viet Cong soldiers in the 1970s. The website www.hin namno.org has excellent information on the human and natural attractions in this area.

In theory, it's possible to reach the village independently (outside of the rainy season, that is), but to arrange anything, you'll need to be able to communicate in Lao or Thai. It's also worth noting that this area has only recently opened to outside tourism, and independent visitors might be subject to scrutiny from overzealous local officials (as we were).

outside of the rainy season. To get there, you'll need to make your way along the approximately 40km of very rough road (passable only during the dry season) from Lang Khang to Bualapha, then via an even rougher road to Ban Nong Ping. This is a trip that can only be done with an off-road vehicle; don't even think about attempting it on the city scooter you hired in Tha Khaek.

Green Discovery (p192) offers two-day (US$375) and three-day (US$454) excursions to the cave for groups of two people. It's also a good idea to check in with the Tourist Information Centre (p193) in Tha Khaek.

🛏 Sleeping & Eating

The dusty crossroads village of Lang Khang is the only place in the Hin Namno NPA area with hotel-style accommodation. Otherwise, you'll be sleeping at the homestays at Ban Thongxam or Ban Nong Ping.

Lang Khang has a couple of basic restaurants, otherwise most of your meals in Hin Namno NPA will be at homestays or by a campfire.

Khoun Pan Ya Guesthouse GUESTHOUSE $
(☏020-55851409; Lang Khang; r 80,000-100,000K; ❄) The only place to stay in Lang Khang (and the only hotel-like accommodation in the area), it doesn't look like much from the outside, but the rooms here are spacious and capable, if plain.

It's located around 250m along the road to Bualapha; look for the sign on the left and contact at the adjacent pharmacy.

ⓘ Getting There & Away

There's very little in terms of public transport in this area. Buses that run from Tha Khaek to Vietnam may be willing to drop you off in Lang Khang. From there, to get to the homestay at Ban Thongxam or to Tham Lot Se Bang Fai, you'll need to arrange 4WD transport.

Nakai–Nam Theun National Park & Around

Nakai–Nam Theun National Park (ບາງກາຍ-ສວນສາຫາລະບະສຸກາແຫງຊາດນ້ຳເທິນ) is the largest and most diverse protected area in Laos. Upgraded to national park status in 2019 and slowly opening its doors to visitors, its 3532 sq km are thought to hold some of the most pristine wilderness in mainland Southeast Asia. The park is home to several important species including elephants, nine types of primates, and even some recently discovered species and animals not seen elsewhere in Laos.

Ban Tha Lang, a scruffy, dusty village at the edge of the vast and post-apocalyptic reservoir created by the Nam Theun 2 Dam, functions as the unlikely jumping-off point for the park.

◉ Sights & Activities

The main attraction in this area is the Nakai–Nam Theun National Park, although it's worth noting that from May to August, water levels are too low for boats to reach the trailheads. The main facilitator is Phosy Tha Lang Guesthouse (p196), from where Amphai leads all-inclusive day hikes (US$100, two-person minimum), two-day trips (US$200) and three-day trips (US$500) up the Nam Xot and deep into the protected zone. Treks can include a stay at a minority village, a visit to a waterfall, and kayaking,

BORDER CROSSINGS

Getting to Vietnam: Na Phao to Cha Lo

Getting to the border Despite the fact that Rte 12 is now fully paved, for *falang* (Westerners) the Na Phao (Laos)/Cha Lo (Vietnam) border crossing (7am to 7pm) remains one of the least used of all Laos' borders. This is partly because transport on both sides is slow and infrequent. The only regular transport through this border are buses from Tha Khaek to Vinh, in Vietnam (100,000K, 9am).

At the border The Lao border offers 30-day tourist visas on arrival. Some nationalities require a Vietnam visa in advance, so check with the Vietnamese embassy (p287). Most regional visitors and Scandinavian, British, French, German, Italian and Spanish visitors do not need a visa for short stays.

Moving on Get back on the same bus, which will wait for you to complete your paperwork before continuing to Vinh.

Getting to Thailand: Tha Khaek to Nakhon Phanom

Getting to the border Crossing the Mekong at the Tha Khaek (Laos)/Nakhon Phanom (Thailand) border is now only possible for locals. Travellers can catch an international bus (18,000K/70B, around 1½ hours) to Nakhon Phanom via the Friendship Bridge from the main bus station in Tha Khaek. Buses run every hour or so from 8.15am to 5pm. If crossing the border after 4pm you'll have to pay an overtime fee.

At the border In Thailand, travellers from most countries are given visa-free, 30-day entry. In Tha Khaek, Lao immigration issues 30-day tourist visas on arrival and there's a BCEL money-exchange service and 24-hour ATM at the immigration office.

Moving on Once in Nakhon Phanom, buses depart regularly for Udon Thani and head to Bangkok at 7.30am and then regularly from 4.30pm to 7.30pm. Faster and almost as cheap are budget flights to Bangkok offered by Air Asia and Nok Air, with several flights per day.

and the park provides a relatively good chance of spotting some wildlife.

Phosy Tha Lang also offers activities in the reservoir including kayaking (50,000K) and an hour-long sunset cruise (per person 50,000K).

🛏 Sleeping & Eating

The sleepy village of Ban Tha Lang functions as the access point for Nakai–Nam Theun National Park, and is home to two basic guesthouses. Within the park, remote minority villages and camping are the only accommodation options.

Ban Tha Lang is home to a couple of guesthouse-based restaurants.

Sabaidee Guesthouse GUESTHOUSE $
(☑020-55429950; Ban Tha Lang; r 50,000-60,000K; 🅿🛜) The characterless yet clean rooms here are set in bungalows in a spacious garden and firepits are lit nightly during peak season.

Phosy Tha Lang Guesthouse BUNGALOW $
(☑020-58804711; Ban Tha Lang; bungalow 70,000-90,000K; 🅿🛜❄) This guesthouse

offers respite in a string of rather small, aged, stuffy bungalows. The more expensive rooms are the only ones worth considering, and the communal areas and sister restaurant are probably more interesting than the accommodation.

Amphai, based here or at the restaurant, is the person to contact regarding visits to Nakai–Nam Theun National Park.

Phosy Tha Lang Restaurant LAO $
(Ban Tha Lang; mains 15,000-70,000K; ⊙6am-10pm) Linked to the guesthouse of the same name and located at the edge of the reservoir created by the Nam Theun 2 Dam, views, tasty Lao food and real coffee make this the best place to eat in the area.

ℹ Getting There & Away

The main transport hub in the area is Nakai, 20km south of Ban Tha Lang. From there, *sŏrngtăaou* head to Tha Khaek at 8.15am and noon (50,000K), and there's two daily *sŏrngtăaou* to Ban Tha Lang, at 10.30am and 2pm (40,000K).

SAVANNAKHET PROVINCE

Savannakhet is the country's most populous province and is home to about 15% of all Lao citizens. The population of around one million includes Lowland Lao, Tai Dam, several small Mon-Khmer groups and communities of Vietnamese and Chinese.

Stretching between the Mekong and Thailand in the west and the Annamite Mountains and Vietnam in the east, it has become an important trade corridor between these two bigger neighbours.

The eponymous provincial capital is one of the more charming cities in Laos, not to mention a natural jumping-off point for the province's protected wildernesses.

There are three NPAs here: Dong Phu Vieng to the south of Rte 9; remote Phu Xang Hae to the north; and Xe Bang Nuan straddling the border with Salavan Province. Eastern Savannakhet is a good place to see remnants of the Ho Chi Minh Trail, the primary supply route to South Vietnam for the North Vietnamese Army during the Second Indochina War.

Savannakhet ສະຫວັນນະເຂດ

♪ 041 / POP 91,000

Languid, time-trapped and somnolent during the sweltering days that batter the old city's plasterwork, Savannakhet is a charming blend of past and present Laos. The highlight is the historic quarter with its impressive display of decaying early-20th-century architecture. There's little to do in town but wander the riverfront and cool off in one of a clutch of stylish restaurants and bijou cafes that are steadily growing in number.

That said, there's plenty to do outside of town and outfits such as Marvelaos (p199) can help you plan intrepid trips into the nearby countryside and NPAs.

⊙ Sights

Much of the charm of Savannakhet is in simply wandering through the quiet streets in the town centre, between the old and new buildings, the laughing children and the slow-moving, *petang*-playing old men. The Tourist Information Centre (p202) produces *Savannakhet Downtown*, a brochure featuring a self-guided tour of the city's most interesting buildings.

⊙ In Town

St Theresa's Catholic Church   CHURCH
(Th Phetsalat; ⊙ daylight hours) **FREE** Built in the 1920s, St Theresa's is a Savannakhet landmark and the largest Catholic church in the city.

Wat Rattanalangsi   BUDDHIST TEMPLE
(ວັດລັດຕະນະລັງສີ; Th Phagnapui; ⊙ daylight hours) **FREE** Wat Rattanalangsi was built in 1951 and houses a monks' primary school. The *sĭm* (ordination hall) is unique in that it has glass windows (most windows in Lao temples are unglazed). Other structures include a rather gaudy Brahma shrine, a modern *săhláh lóng tám* (sermon hall) and a shelter containing a 15m reclining Buddha backed by Jataka (stories of the Buddha's past lives) paintings.

Savannakhet Museum   MUSEUM
(ພິພິດທະພັນແຂວງຊະຫວັນນະເຂດ; Th Khanthabuli; 5000K; ⊙ 8am-noon & 1.30-4pm Mon-Fri) The rather dusty Savannakhet Museum houses old photos, war relics, artillery pieces and inactive examples of the deadly unexploded ordnance (UXO) that has claimed the lives of more than 20,000 Lao since the end of the Secret War.

Musée Des Dinosaures   MUSEUM
(ທ່ພິພິດທະພັນໄດໂນເລົ່າ, Dinosaur Museum; *♪* 041-212597; Th Khanthabuli; 10,000K; ⊙ 8-11.30am & 1-4pm) A major dig in the 1930s near a village 145km east of the city unearthed 110-million-year-old dinosaur fossils. The underwhelming Dinosaur Museum is the place to learn about this history. Savannakhet Province is home to more than a dozen dinosaur sites with bones from six distinct species.

Around Town

Dong Natad   WILDLIFE RESERVE
(ດົງນາຫາດ) Dong Natad is a sacred, semi-evergreen forest within a provincial protected area 15km east from Savannakhet. It's home to two villages that have been coexisting with the forest for about 400 years, with villagers gathering forest products such as mushrooms, fruit, oils, honey, resins and insects. It's possible to visit Dong Natad by bicycle, motorbike or tuk-tuk from Savannakhet.

Marvelaos (p199) and Savannakhet's Tourist Information Centre (p202) offer various programs, ranging from multiday homestays to one-day cycling trips. These

Savannakhet

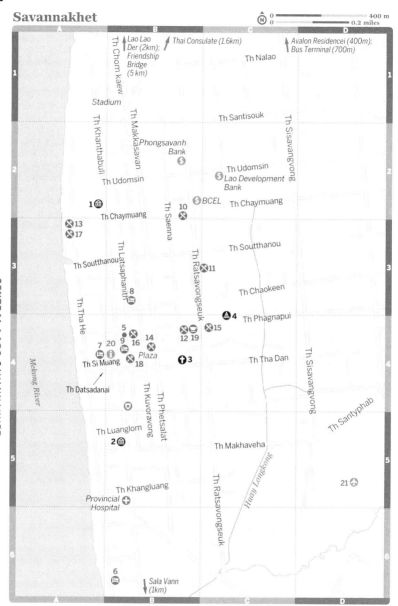

N
0 — 400 m
0 — 0.2 miles

Th Chom kaew

↑ Lao Lao Der (2km); Friendship Bridge (5 km)

↑ Thai Consulate (1.6km)

↑ Avalon Residencei (400m); Bus Terminal (700m)

Th Nalao

Stadium

Th Makkasavan

Th Santisouk

Th Sisavangvong

Th Khanthabuli

Phongsavanh Bank 💲

Th Udomsin

Th Udomsin

💲 Lao Development Bank

Th Udomsin

1 🏛

💲 BCEL

Th Chaymuang

Th Chaymuang

Th Saenna

10 ✕

✕13

✕17

Th Souththanou

Th Latsaphanith

Th Ratsavongseuk

✕11

Th Souththanou

Th Chaokeen

8 🏨

Th Tha He

▲4

Th Phagnapui

5 ✕

14 ✕

✕15

7 20 9 🏨

16

12 19

Mekong River

🏨 ℹ

18

Plaza

3

Th Si Muang

Th Tha Dan

Th Sisavangvong

Th Datsadanai

Th Kuvoravong

Th Phetsalat

⊙

Th Santyphab

Th Luanglom

2 🏛

Th Makhaveha

Huay Longkong

21 ✈

Th Khangluang

Th Ratsavongseuk

Provincial Hospital ✚

6 🏨

↓ Sala Vann (1km)

---

community-based trips have had plenty of positive feedback and the combination of English-speaking guide and village guide proves a great source of information about how the local people live. If you visit, there's a good chance you'll encounter villagers collecting red ants, cicadas or some other critter, depending on the season; all are important parts of their diet and economy. Make arrangements at least a day ahead.

That Ing Hang
BUDDHIST TEMPLE

(ขาดອิງຮັງ; 5000K; ⊙7am-6pm) Thought to have been built in the mid-16th century,

Savannakhet

this well-proportioned, 9m-high *thâat* is the second-holiest religious edifice in southern Laos after Wat Phu Champasak. It's located about 11.5km northeast of Savannakhet via Rte 9, then 3km east and the turn-off is clearly signposted. Going by bicycle or motorbike is the easiest option.

The Buddha is believed to have stopped here when he was sick during his wanderings back in ancient times. He rested by leaning *(ing)* on a hang tree (thus Ing Hang). A relic of the Buddha's spine is reputed to be kept inside the *thâat*.

Not including the Mon-inspired cubical base, That Ing Hang was substantially rebuilt during the reign of King Setthathirat (1548–71) and now features three terraced bases topped by a traditional Lao stupa and a gold umbrella weighing 40 baht (450g). A hollow chamber in the lower section contains a fairly undistinguished collection of Buddha images; by religious custom, women are not permitted to enter the chamber. The French restored That Ing Hang in 1930. The That Ing Hang Festival is held on the full moon of the first lunar month.

Any northbound bus can stop here, or you could haggle with a *sakai-làap* (jumbo) driver to take you here (you'll do well to knock the price down below 100,000K return).

☞ Tours

To get out into the countryside, the city's Tourist Information Centre (p202) and Marvelaos are your best bets for arranging guides and/or transport to the sacred forest at Dong Natad, and destinations further abroad.

★**Marvelaos**   TOURS
(☑ 020-55552927, 030-5873604; www.marvelaos. com; 283 Th Latsapanith; ⊙ 8.30am-6pm Mon-Sat) Enthusiastic and reliable Alex and Tek offer tours of Savannakhet, including guided homestays (for two people, all-inclusive, US$160) and cycling trips (US$175) to Dong Natad, and destinations further abroad, including overnight treks in Dong Phu Vieng NPA (US$360), and by the time you read this, possibly Phu Xang Hae NPA. Highly recommended.

Marvelaos can also help arrange transport, and hire out bicycles (per day 30,000K) and motorcycles (per day 100,000K).

⊟ Sleeping

Savannakhet has decent budget and midrange options but little to excite if you're looking for luxury. Most accommodation is located within walking distance of the attractive old town.

★**Hostel Savan Cafe**   HOSTEL **$**
(☑ 020-91243402; Th Si Muang; dm 70,000K, r 200,000K; ❋ 🛜) This swanky hostel will make you feel like a million bucks on just a few thousand kip. Located right in the heart of 'downtown' Savannakhet, the handsome two- to six-bed dorms (and a couple of private rooms) provide access to a trendy floor-level cafe, leafy lounge zones

WORTH A TRIP

AN EATER'S TOUR OF SAVANNAKHET

Savannakhet is one of the tastiest places to dive directly into real Lao food. And it's also one of the easiest: within four blocks along Th Phagnapui, in the town's French quarter, there's a handful of restaurants and stalls that do excellent versions of nearly all classic Lao dishes.

Start your tour with Lao-style coffee – that is, poured through a sock-like filter onto sweetened condensed milk – at the Lao Coffee Stall (p202); the boisterous owner here does one of the better versions we've come across.

Now you're ready for breakfast. You can head a block east to Mae Bueam, or you could head just west to the Lao Breakfast Corner.

Rest and digest. When you're ready again, head back to Th Phagnapui to the No Name Grill Place. Simply point to whatever looks good on the grill – the options include an excellent fish, chicken or pork belly – and couple it with pounded papaya salad, bamboo soup and a mountain of sticky rice. This is simple Lao food at its best.

We're going to leave dinner up to you, but you'll regret not trying the excellent beef ragout (known in Lao as *lagoo*) at Café Chez Boune (p202).

---

and a tiled rooftop patio with sweeping sunset views of the Mekong.

Pilgrim's Inn　　　　　　　　　GUESTHOUSE **$**
(☑020-22133733; www.facebook.com/pilgrims kitchenandinn; 106 Th Latsaphanith; r US$20-25; ❋ 🛜) Pilgrim's Inn is attached to the popular **Pilgrim's Kitchen** (mains 30,000-50,000K; ⊙7.30am-9pm Mon-Sat; ❋🛜🍴) with English-speaking staff who make you feel at home. Guacamole-green rooms feature clean beds, air-con and attached bathrooms with hot water, although some lack natural light.

★Vivanouk Homestay　　　　HOMESTAY **$$**
(☑020-91606030; www.vivanouk.com; Th Latsaphanith; r without bathroom US$20-40; ♿❋🛜) This funky little place is akin to a boutique homestay. There are just three rooms sharing two bathrooms – one with an alfresco outdoor shower – and delightfully decorated in a contemporary-colonial fusion style. Breakfast is available downstairs in an artsy venue that doubles as a bar by night.

Daosavanh Resort & Spa Hotel　　HOTEL **$$$**
(☑041-252188; www.daosavanh.com; Th Tha He; incl breakfast r 504,000-600,000K, ste 788,000-1,050,000K; ♿❋@🛜🏊) This ostentatious hotel overlooking the Mekong offers a slice of international comfort, and its kidney-shaped pool is very welcome on sweltering days, of which there are many in Savan. Its 53 rooms are large and immaculate, and prices include free airport and border transfers.

🍴 Eating

Savan has one of the liveliest food scenes in the country. In particular, it's a great place for Lao-style breakfast and lunch, and it's possible to hit Western food for dinner.

★No Name Grill Place　　　　　　LAO **$**
(Th Phagnapui; mains from 10,000K; ⊙9am-1pm) Keep your eyes peeled for smoke from the grill and uniformed officials – two signs of a good place to eat in Laos. This tin-roofed, dirt-floored place excels at anything grilled – simply point to what looks good – especially when coupled with sides of spicy papaya salad, hearty bamboo soup and sticky rice.

Mae Bueam　　　　　　　　　　　　LAO **$**
(Th Ratsavongseuk; ⊙5am-9pm) This buzzy vendor does *kòw jee*, Vietnamese-style baguette sandwiches, including options with egg – a great breakfast. There's an English-language menu printed above the counter but no English-language sign; look for the open-fronted shop right at the intersection.

Lao Breakfast Corner　　　　　　LAO **$**
(Th Phagnapui; mains from 10,000K; ⊙5am-1pm) In these two nearly linked knots of vendors, you'll find dishes including *kòw ɓęeak sèn*, *bǎn kǔan* (Lao for *bánh cuôn,* a Vietnamese speciality that is popular in Laos of freshly steamed rice noodle filled with minced pork, mushrooms and carrots), sticky rice-based sweets and deep-fried treats.

Khao Piak Mae Tik LAO $
(020-77744248; Th Ratsavongseuk; mains 10,000K; ⏱24hr) Mae Tik sells a delicious *kòw ḅeeak sèn* in Savannakhet. Look for the tiny roadside shack with the wooden sign.

Lin's Café INTERNATIONAL $
(030-5332188; Th Phetsalat; mains 23,000-60,000K; ⏱8.30am-10pm Mon-Sat; ❄⚹) Savannakhet's original travellers' cafe; come here for a refreshing air-conditioned vibe, a full menu of coffee drinks, and home-made pastries.

Savannakhet Plaza Food Market INTERNATIONAL $
(Savannakhet Plaza; meals 10,000-30,000K; ⏱5-10pm) This nightly food market brings 20 or more stalls to the Savannakhet Plaza area in the heart of the old town. This means barbecued skewers, steaming noodle soups, dim-sum-sushi-tapas confusion and more. Plus Beerlao in plentiful supply.

Riverside Snack & Drink Vendors STREET FOOD $
(⏱5-10pm) The riverside snack and drink vendors are a great place for sundowners,

PROTECTED AREAS IN CENTRAL LAOS

Central Laos is home to the majority of the country's protected areas – both National Protected Areas (NPAs) and national parks – and is possibly the best place to explore its wilderness. As these areas are also home to villages, visits are done via homestays, which means there's also opportunity for a unique cultural experience.

The downside is that many of these areas truly are wild, and lack of infrastructure aside, you'll need help in securing the required permission to visit. In Bolikhamsai and Khammuan Provinces, Tha Khaek's Tourist Information Centre (p193) and Green Discovery (p192) control much of the action, while in Savannakhet, the excellent Marvelaos (p199) is the sole facilitator.

A rundown of the protected areas in central Laos:

Phu Hin Bun NPA (p183) This stunning protected area in Bolikhamsai and Khammuan Provinces includes Tham Kong Lor, so many visitors don't even realise that they've been there. It's really the only protected area in central Laos that visitors can approach independently, although there are guided tours that provide deeper access to the area.

Hin Namno NPA (p194) One of the most beautiful of the protected zones in southern Laos, this candidate for a Unesco Natural World Heritage site is also one of the most rugged and inaccessible, although this is starting to change. The homestay at Ban Thongxam (p195) allows a relatively accessible peek into remote village life and an excursion into some truly wild jungle and fascinating Ho Chi Minh Trail sites, while if you have the time and money, you can mount a virtual expedition to the cave-bound river that is Tham Lot Se Bang Fai (p194). Located in Khammuan Province.

Dong Phu Vieng NPA (p204) The three-day trek offered here is a good balance of nature and culture, and spans hiking in varied jungle, stays at two Katang villages, and a boat ride along the beautiful Se Bang Hiang. In Savannakhet Province.

Nakai–Nam Theun National Park (p195) Granted national park status in 2019 and only recently opening its doors to tourism, this park – the country's largest protected area – is said to be a particularly good place to spot wildlife. In Bolikhamsai and Khammuan Provinces.

Phu Xang Hae NPA (ປ່າສະຫງວນແຫ່ງຊາດຊ້າງແຫ່) There's much potential at this protected area in Savannakhet Province, and at the time of writing, authorities were just starting to investigate ways to open it to tourism. Stay tuned.

Nam Kading NPA (ປ່າສະຫງວນແຫ່ງຊາດນ້ຳກະດິງ) 🍃 In Bolikhamsai Province; unfortunately, at the time of writing, there was little or no infrastructure to accommodate those who want to visit this protected area.

Xe Bang Nuan NPA Straddling Savannakhet and Salavan Provinces, this is the furthest off the beaten track of protected areas in central Laos.

ℹ️ SLEEPING WITH SPIRITS

The Katang villagers of Dong Phu Vieng NPA believe in the myriad spirits that surround them in the forest. One of the most important is the house spirit, which is believed to live in the home of every village family. Over the centuries a series of taboos have been developed in an effort to avoid disturbing this spirit, and as a visitor in a Katang home, it is vitally important you don't break them.

➡ You should never enter the owner's bedroom or touch the spirit place.

➡ Do not sleep beside a person of the opposite sex, even if that person is your spouse. If you really can't be separated tell your guide and he can bring a tent for you.

➡ Sleep with your head pointed towards the nearest outside wall; never point your feet at the outside wall or, spirits forbid, another person's head.

serving cheap big bottles of Beerlao (10,000K) and *sìn daat* (Lao hotpot barbecue) sizzling away on charcoal grills.

Café Chez Boune　　　INTERNATIONAL **$$**
(www.cafechezboune.com; Th Chaymuang; mains 60,000-160,000K; ☀️ 7am-10pm; ❄️🛜) Chez Boune has a French-speaking owner, a handsome wood-decked dining room, and is one of the better places in the area for Western food. If you want to keep it semi-local, opt for the delicious beef ragout (known in Lao as *lagoo*), one of few examples of French-Lao fusion.

Lao Derm　　　LAO **$$**
(☎ 041-212270; mains 30,000-90,000K; ☀️ 10am-11pm) This riverside restaurant is one of the only places in town to offer great Mekong views. The hefty menu spans Lao, Thai and Chinese dishes, but Lao Derm functions equally well as a bar. There's no English-language sign; look for the wooden building and the floating barge.

🍷 Drinking & Nightlife

The riverside snack and drink vendors (p201) opposite Wat Sainyaphum are great for sundowners. It's fair to say Savannakhet is not the top nightlife destination in Laos, but there are a few karaoke bars drawing in the locals and a handful of travellers.

Lao Coffee Stall　　　CAFE
(Th Phagnapui; ☀️ 5am-noon) What better way to start the day than with a group of older gentlemen shooting the breeze, playing dominoes and sipping jet-black Lao-style coffee? A few sips might even provide some insight into Savannakhet. There's no English-language sign here; look for the open-fronted baby-blue building.

Laochaleun Bar　　　BAR
(Th Si Muang; ☀️ 6pm-midnight; 🛜) The atmospheric Laochaleun occupies a strategic corner overlooking Savannakhet Sq and draws a lively crowd from about 7pm onwards. Live music on weekend nights and a bit of a party atmosphere.

ℹ️ Information

MEDICAL SERVICES

Provincial Hospital (☎ 041-212717; Th Khanthabuli; ☀️ 24hr)

MONEY

BCEL (Th Ratsavongseuk; ☀️ 8.30am-4.30pm) and **Lao Development Bank** (Th Udomsin; ☀️ 8.30-11.30am & 1-4.30pm) both have cash exchange, credit-card advances and an ATM. **Phongsavanh Bank** (☎ 041-300888; Th Ratsavongseuk; ☀️ 8.30am-4pm Mon-Fri, to 11.30am Sat) has cash exchange, Western Union and an ATM.

POLICE

Police Station (☎ 041-260173; Th Khanthabuli; ☀️ 24hr)

TOURIST INFORMATION

Marvelao (p199) The best resource for local information.
Tourist Information Centre (☎ 041-212755; Th Si Muang; ☀️ 8-11.30am & 1.30-4pm Mon-Fri) Has a selection aged but well-produced brochures on Savannakhet and its surrounds, but not much else.

ℹ️ Getting There & Away

Savannakhet's **airport** (☎ 041-212140; Th Kaysone Phomvihane) is served solely by Lao Airlines, with connections to Vientiane (from 400,000K, 55 minutes, four weekly), Pakse (from 190,000K, 30 minutes, four weekly) and Bangkok (from US$86, 80 minutes, four weekly). Tickets can be purchased at the **Lao Airlines office** (☎ 041-212140; www.laoairlines.com; Savannakhet Airport; ⏱ 8.30am-4pm Sun, Mon, Wed & Fri) at the airport, online or with travel agents in town.

An alternative option for those wanting to save money on the Bangkok route is to cross the Friendship Bridge and connect with the Fly-Drive services offered with Air Asia or Nok Air via Nakhon Phanom Airport; tickets are available from less than 1000B.

Savannakhet's orderly **bus terminal** (Th Makkasavan), usually called the *khíw* lot, is at the northern edge of town. If you're headed north or south, in addition to the services listed, it's

BORDER CROSSINGS

Getting to Vietnam: Dansavanh to Lao Bao

Getting to the border Crossing the Dansavanh (Laos)/Lao Bao (Vietnam) border (7am to 7.30pm) is a relative pleasure. From Savannakhet's bus terminal, buses leave for Dansavanh (40,000K, five to six hours) at 7am and noon. Alternatively, consider breaking the journey for a night in Sepon, which you can use as a base for seeing the Ho Chi Minh Trail; there are relatively frequent *sŏrngtăaou* to Dansavanh between 7am and 3pm (20,000K, one hour).

The bus station in Dansavanh is about 1km short of the border; Vietnamese teenagers on motorbikes are more than happy to take you the rest of the way for about 10,000K.

At the border The Lao border offers 30-day tourist visas on arrival and has an exchange booth. Some nationalities require a Vietnam visa in advance, so check with the Vietnamese embassy (p287) in Savannakhet. Most regional visitors, Scandinavian visitors, and British, French, German, Italian and Spanish visitors do not need a visa for short stays.

Moving on Once through, take a motorbike (40,000d or US$2) 2km to the Lao Bao bus terminal and transport to Dong Ha (50,000d, two hours) on Vietnam's main north–south highway and railway. Entering Laos, there are buses to Savannakhet (40,000K, five to six hours) at 7am and 9am, as well as regular *sŏrngtăaou* (passenger trucks) to Sepon (30,000K, one hour) from 7am to 5pm. Simple accommodation is available on both sides of the border.

If you're in a hurry, an alternative is to take one of the various direct buses from Savannakhet bound for the Vietnamese cities of Hanoi, Hue and Danang.

Getting to Thailand: Savannakhet to Mukdahan

Since the construction of the second Thai–Lao Friendship Bridge back in 2006, non-Thai and non-Lao citizens are not allowed to cross between Mukdahan and Savannakhet by boat.

Getting to the border The Thai–Lao International Bus crosses the Savannakhet (Laos)/Mukdahan (Thailand) border crossing (6am to 10pm) in both directions. From Savannakhet's bus terminal, the Thai–Lao International Bus (13,000K, 45 minutes) departs approximately every hour from 8.15am to 7pm. It leaves Mukdahan's bus station (50B, 45 minutes) roughly every hour from 7.30am to 7pm and also stops at the border crossing to pick up passengers.

At the border Be sure not to board the Savan Vegas Casino staff bus at the border, as this also stops at the international bus stop but heads out of town to the eponymous casino resort.

The Lao border offers 30-day tourist visas on arrival. If you don't have a photo you'll be charged the equivalent of US$1. An additional US$1 'overtime fee' is charged from 6am to 8am and 6pm to 10pm on weekdays, as well as on weekends and holidays. Most nationalities do not require a visa to cross into Thailand; check with the Thai consulate (p287) in Savannakhet.

Moving on Onward from Mukdahan, there are at least five daily buses bound for Bangkok. Alternatively, to save time, consider a fly-drive option with Air Asia or Nok Air, including an express minivan to Nakhon Phanom Airport and a budget flight to Bangkok.

BUSES TO/FROM SAVANNAKHET

DESTINATION	PRICE (K)	DURATION	FREQUENCY
Attapeu	75,000	8-10hr	9am
Danang (Vietnam)	150,000	12hr	9am Tue, Thu, Sat
Dansavanh	40,000	5-6hr	7am, noon
Hanoi (Vietnam)	250,000	24hr	10am Mon, Wed, Thu, Sat (all sleeper)
Hue (Vietnam)	110,000	10hr	8am
Mukdahan (Thailand)	13,000	45 min	hourly 8.15am-7pm
Pakse	40,000	5-6hr	7am, 5.30pm
Sepon	40,000	4-5hr	7am, noon
Tha Khaek	30,000	2½-4hr	frequently 7am-1pm
Vientiane	75,000-120,000	8-11hr	frequently 6am-1.30pm; 8.30pm (sleeper)

also usually possible to hop on one of the regular buses passing through to/from Vientiane.

ⓘ Getting Around

Savannakhet is just big enough that you might occasionally need a jumbo. A charter around town costs about 15,000K and more like 20,000K to the bus station. Jumbos make the trip from the airport for 30,000K, although rates may start higher for new arrivals fresh off the plane.

Marvelaos (p199) hires out bicycles (per day 30,000K) and motorcycles (per day 100,000K).

Dong Phu Vieng NPA & Around

Formerly off the beaten track, Dong Phu Vieng NPA (ປ່າສະຫງວນແຫ່ງຊາດດົງພູວຽງ) has opened its doors to the outside world. The park spans a mix of forests ranging from dense woodlands to rocky areas with little cover, and animals regularly seen include the rare silver langur, the leaf monkey and the hornbill. It's also home to a number of Katang villages.

Heading east from the park is Sepon, a border area that was an important section of the Ho Chi Minh Trail, which still holds reminders of that era.

The park headquarters are in Muang Phin, but to secure the proper permission, transport and accommodation, you'll need to go through the services of Savannakhet-based Marvelaos (p199). It's created a three-day trek that involves walking through the jungle, overnight stays in Katang villages that include a walk through a sacred forest where you'll see *lak la'puep* (clan posts placed in the jungle by village families), followed by a boat trip along the beautiful Se Bang Hiang. An all-inclusive trek for two runs US$360.

It's worth noting that there is still UXO in the park; do no stray from any clearly marked trails.

Muang Phin is the base for visits to Dong Phu Vieng NPA, but accommodation is via homestays in Katang villages. It is important to read up on traditional Katang culture and sleeping with the spirits (p202) before overnighting.

All food is included on the Dong Phu Vieng treks. Catering for dietary requirements is hard to arrange. Muang Phin is home to basic restaurants and markets.

ⓘ Getting There & Away

There's regular public transport along Rte 9 between Savannakhet and the border at Dansavanh.

Muang Phin is the jumping-off point for any visits to Dong Phu Vieng NPA, but a guided tour will provide transport.

Southern Laos

Best Places to Eat

➡ Nakorn Cafe Restaurant (p218)

➡ Daolin Restaurant (p211)

➡ Le Panorama (p211)

➡ Delta Coffee (p211)

➡ Chez Fred et Lea (p248)

Best Places to Stay

➡ Kingfisher Ecolodge (p224)

➡ Le Jardin (p210)

➡ Sala Done Khone (p247)

➡ Pon Arena Hotel (p239)

Why Go?

Southern Laos is dominated by the Bolaven Plateau, a fertile highland that spreads over four of the region's provinces. It is the site of Laos' thriving coffee plantations and also many of the region's beautiful waterfalls.

Pakse is the 'big smoke', a not-unpleasant mid-sized town tuned in to travellers' needs with accommodation and restaurants. It's the base for tours into the Bolaven Plateau and other destinations, and is well endowed with tour and bike-hire companies. Wat Phu Champasak, a striking remnant of the once-mighty Khmer empire, can be reached from here, or from the small town of Champasak.

The mighty Mekong plunges and spills to its widest point in Si Phan Don, which has established itself as a backpacker place-to-be, but also has some exquisite boutique hotel accommodation. Here are opportunities to take relaxing bicycle rides through the local villages, go kayaking or ziplining, or view the increasingly rare Irrawaddy dolphins.

When to Go
Pakse

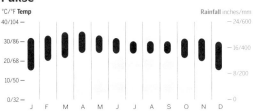

Oct–Nov Ideal time for bike touring, as rains trickle and dust remains manageable.

Dec–Feb Sunny and cooler, and downright cold on the Bolaven Plateau. Ideal for trekking.

May–Sep After the hot season the rains kick in. Travel is more difficult, and impossible in some regions.

Southern Laos Highlights

1 Khon Phapheng (p241)
Taking in one of the Mekong's most spectacular falls, and learning the mystery of the Manikhote tree.

2 Bolaven Plateau (p225)
Gazing in awe at 100m-high waterfalls, sipping fair-trade coffee and soaking in the cool climate.

3 Wat Phu Champasak (p219) Exploring this ancient Khmer temple complex.

4 Si Phan Don (p237)
Cycling the islands, kayaking to spot dolphins, or just watching the Mekong flow by.

5 Kiet Ngong (p223) Taking a trek and a boat trip into the

jungle around the region's premier ecotourism area.

6 Tayicseua (p225) Staying in rustic accommodation and hiking through the forest to amazing waterfalls.

7 Ziplining the Mekong (p245) Gliding over the raging torrent at Tat Somphamit.

PAKSE REGION

While most visitors to the south base themselves in Pakse city, the region's real gems lie in the surrounding countryside. Wat Phu Champasak is a must-see, and the Se Pian NPA is good for nature lovers, while the islands of Don Kho and Don Daeng provide easy insight into Lao culture.

Once part of the Cambodian Angkor empire, Champasak Province was later absorbed into the Lan Xang kingdom and eventually became an independent kingdom from the early 18th century to the beginning of the 19th century. Today it has a population of more than 700,000, including lowland Lao (many of them Phu Thai), Khmers and a host of small upland Mon-Khmer groups, most of whom inhabit the Bolaven Plateau region.

Pakse ປາກເຊ

♪ 031 / POP 68.330

Pakse, the capital of Champasak Province and the gateway to southern Laos, sits at the confluence of the Mekong and the Se Don (Don River). It's a relatively lively town with lots of accommodation and eating options, as well as transport connections, and many travellers base themselves here for forays to surrounding attractions such as the Bolaven Plateau (p225) and Wat Phu Champasak (p219). The many good restaurants, stylish hotels and clued-in tour companies make it a comfortable and convenient home base.

⊙ Sights

Pakse is much more about being a home base rather than a place to take in the sights. Wat Phou Salao is a worthwhile trip (either by tuk-tuk, or on foot if you're fit) for its views, especially at sunset.

Wat Phou Salao VIEWPOINT
(ວັດພູສະເຫຼົ່າ; Rte 16) The centrepiece of this hilltop temple across the Mekong from Pakse is the giant golden Buddha statue looking out over the city. The views from his perch are as fantastic as you'd expect, especially at sunset. To enjoy them, take the first left after the bridge and either climb up the long staircase or take the 4.5km road route up the back. The temple buildings are also a pleasant sight, making it a good place for a wander.

Talat Dao Heuang MARKET
(ຕະຫຼາດດາວເຮືອງ; ⊙5am-6pm) This vast market near the Lao–Japanese Bridge is one of the biggest in the country. It's at its most chaotic in the food zones, but just about anything a person might need – from medicinal herbs to mobile phones – is sold here. It's highly worth a visit.

Sacred Heart Cathedral CHURCH
(ມະຫາວິຫານທີ່ສັກສິດຫົວໃຈ; Th 10; ⊙5.30am-8pm) This modest, tin-roofed building isn't much to look at from the outside, but the one-of-a-kind paintings inside are the reason to visit. They show Jesus in various spots around southern Laos, including Wat Phu Champasak and Khon Phapheng Falls, and having a last supper of sticky rice and traditional Lao foods.

Champasak Historical Heritage Museum MUSEUM
(ພິພິດທະພັນມໍລະດົກປະຫວັດສາດຈຳປາສັກ; Rte 13; 10,000K; ⊙8.30-11.30am & 2-4pm Mon-Fri) Highlights here include ancient bronze drums, stone carvings unearthed up on the Bolaven Plateau, stelae in Tham script dating from the 15th to 18th centuries, Khmer stone carvings, and musical instruments. Also of interest is the textile and jewellery collection from ethnic minorities such as the Nyaheun, Suay and Laven, with large iron ankle bracelets and ivory earplugs.

At the time of research, this museum had just moved to a new location. It's not clear if this is a permanent move, but in any case you may find tuk-tuk drivers unaware of its location. It's near the old swimming pool (*sá wài nâm*) about 7km out of town on Rte 13.

🏃 Activities

Dok Champa Massage MASSAGE
(♪020-54188778; Th 5; massages 60,000-100,000K; ⊙9am-10pm) Dok Champa delivers Lao massage, foot massage, herbal remedies and more. Staff are friendly and professional, and there is a resident *ajahn* (teacher) on hand supervising the staff.

Clinic Keo Ou Don MASSAGE
(Traditional Medicine Hospice; ♪031-251895, 020-5431115; massage 45,000K, sauna 20,000K; ⊙10am-5pm, sauna 4-8pm) Professional and popular, this centre has an air-conditioned massage room and herbal sauna segregated by gender. To get here, head out of town on Th 38 and turn right towards Pakse Golf, 1km east of Champasak Grand Hotel. It's on the

Pakse

0   400 m
0   0.2 miles

Se Don

Russian Bridge

Souphanouvong Bridge

Khaemse Guest House (140m)

(2.5km);
Northern (7km);
Ban Saphai (13km)

VIP Bus Station

Mekong River

Rte 16W

Talat Dao Heuang

2km (500m);
Southern (7km);
Paksong (49km);
Si Phan Don (135km)

Le Jardin (700m);
Kiang Kai (1.7km);
Champasak (30km);
Vang Tao (43km)

Banlao (350m);
Clinic Keo Ou Don (1.2km);
Mekong Paradise Resort (1.5km)

Th 21
Th 14
Th 11
Th 10
Th 9
Th 8
Th 38
Th 36
Th 42
Th 35
Th 34
Th 46
Th 24
Th 1
Th 11
Rte 13

Pakse

right-hand side just a couple of hundred metres down and has both blue and green signs.

Xuan Mai Cooking Class COOKING
(☎020-28058585; Th 5; per person 300,000K) Learn to make one Lao, one Vietnamese and one Thai meal, plus a dessert, in half-day cooking classes with the chef-owner of Xuan Mai Restaurant (p211).

☞ Tours

Most people organise their southern Laos tours and treks in Pakse. Pretty much all hotels and travel agencies sell a standard selection of day trips to the Bolaven Plateau, Wat Phu Champasak and Kiet Ngong. Miss Noy (p212) is probably the best place in town to get tour and travel information.

The cheapest tours are simply transportation; admission fees and meals are not included and there is no guide. For many people this is fine, but for others it's a disappointing surprise. Be sure you know what you are getting before you agree to go.

★ Green Discovery ADVENTURE
(☎031-252908; www.greendiscoverylaos.com; Th 10; 2-day Tree Top Explorer tour 2-/4-person group per person US$399/329; ☉8am-8.30pm) Green Discovery is one of the foremost eco- and adventure-tour companies in Laos. Its

signature trip is the Tree Top Explorer adventure in Dong Hua Sao NPA (p226) near Paksong, consisting of two or three days' ziplining, canopy walking and jungle trekking around waterfalls beyond any roads. Accommodation is in ecofriendly huts set high up above the forest floor.

Green Discovery also runs tours to many other destinations, such as the Phu Xieng Thong and Se Pian NPAs.

Vat Phou Cruises CRUISE
(☎031-251446; www.vatphou.com; just off Th 11; ☉office 8am-5pm Mon-Sat, no cruises in Jun) Operates three-day luxury Mekong cruises between Pakse and Si Phan Don, including visits to Wat Phu Champasak (p219) and Khon Phapheng Falls (p241).

🛏 Sleeping

The tourist centre is on Rte 13 between the Souphanouvong Bridge (formerly the French Bridge) and Th 24. Stay here if you want easy access to travel agencies, motorbike rentals, money changers and touristy restaurants. Around the corner you'll find more hotels and restaurants in the commercial district, which is centred around the Doungdy Plaza (p212). If you're staying anywhere else, rent a motorbike or bicycle to get around.

SOUTHERN LAOS PAKSE

Alisa Guesthouse
GUESTHOUSE **$**

(📞 031-251555; www.alisa-guesthouse.com; Rte 13; r 130,000-160,000K, f 210,000K; ➋ ✳ @ 🛜) Perhaps the best-value lodging in Pakse, Alisa has sparkling rooms, tiled floors, solid wood beds, armoires, working satellite TV and a fridge. Service is good, too. The only significant knock is that some rooms barely catch a wi-fi signal. No surprise, it's often full.

Phi Dao Hotel
HOTEL **$**

(📞 031-215588; phidaohotel@gmail.com; Rte 13; s 100,000-155,000K, d 130,000-155,000K, r 180,000K; ➋ ✳ 🛜) A very solid city-centre choice, the rooms here are among the best in this price range for quality, maintenance and cleanliness, although not the best for value. Street-side rooms are loud, so request something at the back. It has a lively cafe, but breakfast is not included in the room rates.

Khaemse Guest House
GUESTHOUSE **$**

(📞 020-56359292; Th 12; r with fan 40,000-70,000K, r with air-con 100,000-120,000K; ✳ 🛜) With its riverside position and rickety sun deck shipwrecked over the bank, this friendly house at the end of a lane feels far from the city and has a lazy tumbledown charm. The rooms offer great value for money (they're simple but clean, with river views) and the owners are extremely friendly.

★ Le Jardin
BOUTIQUE HOTEL **$$**

(📞 030-9463324; www.lejardindepakse.com; r US$70; ✳ 🛜 🏊) One of the nicest places to stay in Pakse, Le Jardin oozes old colonial charm, with yellow-ochre-and-white-trim walls and floral tiling throughout. The garden adds to the atmosphere, and the rooms are decorated with artworks and stylish touches. It's a bit out of town, just behind Dao Heuang market, but there's a free shuttle into the main restaurant hub every evening at 7pm.

Note that in Lao it's pronounced 'ler jardaeng'.

★ Residence Sisouk
BOUTIQUE HOTEL **$$**

(📞 031-214716; www.residence-sisouk.com; cnr Th 9 & Th 11; r incl breakfast US$60-80; ➋ ✳ @ 🛜) This exquisite boutique hotel occupies a lovely old house and evokes a bit of old France. The rooms enjoy polished hardwood floors, flat-screen TVs, verandas, Hmong bed runners, stunning photography and fresh flowers everywhere. Breakfast is in the penthouse cafe with great views. Paying extra gets you a bigger, brighter room with a balcony in front. Rates drop 30% out of season.

Mekong Paradise Resort
HOTEL **$$**

(📞 031-254120; Ban Non Sawang; r incl breakfast US$38-85; ➋ ✳ 🛜) A riverside spot just 3km southeast of central Pakse that makes for a wonderful escape from the city. Most rooms have unbeatable Mekong sunset views. The superior rooms (US$55) with their private balconies are almost romantic, but the views are actually better from the US$45 Mekong Paradise rooms. The Garden View rooms (US$38) defeat the point of staying out here.

It's a bit far from town, but if a retreat is what you want, this may be just the place.

Champasak Palace Hotel
HOTEL **$$**

(📞 031-212263; www.champasakpalacehotel.com; Rte 13; all incl breakfast r 330,000-350,000K, ste 550,000K; ✳ 🛜) Palace indeed. This vast, wedding-cake-style building was originally built for Chao Boun Oum, the last prince of Champasak and Lao prime minister between 1960 and 1962. The standard rooms are a tad twee, but well kept with comfortable beds, while the graceful restaurant and common areas turn heads with wood columns, louvred windows and touches of flair.

It is worth investing in a huge VIP suite (550,000K), with parquet floors and panoramic views. The cheapest rooms are in the newer Sedone building out back and are far less inspiring.

★ Athena Hotel
HOTEL **$$$**

(📞 031-214888; www.athenahotelpakse.com; Rte 13; r incl breakfast US$60-90; ➋ ✳ @ 🛜 🏊) Athena's subdued style features tasteful timber finishes and a classy ambience. The beds are marshmallowy delights, and dimming inlaid ceiling lights let you illuminate them in many ways. The cosy pool is most welcome after a day out on dusty roads and there's an upmarket thatch-roofed *sala* for relaxing (or photo ops). It's about a 10-minute walk from the tourist centre.

✕ Eating

Two good morning spots for delicious *fĕr* (rice noodles) are the **Noodle Shop Mengky** (Rte 13; noodles 20,000K; ⏱ 6am-1pm) and the more tourist-friendly **Lankham Noodle Shop** (Rte 13; noodles 20,000-50,000K; ⏱ 6am-2pm; 🛜) across the road.

The Pon Sai area at the junction of Th 34 and Th 46 bustles with small shops and street vendors selling *fĕr*, baguettes, *kòw nĕeo bîng* (grilled, egg-dipped sticky rice patties) and many doughy delights. It's best in the morning, but some shops stay open through the day and into the night.

★**Daolin Restaurant** LAO, INTERNATIONAL **$**
(Rte 13; mains 15,000-50,000K; ⏱7am-10pm; 🛜🅿) Overlook the traffic noise – this popular restaurant has great food and service. It has some of the best Thai food in town and is a great introduction to Lao food, with set meals of sticky rice, steamed veggies, chilli sauce and fried fish/chicken/pork. Vegetarians can try Lao food that is usually meat-based, such as pumpkin soup *(om mahk éu)* and mushroom *gôy.*

★**Delta Coffee** CAFE **$**
(Rte 13; mains 25,000-50,000K; ⏱7am-9pm; 🛜) Delta offers a lot more than the name suggests. Owners Alan and Siriporn (he's Chinese, she's Thai) serve coffee from their plantation near Paksong, but also have a menu that includes pizza, spinach lasagne and a full range of Lao and Thai dishes. Recommended.

Sinouk Coffee Shop CAFE **$**
(cnr Th 9 & Th 11; mains 30,000-45,000K; ⏱6.30am-9pm; 🛜) Stylish Sinouk has glass-topped tables inlaid with coffee beans as that's what it's all about – delicious Arabica coffee grown on its plantation in the Bolaven Plateau. If you're after more, then get started on the panini sandwiches, pastries, salads and the usual Thai-Lao mix of dishes. It's one of the pricier spots for a light meal, but the quality is high.

It's run by the same company that operates the Sinouk Coffee Resort (p227) in Paksong.

Ban Tong Night Market MARKET **$**
(Th 1; ⏱4.30-9.30pm) Though small and everything is sold as takeaway, this is the closest thing Pakse has to a Thai-style night market. It's a great place to sample Lao food since you can just point to what you want.

La Terrasse LAO, INTERNATIONAL **$**
(Th 24; mains 20,000-70,000K; ⏱10am-10.30pm; 🛜) A block off the main road on the edge of the tourist strip, La Terrasse attracts a mixed clientele of travellers and expats. The menu is half Lao-Thai and half Western, though the stars are the giant wood-fired pizzas (evenings only) and over-stuffed baguette sandwiches. It also brews its own special fruity *lòw-lów* (rice whisky).

Xuan Mai Restaurant VIETNAMESE, LAO **$**
(Th 5; mains 15,000-40,000K; ⏱7am-10.30pm; 🛜🅿) Vietnamese-run Xuan Mai serves super-fresh *fěr, năam néuang* (pork balls),

kòw Ћǔn (white flour noodles with sweet-spicy sauce) and a house *láhp* that's full of zing. Its set meals are good value if you're dining in a group.

★**Le Panorama** LAO, INTERNATIONAL **$$**
(Th 5; mains 35,000-85,000K; ⏱4.30-10pm; 🛜🅿) The rooftop restaurant of the Pakse Hotel serves up delicious Franco-Asian cuisine and unbeatable 360-degree city views. The menu includes duck breast, pizza and a succulent *Ћah neung het hŏrm* (stuffed fish steamed in banana leaves).

Dok Mai Trattoria Italiana ITALIAN **$$**
(Th 24; mains 30,000-80,000K; ⏱10am-10.30pm; 🛜) Italian-owned, this little gem aims for culinary authenticity with perfectly prepared pasta and eggplant parmigiana, plus a big selection of salads. And it all comes with a fantastic rock-and-roll soundtrack and garden seating in back.

Banlao LAO, THAI **$$**
(Th 11; mains 20,000-80,000K; ⏱10am-10pm) One of several floating restaurants in Pakse, Banlao has a reliable menu of expected favourites but also many dishes you might not have encountered before, such as the seasonal ant-egg *gôy* (*gôy kài mót sòm* – *gôy* is similar to *láhp* but with added blood). For the less adventurous there's mild, central-Thai papaya salad and grilled fish with herbs.

 Drinking & Nightlife

Le Panorama is a required stop for a sunset Beerlao or two. For a more local touch, there are a few floating restaurants, such as Banlao, along the rivers that catch some of the twilight. For the best sunset, cross the Souphanouvong Bridge and walk left to the mouth of the Se Don, or continue to one of the bars on the Mekong River just past it.

Champahom BAR
(Th 11) A chill place to drink and snack, this Thai-owned bar has live music (usually Carabao-style Thai country music) most nights except Sunday from about 7.30pm to 9pm.

Shopping

Coffee from the Bolaven Plateau is the traditional souvenir from the region; pick up a bag at any cafe. Delta Coffee is one that specialises in good coffee. Several shops in Doungdy Plaza (p212) and Talat Dao Heuang (p207) sell typical Lao skirts.

Doungdy Plaza MARKET
(Th 5; ⏰8am-7pm) This modern market sells mostly discount clothing, much of which are brand-name knock-offs, of course, but a few shops stock Lao skirts and fabrics.

Monument Books BOOKS
(Th 5; ⏰9am-8pm Mon-Sat, to 6pm Sun) This modest bookshop is your best stop for maps of Laos and its neighbours, though don't expect much detail, plus postcards and a good range of regional historical and cultural books.

ℹ Information

MEDICAL SERVICES
International Hitech Polyclinic (VIP Clinic; ☎031-214712; ihpc_lao@yahoo.com; cnr Th 1 & Th 10; ⏰24hr) Adjacent to the **public hospital** (☎030-5785709; Th 10; ⏰24hr), it has English-speaking staff and much higher standards of care, service and facilities, plus a pharmacy.

MONEY
Banks, such as the conveniently located **BCEL** (Th 11; ⏰8.30am-3.30pm Mon-Fri) and **Lao Development Bank** (Rte 13; ⏰8.30am-3.30pm Mon-Fri), have the best currency-exchange rates, though the exchange counter at the **Lankham Hotel** (⏰7am-7pm) is good too. All three give cash advances (3% commission) on credit cards. LDB also has Western Union and can exchange US dollar travellers cheques (1%).

ATMs are plentiful in the city centre.

POLICE
Main Police Station (☎031-252127)

TOURIST INFORMATION
Provincial Tourism Office (☎020-9204994; Th 11; ⏰8am-4pm Mon-Fri) Mostly exists to hand out maps and brochures, but some staff can answer questions or help you make bookings for homestays and activities at Kiet Ngong, Don Kho and Don Daeng. Note: at the time of research, the office was planning to move, so may have relocated by the time you read this; enquire locally for the latest.
Miss Noy (☎020-22272278; noy7days@hotmail.com; Rte 13; per day bicycles 10,000K, motorbikes 60,000K; ⏰8am-8pm) The gang here are seriously clued in to the region, especially the Bolaven Plateau.

VISAS
Pakse's **immigration bureau** (Th 10; ⏰8-11am & 2-4pm Mon-Fri) is next to the Foreigner Control Area of the main police station in a low-lying mint-green building. To extend your stay, bring a photocopy of your passport name page and visa, two photos, and 50,000K plus 20,000K per day. An extension for a minimum of three days and a maximum of 30 should be ready the next afternoon.

ℹ Getting There & Away

AIR
The **Pakse International Airport** (Rte 13) is 2.5km northwest of the Souphanouvong Bridge. A tuk-tuk to/from the airport will cost about 40,000K.
Lao Airlines (☎031-212252; www.laoairlines.com; Pakse International Airport; ⏰8am-5pm) has direct flights to the following cities in Asia:
Bangkok US$115, four weekly
Ho Chi Minh City US$105, three weekly
Luang Prabang 1,010,000K, three weekly
Savannakhet 375,000K, four weekly
Siem Reap US$100, five weekly
Vientiane 770,000K, three daily
A better way to fly to Bangkok is to travel overland to Ubon Ratchathani and catch a budget flight from there, which is considerably cheaper.

BOAT
A tourist boat motors from Pakse to Champasak (one way per person 70,000K) at 8.30am, provided there are enough punters – in the low season this usually aren't. It's two hours downstream to Champasak, and a bit longer on the return. Book through Miss Noy or call **Mr Khamlao** (☎020-22705955; per boat US$70), who runs his own separate boat.

BUS & SŎRNGTĂAOU
Pakse, frustratingly, has many bus and *sŏrngtăaou* (passenger truck) stations. The vast majority of tourists simply book bus journeys through their guesthouse or a travel agency, and since these are either special tourist buses that pick you up in the centre or include a free transfer to the relevant departure point, the prices are usually reasonable.

Note that on long-distance routes to Cambodia and Vietnam you'll want to be careful which company you use: choosing the wrong one could cost you several hours and cause a lot of pain. Buy your ticket from a travel agency that actually knows the details of the route, rather than a guesthouse, which probably does not.

There are six main stations:
Southern Bus Terminal (Rte 13) Pakse's main bus station, with departures to most places. Also known as *kîw lot lák þaat* (8km bus terminal) because it's 8km east of town on Rte 13.
Northern Bus Terminal (Rte 13) This is the most orderly of the stations and is usually called *kîw lot lák jét* (7km bus terminal); it's – you guessed it – 7km north of town. Only for northern destinations. The English-language signs on departures are frequently wrong.

Talat Dao Heuang Vans and *sŏrngtăaou* to nearby destinations, such as the Thai border, depart from a very chaotic lot in the southeast corner of the market and also from Th 38 in front of the market.

2km Bus Station (☑ 031-212428; Rte 13) Also known as Sengchalern station after the company that owns it; the office is in the lobby of SL Guest House, which is in front of Friendship Mall.

VIP Bus Station (Th 11) Also called Thasalakham station, it only serves VIP night buses to Vientiane and towns along the way. There are a number of different companies here, all offering the same tickets at the same price.

Kiang Kai Bus Station (off Th 38) This small, hard-to-find station, in a red-and-yellow building set back well off Th 38, is 1.5km past the Japanese bridge. It's used by buses to/from Thailand, though these also use the Southern Bus Terminal, as well as buses to Vientiane.

Vientiane & Points North

Most travellers prefer the comfortable 'VIP' night sleeper buses to Vientiane (170,000K, 10 hours). You can book these through your guesthouse or head to the conveniently located VIP Bus Station, from where there are several nightly departures, all leaving at 8.30pm; or the 2km Bus Station, with one departure at 8pm. It's possible to take these buses to Tha Khaek (130,000K, 4½ hours) and Seno (for Savannakhet; 100,000K, three hours).

If you prefer day travel, slower-moving, ordinary air-con buses (110,000K, 12 to 14 hours) depart throughout the day from the Southern Bus Terminal, stopping occasionally to pick up more passengers at the Northern Bus Terminal. These buses also go to Tha Khaek (60,000K, five hours) and Seno (65,000K, seven hours).

Bolaven Plateau & Points East

Transport to the Bolaven Plateau and points east consists of buses from the Southern Bus Terminal (p212) and the 2km Bus Station

GETTING TO THAILAND: VANG TAO TO CHONG MEK

Getting to the border Other than finding the right counters to use at immigration, crossing at the Vang Tao (Laos)/Chong Mek (Thailand) border (open 6am to 8pm) is straightforward.

The easiest way to get there is on the Thai–Lao International Bus (60,000K, 2½ to three hours, 8.30am and 3pm) between Pakse's Southern Bus Terminal and Ubon Ratchathani's bus station. It picks up more passengers at the little Kiang Kai Bus Station on the way. If you're travelling *to* Pakse (departures from Ubon at 9.30am and 1.30pm, 200B) note that this bus does wait long enough for people to get Lao visas.

There are also frequent minivans from Pakse to Vang Tao (20,000K, 45 minutes) departing from the street in front of Talat Dao Heuang and also *sŏrngtăaou* (passenger trucks) leaving from inside the market until about 4pm. Vans to Vang Tao also depart hourly from the Southern Bus Terminal. You'll be dropped off in a dusty/muddy parking area about 500m from the Lao immigration office.

If you're headed to Bangkok (225,000K, 13 hours), a direct service (that sometimes involves changing buses at Ubon) departs the Southern Bus Terminal daily at 4pm. Pakse travel agents also offer a combination bus/sleeper train ticket to the Thai capital with prices starting at 310,000K for 2nd-class fan carriages and going much higher for better service.

At the border Laos issues visas on arrival (around US$35, or 1500B, depending on which passport you hold), while on the Thai side most nationalities are issued 30-day visa waivers free of charge. You walk between the two countries using a pointless underground tunnel for part of the way.

Although it seems like a scam, there is a legitimate overtime fee on the Laos side after 4pm weekdays and all day on weekends and holidays. The real scam is that the officials demand 100B even though the actual price is 10,000K. Just tell them you want a receipt and you'll pay the correct price.

Moving on Minivans head to Ubon (100B, 1¼ hours, every 30 minutes) from Chong Mek's bus terminal, which is 600m (20B by motorcycle taxi) up the main road. Alternatively, informal taxi drivers hang around immigration and charge 1000B to anywhere in Ubon Ratchathani city.

(p213). The last departures to all cities are at 4pm, except for Sekong from the Southern Bus Terminal, which is at 2.30pm. Buses to Salavan (30,000K, three hours) can drop you at Tat Lo. Buses to Attapeu (50,000K, 3½ to five hours) pass through Paksong (15,000K, 90 minutes) and about half use the long route via Sekong (55,000K, four hours).

Champasak & Si Phan Don

Regular *sŏrngtăaou* leave Talat Dao Heuang (p213) for Champasak (20,000K, one hour) until noon or so – sometimes even as late as 2pm. There's also a morning tourist bus-boat combo to Champasak (65,000K, 1½ hours) offered by most travel agencies. Be sure your ticket includes the boat crossing from Ban Muang. The regular price for the boat is 10,000K per person or 30,000K if you're alone.

For Si Phan Don, tourist buses and minivans – including pick-ups in town and boat transfer to Don Khong (60,000K, 2½ hours), Don Det (75,000K, three hours) and Don Khon (80,000K, 3¼ hours) – are most comfortable and convenient. Book these through any guesthouse or travel agent. All departures are in the morning around 8am.

If you want to leave later in the day, take a *sŏrngtăaou* from the Southern Bus Terminal (p212) to Ban Nakasang (for Don Det and Don Khon; 40,000K, 3½ hours). These depart hourly until 5pm and go via Hat Xai Khun (for Don Khong).

One *sŏrngtăaou* services Kiet Ngong (30,000K, two hours), leaving at 1pm.

Neighbouring Countries

Travelling to Cambodia (p249) is a guaranteed hassle, while entering Thailand (p213) is a breeze. Travelling to Vietnam falls in between.

The most comfortable way to Hué (200,000K, 12 hours) and Danang (230,000K, 14 hours) in Vietnam is to catch one of the morning sleeper buses from the Southern Bus Terminal (p212), which for legal reasons use the long route through the Lao Bao border east of Savannakhet. Note that these do not go every day – sometimes a regular bus goes instead and sometimes there is simply no bus. Up to three hours faster for the same price are the modern, comfortable minibuses that go via Salavan and use the Lalay border (p232), through the drivers tend to be reckless. Then there are the slower and truly crappy cargo buses that only save a few of their seats for passengers. These make for a very uncomfortable and much longer journey. If there is no large bus, some unscrupulous travel agencies will book passengers on these buses without telling them, so be sure you know what vehicle your ticket is really for. For Kom Tun or Ho Chi Minh City you travel via the Bo Y border (p236). Some travel agencies sell direct buses to Ho Chi Minh City (450,000K, 15 hours), but these go via the southern route so you need to buy a Cambodian visa. It takes several hours longer, but is actually much cheaper to travel to Kom Tum and take a connecting bus (240,000d) from there.

ⓘ Getting Around

BICYCLE

Cycling around to the city's few sites can make for a pleasant few hours. Miss Noy (p212) hires bikes.

CAR & MOTORCYCLE

Several shops and guesthouses in the tourist belt along Rte 13 rent motorbikes from 50,000K per day for 100cc bikes, rising to 100,000K for an automatic Honda Scoopy. Safe bets are Miss Noy (p212), which has a nightly planning meeting for those heading to the Bolaven Plateau, and **Pakse Travel** (☐ 020-22277277; Rte 13; ⊘7.30am-8.30pm).

Talk to any travel agency or hotel about hiring a car with driver, which should cost about US$100 (plus fuel) depending on where you want to go. **Avis** (☐ 031-214946; www.avis.la; Th 10; per day from US$75; ⊘8.30am-6pm Mon-Fri, 9am-1pm Sat & Sun) rents out pickups and SUVs with or without drivers and can provide paperwork to allow the cars to go to Thailand and Vietnam (but not Cambodia).

LOCAL TRANSPORT

Local transport in Pakse is expensive by regional standards. Figure on about 10,000K to 20,000K for a short tuk-tuk ride. A ride to the Northern or Southern Bus Terminals costs 15,000K per person shared and 50,000K for a whole tuk-tuk.

AROUND PAKSE

Don Kho, Ban Saphai & Ban Don Khoh

The Mekong-hugging Ban Saphai (Saphai Village; ບ້ານສະພາຍ) and adjacent island of Don Kho (ດອນໂຄ) just north of Pakse are famous for their weaving. Women work on large looms underneath their homes producing silk and cotton dresses and other products, and are happy to show you how. While this is a well-known destination, it's not overrun. The rarely visited Ban Don Khoh (Don Khoh Village; ບ້ານດອນເຂາະ), not far away, does impressive stone carving. These three destinations combine for a good half-day trip out of Pakse and cultural explorers can dig deeper with a night at Don Kho's homestay.

⊙ Sights

These are primarily destinations for those interested in handicrafts, but all three villages also offer a relaxed look at local life.

⊙ Don Kho

There are no cars and hardly any motorcycles on this 450m-wide island and, despite the advent of electricity, it's easy to feel like you're stepping back to a simpler time. The 350 residents live along both shores on the island's northern half and farm rice in the centre. There are no traditional tourist sites on the island, though the women weaving silk under their homes welcome drop-in visitors.

Wat Silattana Satsadalam (aka Wat Don Kho) has a manuscript hall mixing Lao and French styles and a giant tree that locals dubiously claim is 500 years old. For about half the year you can walk out to some beaches and for 50,000K boatmen will take you out for a fishing trip. The 'traditional twin roof house' shown on the map at the landing is gone and it will take some bushwhacking to find the traces of the old village and the cemetery in the mostly forested southern half of the island; and if you do find them, the pay-off is very small.

Though it's small enough to walk, there are bikes (20,000K per day) for hire. Turn left from the landing and ask at the little administration centre where you can also arrange a village homestay.

Believe it or not, Don Kho was briefly the capital of southern Laos following the French arrival in the 1890s. It served as a mooring point for boats steaming the Mekong River between Don Det and Savannakhet.

⊙ Ban Saphai

First stop in this weaving village should be the **Ban Saphai Handicraft Centre** (ສູນຫັດຖກຳບ້ານສະໄຟ; ⊙6am-7pm) next to the boat pier. Several weavers have their looms here and locally woven textiles and other crafts are on sale. Also, you aren't just welcomed, you're openly encouraged to visit women weaving at their homes elsewhere in the village. A map posted outside the Handicraft Centre leads you on a short walking tour to some weaving houses, an old school building at the temple, and the local market.

⊙ Ban Don Khoh

Not to be confused with single-'H' Don Kho island to the north, little-known Ban Don Khoh is a peaceful place to visit. The village has become a home to dozens of stone-carvers, who mostly make Buddha images. Some basic work is done with power tools, but most of the carving is still done with hammer and chisel. The carvers are relaxed as they go about their work and this is a hassle-free atmosphere where you can see images at all different stages of completion. They work all day every day, except when there's a ceremony at the temple or a big *muay thai* fight on TV.

The workshops are in front of **Wat Chomphet**, (ວັດຈອມເພັດ) which has a 30m-tall Buddha image on its grounds. Ban Don Khoh proper is bit to the west along the Mekong River, so this carving community is also known as Ban Chomphet.

🛏 Sleeping & Eating

Don Kho is a great place to experience a village homestay. You'll see a sign for a community guesthouse on the far side of the island, but it's on the verge of collapse.

There are a few proper restaurants in Ban Saphai, there's limited local food on Don Kho, and you're out of luck at Ban Don Khoh.

Don Kho Homestay HOMESTAY $
(per person 30,000K, per meal 20,000K) Don Kho is a great place to experience a village homestay. Just turn up on the island and say 'homestay' and the villagers will sort you out. Meals are taken with the host family and in our experience, the food is delicious. The Provincial Tourism Office (p212) in Pakse can arrange things in advance.

ℹ Information

Some people at the Ban Saphai Handicraft Centre can speak some English. They will call to arrange your homestay and/or activities on Don Kho.

The Provincial Tourism Office (p212) in Pakse can do the same.

ℹ Getting There & Away

Ban Saphai is 16km north of Pakse's Souphanouvong Bridge and the turn-off is clearly signed. *Sŏrngtǎaou* from Pakse to Ban Saphai (20,000K, 45 minutes) leave fairly regularly from the street in front of the Talat Dao Heung (p213).

From Ban Saphai to Don Kho, longtail boats cost 40,000K round trip and can hold up to five people. Set a time for pick-up, or take the boatman's phone number and call when you want to return.

Ban Don Khoh is between Pakse and Ban Saphai, 9km from the Souphanouvong Bridge. The turn is unmarked, but it's the paved road going west just before the bus station.

Phu Xieng Thong NPA

Spread over 1200 sq km in Champasak and Salavan Provinces, **Phu Xieng Thong NPA** (ປ່າສະຫງວນແຫ່ງຊາດພູຊຽງທອງ) is most accessible about 50km upriver from Pakse. The area has a sometimes other-worldly beauty, with oddly eroded outcroppings and exposed sandstone ridges, some of which contain prehistoric paintings. Most of the big wildlife has been eradicated by hunting, but there are still lots of birds, including significant concentrations of green peafowl, and a diversity of wild orchids.

The typical trip, available December to June, through Green Discovery (p209) for US$132 per person (in a group of four or more), begins in the Mekong River village of Ban Mai Singsamphan, where you will do a homestay between two days of moderately challenging trekking. A highlight is the sunset view from the top of Phu Khong (Khong Mountain). The return trip to Pakse includes a boat trip on the Mekong.

Independent travellers are pretty much out of luck since Pakse's provincial tourism office no longer arranges trips here and none of the local guides speak much English. If you get yourself to Ban Mai Singsamphan you can make it happen.

Tat Phasuam

Tat Phasuam (ຕາດຜາສ້ວມ; Rte 20; entrance 10,000K, motorcycle/car 2000/5000K; ☉8am-6pm), a modest but interesting U-shaped waterfall, is 2km from the highway, within the Uthayan Bajiang Nature Resort about 35km from Pakse. Hawkers sell forest produce (such as bee larvae and forest fruits) along the path to the waterfall. Rickety wooden pathways and bridges lead to the falls, but ongoing construction points to big plans for development.

The nearby Tat Mak Ngaew, 200m from Tat Phasuam, is also worth checking out.

CHAMPASAK

🎵 031 / POP 15,440

It's hard to imagine Champasak (ຈຳປາສັກ) as a seat of royalty, but from 1713 until 1946 it was just that. These days the town is a somnolent place, the fountain circle (that no longer hosts a fountain) in the middle of the main street alluding to a grandeur long since departed, along with the former royal family. Scattered French colonial-era buildings share space with traditional Lao wooden stilt houses, and the few vehicles that venture down the narrow main street (which pretty well comprises most of the town) share it with chickens and cows.

With a surprisingly good range of accommodation and several attractions in the vicinity – most notably the Angkor-period ruins of Wat Phu Champasak (p219) – it's easy to see why many visitors to the region prefer staying in Champasak over bustling Pakse.

Just about everything in Champasak is spread along the riverside road, both sides of the fountain circle.

⊙ Sights & Activities

Champasak has a few mildly interesting temples, and soaking up the Mekong scenery and seeing local life along the riverfront road can make for a wonderful day.

Wat Muang Kang   BUDDHIST TEMPLE
(ວັດເມືອງກາງ, Wat Phuthawanaram) About 5km south of town along the Mekong stands the oldest active temple in Champasak, and one of the most interesting in southern Laos. The soaring Thai-style *ubosot* (ordination hall), with its red-tiled roof (under reconstruction during our visit) and ring of pillars, is impressive, but the *hŏr tại* (Tripitaka library), with its elements of Lao, Chinese, Vietnamese and French-colonial architecture, is striking.

The damaged, but still beautiful, tower supposedly holds Buddha images and, if you ask some locals, it has another magical purpose: in the middle of the night, a mystic light beam comes from across the river, bounces through a *gâaou* (crystal) and alights atop Sri Lingaparvata, the holy mountain above Wat Phu Champasak.

Almost all families in Muang Kang village weave bamboo sticky rice and various other baskets.

It's easy enough to reach Wat Muang Kang: head out of Champasak on the

Champasak

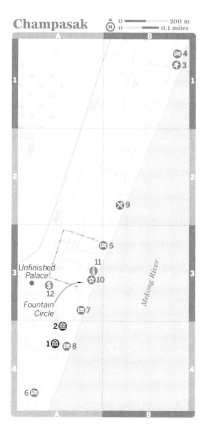

Mekong River

Unfinished Palace

Fountain Circle

Champasak

riverside road and continue south on the dirt road where the main road turns towards Wat Phu. Coming back, if you're on a bike or motorcycle, you can follow the pleasant narrow path directly on the riverfront for part of the way.

Champasak Spa   SPA
(☏ 020-56499739; www.champasak-spa.com; massage 80,000-160,000K; ⊙ 10am-noon & 1-7pm, closed Mon May-Oct, all of Jun) 🍃 Run by Nathalie, this is a fragrant oasis of free tea and sensitively executed treatments using locally grown and sourced organic bio products. And it creates jobs for local residents. A full-day spa package (reservations required) comprising facial, body scrub, hair spa, massage and lunch costs 550,000K.

🛏 Sleeping

Finding a room in Champasak is straightforward enough except during the Wat Phu Champasak Festival (p222; usually in February), when you can camp on the grounds of Wat Phu Champasak. Luxury and homestay accommodation is also available on nearby Don Daeng.

Souchitra Guesthouse   GUESTHOUSE $
(☏ 020-9719877; r with fan/air-con 60,000/ 120,000K; ❄) This ageing guesthouse was undergoing refurbishments when we last visited. It has a pleasant garden fronting onto the main road and backs onto great river views. The rooms are serviceable and look good for the price, though there was no wi-fi.

Saythong Guesthouse   GUESTHOUSE $
(☏ 020-22206215; r with fan/air-con 80,000/ 120,000K; ❄ 🛜) This friendly place has decent rooms that are very good value. The restaurant occupies a pleasant perch with great views over the Mekong.

**★ Nakorn Cafe
Guest House**   GUESTHOUSE $$
(☏ 020-98177964; r US$38-45; ❄ 🛜) This Lao-Belgian-owned spot on the river a tad south of the main drag has the cleanest rooms in town, with private balconies, beautifully tiled interiors and luxurious rain showers. There's a second unit of rooms overlooking the Mekong a few doors down, with a two-level family room (US$70). Optional breakfast at the Nakorn Cafe is US$7 extra.

FORMER ROYAL RESIDENCES

The two standout white buildings 300m south of the fountain circle are Champasak's most enduring reminders of its distant glory. The large 1952 building was the **residence of Chao Boun Oum** (ວັງເຈົ້າບຸນອຸ້ມ; the king's younger brother) while one street over is **Chao Ratsadanai's residence** (ໂຮງເຈົ້າຣັດສະດານໄນ), a faded 1926 French colonial building for his father. Distant relatives of the king still own them today.

★**River Resort**   RESORT **$$$**
(☏020-56850198;   www.theriverresortlaos.com; Ban Phaphinnoy; all incl breakfast garden villas US$130, river-view villas US$180; ⊛✳☎☀) The 12 duplex villas (nine riverfront and three set back along a pond and rice paddies) are outfitted with gargantuan beds, indigenous wall hangings, indoor-outdoor showers, and big balconies with five-star views. Alongside a pair of pools, Thai and Lao massage and a beautiful restaurant, the resort also offers upscale excursions by boat (the sunset trip is fantastic) and other means.

It's 3km north of town, but feels miles away from anything.

★**Residence
Bassac Hotel**   BOUTIQUE HOTEL **$$$**
(☏030-5407587; www.residencebassac.com; r incl breakfast US$86-110; ⊛✳☎) The belle of the river, the Residence has rooms that are a mix of old and new, but all ooze charm and induce relaxation. And all have little touches of luxury – ambient lighting, flat-screen TVs, safes and rain showers – that set them apart from the in-town competition. New rooms were being added at the time of our visit.

✕ Eating & Drinking

Guesthouses here do tend to have good food, but their prime amenity is riverside seating. Champasak with Love wins the best deck award, with **Dokchampa** (☏020-55350910; r incl breakfast with fan/air-con 90,000/200,000K; ✳☎) getting honourable mention.

Relaxing with a Beerlao on your guesthouse's deck in the moonlight is a good way to pass the night.

★**Nakorn Cafe
Restaurant**   LAO, INTERNATIONAL **$**
(mains 20,000-53,000K; ◷7.30am-9.30pm; ☎✎) A pleasant melange of classy and casual, this riverside restaurant has a small mixed menu that covers duck *láhp* to chicken green curry to tuna sandwiches. There are some Belgian beers on the menu, and also plenty of local advice available from the affable owners.

Champasak with Love   LAO, THAI **$**
(☏030-9786757; mains 20,000-40,000K; ◷8am-9pm; ☎✎) The marvellous riverfront patio shaded by a big old ficus tree is alone worth a visit, but the food and service are also good. It has the biggest menu in town, with mostly Thai food but also Lao standards and good brownies, fruit salad, sandwiches and breakfasts.

The basic and slightly overpriced guest rooms (with fan/air-con 40,000/80,000K) in the creaky old house have shared bathrooms.

**Residence Bassac
Restaurant**   LAO, INTERNATIONAL **$$**
(mains 40,000-95,000K; ◷7am-10pm; ☎✎) The Residence's sumptuous low-lit restaurant offers a compelling reason to linger longer in Champasak. It's based in a beautifully renovated Chinese shophouse, with a menu that spans mushroom *láhp* to its creative yellow curry pizza.

☆ Entertainment

**Shadow Puppet
Theatre & Cinema Tuktuk**   CINEMA, PUPPETRY
(☏020-55081109; 50,000K; ◷Nov-Apr) Run by Frenchman Yves Bernard, this magical theatre next to the tourist office tells a story from the *Ramayana* with traditional shadow puppets, while on Wednesday and Saturday it sits creens the Academy Award–nominated silent film *Chang* (1927). What makes it so great is the live musicians providing the soundtrack.

Chang was filmed over 18 months in the jungles of northeast Thailand by the writer and director of Hollywood's original *King Kong*.

❶ Information

Lao Development Bank (◷8.30am-3.30pm Mon-Fri) Has an ATM, changes cash and does Western Union.

Champasak District Visitor Information Centre (☏030-9239673; ◷8am-4.30pm Mon-Fri, also open weekends Sep-Apr) The staff here are friendly and can give information and also arrange boats to, and accommodation on, Don Daeng. Local guides, some of whom speak English, lead day walks around Wat Phu and can accompany you to Uo Moung. You can also arrange boats to Uo Moung here (350,000K), taking in Don Daeng and Wat Muang Kang.

❶ Getting There & Away

Champasak is 30km from Pakse along a beautiful, almost empty sealed road running along the west bank of the Mekong. *Sŏrngtǎaou* to Pakse (20,000K, one hour) depart only in the morning, up to around 8am. There are also the tourist buses and boats direct to/from Pakse, but they don't run often due to lack of demand.

The regular morning tourist buses from Pakse to Champasak (55,000, 1½ hours) are actually the buses heading to Si Phan Don and these drop you at Ban Muang on the eastern bank of the Mekong where a small ferry (20,000K per person, 30,000K for motorbikes) crosses to the village of Ban Phaphin just north of Champasak. Be sure you know whether your ticket includes the ferry or not. (The ferrymen won't rip you off over this, but some of the ticket agents in Pakse have been known to.) None of the tickets include the final 2km into Champasak, so you'll probably need to walk in.

To reach Si Phan Don you can also use the Ban Muang **ferry** route or travel by boat (US$240 private; the Champasak District Visitor Information Centre will know if others are interested in sharing the cost).

❶ Getting Around

All guesthouses rent bicycles (10,000K to 20,000K per day) and a few, including **Anouxa** (☑ 020-55339008), also have motorbikes (from 70,000K per day). Anouxa also has mountain bikes, a rarity in Champasak.

AROUND CHAMPASAK

Wat Phu World Heritage Area

A visit to the ancient Khmer religious complex of Wat Phu (ວັດພູຈຳປາສັກ) is one of the highlights of southern Laos. Stretching 1400m up the slopes of Phu Pasak (also known more colloquially as Phu Khuai or Mt Penis), Wat Phu is small compared with the monumental Angkor-era sites near Siem Reap in Cambodia. However, you know the old adage about location, location, location! The tumbledown pavilions,

ornate Shiva-lingam sanctuary, enigmatic crocodile stone and tall trees that shroud much of the upper walkway in soothing shade give Wat Phu an almost mystical atmosphere. These, and a layout that is unique in Khmer architecture, led to Unesco declaring the Wat Phu complex a World Heritage Site in 2001.

An electric cart shuttles guests from the ticket office area past the *baray* (ceremonial pond; *nǎwng sá* in Lao). After that, you must walk.

⊙ Sights

Wat Phu is situated at the junction of the Mekong plain and Phu Pasak, a mountain that was sacred to the Austro-Asiatic tribes living in this area centuries before the construction of any of the ruins now visible.

South of Wat Phu are three small Angkor-era sites in poor condition that will mainly interest die-hard fans of Khmer architecture. Each stands beside the ancient road to Angkor Wat in Cambodia. On the opposite bank of the Mekong, Uo Moung (p222) is also thought to be related to Wat Phu and is encompassed by the Wat Phu Unesco World Heritage Site.

★**Wat Phu Champasak**   RUINS
(ວັດພູຈຳປາສັກ;   50,000K, motorbike parking 5000K; ⊙ site 8am-6pm, museum to 4.30pm) Bucolic Wat Phu sits in graceful decrepitude, and while it lacks the arresting enormity of Angkor in Cambodia, given its few visitors and more dramatic natural setting, these small Khmer ruins evoke a more soulful response. While some buildings are more than 1000 years old, most date from the 11th to 13th centuries. The site is divided into six terraces on three levels joined by a frangipani-bordered stairway ascending the mountain to the main shrine at the top.

Visit in the early morning for cooler temperatures (it gets really hot during the day, and on the lower levels there isn't any shade) and to capture the ruins in the best light. Make sure to grab a map at the entrance as there is little to no signage here.

➡ **Lower Level**
The electric cart takes you past the great *baray* and delivers you to the large sandstone base of the ancient main entrance to Wat Phu. Here begins a causeway-style ceremonial promenade lined by stone lotus buds and flanked by two much smaller *baray* that

Around Champasak

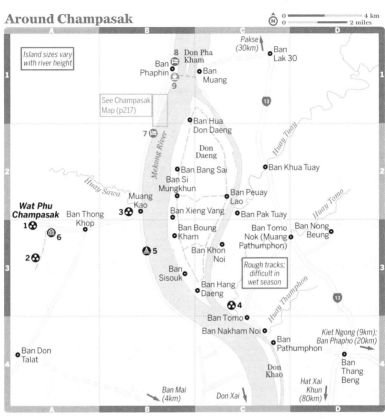

N 0 ———————— 4 km
0 ———————— 2 miles

Island sizes vary with river height

See Champasak Map (p217)

Pakse (30km)

Around Champasak

still fill with water, lotus flowers and the odd buffalo during the wet season.

➡ **Middle Level**

Wat Pu's middle section features two exquisitely carved **quadrangular pavilions** built of sandstone and laterite that are believed to date from the mid-10th or early 11th century. The buildings consist of four galleries and a central open courtyard. Wat Phu was converted into a Buddhist site in later centuries but much of the original Hindu sculpture remains in the lintels, which feature various forms of Vishnu and Shiva.

A good example is the eastern pediment of the north pavilion, which is a relief of Shiva and Parvati sitting on Nandi, Shiva's bull mount.

Next to the southern pavilion stands the much smaller **Nandi Hall** (dedicated to Shiva's mount). It was from here that an ancient royal road once led over 200km to Angkor Wat in Cambodia. In front is a smaller version of the initial causeway, this one flanked by two collapsed galleries, leading to a pair of steep staircases.

At the base of a second stairway is an impressive and now very holy **dvarapala** (sentinel figure) standing ramrod straight with sword held at the ready. Most Thai and Lao visitors make an offering to his spirit before continuing up the mountain. If you step down off the walkway and onto the grassy area just north of here you'll come to the remains of a yoni pedestal, the cosmic vagina-womb symbol associated with Shaivism, and two unusually large, headless and armless **dvarapala statues** half-buried in the grass. These are the largest *dvarapala* found anywhere in the former Angkorian kingdom.

After the *dvarapala* a rough sandstone path ascends quickly to another steep stairway, atop which is a small terrace holding six ruined brick shrines – only one retains some of its original form. From here two final staircases, the second marked by crouching guardians also sans heads and arms, take you to the top, passing through the large terraces you saw clearly from the bottom of the mountain.

Shade is provided along much of this entire middle-level route from *dork jǎmpàh* (plumeria or frangipani), the Lao national tree.

➡ **Upper Level**

On the uppermost level of Wat Phu is the **sanctuary** itself. It has many carvings, notably two guardians and two *apsara*

(celestial dancers), and it once enclosed a Shiva lingam that was bathed, via a system of sandstone pipes, with waters from the **sacred spring** that still flows behind the complex. The sanctuary now contains a set of very old, distinctive Buddha images on an altar. The brick rear section, which might have been built in the 9th century, is a *cella* (cell), where the holy lingam was kept.

Sculpted into a large boulder behind the sanctuary is a Khmer-style **Trimurti**, the Hindu holy trinity of Shiva, Vishnu and Brahma. Further back, beyond some terracing to the south of the Trimurti, is the cave from which the holy spring flowed into the sanctuary. Up a rough path to the north of the Trimurti, a **Buddha footprint** and an elephant are carved into a rock wall.

Just north of the Shiva lingam sanctuary, amid a mess of rocks and rubble, look around for two unique stone carvings known as the **elephant stone** and the **crocodile stone**. Crocodiles were semi-divine figures in Khmer culture, but despite much speculation that the stone was used for human sacrifices, its function – if there was one – remains unknown. The crocodile is believed to date from the Angkor period, while the elephant is thought to date from the 16th century. Also look out for an interesting chunk of a staircase framed by two snakes and some small caves that were probably used for meditation in ancient days.

When you've seen everything here, just sitting and soaking up the wide-angle view of the *baray,* the plains and the Mekong is fantastic. A small shop sells snacks and cool drinks.

Wat Phu Champasak

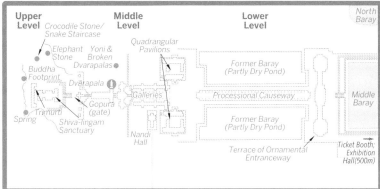

Hong Nang Sida
ARCHAEOLOGICAL SITE

(ໂຮງນາງສິດາ; 8am-4.30pm) **FREE** An easy 2km walk to the south of Wat Phu – follow the signs from near the main gate – stands Nang Sida temple, which probably dates from the middle of the 11th century and might have been the central shrine for a second ancient city. You can walk down the ceremonial causeway to the tower, which has collapsed into an impressively large pile of sandstone blocks. A brick 'library' is off to the side.

Wat Phu Exhibition Hall
MUSEUM

(ຫໍພິພິດຊະພັນວັດພູ; entry with Wat Phu ticket; 8am-4.30pm) The Exhibition Hall near the ticket office showcases dozens of lintels, *naga* (mythical water serpents), Buddhas and other stone work from Wat Phu and its associated sites. Detailed descriptions are in English, plus the building includes clean bathrooms.

Uo Moung
RUINS

(ອູໂມງ, Tomo Temple; 10,000K; 8am-4pm) The Khmer temple ruin of Uo Moung, beside a small tributary of the Mekong, is believed to have been built late in the 9th century during the reign of the Khmer king Yasovarman I. Its exact function is unknown, though its orientation suggests its location was somehow related to Wat Phu Champasak (p219), and thus it's included as part of the Wat Phu World Heritage Site, even though it sits on the east side of the river.

The ruins include an entranceway bordered by lotus-bud carvings, like those found at Wat Phu, and two crumbling *gopura* (ornate entranceways), one still partially standing. Several lintels and other sandstone carvings are displayed on rocks beneath towering dipterocarp trees, but the best art from this site is in the Wat Phu Exhibition Hall, including an unusual lingam-style stone post on which two faces have been carved. It's unusual because *mukhalinga* usually have four *mukha* (faces), while most ordinary lingam have no face at all. The white building at the heart of the site houses a bronze Sukhothai-style Buddha.

Uo Moung is 45km from Pakse. The signed turn-off along Rte 13 is just past the Huay Tomo bridge next to a market where you can look for *săhm-lór* or tuk-tuk if you are travelling by public transport and don't want to walk the 4.5km to the site. It's not worth a trip for everyone, but the forest and excessive moss do give it a 'lost' feeling.

You can also visit Uo Moung by boat from Don Daeng or Champasak on the opposite bank of the Mekong. From Champasak, you're looking at about 400,000K return to charter a boat, including waiting time of an hour or so, to the nearby village of Ban Tomo. The price is about 60,000K or so return from Ban Sisouk at the south end of Don Daeng, although keep in mind that there is a small possibility that no boats will be available.

A good full-day option is to rent a bicycle in Champasak and take a boat first to Don Daeng, then to Ban Tomo, then cross the river back to the western shore (also about 60,000K) and ride back to Champasak.

⚔ Festivals & Events

Bun Wat Phu Champasak
BUDDHIST

(Wat Phu Champasak Festival) The highlight of the year in Wat Phu Champasak is this three-day Buddhist festival, held on Magha Puja day on the full moon of the third lunar month, usually in February. The ceremonies culminate on the full-moon day with an early-morning offering of alms to monks, followed that evening by a candlelit *wéean téean* (circumambulation) of the lower shrines.

Throughout the three days of the festival Lao visitors climb around the hillside, stopping to pray and leave offerings of flowers and incense. The festival is more commercial than it once was, and for much of the time has an atmosphere somewhere between a kids' carnival and music festival. Events include kick-boxing matches, boat races, cockfights, comedy shows and plenty of music and dancing, as bands from as far away as Vientiane arrive. After dark the beer and *lòw-lów* (Lao whisky) flow freely and the atmosphere gets pretty rowdy.

🛏 Sleeping & Eating

It is possible to sleep at a guesthouse near the entrance to Wat Phu, but spending the night next to the Mekong in Champasak town is far superior.

There are restaurants by the entrance to Wat Phu and a small shop selling snacks and cool drinks up at the top.

❶ Getting There & Away

Wat Phu Champasak is 43km from Pakse and 10km from Champasak. It's a flat, easy bike ride from Champasak, though there's not a lot of shade. A tuk-tuk from Champasak will cost around 100,000K return.

MUANG KAO

Under the palm trees and rice paddies 3km south of Champasak town are the remains of a city that was, about 1500 years ago, the capital of the Mon-Khmer Chenla kingdom. The site is known today as **Muang Kao** (ເມືອງເກົ່າ Old City), but scholars believe it was called Shrestapura.

Aerial photographs show the remains of a rectangular city measuring 2.3km by 1.8km, surrounded by double earthen walls on three sides and protected on the east by the Mekong River. Other traces of the old city include small *baray* (a Khmer word meaning 'artificial body of water'), the foundations for circular brick monuments, evidence of an advanced system of irrigation, various Hindu statuary and stone carvings, stone implements and ceramics. The sum of all this is an extremely rare example of an ancient urban settlement in Southeast Asia, one whose design reveals how important religious belief was in the workings of everyday life.

The origin of the city remained a mystery until Southeast Asia's oldest Sanskrit inscription was discovered here. The 5th-century stele stated the city was founded by King Devanika and was then called Kuruksetra; it also mentions the auspicious Sri Lingaparvata nearby, a clear reference to the mountain near Wat Phu Champasak. 'Honoured since antiquity', the mountain was believed to be the residence or the manifestation of the Hindu god Shiva, and even today local people honour the mountain as the place of Phi Intha (the soul or protecting spirit of the mountain).

By the end of the 5th century the city was thriving. It continued as a major regional centre until at least the 7th century, as shown by two Nandi (Shiva's bull mount) pedestal sculptures discovered in 1994–95 bearing inscriptions by King Citrasena-Mahendravarman, the 'conqueror' who later shifted the kingdom's capital to Sambor Prei Kuk in central Cambodia. Archaeological material suggests the city was inhabited until the 16th century.

Ongoing research by Dr Patrizia Zolese and her team has revealed that a second city was built near Wat Phu after the 9th century. She believes the Hong Nang Sida was at the centre of this city, which was probably Lingapura, a place mentioned in many ancient inscriptions but which has not been categorically identified by modern scholars.

Kiet Ngong ບ້ານກ້ຽງໂຍ້ງ

🎵 030

Laos has a few national parks but few of them are carefully managed, and tourist infrastructure is minimal for the most part. The best way to see the Se Pian NPA is to visit the Lao Loum villages of Kiet Ngong.

Kiet Ngong sits at the edge of a bird-rich wetland about 9km from Rte 13. Elephants (which are now used almost exclusively for tourist treks) and an unusually large herd of buffalo give the wetland a safari feel. It's best to sleep here for at least a night, but it also works as a day trip from Pakse or Champasak.

Visitors heading to Kiet Ngong are expected to pay a 25,000K entry fee for Se Pian NPA at the little white building 2km east of Rte 13 that you pass on your way there, though attendance here can be intermittent.

☉ Sights & Activities

The community-run Visitor Information Centre (p224) organises homestays, trekking, birdwatching and other activities. It's best to contact them in advance, although you can usually just show up and arrange things on the spot.

Forest walks and traditional canoe rides (July to March only) in the swamp are the real highlights here. Trips into the jungle of the Se Pian NPA (p224) can range from half-day nature walks to extended overnight treks. Camping gear is available for hire. The wetland, Bueng Kiet Ngong, covers 13.8 sq km and was designated a Ramsar Site (a wetland of international importance) in 2010. It's emerging as a birdwatching destination, with the rare white-winged duck a possible tick.

Guides cost 100,000K per day, with additional costs depending on the particular activity. Things can be arranged either at the Visitor Information Centre or Kingfisher

Ecolodge, although mountain biking (per person 430,000K with two people) is only available from the lodge.

Se Pian NPA
NATIONAL PARK

(ປ່າສະຫງວນແຫ່ງຊາດເຊປຽນ; www.xepian.org) Se Pian NPA is one of the most important protected areas in Laos. The 2400-sq-km park boasts small populations of Asiatic black bears, yellow-cheeked crested gibbons and Siamese crocodiles, and is home to many birds, including the rare sarus crane, vultures and hornbills. Banteng, Asian elephants, gaur and tiger once roamed here, but sightings of these creatures have been rare to nonexistent in recent years.

Stretching from Rte 13 in the west into Attapeu Province in the east, and to the Cambodian border in the south, it is fed by three major rivers: the Se Pian, Se Khampho and Se Kong.

It's almost impossible to visit the park under your own steam, but you can get into the park for either tough multiday jungle treks or short nature walks, bike trips and boat rides through Kiet Ngong village or Green Discovery tour company (p209) in Pakse. If you're feeling really frisky and adventurous, you could try to charter a boat down the Sekong from Sanamsay, on Rte 18A about 35km west of Attapeu. This trip towards the Cambodian border would get you deep into a scenic section of Se Pian NPA.

🛏 Sleeping & Eating

In addition to the excellent Kingfisher Ecolodge, the Kiet Ngong community offers two types of accommodation, both booked through the Visitor Information Centre. Choose from a homestay with a local family or the community guesthouse with dorm-style sleeping in bungalows in a great spot overlooking the wetland. Some, but not all, homestay homes have hot-water showers. Both options cost 40,000K per person, plus 30,000K for meals.

There are a few guesthouses with restaurants in Kiet Ngong village, but it's a matter of luck if they are open. Either way, community meals in homestays (per meal 30,000K) are the better option.

Bounhome Homestay
HOMESTAY $

(☏ 030-5346293; per bed 50,000K) In Ban Phapho (Phapho Village), 10km east of Kiet Ngong, this homestay has four small, ultra-simple rooms in the family's wooden house. The bathroom is shared and there's no hot water, but Mr Bounhome and his family speak some English and French and have been welcoming travellers for well over 20 years.

Order meals of *láhp* and *kòw něeo* (20,000K) in advance. Mr Bounhome can also take you out for forest walks and boat trips.

★ Kingfisher Ecolodge
LODGE $$

(☏ 020-55726315; www.kingfisherecolodge.com; bungalows 800,000K; ☉ closed May & Jun; 🛜) 🌿 Run by a Lao-Italian family, the Kingfisher Ecolodge is set on 7 hectares at the edge of the wetland, about 700m past Kiet Ngong village. It's a beautiful spot. Sitting on your balcony at dawn and watching birds flit across the wetland is a memorable experience and the two-tiered restaurant-bar could easily be in an East African safari lodge.

The seven comfortable bungalows have a great safari feel, with natural timbers and thatched grass, and huge wooden countertops in the bathrooms, polished hardwood pillars and floors, lovely beds and – the coup de grâce – large balconies with hammocks. The economy rooms have more modest balconies and share a spotless bathroom. Air-con rooms and a swimming pool were being planned at the time of research.

Most activities offered by the Visitor Information Centre are also offered here, with the addition of full-day guided mountain-bike tours (per person 430,000K with two people) into Se Pian NPA. And it lives up to the 'eco' in its name by supporting the local school, using solar power and promoting conservation within Se Pian NPA.

Wi-fi is available only in the restaurant.

ℹ Information

Visitor Information Centre (☏ 030-9552120; ☉ 8am-4pm) This community-run centre in the middle of Kiet Ngong arranges activities, accommodation and transport from Rte 13. Placards on the walls have useful information about the various options and also the ecology, history and culture of the area. A few of the guides speak some English. All activities can also be arranged through the excellent Kingfisher Ecolodge.

ℹ Getting There & Away

Kiet Ngong is 56km from central Pakse. Most visitors come here as part of a tour, but travelling independently is fairly easy. One van or *sǒrngtǎaou* (30,000K, two to 2½ hours) leaves Kiet Ngong for Lak 8 bus station in Pakse at about 8am and heads back at 11am. Kiet Ngong is often mispronounced so ask instead for 'Phu Asa'. Alternatively, board anything going south on Rte 13, get off at Ban Thang Beng and call the Visitor Information Centre for a pick-up by motorcycle (25,000K per person) for the last 9km to the village.

BOLAVEN PLATEAU REGION

Spreading across parts of all four southern provinces, the fertile Bolaven Plateau (ພູພຽງບໍລະເວນ; known in Lao as Phu Phieng Bolaven) is famous for its cool climate, dramatic waterfalls and high-grade coffee.

The French started planting coffee, rubber and bananas in the early 20th century, but many left following independence in the 1950s and the rest followed when US bombardment began in the late '60s. Controlling the Bolaven Plateau was considered strategically vital to both the Americans and North Vietnamese, as evidenced by the staggering amount of unexploded ordnance (UXO) still lying around. But where it has been cleared, both local farmers and large companies are busy cultivating coffee. Other local products include fruit, cardamom, rattan and, more recently, avocados.

The largest ethnic group on the plateau is the Laven (Bolaven means 'Home of the Laven'). Several other Mon-Khmer ethnic groups, including the Alak, Katu, Tahoy and Suay, also live on the plateau and its escarpment.

Paksong Area

Paksong, Laos' coffee capital, is not much to look at, most of it having been obliterated in a storm of bombs during the Second Indochina War. Other than doing a coffee tour or buying a fresh cuppa, you probably won't want to stop here. While many of the waterfalls near the town definitely should be part of your Bolaven itinerary, they can easily be reached from Pakse.

⊙ Sights

Many spectacular cascades sit within striking distance of Paksong, the most popular of which are Tat Fan and Tat Nyeuang (p226),

though the less-visited and more-distant clutch of cascades at Tayicseua are the best of the bunch. All are signed from the main road and buses can drop you at the turn-offs. Women swimming at any of the falls should wear a shirt or a sarong.

Coffee plantations of varying sizes blanket the plateau, and from November to February you'll see the beans out drying in the sun. Many families along the road between Pakse and Paksong encourage you to stop in for a quick visit. For something more formal, you can take a coffee tour (p227).

★ Tayicseua   WATERFALL
(ຕາຍິກເສືອ; 5000K, parking 5000K) There are seven significant waterfalls (none of them named Tayicseua) and several smaller ones at this remote but easily accessible private nature reserve. Some sit right near the restaurant-parking area while others, such as postcard-worthy Tat Halang (aka Tat Alang), are down in the forest along a good set of trails, which you can walk without a guide. It's in the early stages of growing into a proper resort but, for now, crowds remain rare.

Due to the size of the area and the serene setting, the best way to visit is to spend the night at Tayicseua Guesthouse (p227).

Tayicseua sits off the main paved road 43km from Paksong. Coming from the east it's 4km from the paved road to the signed entrance. For the most part, this dirt road is fine, but there are some steep, rough spots that require care on a motorcycle, especially in the rainy season. The longer dirt road from the west is much smoother.

★ Tat Fan   WATERFALL
(ຕາດຟານ; Tad Fane; Rte 16, Km 38; 10,000K, motorcycle/car 3000/5000K) Tat Fan is one of the most spectacular waterfalls in Laos. Twin streams plunge out of dense forest and tumble down more than 120m to form the Huay Bang Lieng. Early morning and late afternoon have the best sunlight, but the falls are often shrouded in fog. The viewing point is at Tad Fane Resort (p227), a jungle lodge atop the cliff opposite the falls, and it's a near-mandatory stop for anyone in the area.

One way to beat the crowds is to take a trek to the top or bottom. The price is US$10/15 per person for a half-/full-day hike, and this includes the national-park entrance fee. The half-day walk includes a visit to nearby Tat Nyeuang (p226) and an abandoned temple.

The access road to the falls is in Ban Lak 38, which is 12km from Paksong.

Tat Champee
WATERFALL

(ຕາດຈຳປີ; Rte 16, Km 38; 5000K, motorcycle/car 3000/5000K) Not to be confused with the far inferior waterfall of the same name along Rte 20 on the way to Tat Lo, this is the smallest of the four waterfalls west of Paksong, but it's the most fun to visit. A good set of concrete steps leads down to an up-close viewpoint, then a sketchy wooden staircase or a longer footpath takes you down to the river, where you can swim and even go behind the waterfall.

The 2km road leading to it (which begins directly across from the road to Tat Fan) is a bit rough, so it's the only waterfall around Paksong that doesn't get crowded. The access road is 12km from Paksong.

Dong Hua Sao NPA
NATIONAL PARK

(ປ່າສະຫງວນແຫ່ງຊາດດົງຫົວສາວ) The 1100-sq-km Dong Hua Sao NPA, south of Paksong, is home to large tracts of pristine jungle, where you might spot monkeys, large butterflies and rare hornbills. Poaching is a problem, as is illegal logging to plant coffee. Adventure specialist Green Discovery (p209) runs its Tree Top Explorer trips here, which are an excellent way to experience the park, though bookings must be made in Pakse. Treks run by Tad Fane Resort also get you into the park.

Tat E-Tu
WATERFALL

(ຕາດອີຕູ້; Rte 16, Km 35; 5000K, motorcycle/car 3000/5000K) Just 1km north of the main road (Rte 16), this is the first large waterfall you reach on the drive up from Pakse. The waterfall is beautiful, and its 40m drop impressive, though it's less visited than some other waterfalls nearby. It's a short walk to the viewpoint from the parking area, with steep but solid steps leading to the bottom of the falls.

The access road is 15km from Paksong.

ⓘ WARNING: TAT KATAMTOK

At the time of research there had been numerous reports of accidents and violence along the road into Tat Katamtok, and tour operators had ceased going there for a number of years. For that reason it is not advised to travel to this waterfall until the situation changes.

Tat Nyeuang
WATERFALL

(ຕາດເຍືອງ; Rte 16, Km 40; 10,000K, motorcycle/car 10,000K; ⊙ticket booth 8am-5pm, falls to 6.30pm) Probably the most developed of the Bolaven Plateau waterfalls, Tat Yuang, as some signs spell it, is impressive, with its twin torrents falling about 40m into lush jungle. It's very popular with day trippers and there's a bit of a festive atmosphere on weekends, with handicraft shops and food stalls lining the path to the waterfall.

A fun stairway leads through the forest to other viewpoints and a path leads all the way to the bottom. Swimming at the top is fine year-round, but don't try to swim at the bottom in the rainy season.

The turnoff is about 1km past Ban Lak 38, then 1.2km from the highway to the park.

🏃 Activities & Tours

Rafting and kayaking trips are possible on Huay Bang Lieng, the river that feeds Tat Fan, during the wet season from July to November. For details speak to Green Discovery (p209) in Pakse.

Tad Fane Zipline
ADVENTURE SPORTS

(Tad Fane Resort, Rte 16, Km 38; US$40) This exhilarating zipline is not for the faint-hearted! The ride takes you over 250m above the forest below, with spectacular views of the twin falls of Tat Fan. It's split into four sections and includes some forest walking. Guides are on hand to give assistance if required.

Koffie's Coffee Tours
TOURS

(☑020-22760439; www.paksong.info; per person coffee tour 50,000K, tour incl roasting workshop 180,000K) 'Mr Koffie', an expat Dutch coffee connoisseur, leads coffee tours around Paksong. The two-hour tour looks at growing, harvesting and processing coffee, and samples local brews. At the afternoon roasting workshop you'll finish the day with a cup you brewed yourself and a bag of beans to take home. Tours start at 10am at Won Coffee (p228).

🛏 Sleeping

While many travellers base themselves in Pakse and make day trips to destinations in the Bolaven Plateau, there are also many rustic accommodation options in the Paksong area, where the major waterfalls are. There's little need for air-con up here, and indeed most resorts don't even offer it. But you have the advantage of seclusion, plus

LAO COFFEE

The high, flat ground, fertile, mineral-rich volcanic soils and heavy rainfall of the Bolaven Plateau are ideal for growing coffee, and the region produces some of the best and most expensive beans on earth: arabica, arabica typica and robusta are all grown here. The 'coffee town' of Paksong is at the centre of it all.

The French introduced coffee to the Bolaven Plateau in the early 1900s and the arabica typica shipped home became known as the 'champagne of coffee'. The carpet bombing of the '60s and '70s put the brakes on the business, but things began to pick up in the 1990s and now nearly 30,000 tonnes of green coffee beans – 90% of all coffee produced in Laos – are grown in Paksong and the adjacent Tha Taeng districts.

Though the money provided by growing coffee has benefited thousands of people in the area, particularly women, water pollution and deforestation are serious downsides to the coffee boom.

The largest producer is Pakse-based Dao Heung. You'll see the factory on the drive up to Paksong, as well as the owner's outrageous mansion in Pakse, next to the Japanese bridge.

Two very different coffee shops in Paksong, Won Coffee (p228) and Jhai Coffee House (p228) (just 200m from each other, on the south side of the road in the centre of Paksong near the hospital), offer top-shelf brews, and Won Coffee offers educational coffee tours. These tours should be booked in advance, but you can try your luck just showing up.

some of the most beautiful scenery on the plateau.

★Tayicseua Guesthouse   GUESTHOUSE $
(☎020-95399789; www.tayicseua.com; off Rte 16; dm 60,000K, r 120,000K; ☜) This friendly spot surrounded by seven large waterfalls (p225) deserves its rave reviews. You'll fall asleep to tumbling water and wake up to birdsong from under mosquito nets in rustic bamboo huts (or your own tent), or more substantial timber bungalows. A communal lodge overlooks the distant mists of Tat Jariem deep in the valley below. Simple meals cost 20,000K.

Everything is very basic, but all things considered, this place is perfect for those OK with roughing it a bit.

Mystic Mountain Coffee   HOMESTAY $
(☎020-99661333; www.mysticmountain.coffee; r per person 25,000K) Friendly Mr Khamsone has built a couple of simple rooms with two beds at his remote coffee plantation. Though facilities are rustic, you'll be well cared for. Tours (from US$60 per person) are the main focus. Meals are free if you book a tour, otherwise they're 20,000K. It's about 12km north of Paksong on the rough road to Lao Ngam. Reservations required.

Tad Fane Resort   RESORT $$
(☎020-56693366; www.tadfaneresort.com; Rte 16, Km 38; r incl breakfast US$30-50; ☜) This jungle lodge has a one-of-a-kind location, overlooking Tat Fan and nestled in a cool forest

setting. The rustic duplex cottages let you enjoy the nightly symphony of forest sounds and get up to see the falls before the crowds arrive. A few of the cottages at the back even have partial waterfall views.

A big attraction here is the zip line (p226), but the resort also offers half-day (US$10) and one-day (US$15) guided forest walks to Tat Nyeaung, among other places.

Baan E-Tu Waterfall Resort   RESORT $$
(☎020-22769769, in Thailand 020-28347766; www.etuwaterfall.com; Rte 16, Km 35; all incl breakfast r 320,000-350,000K, bungalows 420,000K; ❄☜) Set on a former coffee and tea plantation 15km west of Paksong, the smart bungalows at this sprawling resort have polished wooden floors, ultrasoft beds and – in the priciest rooms – large balconies within earshot of Tat E-Tu.

Sinouk Coffee Resort   BOUTIQUE HOTEL $$$
(☎030-9558960; https://sinouk-resort.business. site; Rte 16; r incl breakfast US$70-100; ➡❄@☜) Set beside a babbling brook on a working coffee plantation 32km northeast of Paksong on the road to Tha Taeng, there's a hill-station feel here. Like its sister lodge, Pakse's Residence Sisouk (p210), it's loaded with indigenous textiles, period furniture and framed old-world photos. It's also worth stopping in for a meal (mains 25,000K to 75,000K) amidst the manicured gardens if you're passing by.

SOUTHERN LAOS PAKSONG AREA

✖️ Eating & Drinking

There are restaurants at all the waterfalls, which is where you should eat, and also Paksong town if you need them.

Tad Fane Restaurant
LAO $

(📞 020-56693366; Tad Fane Resort, Rte 16, Km 38; mains 25,000-40,000K; ⏰ 7.30am-10.30pm; 📶) The restaurant at the Tad Fane Resort (p227) may look deserted when you visit but it is open to visitors as well as the resort's guests. Dishes cover the usual gamut of Western and Lao choices.

Tat Nyeuang Restaurant
LAO $

(📞 020-56365324; Rte 16, Km 40; mains 30,000-50,000K; ⏰ 7am-6pm) If you're visiting Tat Nyeuang (p226) you won't go wrong visiting its namesake restaurant, an open wooden building with novelty music blaring and some good Lao dishes on offer, including its signature two-colour sticky rice.

Jhai Coffee House
COFFEE

(www.jhaicoffeehouse.com; Rte 16, Paksong; ⏰ 8am-5.30pm; 📶) 🍴 Billing itself as the world's first completely philanthropic coffee roaster and cafe located at the source, Jhai buys its beans at fair-trade prices from the Jhai Coffee Farmer Cooperative and puts 100% of profits back into local water and hygiene projects and children's education needs. It's a surprising little oasis with perfect coffee (12,000K to 15,000K) in the centre of Paksong town.

Won Coffee
COFFEE

(Rte 16, Paksong; ⏰ 7am-5.30pm; 📶) Though run in part by 'Mr Koffie' (p226), this is very much a local spot. Besides regular organic coffees (from 10,000K), he produces his own civet-excreted *kopi luwak* (30,000K per cup or 250,000K per 100g) and leads coffee tours. It's in the centre of town. Look out for the 'Won Coffee' sign.

ℹ️ Getting There & Away

Travel by hired motorcycle is best, but all buses heading east from Pakse can drop you in Paksong (15,000K, 90 minutes) or near any of the waterfalls to the west of town. For Tayicseua, take an Attapeu bus, but make sure it's one using the direct route rather than going via Sekong.

Tat Lo
ຕາດເລາະ

♪ 030

Tat Lo (pronounced *dàht ló*) has taken a place on the backpacker trail thanks to an attractive setting, cheap accommodation

and some beautiful waterfalls. It lacks the party scene of Don Det and Vang Vieng, and locals are set on it staying this way. Thankfully, several Westerners who have settled here and opened businesses are in full agreement. The result is a serenity that sees many visitors stay longer than they planned.

The availability of day treks, along with widespread use of English, makes Tat Lo by far the best base for getting to know the Bolaven Plateau, even though it actually sits against the foot of it, rather than up on top of it. The real name of Tat Lo village is Ban Saen Vang, but these days everybody just calls it Tat Lo.

👁️ Sights

There are actually three waterfalls on this stretch of river: Tat Lo, Tat Hang and Tat Soung. Tat Lo, ironically, is the least impressive. In fact, all three are much less beautiful than they once were due to the building of a new dam.

Note that dam authorities upstream release water in the evening and being in its path could be fatal. Check with locals about the release time before you visit the falls.

⭐ Tat Soung
WATERFALL

(ຕາດສູງ; parking 5000K) Tat Soung is a 50m drop over the edge of the Bolaven Plateau, and though the dam has affected these falls more than the others – slowing them to a trickle for most of the year – you can walk around the rocky top of the falls from where the views are fantastic. During heavy rains from August to October, when they reach their full width, the falls themselves are quite spectacular too.

Tat Soung is 8km south of Tat Lo town, uphill almost the entire way. Along the way, 3.5km out of Tat Lo, you'll pass a sign for the bottom of the falls at Ban Kiang Tat Soung (Kiang Tat Soung Village). (Note that the sign inside the village saying 'top' is a mistake.) It's a fun walk and a beautiful destination, and young guides will offer to walk you there for a small tip. It's a round trip of about 1.5km. Definitely don't leave anything in your motorcycle basket; chances are it won't be there when you get back.

Ban Houay Houn
VILLAGE

(ບ້ານຫ້ວຍຫຸນ) You'll know you've arrived in this village, 24km from Tat Lo, by the 'Katu Weavers' sign or the tourists gathered around the traditional community meeting hall. The women here weave cotton textiles using back-strap looms held taut with their feet. Bold patterns are added with white beads. While red and black are the Katu tribe's traditional colours, they now weave from the whole rainbow to match tourist demand.

Although this is certainly not a traditional village experience, and this type of weaving is done in many other villages, it's worth a stop since at least one woman comes to sell and weave daily so you can be sure of seeing it. There's no guarantee you'll have such luck elsewhere.

Tat Lo   WATERFALL

(ຕາດເລາະ) FREE Tat Lo, about 500m up-river from Tat Hang, is a little bigger than its neighbour, but probably won't knock your socks off. To get here, walk past Saise Resort's bungalows and follow the road to the end, then you need to scramble over some rocks. To reach the top of the falls, it's 1km up the eastern road from the village's junction to the signed turn-off.

Tat Hang   WATERFALL

(ຕາດຮັງ) FREE Tat Hang is the waterfall you see from the bridge in town and some guest-houses. It's about 6m tall and wide, with several steps making it quite beautiful even in low flow. You can swim here; often along with hordes of locals.

✈ Activities

The Tat Lo Guides Association, operated out of the Tat Lo Tourism Information Centre, offers highly recommended walks (half-/full day 80,000/160,000K per person) combining all three waterfalls – Tat Hang, Tat Lo and Tat Soung – with visits to Katu, Tahoy and/or Suay ethnic-minority villages.

For something more adventurous they can also lead you to some more distant waterfalls and cultural stops, such as a cave with ancient stone caskets. Or, consider the two-day excursion to **Phou Tak Khao** mountain, with an overnight in an ethnic Suay village. This costs US$100/60 per person for a group of two/four people with local guides; English-speaking guides cost extra.

🛏 Sleeping & Eating

If you book a room in advance, ask your guesthouse about free transfers from the highway (Rte 20). The Tat Lo Tourism Information Centre can arrange homestays for 25,000K per person.

Generally people just eat at their guesthouses, though there are several small non-affiliated restaurants around.

★ Mr Vieng Coffee
& Homestay   HOMESTAY $

(☑ 020-99837206; Ban Houay Houn; per person 20,000K, per meal 15,000K) This fun, friendly homestay on a coffee plantation in Ban Houay Houn sits just in from Rte 20, 19km southwest of Tat Lo. Rooms are simple, but quite good for the price, and the ethnic Katu couple who run it give plantation tours (15,000K per person), and make and sell weavings. A grass-roofed pavilion to showcase weaving and other products was underway at the time of research.

Tadlo Lodge   RESORT $$

(☑ 020-99352198; souriyavincent@yahoo.com; r/ste incl breakfast from US$50/100; ❀ 🛜) Situated above Tat Hang, this is the only semi-fancy lodging around. The main building exudes some classic Lao style, while rooms are stylish and comfortable with decks out front. The views of the falls from the restaurant are excellent. Only the suite has air-conditioning. Animal lovers should note that the hotel keeps trekking elephants chained up most of the day.

Saise Resort   RESORT $$

(☑ 020-59156666; r 150,000-250,000K; ❀ 🛜) Set in the forest right up against Tat Hang, this is probably the best place in the area in terms of location, although staff are a bit indifferent, and the rooms are fairly basic. If you get one with a view of the falls it might be worth it.

Saise Resort   LAO, THAI $

(mains 20,000-60,000K; ☉ 7am-9pm; 🛜) Saise Resort has good food (mostly Thai) served on a great deck with an awesome view of Tat Hang. It's worth making one trip out here during your stay for the views alone.

ℹ Information

The only financial resource in this area is an ATM up at the highway, though guesthouses change money at terrible rates; you're better off changing money before you arrive.

Tat Lo Tourism Information Centre (☑ 020-54455907; kouka222@hotmail.com; ☉ 8-11.30am & 1.30-4.30pm Mon-Fri, daily Nov-Feb) This helpful centre runs the Tat Lo Guides Association. It should be your first stop if you need a guide or info on local excursions, or plan to venture deeper into Salavan Province and beyond. It can also help you with public transport options around the Bolaven Plateau. Maps and brochures on the region are available. Kouka speaks English and is worth contacting in advance to book as an English-speaking guide.

❶ Getting There & Away

Just say 'Tat Lo' at Pakse's Southern Bus Terminal (p212) and you'll be pointed to one of the nine daily buses to Salavan that stop on Rte 20 at Ban Khoua Set (30,000K, two hours), from where it's a 1.5km walk or moto-taxi ride (10,000K) to Tat Lo.

For Sekong (20,000K, one hour) or Attapeu (40,000K, three hours), your best bet is the morning bus that passes through Ban Beng, which is a 15,000K moto-taxi ride away from Tat Lo. In Ban Beng you can also catch some minibuses and *sŏrngtăaou* to Sekong and passing buses to Paksong (20,000K, one hour). The Tat Lo Tourism Information Centre (p229) can call to have buses to Vietnam stop and pick you up at Ban Khoua Set.

Salavan   ສາລະວັນ

🎵 034 / POP 12,700

Salavan (spelt various ways, including Saravan and Saravane) is just 30km from popular Tat Lo, but is not heavily visited. The town is rather pleasant but has no outstanding sights. The best thing visitors can do here is get out and explore the ethnic diversity of the countryside.

While more than half of the population of Salavan Province is ethnically Lao (Loum and Soung), few are native to this area. The remainder of the 350,000 inhabitants belong to various Mon-Khmer groups, including the Tahoy, Lavai, Alak, Laven, Ngai, Tong, Pako, Kanay, Katu, Kado and Katang, the last being expert weavers.

◎ Sights

The most appealing of Salavan's meagre attractions is its market, but anyone with an interest in Buddhist art will also enjoy a quick jaunt around town. A provincial museum has been built, but had not yet opened at the time of research.

Better than anything in town, although a bit of a challenge to get to, is the ruined Prince Souphanouvong's Bridge, about 18km away, and the weaving villages around Toumlan.

Salavan Market   MARKET

(ຕະຫຼາດສາລະວັນ; ⊙6am-6.30pm) Many women come in to this market from the surrounding villages to sell foods they've collected or caught in the forest, such as mushrooms, bamboo shoots, ant eggs and monitor lizards.

Wat Kang Salavan   BUDDHIST TEMPLE

(ວັດກາງສາລະວັນ, Wat Simongkhoun) Founded over two centuries ago, this temple, 700m northeast of the market, has a very large *hŏr dąi* – a building dedicated to Buddhist scriptures – located in a pond, to prevent termites from eating the holy manuscripts stored inside. It is supported by 57 pillars and has been undergoing renovation for some time. The gold finishing and dark wooden pillars are striking.

Much of the temple was destroyed in 1972 and brick remains of the former *sĭm* (hall) and stupa are hidden by brush across the road.

○ Around Town

Prince Souphanouvong's Bridge   RUINS

(Ban Dan Bridge; Rte 23) Really only of interest to dedicated bike riders, this ruin of a bridge is way off the beaten track, about 10km west of Salavan and then 10km north. The 150m-long bridge was blown up by American bombers in 1968 due to its position on a supply branch of the Ho Chi Minh Trail. Only some concrete supports and a part of the steel span remain. The contrast between heavy war damage and the peaceful setting makes it quite interesting.

The bridge is named after its builder, the 'Red Prince' Souphanouvong, who was a trained engineer.

You can take a ferry (10,000K) to visit the other side; in dry months you can just walk across the river.

Pretty well the only way to get here is by motorcycle. You can continue on to Toumlan, though there are lots of missing small bridges, so enquire in Salavan before attempting this route in the rainy season. The trip is interesting as it affords a beautiful drive following the mountains of the Se Ban Nuan NPA.

Toumlan   VILLAGE

(ບ້ານຕຸ້ມລານ) Toumlan, 50km north of Salavan, is a slapped-together boom town with some small shops and restaurants and several oversized, out-of-place government buildings. The surrounding Katang villages comprise one of Laos' most important **weaving** regions. Women here weave a variety of silk and cotton styles, including some *mat-mee* (ikat or tie-dye), using large wooden floor looms instead of the back-strap looms typical in the Bolaven region.

Although virtually no English or Thai is spoken, if you see someone weaving you will almost certainly be welcome to stop and watch, as long as you're polite and friendly – this includes not turning your visit into a photo shoot. The best place to look is along the highway east of Toumlan proper where seemingly every house has a loom under it. Many of these villages raise their own silkworms.

The famous Lapup buffalo sacrifice festival is usually held in late February.

There's no public transport up here, but Rte 15A is paved and in good condition, or you can take the adventurous way using Rte 23 past Prince Souphanouvong's Bridge.

Ta-Oy   VILLAGE

(ບ້ານຕາໂອ້ຍ) Though it's hard to justify a trip all the way to Ta-Oy on its own, it makes a good add-on if you'd like to turn a half-day trip to Toumlan into a full-day journey. The route here crosses a remote mountainous area with few villages, and – though most of the area has been intensively logged – there are still some beautiful moments. Ta-Oy was once an important marker on the Ho Chi Minh Trail and two major branches split off here.

This is a centre for the Tahoy ethnic group, who number around 30,000 spread across the eastern areas of Salavan and Sekong Provinces. Other groups in this region include Katang, Pako, Kado and Kanay. The Tahoy live in forested mountain valleys and, like many Mon-Khmer groups in southern Laos, they practise a combination of animism and shamanism; during village ceremonies, the Tahoy put up diamond-patterned bamboo totems to warn outsiders not to enter. Keep your eyes peeled for some of their enormous **longhouses** in and around town. You'll see some in a village just before crossing the large bridge into Ta-Oy. Down below the town, upstream from the bridge, are beautiful **rapids** that can be easily reached by a short footpath.

Ta-Oy is 80km from Salavan on a good paved road, and you could double the distance and continue to Samouy near the Vietnamese border. Both are small but

OFF THE BEATEN TRACK

VISITING PROTECTED AREAS

Though much of the province is still covered by natural forest, visiting the protected areas is really tough since they have almost no tourist infrastructure. The tourism office (p232) in Salavan can organise treks and arrange guides. It can also help out with homestays. Contact the office in advance for all of these. Truthfully, though, you'd probably have better luck arranging it through the Tat Lo Tourism Information Centre (p229).

developed towns with a few guesthouses as well as places to eat and fuel up.

🛏 Sleeping & Eating

Most lodging is on Rte 15 west of the centre and there are some more choices on the way into town from the south.

Despite its size, Salavan is one of Laos' most culinarily challenged towns. That said, Sabaidee Salavan is pretty good and has an English menu.

Phonexay Hotel   HOTEL $
(☏ 020-91999655; Rte 15; r with fan 780,000K; r with air-con 120,000-200,000K; ✳ 🛜) As the main building is fairly newish and the rooms have wi-fi, this mostly clean place 1.5km west of the market is the best lodging choice in town. Rooms in the newer building are large, spotless and well appointed, although wi-fi was patchy when we visited.

Jindavone Guesthouse   GUESTHOUSE $
(☏ 034-211065; r with fan/air-con 70,000/100,000K; ✳) This eye-catching blue building just off the southeast corner of the market is cheap and central, and has a nice feel to it. Rooms on the 2nd floor can catch a bit of a breeze. The friendly family who run it speak a little English.

Phoufa Hotel   HOTEL $
(☏ 030-5370799; Rte 20; r 60,000-150,000K; ✳ 🛜) An older, but overall good hotel with a variety of clean and fairly well-maintained bungalows surrounded by pleasant gardens with some tall trees. It's along Rte 20, 1.5km before you enter town.

Sabaidee Salavan   LAO, THAI $
(mains 15,000-50,000K; ⏱ 7am-8.30pm) One of the few dining options in town with an

English menu, Sabaidee does a good job with all the standard Lao and Thai dishes, and also offers sukiyaki. The food is delicious and the Thai pop music not too loud. It's located off Rte 15, around the corner from the Phonexay Hotel.

ℹ️ Information

UXO remains a serious problem in rural areas, so exercise caution if you go out exploring the province beyond main roads: stick to established tracks and trails.

There are several banks and ATMs in town, including some around the market.

Salavan Tourism Centre (📞 034-211528; ⏰ 8am-4pm Mon-Fri) Staff are eager to help and some are knowledgeable about tourism in the area. It's south of the market, next to the large, glass-fronted Phongsavanh Bank building.

ℹ️ Getting There & Away

Salavan's bus terminal is 2km west of the town centre, where Rte 20 meets Rte 15. There are nine daily buses to Pakse (30,000K, three hours), with three (8.30am, 4pm, 4.30pm) continuing on to Vientiane (regular/sleeper 130,000/190,000K, 12 to 14 hours), and one bus to Attapeu (50,000K, 4½ hours).

No buses to Vietnam originate here, but you can hope one passing through from Pakse has empty seats.

Attapeu ອັດຕະປື

📞 036 / POP 15,900

Attapeu, the capital of Attapeu Province, is set where the Se Kong (Kong River) and the smaller Se Kaman (Kaman River) meet. It is an unexciting but not unpleasant place. Around Laos it is known as the 'garden village' for its abundant trees and shrubbery.

Despite any hope inspired by the greenery, the town itself is short on attractions, though the nearby temples at Saisettha and war junk in Pa-Am are interesting.

The province became news in 2018 when part of one of the many hydroelectricity dams being built in Laos collapsed, causing the destruction of several villages and significant loss of life.

A Vietnamese phrasebook will be just as useful here as a Lao dictionary since about half the population is Vietnamese.

⊙ Sights

Attapeu's standard attractions are pretty ho-hum, but the sunsets down by the river can be fantastic. Indeed, the city's most interesting sights are not in Attapeu at all: a visit to the villages of Saisettha and Pa-Am (p234) makes a great half-day trip, while the beautiful volcanic crater lake Nong Fa (Sky Blue Lake) in Dong Amphan NPA (p235) is more challenging to reach, but worth the effort.

The town has been promoting two rather spectacular waterfalls that lie about 40km out of town, Tat Sae Pha and Tat Sae Pong Lai. The 2018 hydroelectricity dam collapse stymied those efforts, but rebuilding has since got under way.

Attapeu Provincial Museum MUSEUM (ຫໍພິພິດທະພັນແຂວງອັດຕະປື; Samakhy Rd; ⏰ 8.30-11.30am & 1.30-4pm Mon-Fri) FREE This large, elegant building holds a small collection of rural and tribal artefacts, tools such

GETTING TO VIETNAM: LA LAY TO LALAY

Getting to the border Most people travelling from Pakse to Hué and Danang use sleeper buses, which go through the Lao Bao border crossing east of Savannakhet. The faster minibuses, on the other hand, go via Salavan and cross at La Lay (Laos)/Lalay (Vietnam). If you're in Salavan, you don't need to backtrack to Pakse. There are usually seats available when the buses from Pakse pass through. There isn't much traffic on this route, so doing the trip in stages is not recommended, but if you're set on it, start with the 7.30am minibus to Samouy (35,000K, 3½ hours), which is very near the border.

At the border The border is open from 6am to 7pm and though it's little more than a shack you will probably not have any hassles (other than the usual Lao 'overtime fee'), assuming you have your Vietnamese visa already, or don't need one. In the reverse, you can get a Lao visa at the border.

Moving on For those going in stages, most of the traffic here is trucks, so you should be able to buy an onward ride, though be sure you know whether the driver will be taking a right at the junction to Hué and Danang or turning left to Đông Hà.

ATTAPEU DAM COLLAPSE

On 23 July 2018 at around 8pm the Saddle Dam D portion of a large hydroelectric project in southern Laos, under pressure from more intense than usual seasonal rainfall in the form of tropical storm Son-Tinh, collapsed, causing a flash flood of billions of litres of water to wash into Attapeu's Sanamsai district. The result was a virtual tsunami, a wall of water, mud, trees and rocks (some as big as trucks) that smashed into and over a number of villages, including Hinlat, Ban Mai, Tha Hin and Samong, which were destroyed.

While officials had been aware of the imminence of the collapse and made efforts to warn people, some of the villagers only became aware of the event when they saw the mass of destruction racing towards them, as they attempted to flee in whatever way possible, clambering up trees with children in their arms or seeking high roofs (not all of which were safe: the school house in Ban Mai ended up with a massive 20m-long tree trunk atop its smashed roof). An estimated 120 people died or went missing as a result of the tragedy, and thousands were displaced. Moreover, one year later the recovery was still under way. As of mid-2019 many people were still living in temporary, refugee-like accommodation while awaiting relocation to new villages being built on higher ground. Returning to their former villages is not an option – the thick silt dumped over the flooded ground has rendered the land useless for farming.

as a rice husker, models of various kinds of tribal houses and some weapons, as well as countless photos of local dignitaries. It's worth a peek if you have nothing else to do, although bear in mind that the building does leak badly in heavy rain.

Lak 3 Market MARKET
(ຕະຫຼາດຫຼັກ 3) A lively market selling fresh foods, baguettes and other snacks.

Around Town

Tat Sae Pha WATERFALL
(ຕາດແຊພະ) One of the most beautiful waterfalls in Laos, Tat Sae Pha, about 40km from Attapeu, is way off the beaten track and pretty well impossible to access in the rainy season, but in the drier months it's well worth the journey. Cascading down 20m in a broad horseshoe shape, the falls form a spectacular sight. It's possible to get close to the water and there are small pools for a refreshing paddle.

Contact the Attapeu tourism office (p236) for an update on current travel options.

A guesthouse and restaurant had been built here and access roads improved in preparation for opening it up to tourism, but the 2018 Attapeu Dam collapse effectively washed away everything that had been constructed and put the project back to square one. At the time of research rebuilding efforts were underway. The falls are destined for a much higher profile on the traveller circuit once the infrastructure is improved.

To get here, take Rte 18A to Hua Se Pien village, then take a right on Rte 9005 to Paksong. This route will take you through the villages that were devastated in the dam collapse, namely Hinlat, Ban Mai and Ban Samong, before reaching the falls, about 9km past Samong village.

Tat Sae Pong Lai WATERFALL
(ຕາດແຊປ່ອງໄລ) This spectacular waterfall was unfortunately heavily affected by the 2018 Attapeu Dam collapse. It's difficult to reach, lying about 7km north of Tat Sae Pha. Before the dam collapse, it was more appealing than Tat Sae Pha, but the deluge deposited masses of now-hardened silt around the base of the waterfall, although it is still a beautiful sight.

Until approaching roads are improved, it's only reachable by motorbike or 4WD. Contact the Attapeu tourism office (p236) before attempting to get here.

Saisettha VILLAGE
(ໄຊເຊດຖາ) Saisettha, 11km east of Attapeu on Rte 18B, is a sizeable village on the north bank of the Se Kaman (Kaman River). It used to be a small, quiet village with a good vibe, but it's mostly outgrown that; however, art lovers will appreciate some of the temples here.

Just past the Houay Phateun Bridge, turn right to the peaceful riverfront **Wat Silia-wat That Inping** (aka Wat Fang Daeng), which has a large octagonal stupa. Inside the adjacent hall is a rather complete set of

Attapeu

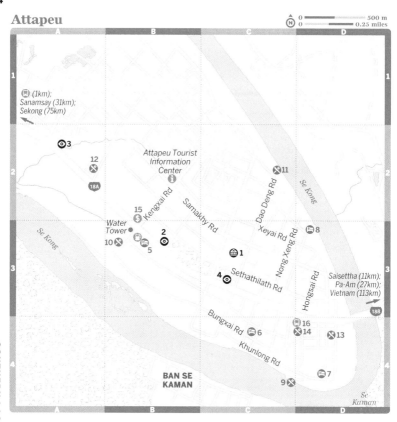

A-1 🖼 (1km);
Sanamsay (31km);
Sekong (75km)

A-2 ◉3
12 ✕
18A

Attapeu Tourist
Information
Center ℹ

✕11 B-2
Se Kong

Dao Deng Rd

Kengxai Rd
Samakhy Rd
Xeyai Rd

15 🏦
Water
Tower •
10 ✕
5 🏨 2 ◉
🏛 1

Nong Xeng Rd

🖼 8

Se Kong

4 ◉
Sethathilath Rd

Hongsai Rd

Saisettha (11km);
Pa-Am (27km);
Vietnam (113km)
18B

Bungxai Rd
🖼 6
🖼 16
✕14 ✕13

Khunlong Rd

🖼 7

**BAN SE
KAMAN**

9 ✕

Se
Kaman

paintings telling the Wetsandon Jataka (the Buddha's penultimate birth) tale.

Just over a kilometre to the east, at the end of the road, the *sala* (open-sided shelter) of **Wat Ban Xai** has more adroit mural paintings, focusing mostly on the Buddha's life story. The old *ubosot* (ordination hall) has some original floral stucco work on the front.

From Wat Ban Xai, go back to the highway and continue east. Take a sharp right at the first large road after crossing the Se Kaman bridge and continue to the second temple you meet (6.5km total) in Muang Kao (Old City). This is **Wat Luang**, famous because the Lan Xang King Setthathirat, for whom the district is named, is buried here. The temple was supposedly founded in 1571, the year of his death, and the stupa in which he is interred was erected soon after, though it has been rebuilt since then. There's also a crumbling old *wihǎhn* (temple hall) with a large Buddha inside and some original

woodcarving on the front gable and door. The little *ubosot* in front is in better shape.

Pa-Am   VILLAGE

(ພະອໍາ) The area east of Attapeu was an integral part of the Ho Chi Minh Trail – two main branches, the Sihanouk Trail continuing south into Cambodia and the Ho Chi Minh Trail veering east towards Vietnam, split here – and as such was heavily bombed during the war. One of the few visible reminders of this time is a Russian-made surface-to-air missile (SAM) set up in the village of Pa-Am (aka Ban Sombun) by the North Vietnamese to defend against aerial attack.

It has survived the scrap hunters and, by government order, is now on display, surrounded by a barbed-wire fence held up, in part, by cluster-bomb casings.

Next to the missile is a small handicraft shop with textiles and baskets woven by local Talieng women. If you drive around the

Attapeu

village you might get lucky and see some women weaving.

Pa-Am is 16km past Saisettha (follow the signs for San Xai off Rte 18B) and the two villages make a great half-day trip from Attapeu if you have your own wheels. There is no public transport to Pa-Am.

North of Pa-Am the road quickly turns rocky and continues on to Chaleun Xai, 38km north, then northwest to Sekong. This route has been improved somewhat, but it's still rough and recommended for dry-season travel only.

Dong Amphan NPA   NATIONAL PARK
(ປ່າສະຫງວນແຫ່ງຊາດດົງອຳພານ) The highlight of this 1975-sq-km protected area in eastern Attapeu Province is the fabled **Nong Fa** (Sky Blue Lake). This beautiful volcanic crater lake, also known as Nong Kai Ork, sits at an elevation of about 1500m. The view looking back away from the lake is just as beautiful as the lake itself. Unfortunately, until infrastructure is improved, travel to the lake is difficult if not impossible. Ask at the Attapeu tourism office (p236) about getting here.

Used by the North Vietnamese as an R&R (rest and recuperation) spot for soldiers hurt on the Ho Chi Minh Trail, this beautiful lake was once only able to be reached via a difficult five-day trek. New roads mean you can make it here and back from Attapeu in a day if you have a 4WD (available through Dokchampa Hotel) or an enduro motorcycle. Typically, it's visited on a two-day trip, with your guide arranging an informal homestay near the lake.

The park itself was, until recently, one of the most intact ecosystems in the country. However, logging, gold mining, wildlife poaching and hydroelectric projects on the Se Kaman and Se Su (Su River) have taken a toll on the pristine environment. Still, gaur, tiger, elephant and some 280 bird species, including the beautiful crested argus, inhabit the forests of Dong Amphan NPA.

The 65km of dirt track off Rte 18B from Attapeu to the park has steep hills, lots of rock, and some streams to cross, making it tough in the dry season and impossible for much of the rainy season. Theoretically you could get here on your own, but it's a very remote route and you risk being turned back by officials before you reach your goal.

🛏 Sleeping

Attapeu has no great hotels, but several reasonable ones.

★ **Sokpaserd Riverside**   GUESTHOUSE $
(📋020-22291223; Khunlong Rd; r 100,000K; ❄🛜) Probably the best value for the price you can get in Attapeu, the Sokpaserd has decent air-con rooms in a couple of buildings with a nice garden, friendly service and a pleasant atmosphere. Though it's across the street from, rather than on, the Se Kong, you can see the river through the trees from the 2nd floor.

Dokchampa Hotel   HOTEL $
(📋036-211069; www.dokchampakham.weebly.com; Rte 18A; r incl breakfast 129,000-259,000K; ❄🛜) The cheaper rooms in the older wing are dark and dingy, but the more expensive newer wing is much better, with large beds, fridge and the usual conveniences (though no TV). The 'breakfast' is very basic. On the plus side, it's quiet.

The hotel has signs advertising itself as a travel service, and the website says something similar, but don't expect much on that front.

Soukdaoxay Guesthouse GUESTHOUSE $
(☏ 020-22900054; r/d 100,000/200,000K; ❀ 🛜) The rooms in this eye-catching pink building on the Se Kong north of the centre are relatively new and good value. Three of the 2nd-floor rooms in back have nice river views.

🍴 Eating

Vendors hawk baguette sandwiches, *fĕr* and other street foods during the morning at **Talat Samakhixay** (Talat Nyai; Khunlong Rd), near the bridge. Vietnamese food is, of course, common in Attapeu; English menus, however, are not. There are one or two good Lao restaurants.

There are several simple joints along the Se Kong at the south end of town where locals linger over beer after dinner.

Kiengnoi Attapeu LAO, THAI $
(mains 20,000-50,000K; ⊙ 7am-10pm; 🛜) Many of the eateries in Attapeu are drinking spots or hot-pot shops. This is a solid rice-and-curry joint that sells just about everything and the quality is good. Because it is *ah-hăhn dahm sang* (food to order), you can mix-and-match or order things that aren't on the menu. The owner is a friendly woman who takes pride in her cooking.

Huean Phae Nang Gulap LAO, THAI $
(Khunlong Rd; mains 20,000-70,000K; ⊙ 9am-11pm; 🛜) It's a bit of a climb down the stairs to get to this floating 'raft restaurant', but 'Ms Rose's Raft' is great for a sundowner with beautiful views. The food is good. Just order any common Lao or Thai dish and they can probably make it. The spicy *đôm*

sòm with fish (labelled as 'a sweet and sour soup') is a good choice.

SP Coffee CAFE $
(☏ 020-22293281; mains 15,000-25,000K; ⊙ 7am-10pm; 🛜) Attapeu is pretty light-on with air-con coffee shops, so if you're on the hunt for a quick caffeine fix, this is the spot. The coffee is decent, and there are also reasonably priced Thai and Lao dishes on the menu. At night it becomes a bar and occasional karaoke joint.

Thi Thi Restaurant VIETNAMESE $
(Rte 18A; mains 15,000-35,000K; ⊙ 6am-9pm; 🛜) The Dúc Lôc Hotel's restaurant serves some of the best Vietnamese food in town. Various fish dishes and soups, plus fried rice and *fĕr* grace the menu.

Sabaidee Attapeu LAO $$
(mains 30,000-70,000K; ⊙ 8am-9pm; 🛜) It's all about the setting here, in a converted wooden house with a broad deck overlooking the Se Kong and the distant mountains. The menu features grilled and fried meats galore, but also lighter dishes such as a delicious spicy papaya salad.

ℹ️ Information

Banks, including the full-service **BCEL** (Rte 18A; ⊙ 8.30am-3.30pm Mon-Fri), line Rte 18A, but there are no ATMs in the city centre. More convenient than the banks is **Thi Thi Money Exchange** (Rte 18A; ⊙ 6am-8pm).

There is an official **Attapeu Tourist Information Center** (☏ 020-92265123; Kengxai Rd; ⊙ 8-11.30am & 1.30-4pm Mon-Fri). Staff here are very helpful but the literature available (eg brochures and maps) is limited. Guides can be

---

GETTING TO VIETNAM: PHOU KEUA TO BO Y

Getting to the border Though few foreigners take this route, there are several morning minibuses daily from Pakse to Kon Tum (160,000K, nine hours), all of which stop for a quick break in Attapeu about 10am. All of the companies pick up more passengers in Attapeu (to Kon Tum 60,000K, four hours), mostly at or near the **Dúc Lôc Hotel**, which is the base for Mai Linh Express. Rte 18B after Attapeu is a dramatic mountain road that runs 113km to the Bo Y (Vietnam)/Phou Keua (Laos) crossing. The second half is all uphill and landslides are common during the wet season.

At the border The Vietnamese side of the border (open 6am to 7pm) is built up while the Lao side is utilitarian. Formalities on both sides are easy since there is little traffic. Most people need to get a Vietnamese visa beforehand. In the other direction, Lao visas are available to all.

Moving on From Kon Tum there are connections to pretty much everywhere, including Hué and Ho Chi Minh City.

arranged. Ask here about travelling to some of the region's more remote waterfalls.

ℹ️ Getting There & Away

Buses to/from Pakse (50,000K, 3½ to five hours) run hourly, with about half using the direct Paksong (35,000K, 2½ hours) route and half passing through Sekong (20,000K, two hours). Five of them go all the way to Vientiane (regular 140,000K to 170,000K, sleeper 220,000K, 16 to 18 hours). There's also a morning bus to Salavan (50,000, 4½ hours). All buses leave from the **station** (Rte 11).

Mai Linh Express (📞 020-98302222; Rte 18A), at the Dúc Lôc Hotel, also has morning minibuses to Kon Tum (60,000K, five hours), Danang (150,000K, nine hours) and Hué (140,000K, 12 hours).

ℹ️ Getting Around

There are not many tuk-tuks in Attapeu, but one from the bus station to the city centre costs 10,000K per person, or 20,000K if you're alone. **Phoutthavong Guesthouse** (📞 020-5551 7870) hires bicycles for 20,000K per day.

There's a **petrol station** near the centre of town.

SI PHAN DON

📄 031

Si Phan Don (ສີ່ພັນດອນ) is where Laos becomes the land of the lotus-eaters, an archipelago of islands where the pendulum of time swings slowly and postcard-worthy views are the rule rather than the exception. Many a traveller has washed ashore here, succumbed to its charms and stayed longer than expected.

Down here the Mekong bulges to a breadth of 14km – the river's widest reach along its 4350km journey from the Tibetan Plateau to the South China Sea – and if you count every islet and sandbar that emerges in the dry months the name, which literally means 'Four Thousand Islands', isn't that much of an exaggeration.

Don Khong   ດອນໂຂງ

📄 031 / POP 55,000

Life moves slowly on Don Khong (Khong Island), like a boat being paddled against the flow on the Mekong. It's a pleasant place to spend a day or two, wandering past fishing nets drying in the sun, taking a sunset boat ride, pedalling about on a bicycle or just chilling and reading by the river. Some of the accommodation options here make a stay worthwhile in their own right.

Don Khong measures 18km long by 8km at its widest point. Most of the islanders live on the perimeter and there are only two proper towns: lethargic Muang Khong on the eastern shore and the charmless market town of Muang Saen on the west; an 8km road links the two.

Khamtay Siphandone, the postman who went on to serve as president of Laos from 1998 to 2006, was born in Ban Hua Khong at the north end of Don Khong in 1924.

👁️ Sights

Don Khong is a pretty island with rice fields and low hills in the centre and simple-life villages around the perimeter, and a bike trip around the island makes for a fantastic day for cultural travellers. The road around the island is paved, though heavily potholed, the whole way. The temples in Ban Hin Siew (Hin Siew Village) and Ban Hang Khong (Hang Khong Village) on the southern end of the island have old buildings that are worth a quick peek if you happen to be passing by.

A bridge in Ban Hua Khong Lem makes it easy to extend your exploration from Don Khong to sparsely populated and rarely visited Don San. A frequently rough dirt track follows the east side 6km to the very tip of the island where, when the river is low, a beach emerges. This is Si Phan Don's northernmost point.

Ban Hin Siew Tai Palm Sugar Trees   FARM
(ຕົ້ນຕານບ້ານຫິນສ່ຽວໃຕ້; Map p238) Although sugar palms can be seen across the island, Ban Hin Siew Tai is southern Laos' sugar capital. Many farmers here climb the trees twice a day to collect the juice and then boil it down to sugar, and if you see them working you are welcome to pop in for a visit. The sugar season is from November to February and early morning is the best time to go.

Don Khong History Museum   MUSEUM
(ພິພິດທະພັນປະຫວັດສາດດອນໂຂງ; Map p238; Muang Khong; 5000K; ⏰ 8.30-11.30am & 1-4pm Mon-Fri) When the local governor built this two-storey French colonial-style home in 1935, he was so proud of himself that he christened it Sathanavoudthi, which means 'Garden of Eden' in an old Lao dialect. Level-headed locals just called it 'The Brick House'. In 2010 it was restored and now

Si Phan Don

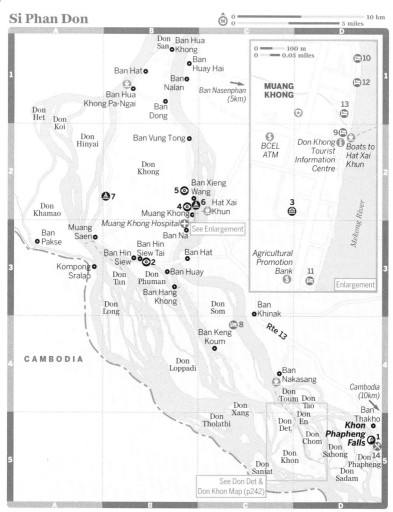

houses one of Laos' smallest museums. But the musical instruments, animal traps and photos of the Don Khon railway are worth a few minutes of your time.

It is usually kept shut, but go around the back and someone will open it for you.

Wat Jom Thong   BUDDHIST TEMPLE
(ວັດຈອມທອງ; Map p238; Muang Khong) At the northern end of Muang Khong is Wat Jom Thong, the oldest temple on the island, dating from the Chao Anou period (1805–28). The *wihǎhn* (temple hall) features a cruciform floor plan, a unique triple-gated entrance, carved wooden doors and shutters,

and a bevy of mythical Hindu-Buddhist creatures adorning the roof and gables.

Tham Phu Khiaw   CAVE
(ຖ້ຳພູຂຽວ; Map p238) Two kilometres north of Muang Khong a trail leads to Green Mountain Cave, a small, shallow shelter in the middle of the forest. It holds some fairly crude Buddha images and bits of broken pottery and is the object of an annual pilgrimage, usually in June. It's definitely more about the journey than the destination.

It's only a 15-minute walk, mostly uphill. Follow the main trail to the second rocky opening in the forest and then veer

Si Phan Don

south (left) to the little cliff. The trailhead is marked by a blue sign. If you wish to continue past the cave to the viewpoint or even all the way across the island, you'll need a guide.

Wat Phu Khao Kaew   BUDDHIST TEMPLE
(ວັດພູເຂົາແກ້ວ; Map p238) About 6.5km northeast of Muang Saen, Wat Phu Khao Kaew was built on the site of some presumed pre-Khmer ruins, making it a holy spot for locals. Nothing of that era is visible; now there is a bright red and gold modern stupa and a large reclining Buddha in the arm-down, 'Entering Nirvana' posture. It sits atop some exposed bedrock and the beautiful Mekong-side perch is more of a reason to stop than any of the structures.

It is also believed to be home to a *naga* (river serpent), though the entrance to its lair is covered. Don't be confused by the sign on the road that misspelt the last word as 'Kae'.

🎉 Festivals & Events

Bun Suang Heua   BOAT RACING
(Bun Nam; ⊙Nov/Dec) A boat-racing festival is held on Don Khong in early December or late November around National Day. Four days of carnival-like activity include longboat races opposite Muang Khong, much closer to the shore than in larger towns.

🛏 Sleeping

The island has some of the best accommodation in Si Phan Don, though if you're looking for waterfront bungalows, or a party scene,

you're better off heading further south to Don Det and Don Khon.

★**Don Som Riverside**
Guesthouse   GUESTHOUSE $
(Map p238; ☑030-9434108; Don Som; r with/without bathroom 85,000/58,000K) This guesthouse, run by a friendly Dutch-Lao couple, is deservedly popular because of its stunning location on Don Som, which is a short ferry ride from Don Khong. There is no wi-fi, so the emphasis is on simple living. Rooms are in rustic but attractive and neat wooden bungalows, one of which has a shared bathroom.

There is a restaurant and Lao cooking courses are also available.

Khong View Guesthouse   GUESTHOUSE $
(Map p238; ☑030-95666634; Muang Khong; r with fan 60,000K, r with air-con 100,000-120,000K; ❄🛜) It's hard to beat the location of this place. It's near, but serenely separate from, the tourist strip and the big, breezy 2nd-floor deck provides the best Mekong views in town. The friendly owners give it a homestay feel. There's no restaurant, but sometimes they will cook food for guests.

Done Khong Guesthouse   GUESTHOUSE $
(Map p238; ☑020-52535999; donekhong.gh @gmail.com; Muang Khong; r with fan/air-con 70,000/100,000K; ❄🛜) The first place you'll see when you get off the boat, Done Khong has dark rooms with tiled floors and homely furnishings in an old house run by an English-speaking man. Try to bag a 2nd-floor room with a river-facing balcony. The riverside restaurant, with a mostly Lao menu, is a good place to chill and the staff are a good source of island info.

★**Mekong Inn**   HOTEL $$
(Map p238; ☑031-213668; www.gomekonginn. com; Muang Khong; r incl breakfast US$35; ⊜❄🛜🏊) This Lao-Canadian-owned spot a bit south of the centre is more upmarket than a typical guesthouse, but it's a very welcoming place. Rooms, which are solid and spacious with wonderful river views, are in two buildings, one of which fronts the pool. When we passed through they were conducting a Lao dancing class for the guests.

★**Pon Arena Hotel**   BOUTIQUE HOTEL $$
(Map p238; ☑031-515018, 020-22270037; Muang Khong; r incl breakfast US$50-85; ❄🛜🏊) This upscale hotel has a great location right on the river and beautifully designed rooms

SOUTHERN LAOS DON KHONG

with soft beds, neat wood trim and flat-screen TVs, plus two swimming pools, one of which is so close to the river it actually sticks out over it. There are a number of buildings, and at the time of our visit the hotel was expanding.

Eating & Drinking

There are few restaurants in Muang Khong other than those attached to accommodation (which all have similar menus and food quality). But it's still easy to eat local as there are some simple joints along the big road behind the guesthouses. There's also some cooked food available at the **market** (ຕະຫຼາດເມືອງໂຂງ; Map p238; Muang Khong; ⊙5.30am-8am) for an early breakfast.

Many guesthouse restaurants serve Don Khong's famous handmade *lòw-lów* (rice whisky), which is often cited as the smoothest in the country.

ⓘ Information

MEDICAL SERVICES
Muang Khong Hospital (Map p238; Muang Khong; ⊙24hr) At the far southern edge of town. There are some English-speaking staff.

MONEY
Agricultural Promotion Bank (Map p238; Muang Khong; ⊙8am-3.30pm Mon-Fri) Exchanges major currencies and has an ATM out front.

BCEL ATM (Map p238; Muang Khong) Below the Lao Telecom tower.

POLICE
Police Station A block back from the river in Muang Khong.

TOURIST INFORMATION
Don Khong Tourist Information Centre (Map p238; ✆030-9682036, 020-29250303; bkouam1960@yahoo.com; Muang Khong; ⊙8am-4pm Mon-Fri) Near the boat landing, this office is run by helpful Mr Phan and Mr Boun. There's information for the whole Si Phan Don region and they can set you up with a local guide for 80,000K per day.

ⓘ Getting There & Away

BOAT
The Don Khong boatmen's association runs a boat most days to Don Det and Don Khon (one way/return per person 40,000/60,000K) at 8.30am and departing Don Det at 3pm. It's 1½ hours downstream and two hours back. The rate rises if there are fewer than six people as there is a fixed price per boat of 250,000K. You can

book this trip through any guesthouse. The boat landing is easy to spot, right opposite the tourist information centre.

BUS
The vast majority of travellers ride the tourist bus, which always includes getting dropped off on Rte 13 with a connecting leg to the island. Sometimes you will get dropped off at the road to the bridge and head to Muang Khong by tuk-tuk. Other times you will be dropped off at Hat Xai Khun on the mainland (1km from the highway) and then squeezed into a small **ferry** (Map p238). If you need the **boat** (Map p238) or tuk-tuk on your own, the price is 15,000K per head with a 30,000K minimum.

For leaving the island, tourist transport heading south to Don Det (70,000K) and Don Khon (80,000K including boat transfers, two hours) passes by Hat Xai Khun about 10am, while pick-up for going north to Pakse (70,000K, two hours) is about noon.

There are also non-air-conditioned buses (50,000K, three hours) from Muang Khong to Pakse's Southern Bus Terminal (p212) leaving between 6am and 9.30am. They pick up passengers in Muang Khong on the way. At other times, you can go to Rte 13 and wait for the hourly Pakse–Nakasang *sŏrngtǎaou*.

BICYCLE & MOTORBIKE
If you're up for some adventure, you can walk, cycle or motorbike 15km across Don Som down to Don Det with a **ferry ride** (Map p238; 10,000K per person) at each end. In the rainy season this trip ranges from tough to impossible due to mud. People in Muang Khong will have only a rough idea what the conditions are at any particular time, but the ferryman will know everything for certain.

ⓘ Getting Around

Motorbikes (from 60,000K to 80,000K per day) that are real clunkers and newish bicycles (10,000K per day) can be hired at several places on the tourist strip in Muang Khong.

Don Det & Don Khon

The vast majority of travellers to Si Phan Don end up on these twin islands. Don Det (ດອນເດດ) is defined by its hippyesque party scene, though it's really quite mild and there's nothing stronger than grass in the 'happy' snacks sold openly at some bars.

Of course there's much more to these two islands. Heading south from Ban Hua Det (Hua Det Village), the guesthouses thin out and the icons of rural island life – fishermen, rice farmers, weavers, buffalo, sugar palms

– are on full display. Chill in a hammock, wander aimlessly around the islands or languidly drift downstream in an inner tube in the turquoise arms of the Mekong.

The serenity continues across the French bridge on Don Khon (ດອນຄອນ), but down here there are also some gorgeous waterfalls to visit, sandy beaches to lounge on, dolphins to spot and even a little patch of wilderness to explore.

⊙ Sights

These twin islands are famous for soaking up low-key village life rather than ticking off a list of attractions. Don Det in particular doesn't have any attractions to speak of, but the dolphins and waterfalls on Don Khon are genuinely wonderful destinations.

★Khon Phapheng Falls WATERFALL
(ຕາດຄອນພະເພັ້ງ; Map p238; 55,000K; ⊙8am-5pm) More a glorified set of rapids than a waterfall, but oh, how glorious it is. The largest and by far the most awesome waterfall anywhere along the Mekong, Khon Phapheng is pure, unrestrained aggression, as millions of litres of water crash over the rocks. While pricier than the similar Tat Somphamit, this place, with its gardens and walking paths, is more attractive. You can also get down closer to the rapids.

There are several viewpoints in resort-like grounds, plus many restaurants and snack shops. With luck you can catch some rainbows in the early-morning mist. And like all the waterfalls in this area, there's a shaky network of bamboo scaffolds on the rocks next to the falls used by daring fishermen. A free shuttle runs continuously between both ends of the park – a 500m trip.

Be sure to check out the pavilion for the legendary Manikhote tree (p245), which is 150m or so in from the entrance. You can't miss it, actually.

Khon Phapheng is at the eastern shore of the Mekong near Ban Thakho. From Ban Nakasang it's 3km out to Rte 13, then 8.5km southeast to the turn-off and another 1.5km to the falls. A tuk-tuk from Nakasang costs about 50,000K return with an hour wait time. You can also easily motorcycle down from Don Khong. The falls are included in kayak tours out of Don Det and Don Khon. Since amateurs can't kayak anywhere near these falls, you'll be taken there by vehicle as your kayaks are driven up to Ban Nakasang.

★Tat Somphamit WATERFALL
(ຕາດສົ້ມພະມິດ, Li Phi Falls; Map p242; Don Khon; 35,000K; ⊙ticket booth 8am-5pm) Now billing itself as the Don Khone Somphamit Waterfalls Park, vast Tat Somphamit (also called Li Phi) is a gorgeous set of raging rapids. Recent developments include clear walking paths and the Mekong Fly zipline (p245). While local fishermen risk their skin edging out onto rocks, don't try this yourself – the rapids are extremely dangerous, and there have been deaths.

At the back end of the park, below the falls, is little Li Phi Beach (under water in the rainy season). A fundamental fear of ghosts means you'll never see locals swimming here. But even rationalists need to be wary as the current runs fast. Xai Kong Nyai Beach (p242), a kilometre downriver, is a safer, year-round swimming option.

Above the beach is a lovely thatched-roof restaurant and though it stops serving at 5pm, you can stick around to watch the sunset. There are lots of other, cheaper restaurants set back away from the falls.

Ban Hang Khon Viewpoint VIEWPOINT
(ຈຸດຊົມວິວບ້ານຫາງຄອນ; Map p242; Ban Hang Khon, Don Khon) Near the old French port in Ban Hang Khon, 150 steps take you up to a good viewpoint of the Mekong.

Khon Pa Soi Falls WATERFALL
(ຕາດຄອນປາສ່ອຍ; Map p242; Don Khon) **FREE** Although it's not the largest waterfall on the islands, Khon Pa Soi Falls is still pretty impressive, and it never gets crowded due to its isolated location. From the little **restaurant** (sometimes only serving cold drinks) cross the big, fun (or scary, depending on the person) wooden suspension bridge to Don Pa Soi island and follow the roar 200m to the main waterfall.

You can find bathing spots when the river is low, but be seriously careful here and don't get caught in the current.

A second smaller bridge takes you to some of the old logging diversion walls the French built in the Mekong for their logging operations.

Ban Hang Khon Steam Locomotive HISTORIC SITE
(ຫົວລົດໄຟຈັກອາຍບ້ານຫາງຄອນ; Map p242; Don Khon) The less intact of the two rusting locomotives sitting at opposite ends of the main cross-island road, which follows the old railway route. Placards detail the history of the railway.

Don Det & Don Khon

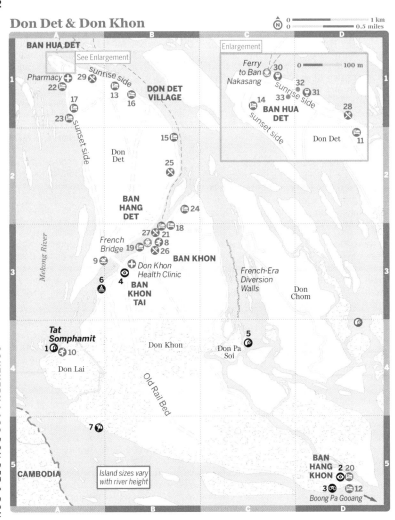

Ban Khon Steam Locomotive HISTORIC SITE
(ຫົວລົດໄຟຈັກຮ້ອຍນ້ຳບ້ານຄອນ; Map p242; Don Khon) This is the second of the two locomotives for the railway, which the French built in the late 1800s as a way of transporting supplies around the impassable falls. The railway has been out of use since WWII (when the Japanese briefly operated it) as new roads made it redundant, and the track has long since been carted off.

Across the old tracks from the Ban Khon locomotive is a small **Christian cemetery**.

Xai Kong Nyai Beach BEACH
(ຫາດຊາຍກອງໃຫຍ່, Tha Sanam; Map p242; Don Khon) If a beach towel is more your style than a hammock, then this little stretch of sand will satisfy. Swimming is possible year-round, but you need to be careful of fast currents away from the shore. There are three simple **restaurants** with cold drinks, and fishermen here will take you out to see waterfalls, dolphins or the sunset in their small longtail boats. They have no sunshades, life jackets or fixed prices.

Don Det & Don Khon

Wat Khon Tai   BUDDHIST TEMPLE
(ວັດຄອນໃຕ້; Map p242; Don Khon) Don Khon's main Buddhist temple was built on the site of an ancient Khmer shrine. Hidden behind the old ordination hall, which is itself tucked away behind a modern building, is an old, beautifully decrepit stupa and a Khmer-era shiva lingam. Other ancient stone blocks lie scattered around the grounds. Also take a look at the long racing boats stored nearby.

 Activities

Water Sports

Kayaking around the islands is very popular, and for good reason considering the sublime beauty of the Mekong in these parts. Full-day trips (180,000K per person) paddle to Khon Pa Soi Falls (p241) and then down to the dolphin pool – unlike the regular dolphin-watching trips, seeing them while on a kayak tour is hit or miss – before you visit Khon Phapheng Falls (p241) by vehicle. Prices are sometimes negotiable – mostly in the low season – or in lieu of a discount, some guesthouses will give you free breakfast the morning of the tour if you book it through them.

Due to the potential dangers, most businesses are unwilling to just rent out kayaks. Tubing (10,000K), however, is a big thing here. But don't float past the French bridge or you'll hit the fast currents that feed into the lethal falls. You could also have a boat take you upstream so you float back to Don Det. December to July is the best season, but you can go any time.

A relaxing alternative to the kayak tours are the afternoon BBQ boat tours (55,000K per person or 40,000K just for transport), such as that offered by Souksan Guesthouse (p247). All guesthouses can also arrange other sorts of boat tours: sunset cruises, full-day island hops, morning birdwatching trips, fishing – you name it.

Dolphin-Watching

A small and diminishing pod of severely endangered Irrawaddy dolphins (p247) lives along the southern shore of Don Khon and spotting these rare creatures in the wild is a highlight of any trip to southern Laos. The population has dropped to just three as some have died and others have gone south. Though nothing in nature is guaranteed, sightings here are virtually certain.

LOCAL KNOWLEDGE

DON KHON RAILWAY

A railway on Don Khon? As strange as it seems, there was indeed a railway of sorts on the island, as testified by the two mini-locomotives, all that remain of the railway, on display in Ban Khon and Ban Hang Khon.

The railway was opened in 1893. At that time roads in Laos were scarce, and the Mekong, which had been used for centuries as the main avenue of transport for Lao, Chinese and Cambodian traders, was seen by the French as a vital link for commerce between Cambodia and China. They had tried to ply their vessels up the Mekong's rapids a number of times but without success. In the end they struck upon the idea of a railway to transport vessels, freight and passengers for the length of Don Khon, and so bypass the impassable rapids. During the early stages goods were transported partly by manpower, with teams of Vietnamese labourers hauling them along the rails, but in 1897 the steam locomotives were brought in.

In the 1920s the railway was extended to Don Det, although nothing remains of it now. Trains could have up to 12 cars, and it would take two trainloads to transport an average vessel. The railway continued to function until 1940, when WWII put its operations on hold, from which it never recovered.

Boats are chartered (70,000K, maximum four people) from the old French landing pier in Ban Hang Khon. The pier itself is worth a trip just for the spectacular views of the Mekong, which spreads wide on either side of you, with vistas out over to Cambodia. Where you go depends on where the dolphins are. In the hot season they stay close to the village, but when the river runs high they can travel further away. You may be able to see them from your boat, or you may need to disembark in Cambodia and walk to a spot that overlooks the conservation zone. This may require a 20,000K payment to the officials there. Try to go in the early morning or early evening to avoid the heat.

The boat trips from Bang Hang Khon can combine dolphin-watching with Khon Phapheng Falls (p241) (250,000K) or little **Nook Xume** (100,000K) waterfall.

Cycling

A bike trip around Don Khon is a pure delight. Begin in Ban Khon (Khon Village) and take the paved path to Ban Don Khon Neua temple, then follow the twisting little paths through the rice paddies until you reach the riverbank.

Head south and you'll soon see large portions of the concrete **diversion walls** the French built to direct logs. Usually sent down from forests in Sainyabuli Province, west of Vientiane, the logs were lashed together into rafts of three. To prevent them going off course, a Lao 'pilot' would board the raft and steer it through the maze of islands. When they reached the critical area at the north end of Don Khon, the pilots were required to guide the raft onto a reinforced concrete wedge, thus splitting the binds and sending the logs into the correct channel. The pilot would jump for his life moments before impact.

Turn at the sign for Khon Pa Soi Falls (p241), which is reached by a big wooden suspension bridge that would be worth a visit even if there was no waterfall here. The path used to continue on to the south of the island but the bridges have been washed out. For now you will have to backtrack until you see a road diverging left, which will take you to the old railbed road. This will take you down to the southern point, Ban Hang Khon, where there is the ruin of an old **French port** and a spectacular view of the Mekong at the southern tip of the island. Dolphin-watching tours are offered from here.

The village also has a hilltop viewpoint (p241), a decrepit old French colonial-era steam locomotive (p241), several restaurants and a real village homestay (p247).

Head back north along the old railbed 5km across the island to Ban Khon Tai. Next to the photogenic **French Bridge** sits another, better-preserved French steam locomotive (p242). From here, head southwest, taking either the road around or through historic Wat Khon Tai (p243) to finish your trip at the impressive waterfall Tat Somphamit (p241).

Be sure to ask about the conditions before setting off in the rainy season as the dusty roads often turn into chocolate pudding.

Other Activities

★ Mekong Fly ZIPLINING
(Map p242; ☑ 030-4999989; Don Khon; 250,000K;
☺ 8am-5pm) For an exhilarating soar over the
raging rapids of Tat Somphamit (p241), this
offering can't be beat. The zipline has seven
platforms and includes some walking and
bridge-crossing as well. Staff are on hand to
help with the experience and ensure safety.
The ride begins at the falls restaurant, where
you can also view videos of the experience.
Selfie-taking seems to be de rigueur.

The company also runs kayaking dolphin-
watching tours (150,000K) in the high
season.

**Long Island Resort
Swimming Pool** SWIMMING
(Map p242; Don Det; 25,000K) This attractive
pool in the south of Don Det feels a bit out
of place amid the rice paddies. There's also a
bar and plenty of sun lounges and towels are
included in the high-season price.

Lao's Massage MASSAGE
(Map p242; Ban Khon; Lao massage 60,000K;
☺ 9am-10pm) Restful treatments in an air-
con room on Don Khon include foot massages, oil massages and body scrubs.

🛏 Sleeping

The common wisdom is to stay on Don Det
to party, and Don Khon to get away from it
all. But in fact the party is confined to the
northern tip of Don Det, and the quietest
and most isolated guesthouses in all of Si
Phan Don are actually on the southern portion of Don Det.

Many places offer low-season discounts;
sometimes it's automatic and sometimes
you need to ask.

Don Det

Don Det's best accommodation – and highest prices – is on the sunrise side, though
there are still plenty of good budget beds
here too. Flimsy bamboo bungalows pre-
dominate on the sunset side, with some
pleasant exceptions. The drawback here is
that late in the day rooms become furnace-
like after baking in the afternoon sun. On
the other hand, there's less boat traffic (ie
noise) here.

On both sides of the island, walk far
enough (on the sunrise side this means
going past the old French port in Don Det
village) and the modest party scene of Ban
Hua Det feels light years away. The sunset
side gets downright rural after a kilometre.

THE WEIRD & WONDERFUL MANIKHOTE TREE

As you enter the manicured grounds of the Khon Phapheng Falls (p241), the path eventually leads you to a lavish spired Lao-style pavilion. This is the shrine to the legendary
Manikhote tree, which once stood, solitary, mysterious and unreachable, on a rocky rise
in the centre of the raging torrent of Khon Phapheng.

The tree's unusual appearance gave rise to much folklore. It was said that the tree was
the sole member of its species, and that its roots reached skyward while its branches
were rooted on the rock (indeed, it did look that way). Furthermore, it was said that when
it fruited, it delivered three different kinds of fruits, depending on the branch the fruit appeared on. Some of the fruits would give the eater eternal life, others would turn you into
a monkey. Of course, no one ever ate any of the fruits because the tree was inaccessible.

The tree had stood at its location for as long as anyone could remember, and had
been the subject of legend for many generations. Some said that it was mentioned in the
ancient Indian epic, the *Ramayana*. But on 19 March 2012, Manikhote toppled and died.
Efforts were made to retrieve it. The first attempt was unsuccessful, but did manage
to secure the tree to the rock so that it wouldn't wash away. It was finally 'rescued' by
helicopter and an army team on 13 January 2013. Apparently the tree was only able to
be moved once a shaman had made a promise to it that they would not be taking it away
from the falls, and even then only after seven days and nights of chanting.

Not all of the tree could be salvaged. What remains of it now lies in a Perspex 'coffin',
the central part of the shrine, an object of devotion and offerings from Lao people from
all corners of the country.

Seng Thavan 2 Guesthouse GUESTHOUSE $
(Map p242; ☏ 020-98622348; sunset side; r with/
without bathroom 150,000/80,000K; 🛜) This
riverside guesthouse offers a number of different basic options, ranging from simple
timber constructions to rooms in a large
new concrete building, plus at the time of research new rooms were under construction.
There's a restaurant with river views and
some floral decoration, making it a pleasant
place to sit.

Mama Piang GUESTHOUSE $
(Map p242; ☏ 020-58186049; sunrise side; r
50,000K) If there is a more fun and friendly host in Si Phan Don than Mama Piang –
who proudly calls herself 'crazy' – we didn't
meet her. There are six cold-water fan rooms
across the road from her riverfront **restaurant**. She's rightfully pretty proud of her
cooking.

Crazy Gecko GUESTHOUSE $
(Map p242; ☏ 020-97193565; www.crazygecko.ch;
sunrise side; r 170,000-240,000K; 🛜) In a stilted
structure made of solid wood, Crazy Gecko's
three tidy rooms surround a balcony that's
equal parts funky and functional. Festooned
with hammocks and random decoration, it's
a superior place to relax (if a bit overpriced).
There's a pool table and board games down
below and across the road is a recommended restaurant on a deck over the water.

Mama Leuah Guesthouse GUESTHOUSE $
(Map p242; ☏ 020-59078792; www.mamaleuah-
dondet.com; sunrise side; r 100,000K; 🛜) The
rooms are super-basic, but it's a quiet and
beautiful location with some surrounding
gardens, unusual for Don Det. The restaurant

(p248) serves excellent Thai cuisine as well
as some unexpected Swiss dishes.

Seng Thavan 1 Guesthouse GUESTHOUSE $
(Map p242; ☏ 020-56132696; sunset side; r
100,000K; 🛜) A good choice in the budget
range on the sunset side, Seng Thavan's
four en suite rooms are old but fastidiously
clean. They're off the river, but you get great
views from its low-key cafe, full of recliner
cushions.

★ **Baba Guesthouse** GUESTHOUSE $$
(Map p242; ☏ 020-98893943; www.dondet.net;
sunrise side, Ban Hua Det; r 350,000K; ❄🛜) This
solid guesthouse looks out at the Mekong on
one side, and emerald paddy fields on the
other. The price is a bit above average for
this area, but you get more for your money
here. Rooms are sleekly white and almost
luxurious, with private balcony, tasteful de-
cor, mosquito net and spotless bathroom.
There's also an attached restaurant (open
7am to noon).

The terraced restaurant over the river is
as classy as the guesthouse and is a great
breakfast spot. Owner Basil and his wife are
the perfect hosts. They offer steep discounts
out of season.

Moon by Night GUESTHOUSE $$
(Map p242; ☏ 020-95767543; sunset side; ❄🛜)
Run by an Aussie expat, this new place has
stylish concrete rooms, immaculately detailed with some of the most comfortable
beds you'll find on the island, and spacious
bathrooms. There is no attached restaurant (unusual for this region), although the

---

ℹ **RESPONSIBLE TRAVEL IN SI PHAN DON**
....

The islanders are benefiting from the income tourism brings, but there are a few things
you can do on Don Det and Don Khon to keep the smiles genuine and your footprint
positive.

Marijuana is fairly common on Don Det, but that does not mean locals have simply
accepted its prevalence. In fact, many are completely unaware what 'happy' means. And
even those who do know and don't care prefer that it's an incidental part of a visit rather
than the sole reason for coming. If you do partake, be discreet.

The beach on Ban Hua Det has become a cool spot for sunbathing and nightly bonfires, but make sure you pick up your litter afterwards.

To avoid putting additional strain on the islands' environment, you can pay to refill
a water bottle at many shops and guesthouses on Don Det. This service hasn't quite
caught on yet on Don Khon.

And please don't hand out candies, pens, coins etc to children. This has already led
some kids on Don Khon to start begging, which is not only bad for them in the long run,
but it brings shame to their families.

DOLPHINS ENDANGERED

The Irrawaddy dolphin (*Orcaella brevirostris*, called *pạa khaa* in Lao) is one of the Mekong River's most fascinating creatures, and one of its most endangered. The dark-blue to grey cetaceans grow to 2.75m long and are recognisable by their bulging foreheads, perpetual grins and small dorsal fins. They are unusually adaptable and can live in freshwater, brackish-water estuaries or semi-enclosed saltwater bodies such as bays.

Among the Lao and Khmer, Irrawaddy dolphins are traditionally considered reincarnated humans and there are many stories of dolphins having saved the lives of fishermen or villagers who have fallen into the river or been attacked by crocodiles. These cultural beliefs mean neither the Lao nor the Khmer intentionally capture dolphins for food or sport.

But gill netting and years of destructive fishing practices such as dynamite fishing in Cambodia have inevitably taken their toll on the dolphins. Education and conservation programs to save the dolphins continue, particularly in Cambodia, but gill netting remains a constant threat – dolphins need to surface and breathe every two to three minutes, and will usually drown before fishermen even know they are in the nets.

In Laos, dolphins used to travel up the Se Kong (Kong River), but these days they are largely confined to a 600m-wide, 50m-deep (in the wet season) pool on the Cambodian border known in Lao as Boong Pa Gooang and in Cambodian as Anlong Cheuteal. Only three dolphins survive in this pool.

owner also runs the Street View Restaurant (p248) on the sunrise side.

Little Eden
HOTEL **$$**
(Map p242; ☏020-77739045; www.littleeden dondet.com; sunset side, Ban Hua Det; r incl breakfast US$41-50; ➠❄🛜🖳) Don Det's most luxurious complex is set on a large plot on its northern tip. Fragrant rooms tempt with contemporary dark-wood furniture and polished wood floors, plus plenty of mod cons. Also, the hotel has a beautiful 18m-long swimming pool, a bar and a sunset-perfect restaurant. You will feel like you have escaped Ban Hua Det.

Don Khon

There's a good mix of both budget and better places here. Except for the village homestay (Map p242; ☏020-98893204; Ban Hang Khon, Don Khon; per person 36,000K, per meal 30,000K) and Pomelo Guesthouse in Ban Hang Khon, all Don Khon accommodation is in Ban Khon village facing Don Det. It's a pretty peaceful town (no partying here) but it's not exactly oozing an island vibe.

Pa Kha Guesthouse
GUESTHOUSE **$**
(Map p242; ☏020-55841522; r with fan/air-con 80,000/120,000K; ❄🛜) Great-value digs with welcoming, clean rooms, good service and a quiet location. The cheapest rooms are on the river; the newer air-con rooms are across the road, as is the restaurant.

Souksan Guesthouse
GUESTHOUSE **$**
(Map p242; ☏020-91808944; r with fan 50,000-60,000K; 🛜) Souksan has so-so rooms set in a bungalow block with a great shared riverview terrace. Next door is the restaurant, with cushion seating right over the water. Bathrooms have only cold water. Mr Souksan's BBQ boat tours (to Khon Phapheng 100,000K, to Don Som 55,000K) are popular and fun.

★Pomelo Guesthouse
GUESTHOUSE **$$**
(Map p242; ☏020-97925893; Ban Hang Khon; r US$25; 🛜) Run by a Thai chef and his Swiss girlfriend, this rustic and tasteful guesthouse boasts a stunning location over the river in Ban Hang Khon. There are two spacious rooms in a traditional stilt home with rain showers and sweeping views, as well as two bungalows. There's a private swimming platform and a kayak free for guests.

★Sala Done Khone
BOUTIQUE HOTEL **$$**
(Map p242; ☏031-515050; www.salalaoboutique. com; r incl breakfast US$60-80; ➠❄🛜🖳) 🖊 Five hotels in one, Sala Done Khone has both the classiest and the most original rooms in Si Phan Don. Its signature unit, the French Residence, is a renovated 1896 trading headquarters with timbered interiors, beautiful original tiled floors and louvred blinds, while out on the river the Sala Phae wing features floating cottages with bio-safe toilets and private decks.

The newest Ban Din rooms are built of clay and other eco-friendly materials, and are just as lovely and comfortable as the others.

Pan's Residence
GUESTHOUSE $$

(Map p242; ☑ 020-23655151; www.pansresidence.com; Ban Khon; r incl breakfast US$28-35; ❋🛜❄) Enticing bungalows sitting in a garden flickering with butterflies or along the river are finished in solid stained wood with creamy-white interiors, immaculate bathrooms and balconies slung with hammocks. The travel office here is dependable and breakfast is included in the rates.

✕ Eating

Most guesthouses serve a range of Lao, Thai and Western favourites from virtually identical menus. Stand-alone restaurants are usually a step above the guesthouses and the extra 5000K to 10,000K per dish that they charge is worth it. Generally the best dining is on Don Khon and the sunrise side of Don Det just south of Ban Hua Det.

★ Chez Fred et Lea
INTERNATIONAL, LAO $

(Map p242; ☑ 020-22128882; Ban Khon, Don Khon; mains 20,000-50,000K; ⊙7am-10pm; 🛜) This cafe and 'salon de thé' serves organic coffees and teas, as well as top-quality Lao and Western cuisine that you won't find elsewhere on the island. There are no river views, but the Lao-French couple who run the place make up for it with inviting tunes and the freshest of ingredients. Try a Lao or French set menu for 80,000K.

Mr Mo's Restaurant
LAO, WESTERN $

(Map p242; ☑ 030-55759252; Ban Hua Det, Don Det, sunrise side; mains 20,000-50,000K; ⊙7am-11pm; 🛜) You can't fail to see signs advertising Mr Mo's tours as soon as you get off the ferry, and his restaurant quickly comes into view. Unlike some of the pokier restaurants on the island, this one is big, bright and breezy. The food is consistently good, as is the coffee.

The rooms (double/triple 100,000/150,000K) across the street are serviceable, if nothing special.

The Gardens
LAO, THAI $

(Map p242; Ban Khon, Don Khon; mains 20,000-65,000K; ⊙9am-10pm; 🍴) Taking freshness seriously, this thatched-roof, open-kitchen restaurant is a good place for the uninitiated to sample Lao foods, such as spicy papaya

salad and grilled Mekong River fish. It also serves all the usual traveller comfort foods and the cook's personal version of lemongrass chicken.

Chanthoumma's Restaurant
LAO $

(Map p242; Ban Khon, Don Khon; mains 25,000-70,000K; ⊙6.30am-10pm; 🍴) The friendly family here has been serving good food, including spring rolls, papaya salads and veggie options, from in front of their tumbledown home for many years.

★ Mama Lueah Guesthouse Restaurant
THAI, SWISS $$

(Map p242; sunrise side, Don Det; mains 20,000-50,000K; 🍴) This guesthouse restaurant serves excellent Thai cuisine along with Swiss surprises such as *Zürcher geschnetzeltes* (pork with creamy mushroom sauce) and a favourite dish with local expats, *cordon bleu*.

★ Little Eden Restaurant
LAO, INTERNATIONAL $$

(Map p242; sunset side, Ban Hua Det, Don Det; mains 35,000-140,000K; 🛜) Catching the breeze from the tip of the island, Little Eden's perfectly placed waterfront restaurant is one of the best spots to eat upmarket Lao and Western cuisine. Think tender *duck à l'orange*, spaghetti bolognese and fish *láhp* using Mekong catfish.

Street View Restaurant
PIZZA $$

(Map p242; ☑ 020-98779177; sunrise side, Don Det; mains 35,000-65,000K; ⊙8am-11pm; 🛜) This attractive wooden riverside haunt has decks for chilling on, a long, well-stocked bar and a good reputation. Tuck into mouthwatering wood-fired pizza, barbecued chicken, Mekong fish, pork chops, burgers, salads and healthy breakfasts. Prices are higher than average, but worth it.

Four Thousand Sunsets
FUSION $$

(Map p242; Don Khon; mains 25,000-80,000K; ⊙7am-10pm; 🛜🍴) Aptly named, this high-class floating restaurant lowers your pulse with the metronomic flow. The menu is a big break from the usual, with many dishes you won't find elsewhere in the islands, such as northern Thai *hinlay* curry. There's also steamed and grilled fresh river fish, Lao 'smoking' herbal sausages and many stir-fries.

Treat yourself to a vodka martini as you drink up the amber sunset.

View Restaurant   LAO $$
(Map p238; Khon Phapheng; mains 30,000-80,000K; ⊙ 7.30am-5pm) The restaurant at Khon Phapheng Falls (p241) has a wide range of dishes on offer and is worth a stop while visiting the falls. But the best thing on the menu is the view, which is spectacular. Service can be a bit lethargic, but you're in no hurry, right?

Boathouse   FISH $$
(Map p242; Don Det; mains 20,000-65,000K; ⊙ 7am-11pm) Run by a German former fisherman married to a local gal, this place has an emphasis on freshly made Mekong fish dishes. Try the catfish *mók* (steamed in banana leaf) or the fish barbecue, which needs to be ordered in advance. It's in a sturdy raised structure off the river in the south of Don Det, about 1km beyond the village.

 Drinking & Nightlife

Ban Hua Det is where the action is. There's a semi-solid midnight curfew when the bars wind down and the action moves to the

---

GETTING TO CAMBODIA: NONG NOK KHIENE TO TRAPAENG KRIEL

Getting to the border The Nong Nok Khiene (Laos)/Trapaeng Kriel (Cambodia) border (open 6am to 6pm) is a popular route for backpackers on the Indochina overland circuit, and it is always a real hassle.

The Cambodian company Sorya Transport runs the Pakse–Phnom Penh route from the Southern Bus Terminal (p212) (7.30am, 220,000K) and is the best choice. Sengchalern bus company provides daily service from Pakse to Phnom Penh (230,000K, 12 to 14 hours) via Stung Treng (120,000K, six hours) and Kratie (160,000K, nine hours), but the method of travel varies. Sometimes it sends a big bus that goes direct the whole way, other times it sends you to the border in a minibus and you change vehicles there, and you might even have to change a third time at Stung Treng. These vehicle changes often lead to long delays. Regardless of which vehicle, departures are at 7am from the 2km Bus Station (p213), with a stop to pick up more passengers at the Southern Bus Terminal. Tickets for this route sold from the islands in Si Phan Don will include the ferry from the island and, if needed, a minivan to take you to the connecting point.

Sengchalern at the 2km Bus Station also sells tickets to Siem Reap (280,000K), but this extra long trip is not recommended. Better to use reliable **Asia Van Transfer** (AVT; www.asiavantransfer.com), which departs from the border at 11.30am and takes the new northern route to Siem Reap (US$20) arriving at about 7pm. The price includes a tuk-tuk ride to your hotel. It takes internet bookings, but this means you have to get yourself to the border. In Don Det, Green Paradise Travel (p250) and a few guesthouses sell combo tickets for AVT (270,000K) that include the boat to Nakasang and a minivan to the border. A similar ticket from a travel agency in Pakse costs 260,000K. **Wonderful Tours** (Map p242; ☑ 020-55705173; Ban Hua Det, Don Det; ⊙ 7am-9.30pm) also specialises in tickets to Cambodia, but uses Cambodian local transport.

At the border Both Lao and Cambodian visas are available on arrival, while bribes, scams and rudeness are a mandatory part of the process. In Laos, you'll pay a US$2 (or the equivalent in kip or baht) 'overtime' or 'processing' fee, depending on when you cross, upon both entry and exit. In Cambodia, they jack up the price of a visa to US$35 from the actual US$30. In addition, the Cambodians charge US$1 for a cursory medical inspection upon arrival in the country, and levy a US$2 processing fee upon exit. All of these fees can be avoided if you are willing to wait it out, but this will probably take so long that your bus may leave without you. The bus companies want their cut too, so they charge an extra US$5 or more to handle your paperwork with the border guards, even if you already have a visa. Technically this isn't a scam, since you are getting a service in return for your money, but they will not tell you this service is optional. To avoid this fee, insist on doing your own paperwork and walk through immigration on your own; it's not hard.

Moving on Aside from the buses mentioned above, there's virtually zero traffic here. If you're dropped at the border, expect to pay about US$45 for a private taxi heading south to Stung Treng, or 150,000/60,000K for a taxi/*sǎhm-lór* (three-wheeled padicab) heading north to Ban Nakasang.

'beach' (under water in the rainy season), where bonfires and midnight dips are not unheard of.

4000 Island Bar   BAR

(Map p242; ✆020-96476088; sunrise side, Ban Hua Det, Don Det; ⊙7am-11pm; �) Good Western and Indian food, cold drinks, friendly service and a soothing vibe combine to make this a perennial favourite among travellers. You can make new friends around the pool table, throw some darts, play your favourite tunes or just kick back, relax and enjoy the view.

Adam's Bar   BAR

(Map p242; sunrise side, Ban Hua Det, Don Det; ⊙7am-11pm) Staff are upfront about their special 'secret' ingredients, so if that's your kind of scene then this is your kind of place. Has a full menu of Lao and Western food (mains 20,000K to 55,000K) and helpful advice about the islands, too.

ⓘ Information

MEDICAL SERVICES

Don Khon has a simple **health clinic** (Map p242; Ban Khon) while Don Det has just a small **pharmacy** (Map p242; sunset side, Ban Hua Det). These services can also be found in Ban Nakasang on the mainland. The nearest proper health facility is on Don Khong, but for anything serious you should head straight to Pakse.

MONEY

There are no banks on the islands, though an increasing number of businesses accept plastic. Cash can be exchanged, at generally poor rates, at most guesthouses and some, including Baba (p246) on Don Det, do cash advances on credit cards for a 6% commission. There's an Agricultural Promotion Bank and a BCEL with ATMs on the main drag in Ban Nakasang. Kayaking tours budget enough time at the end of the trip for people to make an ATM stop.

TOURIST INFORMATION

There is no tourism office on these islands, so you're left with guesthouses and travel agencies, which in fact do a lot more than most tourist offices. The Baba Guesthouse (p246) website (www.dondet.net) has lots of helpful information.

ⓘ Getting There & Away

Boat prices between **Ban Nakasang** (Map p238) and the islands are fixed by a local boat association, and there are very few running each day on a shared basis. Expect to pay 15,000K per person (or 30,000K if travelling on your own) to Don Det, and 20,000K per person (or 60,000K if travelling alone) to **Don Khon** (Map p242).

For Pakse, most travellers book tickets on the island, which includes the local boat and a noon bus or minibus (60,000K, three hours). If you want to leave at another time there are *sŏrngtăaou* from Ban Nakasang to the Southern Bus Terminal (p212) in Pakse (40,000K, 3½ hours) every hour until noon. One shared boat always leaves the islands in time for the 8am *sŏrngtăaou*. These all stop in Hat Xai Khun (for Don Khong).

Even in the best of circumstances, travel to Cambodia (p249) from the islands by public transport is a hassle. **Green Paradise Travel** (Map p242; ✆020-99533939, 020-55494928; greenparadisetours99@gmail.com; sunrise side, Ban Hua Det, Don Det; ⊙7am-9.30pm) has a decent service that includes boat and vehicle transfers to the border.

River travel to Don Khong (500,000K) and Champasak (US$200) is only available by chartered boat, but very often there are other people willing to join together to share the cost. For Don Khong you could also call Done Khong Guesthouse (p239) or Pon's Riverside Guesthouse (✆020-55406798) on that island to see if a boat is coming from there in the morning. If so, you can probably buy a seat (50,000K) for the return journey.

ⓘ Getting Around

With virtually no traffic and only a few small hills, Don Det and Don Khon are ideally explored by bicycle (hired from just about any guesthouse for 10,000K per day), though they are small enough that everything is also walkable.

There are some tuk-tuk available in Ban Hua Det and Ban Khon. It's 100,000K for a trip from Ban Hua Det to see the dolphins and Tat Somphamit, including sufficient waiting time, and 70,000K just to travel between Ban Hua Det and Ban Khon.

Understand Laos

History

Laos first emerged as Lan Xang, the 'Kingdom of a Million Elephants', in the 14th century. Despite bursts of independence, the kingdom generally found itself paying tribute to more powerful neighbours, including the Siamese and Vietnamese. Geography ensured Laos was sucked into the Vietnam War and a lengthy civil war culminated in a communist takeover in 1975. After years of isolation, Laos began to experiment with economic reforms in the 1990s, but political reform remains a distant dream for most.

Prehistory & Tai-Lao Migration

The first modern humans *(Homo sapiens)* arrived in Southeast Asia around 50,000 years ago. A Neolithic culture evolved about 8000 BC, and hunter-gatherers spread throughout the region, including Laos. These people were the ancestors of the present-day upland minorities, collectively known as the Lao Thoeng (Upland Lao), the largest group of which are the Khamu of northern Laos.

The earliest kingdom in southern Laos was identified in Chinese texts as Chenla, dating from the 5th century. One of its capitals was close to Champasak, near the site that later housed the Khmer temple of Wat Phu. A little later Mon people (speaking another Austro-Asiatic language) established kingdoms on the middle Mekong – Sri Gotapura (Sikhottabong in Lao) with its capital near Tha Khaek, and Chanthaburi in the vicinity of Viang Chan (Vientiane).

Tai peoples probably began migrating out of southern China in about the 8th century. They included the Tai-Lao of Laos, the Tai-Syam and Tai-Yuan of central and northern Thailand, and the Tai-Shan of northeast Burma. They are called Tai to distinguish them from the citizens (Thai) of modern Thailand. All spoke closely related Tai languages, practised wet-rice cultivation along river valleys, and organised themselves into small principalities, known as *meuang,* each presided over by a hereditary ruler, or *jow meuang* (lord of the *meuang*). The Tai-Lao, or Lao for short, moved slowly down the rivers of northern Laos until they arrived at the Mekong, the Great River.

TIMELINE	AD 500	1181	1256
	The early Mon-Khmer Chenla capital of Shrestapura is a thriving city based around the ancient temple of Wat Phu Champasak.	King Jayavarman VII vanquishes the Chams from Angkor and becomes the most powerful ruler of the Khmer empire, extending its boundaries to include most of modern-day Laos.	Kublai Khan sacks the Tai state of Nan Chao, part of the Xishuangbanna region of modern-day Yunnan in China. This sparks the southern exodus of the Tai people.

The Kingdom of Lan Xang

The first extended Lao kingdom dates from the mid-14th century, a time of many changes in mainland Southeast Asia. The great Khmer empire of King Jayavarman VII, who had built the city of Angkor Thom, had ceased its expansion into the middle Mekong and was in retreat. Filling the vacuum, King Ramkhamhaeng founded the Tai-Syam kingdom of Sukhothai, while to his north, Mangray founded the Tai-Yuan kingdom of Lanna (meaning 'A Million Rice Fields'), with his capital at Chiang Mai. Other smaller Tai kingdoms were established at Phayao and Xiang Dong Xiang Thong (Luang Prabang). In southern Laos and eastern Thailand, however, the Khmer still held on to power.

The Cambodian court looked around for an ally, and found one in the form of a young Lao prince, Fa Ngum, who was being educated at Angkor. Fa Ngum's princely father had been forced to flee Xiang Dong Xiang Thong after he seduced one of his own father's concubines. So Fa Ngum was in direct line for the throne.

The Khmer gave Fa Ngum a Khmer princess and an army, and sent him north to wrest the middle Mekong from the control of Sukhothai, and so divert and weaken the Tai-Syam kingdom. He was successful, and Fa Ngum was pronounced king in Xiang Dong Xiang Thong, before forcibly bringing Viang Chan into his growing empire. He named his new kingdom Lan Xang Hom Khao, which means 'A Million Elephants and the White Parasol'. Fa Ngum built a fine capital at Xiang Dong Xiang Thong and set about organising his court and kingdom, introducing Khmer Theravada Buddhism at the request of his wife.

When Fa Ngum began to seduce the wives and daughters of his court nobles, they decided to replace him, and he was sent into exile in Nan (now in Thailand), where he died within five years. His legacy, however, stood the test of time. The kingdom of Lan Xang remained a power in mainland Southeast Asia until early in the 18th century.

Fa Ngum was succeeded by his son Un Heuan (Samsenthai), who married princesses from the principal Tai kingdoms (Lanna and Ayutthaya, which had replaced Sukhothai), consolidated the kingdom and developed trade. With his wealth he built temples and beautified his capital.

Following Samsenthai's long and stable reign of 42 years, Lan Xang was shaken by succession disputes. The throne eventually passed to Samsenthai's youngest son, who took the throne name Xainya Chakkaphat (Universal Ruler). It was an arrogant claim, but he ruled wisely and well.

Lan Xang suffered its first major invasion when the Vietnamese captured and sacked Xiang Dong Xiang Thong. Xainya Chakkaphat fled

By naming his kingdom Lan Xang Hom Khao, Fa Ngum was making a statement about power and kingship. Elephants were the battle tanks of Southeast Asian warfare, so to claim to be the 'Kingdom of a Million Elephants' was to issue a warning to surrounding kingdoms.

HISTORY THE KINGDOM OF LAN XANG

1353	1421	1501	1560
Fa Ngum establishes the Lao kingdom of Lan Xang and builds a capital at Xiang Dong Xiang Thong.	King Fa Ngum's son and successor Samsenthai dies and Lan Xang implodes into warring factions for the next century.	King Visoun comes to the throne and rebuilds the Lao kingdom, marking a cultural renaissance for Lan Xang. He installs the Pha Bang Buddha image in Luang Prabang.	King Setthathirat, grandson of King Visoun, moves the capital to Viang Chan because of the threat from Burma, a rising power in the region.

FIRST CONTACT

The first European to have left an account of the Lao kingdom arrived in Viang Chan (Vientiane) in 1641. He was a merchant by the name of Gerrit van Wuysthoff, an employee of the Dutch East India Company, who wanted to open a trade route down the Mekong. He and his small party were royally accommodated and entertained during their eight-week stay in the Lao capital. Van Wuysthoff had more to say about the prices of trade goods than about Lao culture or religion, but he was followed a year later by a visitor who can offer us more insight into 17th-century Viang Chan. This was the Jesuit missionary Giovanni-Maria Leria, who stayed in Viang Chan for five years. During that time he had singularly little success in converting anyone to Christianity and eventually gave up in disgust. But he liked the Lao people (if not the monks) and has left a wonderful description of the royal palace and the houses of the nobility.

and the Lao mounted a guerrilla campaign. Eventually the Vietnamese were forced to withdraw, their forces decimated by malaria and starvation. So great were their losses that the Vietnamese vowed never to invade Lan Xang again.

The Lao kingdom recovered under one of its greatest rulers, who came to the throne in 1501. This was King Visoun, who had previously been governor of Viang Chan. He built the magnificent temple known as Wat Wisunarat (Wat Visoun), which, though damaged and repaired over the years, still stands in Luang Prabang.

King Visoun's grandson, King Setthathirat (r 1546–71), became the greatest builder in Lao history. Not only did he construct or refurbish several monasteries in Luang Prabang, including the beautiful Wat Xieng Thong, but he also did the same in Viang Chan, where he moved the capital in 1560 due to the threat of rising Burmese power. He left behind the sacred Buddha image Pha Bang, and changed the name of Xiang Dong Xiang Thong to Luang Prabang in its honour. With him he took what he believed to be an even more powerful Buddha image, the Pha Kaew (Emerald Buddha), now housed in Bangkok. His most important building projects, apart from a new palace on the banks of the Mekong, were the great That Luang stupa, a temple for the Emerald Buddha (Wat Pha Kaeo) and endowment of a number of royal temples in the vicinity of the palace.

It was more than 60 years before another great Lao king came to the throne, a period of division, succession disputes and intermittent Burmese domination. In 1638 Suriya Vongsa was crowned king. He would rule for 57 years, the longest reign in Lao history and a 'golden age' for the kingdom of Lan Xang. During this time, Lan Xang was a powerful

1695	1707–13	1769	1778
King Suriya Vongsa dies and Lan Xang once again fractures into competing kingdoms.	Lan Xang is divided into three smaller and weaker kingdoms: Viang Chan, Luang Prabang and Champasak.	Burmese armies overrun northern Laos and annex the kingdom of Luang Prabang.	Thai forces invade southern Laos and conquer the kingdom of Champasak.

kingdom and Viang Chan was a great centre of Buddhist learning, attracting monks from all over mainland Southeast Asia.

The Kingdom Divided

When King Suriya Vongsa died in 1695 a succession dispute wracked the kingdom, with the result that Lan Xang was divided. First the ruler of Luang Prabang declared independence from Viang Chan, followed a few years later by Champasak in the south.

The once-great kingdom of Lan Xang was reduced to regional kingdoms, none of which was able to withstand the growing power of the Tai-Syam kingdom of Ayutthaya. While the Siamese were distracted over the next half century by renewed threats from Burma, culminating in the sack of Ayutthaya, it did not take them long to recover. The inspiring leadership of a young military commander called Taksin rallied the Siamese and drove the Burmese out. After organising his kingdom and building a new capital, Taksin sought new fields of conquest. The Lao kingdoms were obvious targets. By 1779 all three had surrendered to Siamese armies and accepted the suzerainty of Siam. The Emerald Buddha was carried off by the Siamese and all Lao kings had to present regular tribute to Bangkok.

When Chao Anou succeeded his two older brothers on the throne of Viang Chan, he was determined to assert Lao independence. First he made merit by endowing Buddhist monasteries and building his own temple (Wat Si Saket). Then in 1826 he made his move, sending three armies down the Mekong and across the Khorat plateau. The Siamese were taken by surprise, but quickly rallied. Siamese armies drove the Lao back and seized Viang Chan. Chao Anou fled, but was captured when he tried to retake the city a year later. This time the Siamese were ruthless. Viang Chan was thoroughly sacked and its population resettled east of the Mekong. Only Wat Si Saket was spared. Chao Anou died a caged prisoner in Bangkok.

For the next 60 years the Lao *meuang*, from Champasak to Luang Prabang, were tributary to Siam. At first these two remaining small kingdoms retained a degree of independence, but increasingly they were brought under closer Siamese supervision. One reason for this was that Siam itself was threatened by a new power in the region and felt it had to consolidate its empire. The new power was France, which had declared a protectorate over most of Cambodia in 1863.

Four years later a French expedition sent to explore and map the Mekong River arrived in Luang Prabang, then the largest settlement upstream from Phnom Penh. In the 1880s the town became caught up in a struggle that pitted Siamese, French and roving bands of Chinese brigands (known as Haw) against each other. In 1887 Luang Prabang

The Lao believe most *naga* (snake deities; *nàhk* in Lao) have been converted to become serpent protectors of Buddhism. They still require propitiation, however, and annual boat races are held for their amusement. Many Buddhist temples have protective *naga* balustrades.

1826–28	1867	1885	1893
Chao Anou succeeds his two older brothers on the throne of Viang Chan and wages war against Siam for Lao independence. He is captured and Viang Chan is sacked by the Siamese armies.	Members of the French Mekong expedition reach Luang Prabang. Over the next 20 years the town is caught up in a struggle which sees the king offered protection by France.	Following centuries of successive invasions by neighbouring powers, the former Lan Xang is broken up into a series of states under Siamese control.	A French warship reaches Bangkok, guns trained on the palace. This forces the Siamese to give France sovereignty over all Lao territories east of the Mekong.

was looted and burned by a mixed force of Upland Tai and Haw. Only Wat Xieng Thong was spared. The king escaped downstream. With him was a French explorer named Auguste Pavie, who offered him the protection of France.

Southeast Asian kingdoms were not states in the modern sense, with fixed frontiers, but varied in extent depending on the power of the centre. Outlying meuang (principalities) might transfer their allegiance when the centre was weak. Scholars prefer the term mandala (montón in Lao), meaning 'circle of power' in Sanskrit.

French Rule

In the end French rule was imposed through gunboat diplomacy. In 1893 a French warship forced its way up the Chao Phraya River to Bangkok and trained its guns on the palace. Under duress, the Siamese agreed to transfer all territory east of the Mekong to France. Thus Laos became a French colony, with the kingdom of Luang Prabang as a protectorate and the rest of the country directly administered.

In 1900 Viang Chan (Vientiane) was re-established as the administrative capital of Laos, although real power was exercised from Hanoi, the capital of French Indochina. In 1907 a further treaty was signed with Siam adding two territories west of the Mekong to Laos (Sainyabuli Province and part of Champasak). Siem Reap and Battambang Provinces were regained by Cambodia as part of the deal.

Despite French plans for economic exploitation, Laos was always a drain on the budget of Indochina. Corvée labour was introduced, particularly to build roads, and taxes were heavy, but the colony never paid its own way. Some timber was floated down the Mekong, and tin was discovered in central Laos, but returns were meagre. Coffee was grown in southern Laos, and opium in the north, most of it smuggled into China.

Nationalism & Independence

The independence movement was slow to develop in Laos. The French justified their colonial rule as protecting the Lao from aggressive neighbours, particularly the Siamese. Most of the small Lao elite, aware of their own weakness, found this interpretation convincing, even though they resented the presence of so many Vietnamese. The Indochinese Communist Party (ICP), founded by Ho Chi Minh in 1930, did not espouse separate independence for Vietnam, Laos and Cambodia, and only managed to recruit its first two Lao members in 1935.

Naga Cities of Mekong (2006), by Martin Stuart-Fox, provides a narrative account of the founding legends and history of Luang Prabang, Vientiane and Champasak, and a guide to their temples.

It took the outbreak of war in Europe to weaken the French position in Indochina. A new aggressively nationalist government in Bangkok took advantage of this French weakness to try to regain territory 'lost' 50 years before. It renamed Siam Thailand, and opened hostilities. A Japanese-brokered peace agreement deprived Laos of its territories west of the Mekong, much to Lao anger.

To counter pan-Tai propaganda from Bangkok, the French encouraged Lao nationalism. Under an agreement between Japan and the Vichy French administration in Indochina, French rule continued, although

1904	1907	1945	1946
King Sisavang Vong founds the modern royal family.	The present borders of Laos are established by international treaty. Vientiane (the French spelling of Viang Chan) becomes the administrative capital.	The Japanese occupy Laos then force the king to declare independence; a nationalist resistance movement, the Lao Issara, takes shape and forms an interim government.	The French reoccupy Laos, sending the Lao Issara government into exile.

Japanese forces had freedom of movement. The Japanese were in place, therefore, when in early 1945 they began to suspect the French of shifting their allegiance to the allies. On 9 March the Japanese struck in a lightning coup de force throughout Indochina, interning all French military and civilian personnel. Only in Laos did a few French soldiers manage to slip into the jungle to maintain some resistance, along with their Lao allies.

The Japanese ruled Laos for just six months before the atomic bombing of Hiroshima and Nagasaki brought WWII to an end. During this time they forced King Sisavang Vong to declare Lao independence, and a nationalist resistance movement took shape, known as the Lao Issara (Free Lao). When the Japanese surrendered on 15 August, the Lao Issara formed an interim government, under the direction of Prince Phetsarat, a cousin of the king. For the first time since the early 18th century, the country was unified. The king, however, repudiated his declaration of independence in the belief that Laos still needed French protection, then dismissed Phetsarat as prime minister. As a result, the provisional National Assembly of 45 prominent nationalists passed a motion deposing the king.

Behind these tensions were the French, who were determined to regain their Indochinese empire. In March 1946, while a truce was held in Vietnam between the Viet Minh and the French, French forces struck north to seize control of Laos. The Lao Issara government was forced to flee to exile in Bangkok, leaving the French to sign a modus vivendi with the king reaffirming the unity of Laos and extending the king's rule from Luang Prabang to all of Laos. West Bank territories seized by Thailand in 1940 were returned to Laos.

By 1949 something of a stalemate had developed between the French and the Viet Minh in the main theatre of war in Vietnam. In order to shore up their position in Laos, the French granted the Lao a greater measure of independence. A promise of amnesty for Issara leaders attracted most back to take part in the political process in Laos. Among the returnees was Souvanna Phouma, a younger brother of Phetsarat, who remained in Thailand. Meanwhile, Souphanouvong, a half-brother of the two princes, led his followers to join the Viet Minh and keep up the anticolonial struggle.

Paths to Conflagration: Fifty Years of Diplomacy and Warfare in Laos, Thailand and Vietnam, 1778–1828 (1998), by Mayoury Ngaosyvathn and Pheuiphanh Ngaosyvathn, provides the best account of the Lao revolt against Bangkok, from a Lao perspective.

Rise of the Pathet Lao

The decisions of the three princes to go their separate ways divided the Lao Issara, with some returning to Laos to continue to work for Lao independence within a legal framework and some joining the Viet Minh to work for the expulsion of the French and formation of a Marxist regime. Their movement became known as the Pathet Lao (Land of the Lao).

1950	1953	1955	1957
Lao communists (the Pathet Lao) form a 'Resistance Government'. Souphanouvong becomes the public face of the Resistance Government and president of the Free Laos Front.	The Franco–Lao Treaty of Amity and Association grants full independence to Laos and a Lao delegation attends a conference in Geneva where a regroupment area is set aside for Pathet Lao Forces.	Pathet Lao leaders form the Lao People's Party (later the Lao People's Revolutionary Party) with a broad political front called the Lao Patriotic Front (LPF).	The First Coalition Government of National Union is formed and collapses after a financial and political crisis.

The first French-man to arrive in Laos was Henri Mouhot, an explorer and naturalist who died of malaria in 1861 near Luang Prabang (where his tomb can still be seen).

The architect of the Lao Issara–Viet Minh alliance was Prince Souphanouvong, who became the public face of the Resistance Government and president of the Free Laos Front (Naeo Lao Issara), successor to the disbanded Lao Issara. Real power lay, however, with Kaysone Phomvihane, in charge of defence, and Nouhak Phoumsavan, in charge of economy and finance, who were both members of the ICP.

By this time the whole complexion of the First Indochina War had changed with the 1949 victory of communism in China. As Chinese weapons flowed to the Viet Minh, the war widened and the French were forced onto the defensive, surrendering on 7 May 1954. The following day a conference opened in Geneva that eventually brought the curtain down on the French colonial period in Indochina.

Division & Unity

At the Geneva Conference in May 1954 it was agreed to temporarily divide Vietnam into north and south, Cambodia was left undivided, and in Laos two northeastern provinces (Hua Phan and Phongsali) were set aside as regroupment areas for Pathet Lao forces. There the Pathet Lao consolidated their political and military organisation, while negotiating with the Royal Lao Government (RLG) to reintegrate the two provinces into a unified Lao state.

The first thing Pathet Lao leaders did was to establish the Marxist-leaning Lao People's Party (LPP) in 1955 (later renamed the Lao People's Revolutionary Party; LPRP). It remains the ruling party of the Lao PDR (Lao People's Democratic Republic) today. The LPP established a broad political front, called the Lao Patriotic Front (LPF), with Souphanouvong as its president and Kaysone secretary-general. Together with other members of the 'team' they led the Lao revolution throughout its '30-year struggle' (1945 to 1975) for power.

The first priority for the RLG was to reunify the country with a political solution palatable to the Pathet Lao. In its remote base areas, the Pathet Lao was entirely dependent for weapons and most other kinds of assistance on the North Vietnamese. Meanwhile, the RLG became increasingly dependent on the US, which soon took over from France as its principal aid donor. Thus Laos became the cockpit for Cold War enmity.

The Lao politician with the task of finding a way through both ideological differences and foreign interference was Souvanna Phouma. As prime minister of the RLG, he negotiated a deal with his half-brother Souphanouvong which saw two Pathet Lao ministers and two deputy ministers included in a coalition government. The Pathet Lao provinces

1958	1960	1961	1962
The government falls and comes under the control of the right-wing, US-backed Committee for the Defence of National Interests (CDNI).	Guerrilla warfare covers large areas. A neutralist coup d'état is followed by the battle for Vientiane.	Orders are given to the Central Intelligence Agency (CIA) to form a 'secret army' in northern Laos with links to the American war in Vietnam.	The Geneva Agreement on Laos establishes the second coalition government that balances Pathet Lao and rightist representation with neutralist voting powers.

were returned to the royal administration. Elections were held, in which the LPF did surprisingly well. And the US was furious.

Between 1955 and 1958, the US had given Laos US$120 million, or four times what France had provided over the previous eight years. Laos was almost entirely dependent, therefore, on American largesse to survive. When that aid was withheld, as it was in August 1958 in response to the inclusion of Pathet Lao ministers in the government, Laos was plunged into a financial and political crisis. As a result, the first coalition government collapsed after just eight months.

As guerrilla warfare resumed over large areas, moral objections were raised against Lao killing Lao. On 9 August 1960, the diminutive commanding officer of the elite Second Paratroop Battalion of the Royal Lao Army seized power in Vientiane while almost the entire Lao government was in Luang Prabang making arrangements for the funeral of King Sisavang Vong. Captain Kong Le announced to the world that Laos was returning to a policy of neutrality, and demanded that Souvanna Phouma be reinstated as prime minister. King Sisavang Vatthana acquiesced, but military strongman General Phoumi Nosavan refused to take part, and flew to central Laos where he instigated opposition to the new government.

In this, he had the support of the Thai government and the US Central Intelligence Agency (CIA), which supplied him with cash and weapons. The neutralist government still claimed to be the legitimate government of Laos, and as such received arms, via Vietnam, from the Soviet Union. Most of these found their way to the Pathet Lao. Throughout the country large areas fell under the control of communist forces. The US sent troops to Thailand, in case communist forces should attempt to cross the Mekong, and it looked for a while as if the major commitment of US troops in Southeast Asia would be to Laos rather than Vietnam.

The Second Indochina War

At this point the new US administration of President John F Kennedy had second thoughts about fighting a war in Laos. In an about-face it decided instead to back Lao neutrality. In May 1962 a new conference on Laos was convened in Geneva, where an international agreement was signed guaranteeing Lao neutrality and forbidding the presence of all foreign military personnel. In Laos the new coalition government took office buoyed by popular goodwill and hope.

Pressures created by the war in Vietnam, however, caused cracks to appear in the coalition. Despite the terms of the Geneva Agreements, both the US and the North Vietnamese continued to provide their respective clients with arms and supplies.

During the Second Indochina War, Chinese military engineers built a network of roads into northern Laos. Though these roads assisted the Pathet Lao, they were never bombed by American aircraft, for fear that Chinese troops might join the war in northern Laos.

1964	1964–73	1974	1975
The US begins an air war against ground targets in Laos, mostly against communist positions on the Plain of Jars.	The Second Indochina War spills over into Laos. Both the North Vietnamese and US presence increases dramatically and bombing extends along the length of Laos.	Finally a 1973 ceasefire in Vietnam means an end to fighting in Laos and the formation of the third coalition government.	Communists seize power and declare the Lao People's Democratic Republic (Lao PDR). This ends 650 years of the Lao monarchy.

By the end of 1963, as each side denounced the other for violating the Geneva Agreements, the second coalition government had irrevocably broken down. It was in the interests of all powers, however, to preserve the facade of Lao neutrality, and international diplomatic support was brought to bear for Souvanna Phouma to prevent rightist generals from seizing power in coups mounted in 1964 and 1965.

In 1964 the US began its air war over Laos, with strafing and bombing of communist positions on the Plain of Jars. As North Vietnamese infiltration picked up along the Ho Chi Minh Trail, bombing was extended across all of Laos. According to official figures, the US dropped 2,093,100 tonnes of bombs in 580,944 sorties. The total cost was US$7.2 billion, or US$2 million a day for nine years. No one knows how many people died, but one-third of the population of 2.1 million became internal refugees.

During the 1960s both the North Vietnamese and the US presence increased exponentially. By 1968 an estimated 40,000 North Vietnamese regular army troops were based in Laos to keep the Ho Chi Minh Trail open and support some 35,000 Pathet Lao forces. The Royal Lao Army then numbered 60,000 (entirely paid for and equipped by the US), the Hmong forces led by Vang Pao were half that number (still under the direction of the CIA) and Kong Le's neutralists numbered 10,000. Lao forces on both sides were entirely funded by their foreign backers. For five more years this proxy war dragged on, until the ceasefire of 1973.

The 1968 Tet Offensive was a turning point in the war in Vietnam, with the American people convinced of the need for a political solution. The effect in Laos, however, was to intensify both the air war and fighting on the Plain of Jars. When bombing was suspended over North Vietnam, the US Air Force concentrated all its efforts on Laos. The Pathet Lao leadership was forced underground, into the caves of Vieng Xai.

Backfire: The CIA's Secret War in Laos and Its Link to the War in Vietnam (1995), by Roger Warner, provides an informed account of the range of CIA activity in Laos.

By mid-1972, when serious peace moves were underway, some four-fifths of the country was under communist control. In peace as in war, what happened in Laos depended on what happened in Vietnam. Not until a ceasefire came into effect in Vietnam in January 1973 could the fighting end in Laos. Then the political wrangling began. In September an agreement was reached on the composition of the third coalition government and how it would operate.

Revolution & Reform

In April 1975, first Phnom Penh and then Saigon fell to communist forces. Immediately the Pathet Lao brought political pressure to bear on the right in Laos. Escalating street demonstrations forced leading rightist politicians and generals to flee the country. Town after town was

1986	1987	1991	1997
The 'New Economic Mechanism' opens the way for a market economy and foreign investment.	A three-month border war breaks out between Laos and Thailand, ending in a truce in February 1988.	The constitution of the Lao PDR is proclaimed. General Khamtay Siphandone becomes prime minister.	Laos joins the Association of Southeast Asian Nations (Asean).

RE-EDUCATION

Re-education camps were all in remote areas. Inmates laboured on road construction, helped local villagers and grew their own vegetables. Food was nevertheless scarce, work hard and medical attention inadequate or nonexistent. Except for a couple of high-security camps for top officials and army officers, inmates were allowed some freedom of contact with local villagers. Some even took local women as partners. Escape was all but impossible, however, because of the remoteness of the camps. Only those showing a contrite attitude to past 'crimes' were released, some to work for the regime, but most to leave the country to join families overseas.

peacefully 'liberated' by Pathet Lao forces, culminating with Vientiane in August.

Souvanna Phouma, who could see the writing on the wall, cooperated with the Pathet Lao in order to prevent further bloodshed. Hundreds of senior military officers and civil servants voluntarily flew off to remote camps for 'political re-education'.

In November an extraordinary meeting of what was left of the third coalition government bowed to the inevitable and demanded formation of a 'popular democratic regime'. Under pressure, the king agreed to abdicate, and on 2 December a National Congress of People's Representatives assembled by the party proclaimed the end of the 650-year-old Lao monarchy and the establishment of the Lao People's Democratic Republic (Lao PDR). Kaysone Phomvihane became prime minister in the new Marxist–Leninist government. Souphanouvong was named state president.

The new regime was organised in accordance with Soviet and North Vietnamese models. The government and bureaucracy were under the strict direction of the Party and its seven-member politburo. Immediately the Party moved to restrict liberal freedoms of speech and assembly, and to nationalise the economy. As inflation soared, price controls were introduced. In response, around 10% of the population, including virtually all the educated class, fled across the Mekong to Thailand as refugees, setting Lao development back at least a generation.

The Hmong insurgency dragged on for another 30 years. In 1977, fearing the king might escape his virtual house arrest to lead resistance, the authorities arrested him and his family and sent them to Vieng Xai, the old Pathet Lao wartime headquarters. There they were forced to labour in the fields. The king, queen and crown prince all eventually died, probably of malaria and malnutrition, although no official explanation of their deaths has ever been offered.

HISTORY REVOLUTION & REFORM

1998–2000	2000	2004	2006
The Asian economic crisis seriously impacts on the Lao economy. China and Vietnam come to the country's aid with loans and advice.	The economic crisis sparks some political unrest. Anti-government Lao rebels attack a customs post on the Thai border. Five are killed.	Security is still tight when Laos hosts the 10th Asean summit in Vientiane, the largest gathering of world leaders ever assembled in Laos.	The Eighth Congress of the Lao People's Revolutionary Party and National Assembly elections endorse a new political leadership.

By 1979 it was clear that policies had to change. Kaysone announced that people could leave cooperatives and farm their own land, and that private enterprise would be permitted. Reforms were insufficient to improve the Lao economy. The Soviet Union, embarking on its own momentous reforms, was getting tired of propping up the Lao regime. Eventually Kaysone convinced the Party in 1986 to follow the Chinese example and open the economy up to market forces while retaining a tight monopoly on political power.

Economic improvement was slow in coming, partly because relations with Thailand remained strained. In August 1987 the two countries fought a brief border war over disputed territory, which left 1000 people dead. The following year, relations with both Thailand and China were patched up. The first elections for a national assembly were held, and a constitution at last promulgated. Slowly a legal framework was put into place, and by the early 1990s, foreign direct investment was picking up and the economy was on the mend.

The Politics of Ritual and Remembrance: Laos Since 1975 (1998), by Grant Evans, provides a penetrating study of Lao political culture, including attitudes to Buddhism and the 'cult' of communist leader Kaysone.

Modern Laos

Kaysone Phomvihane died in 1992. He had been the leading figure in Lao communism for more than a quarter of a century. General Khamtay Siphandone became both president of the LPRP and prime minister. His rise signalled control of the Party by the revolutionary generation of military leaders. When Khamtay stepped down in 2006, he was succeeded by his close comrade, General Chummaly Sayasone.

The economic prosperity of the mid-1990s rested on increased investment and foreign aid, on which Laos remained very dependent. The Lao PDR enjoyed friendly relations with all its neighbours. In 1997 Laos joined the Association of Southeast Asian Nations (ASEAN).

With the Asian economic crisis of the late 1990s, the collapse of the Thai baht led to inflation of the Lao kip, to which it was largely tied. The economic crisis sparked some political unrest. A small student demonstration calling for an end to the monopoly of political power by the LPRP was ruthlessly crushed and its leaders given long prison sentences.

A Short History of Laos, the Land in Between (2002), by Grant Evans, gives a very readable and insightful coverage of the country's history up to the year 2000.

In 2003 Western journalists for the first time made contact with Hmong insurgents. Their reports revealed an insurgency on the point of collapse. Renewed military pressure forced some Hmong to surrender, while others made their way to refuge in Thailand. However, the Thai classified the Hmong as illegal immigrants; negotiations for resettlement in third countries stalled, and in December 2009, despite widespread international condemnation, some 4000 Hmong were forcibly repatriated to Laos.

2009	2010	2012	2013
Laos hosts the 25th Southeast Asia Games. Four thousand Hmong refugees are forcibly repatriated from Thailand.	The Nam Theun 2 hydropower dam, the largest in mainland Southeast Asia, begins production.	Internationally acclaimed community-development worker Sombath Somphone disappears. The Lao government denies responsibility for his disappearance.	Work begins on the Xayaboury Dam, the first dam to be built on the Mekong River in Laos. Cambodia and Vietnam raise objections.

In the decade to 2010, China greatly increased investment in Laos to equal that of Thailand. Japan remained the largest aid donor. However, Chinese companies invested in major projects in mining, hydropower and plantation agriculture and timber. Meanwhile, cross-border trade grew apace. Increased economic power brought political influence at the expense of Vietnam, though Lao–Vietnamese relations remained close and warm. Senior Lao Party cadres still take courses in Marxism–Leninism in Vietnam, although their economic inspiration more likely comes from Laos' mighty northern neighbour, China.

In April 2016 vice president Bounnhang Vorachith became president of the Lao PDR, establishing himself as a force against corruption. Calling for a halt on logging, making a pledge to reforest 70% of Laos by 2020 and (allegedly) sacking many of his ministers and replacing them with people he could trust, he set the stage for the August gathering of Asean, held in Laos and attended by US President Barack Obama. This followed high-profile visits from John Kerry earlier in the year and Hillary Clinton in 2012. America seemed keen to signal to China it intended to take an interest in Laos' future; the Asian superpower continues funding dams and high-speed rail lines into Laos, placing the diminutive country ever more in its debt, as a key conduit to Southeast Asia in its 'new Silk Road' trade strategy. The 2018 collapse of Saddle Dam D was a grim reminder of the costs this kind of progress can have, and the challenges that face the government.

Bamboo Palace: Discovering the Lost Dynasty of Laos (2003), by Christopher Kremmer, builds on his personal travelogue told in *Stalking the Elephant Kings* (1997) to try to discover the fate of the Lao royal family.

2015	2016	2016	2018
Ten-yearly census is conducted, putting population of Laos at 6,492,000.	Vice President of Laos, Bounnhang Vorachith, becomes Laos' new supreme leader.	US President Barack Obama becomes the first sitting president to visit Laos, pledging US$90 million over the next three years for UXO (land-mines) clean-up.	Saddle Dam D in Attapeu collapses, causing up to 100 deaths and displacement of thousands of villagers.

People & Culture

It's hard to think of any other country with a population as laid-back as Laos – *bor ɓen nyǎng* (no problem) could be the national motto. On the surface at least, nothing seems to faze the Lao, whose national character is a complex combination of culture, environment and religion. It takes visitors a little time to settle into the local rhythm.

The National Psyche

To a large degree 'Lao-ness' is defined by Buddhism, specifically Theravada Buddhism, which emphasises the cooling of human passions. Thus strong emotions are a taboo in Lao society. *Kamma* (karma; intentional action), more than devotion, prayer or hard work, is believed to determine one's lot in life, so the Lao tend not to get too worked up over the future. It's a trait often perceived by outsiders as a lack of ambition.

Lao commonly express the notion that 'too much work is bad for your brain' and they often say they feel sorry for people who 'think too much'. Education in general isn't highly valued, although this attitude is changing with modernisation and greater access to opportunities beyond the country's borders. Avoiding any undue psychological stress, however, remains a cultural norm. From the typical Lao perspective, unless an activity – whether work or play – contains an element of *móoan* (fun), it will probably lead to stress.

The contrast between the Lao and the Vietnamese is an example of how the Annamite Chain has served as a cultural fault line dividing Indo-Asia and Sino-Asia, as well as a geographic divide. The French summed it up as: 'The Vietnamese plant the rice, the Cambodians tend the rice and the Lao listen to it grow.' And while this saying wasn't meant as a compliment, a good number of French colonialists found the Lao way too seductive to resist, and stayed on.

The Lao have always been quite receptive to outside assistance and foreign investment, since it promotes a certain degree of economic development without demanding a corresponding increase in productivity. The Lao government wants all the trappings of modern technology – the skyscrapers seen on socialist propaganda billboards – without having to give up Lao traditions, including the *móoan* philosophy. The challenge for Laos is to find a balance between cultural preservation and the development of new attitudes that will lead the country towards a measure of self-sufficiency.

Laos: Culture and Society (2000), edited by Grant Evans, brings together a dozen essays on Lao culture, among them a profile of a self-exiled Lao family that eventually returned to Laos, and two well-researched studies of the modernisation and politicalisation of the Lao language.

Lifestyle

Maybe it's because everything closes early, even in the capital, that just about everyone in Laos gets up before 6am. Their day might begin with a quick breakfast, at home or from a local noodle seller, before work. In Lao Loum (Lowland Lao) and other Buddhist areas, the morning also sees monks collecting alms, usually from women who give rice and other foods outside their homes in return for a blessing.

School-age children will walk to a packed classroom housed in a basic building with one or two teachers. Secondary students often board during the week because there are fewer secondary schools and it can be too far to commute. Almost any family who can afford it pays for their kids to learn English, which is seen as a near-guarantee of future employment.

Given that most Lao people live in rural communities, work is usually some form of manual labour. Depending on the season, and the person's location and gender (women and men have clearly defined tasks when it comes to farming), work might be planting or harvesting rice or other crops. Unlike neighbouring Vietnam, the Lao usually only harvest one crop of rice each year, meaning there are a couple of busy periods followed by plenty of time when life can seem very laid-back.

During these quiet periods, men will fish, hunt and repair the house, while women might gather flora and fauna from the forest, weave fabrics and collect firewood. At these times there's something wonderfully social and uncorrupted about arriving in a village mid-afternoon, sitting in the front of the local 'store' and sharing a *lòw-lów* (rice whisky) or two with the locals, without feeling like you're stealing their time.

Where vices are concerned, *lòw-lów* is the drug of choice for most Lao, particularly in rural areas where average incomes are so low that Beerlao is beyond most budgets. Opium is the most high-profile of the other drugs traditionally used – and tolerated – in Laos, though recent crop-clearing has made it less available. In cities, *yaba* (methamphetamine), in particular, has become popular among young people.

Because average incomes are low in Laos, despite the minimum wage being increased to US$130 per month in 2018, the Lao typically socialise as families, pooling their resources to enjoy a *bun wat* (temple festival) or picnic at the local waterfall together. The Lao tend to live in extended families, with three or more generations sharing one house or compound, and dine together sitting on mats on the floor with rice and dishes shared by all.

Most Lao don some portion of the traditional garb during ceremonies and celebrations: the men a *pàh bęeang* (shoulder sash), the women a similar sash, tight-fitting blouse and *pàh nung* (sarong). In everyday life men wear neat but unremarkable shirt-and-trousers combinations. However, it's still normal for women to wear the *pàh nung* or *sìn* (sarong). Other ethnicities living in Laos, particularly Chinese and Vietnamese women, will wear the *pàh nung* when they visit a government office, or risk having any civic requests denied.

Population

Laos has one of the lowest population densities in Asia, but the number of people has more than doubled in the last 30 years, and continues to grow quickly. One-third of the country's seven million inhabitants live in cities in the Mekong River valley, chiefly Vientiane, Luang Prabang, Savannakhet and Pakse. Another one-third live along other major rivers.

This rapid population growth comes despite the fact that about 10% of the population fled the country after the 1975 communist takeover. Vientiane and Luang Prabang lost the most inhabitants, with approximately a quarter of the population of Luang Prabang going abroad. During the last couple of decades this emigration trend has been reversed so that the influx of immigrants (mostly repatriated Lao, but also Chinese, Vietnamese and other nationalities) now exceeds the number of émigrés.

Most Westerners living in Laos are temporary employees of multilateral and bilateral aid organisations. A smaller number are employed by foreign companies involved in mining, petroleum, hydropower and the tourism industry.

Feature-film making resumed in Laos in 1997 with the release of *Than Heng Phongphai* (The Charming Forest) directed by Vithoun Sundara. This was followed in 2001 by *Falang Phon* (Clear Skies After Rain), and in 2004 by *Leum Teua* (Wrongfulness), also directed by Sundara.

Ethnic Groups

Laos is often described as less a nation state than a conglomeration of tribes and languages. And depending on who you talk with, that conglomeration consists of between 49 and 134 different ethnic groups. The lower figure is officially used by the government.

While the tribal groups are many and varied, the Lao traditionally divide themselves into four categories: Lao Loum, Lao Tai, Lao Thoeng and Lao Soung. These classifications loosely reflect the altitudes at which the groups live, and, by implication (it's not always accurate), their cultural proclivities. To address some of these inaccuracies, the Lao government recently reclassified ethnic groups into three major language families: Austro-Tai, Austro-Asiatic and Sino-Tibetan. However, many people do not know which language family they come from, so here we'll stick with the more commonly understood breakdown.

Article 9 of the current Lao constitution forbids all religious proselytising, and the distribution of religious materials outside churches, temples or mosques is illegal. Foreigners caught distributing religious materials may be arrested and expelled from the country.

Just over half the population are ethnic Lao or Lao Loum, and these are clearly the most dominant group. Of the rest, 10% to 20% are tribal Tai; 20% to 30% are Lao Thoeng ('Upland Lao' or lower-mountain dwellers, mostly of proto-Malay or Mon-Khmer descent); and 10% to 20% are Lao Soung ('Highland Lao', mainly Hmong or Mien tribes who live higher up).

The Lao government has an alternative three-way split, in which the Lao Tai are condensed into the Lao Loum group. This triumvirate is represented on the back of every 1000 kip bill, in national costume, from left to right: Lao Soung, Lao Loum and Lao Thoeng.

Small Tibeto-Burman hill-tribe groups in Laos include the Lisu, Lahu, Lolo, Akha and Phu Noi. They are sometimes classified as Lao Thoeng, but like the Lao Soung they live in the mountains of northern Laos.

Lao Loum

The dominant ethnic group is the Lao Loum (Lowland Lao), who live in the fertile plains of the Mekong River valley or lower tributaries of the Mekong. Thanks to their superior numbers and living conditions, they have dominated the smaller ethnic groups for centuries. Their language is the national language; their religion, Buddhism, is the national religion; and many of their customs, including the eating of sticky rice and the *bąasìi* (sacred string-tying ceremonies), are interpreted as those of the Lao nation, even though they play no part in the lives of many other ethnic groups.

Lao Loum culture has traditionally consisted of a sedentary, subsistence lifestyle based on wet-rice cultivation. The people live in raised homes and, like most Austro-Tais, are Theravada Buddhists who retain strong elements of animist spirit worship.

The distinction between 'Lao' and 'Thai' is a rather recent historical phenomenon, especially considering that 80% of all those who speak a language recognised as 'Lao' reside in northeastern Thailand. Even Lao living in Laos refer idiomatically to different Lao Loum groups as 'Tai' or 'Thai', such as Thai Luang Phabang (Lao from Luang Prabang).

Lao Tai

Although they're closely related to the Lao, these Tai (or sometimes Thai) subgroups have resisted absorption into mainstream Lao culture and tend to subdivide themselves according to smaller tribal distinctions. Like the Lao Loum, they live along river valleys, but the Lao Tai have chosen to reside in upland valleys rather than in the lowlands of the Mekong floodplains.

Depending on their location, they cultivate dry (mountain) rice as well as wet (irrigated) rice. The Lao Tai also mix Theravada Buddhism and animism, but tend to place more importance on spirit worship than do the Lao Loum.

Generally, the various Lao Tai groups are distinguished from one another by the predominant colour of their clothing, or by the general area of habitation; for example, Tai Dam (Black Tai), Tai Khao (White Tai), Tai Pa (Forest Tai), Tai Neua (Northern Tai) and so on.

Lao Thoeng

The Lao Thoeng (Upland Lao) are a loose affiliation of mostly Austro-Asiatic peoples who live on mid-altitude mountain slopes in northern and southern Laos. The largest group is the Khamu, followed by the Htin, Lamet and smaller numbers of Laven, Katu, Katang, Alak and other Mon-Khmer groups in the south. The Lao Thoeng are also known by the pejorative term *kàh*, which means 'slave' or 'servant'. This is because they were used as indentured labour by migrating Austro-Thai peoples in earlier centuries and more recently by the Lao monarchy. They still often work as labourers for the Lao Soung.

The Lao Thoeng have a much lower standard of living than any of the three other groups. Most trade between the Lao Thoeng and other Lao is carried out by barter.

The Htin (also called Lawa) and Khamu languages are closely related, and both groups are thought to have been in Laos long before the arrival of the Lowland Lao, tribal Tai or Lao Soung. During the Lao New Year celebrations in Luang Prabang the Lowland Lao offer a symbolic tribute to the Khamu as their historical predecessors and as 'guardians of the land'.

Lao Soung

The Lao Soung (Highland Lao) include the hill tribes who live at the highest altitudes. Of all the peoples of Laos, they are the most recent immigrants, having come from Myanmar (Burma), southern China and Tibet within the last 150 years.

The largest group is the Hmong, also called Miao or Meo, who number more than 300,000 in four main subgroups: the White Hmong, Striped Hmong, Red Hmong and Black Hmong. The colours refer to certain clothing details and these groups are found in the nine provinces of the north, plus Bolikhamsai in central Laos.

The agricultural staples of the Hmong are dry rice and corn raised by the slash-and-burn method. The Hmong also breed cattle, pigs, water buffalo and chickens, traditionally for barter rather than sale. For years their only cash crop was opium, and they grew and manufactured more than any other group in Laos. However, an aggressive eradication program run by the government, with support from the US, has eliminated most of the crop. The resulting loss of a tradeable commodity has hit many Hmong communities very hard. The Hmong are most numerous in Hua Phan, Xieng Khuang, Luang Prabang and northern Vientiane Provinces.

The second-largest group are the Mien (also called Iu Mien, Yao and Man), who live mainly in Luang Namtha, Luang Prabang, Bokeo, Udomxai and Phongsali. The Mien, like the Hmong, have traditionally cultivated opium poppies. Replacement crops, including coffee, are taking time to bed in and generate income.

The Mien and Hmong have many ethnic and linguistic similarities, and both groups are predominantly animist. The Hmong are considered more aggressive and warlike than the Mien, however, and as such were perfect for the CIA-trained special Royal Lao Government forces in the 1960s and early 1970s. Large numbers of Hmong–Mien left Laos and fled abroad after 1975.

Due to Laos' ethnic diversity, 'Lao culture' only exists among the Lao Loum (Lowland Lao), who represent about half the population. Lao Loum culture predominates in the cities, towns and villages of the Mekong River valley.

PEOPLE & CULTURE ETHNIC GROUPS

Ethnic Groups of Laos, Vols 1–3 (2003), by Joachim Schliesinger, is a well-respected modern ethnography of Laos. Schliesinger's scheme enumerates and describes 94 ethnicities in detail.

Other Asians

As elsewhere in Southeast Asia, the Chinese have been migrating to Laos for centuries to work as merchants and traders. Most come directly from Yunnan but more recently many have also arrived from Vietnam. Estimates of their numbers vary from 2% to 5% of the total population. At least half of all permanent Chinese residents in Laos are said to live in Vientiane and Savannakhet. There are also thousands of Chinese migrant workers in the far north.

Substantial numbers of Vietnamese live in all the provinces bordering Vietnam and in the cities of Vientiane, Savannakhet and Pakse. For the most part, Vietnamese residents in Laos work as traders and own small businesses, although there continues to be a small Vietnamese military presence in Xieng Khuang and Hua Phan Provinces. Small numbers of Cambodians live in southern Laos.

Religion

Buddhism

About 60% of the people of Laos are Theravada Buddhists, the majority being Lao Loum, with a sprinkling of tribal Tais. Theravada Buddhism was apparently introduced to Luang Prabang (then known as Muang Sawa) in the late 13th or early 14th centuries, although there may have been contact with Mahayana Buddhism during the 8th to 10th centuries and with Tantric Buddhism even earlier.

King Visoun, a successor of the first monarch of Lan Xang, King Fa Ngum, declared Buddhism the state religion after accepting the Pha Bang Buddha image from his Khmer sponsors. Today the Pha Bang is kept at the Royal Palace in Luang Prabang. Buddhism was fairly slow to spread throughout Laos, even among the lowland peoples, who were reluctant to accept the faith instead of, or even alongside, *pĕe* (earth spirit) worship.

Theravada Buddhism is an earlier and, according to its followers, less corrupted school of Buddhism than the Mahayana schools found in east Asia and the Himalayas. It's sometimes referred to as the 'southern' school since it took the southern route from India through Sri Lanka and Southeast Asia.

Theravada doctrine stresses the three principal aspects of existence: *dukkha* (suffering, unsatisfactoriness, disease), *anicca* (impermanence, transience of all things) and *anatta* (nonsubstantiality or nonessentiality of reality; no permanent 'soul'). Comprehension of *anicca* reveals that no experience, state of mind or physical object lasts. Trying to hold onto experience, states of mind and physical objects that are constantly changing creates *dukkha*. *Anatta* is the understanding that there is no part of the changing world we can point to and say 'This is me' or 'This is God' or 'This is the soul'.

The ultimate goal of Theravada Buddhism is *nibbana* (nirvana in Sanskrit), which literally means the 'blowing-out' or 'extinction' of all causes of *dukkha*. Effectively it means an end to all corporeal or even heavenly existence, which is forever subject to suffering and which is conditioned from moment to moment by *kamma*. In reality, most Lao Buddhists aim for rebirth in a 'better' existence rather than the goal of *nibbana*. By feeding monks, giving donations to temples and performing regular worship at the local wat, Lao Buddhists acquire enough 'merit' (Pali *puñña;* Lao *bun*) for their future lives. And it's in the pursuit of merit that you're most likely to see Lao Buddhism 'in action'. Watching monks walking through their neighbourhoods at dawn to collect offerings of food from people who are kneeling in front of their homes is a memorable experience.

Lao Buddhists don't visit the wat on a set day. Most often they'll visit on a *wan sĭn* (ວັນສິນ), meaning 'Precept Day' (or rule day), which occur with every full, new and quarter moon (roughly every seven days). On such a visit, typical activities include the offering of lotus buds, incense and candles at various altars and bone reliquaries, offering food to the monks, meditating, and attending a *táirt* (*Dhamma* talk) by the abbot.

Monks & Nuns

Unlike other religions in which priests or nuns make a lifelong commitment to their religious vocation, being a Buddhist monk or nun can be a much more transient experience. Socially, every Lao Buddhist male is expected to become a *kŏo-bạh* (monk) for at least a short period in his life, optimally between the time he finishes school and starts a career or marries. Men or boys under 20 years of age may enter the Sangha (monastic order) as *náirn* (novices) and this is not unusual since a family earns merit when one of its sons takes robe and bowl. Traditionally, the length of time spent in the wat is three months, during the *pansăh* (Buddhist lent), which coincides with the rainy season. However, nowadays men may spend as little as a week or 15 days to accrue merit as monks or novices. There are, of course, some monks who do devote all or most of their lives to the wat.

There is no similar hermetic order for nuns, but women may reside in temples as *náhng sée* (lay nuns), with shaved heads and white robes.

Spirit Cults

No matter where you are in Laos the practice of *pĕe* (spirit) worship, sometimes called animism, won't be far away. *Pĕe* worship predates Buddhism and despite being officially banned it remains the dominant non-Buddhist belief system. But for most Lao it is not a matter of Buddhism *or* spirit worship. Instead, established Buddhist beliefs coexist peacefully with respect for the *pĕe* that are believed to inhabit natural objects.

An obvious example of this coexistence is the 'spirit houses', which are found in or outside almost every home. Spirit houses are often ornately decorated miniature temples, built as a home for the local spirit. Residents must share their space with the spirit and go to great lengths to keep it happy, offering enough incense and food that the spirit won't make trouble for them.

In Vientiane, Buddhism and spirit worship flourish side by side at Wat Si Muang. The central image at the temple is not a Buddha figure but the *lák méuang* (city pillar from the time of the Khmer empire), in which the guardian spirit for the city is believed to reside. Many local residents make daily offerings before the pillar, while at the same time praying to a Buddha figure. A form of *pĕe* worship visitors can partake in is the *bạasĭi* ceremony.

Outside the Mekong River valley, the *pĕe* *c*ult is particularly strong among the tribal Tai, especially the Tai Dam, who pay special attention to a class of *pĕe* called *ten*. The *ten* are earth spirits that preside not only over the plants and soil, but over entire districts as well. The Tai Dam also believe in the 32 *kwăn* (guardian spirits). *Mŏr* (master/shaman), who are specially trained in the propitiation and exorcism of spirits, preside at important Tai Dam festivals and ceremonies. It is possible to see some of the spiritual beliefs and taboos in action by staying in a Katang village during a trek into the forests of Dong Phu Vieng NPA.

The Hmong–Mien tribes also practise animism, plus ancestral worship. Some Hmong groups recognise a pre-eminent spirit that presides over all earth spirits; others do not. The Akha, Lisu and other Tibeto-Burman groups mix animism and ancestor cults.

Festivals of Laos (2010), by Martin Stuart-Fox and Somsanouk Mixay, covers the full annual cycle of Lao festivals, from New Year to That Luang, with the added bonus of Steve Northup's stunning photographs.

Other Religions

A small number of Lao, mostly those of the remaining French-educated elite, are Christians. An even smaller number of Muslims live in Vientiane, mostly Arab and Indian merchants whose ancestry as Laos residents dates as far back as the 17th century. Vientiane also harbours a small community of Chams, Cambodian Muslims who fled Pol Pot's Kampuchea in the 1970s. In northern Laos there are pockets of Muslim Yunnanese, known among the Lao as *jĕen hór*.

Women in Laos

For the women of Laos, roles and status vary significantly depending on their ethnicity, but it's fair to say that whatever group they come from they are seen as secondary to men. As you travel around Laos the evidence is overwhelming. While men's work is undoubtedly hard, women always seem to be working harder, for longer and with far less time for relaxing and socialising.

Lao Loum women gain limited benefits from bilateral inheritance patterns, whereby both women and men can inherit land and business ownership. This derives from a matrilocal tradition, where a husband joins the wife's family on marriage. Often the youngest daughter and her husband will live with and care for her parents until they die, when they inherit at least some of their land and business. However, even if a Lao Loum woman inherits her father's farmland, she will have only limited

POST-REVOLUTION BUDDHISM

During the 1964–73 war years, both sides sought to use Buddhism to legitimise their cause. By the early 1970s, the Lao Patriotic Front (LPF) was winning this propaganda war as more and more monks threw their support behind the communists.

Despite this, major changes were in store for the Sangha (monastic order) following the 1975 takeover. Initially, Buddhism was banned as a primary-school subject and people were forbidden to make merit by giving food to monks. Monks were also forced to till the land and raise animals, in direct violation of their monastic vows.

Mass dissatisfaction among the faithful prompted the government to rescind the ban on the feeding of monks in 1976. By the end of that year, the government was not only allowing traditional giving of alms, it was offering a daily ration of rice directly to the Sangha.

In 1992, in what was perhaps its biggest endorsement of Buddhism since the Revolution, the government replaced the hammer-and-sickle emblem that crowned Laos' national seal with a drawing of Pha That Luang, the country's holiest Buddhist symbol.

Today the Department of Religious Affairs (DRA) controls the Sangha and ensures that Buddhism is taught in accordance with Marxist principles. All monks must undergo political indoctrination as part of their monastic training, and all canonical and extracanonical Buddhist texts have been subject to 'editing' by the DRA. Monks are also forbidden to promote *pĕe* (earth spirit) worship, which has been officially banned in Laos along with *săinyasąht* (magic). The cult of *kwăn* (the 32 guardian spirits attached to mental/physical functions), however, has not been tampered with.

One major change in Lao Buddhism was the abolition of the Thammayut sect. Formerly, the Sangha in Laos was divided into two sects, the Mahanikai and the Thammayut (as in Thailand). The Thammayut is a minority sect that was begun by Thailand's King Mongkut. The Pathet Lao saw it as a tool of the Thai monarchy (and hence US imperialism) for infiltrating Lao political culture.

For several years all Buddhist literature written in Thai was also banned, severely curtailing the teaching of Buddhism in Laos. This ban has since been lifted and Lao monks are even allowed to study at Buddhist universities throughout Thailand. However, the Thammayut ban remains and has resulted in a much weaker emphasis on meditation, considered the spiritual heart of Buddhist practice in most Theravada countries. Overall, monastic discipline in Laos is far more relaxed than it was before 1975.

control over how it is used. Instead, her husband will have the final say on most major decisions, while she will be responsible for saving enough money to see the family through any crisis.

This fits with the cultural beliefs associated with Lao Buddhism, which commonly teaches that women must be reborn as men before they can attain nirvana, hence a woman's spiritual status is generally less than that of a man. Still, Lao Loum women enjoy a higher status than women from other ethnic groups, who become part of their husband's clan on marriage and rarely inherit anything.

Women in Laos face several other hurdles: fewer girls go to school than boys; women are relatively poorly represented in government and other senior positions; and although they make up more than half the workforce, pay is often lower than male equivalents. If a Lao woman divorces, no matter how fair her reasons, it's very difficult for her to find another husband unless he is older or foreign.

In the cities, however, things are changing as fast as wealth, education and exposure to foreign ideas allows, and in general women in cities are more confident and willing to engage with foreigners than their rural counterparts. Women are gradually pushing into more responsible positions, such as Pany Yathotou, a Hmong woman chosen as President of the National Assembly.

Arts

The focus of most traditional art in Lao culture has been religious, specifically Buddhist. Yet, unlike the visual arts of Thailand, Myanmar and Cambodia, Lao art never encompassed a broad range of styles and periods, mainly because Laos has a much more modest history in terms of power and because it has only existed as a political entity for a short period. Furthermore, since Laos was intermittently dominated by its neighbours, much of the art that was produced was either destroyed or, as in the case of the Emerald Buddha, carted off by conquering armies.

Laos' relatively small and poor population, combined with a turbulent recent history, also goes some way towards explaining the absence of any strong tradition of contemporary art. This is slowly changing, and in Vientiane and Luang Prabang modern art in a variety of media is finding its way into galleries and stores.

Weaving is the one art form that is found almost everywhere and has distinct styles that vary by place and tribal group. It's also the single most accessible art the traveller can buy, often directly from the artist.

Lao Buddha: The Image and Its History (2000), by Somkiart Lopetcharat, is a large coffee-table book containing a wealth of information on the Lao interpretation of the Buddha figure.

Literature & Film

Pha Lak Pha Lam, the Lao version of the Indian epic the Ramayana, is the most pervasive and influential of all classical Lao literature. The Indian source first came to Laos with the Hindu Khmer as stone reliefs at Wat Phu Champasak and other Angkor-period temples. Oral and written versions may also have been available; later the Lao developed their own version of the epic, which differs greatly both from the original and from Cambodia's *Reamker.*

Of the 547 Jataka tales in the *Pali Tipitaka,* each chronicling a different past life of the Buddha, most appear in Laos nearly word-for-word as they were first inscribed in Sri Lanka. A group of 50 'extra' or apocryphal stories, based on Lao-Thai folk tales of the time, were added by Pali scholars in Luang Prabang between 300 and 400 years ago.

Contemporary literature has been hampered by decades of war and communist rule. The first Lao-language novel was printed in 1944, and only in 1999 was the first collection of contemporary Lao fiction, Ounthine Bounyavong's *Mother's Beloved: Stories from Laos,* published in a bilingual Lao and English edition. Since then, a growing number of Lao novels and short stories have been translated into Thai, but very few have seen English-language translations. One of the most popular was 2009's *When the Sky Turns Upside Down: Memories of Laos,* a translation of short stories, some of which date back 60 years, by prominent Lao authors Dara Viravongs Kanlaya and Douangdeuane Bounyavong.

Not surprisingly, Laos also has one of the quietest film industries in Southeast Asia, and 2008's *Good Morning, Luang Prabang* is only one of a handful of feature films produced in the country since 1975. Starring Lao-Australian heart-throb Ananda Everingham and led by Thai director Sakchai Deenan, the film features a predictably 'safe' plot that nonetheless required the close attention of the Lao authorities during filming.

The Betrayal – Nerakhoon (2008) is a documentary directed by American Ellen Kuras, with the help of the film's main subject, Thavisouk Phrasavath. Shot over a 23-year period, the film documents the Phrasavath family's experience emigrating from Laos to New York City after the communist revolution.

In 2013, *The Rocket,* the story of a young Lao boy who builds a rocket to regain his family's trust, was released.

The year 2015 saw the release of *Banana Pancakes and the Children of Sticky Rice,* a gentle and touching story of two cultures colliding with the meeting of a Lao boy and Western girl in northern Laos.

Finally, 2016's *Dearest Sister* is a disturbing and well-wrought horror set in Laos, directed and written by Laos' first female film director Mattie Do, and tells the story of a rural girl looking after her cousin in Vientiane who goes blind but gains the ability to talk to the dead.

Two slim volumes of *Lao Folktales,* collected by Steve Epstein, retell some of Laos' better-known folklore. They're great for kids and offer an interesting insight into Lao humour and values.

Music & Dance

Lao classical music was originally developed as court music for royal ceremonies and classical dance-drama during the 19th-century reign of Vientiane's Chao Anou, who had been educated in the Siamese court in Bangkok. The standard ensemble for this genre is the *sep nyai* and consists of *kôrng wóng* (a set of tuned gongs), the *ranyâht* (a xylophone-like instrument), the *kooi* (bamboo flute) and the *Ƀee* (a double-reed wind instrument similar to the oboe).

The practice of classical Lao music and drama has been in decline for some time, as 40 years of intermittent war and revolution simply made this kind of entertainment a low priority among most Lao. Generally, the only time you'll hear this type of music is during the occasional public performance of the *Pha Lak Pha Lam.*

Not so with Lao folk and pop, which have always stayed close to the people. The principal instrument in folk, and to a lesser extent in pop, is the *káan* (common French spelling: *khene*), a wind instrument that is made of a double row of bamboo-like reeds fitted into a hardwood soundbox and made airtight with beeswax. The rows can be as few as four or as many as eight courses (for a total of 16 pipes), and the instrument can vary in length from around 80cm to about 2m. An adept player can produce a churning, calliope-like dance music.

When the *káan* is playing locals dance the *lám wóng* (circle performance), easily the most popular folk dance in Laos. Put simply, in the *lám wóng* couples dance circles around one another until there are three circles in all: a circle danced by the individual, a circle danced by the couple, and one danced by the whole crowd.

Mŏr Lám

The Lao folk idiom also has its own musical theatre, based on the *mŏr lám* tradition. *Mŏr lám* is difficult to translate but roughly means 'master of verse'. Led by one or more vocalists, performances always feature a witty, topical combination of talking and singing that ranges across themes as diverse as politics and sex. Very colloquial, even bawdy, language is employed. This is one art form that has always bypassed government censors and it continues to provide an important outlet for grassroots expression.

There are several different types of *mŏr lám,* depending on the number of singers and the region the style hails from. *Mŏr lám koo* (couple *mŏr lám*) features a man and woman who engage in flirtation and verbal repartee. *Mŏr lám jót* (duelling *mŏr lám*) has two performers of the same gender who 'duel' by answering questions or finishing an incomplete story issued as a challenge, similar to freestyle rap.

Northern Lao *kàan*-based folk music is usually referred to as *kàp* rather than *lám.* Authentic live *mŏr lám* can be heard at temple fairs and on Lao radio. Born-and-bred American artist Jonny Olsen (also known as Jonny Khaen) has become a celebrity in Laos for his *kàan*-based music.

Traditional Music of the Lao (1985), by Terry Miller, although mainly focused on northeast Thailand, is the only book-length work yet to appear on Lao music, and is very informative.

Lao Pop

Up until 2003 performing 'modern' music was virtually outlawed in Laos. The government had decided it just wasn't the Lao thing, and bands such as local heavy-metal outfit Sapphire, who chose to play anyway, were effectively shut down. Instead, the youth listened to pirated Thai and Western music, while Lao-language pop was limited to the *look tûng,* syrupy arrangements combining cha-cha and bolero rhythms with Lao-Thai melodies.

Then the government decided that if Lao youth were going to listen to modern pop, it might as well be home-grown. The first 'star' was Thidavanh Bounxouay, a Lao-Bulgarian singer more popularly known as Alexandra. Her brand of pop wasn't exactly radical, but it was decidedly upbeat compared with what went before. Other groups have followed, including girl band Princess and pop-rock group Awake.

Slightly edgier rock bands have also emerged, such as Crocodile and Leprozy, the latter of which have even played relatively high-profile gigs in Thailand. The hard-rock band Cells is another example of a Lao band for whom success has been much more rewarding in Thailand, where they've played big and relatively lucrative gigs in Bangkok.

There's also a tiny but burgeoning school of Lao-language hip-hop that until recently was almost exclusively associated with Los Angeles and that city's Lao diaspora. However, a domestic scene has developed around home-grown acts such as Hip Hop Ban Na and L.O.G.; the latter scored a chart-topping hit in Thailand.

In Vientiane, recordings by many if not all of the artists mentioned above are available at the open-air market near Pha That Luang and at Talat Sao mall. Some can also be caught live at venues in Vientiane, though you're more likely to see them at outdoor gigs to celebrate major holidays.

North Illinois University has pages of information on Lao culture, language, history, folklore and music, including recordings of the *kàan,* at www.seasite.niu.edu/lao.

Architecture

As with all other artistic endeavours, for centuries the best architects in the land have focused their attention on Buddhist temples. The results are most impressive in Luang Prabang.

However, it's not only in temples that Laos has its own peculiar architectural traditions. The *that* (stupas) found in Laos are different to those found anywhere else in the Buddhist world. Stupas are essentially monuments built on top of a reliquary which itself was built to hold a relic of the Buddha, commonly a hair or fragment of bone. Across Asia they come in varying shapes and sizes, ranging from the multilevel-tiered pagodas found in Vietnam to the buxom brick monoliths of Sri Lanka. Laos has its own unique style combining hard edges and comely curves.

The most famous of all Lao stupas is the golden Pha That Luang in Vientiane, which doubles as the national symbol.

Traditional housing in Laos, whether in the river valleys or in the mountains, consists of simple wooden or bamboo-thatch structures with leaf or grass roofing. Among Lowland Lao, houses are raised on stilts to avoid flooding during the monsoons and allow room to store rice underneath, while the highlanders typically build directly on the ground. The most attractive Lowland Lao houses often have a starburst pattern in the architraves, though these are increasingly difficult to find.

Colonial architecture in urban Laos combined the classic French provincial style – thick-walled buildings with shuttered windows and pitched tile roofs – with balconies and ventilation to promote air circulation in the stifling Southeast Asian climate. Although many of these structures were torn down or allowed to decay following independence from France, today they are much in demand, especially by foreigners. Luang Prabang and Vientiane both boast several lovingly restored buildings from this era. By contrast, in the Mekong River towns of Tha Khaek, Savannakhet and Pakse, French-era buildings are decaying at a disturbing rate.

Buildings erected in post-Revolution Laos followed the socialist realism school that was enforced in the Soviet Union, Vietnam and China. Straight lines, sharp angles and an almost total lack of ornamentation were the norm. More recently, a trend towards integrating classic Lao architectural motifs with modern functions has taken hold. Prime examples of this include Vientiane's National Assembly and the Luang Prabang airport, both of which were designed by Havana- and Moscow-trained architect Hongkad Souvannavong. Other design characteristics, such as those represented by the Siam Commercial Bank on Th Lan Xang in Vientiane, seek to gracefully reincorporate French colonial-era features ignored for the last half-century.

Sculpture

Perhaps most impressive of all the traditional Lao arts is Buddhist sculpture from the 16th to 18th centuries, the heyday of the kingdom of Lan Xang. Sculptural media usually included bronze, stone or wood, and the subject was invariably the Lord Buddha or figures associated with the Jataka (*sáh-dók;* stories of the Buddha's past lives). Like other Buddhist sculptors, the Lao artisans emphasised the features thought to be peculiar to the historical Buddha, including a beak-like nose, extended earlobes and tightly curled hair.

Two types of standing Buddha image are distinctive to Laos. The first is the 'Calling for Rain' posture, which depicts the Buddha standing with hands held rigidly at his side, fingers pointing towards the ground. This posture is rarely seen in other Southeast Asian Buddhist art traditions. The slightly rounded, 'boneless' look of the image recalls Thailand's Sukhothai style, and the way the lower robe is sculpted over the hips looks vaguely Khmer. But the flat, slab-like earlobes, arched eyebrows and aquiline nose are uniquely Lao. The bottom of the figure's robe curls upward on both sides in a perfectly symmetrical fashion that is also unique and innovative.

The other original Lao image type is the 'Contemplating the Bodhi Tree' Buddha. The Bodhi tree (Tree of Enlightenment) refers to the large banyan tree that the historical Buddha purportedly was sitting beneath when he attained enlightenment in Bodhgaya, India, in the 6th century BC. In this image the Buddha is standing in much the same way as in the 'Calling for Rain' pose, except that his hands are crossed at the wrists in front of his body.

The finest examples of Lao sculpture are found in Vientiane's Haw Pha Kaeo and Wat Si Saket, and in Luang Prabang's Royal Palace Museum.

Traditional Khamu houses often have the skulls of domestic animals hanging on a wall with an altar beneath. The skulls are from animals the family has sacrificed to their ancestors, and it is strictly taboo to touch them.

Today the traditional art is alive and well, and can be seen in action at Ban Don Khoh near Pakse, where almost the entire village makes a living sculpting Buddha images from stone.

Handicrafts

Mats and baskets woven of various kinds of straw, rattan and reed are common and are becoming a small but important export. Minority groups still wear these baskets, affirming that until recently most Lao handicrafts were useful as well as ornamental. In villages it's possible to buy direct from the weaver. Among the best baskets and mats are those woven by the Htin (Lao Thoeng).

Among the Hmong and Mien hill tribes, silversmithing plays an important role in 'portable wealth' and inheritances. In years past, the main source of silver was French coins, which were either melted down or fitted straight into the jewellery of choice. In northern villages it's not unusual to see newer coins worn in elaborate headdresses.

The Lowland Lao also have a long tradition of silversmithing and goldsmithing. While these arts have been in decline for quite a while now, there are still plenty of jewellers working over flames in markets around the country.

Paper handcrafted from *sǎh* (the bark of a mulberry tree) is common in northwestern Laos, and is available in Vientiane and Luang Prabang. Environmentally friendly *sǎh* is a renewable paper resource that needs little processing compared with wood pulp.

TEMPLE ARCHITECTURE: A TALE OF THREE CITIES

The *sǐm* (ordination hall) is usually the most important structure in any Theravada Buddhist wat. The high-peaked roofs are layered to represent several levels (usually three, five, seven or occasionally nine), which correspond to various Buddhist doctrines. The edges of the roofs almost always feature a repeated flame motif, with long, finger-like hooks at the corners called *chôr fâh* (sky clusters). Umbrella-like spires along the central roof-ridge of a *sǐm,* called *nyôrt chôr fâh* (topmost *chôr fâh*), sometimes bear small pavilions featuring naga (mythical water serpents) in a double-stepped arrangement representing Mt Meru, the mythical centre of the Hindu-Buddhist cosmos.

There are basically three architectural styles for such buildings: the Vientiane, Luang Prabang and Xieng Khuang styles.

The front of a *sǐm* in the Vientiane style usually features a large verandah with heavy columns supporting an ornamented overhanging roof. Some will also have a less ornamented rear verandah, while those that have a surrounding terrace are Bangkok-influenced.

In Luang Prabang, the temple style is akin to that of the northern Siamese (Lanna) style, hardly surprising as for several centuries Laos and northern Thailand were part of the same kingdoms. Luang Prabang temple roofs sweep very low, almost reaching the ground in some instances. The overall effect is quite dramatic, as if the *sǐm* were about to take flight. The Lao are fond of saying that the roof line resembles the wings of a mother hen guarding her chicks.

Little remains of the Xieng Khuang style of *sǐm* architecture because the province was so heavily bombed during the Second Indochina War. Pretty much the only surviving examples are in Luang Prabang and to look at them you see aspects of both Vientiane and Luang Prabang styles. The *sǐm* raised on a multilevel platform is reminiscent of Vientiane temples, while wide sweeping roofs that reach especially low are similar to the Luang Prabang style, though they're not usually tiered. Cantilevered roof supports play a much more prominent role in the building's overall aesthetic, giving the *sǐm's* front profile a pentagonal shape.

Textiles

Silk and cotton fabrics are woven in many different styles according to the geographic provenance and ethnicity of the weavers. Although Lao textiles do have similarities with other Southeast Asian textiles, Lao weaving techniques are unique in both loom design and weaving styles, generating fabrics that are very recognisably Lao.

Southern weavers, who often use foot looms rather than frame looms, are known for the best silk weaving and for intricate *mat-mee* (ikat or tie-dye) designs that include Khmer-influenced temple and elephant motifs. The result is a soft, spotted pattern similar to Indonesian ikat. *Mat-mee* cloth can be used for different types of clothing or wall hangings. In Sekong and Attapeu Provinces some fabrics mix beadwork with weaving and embroidery. One-piece *pàh nung* are more common than those sewn from separate pieces.

In central Laos, typical weavings include indigo-dyed cotton *mat-mee* and minimal weft brocade (*jók* and *kit*), along with mixed techniques brought by migrants to Vientiane.

Generally, the fabrics of the north feature a mix of solid colours with complex geometric patterns – stripes, diamonds, zigzags, animal and plant shapes – usually in the form of a *pàh nung* or *sin* (a woman's wrap-around skirt). Sometimes gold or silver thread is woven in along the borders. Another form the cloth takes is the *pàh bęeang,* a narrow Lao-Thai shawl that men and women wear singly or in pairs over the shoulders during weddings and festivals.

Gold and silver brocade is typical of traditional Luang Prabang patterns, along with intricate patterns and imported Tai Lü designs. Northerners generally use frame looms; the waist, body and narrow *sín* (bottom border) of a *pàh nung* are often sewn together from separately woven pieces.

In northeastern Laos, tribal Tai produce *yìap ko* (weft brocade) using raw silk, cotton yarn and natural dyes, sometimes with the addition of *mat-mee* techniques. Large diamond patterns are common.

Among the Hmong and Mien tribes, square pieces of cloth are embroidered and quilted to produce strikingly colourful fabrics in apparently abstract patterns that contain ritual meanings. In Hmong these are called *pandau* (flowercloth). Some larger quilts feature scenes that represent village life, including both animal and human figures.

Many tribes among the Lao Soung and Lao Thoeng groups produce woven shoulder bags in the Austro-Thai and Tibetan-Burmese traditions, such as those seen all across the mountains of South Asia and Southeast Asia. In Laos, these are called *nyahm*. Among the most popular *nyahm* nowadays are those made with older pieces of fabric from 'antique' *pàh nung* or from pieces of hill-tribe clothing. Vientiane's Talat Sao is one of the best places to shop for this kind of accessory.

Natural sources for Lao dyes include ebony (both seeds and wood), tamarind (seeds and wood), red lacquer extracted from the *Coccus iacca* (a tree-boring insect), turmeric (from a root) and indigo. A basic palette of five natural colours – black, orange, red, yellow and blue – can be combined to create an endless variety of other colours. Other unblended, but more subtle, hues include khaki (from the bark of the Indian trumpet tree), pink (sappanwood) and gold (jackfruit and breadfruit woods).

Lao Textiles and Traditions (1997), by Mary F Connors, is useful to visitors interested in Lao weaving; it's the best overall introduction to the subject.

Environment

Laos is not blessed with large amounts of minerals or oil, but it does have a lot of natural resources in timber and water, and these have fed its economy. Illegal logging has been given temporary respite with the recent ban on logging, but the widespread construction of hydroelectric dams is exerting considerable stress on the land. The popularity of ecotourism in Laos may be the key to preserving its remaining natural areas, but currently commerce seems to be winning against conservation.

The Land

Covering an area slightly larger than Great Britain, landlocked Laos shares borders with China, Myanmar (Burma), Thailand, Cambodia and Vietnam. Rivers and mountains dominate, folding the country into a series of often-spectacular ridges and valleys, rivers and mountain passes, extending westward from the Laos–Vietnam border.

Mountains and plateaus cover more than 70% of the country. Running about half the length of Laos, parallel to the course of the Mekong River, is the Annamite Chain, a rugged mountain range with peaks averaging between 1500m and 2500m in height. Roughly in the centre of the range is the Khammuan Plateau, a world of dramatic limestone grottoes and gorges where vertical walls rise hundreds of metres from jungle-clad valleys. At the southern end of the Annamite Chain, covering 10,000 sq km, the Bolaven Plateau is an important area for the cultivation of high-yield mountain rice, coffee, tea and other crops that flourish in the cooler climes found at these higher altitudes.

The larger, northern half of Laos is made up almost entirely of mountain ranges. The highest mountains are found in Xieng Khuang Province, including Phu Bia, the country's highest peak at 2820m, though this remains off limits to travellers for now. Just north of Phu Bia stands the Xieng Khuang plateau, the country's largest mountain plateau, which rises 1200m above sea level. The most famous part of the plateau is the Plain of Jars, a mysterious area of rolling hills, pockmarked with bomb craters, that's named for the huge prehistoric stone jars that dot the landscape.

Much of the rest of Laos is covered by forest, most of which is mixed deciduous. This forest enjoys a complex relationship with the Mekong and its tributaries, acting as a sponge for the monsoon rains and then slowly releasing the water into both streams and the atmosphere during the long dry season.

The Mekong & Other Rivers

Springing forth nearly 5000km from the sea, high up on the Tibetan Plateau, the Mekong River so dominates Lao topography that, to a large extent, the entire country parallels its course. Although half of the Mekong's length runs through China, more of the river's volume courses through Laos than through any other Southeast Asian country. At its widest, near Si Phan Don in the south, the river can expand to 14km

The Mekong River is known as Lancang Jiang (Turbulent River) in China; Mae Nam Khong (the Mother of Water) in Thailand, Myanmar (Burma) and Laos; Tonle Thom (Great Water) in Cambodia; and Cuu Long (Nine Dragons) in Vietnam.

across during the rainy season, spreading around thousands of islands and islets on its inevitable course south.

The Mekong's middle reach is navigable year-round, from Heuan Hin (north of the Khemmarat Rapids in Savannakhet Province) to Kok Phong in Luang Prabang. However, these rapids, and the brutal falls at Khon Phapheng in Si Phan Don, have prevented the Mekong from becoming the sort of regional highway that other great rivers have been.

The fertile Mekong River flood plain, running from Sainyabuli to Champasak, forms the flattest and most tropical part of Laos. Most of the domestic and export rice is grown here, and other large-scale farming takes place here as well. The Mekong and, just as importantly, its tributaries are also an important source of fish, a vital part of the diet for most people living in Laos.

Major tributaries of the great river include the Nam Ou (Ou River) and the Nam Tha, both of which flow through deep, narrow limestone valleys from the north, and the Nam Ngum, which flows into the Mekong across a broad plain in Vientiane Province. The Nam Ngum is the site of one of Laos' oldest hydroelectric plants, which provides power for Vientiane-area towns and Thailand. The Se Kong (Kong River) flows through much of southern Laos before eventually reaching the Mekong in Cambodia, and the Nam Kading and Nam Theun are equally important in central Laos.

All the rivers and tributaries west of the Annamite Chain drain into the Mekong, while waterways east of the Annamites (in Hua Phan and Xieng Khuang Provinces only) flow into the Gulf of Tonkin off the coast of Vietnam.

The Mekong: Turbulent Past, Uncertain Future (2000), by Milton Osborne, is a fascinating cultural history of the Mekong that spans 2000 years of exploration, mapping and war.

Wildlife

Laos still boasts one of the least disturbed ecosystems in Asia due to its overall lack of development and low population density. Least disturbed, however, does not mean undisturbed, and for many species like the tiger and Asian elephant the future looks very dark indeed.

Animals

The mountains, forests and river networks of Laos are home to a range of animals both endemic to the country and shared with its Southeast Asian neighbours. Nearly half of the animal species native to Thailand are shared by Laos, with the higher forest cover and fewer hunters

RESPONSIBLE TRAVEL & WILDLIFE

While subsistence hunting is permitted by the Lao government for local rural villagers, the sale and purchase of *any* wildlife is illegal in Laos. Here are a few pointers to make sure you're not contributing to the downfall of endangered species:

➡ Never buy a wild animal – dead or alive – at a market.

➡ Though they are available on some menus, avoid eating endangered species or prey of endangered species, such as soft-shelled turtles, rat snakes, mouse deer, sambar deer, squirrels, bamboo rats, muntjac deer and pangolins.

➡ No matter the macabre value, avoid buying necklaces made from animal teeth; stuffed animals; spiders in glass frames; and witchy bottles of alcohol with snakes, birds, or insects inside.

➡ Keep an eye out for products with a label stating they are certified by the Convention on International Trade in Endangered Species of Wild Fauna and Flora (CITES). These are legal to buy in Laos and take home.

For more information visit the Wildlife Conservation Society (https://laos.wcs.org) website.

meaning that numbers are often greater in Laos. Almost all wild animals, however, are threatened to some extent by hunting and habitat loss.

In spite of this Laos has seen several new species discovered in recent years, such as the bent-toed gecko and long-toothed pipistrelle bat, while others thought to be extinct have turned up in remote forests. Given their rarity, these newly discovered species are on the endangered list.

As in Cambodia, Vietnam, Myanmar and much of Thailand, most of the fauna in Laos belongs to the Indochinese zoogeographic realm (as opposed to the Sundaic domain found south of the Isthmus of Kra in southern Thailand or the Palaearctic to the north in China).

Notable mammals endemic to Laos include the lesser panda, raccoon dog, Lao marmoset rat, Owston's civet and the pygmy slow loris. Other important exotic species found elsewhere in the region include the Malayan and Chinese pangolins, 10 species of civet, marbled cat, Javan and crab-eating mongoose, the serow (sometimes called Asian mountain goat) and goral (another type of goat-antelope), and cat species including the leopard cat and Asian golden cat.

Among the most significant of Laos' wildlife are the primates. Several smaller species are known, including Phayre's leaf monkey, François' langur, the Douc langur and several macaques. Two other primates that are endemic to Laos are the concolour gibbon and snub-nosed langur. It's the five species of gibbon that attract most attention. Sadly, the black-crested gibbon is endangered, being hunted both for its meat and to be sold as pets in Thailand. Several projects are underway to educate local communities to set aside safe areas for the gibbons.

The World Conservation Union believes wildlife in Laos has a much better chance of surviving than in neighbouring Vietnam. Lending weight to this is the discovery of the Vietnam warty pig (*Sus bucclentus*), a species found in Laos but last recorded in Vietnam in 1892 and until recently considered extinct.

Elephants

It's a sad statistic that for every 10 elephants born in captivity in Laos, according to the Elephant Conservation Center in Sainyabuli, only two survive. Veterinary care and the ability to give their working female elephant three to four years to gestate, birth, lactate and rear her calf is more time than the average mahout can afford. About four years too much. So no wonder the population is withering.

Laos might once have been known as the land of a million elephants, but these days only about 800 remain in total, of which about 300 to 400 roam wild in open-canopy forest areas, predominantly in Sainyabuli Province west of Vientiane, Bolikhamsai Province in the Phu Khao Khuay NPA, and along the Nakai Plateau in central eastern Laos.

Hunting and habitat loss are their main threats. In areas such as the Nakai Plateau, Vietnamese poachers kill elephants for their meat and hides, while the Nam Theun 2 Hydropower Project in Khammuan Province has swallowed up a large chunk of habitat. The Wildlife Conservation Society (WCS) has an ongoing project in this area, with a long-term aim of establishing a 'demonstration site that will serve as a model for reducing human-elephant conflict nationwide'.

Working, domesticated elephants, totalling around 400, are also found in a number of provinces. Logging elephants are put in extreme danger on the sides of mountains trying to access the last available hardwood. Since the 2016 logging ban, many mahouts and their elephants have been out of a job. Given the considerable funds needed to feed an elephant (about US$250 per week), their only alternative is finding income through tourism, where ex-logging pachyderms give rides to tourists with a howdah (chair) strapped on their backs. Because the spine of an elephant is jagged and convex this is extremely painful. Most travellers are also unaware that to subjugate a young elephant to the point they can be trusted to carry travellers, it must first be subjected to the 'crush', a cage where it is broken down and starved, with regular beatings by a bull-hook. It is this fear of the bull-hook as an adult that makes them do as they are told.

A further concern is that many of these logging elephants in search of a job are males. Because of musting, during which a huge release of testosterone occurs, their tempers can be mercurial to put it lightly, and they can become dangerous to ride on. The mahout cannot argue with his employer who runs the camp if he insists on working the elephant through this lethal period. And fatal events do occur with frightening regularity, such as in Thailand in 2015 when a musting elephant killed his mahout and a Scottish man and his daughter.

There are positive ways to encounter elephants in Laos that do not involve riding. The impressive Elephant Conservation Center (p136) near Sainyabuli offers an immersive elephant experience for visitors which focuses on observing them in a natural area.

Endangered Species

All wild animals in Laos are endangered due to widespread hunting and gradual but persistent habitat loss. Laos ratified the UN Convention on International Trade in Endangered Species of Wild Fauna and Flora (CITES) in 2004, which, combined with other legal measures, has made it easier to prosecute people trading species endangered as a direct result of international trade. But in reality you won't need 20/20 vision to pick out the endangered species, both dead and alive, on sale in markets around the country. Border markets, in particular, tend to attract the most valuable species, with Thais buying gibbons as pets, and Chinese and Vietnamese shopping for exotic food and medicines.

Of the hundreds of species of mammals known in Laos, several dozen are endangered according to the IUCN Red List (www.iucnredlist.org). These range from bears, including the Asiatic black bear and Malayan sun bear, through to less glamorous wild cattle such as the gaur and banteng, to high-profile cats like the tiger, leopard and clouded leopard. Exactly how endangered they are is difficult to say. Camera-trapping projects (setting up cameras in the forest to take photos of anything that wanders past) are being carried out by various NGOs and, in the Nakai–Nam Theun National Park, by the Nam Theun 2 dam operators themselves.

In the Nam Et/Phou Louey National Park there are said to be nine tigers remaining, perhaps the last in Laos. The WCS (www.wcs.org) employs 150 staff consisting of foresters, military officers, locals and biologists, and has also set up a successful ecotourism community outreach program – Nam Nern Night Safari (p96) – to maintain this most delicate of populations. The WCS is also focusing its conservation activities on species including the Asian elephant, Siamese crocodile, western black-crested gibbon and Eld's deer.

Some endangered species are so rare they were unknown until very recently. Among these is the spindlehorn (*Pseudoryx nghethingensis;* known as the *saola* in Vietnam, *nyang* in Laos), a horned mammal found in the Annamite Chain along the Laos–Vietnam border in 1992. The spindlehorn, which was described in 14th-century Chinese journals, was long thought not to exist, and when discovered it became one of only three land mammals to earn its own genus in the 20th century. Unfortunately, horns taken from spindlehorn are a favoured trophy among certain groups on both sides of the border.

In 2005 WCS scientists visiting a local market in Khammuan Province discovered a 'Laotian rock rat' laid out for sale. But what was being sold as meat turned out to be a genetically distinct species named the *Laonastes aenigmamus*. Further research revealed the species to be the sole

Odd-shaped rocks are venerated across Laos. Even in what appears to be the middle of nowhere, you'll see saffron robes draped over rocks that look vaguely like turtles, fishing baskets or stupas. Local legends explain how the rocks came to be, and some are famous around the country.

survivor of a prehistoric group of rodents that died out about 11 million years ago. If you're very lucky you might see one on the cliffs near the caves off Rte 12 in Khammuan Province.

Among the most seriously endangered of all mammals is the Irrawaddy dolphin, in Laos found in increasingly small pockets of the Mekong River near the Cambodian border. Gill-net fishing has brought the animals here to what is referred to by the WWF as 'functional extinction' (ie there are no longer sufficient numbers to ensure the breed survives).

Birds

The forests and mountains of Laos harbour a rich selection of resident and migrating bird species. Surveys carried out by a British team of ornithologists in the 1990s recorded 437 species, including eight globally threatened and 21 globally near-threatened species. Some other counts rise as high as 650 species.

Notable among these are the Siamese fireback pheasant, green peafowl, red-collared woodpecker, brown hornbill, tawny fish-owl, Sarus crane, giant ibis and the Asian golden weaver. Hunting keeps urban bird populations noticeably thin. In 2008, scientists from the WCS and the University of Melbourne conducting research in central Laos discovered a new bird species, the bare-faced bulbul, the first bald songbird to be spotted in mainland Asia, and the first new bulbul to have been discovered in the last century.

Until relatively recently, it wasn't uncommon to see men pointing long-barrelled muskets at upper tree branches in cities as large as Savannakhet and Vientiane. Those days are now gone, but around almost every village you'll hear hunters doing their business most afternoons.

Plants

According to the UN Food and Agriculture Organization, in 2005 forest covered more than 69% of Laos. Current figures linger at around 45%. Of these woodlands, about 11% can be classified as primary forest.

Most indigenous vegetation in Laos is associated with monsoon forests, as is common in areas of tropical mainland Southeast Asia that experience dry seasons lasting three months or longer. Rainforests, which are typically evergreen, don't exist in Laos, although non-indigenous rainforest species such as the coconut palm are commonly seen in the lower Mekong River valley. There are undoubtedly some big trees in Laos, but don't expect the sort of towering forests found in some other parts of Southeast Asia. The conditions do not, and never have, allowed these sorts of giants to grow here.

Instead the monsoon forests of Laos typically grow in three canopies. Dipterocarps – tall, pale-barked, single-trunked trees that can grow beyond 30m high – dominate the top canopy of the forest, while a middle canopy consists of an ever-dwindling population of prized hardwoods, including teak, padauk (sometimes called 'Asian rosewood') and mahogany. Underneath there's a variety of smaller trees, shrubs, grasses and, along river habitats, bamboo. In certain plateau areas of the south, there are dry dipterocarp forests in which the forest canopies are more open, with less of a middle layer and more of a grass-and-bamboo undergrowth. Parts of the Annamite Chain that receive rain from both the southwestern monsoon as well as the South China Sea are covered by tropical montane evergreen forest, while tropical pine forests can be found on the Nakai Plateau and Sekong area to the south.

In addition to the glamour hardwoods, the country's flora includes a toothsome array of fruit trees, bamboo (more species than any country outside Thailand and China) and an abundance of flowering species such as the orchid. However, in some parts of the country orchids are

ENVIRONMENT WILDLIFE

Wildlife Trade in Laos: The End of the Game (2001), by Hanneke Nooren and Gordon Claridge, is a frightening description of animal poaching in Laos.

The giant Mekong catfish may grow up to 3m long and weigh as much as 300kg. Due to Chinese blasting of shoals in the Upper Mekong and the building of dams, it now faces extinction in Laos.

being stripped out of forests (often in protected areas) for sale to Thai tourists; look for the markets near the waterfalls of the Bolaven Plateau to see them. In the high plateaus of the Annamite Chain, extensive grasslands or savannahs are common.

Around 85% of Laos is mountainous terrain and less than 4% is considered arable.

National Protected Areas (NPAs)

Laos boasts one of the youngest and most comprehensive protected-area systems in the world. In 1993 the government set up 18 National Biodiversity Conservation Areas, comprising a total of 24,600 sq km, or just over 10% of the country's land mass. Most significantly, it did this following sound scientific consultation rather than creating areas on an ad hoc basis (as most other countries have done). Two more were added in 1995, for a total of 20 protected areas covering 14% of Laos. A further 4% of Laos is reserved as Provincial Protected Areas, making Laos one of the most protected countries on earth.

The areas were renamed NPAs a few years ago. And while the naming semantics might seem trivial, they do reflect some important differences. The main one is that an NPA has local communities living within its boundaries, unlike a national park, where only rangers and those working in the park are allowed to live and where traditional activities such as hunting and logging are banned. Indeed, forests in NPAs are divided into production forests for timber, protection forests for watershed, and conservation forests for pure conservation.

The largest protected areas are in southern Laos, which, contrary to popular myth, bears a higher percentage of natural forest cover than the north. Nakai–Nam Theun National Park, the largest of the protected areas, covers 3710 sq km and is home to the recently discovered spindlehorn, as well as several other species unknown to the scientific world until not that long ago.

The wildlife in these areas, from rare birds to wild elephants, is relatively abundant. The best time to view wildlife in most of the country is just after the monsoon in November. However, even at these times you'll be lucky to see very much. There are several reasons for this, the most important of which is that ongoing hunting means numbers of wild animals are reduced and those living are instinctively scared of humans. It's also difficult to see animals in forest cover at the best of times, and many animals are nocturnal. Teaming up with a recommended outfit will increase your chances of seeing wildlife.

Unfortunately, due to lack of funding, NPAs, and indeed many nature-tourism sites, suffer from lack of management and resources. A common refrain is that there is no budget for their maintenance. As a result, nature tourism sites such as waterfalls are usually managed by private concessions, who are licensed by the government to run them. Occasionally these licences are revoked, leaving the site in a state of limbo. In addition, many NPAs are very difficult to access by independent travel. Most travellers rely on adventure-tour companies.

For more information on all of Laos' National Protected Areas (NPAs), see the comprehensive website www.ecotourismlaos.com.

In an effort to redress these shortcomings, the government in 2018 began establishing national parks, which differ from NPAs in that they will have better levels of management and financing. Currently Nakai–Nam Theun and Nam Et/Phou Louey have both been designated as national parks, and it is planned to upgrade another eight NPAs to national park status over the next five years.

Environmental Issues

Flying over Laos it's easy to think that much of the country is blanketed with untouched wilderness. But first impressions can be deceiving. What that lumpy carpet of green conceals is an environment facing several interrelated threats.

For the most part they're issues of the bottom line. Hunting endangers all sorts of creatures of the forest but it persists because the hunters can't afford to buy meat from the market. Overfishing is also an ongoing problem, as increasing human population and export demands place a heavier toll on the rivers. Forests are logged at unsustainable rates because the timber found in Laos is hugely valuable and loggers see more profit in cutting than not. And hydropower projects affect river systems and their dependent ecologies, including the forests, because Laos needs the money hydroelectricity can bring, and it's relatively cheap and easy for energy companies to develop in Laos.

Laws do exist to protect wildlife and plenty of Laos is designated as NPAs. But most Lao people are completely unaware of global conservation issues and there is little will and less money to pay for conservation projects, such as organised park rangers, or to prosecute offenders. Lack of communication between national and local governments and poor definitions of authority in conservation areas add to the issues.

One of the biggest obstacles facing environmental protection in Laos is corruption (Laos is ranked 132 out of 180 nations in the Transparency International Corruption Perceptions Index 2018). Fortunately, with the support of several dedicated individuals and NGOs, ecotourism is growing to the point where some local communities are beginning to understand – and buying into – the idea that an intact environment can be worth more money than an exhausted one.

One long-standing environmental problem has been the unexploded ordnance (UXO) contaminating parts of eastern Laos where the Ho Chi Minh Trail ran during the Second Indochina War. Bombs are being found and defused at a painstakingly slow rate; however, on his 2016 visit former US President Barack Obama pledged US$90 million over a three-year period to speed up the process.

The major challenges facing Laos' environment are, therefore, the internal pressures of economic growth as well as external pressures from the country's more populated and affluent neighbours, particularly China, Vietnam and Thailand, who all benefit from Laos' abundant resources, be it hardwood, copper or hydroelectric power.

Conservation Websites

ElefantAsia (www.elefantasia.org)

Traffic East Asia (www.traffic.org)

Wildlife Conservation Society (www.wcs.org)

International Union for Conservation of Nature (www.iucn.org/lao)

World Wildlife Fund (www.panda.org)

Elephant Conservation Center (www.elephantconservationcenter.com)

ECOTOURISM IN LAOS

With forests covering about half of the country, two national parks, 18 National Protected Areas (NPAs), 49 ethnic groups, over 650 bird species and hundreds of mammals, Laos has some of Southeast Asia's healthiest ecosystems.

Following the success of the Nam Ha Ecotourism Project in Luang Namtha Province, which began in 1999, the ecotourism industry has grown using a sustainable, internationally developed blueprint which seeks to protect and preserve the interests of ethnic people, wildlife and forests.

Many tour companies in Laos have endured since the inception of ecotourism because they have honoured their pledges to local tribes and conservation. Before splashing out on a trek ask the following questions:

➡ Are you in a small group that will not disturb village life?

➡ Will you be led by a local guide?

➡ Will your trip directly benefit local people whose forests/village you are passing through?

➡ Does the company channel some of its profits into conservation or local education charities, or is it directly affiliated with organisations such as the WWF and WCS?

See www.ecotourismlaos.com for further information on environmentally sustainable tourism in Laos.

Damming the Mekong for Hydroelectric Power

For millennia the Mekong River has been the lifeblood of Laos and the wider Mekong region. It's the region's primary artery, and about 60 million people depend on the rich fisheries and other resources provided by the river and its tributaries. The Mekong is the world's 12th-longest river and 10th largest in terms of volume. But unlike other major rivers, a series of rapids have prevented it from developing into a major transport and cargo thoroughfare, or as a base for large industrial cities.

When the Nam Theun 2 dam in Khammuan Province was approved by the World Bank in 2005, it was the equivalent of opening hydropower's Pandora's box. Since then hydropower has become an important contributor to Laos' economic growth. Six big dams are already in operation, seven are currently under construction, at least 12 more are planned, and development deals are ready to go on another 35.

The negative impacts associated with these dams have so far included forced displacement of local communities and the uprooting of their traditional riverine culture, flooding upstream areas, reduced sediment flows, and increased erosion downstream with resulting issues for fish stocks and those who work the rivers.

The most catastrophic consequence of dam building was the collapse of Saddle Dam D (p233) in Attapeu Province in 2018. This led to the outright destruction of villages, loss of human life and livestock, and displacement of thousands of villagers. While the government has attempted to deal with the fallout, there has been little questioning of the ongoing policy.

Less immediately visible, but with a potentially much greater influence in the long term, are the changes these dams will have on the Mekong's flood pulse, especially the Tonlé Sap Lake in Cambodia, which is critical to the fish spawning cycle, and thus the food source of millions of people.

More information can be found online, including through the Mekong River Commission (www.mrcmekong.org), which oversees the dam developments; Save the Mekong Coalition (https://savethemekong.net); and the WWF (www.panda.org).

Deforestation

In 2016 the new president of Laos banned the export of timber and logs, throwing long-established illegal smuggling operations into panic. Since the ban, truckloads of hardwood have been seized from forest hideouts and sawmills across the country. In 2015 Radio Free Asia exposed a Lao politburo member's son as a smuggling kingpin of hardwood trees across the border into China via Mohan, and it's widely alleged that illegal logging has been clandestinely run by elements of the Lao Army, such as in Khammuan Province and remote areas of the country's far south.

The national electricity-generating company also profits from the timber sales each time it links a Lao town or village with the national power grid, as it clear-cuts along Lao highways. Large-scale plantations and mining, as well as swidden (slash-and-burn) methods of cultivation, are also leading to habitat loss. This can have a knock-on effect in rural communities: in some rural areas 70% of non-rice foods come from the forest.

The current president has pledged to recover forest levels to 70% by 2020 or resign. It remains to be seen how successful the government will be in carrying out this pledge.

While opium has been cultivated and used in Laos for centuries, the country didn't become a major producer until the passing of the 1971 Anti-Narcotics Law. Having almost been eradicated, opium is allegedly being grown again in remote parts of northern Laos.

Marco Polo was probably the first European to cross the Mekong, in the 13th century, and was followed by a group of Portuguese emissaries in the 16th century. Dutch merchant Gerrit van Wuysthoff arrived by boat in the 17th century.

Survival
Guide

Directory A–Z

Accessible Travel

With its lack of paved roads or footpaths (sidewalks), Laos presents many obstacles for people with mobility or vision impairments. Wheelchair users will need to use the roads, along with other wheeled transportation of all kinds. Rarely do public buildings feature ramps or other access points for wheelchairs, nor do many hotels provide access for travellers with disabilities, the few exceptions being at the top end in Vientiane and Luang Prabang, which are also the only places you'll find an accessible toilet. Most sights also lack accessibility. Public transport is particularly crowded and difficult, even for the fully ambulatory.

For anyone with access needs, a trip to Laos will require a good deal of advance planning, fortitude and the willingness to improvise. As in most developing countries, a lack of infrastructure can often be overcome with people power: wheelchairs and their users can be lifted over obstacles or into vehicles if you're willing to take the risk. Reports from wheelchair-using travellers to the country, however, suggest that locals may be less quick to offer assistance than in other Southeast Asian nations.

There's not much in the way of useful online resources, but the Lao Disabled People's Association (http://ldpa.org.la) lists organisations affiliated with particular disabilities that may be able to offer travel advice.

Download Lonely Planet's free Accessible Travel guides from http://lptravel.to/AccessibleTravel.

Bargaining

Bargaining in most places in Laos is not nearly as tough as in other parts of Southeast Asia. Lao-style bargaining is generally a friendly transaction where two people try to agree on a price that is fair to both of them. Good bargaining, which takes practice, is one way to cut costs.

Most things bought in a market can be bargained for, but in shops prices are mostly fixed. The first rule to bargaining is to have a general idea of the price. Ask around at a few vendors to get a ballpark figure. Once you're ready to buy, it's generally a good strategy to start at 50% of the asking price and work up from there. In general, keeping a friendly, flexible demeanour throughout the transaction will almost always work in your favour. Don't get angry or upset over a few thousand kip. The locals, who invariably have less money than foreign visitors, never do this.

Climate

The annual monsoon cycles that affect all of mainland Southeast Asia produce a dry and wet monsoon climate, with three basic seasons for most of Laos. The southwest monsoon arrives in Laos between May and July and lasts into November.

The monsoon is followed by a dry period (from November to May), beginning with lower relative temperatures and cool breezes created by Asia's northeast monsoon (which bypasses most of Laos) and lasting until mid-February. Exceptions to this general pattern include Xieng Khuang, Hua Phan and Phongsali Provinces, which may receive rainfall coming from Vietnam and China during the months of April and May.

Temperatures also vary according to altitude. In the humid, low-lying Mekong River valley, temperatures range from 15°C to 38°C, while in the mountains of the far north they can drop to 0°C at night. Particularly cold years see snow falling in the mountains.

See the climate map on p16. and the climate charts in the On the Road chapters.

Electricity

Type A
120V/60Hz

Type C
220V/50Hz

Embassies & Consulates

There are about 25 embassies and consulates in Vientiane. Many nationalities are served by their embassies in Bangkok (eg New Zealand and the Netherlands), Hanoi (eg Ireland) or Beijing.

Australian Embassy (Map p146; ☑021-353800; www.laos.embassy.gov.au; Km 4, Rue Tha Deua, Vientiane; ⊙8.30am-5pm Mon-Fri) Also represents nationals of Canada.

Cambodian Embassy (Map p146; ☑021-314952; www.cambodianembassy-laos.com; Km 3, Rue Tha Deua, Vientiane; ⊙8am-noon & 2-5pm Mon-Fri) Issues visas for US$30.

Chinese Embassy (Map p146; ☑021-315100; http://la.china-embassy.org/eng; Rue Wat Nak Nyai, Vientiane; ⊙8-11.30am Mon-Fri) Issues visas in four working days (less for a fee). Some travellers report sudden and unannounced 'changes in policy' preventing them from applying for visas.

French Embassy (Map p152; ☑021-267400; www.ambafrance-laos.org; Rue Setthathi-rath, Vientiane; ⊙9am-12.30pm & 2-5.30pm Mon-Fri)

German Embassy (Map p146; ☑021-312110; www.vientiane.diplo.de; Rue Sok Pa Luang, Vientiane; ⊙9am-noon Mon-Thu)

Myanmar Embassy (Map p146; ☑021-314910; Rue Sok Pa Luang, Vientiane; ⊙8.30am-noon Mon-Fri) Issues tourist visas in three working days for US$40, but can turn a visa around the same day on request if you already have a ticket to travel.

Thai Embassy (Map p146; ☑021-214581; http://vientiane.thaiembassy.org/en/; Rue Kaysone Phomvihane, Vientiane; ⊙8.30am-noon & 1-4.30pm Mon-Fri) For visa renewals and extensions, head to the consulates in **Vientiane** (Map p146; ☑021-415335; http://vientiane.thaiembassy.org/en/; 15 Rue Bourichane; ⊙8.30-noon & 1-3pm Mon-Fri) or **Savannakhet** (☑041-212373; Rte 9; ⊙8.30am-4.30pm Mon-Fri), which issue tourist and nonimmigrant visas (1000B).

UK Embassy (Map p146; ☑030-7700000; www.gov.uk/world/organisations/british-embassy-vientiane; Rue Yokka-bat, Vientiane; ⊙8.30-11.30am Mon-Fri)

US Embassy (☑021-487000; https://la.usembassy.gov; Km 9, Rue Tha Deua, Vientiane; ⊙7.30am-4pm Mon-Fri) Based in a new building to the south of the city.

Vietnamese Embassy (Map p146; ☑021-451990; www.mofa.gov.vn/vnemb.la; 85 Rue 23 Singha, Vientiane; ⊙8.30-11.30am & 1.30-5pm Mon-Fri) Issues tourist visas in three working days for US$55, or in one day for US$65. The **Luang Prabang consulate** (Map p48; www.vietnamconsulate-luangprabang.org; Th Phothisarat; ⊙8-11.30am & 1.30-5pm Mon-Fri) issues tourist visas for US$50 in 24 hours or US$40 if you wait three days. At the consulate in **Pakse** (Map p208; ☑020-99691666; https://vnconsulate-pakse.mofa.gov.vn; Th 21; ⊙8.30-11.30am & 2.30-4.30pm Mon-Fri), visas cost US$60.

Etiquette

The Lao people are generally very gracious hosts, but there are some important spiritual and social conventions to observe.

Buddhism When visiting temples, cover up to the knees and elbows, and remove your shoes and any head covering. Sit with your feet tucked behind you to avoid pointing them at Buddha images. Women should never touch a monk or his belongings; step out of the way and don't sit next to them on public transport.

Local greeting Called the *nop*, the local greeting in Laos involves putting your hands together in a prayer-like manner. Use this when being introduced to new Lao friends.

Modesty Avoid wearing swimsuits or scanty clothing when walking around towns, particularly after tubing in Vang Vieng. Wear a sarong or similar to cover up.

Saving face Never get into an argument with a Lao person. It's better to smile through any conflict.

PRACTICALITIES

Vientiane Times (www.vientianetimes.org.la) The country's only English-language newspaper follows the party line. Published Monday to Saturday.

Le Rénovateur (www.lerenovateur.la) A government mouthpiece in French; similar to the *Vientiane Times*.

Lao National Radio (LNR; www.lnr.org.la) Broadcasts sanitised English-language news twice daily.

TV Lao National TV is so limited that most people watch Thai TV and/or karaoke videos.

Weights & Measures The metric system is used for measurements. Gold and silver are sometimes weighed in baht (15g).

Smoking While a large number of people smoke in rural Laos, towns and cities are becoming increasingly smoke-free. Almost all hotels in Laos offer nonsmoking rooms and there is a ban on smoking in cafes and restaurants in Vientiane and Luang Prabang.

Insurance

A good travel insurance policy, as always, is a wise investment. Laos is generally considered a high-risk area, and with limited medical services it's vital to have a policy that covers being evacuated (medevaced), by air if necessary, to a hospital in Thailand. Read the small print in any policy to see if hazardous activities are covered; rock climbing, rafting and motorcycling are often not.

If you undergo medical treatment in Laos or Thailand, be sure to collect all receipts and copies of the medical report, in English if possible, for insurance purposes.

Worldwide travel insurance is available at www.lonelyplanet.com/travel-insurance. You can buy, extend and claim online anytime – even if you're already on the road.

Internet Access

Free wi-fi is pretty standard these days and available in most guesthouses, hotels and cafes in the main tourist destinations around Laos. Internet cafes are still around in Vientiane but are increasingly rare elsewhere. If you can find one, it's generally possible to get online

from 5000K to 10,000K per hour.

Legal Matters

Although Laos guarantees certain rights, the reality is that you can be fined, detained or deported for any reason, as has been demonstrated repeatedly in cases involving foreigners.

If you stay away from anything you know to be illegal, you should be fine. If not, things might get messy and expensive. Drug possession and using prostitutes are the most common crimes for which travellers are caught, often with the dealer or consort being the one to inform the authorities. Sexual relationships between foreigners and Lao citizens who are not married are illegal; penalties for failing to register a relationship range from fines of US$500 to US$5000, and possibly imprisonment or deportation.

If you are detained, ask to call your embassy or consulate in Laos, if there is one. A meeting or phone call between Lao officers and someone from your embassy or consulate may result in quicker adjudication and release.

Police sometimes ask for bribes for traffic violations and other petty offences.

LGBT+ Travellers

For the most part Lao culture is pretty tolerant of homosexuality, although lesbianism is often either denied completely or misunderstood. In any case, public displays of affection, whether heterosexual or homosexual, are frowned upon.

While there are no laws criminalising homosexuality, the gay and lesbian scene is certainly more hidden these days and not nearly as prominent as in neighbouring Thailand. Authorities sometimes shut down drag shows in Vientiane and have banned gay-friendly establishments from marketing themselves as such with rainbow flags. That doesn't mean they've disappeared!

Check out **Utopia** (www.utopia-asia.com) for gay travel information and contacts in Laos, including some local gay terminology.

Money

The official national currency in Laos is the Lao kip (K), but Thai baht (B) and US dollars (US$) are also commonly accepted.

ATMs

ATMs are now found all over Laos. But before you get too excited, ATMs dispense a maximum of 700,000K to 2,000,000K (about US$85 to US$250) per transaction, depending on the bank, not to mention a variable withdrawal fee. If you also have to pay extortionate charges to your home bank on each overseas withdrawal, this can quickly add up.

Credit Cards

A growing number of hotels, upmarket restaurants and gift shops in Vientiane and Luang Prabang accept Visa and MasterCard, and, to a much lesser extent, Amex and JCB. However, many places will also pass on the transaction fee to the customer, usually around 3%. Outside of the main towns, credit cards are virtually useless.

Banque pour le Commerce Extérieur Lao (BCEL) branches in most major towns offer cash advances/withdrawals on MasterCard and Visa credit/debit cards for a 3% transaction fee. Other banks may have slightly different charges, so it might be worth shopping around in Vientiane.

Currency

Laos relies heavily on the Thai baht and the US dollar for the domestic cash economy. An estimated one-third of all cash circulating in Vientiane, in fact, bears the portrait of the Thai king, while another third celebrates US presidents. Kip is usually preferred for small purchases, while more expensive items and services may be quoted in kip, baht or US dollars. Anything costing the equivalent of US$100 or more is likely to be quoted in US dollars.

The majority of transactions will be carried out in kip, however, so it's always worth having a wad in your pocket. Notes come in denominations of 500, 1000, 2000, 5000, 10,000, 20,000, 50,000 and 100,000 kip. Small vendors, especially in rural areas, will struggle to change 100,000K notes.

Moneychangers

After years of volatility the kip has in recent times remained fairly stable at about 8500K to the US dollar. Don't, however, count on this remaining the same.

Generally, exchange rates are virtually the same whether you're changing at a bank or a moneychanger. Both are also likely to offer a marginally better rate for larger bills (US$50 and US$100) than smaller bills (US$20 and less). Banks in Vientiane and Luang Prabang can generally change UK pounds, euros, Canadian, US and Australian dollars, Thai baht and Japanese yen. Elsewhere most provincial banks usually change only US dollars or baht.

Licensed moneychangers maintain booths around Vientiane (including at Talat Sao) and at some border crossings. Their rates are similar to the banks, but they stay open longer.

There's no real black market in Laos and unless there's an economic crash, that's unlikely to change.

Tipping

Tipping is not customary in Laos except in tourist-oriented restaurants, where 10% of the bill is appreciated, but only if a service charge hasn't already been added.

Photography

Lao officials are sensitive about photography of airports and military installations.

In rural areas people are often not used to having their photos taken, so ask if they mind before taking any shots. In tribal areas always ask permission before photographing people or religious totems when trekking, as photography of people is taboo among several tribes. Breaking such taboos might not seem like a big deal to you, but it is important to respect local customs.

Post

Sending post from Laos is not all that expensive and is fairly reliable, but people still tend to wait until they get to Thailand to send parcels. If heading to Cambodia, it's probably smarter to post your parcels from Laos.

Leave packages open for inspection by a postal officer. Incoming parcels might also need to be inspected and there may be a small charge for this mandatory 'service'.

The main post office in **Vientiane** (Map p152; ☏021-216425; Rue Saylom; ⊙8am-5pm Mon-Fri) has a poste restante service.

Public Holidays

Schools and government offices are closed on the following official holidays, and the organs of state move pretty slowly, if at all, during festivals.

International New Year 1 January

Army Day 20 January

International Women's Day 8 March

EATING PRICE RANGES

Virtually all restaurants in Laos are inexpensive by international standards. The following price ranges refer to a main course.

$ less than US$5 (40,000K)

$$ US$5–15 (40,000–120,000K)

$$$ more than US$15 (120,000K)

GOVERNMENT TRAVEL ADVICE

The following government websites offer travel advisories and information on current hotspots.

Australian Department of Foreign Affairs (www.smartraveller.gov.au)

Canadian Government (www.voyage.gc.ca)

German Foreign Office (www.auswaertiges-amt.de)

Japanese Ministry of Foreign Affairs (www.anzen.mofa.go.jp)

Netherlands Government (www.minbuza.nl)

New Zealand Ministry of Foreign Affairs (www.safetravel.govt.nz)

UK Foreign Office (www.gov.uk/foreign-travel-advice)

US Department of State (www.travel.state.gov)

Lao New Year 14–16 April
International Labour Day 1 May
International Children's Day 1 June
Lao National Day 2 December

Safe Travel

Over the last couple of decades Laos has earned a reputation among visitors as a remarkably safe place to travel, with little crime reported and few of the scams often found in more touristed places such as Vietnam, Thailand and Cambodia. However, in more recent years, there has been a small rise in petty crimes, such as theft and low-level scams, which are more annoying than dangerous.

Drugs

Most of the more obvious drugs are found in Laos, but are also illegal, carrying the risk of stiff fines or, in the case of stronger substances, a lengthy prison sentence. Travellers may commonly dabble in a happy shake (a shake made with marijuana or magic mushrooms) and occasionally opium where it is still found in remote areas. However, police set-ups and police busts are not unknown, leading to large fines and deportation or imprisonment.

So proceed with caution or stick to the Beerlao.

Queues

The Lao people follow the usual Southeast Asian method of queuing for services, which is to say they don't form a line at all but simply push en masse towards the counter or doorway. The system is 'first seen, first served'. Learn to play the game the Lao way, by pushing your money, passport, letters or whatever to the front of the crowd as best you can. That said, it is nowhere near as chaotic as in some of the bigger neighbouring countries.

Road & River Travel

Better roads, better vehicles and fewer insurgents mean road travel in Laos is quite safe, if not always comfortable. However, while the scarcity of traffic in Laos means there are far fewer accidents than in neighbouring countries, accidents are still the main risk for travellers.

As motorbikes become increasingly popular among travellers, the number of accidents is rising. Even more likely is the chance of earning yourself a Lao version of the 'Thai tattoo' – that scar on the calf caused by a burn from a hot exhaust pipe.

The speedboats that career along the Mekong in northern Laos are as dangerous as they are fast. We recommend avoiding all speedboat travel unless absolutely necessary.

Theft

While theft is much less common than elsewhere in Southeast Asia, it has been on the rise in recent years. Most of the reports we've heard involve opportunistic acts that are fairly easily avoided.

Money or items going missing from rooms is becoming more common, particularly in rural bungalows, so don't leave cash or other tempting belongings on show. If you're on a crowded bus, watch your luggage and don't keep money in loose trouser pockets. When riding a bicycle or motorcycle in Vientiane, don't place anything of value in the basket, as thieving duos on motorbikes may ride by and snatch a bag.

Motorcycle theft is a growing problem. Always lock up your bike when out in the countryside or at night, and pay for parking whenever you can.

Unexploded Ordnance (UXO)

Large areas of eastern and southern Laos are contaminated by unexploded ordnance (UXO). According to surveys by the Lao National UXO Programme (UXO Lao) and other nongovernment UXO clearance organisations, the provinces of Salavan, Savannakhet and Xieng Khuang are the most severely affected, followed by Champasak, Hua Phan, Khammuan, Luang Prabang, Attapeu and Sekong.

Statistically, the UXO risk for foreign visitors is low, but travellers should exercise caution when considering off-road wilderness travel in the aforementioned provinces. Stick only to marked paths. And never touch an object that may be UXO, no matter how old and defunct it may appear.

Telephone

With a local SIM card and a 3G/4G or wi-fi connection, the cheapest option is to use internet-based messaging and call apps. Topping up a phone for as little as 50,000K can give you enough data to last a month.

International calls can be made from Lao Telecom offices or the local post office in most provincial capitals and are charged on a per-minute basis, with a minimum charge of three minutes. Calls to most countries cost about 2000K to 4000K per minute. Office hours typically run from about 7.30am to 9.30pm.

Mobile Phones

Lao Telecom and several private companies offer mobile phone services on the GSM and 3G/4G systems. Competition is fierce and you can buy a local SIM card for as little as 10,000K from almost anywhere. Calls are cheap and recharge cards are widely available. Network coverage varies depending on the company and the region.

Phone Codes

The country code for calling Laos is ☑856. For long-distance calls within the country, dial ☑0 first, then the area code and number. For international calls dial ☑00 first, then the country code, area code and number.

All mobile phones have a ☑020 code at the beginning of the number. Similar to this are WIN satellite phones, which begin with ☑030.

Time

Laos is seven hours ahead of GMT/UTC. Thus, noon in Vientiane is 10pm the previous day in San Francisco, 1am in New York, 5am in London and 3pm in Sydney. There is no daylight saving time.

Toilets

While Western-style toilets are now found in most mid-range and top-end accommodation, budget travellers should expect squat toilets when staying in some guesthouses and particularly homestays.

In places where sit-down toilets are installed, the plumbing may not be designed to take toilet paper. In such cases there will usually be a rubbish bin for used paper.

Public toilets are uncommon as soon as you leave the main north to south tourist trail and head into more remote areas. While on the road between towns and villages, it's perfectly acceptable to go behind a tree or use the roadside.

Tourist Information

The Department of Tourism Marketing, part of the Ministry of Information, Culture and Tourism (MICT), has tourist offices all over Laos, with the ones in Vientiane and Luang Prabang particularly helpful.

Many offices are well-stocked with brochures and maps, and have easily understood displays of their provincial attractions and English-speaking staff to answer your questions. Offices in Tha Khaek, Savannakhet, Pakse, Luang Namtha, Sainyabuli, Phongsali and Sam Neua are all pretty good, with staff trained to promote treks and other activities in the area and able to hand out brochures and first-hand knowledge. They should also be able to help with local transport options and bookings. Alternatively, you can usually get up-to-date information from a popular guesthouse.

The MICT also runs three very good websites that offer valuable pre-departure information:

Central Laos Trekking (www.trekkingcentrallaos.com)

Ecotourism Laos (www.ecotourismlaos.com)

Ministry of Information, Culture and Tourism (www.tourismlaos.org)

Visas

Thirty-day tourist visas are readily available on arrival at international airports and most land borders.

Tourist Visa on Arrival

The Lao government issues 30-day tourist visas on arrival at all international airports and most international border crossings.

The whole process is very straightforward. You need between US$30 and US$42 in cash, one passport-sized photo and the name of a hotel or guesthouse. Those without a photo, or who are arriving on a weekend, holiday or after office hours, will have to pay an additional one or two dollars.

The visa fee varies depending on the passport of origin, with Canadians having to fork out the most (US$42) and most other nationalities paying between US$30 and US$35. It's cheaper to pay in US dollars as a flat rate of 1500B (around US$45) is applicable in Thai baht. No other foreign currencies are accepted.

Tourist Visas

For those not eligible for a visa on arrival, Lao embassies and consulates abroad offer 30-day tourist visas. The process involves roughly the same cost and documentation and generally takes three working days. In Bangkok you can get your visa on the same day for an additional 200B express fee.

Business Visas

Business visas, valid for 30 days, are relatively easy to obtain as long as you have a sponsoring agency in Laos. A business visa can be extended by up to a year.

Visa Extensions

The 30-day tourist visa can be extended for an additional 90 days at a cost of 20,000K per day, but only in major cities such as Vientiane, Luang Prabang, Pakse and Savannakhet.

Overstaying Your Visa

Overstaying a visa is not a major crime, but it is expensive. It costs US$10 for each day overstayed, paid at the immigration checkpoint on departure.

Volunteering

Volunteers have been working in Laos for years, usually on one- or two-year contracts that include a minimal monthly allowance. Volunteers are often placed with a government agency and attempt to help advance development in the country. These sorts of jobs can lead to nonvolunteer work within the nongovernment organisation (NGO) community.

The alternative approach to volunteering, where you actually pay to be placed in a 'volunteer' role for a few weeks or months, has yet to arrive in Laos in any great capacity. A couple of groups in Luang Prabang need volunteers occasionally, and there are also local projects in places as diverse as Huay Xai, Muang Khua and Sainyabuli.

Australian Volunteers International (www.australianvolun teers.com) Places qualified Australian residents on one- to two-year contracts.

Voluntary Service Overseas (VSO; www.vsointernational.org) Places qualified and experienced volunteers for up to two years.

Women Travellers

Laos is generally an easy country for women to travel around, although it is necessary to be more culturally sensitive when compared with Southeast Asia's more developed destinations, as much of rural Laos is still very traditional. Violence against women travellers is extremely rare, but if travelling solo, it may be useful to team up with other travellers on long overland journeys into remote areas of the country.

It's highly unusual for Lao women to wear tank tops, short skirts or shorts. It may be common to see foreign visitors dressed like this in places like Vang Vieng for river tubing or at the Kuang Si Falls, but in most rural areas it is best to dress more conservatively to avoid people staring. If you're planning on bathing in a village or river, a sarong is essential.

Traditionally women didn't sit on the roofs of riverboats, because this was believed to bring bad luck. These days most captains aren't so concerned, but if you are asked to get off the roof while men are not, this is why.

Work

With a large number of aid organisations and a fast-growing international business community, especially in energy and mining, the number of jobs available to foreigners is increasing, but still relatively small. The greatest number of positions are in Vientiane.

Possibilities include teaching English privately or at one of the handful of language centres in Vientiane. Certificates or degrees in English teaching aren't absolutely necessary, but they do help attract a better rate of pay.

If you have technical expertise or international volunteer experience, you might be able to find work with a UN-related program or an NGO providing foreign aid or technical assistance to Laos. These jobs are difficult to find; your best bet is to visit the Vientiane offices of each organisation and enquire about personnel needs and vacancies. For a list of NGOs operating in Laos, see the excellent www. directoryofngos.org.

Transport

GETTING THERE & AWAY

Many travellers enter or exit Laos via the country's numerous land and river borders. Flying into Laos is a relatively easy option as there is only a small number of airlines serving Laos and prices don't vary much. Flights and tours can be booked online at www.lonely planet.com/bookings.

Air

Laos has air connections with regional countries including Thailand, Vietnam, Cambodia, Malaysia, Singapore, China and South Korea. The most convenient international gateway to Laos is Bangkok and there are plenty of flights to the Thai capital. If heading to Laos for a shorter holiday, it is cheaper to take an indirect flight to Bangkok with a stop

on the way. Once in Bangkok, there are planes, trains and buses heading to Laos.

There are four international airports in Laos: **Wattay International Airport** (VTE; Map p146; ☏021-512165; www.vientianeairport.com; Rte 13) in Vientiane, **Luang Prabang International Airport** (LPQ; ☏071-212173; www.luangprabangairport.com; ☏). **Savannakhet International Airport** (Map p198; ☏041-212140; Th Kaysone Phomvihane) and **Pakse International Airport** (Rte 13).

Air Asia (www.airasia.com) Flights from Vientiane to Bangkok daily and Kuala Lumpur several times per week, plus Luang Prabang to Bangkok and Kuala Lumpur.

Bangkok Airways (www.bangkokair.com) Daily flights between Bangkok and Vientiane and Luang Prabang.

China Eastern Airlines (www.ceair.com) Flies daily to Kunming and Nanning from Vientiane,

plus Luang Prabang to Kunming several times per week.

Jeju Air (www.jejuair.net) Daily flights to Seoul.

Lao Airlines (www.laoairlines.com) National carrier. The extensive international flight network includes Vientiane to Bangkok, Busan, Changsha, Changzhou, Guangzhou, Hanoi, Kunming and Seoul; Luang Prabang to Bangkok, Chengdu, Chiang Mai, Hanoi and Jinghong; Pakse to Ho Chi Minh City and Siem Reap; and Savannakhet to Bangkok.

Scoot (www.flyscoot.com) One daily flight connecting both Vientiane and Luang Prabang with Singapore.

Thai Airways (www.thaiairways.com) Vientiane to Bangkok and Luang Prabang daily, including cheaper options with Thai Smile subsidiary.

Vietnam Airlines (www.vietnamairlines.com) Connects Vientiane with Hanoi and Phnom Penh, plus Luang Prabang with Hanoi and Siem Reap.

CLIMATE CHANGE & TRAVEL

Every form of transport that relies on carbon-based fuel generates CO_2, the main cause of human-induced climate change. Modern travel is dependent on aeroplanes, which might use less fuel per kilometre per person than most cars but travel much greater distances. The altitude at which aircraft emit gases (including CO_2) and particles also contributes to their climate change impact. Many websites offer 'carbon calculators' that allow people to estimate the carbon emissions generated by their journey and, for those who wish to do so, to offset the impact of the greenhouse gases emitted with contributions to portfolios of climate-friendly initiatives throughout the world. Lonely Planet offsets the carbon footprint of all staff and author travel.

Land

Laos shares land and/or river borders with Thailand, Myanmar (Burma), Cambodia, China and Vietnam. Border-crossing details change regularly, so ask around and check Thorn Tree (lonelyplanet.com/thorntree) before setting off.

It's possible to bring a car or motorcycle into Laos from Cambodia and Thailand with the right paperwork, but not from Vietnam, China or Myanmar. Lao customs does not object to visitors bringing bicycles into the country.

Cambodia

There are daily buses and minibuses connecting Pakse with Stung Treng (four hours), Kratie (six hours) and Phnom Penh (11 hours). These also stop at Ban Nakasang and Ban Hat Xai in both directions for travellers planning to relax in Si Phan Don. It's best to take one of these through-buses, as it's pretty tough to arrange transport at the Non Nok Khiene (Laos)/Trapeang Kriel (Cambodia) border.

China

Handy through-buses link major towns in Yunnan to northern Laos. Routes include Luang Namtha–Jinghong (six hours), Udomxai–Mengla (five hours) and Kunming–Luang Prabang (around 24 hours on a Chinese sleeper bus). It's also perfectly feasible to make the journey in hops via Boten, the main

China–Lao border crossing currently open to foreigners. From Mohan on the Chinese side it's around a two-hour minibus ride to Mengla, the nearest large town.

Myanmar

The first Lao–Myanmar Friendship Bridge officially opened in 2016 connecting Xieng Kok in Luang Namtha Province with Tachelik District in Shan State. However, border demarcation disagreements have delayed it opening for international traffic. Check in Vientiane or Luang Namtha before setting off this way or play it safe and transit through Thailand, via Chiang Khong and Mae Sai, to the Burmese town of Tachilek.

Thailand

There are eight crossings to Thailand open to foreigners. Some involve taking a boat across the Mekong, or crossing the river on one of the Friendship Bridges.

THAILAND TO VIENTIANE

Through-buses run regularly between Vientiane and the Thai towns of Khon Kaen (four hours), Nakhon Ratchasima (seven hours), Nong Khai (1½ hours) and Udon Thani (2½ hours) via the Friendship Bridge. There are also several daily trains (www.railway.co.th/english) from Bangkok to Nong Khai (about 12 hours), as well as daily departures between Nong Khai and Vientiane's Dongphasy Station. From Udon Thani there are budget flights to Bangkok and other domestic destinations in Thailand.

THAILAND TO NORTHERN LAOS

The majority of visitors are heading to or from Luang Prabang. There are three main options but no route allows you to make the trip in a single journey. The

Chiang Rai–Huay Xai–Luang Prabang route is by far the most tourist-friendly and potentially the quickest route (around 24 hours using buses, or two days by bus-boat combination).

Travel this way is via Chiang Khong/Huay Xai. Departing from Chiang Rai on the first bus of the day, it is possible to connect with the slowboat from Huay Xai to Luang Prabang, arriving the following evening. Or leave Chiang Rai at lunchtime and connect with the 5pm overnight bus (faster but not recommended when compared with the beautiful boat journey), arriving in Luang Prabang late the next morning. Through-tickets from Chiang Mai or Chiang Rai agencies are generally overpriced.

Other possibilities are perfectly feasible but see almost no foreign tourists, so you'll need to be comfortable with local languages or sign language. These routes can also take several days due to limited transport and poor roads. Choose from the Nan–Muang Ngeun–Luang Prabang route or the even more remote Loei–Pak Lai–Sainyabuli option.

THAILAND TO CENTRAL LAOS

Although relatively few tourists use them, the border crossings that straddle the Mekong between northeastern Thailand and central Laos are almost universally convenient and straightforward.

The river crossing between Nakhon Phanom and Tha Khaek is a breeze. There are several daily buses between Bangkok and Nakhon Phanom (12 hours), but it's almost as cheap and much faster to use the budget airlines.

The bridge between Mukdahan and Savannakhet is the southernmost

DEPARTURE TAX

There is a departure tax of US$10 on all international flights, but it is included in the ticket price at the time of purchase.

LAOS BORDER CROSSINGS

CAMBODIA

BORDER CROSSING	CONNECTING TOWNS	VISA AVAILABLE ON ARRIVAL
Non Nok Khiene (L)/Trapeang Kriel (C)	Si Phan Don (L), Stung Treng (C)	Yes

CHINA

BORDER CROSSING	CONNECTING TOWNS	VISA AVAILABLE ON ARRIVAL
Boten (L)/Mohan (C)	Luang Nam Tha (L), Mengla (C)	Laos only

MYANMAR

BORDER CROSSING	CONNECTING TOWNS	VISA AVAILABLE ON ARRIVAL
Houy Koum (L)/Kainglek (M)	Luang Namtha (L), Tachilek (M)	No

THAILAND

BORDER CROSSING	CONNECTING TOWNS	VISA AVAILABLE ON ARRIVAL
Tha Na Leng (L)/Nong Khai (T)	Vientiane (L), Nong Khai (T)	Yes
Paksan (L)/Beung Kan (T)	Paksan (L), Beung Kan (T)	No
Huay Xai (L)/Chiang Khong (T)	Huay Xai (L), Chiang Rai (T)	Yes
Tha Khaek (L)/Nakhon Phanom (T)	Tha Khaek (L), Nakhon Phanom (T)	Yes
Savannakhet (L)/Mukdahan (T)	Savannakhet (L), Mukdahan (T)	Yes
Vang Tao (L)/Chong Mek (T)	Pakse (L), Ubon Ratchathani (T)	Yes
Muang Ngeun (L)/Huay Kon (T)	Hongsa (L), Phrae (T)	Yes
Kaen Thao (L)/Tha Li (T)	Pak Li (L), Loei (T)	Yes

VIETNAM

BORDER CROSSING	CONNECTING TOWNS	VISA AVAILABLE ON ARRIVAL
Dansavanh (L)/Lao Bao (V)	Savannakhet (L), Dong Ha (V)	Laos all/Vietnam some
Phou Keua (L)/Bo Y (V)	Attapeu (L), Kontum (V)	Laos all/Vietnam some
Na Phao (L)/Cha Lo (V)	Tha Khaek (L), Dong Hoi (L)	Laos all/Vietnam some
Nong Haet (L)/Nam Can (V)	Phonsavan (L), Vinh (V)	Laos all/Vietnam some
Nam Phao (L)/Cau Treo (V)	Tha Khaek (L), Vinh (V)	Laos all/Vietnam some
Na Meo (L)/Nam Soi (V)	Sam Neua (L), Thanh Hoa (V)	Laos all/Vietnam some
Pang Hok (L)/Tay Trang (V)	Muang Khua (L), Dien Bien Phu (V)	Laos all/Vietnam some

Mekong River crossing open to non-Thai and non-Lao nationals. Several buses link Bangkok and Mukdahan (about 10 hours), and the Thai-Lao International Bus runs between the latter and Savannakhet's bus station (45 minutes). There are also fly-drive options available via Nakhon Phanom airport with budget airlines.

The river crossing between Beung Kan and Paksan is the weak link with a dearth of regular transport on the Thai side.

THAILAND TO SOUTHERN LAOS
International buses connect Pakse with Ubon Ratchathani (four hours including crossing) via the Vang Tao (Laos) and Chong Mek (Thailand) border twice daily, plus there is one

Laos Border Crossings

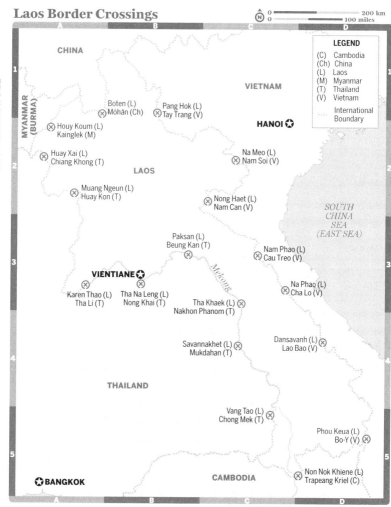

N
0   200 km
0   100 miles

CHINA

VIETNAM

MYANMAR (BURMA)

Boten (L)
⊗ Móhān (Ch)

Pang Hok (L)
⊗ Tay Trang (V)

HANOI ✪

⊗ Houy Koum (L)
Kainglek (M)

⊗ Huay Xai (L)
Chiang Khong (T)

LAOS

Na Meo (L)
⊗ Nam Soi (V)

⊗ Muang Ngeun (L)
Huay Kon (T)

⊗ Nong Haet (L)
Nam Can (V)

SOUTH
CHINA
SEA
(EAST SEA)

Paksan (L)
Beung Kan (T)
⊗

Nam Phao (L)
⊗ Cau Treo (V)

VIENTIANE ✪

⊗   ⊗

Karen Thao (L)
Tha Li (T)

Tha Na Leng (L)
Nong Khai (T)

Mekong

Na Phao (L)
⊗ Cha Lo (V)

Tha Khaek (L) ⊗
Nakhon Phanom (T)

Savannakhet (L) ⊗
Mukdahan (T)

Dansavanh (L) ⊗
Lao Bao (V)

THAILAND

Vang Tao (L) ⊗
Chong Mek (T)

Phou Keua (L)
Bo-Y (V) ⊗

✪ BANGKOK

CAMBODIA

Non Nok Khiene (L)
⊗ Trapeang Kriel (C)

LEGEND
(C)   Cambodia
(Ch)   China
(L)   Laos
(M)   Myanmar
(T)   Thailand
(V)   Vietnam
·········   International Boundary

through-service a day to Bangkok. Combination bus and train tickets can also be purchased in Pakse.

Vietnam

At the time of writing, foreigners could cross between Laos and Vietnam at seven different border posts. Laos issues 30-day tourist visas at all of these, but Vietnamese visas must be arranged in advance in Luang Prabang, Vientiane, Savannakhet or Pakse for

some nationals. Exceptions are Association of Southeast Asian Nations (Asean) countries, Japan and South Korea, plus some European countries such as Scandinavia, France, Italy, Spain, Germany and the UK. In every case we recommend using a through-bus rather than trying to make the trip in hops, as it can be very difficult to arrange onward transport from the remote border posts.

GETTING AROUND

Transport in Laos is generally very good value, but journeys can take a lot longer than distances on a map might suggest.

Air Laos has an extensive domestic flight network and this can save considerable time on a short visit.

Boat Rivers are the lifeblood of Laos, making boat journeys an important element of the transport network.

Bus Laos has some smart buses operating on major routes out of Vientiane, but venture into remote areas and vehicles are as old as the hills.

Car For those with a more flexible budget, a rented car with driver is the smoothest way to cover a lot of ground in a limited amount of time.

Air

Domestic flights to smaller airports suffer fairly frequent cancellations due to fog and, in March, heavy smoke during the slash-and-burn season. During the holiday season it's best to book ahead as flights can fill fast. At other times, when flights are more likely to be cancelled, confirm your flight is still departing a day or two before.

Lao Airlines (www.laoairlines. com) The main airline in Laos handling domestic flights, including between Vientiane and Luang Prabang, Luang Nam Tha, Pakse, Phonsavan, Savannakhet and Udomxai.

Lao Skyway (www.laoskyway. com) A newer domestic airline with flights from Vientiane to Udomxai, Luang Prabang, Huay Xai, Phonsavan, Luang Namtha, Phongsali and Sam Neua. Note that some services such as flights to Phongsali and Sam Neua do not appear on the airline website and can only be booked via the Lao Skyway offices.

With the exception of Lao Airlines offices in major cities, where credit cards are accepted for both international and domestic tickets, it is necessary to pay cash in US dollars if not booking online.

Bicycle

The stunningly beautiful roads and light, relatively slow traffic in most towns and on most highways make Laos arguably the best country for cycling in Southeast Asia.

Simple single-speed bicycles can be hired in most places that see a decent number of tourists, usually costing about 20,000K per day. Better mountain bikes will cost from 30,000K to 80,000K per day.

Boat

More than 4600km of navigable rivers are the highways and byways of traditional Laos, the main thoroughfares being the Mekong, Nam Ou, Nam Khan, Nam Tha, Nam Ngum and Se Kong. The Mekong is the longest and most important route and is navigable year-round between Huay Xai in the north and Savannakhet in the south, though new dams make this increasingly difficult without changing boats. Smaller rivers accommodate a range of smaller boats, from dugout canoes to 'bomb boats' made from war detritus.

Whether it's on a tourist boat from Huay Xai to Luang Prabang or on a local boat you've rustled up in some remote corner of the country, it's still worth doing at least one river excursion while in Laos.

River Ferry (Slowboat) & River Taxi

The slowboat between Huay Xai and Luang Prabang is the most popular river trip in Laos. It is still a daily event and relatively cheap at about 250,000K or US$30 per person for the two-day journey. From Huay Xai, these basic boats are often packed, while travelling in the other direction from Luang Prabang there seems to be more room. Passengers sit, eat and sleep on the wooden decks. The toilet (if there is one) is an enclosed hole in the deck at the back of the boat.

For shorter river trips, such as Luang Prabang to the Pak Ou Caves, it's usually best to hire a river taxi. The *héua hǎhng nyáo* (longtail boats) are the most common and cost around US$10 an hour.

Along the upper Mekong River between Huay Xai and Vientiane, Thai-built *héua wái* (speedboats) are common. They can cover a distance in six hours that might take a ferry two days or more. Charters cost at least US$30 per hour, but

TYPES OF BOAT

Following are some of the *héua* (boats) that you may encounter in your adventures along Laos' many waterways:

Héua sáh (double-deck slowboats) Big, old boats; almost extinct.

Héua dooan (express boat) Roofed cargo boats, common on the Huay Xai–Luang Prabang route. Still slow, but faster than double-deck boats.

Héua wái (speedboat) These resemble a surfboard with a car engine strapped to the back: very fast, exhilarating, deafeningly loud, uncomfortable and rather dangerous. Not recommended.

Héua hǎhng nyáo (longtail boat) Boats with the engine gimbal-mounted on the stern; found all over Laos.

Héua pái (rowboat) Essentially a dugout; common in Si Phan Don.

MOTORCYCLE TIPS

There are few more liberating travel experiences than renting a motorbike and setting off; stopping where you want, when you want. The lack of traffic and stunningly beautiful roads make Laos one of the best places in the region to do it. There are, however, a few things worth knowing before you hand over your passport as collateral to rent a bike.

The bike Price and availability mean that the vast majority of travellers rent Chinese 110cc bikes. No 110cc bike was designed to be used like a dirt bike, however – Japanese bikes deal with the roads better and are worth the extra few dollars a day.

The odometer Given that many roads have no kilometre stones and turn-offs are often unmarked, it's worth getting a bike with a working odometer. Most bike shops can fix an odometer in about 10 minutes for a few dollars. Money well spent, as long as you remember to note the distance when you start.

The gear Don't leave home without sunscreen, a hat, a plastic raincoat or poncho, a bandanna and sunglasses. Even the sealed roads in Laos get annoyingly dusty, so these last two are vital. A helmet is essential (ask for one if they don't offer), as is wearing trousers and shoes, lest you wind up with the ubiquitous leg burn from the exhaust.

The problems Unless you're very lucky, something will go wrong. Budget some time for it.

The responsibility In general, you can ride a motorbike in Laos without a licence, a helmet or any safety gear whatsoever, but for all this freedom you must take all the responsibility. If you have a crash, there won't be an ambulance to pick you up, and when you get to the hospital, facilities will be basic. Carrying a basic medical kit and phone numbers for hospitals in Thailand and your travel insurance provider is a good idea. The same goes for the bike. If it really dies you can't just call the company and get a replacement. You'll need to load it onto the next pick-up or *sŏrngtăaou* and take it somewhere they can fix it. Don't abandon it by the road, or you'll have to pay for another one.

some ply regular routes so the cost can be shared among passengers. They are, however, rather dangerous and we recommend taking one only if absolutely necessary.

Tours

With public boat routes becoming increasingly hard to find, tour companies are offering kayaking and rafting trips on some of the more scenic stretches of river. The best places to organise these are Luang Namtha, Luang Prabang, Nong Khiaw, Vang Vieng, Tha Khaek and Pakse.

For something a bit more luxurious, **Mekong Cruises** (www.mekong-cruises.com) and **Mekong River Cruises** (Map p52; ☑071-254768; www.cruisemekong.com; 22/2 Th Sakkarin, Ban Xieng Thong; 6-day all-inclusive cruise per person from $1080; ◷8.30am-6pm Mon-Fri) offer multiday cruises along the Mekong on refurbished river barges.

Bus

Long-distance public transport in Laos is either by bus or *sŏrngtăaou* (literally 'two rows'), which are converted pick-ups or trucks with benches down either side. Private operators have established VIP buses on some busier routes, offering faster and more luxurious air-con services that cost a little more than normal buses. Many guesthouses can book tickets for a small fee.

Sŏrngtăaou usually service shorter routes within a given province, though these vehicles are slowly being phased out across Laos and replaced with minivans.

Many decent-sized villages still have at least one *sŏrngtăaou*, which will run to the provincial capital and back most days.

Car & Motorcycle

Driving in Laos is easier than it looks. Sure, the road infrastructure is pretty basic, but outside of the large centres there are so few vehicles that it's a doddle compared to Vietnam, China or Thailand.

Motorcyclists planning to ride through Laos should check out the wealth of information at **Golden Triangle Rider** (www.gt-rider.com). Doing some sort of motorbike loop out of Vientiane, Vang Vieng or Tha Khaek is becoming increasingly popular among travellers.

Bring Your Own Vehicle

Bringing a vehicle into Laos is easy enough if you have proof of ownership and a carnet. Simply get the carnet stamped at any international border and there is no extra charge or permit required.

As Thailand doesn't recognise the carnet system, an International Transport Permit, known in Thailand as the *lêm sĕe môoang* (purple book), is required. This is available at Nong Khai's **Land Transport Office** (☑042-411591, ext 103; ⊘8.30am-4.30pm). Bring your vehicle's official registration book and tax receipts, passport and an international driving permit or Thai driver's licence.

On the Lao side you'll need all the documents mentioned above and will also need to arrange Lao vehicle insurance (about 300B for a week).

Exiting into Thailand or Cambodia is fairly hassle-free if your papers are in order. Vietnam is a different story and it is probably best not to even consider a crossing. Heading to China it's virtually impossible to drive a vehicle larger than a bicycle across the border.

Driving Licence

Officially at least, to drive in Laos a valid international driving permit is required. If you're only renting motorbikes you'll never be asked for any sort of licence.

Fuel & Spare Parts

At the time of research fuel cost about US$1 a litre for petrol, slightly less for diesel. Fuel for motorcycles is available from drums or Beerlao bottles in villages across the country, although prices are almost always higher than at service stations. Diesel is available in most towns. It's best to fuel up in bigger towns at big-brand service stations because the quality of fuel can be poor in remote areas.

Spare parts for four-wheeled vehicles are expensive and difficult to find, even in Vientiane.

Hire

Chinese- and Japanese-made 100cc and 110cc step-through motorbikes can be hired for approximately 40,000K to 120,000K per day in most large centres and some smaller towns, although the state of the bikes can vary greatly. No licence is required, though you will have to leave your passport as collateral. Try to get a Japanese bike if travelling any distance out of town. In Vientiane, Luang Prabang, Vang Vieng, Tha Khaek and Pakse, 250cc dirt bikes are available from around US$25 to US$50 per day.

It's possible to hire a self-drive vehicle, but when you consider that a driver usually costs little more, takes responsibility for damage and knows where he's going, it seems less appealing. Costs run from US$40 to US$100 per day, depending on the route.

Vientiane-based **Avis-Budget** (Map p152; ☑020-22861415; www.avis.la; Rue Setthathirath; ⊘8.30am-6pm

ROAD DISTANCES (KM)

	Attapeu	Luang Namtha	Luang Prabang	Muang Khong	Nong Haet	Pakse	Phongsali	Phonsavan	Sam Neua	Savannakhet	Tha Khaek	Udomxai	Vang Vieng
Luang Namtha	1400												
Luang Prabang	1130	270											
Muang Khong	190	1380	1110										
Nong Haet	1280	580	350	1260									
Pakse	210	1250	980	120	1130								
Phongsali	1550	360	410	1520	720	1390							
Phonsavan	1170	470	250	1150	110	1020	620						
Sam Neua	1350	450	460	1320	300	1190	590	180					
Savannakhet	410	1050	780	390	930	250	1190	820	990				
Tha Khaek	480	920	650	460	800	370	1070	690	870	130			
Udomxai	1290	110	180	1270	470	1140	250	360	440	940	820		
Vang Vieng	970	440	170	940	320	810	580	220	480	650	490	350	
Vientiane	810	680	390	790	470	660	810	380	620	500	330	580	150

Mon-Fri, to 1pm Sat & Sun) is a reliable option for car hire.

When it comes to motorbikes, try **Driven By Adventure** (☑020-58656994; www.hochiminhtrail.org; rental per day US$38-95, tours per day from US$190) or **Fuark Motorbike Service** (Map p146; ☑021-261970; fuarkmotorcross@yahoo.com; Rue T2; ◔9am-6pm) in Vientiane.

Insurance

Car-hire companies will provide insurance, but be sure to check exactly what is covered. Note that most travel-insurance policies don't cover use of motorcycles.

Road Conditions

While the overall condition of roads is poor, work over the last couple of decades has left most of the main roads in reasonable shape.

Elsewhere, unsurfaced roads are the rule. Laos has about 23,000km of classified roads and less than a quarter are sealed. Unsurfaced roads are particularly tricky in the wet season when many routes are impassable to all but 4WD vehicles and motorbikes, while in the dry season the clouds of dust kicked up by passing traffic makes travel highly uncomfortable, especially in a *sŏrngtăaou* or by motorbike. Bring a face mask. Wet or dry, Laos is so mountainous that relatively short-distance road trips can take forever.

Road Hazards

Try to avoid driving at dusk and after dark: cows, buffaloes, chickens and dogs, not to mention thousands of people, head for home on the unlit roads, turning them into a dangerous obstacle course.

Road Rules

The single most important rule to driving in Laos is to expect the unexpected. Driving is on the right side, but it's not unusual to see Lao drivers go the wrong way down the left lane before crossing over to the right, a potentially dangerous situation if you're not ready for it. At intersections it's normal to turn right without looking left.

Local Transport

Although most town centres are small enough to walk around, even relatively small settlements often place their bus stations several kilometres out of town.

Bus

Vientiane is the only city with a network of local buses, though, with the exception of a few key recommended routes, they're not much use to travellers.

Sŏrngtăaou, Jumbo, Săhm-lór, Sakai-làep & Tuk-tuk

The various pick-ups and three-wheeled taxis found in Vientiane and provincial capitals have different names depending on where you are. Largest are the *sŏrngtăaou*, which double as buses in some areas and as local buses around bigger towns.

Larger three-wheelers are called *jąmbǫh* (jumbo) and can hold four to six passengers on two facing seats. In Vientiane they are sometimes called tuk-tuks as in Thailand (though traditionally in Laos this refers to a slightly larger vehicle than the jumbo). These three-wheeled conveyances are also labelled simply *taak-see* (taxi) or, usually for motorcycle sidecar-style vehicles, *săhm-lór* (three-wheels). The old-style bicycle *săhm-lór* (pedicab), known as a *cyclo* elsewhere in Indochina, is an endangered species in Laos.

Taxi

Vientiane has a handful of taxis that are used by foreign business people and the occasional tourist, while in other cities a taxi of sorts can be arranged. They can be hired by the trip, by the hour or by the day. Typical all-day hire within a town or city costs between US$35 and US$50, subject to negotiations.

Train

Currently Laos has just 3km of railway line connecting Nong Khai in Thailand to Vientiane Prefecture via the Friendship Bridge. Plans are underway to extend this line to central Vientiane, and eventually connect with a Chinese-funded railway line from Kunming to Vientiane via Luang Prabang. This high-speed train service, with speeds exceeding 300km/h, is currently under construction and due to be completed around 2022.

Health

Health issues and the quality of medical facilities vary enormously depending on where and how you travel in Laos. Travellers tend to worry about contracting infectious diseases when in the tropics, but infections are a rare cause of serious illness or death in travellers. Pre-existing medical conditions such as heart disease and accidental injury account for most of the life-threatening problems. Falling ill in some way, however, is relatively common. Fortunately, most common illnesses can either be prevented with common-sense behaviour or treated easily with a well-stocked traveller's medical kit.

BEFORE YOU GO

Insurance

Even if you are fit and healthy, don't travel without health insurance, as accidents do happen. Declare any existing medical conditions you have: the insurance company *will* check if your problem is pre-existing and will not cover you if it is undeclared. You may require extra cover for adventure activities such as rock climbing. If your health insurance doesn't cover you for medical expenses abroad, consider getting extra insurance: check www.lonelyplanet.com/travel-insurance for more information. If you're uninsured, emergency evacuation is extremely expensive.

Find out in advance if your insurance plan will make payments directly to providers or reimburse you later for overseas health expenditures. In Laos, most doctors expect payment in cash. If you have to claim later, keep all the documentation.

Medical Checklist

The following are some recommended items for a personal medical kit:

➡ antibacterial cream, eg Muciprocin

➡ antibiotics for diarrhoea, eg Norfloxacin or Ciprofloxacin; Azithromycin for bacterial diarrhoea; and Tinidazole for giardiasis or amoebic dysentery

➡ antifungal cream, eg Clotrimazole

➡ antihistamines for allergies, eg Cetirizine for daytime and Promethazine for night

➡ anti-inflammatories, eg Ibuprofen

➡ antinausea medication, eg Prochlorperazine

➡ antiseptic for cuts and scrapes, eg Betadine

➡ antispasmodic for stomach cramps, eg Buscopan

➡ contraceptives

➡ decongestant for colds and flus, eg Pseudoephedrine

➡ DEET-based insect repellent

➡ diarrhoea 'stopper', eg Loperamide

➡ first-aid items such as scissors, plasters (Band Aids), bandages, gauze, thermometer (electronic, not mercury), sterile needles and syringes, and tweezers

➡ indigestion medication, eg Quick Eze or Mylanta

➡ iodine tablets to purify water

➡ oral-rehydration solution for diarrhoea, eg Gastrolyte

➡ paracetamol for pain

➡ permethrin (to impregnate clothing and mosquito nets) for repelling insects

➡ sunscreen and hat

➡ throat lozenges

➡ thrush (vaginal yeast infection) treatment, eg Clotrimazole pessaries or Diflucan tablet

Medication

Pack medications in their original, clearly labelled, containers. A signed and dated letter from your physician describing your medical conditions and medications, including generic names, is also a good idea. If carrying syringes or needles, be sure to have a physician's letter documenting their medical necessity.

If you happen to take any regular medication, bring double your needs in case of loss or theft. In Laos it can be difficult to find some newer drugs, particularly the latest antidepressant drugs, blood-pressure medications and contraceptive pills.

Websites

There is a wealth of travel health advice on the internet.

World Health Organization (WHO; www.who.int/ith) WHO publishes a superb book called *International Travel & Health*, which is revised annually and is available online for free.

Centers for Disease Control & Prevention (CDC; www.cdc.gov) Good general information.

Health Advisories

It's usually a good idea to consult your government's travel-health website before departure, if one is available.

Australia (www.smartraveller. gov.au)

Canada (www.travelhealth.gc.ca)

New Zealand (www.safetravel. govt.nz)

UK (www.gov.uk/foreign-travel-advice)

USA (www.cdc.gov/travel)

IN LAOS

Availability & Cost of Healthcare

Laos has no facilities for major medical emergencies. The state-run hospitals and clinics are among the most basic in Southeast Asia in terms of the standards of hygiene, staff training, supplies and equipment.

For minor to moderate conditions, including malaria, Mahasot Hospital's **International Clinic** (Map p146; ☑021-214024; Mahosot Hospital, Rue Fa Ngoum; ⏲24hr) in Vientiane has a

decent reputation. Some foreign embassies in Vientiane also maintain small but professional medical centres, including the **French Embassy Medical Center** (Map p146; ☑021-214150; cnr Rue Khu Vieng & Rue Simeuang; ⏲8.30am-noon & 1.30-7pm Mon-Tue & Thu-Fri, 8.30am-noon & 1.30-5pm Wed, Sat & Sun).

For any serious conditions, Thailand is the destination of choice. If a medical problem can wait until Bangkok, then all the better, as there are excellent hospitals there.

For medical emergencies that can't be delayed before reaching Bangkok, ambulances can be arranged from nearby Nong Khai or Udon Thani in Thailand. **Nong Khai Wattana General Hospital** (☑042-465201) is the closest. The better **Aek Udon Hospital** (☑042 342555; Th Phosri) in Udon Thani is an hour further from the border by road.

Buying medication over the counter is not recommended, as fake medications and poorly stored or out-of-date drugs are common in Laos.

Infectious Diseases

Dengue Fever

This mosquito-borne disease is becoming increasingly problematic throughout Laos, especially in the cities. As there is no vaccine it can only be prevented by avoiding mosquito bites. The mosquito that carries dengue bites day and night, so use insect avoidance measures at all times. Symptoms include high fever, severe headache and body ache (dengue was once known as 'breakbone fever'). Some people develop a rash and diarrhoea. There's no specific treatment, just rest and paracetamol. Do not take aspirin as it increases the

likelihood of haemorrhaging. See a doctor to be diagnosed and monitored.

Hepatitis A

A problem throughout the region, this food- and water-borne virus infects the liver, causing jaundice (yellow skin and eyes), nausea and lethargy. There is no specific treatment for hepatitis A – you just need to allow time for the liver to heal. All travellers to Southeast Asia should be vaccinated against hepatitis A.

Hepatitis B

The only sexually transmitted disease that can be prevented by vaccination, hepatitis B is spread by body fluids, including sexual contact. In some parts of Southeast Asia, up to 20% of the population are carriers of hepatitis B, and usually are unaware of this. The long-term consequences can include liver cancer and cirrhosis.

Hepatitis E

Hepatitis E is transmitted through contaminated food and water and has similar symptoms to hepatitis A, but it is far less common. It is a severe problem in pregnant women and can result in the death of both mother and baby. There is currently no vaccine; prevention is by following safe eating and drinking guidelines.

HIV

According to Unaids and WHO, Laos remains a 'low HIV prevalence country'. However, it's estimated that only about one-fifth of all HIV cases in Laos are actually reported. Heterosexual sex is the main method of transmission in Laos. The use of condoms greatly decreases but does not eliminate the risk of HIV infection.

Malaria

Many parts of Laos, particularly populated areas, have minimal to no risk of malaria,

RECOMMENDED VACCINATIONS

The only vaccine required by international regulations is yellow fever. Proof of vaccination will only be required if you have visited a country in the yellow-fever zone within the six days prior to entering Southeast Asia.

Specialised travel-medicine clinics are the best source of information on vaccines and will be able to give tailored recommendations.

Most vaccines don't produce immunity until at least two weeks after they're given, so visit a doctor four to eight weeks before departure. Ask the doctor for an International Certificate of Vaccination (otherwise known as the yellow booklet), which will list all the vaccinations received.

and the risk of side effects from antimalaria medication may outweigh the risk of getting the disease. For some rural areas, however, the risk of contracting the disease far outweighs the risk of any tablet side effects. Remember that malaria can be fatal.

Malaria is caused by a parasite transmitted by the bite of an infected mosquito. The most important symptom of malaria is fever, but general symptoms such as a headache, diarrhoea, cough or chills may also occur. Diagnosis can only be made by taking a blood sample.

Two strategies should be combined to prevent malaria: mosquito avoidance and antimalarial medications. Most people who catch malaria are taking inadequate or no antimalarial medication.

Travellers are advised to prevent mosquito bites by taking these steps:

➡ Choose accommodation with screens and fans.

➡ Impregnate clothing with Permethrin in high-risk areas.

➡ Sleep under a mosquito net impregnated with Permethrin.

➡ Spray your room with insect repellent before going out for your evening meal.

➡ Use an insect repellent containing DEET on exposed skin.

➡ Wear long sleeves and trousers in light colours.

Opisthorchiasis (Liver Flukes)

These are tiny worms that are occasionally present in freshwater fish in Laos. The main risk comes from eating raw or undercooked fish. Travellers should in particular avoid eating uncooked ♭ạh dàak (an unpasteurised fermented fish used as an accompaniment for many Lao foods) when travelling in rural Laos.

A rarer way to contract liver flukes is by swimming in the Mekong River or its tributaries around Don Khong in the far south of Laos.

At low levels, there are virtually no symptoms at all; at higher levels, an overall fatigue, low-grade fever and swollen or tender liver (or general abdominal pain) are the usual symptoms, along with worms or worm eggs in the faeces. Opisthorchiasis is easily treated with medication.

Rabies

This uniformly fatal disease is spread by the bite or lick of an infected animal, most commonly a dog or monkey. You should seek medical

advice immediately after any animal bite and commence post-exposure treatment. Having a pre-travel vaccination means the post-bite treatment is greatly simplified. If an animal bites you, gently wash the wound with soap and water, and apply iodine-based antiseptic. If you are not vaccinated you will need to receive rabies immunoglobulin as soon as possible.

STDs

Sexually transmitted diseases (STDs) most common in Laos include herpes, warts, syphilis, gonorrhoea and chlamydia. People carrying these diseases often have no signs of infection. Condoms will prevent gonorrhoea and chlamydia but not warts or herpes. If after a sexual encounter you develop any rash, lumps, discharge or pain when passing urine, seek immediate medical attention. If you have been sexually active during your travels, have an STD check on your return home.

Tuberculosis

Tuberculosis (TB) is very rare in short-term travellers. Medical and aid workers, and long-term travellers who have significant contact with the local population, should take precautions, however. Vaccination is usually only given to children under the age of five, but adults at risk are advised to get pre- and post-travel TB testing. The main symptoms are fever, cough, weight loss, night sweats and tiredness.

Typhoid

This serious bacterial infection is also spread via food and water. It causes a high, slowly progressive fever and headache, and may be accompanied by a dry cough and stomach pain. It is diagnosed by blood tests and treated with antibiotics. Vaccination is

TAP WATER

➡ Never drink tap water.

➡ Bottled water is generally safe, but check the seal is intact at purchase.

➡ Boiling water is the most efficient method of purifying it.

➡ The best chemical purifier is iodine. It should not be used by pregnant women or people who suffer with thyroid problems.

➡ Water filters should protect against viruses. Ensure your filter has a chemical barrier such as iodine and a small pore size.

recommended for all travellers spending more than a week in Southeast Asia, or travelling outside of the major cities.

Traveller's Diarrhoea

Traveller's diarrhoea is by far the most common problem affecting travellers. Somewhere between 30% and 50% of people will suffer from it within two weeks of starting their trip.

Traveller's diarrhoea is defined as the passage of more than three watery bowel actions within 24 hours, plus at least one other symptom such as fever, cramps, nausea, vomiting or feeling generally unwell.

Treatment consists of staying well hydrated. Rehydration solutions like Gastrolyte are the best for this. Antibiotics such as Norfloxacin, Ciprofloxacin or Azithromycin will kill the bacteria quickly.

Loperamide is just a 'stopper' and doesn't get to the cause of the problem, but it can be helpful when taking a long bus ride. Don't take Loperamide if you have a fever, or blood in your stools. Seek medical attention quickly if you do not respond to an appropriate antibiotic.

AMOEBIC DYSENTERY

Amoebic dysentery is very rare in travellers but is often misdiagnosed by poor-quality labs in Southeast

Asia. Symptoms are similar to bacterial diarrhoea, ie fever, bloody diarrhoea and generally feeling unwell. You should always seek reliable medical care if you have blood in your diarrhoea. Treatment involves two drugs: Tinidazole or Metronidazole to kill the parasite in your gut and then a second drug to kill the cysts. If left untreated, complications such as liver or gut abscesses can occur.

GIARDIASIS

Giardia lamblia is a parasite that is relatively common in travellers. Symptoms include nausea, bloating, excess gas, fatigue and intermittent diarrhoea. The parasite will eventually go away if left untreated but this can take months. The treatment of choice is Tinidazole, with Metronidazole being a second-line option.

Environmental Hazards

Food

Eating in restaurants is the biggest risk factor for contracting traveller's diarrhoea. Ways to avoid it include eating only freshly cooked food, and avoiding shellfish and food that has been sitting around in buffets. Peel all fruit and cook all vegetables. Eat in busy restaurants with a high turnover of customers.

Heat

Many parts of Southeast Asia are hot and humid throughout the year and it takes time to adapt to the climate. Swelling of the feet and ankles is common, as are muscle cramps caused by excessive sweating. Prevent these by avoiding dehydration and excessive activity in the heat.

Dehydration is the main contributor to heat exhaustion. Symptoms include feeling weak, headache, irritability, nausea or vomiting, sweaty skin, a fast, weak pulse and a normal or slightly elevated body temperature. Treatment involves getting out of the heat and/or sun, fanning the victim and applying cool wet cloths to the skin and rehydrating with water containing a quarter of a teaspoon of salt per litre. Recovery is usually rapid, though it is common to feel weak for some days afterwards.

Heatstroke is a serious medical emergency. Symptoms come on suddenly and include weakness, nausea, a hot dry body with a body temperature of over 41°C, dizziness, confusion, loss of coordination, seizures and eventually collapse and loss of consciousness. Seek medical help and commence cooling by getting the person out of the heat, removing their clothes, fanning them and applying cool wet cloths or ice to their body, especially to the groin and armpits.

Prickly heat is a common skin rash in the tropics, caused by sweat being trapped under the skin. The result is an itchy rash of tiny lumps. Treat by moving out of the heat and into an air-conditioned area for a few hours and by having cool showers. Locally bought prickly heat powder can be helpful.

Insect Bites & Stings

Bedbugs don't carry disease but their bites are very

itchy. They live in the cracks of furniture and walls and then migrate to the bed at night to feed on you. You can treat the itch with an antihistamine.

Ticks are contracted during walks in rural areas. They are commonly found behind the ears, on the belly and in armpits. If you have had a tick bite and experience symptoms such as a rash, fever or muscle aches, then see a doctor. Doxycycline prevents tick-borne diseases.

Leeches are found in humid forest areas. They do not transmit any disease but their bites are often intensely itchy for weeks afterwards and can easily become infected. Apply an iodine-based antiseptic to any leech bite to help prevent infection.

Bee and wasp stings mainly cause problems for people who are allergic to them. Anyone with a serious bee or wasp allergy should carry an injection of adrenaline (eg an Epipen) for emergency treatment.

Skin Problems

Fungal rashes are common in humid climates. Watch out for moist areas that get less air, such as the groin, armpits and between the toes. The problem starts as a red patch that slowly spreads and is usually itchy. Treatment involves keeping the skin dry, avoiding chafing and using an antifungal cream such as Clotrimazole or Lamisil.

Cuts and scratches become easily infected in humid climates. Take meticulous care of any cuts and scratches to prevent complications such as abscesses. Immediately wash all wounds in clean water and apply antiseptic.

Snakes

Southeast Asia is home to many species of both poisonous and harmless snakes. Assume all snakes are poisonous and never try to catch one. Always wear boots and long pants if walking in an area that may have snakes. First aid in the event of a snakebite involves pressure immobilisation via an elastic bandage firmly wrapped around the affected limb, starting at the bite site and working up towards the chest. The bandage should not be so tight that the circulation is cut off, and the fingers or toes should be kept free so the circulation can be checked. Do not use tourniquets or try to suck the venom out.

Sunburn

Even on a cloudy day, sunburn can occur rapidly. Always use a strong sunscreen (at least factor 30), making sure to reapply after a swim, and always wear a wide-brimmed hat and sunglasses outdoors. Avoid lying in the sun during the hottest part of the day (from 10am to 2pm). If you are sunburnt stay out of the sun until you have recovered.

Women's Health

In urban areas, supplies of sanitary products are readily available. Birth control options may be limited though, so bring adequate supplies of your own form of contraception. Heat, humidity and antibiotics can all contribute to thrush. Treatment is with antifungal creams and pessaries such as Clotrimazole. A practical alternative is a single tablet of Fluconazole (Diflucan).

Pregnant women should receive specialised advice before travelling. The ideal time to travel is in the second trimester (between 16 and 28 weeks), when the risk of pregnancy-related problems is lowest and pregnant women generally feel at their best. Always carry a list of quality medical facilities available at your destination and ensure you continue your standard antenatal care at these facilities. Most of all, ensure travel insurance covers all pregnancy-related possibilities, including premature labour.

Malaria is a high-risk disease during pregnancy. None of the more effective antimalarial drugs are completely safe in pregnancy.

Traditional Medicine

Throughout Southeast Asia, traditional medical systems are widely practised. There is a big difference between these traditional healing systems and 'folk' medicine. Folk remedies should be avoided, as they often involve rather dubious procedures with potential complications. In comparison, traditional healing systems such as traditional Chinese medicine are well respected, and aspects of them are being increasingly used by Western medical practitioners.

All traditional Asian medical systems identify a vital life force, and see blockage or imbalance as causing disease. Techniques such as herbal medicines, massage and acupuncture are utilised to bring this vital force back into balance, or to maintain balance. These therapies are best used for treating diseases such as chronic fatigue, arthritis, irritable bowel syndrome and some chronic skin conditions. Traditional medicines should be avoided for treating serious acute infections such as malaria.

Language

The official language of Laos is the dialect spoken and written in Vientiane. As an official language, it has successfully become the lingua franca between all Lao and non-Lao ethnic groups in the country.

In Lao, many identical syllables are differentiated by their tone only. Vientiane Lao has six tones. Three of the tones are level (low, mid and high) while three follow pitch inclines (rising, high falling and low falling). All six variations in pitch are relative to the speaker's natural vocal range, ie one person's low tone is not necessarily the same pitch as another person's.

➡ **low tone** – Produced at the relative bottom of your conversational tonal range – usually flat level, eg dęe (good).

➡ **mid tone** – Flat like the low tone, but spoken at the relative middle of your vocal range. No tone mark is used, eg het (do).

➡ **high tone** – Flat again, this time at the relative top of your vocal range, eg héu·a (boat).

➡ **rising tone** – Begins a bit below the mid tone and rises to just at or above the high tone, eg săhm (three).

➡ **high falling tone** – Begins at or above the high tone and falls to the mid level, eg sŏw (morning).

➡ **low falling tone** – Begins at about the mid level and falls to the level of the low tone, eg kòw (rice).

WANT MORE?

For in-depth language information and handy phrases, check out Lonely Planet's *Lao Phrasebook*. You'll find it at **shop.lonelyplanet.com**, or you can buy Lonely Planet's iPhone phrasebooks at the Apple App Store.

There is no official method of transliterating the Lao language, though the public and private sectors in Laos are gradually moving towards a more internationally recognisable system along the lines of Royal Thai General Transcription (RTGS), since Thai and Lao have very similar writing and sound systems. This book uses a custom system of transliteration.

In our coloured pronunciation guides, the hyphens indicate syllable breaks within words, eg àng·gít (English). Some syllables are further divided with a dot to help you pronounce compound vowels, eg kĕe·an (write).

The pronunciation of vowels goes like this: i as in 'it'; ee as in 'feet'; ai as in 'aisle'; ah as the 'a' in 'father'; a as the short 'a' in 'about'; aa as in 'bad'; air as in 'air'; er as in 'fur'; eu as in 'sir'; u as in 'put'; oo as in 'food'; ow as in 'now'; or as in 'jaw'; o as in 'phone'; oh as in 'toe'; ee·a as in 'ian'; oo·a as in 'tour'; ew as in 'yew'; and oy as in 'boy'.

Most consonants correspond to their English counterparts. The exceptions are đ (a hard 't' sound, a bit like 'dt') and ɓ (a hard 'p' sound, a bit like 'bp').

BASICS

Hello.	ສະບາຍດີ	sábại-dĕe
Goodbye.	ສະບາຍດີ	sábại-dĕe
Excuse me.	ຂໍໂທດ	kŏr tôht
Sorry.	ຂໍໂທດ	kŏr tôht
Please.	ກະລຸນາๆ	ga-lú-náh
Thank you.	ຂອບໃຈ	kòrp jại
Yes./No.	ແມນ/ບໍ່	maan/bor

How are you?
ສະບາຍດີບໍ່   sábại-dĕe bor

I'm fine, and you?
ຂ້ອຍສະບາຍດີ ເຈົ້າເດ້   kòy sábại-dĕe jôw dâir

What's your name?
ເຈົ້າຊື່ຫຍັງ   jôw seu nyǎng

My name is ...
ຂ້ອຍຊື່ ...   kòy seu ...

Do you speak English?
ເຈົ້າປາກ   jôw bàhk
ພາສາອັງກິດໄດ້ບໍ່   páh-sǎh ang-kít dâi bor

I don't understand.
ຂ້ອຍບໍ່ເຂົ້າໃຈ   kòy bor kòw jai

ACCOMMODATION

hotel	ໂຮງແຮມ	hóhng háam
guesthouse	ທີ່ຮັບແຂກ	hör hap káak

Do you have a room?
ມີຫ້ອງບໍ່   mée hòrng bor

single room
ຫ້ອງນອນຕຽງດ່ຽວ   hòrng nórn đěe·ang dee·o

double room
ຫ້ອງນອນຕຽງຄູ່   hòrng nórn đěe·ang koo

How much ...?	... ເທົ່າໃດ	... tow đại
per night	ຄືນລະ	kéun-la
per week	ອາທິດລະ	ah-tit-la

air-con	ແອເຢັນ	aa yen
bathroom	ຫ້ອງນ້ຳ	hòrng nâm
fan	ພັດລົມ	pat lóm
hot water	ນ້ຳຮ້ອນ	nâm hôrn

DIRECTIONS

Where is the ...?
... ຢູ່ໃສ   ... yòo sǎi

Which (street) is this?
ບ່ອນນີ້ (ຖະໜົນ) ຫຍັງ   born nêe (ta-nǒn) nyǎng

How far?
ໄກເທົ່າໃດ   kai tow đại

Turn left/right.
ລ້ຽວຊ້າຍ/ຂວາ   lêe·o sài/kwǎh

straight ahead
ໄປຊື່ໆ   bại seu-seu

EATING & DRINKING

What do you have that's special?
ມີຫຍັງພິເສດບໍ່   mée nyǎng pi-sèt bor

I'd like to try that.
ຂ້ອຍຢາກລອງກິນເບິ່ງ   kòy yàhk lórng gin berng

I eat only vegetables.
ຂ້ອຍກິນແຕ່ຜັກ   kòy gin đaa pák

I (don't) like it hot and spicy.
ຂອຍ (ບໍ່) ມັກເຜັດ   kòy (bor) mak pét

I didn't order this.
ຂ້ອຍບໍ່ໄດ້ສັ່ງແນວນີ້   kòy bor dâi sang náa·ou nêe

Please bring the bill.
ໄລ່ເງິນແດ່   lai ngern đaa

Key Words

bottle	ແກ້ວ	kâa·ou
bowl	ຖ້ວຍ	tòo·ay
chopsticks	ໄມ້ທູ່	mâi too
fork	ສ້ອມ	sôrm
glass	ຈອກ	jòrk
knife	ມິດ	mêet
menu	ລາຍການ	lái-gạhn
	ອາຫານ	ah-hǎhn
plate	ຈານ	jahn
spoon	ບ່ວງ	boo·ang

Meat & Fish

beef	ຊິ້ນງົວ	sèen ngóo·a
chicken	ໄກ່	kai
crab	ປູ	boo
fish	ປາ	bah
pork	ຊິ້ນໝູ	sèen mǒo
seafood	ອາຫານທະເລ	ah-hǎhn ta-láir
shrimp/prawn	ກຸ້ງ	gûng

Fruit & Vegetables

banana	ໝາກກ້ວຍ	màhk gôo·ay
bean sprouts	ຖົ່ວງອກ	too·a ngôrk
beans	ຖົ່ວ	too·a
cabbage	ກະລ່ຳປີ	gá-lam bẹe
cauliflower	ກະລ່ຳປີດອກ	gá-lam bẹe dòrk
coconut	ໝາກພ້າວ	màhk pôw
cucumber	ໝາກແຕງ	màhk đạang
eggplant	ໝາກເຂືອ	màhk kěua
garlic	ຫົວຜັກທຽມ	hǒo·a pák tée·am

green beans	ถิ่วยาว	too·a nyów
guava	ໝາກສິດາ	màhk sĕe-dah
jackfruit	ໝາກມີ້	màhk mêe
lettuce	ຜັກສະລັດ	pák sá-lat
lime	ໝາກນາວ	màhk nów
longan	ໝາກຍ່າໄຍ	màhk nyám nyái
lychee	ໝາກລິ້ນຈີ່	màhk lín-jee
mandarin	ໝາກກ້ຽງ	màhk gêe-ang
mango	ໝາກມ່ວງ	màhk moo-ang
onion (bulb)	ຫົວຜັກບົ່ວ	hŏoa pák boo-a
onion (green)	ຕົ້ນຜັກບົ່ວ	đôn pák boo-a
papaya	ໝາກຫຸ່ງ	màhk hung
peanuts	ໝາກຖົ່ວດິນ	màhk too-a dịn
pineapple	ໝາກນັດ	màhk nat
potato	ມັນຝລັ່ງ	mán fa-lang
rambutan	ໝາກເງາະ	màhk ngo
sugarcane	ອ້ອຍ	ôy
tomato	ໝາກເລັ່ນ	màhk len
vegetables	ຜັກ	pak
watermelon	ໝາກໂມ	màhk móh

Other

bread (plain)	ເຂົ້າຈີ່	kòw jẹe
butter	ເບີ	bẹr
chilli	ໝາກເຜັດ	màhk pét
egg	ໄຂ່	kai
fish sauce	ນ້ຳປາ	nâm bạh
ice	ນ້ຳກ້ອນ	nâm gôrn
rice	ເຂົ້າ	kòw
salt	ເກືອ	gẹua
soy sauce	ນ້ຳສະອິ້ວ	nâm sá-éw
sugar	ນ້ຳຕານ	nâm-đạhn

Drinks

beer	ເບຍ	bẹe·a
coffee	ກາແຟ	gạh-fáir
draught beer	ເບຍສົດ	bẹe·a sót
drinking water	ນ້ຳດື່ມ	nâm deum
milk (plain)	ນ້ຳນົມ	nâm nóm
orange juice	ນ້ຳໝາກກ້ຽງ	nâm màhk gêe-ang
rice whisky	ເຫຼົ້າລາວ	lòw-lów
soda water	ນ້ຳໂສດາ	nâm sŏh-dạh

| tea | ຊາ | sáh |
| yoghurt | ນົມສົ້ມ | nóm sòm |

EMERGENCIES

| Help! | ຊ່ວຍແດ່ | soo·ay daa |
| Go away! | ໄປເດີ້ | bại dêr |

Call a doctor!
ຊ່ວຍຕາມຫາໝໍ soo·ay đạhm hăh mŏr
ໃຫ້ແດ່ hài daa

Call the police!
ຊ່ວຍເອີ້ນຕຳຫລວດແດ່ soo·ay êrn đam-lòo·at daa

Where are the toilets?
ຫ້ອງນ້ຳຢູ່ໃສ hòrng nâm yoo sǎi

I'm lost.
ຊ້ອຍຫຼົງທາງ kòy lŏng táhng

I'm not well.
ຊ້ອຍບໍ່ສະບາຍ kòy bor sá-bại

SHOPPING & SERVICES

I'm looking for ...
ຊ້ອຍຊອກຫາ ... kòy sòrk hǎh ...

How much (for) ...?
... ເທົ່າໃດ ... tow dại

The price is very high.
ລາຄາແພງຫລາຍ láh-káh páang lăi

I want to change money.
ຊ້ອຍຢາກປ່ຽນເງິນ kòy yàhk bee·an ngérn

bank	ທະນາຄານ	ta-náh-káhn
bookshop	ຮ້ານຂາຍປຶ້ມ	hâhn kǎi beum
pharmacy	ຮ້ານຂາຍຢາ	hâhn kǎi yạh
post office	ໄປສະນີ	bại-sá-née
	(ໂຮງສາຍ)	(hóhng sǎi)

TIME & DATES

What time is it?
ເວລາຈັກໂມງ wáir-láh jàk móhng

this morning	ເຊົ້ານີ້	sôw nêe
this afternoon	ບ່າຍນີ້	bai nêe
tonight	ຄືນນີ້	kéun nêe
yesterday	ມື້ວານນີ້	mêu wáhn nêe
today	ມື້ນີ້	mêu nêe
tomorrow	ມື້ອືນ	mêu eun

Monday	ວັນຈັນ	wán jạn
Tuesday	ວັນອັງຄານ	wán ạng-káhn
Wednesday	ວັນພຸດ	wán put
Thursday	ວັນພະຫັດ	wán pa-hát
Friday	ວັນສຸກ	wán súk
Saturday	ວັນເສົາ	wán sŏw
Sunday	ວັນອາທິດ	wán ạh-tit

TRANSPORT

boat	ເຮືອ	héu·a
bus	ລົດເມ	lot máir
minivan	ລົດຕູ້	lot dôo
plane	ເຮືອບິນ	héu·a bïn

airport
ສະໜາມບິນ — sá-nǎhm bïn

bus station
ສະຖານີລົດປະຈຳທາງ — sa-tǎh-nee lot bá-jạm táhng

bus stop
ບ່ອນຈອດລົດປະຈຳທາງ — born jòrt lot bá-jạm táhng

taxi stand
ບ່ອນຈອດລົດແທກຊີ — born jòrt lot taak-sêe

I want to go to ...
ຂ້ອຍຢາກໄປ ... — kòy yàhk bại ...

I'd like a ticket.
ຂ້ອຍຢາກໄດ້ປີ້ — kòy yàhk dâi bêe

Where do we get on the boat?
ລົງເຮືອຢູ່ໃສ — lóng héu·a yoo sǎi

What time will the ... leave?
... ຈະອອກຈັກໂມງ — ... já òrk ják móhng

What time does it arrive there?
ຈະໄປຮອດພຸ້ນຈັກໂມງ — já bại hôrt pûn ják móhng

Can I sit here?
ນັ່ງບ່ອນນີ້ໄດ້ບໍ່ — nang born nêe dâi bor

Please tell me when we arrive in ...
ເວລາຮອດ ... — wáir-láh hôrt ...
ບອກຂ້ອຍແດ່ — bòrk kòy daa

Stop here.
ຈອດຢູ່ນີ້ — jòrt yoo nêe

I'd like to hire a ...
ຂ້ອຍຢາກເຊົ່າ ... — kòy yàhk sôw ...

Numbers

1	ໜຶ່ງ	neung
2	ສອງ	sŏrng
3	ສາມ	sǎhm
4	ສີ່	see
5	ຫ້າ	hàh
6	ຫົກ	hók
7	ເຈັດ	jét
8	ແປດ	bàat
9	ເກົ້າ	gôw
10	ສິບ	síp
11	ສິບເອັດ	síp-ét
12	ສິບສອງ	síp-sŏrng
20	ຊາວ	sów
21	ຊາວເອັດ	sów-ét
22	ຊາວສອງ	sów-sŏrng
30	ສາມສິບ	sǎhm-síp
40	ສີ່ສິບ	see-síp
50	ຫ້າສິບ	hàh-síp
60	ຫົກສິບ	hók-síp
70	ເຈັດສິບ	jét-síp
80	ແປດສິບ	bàat-síp
90	ເກົ້າສິບ	gôw-síp
100	ຮ້ອຍ	hôy
200	ສອງຮ້ອຍ	sŏrng hôy
1000	ພັນ	pán
10,000	ໝື່ນ(ສິບພັນ)	meun (síp-pán)
100,000	ແສນ(ຮ້ອຍພັນ)	sǎen (hôy pán)
1,000,000	ລ້ານ	lâhn

bicycle	ລົດຖີບ	lot tèep
car	ລົດ(ໂອໂຕ)	lot (ŏh-đŏh)
motorcycle	ລົດຈັກ	lot ják
passenger truck	ສອງແຖວ	sŏrng-tǎa·ou
pedicab	ສາມລໍ້	sǎhm-lôr
taxi	ລົດແທກຊີ	lot tâak-see
tuk-tuk	ຕຸກ ຕຸກ	đuk-đuk

GLOSSARY

ąahaan – food

anatta – Buddhist concept of nonsubstantiality or nonessentiality of reality, ie no permanent 'soul'

anicca – Buddhist concept of impermanence, the transience of all things

Asean – Association of South East Asian Nations

bâhn – the general Lao word for house or village; written Ban on maps

bąhsěe – sometimes spelt basi or *baci*; a ceremony in which the 32 *kwǎn* (guardian spirits) are symbolically bound to the participant for health and safety

baht – *(bàht)* Thai unit of currency, commonly negotiable in Laos; also a Lao unit of measure equal to 15g

BCEL – Banque pour le Commerce Extérieur Lao; in English, Lao Foreign Trade Bank

bęea – beer; *bęea sót* is draught beer

bun – pronounced *bųn*, often spelt boun; a festival; also spiritual 'merit' earned through good actions or religious practices

corvée – enforced, unpaid labour

đàht –waterfall; also *nâm tók*; written Tat on maps

đalàht – market; *talàat sâo* is the morning market; *talàat mèut* is the free, or 'black', market; written Talat on maps

Don – pronounced *dąwn*; island

dukkha – Buddhist concept of suffering, unsatisfactoriness, disease

falang – from the Lao *falangsèht* or 'French'; Western, a Westerner

fěr – rice noodles, one of the most common dishes in Laos

hǎi – jar

héua – boat

héua hǎhng nyáo – longtail boat

héua pái – row boat

héua wái – speedboat

hǒr đại – monastery building dedicated to the storage of the Tripitaka (Buddhist scriptures)

hùay – stream; written Huay on maps

Jataka – (Pali-Sanskrit) mythological stories of the Buddha's past lives; *sáa-dók* in Lao

jęen hór – Lao name for the Muslim Yunnanese who live in Northern Laos

jęhdii – a Buddhist stupa; also written Chedi

jumbo – a motorised three-wheeled taxi, sometimes called tuk-tuk

káan – a wind instrument devised of a double row of bamboo-like reeds fitted into a hardwood soundbox and made air-tight with beeswax

kanǒm – pastry or sweet

kip – pronounced gèep; Lao unit of currency

kòw – rice

kòw jee – bread

kòw něeo – sticky rice, the Lao staple food

kóo-bąh – Lao Buddhist monk

kwǎn – guardian spirits

láhp – a spicy Lao-style salad of minced meat, poultry or fish

lák méuang – city pillar

lám wóng – 'circle dance', the traditional folk dance of Laos, as common at discos as at festivals

Lao Issara – Lao resistance movement against the French in the 1940s

lòw-lów – distilled rice liquor

Lao Loum – 'lowland Lao', ethnic groups belonging to the Lao–Thai Diaspora

Lao Soung – 'highland Lao', hill tribes who make their residence at higher altitudes, such as Hmong, Mien; also spelt Lao Sung

Lao Thoeng – 'upland Lao', a loose affiliation of mostly Mon-Khmer peoples who live on midaltitude mountain slopes

lingam – a pillar or phallus symbolic of Shiva, common in Khmer-built temples

LNTA – Lao National Tourism Administration

LPDR – Lao People's Democratic Republic

LPRP – Lao People's Revolutionary Party

maa nâm – literally, water mother; river; usually shortened to *nâm* with river names, as in Nam Khong (Mekong River)

meuang – pronounced *méuang*; district or town; in ancient times a city state; often written Muang on maps

moo bâhn – village

móoan – fun, which the Lao believe should be present in all activities

mǒr lám – Lao folk musical theatre tradition; roughly translates as 'master of verse'

Muang – see *meuang*

naga – *nâa-kha* in Lao; mythical water serpent common to Lao–Thai legends and art

náhng sée – Buddhist nuns

náirn – Buddhist novice monk; also referred to as *samanera*

nâm – water; can also mean 'river', 'juice', 'sauce': anything of a watery nature

NGO – nongovernmental organisation, typically involved in the foreign-aid industry

nibbana – 'cooling', the extinction of mental defilements; the ultimate goal of Theravada Buddhism

NPA – National Protected Area, a classification assigned to 20 wildlife areas throughout Laos

NVA – North Vietnamese Army

þąh – fish

þąh dàak – fermented fish sauce, a common accompaniment to Lao food

pa – holy image, usually referring to a Buddha; venerable

pàh – cloth

pàh bẹeang – shoulder sash worn by men

pàh nung – sarong, worn by almost all Lao women

pàh salóng – sarong, worn by Lao men

Pathet Lao – literally, Country of Laos; both a general term for the country and a common journalistic reference to the military arm of the early Patriotic Lao Front (a cover for the Lao People's Party); often abbreviated to PL

Pha Lak Pha Lam – the Lao version of the Indian epic, the Ramayana

phúu – hill or mountain; also spelt phu

sǎhláh lóng tám – a sala (hall) where monks and lay people listen to Buddhist teachings

sǎhm-lór – a three-wheeled pedicab

sakai-làap – alternative name for jumbo in southern Laos due to the perceived resemblance to a space capsule (Skylab)

sala – pronounced *sǎa-lǎa;* an open-sided shelter; a hall

samana – pronounced *sǎamanáa;* 'seminar'; euphemism for labour and re-education camps established after the 1975 Revolution

samanera – Buddhist novice monk; also referred to as náirn

se – also spelt *xe;* Southern Laos term for river; hence Se Don means Don River and Pakse means *pàak* (mouth) of the river

sěe – sacred; also spelt *si*

shophouse – two-storey building designed to have a shop on the ground floor and a residence above

sǐm – ordination hall in a Lao Buddhist monastery; named after the *sima,* (pronounced *siimáa;* sacred stone tablets, which mark off the grounds dedicated for this purpose)

soi – lane

sǒrngtǎaou – literally two-rows; a passenger truck

taak-sée – taxi

tanǒn – street/road; often spelt Thanon on maps; shortened to 'Th' as street is to 'St'

tâht – Buddhist stupa or reliquary; written That on maps

tuk-tuk – see jumbo

UXO – unexploded ordnance

Viet Minh – the Vietnamese forces who fought for Indochina's independence from the French

vipassana – insight meditation

wat – Lao Buddhist monastery

wihǎhn – (Pali-Sanskrit vihara) a temple hall

Behind the Scenes

SEND US YOUR FEEDBACK

We love to hear from travellers – your comments keep us on our toes and help make our books better. Our well-travelled team reads every word on what you loved or loathed about this book. Although we cannot reply individually to your submissions, we always guarantee that your feedback goes straight to the appropriate authors, in time for the next edition. Each person who sends us information is thanked in the next edition – the most useful submissions are rewarded with a selection of digital PDF chapters.

Visit **lonelyplanet.com/contact** to submit your updates and suggestions or to ask for help. Our award-winning website also features inspirational travel stories, news and discussions.

Note: We may edit, reproduce and incorporate your comments in Lonely Planet products such as guidebooks, websites and digital products, so let us know if you don't want your comments reproduced or your name acknowledged. For a copy of our privacy policy visit lonelyplanet.com/privacy.

OUR READERS

Many thanks to the travellers who used the last edition and wrote to us with helpful hints, useful advice and interesting anecdotes:

Andra Mijares, Anthony Marx, Attila Elitez, Brett Yeats, Catherine Wartmann, Clint Rooijakkers, Dan Stevens, David Hagen, David Joseph DAngelo, Derry McCarthy, Emiliano Costagli, Gregory Kipling, Ian Prosser, Ikuko Kunitsuka, Jo Lurie, Kaz von Freiburg, Kit Oi Chung , Larissa Hofmann, Lorenzo Facinelli, Lorna Brown, Louise Brown, Meaghan Stolk, Melvyn Buzza, Rahul Samant, Richard Breedon, Robert Marten, Sheila Miller, Stephen Drewe, William Ayres, Wytse van Dijk

WRITER THANKS

Austin Bush

I'd like to thank my DE James Smart, Angela Tinson, my co-authors Nick Ray and Bruce Evans, and the helpful people on the ground in Laos, especially Manilla, Paul Eshoo, Tek and Alex at Marvelao, Mr Somkiad at Tha Khaek's Tourism Information Centre, Amphai at Phosy Tha Lang, Inthy Deuansavanh and Ivan Scholte.

Bruce Evans

On this trip I have to give a big shout out to the Lao people, whose friendliness and earthiness made the trip so much fun, and also to my fellow authors, Nick and Austin. In addition, Vientiane expat David Wharton, Frédéric Gousset on Don Khon, Boun at Green Discovery, Yves at Noi's Bikes in Pakse, Mr Khamphan at the Attapeu tourist office, Paul Eshoo and Don Duvall.

Nick Ray

A heartfelt thanks to the people of Laos, whose warmth, strength and spirit make it such a fascinating place to visit. Biggest thanks are for my lovely wife Kulikar Sotho and our children Julian and Belle. Thanks to Mum and Dad for giving me a taste for travel. Thanks to those in Laos who have helped shaped my knowledge and experience in this country. You know who you are. Thanks also to my co-authors Austin Bush and Bruce Evans, and to the Lonely Planet team behind this title.

ACKNOWLEDGEMENTS

Climate map data adapted from Peel MC, Finlayson BL & McMahon TA (2007) 'Updated World Map of the Köppen-Geiger Climate Classification', *Hydrology and Earth System Sciences*, 11, 1633–44.

Cover photograph: Pha That Luang in Vientiane, Travel Pix Collection/AWL Images ©

The History section was originally written by Professor Martin Stuart-Fox, Emeritus Professor at the University of Queensland, Australia.

THIS BOOK

This 10th edition of Lonely Planet's Laos guidebook was researched and written by Austin Bush, Bruce Evans and Nick Ray. The previous edition was written by Kate Morgan, Tim Bewer, Nick Ray and Richard Waters. This guidebook was produced by the following:

Destination Editor James Smart

Senior Product Editors Kate Chapman, Kathryn Rowan, Victoria Smith

Regional Senior Cartographer Diana Von Holdt

Product Editors Hannah Cartmel, Barbara Delissen

Book Designer Jessica Rose

Assisting Editors Laura Crawford, Rosie Nicholson, Mani Ramaswamy

Assisting Cartographer Rachel Imeson

Cover Researcher Naomi Parker

Thanks to Charlotte Orr, Angela Tinson, Manivone Watson

Index

EMMA NEUVONEN

LONELY PLANET IN THE WILD

Map Legend

Sights

- Beach
- Bird Sanctuary
- Buddhist
- Castle/Palace
- Christian
- Confucian
- Hindu
- Islamic
- Jain
- Jewish
- Monument
- Museum/Gallery/Historic Building
- Ruin
- Shinto
- Sikh
- Taoist
- Winery/Vineyard
- Zoo/Wildlife Sanctuary
- Other Sight

Activities, Courses & Tours

- Bodysurfing
- Diving
- Canoeing/Kayaking
- Course/Tour
- Sento Hot Baths/Onsen
- Skiing
- Snorkelling
- Surfing
- Swimming/Pool
- Walking
- Windsurfing
- Other Activity

Sleeping

- Sleeping
- Camping
- Hut/Shelter

Eating

- Eating

Drinking & Nightlife

- Drinking & Nightlife
- Cafe

Entertainment

- Entertainment

Shopping

- Shopping

Information

- Bank
- Embassy/Consulate
- Hospital/Medical
- Internet
- Police
- Post Office
- Telephone
- Toilet
- Tourist Information
- Other Information

Geographic

- Beach
- Gate
- Hut/Shelter
- Lighthouse
- Lookout
- Mountain/Volcano
- Oasis
- Park
- Pass
- Picnic Area
- Waterfall

Population

- Capital (National)
- Capital (State/Province)
- City/Large Town
- Town/Village

Transport

- Airport
- Border crossing
- Bus
- Cable car/Funicular
- Cycling
- Ferry
- Metro/MRT/MTR station
- Monorail
- Parking
- Petrol station
- Skytrain/Subway station
- Taxi
- Train station/Railway
- Tram
- Underground station
- Other Transport

Routes

- Tollway
- Freeway
- Primary
- Secondary
- Tertiary
- Lane
- Unsealed road
- Road under construction
- Plaza/Mall
- Steps
- Tunnel
- Pedestrian overpass
- Walking Tour
- Walking Tour detour
- Path/Walking Trail

Boundaries

- International
- State/Province
- Disputed
- Regional/Suburb
- Marine Park
- Cliff
- Wall

Hydrography

- River, Creek
- Intermittent River
- Canal
- Water
- Dry/Salt/Intermittent Lake
- Reef

Areas

- Airport/Runway
- Beach/Desert
- Cemetery (Christian)
- Cemetery (Other)
- Glacier
- Mudflat
- Park/Forest
- Sight (Building)
- Sportsground
- Swamp/Mangrove

Note: Not all symbols displayed above appear on the maps in this book

OUR STORY

A beat-up old car, a few dollars in the pocket and a sense of adventure. In 1972 that's all Tony and Maureen Wheeler needed for the trip of a lifetime – across Europe and Asia overland to Australia. It took several months, and at the end – broke but inspired – they sat at their kitchen table writing and stapling together their first travel guide, *Across Asia on the Cheap*. Within a week they'd sold 1500 copies. Lonely Planet was born.

Today, Lonely Planet has offices in Franklin, London, Melbourne, Oakland, Dublin, Beijing and Delhi, with more than 600 staff and writers. We share Tony's belief that 'a great guidebook should do three things: inform, educate and amuse'.

OUR WRITERS

Austin Bush

Vientiane, Vang Vieng & Around, Central Laos Austin originally came to Thailand in 1999 as part of a language study program hosted by Chiang Mai University. The lure of city life, employment and spicy food eventually led him to Bangkok. City life, employment and spicy food have kept him there since. These days, he works as a writer and photographer, and in addition to having contributed to numerous books, magazines and websites, he has contributed text and photos to more than 20 Lonely Planet titles including *Bangkok;* the *Food Book; Food Lover's Guide to the World; Laos; Malaysia, Singapore & Brunei; Myanmar (Burma); Pocket Bangkok; Thailand; Thailand's Islands & Beaches; Vietnam, Cambodia, Laos & Northern Thailand;* and *The World's Best Street Food.*

Bruce Evans

Southern Laos After travelling the hippie trail in the 1970s, Bruce lived in Thailand for more than two decades, much of that in a Buddhist monastery. When he returned to Australia he worked as an editor at Lonely Planet for many years. Since 2013 he has worked as a freelance editor and translator. He specialises in the Southeast Asia region, where he feels very much at home. This trip to Laos was his second authoring job for Lonely Planet. Bruce also wrote the Understand chapters.

Nick Ray

Luang Prabang & Around, Northern Laos A Londoner of sorts, Nick currently lives in Phnom Penh and has written countless guidebooks on the countries of the Mekong region, including contributing to Lonely Planet's *Cambodia, Myanmar* and *Vietnam* books. When not writing, he is often out exploring the remote parts of the region as a location scout or line producer for the world of television and film, including anything from *Tomb Raider* to *Top Gear*. Laos is one of his favourite destinations and he was excited to get back to some remote corners of the far north. Nick also wrote the Plan and Survival chapters.

Published by Lonely Planet Global Limited
CRN 554153
10th edition – June 2020
ISBN 978 1 78701 408 4
© Lonely Planet 2020   Photographs © as indicated 2020
10 9 8 7 6 5 4 3 2 1
Printed in Singapore